CULTURAL RELEVANCE
AND EDUCATIONAL ISSUES

CULTURAL RELEVANCE AND EDUCATIONAL ISSUES

Readings in Anthropology and Education

Edited by

FRANCIS A. J. IANNI
Teachers College, Columbia University

EDWARD STOREY
Georgia State University

LITTLE, BROWN AND COMPANY Boston

PREFACE

Anthropologists experience the processes, structural variety, and problematic aspects of teaching and learning by intensive, first-hand observation of what goes on in schools and in less formal situations of instruction. Yet few anthropologists otherwise identify with schools. There are school psychologists, a growing number of school sociologists, but no school anthropologists. The demand, and possibly the fashion, for anthropological knowledge and insight in American schools shows no sign of slacking; yet most anthropologists are content to let the popular conception of what anthropology is, how it is done, and what it has to say stand. Education, formal and informal, is the chief medium of the transmitted behaviors anthropologists call "culture," the fundamental idea of the discipline. Yet relatively little is anthropologically known of American public schooling, such related phenomena as "street academies," and the extent to which cultural assumptions and culturally defined expectations bias the American teaching and learning experience.

These apparent contradictions derive from, first, the traditional insistence of anthropologists on research in societies other than our own; second, the numerical scarcity of anthropologists; and, third, from conventional attitudes of the profession that consider the practical effects of anthropology to be secondary to its theoretical advance. Serious and sustained application of the discipline to the human opportunities and dilemmas of teaching and learning is anathema to most anthropologists. Much impetus for including anthropology and anthropological perspectives in our schools comes not from the profession of anthropology but from interested public (and private) school personnel.

It should not be surprising then to learn that an overview of anthropology and education, reprinted here, could have referred to the ground shared by anthropology and education as a "frontier area." Although the seeming discrepancies are yet to be resolved, surprisingly or not the

vii

frontier has received a thorough exploration since Spindler's assessment was published. In the past fifteen years or so a relative, if not irregular, outpouring of writing has occurred: curricula and related instructional materials; classroom studies; and a swelling series of anthropological approaches to practically everything educational — the teaching of reading, the context of school and community, bilingual instruction, comparative educational development, innovation, and even the ritual aspect of graduation ceremonies. Also, a good deal of healthy argument inside and out of anthropology has been devoted to how *anthropological* (or educational, as the case may be) are various items in this outpouring.

Indeed, the recent activity of anthropologists whose primary interests are in education and of educators whose orientation is anthropological suggests a division of labor about which much of current involvement distributes. The first division, *anthropology and education*, is the most expansive and the least specific. It is the generic relationship; it represents the large-scale interests of anthropology in the structures, processes, and functions of teaching and learning, in the diverse philosophies and practice of these, in their considerable influence upon man and particular societies of men, and in the force of culture upon what is taught, to whom, and when and where.

A second, *anthropology in education* concerns the anthropological presence, whether expressed as a substantive body of understandings, as curriculum, as programs for teacher training, or as a kind of sensitivity toward humankind and the human variety. The *anthropology of education*, third, represents anthropological *inquiry* into the behaviors we call education; into the organization of education — social, political, and economic; into the actual conduct of teaching and learning; into the credibility of educational research methods and findings; and into the announced aims and recognized needs of educational futures, wherever and in the experience of whatever human group these are being acted upon.

A fourth, and most visible, focus in current anthropology and education is upon education as one of a roster of social problems. The *anthropology of social problems*, commands the attention of critical, engaged anthropologists whose basic interest is the dignity of human difference; social, political, and economic inequity; and the practical effects of anthropology in the *solution* of human problems.

Four anthropologies do not in themselves make a pervasive, or even convincing, influence. Nor are these areas yet well articulated, one to another or all together. They do establish a structure for comprehending the diversity, vigor, and occasional disputes of frontier life in anthropology and education, however; in so doing they remark some meaningful developments that are taking place in relationships *between* anthropology and education, applied and theoretical.

It is said that a book of readings inevitably suffers from a lack of, or weaknesses in, internal logic. What satisfactorily integrates ten, twenty, or forty articles written at different times by as many authors? In some cases, a single topic; in others, as here, a range of topics chosen to signify the scope and the extent of accomplishment of a single field of study. The design of this book, its internal logic, is to inform its readers of the scope and accomplishments of anthropology and education by relating these to the four areas just briefly described, and to a fifth, which represents anthropological accounts of education in cultures not necessarily our own.

Part One of the book, thus, exemplifies the general character of anthropology and education. Part Two represents anthropology *in* education, whereas the articles of Part Three represent activity we have identified as the anthropology *of* education. Part Four includes a selection of field studies of education in and across cultures. In the fifth, and concluding, part, we exemplify anthropological approaches to education as a social problem and stress the vitality of the discipline in problem-solving as well as in social advocacy.

The writings here, in addition to demonstrating the depth and style of anthropological involvement in education — which is, after all, to proselytize — serve another and more basic function. It is the conviction of the editors that the primary value of the articles that follow is the insights into and substantive understandings of *American* education that derive from them. Particularizing the worth of a resource such as this book to any society or people is to fly in the face of the time-honored use of anthropology; it is to be ethnocentric, where anthropology is seen by many to be a continuing (and occasionally dramatic) indictment of ethnocentrism. The decision to favor applications of what is written here to American education is intended less to overthrow disciplinary tradition than it is to recognize the critical need for informed questioning of educational policies and practices in our society. It is also meant to assert the absolute relevance of anthropology — its concepts, perspective, and ways of knowing — to such questioning.

The questions that need constant raising in American education today are not only those which probe new areas of knowledge. They include questions that compromise (and perhaps bully) *conventional* explanation of educational phenomena. Our objective should be clarity in what we do know as well as minds opened to what is not yet known, to what we need to know, and to alternative ways of knowing. Much of the stated rationale for educational policies and practices in America, accounting even for local variation, suffices as its own, best explanation; and much of what we say we are doing is, as a result, inarticulate. Moreover, much of what we say we are doing, we are not doing — the credibility gap. No matter, because a generous part of what we are in fact doing with, and to, children in our schools stands as our major reason for continuing to do it. And much of what is happening in American public education, as a result, does victimize children — particularly those who differ from the American model child generalized throughout public schools.

Many established goals, procedures, and remedies in public education thereby escape serious questioning. They are, as a hidden structure, energized by a system of values that influences even the process of asking questions. Improvements in appearance may little affect underlying structure; questioning educational policies and practices for their improvement or modification, may be to question the wrong things, if not in effect to ask the wrong questions. It is a notorious tendency for fresh points of view, novel solutions, and marvelously complicated analyses to trumpet old structure. The more things change in American education, the more indeed they seem to remain the same.

Less a mission to reduce or redress the balance of ethnocentrism, anthropology can be seen as a science of human alternatives. It can be taken to be the systematic study of *humanly* different ways of being Man. This argues that anthropology is unusually gifted in elaborating alternatives, which is as much as to say that anthropology is disposed to feel few constraints on what it asks, of whom, and where — and fewer still upon the array of solutions to human problems it generates. The latter, positive experience has its negative aspects. Anthropology has a deserved reputation for being inconclusive, if not exasperatingly vague, on specific solutions to specific human problems. This is a direct occupational hazard, and its occasion in anthropology and education is quite regular.

Anthropology and education, as the meeting of two professions, ideally are concerned equally with problem-finding and problem-solving. To those who are less than familiar with anthropology, including most working educators, anthropology is assumed to be a bank of data (and, somewhere, a special drawer of understandings) so comprehensive and sure that it is uniquely suited to problem-solving. Yet the discipline, by the imperatives of its logic, tends toward problem-finding; further, *it* assumes education for the most part to stress problem-solving. It is also inclined to believe education, as a profession, is not fully capable of identifying its "true" problems, that is, of "seeing" these in the broader context of sociocultural process.

If anthropology and education are indeed to maintain a balanced interest in both finding and solving problems, these dispositions need to be altered. How the child of "Z" tribe learns and is taught is not always relevant to contemporary American education. Schoolchildren who are "culturally" different, on the other hand, are not in every case best understood as alien, as being so different as to be more remnants of obscure tribal histories than as American citizens, or as mysteries only an anthropologist can fathom. To be effective, anthropology and education must together develop lines of inquiry and open routes to problem-solving that neither compromise the main interests of their parent professional bodies nor bypass areas of greatest benefit to teachers and learners — the chief beneficiaries of the activity of anthropology and education.

This book tests the present and future limits to what anthropology *can*, or *could*, supply as solutions to educational problems, general and specific. At the same time it indicates the kinds of problems anthropologists seek in educational settings or transactions and those the authors here, at least, have found. It follows that the book is intended as much for educators as it is for anthropologists, if the problematic aspects of education variously treated here are as important to them as are matters parochial to education.

That understood, it is well to add that a view of education as a social problem impels this book as does nothing else, and accounts for its title. Some issues in education are plain to see; others are less obvious. Some are continuous; others are transient or peculiar to localities. Most respond finally to the public sense of what is happening in schools, or of what should be. And it is changes in social life and its condition — rapid changes — that assist issues to the crisis levels some today occupy. The surging interest in the *technological* relevance of schools and schoolwork, commonly dated to the event of Sputnik, has now diminished before present concerns about both the *social costs of technology* and drives for more equitable distribution of American resources among her peoples, including opportunities for quality in the lives of American minorities: Chicano, poor white, black, American Indian, female, and the rest.

During this recent social movement, whether contemporary American education is "helping" or "hurting" has been persistently questioned. Are our schools, in form or in function, relevant? Is public education any longer a critical item in resolving social ills, or has it become part of the problem? Do we retain our educational apparatus, or are we *seriously* to consider alternative approaches to teaching and learning — "voucher" systems, private academies, elaborate extensions of home learning, "open" classrooms, and "free" universities?

True, American public education has been uncovering some of its more outrageous technical defects, professional incompetencies, and structural faults. It is in fact more aware of its role in promoting inequitable distributions of resources, education itself being one of the most basic. Public education is now vulnerable to communities of "have nots" as well as to organized interest groups of the "haves." Yet, the measure of such changes is still that of established perceptions of the "school as a socializing agency," and of the teaching and learning experience as a formal transaction. In the crucial middle years of public schooling, midway between innovative preschool programs and increasingly liberated higher education, the old structure stands pat at the point where normative testing regularly discloses awesome deficiencies in the rates of achievement by large groups of American schoolchildren.

It can be argued that only appearances have changed, just as it can be said that by firing up both ends of the career of the American schoolchild, the middle will inevitably change. In neither case, however, is there convincing evidence of the restructuring due American public education, of a meaningful shift in the traditional values that underlie it. No "outside" profession can claim to have constructed a new, and more viable, educational structure; nor can anyone point with demonstrable certainty to educational processes that are truly alternative to those current in our schools. The disciplines — anthropology included — are brutalized themselves by the *same* educational conventions several contend they are, in part, working to abuse.

What is to be gained, then, from the activity of anthropology and education, accepting that its main efforts are directed to American education and to providing practical solutions to educational problems, general and specific, even as these problems or issues are variously defined by anthropology and by education? How are anthropology and education able to benefit teachers and learners? And how are they, finally, to effect meaningful change, which is to say, in what ways can they help resolve those problems or issues which have reached crisis levels?

In three ways: by informing educational problem-solvers and policymakers; by urging upon teachers and learners a sense of human alternatives, a respect for the dignity of human difference, and a willingness to engage alternatives; and by questioning — by acting as a sort of guerrilla humanism even while performing as the science of *the ways Man becomes human* (we borrow the phrase from Jerome Bruner) — will anthropology and education live up to their potential. Much of that potential is elusive, like any; the larger part of it is represented by a kind of public faith in what all the academic professions will some day accomplish.

It is to deserve that faith, to capture some of the potential of anthropology and education, and to better prepare both anthropologists and educators for decisive action on *their* opportunities to match potential with humane accomplishment, that this book has been made available.

ACKNOWLEDGMENTS

A number of persons directly or indirectly assisted the preparation of this book. Of these, Helen Hardy, and, as well, Sally Ganswich, Sue Gilman, and Dawn Reynolds are due special mention. Their generous share of the work and continuing interest in the development of the book is here gratefully acknowledged.

CONTENTS

xiii

CULTURAL RELEVANCE
AND EDUCATIONAL ISSUES

PART ONE

ANTHROPOLOGY AND EDUCATION: SOME RELATIONSHIPS

The usual relationship between anthropology and education centers about the concept "culture." "Culture" refers to behavior; the concept is an organization of ideas about the phenomena of patterned, socially learned behavior among animal species, including man, which is transmitted through generations. Culture is expressed both as the set of patterned, socially learned behaviors distinctive of a human (or other animal) group and as the continuous influence of patterned, socially learned behaviors upon involuntary (or instinctual) behavior, upon social proceeding, altogether, and upon particular human interactions, such as relations between man and his environment. In the latter sense, culture is adjectival, and we speak of cultural change, cultural ways of doing this or that, and of cultural beliefs. In the former expression, culture is the distinctive *complex* of beliefs, ways of doing things, and, but not exclusively, social arrangements which serves to differentiate one human group from another; thus we refer to the culture of "Z" tribe, or to "Z" culture.

The two uses of the concept occur mainly in description. Occasionally they merge. Culture conflict, for example, sometimes refers to observable oppositions of sets of patterned, socially learned behaviors, such as an African desert tribesman might experience were he to reside in Japanese society for a prolonged period. At other times, culture conflict relates the personal, group, or institutional *distress* in being subject to differing and often contradictory behavior influences, such as those encountered at home and in school, in the case of many American schoolchildren. The two uses of the concept "culture" are in some instances so close in practice as to be one general application, the assumption being that distinctive sets of patterned, socially learned behaviors by definition comprise con-

1

tinuous influences upon human action, especially in terms of human organization and meaning.

The relationship between anthropology and education is not constrained to the concept culture, central as that usually is. Other concepts — including learning, role, age-grading, perception, and social structure — are variously emphasized in the common interests of anthropology and education, which, after all, relate as intellectual activity. Both anthropology and education are professions; each is a disciplined attempt to apply a body of knowledge and understandings to either self-defined tasks meant to accumulate or revise knowledge and understanding, or to the natural world of phenomena itself. Each profession is prepared to "see" the extension of "its" knowledge and understanding as a product mainly of "its" way of "knowing," called — sometimes casually — "method."

The two professions relate in "seeing" many of the same phenomena; further, each of their ways of "knowing" involves approaches to human learning. To the degree that anthropology and education are occupied by the same or similar problems, Mrs. Cazden, here, identifies the joint interests of the two disciplines in matters of language and systems of speech, while Miss Mead discusses the sociocultural context of formal educational structure in seeking credible directions for future secondary education.

While Mr. Musgrove's account utilizes the concept "culture" as it refers to distinctive sets of patterned, socially learned behavior in drawing relationships between anthropology and education, Mr. Gearing, in his article, stresses the utility of the concept "culture" as it expresses behavioral influences, especially those which sensitize us to the dignity of human difference. Mr. Herskovits supplies definition to processes fundamental to the articulation of anthropology and education. In doing so, he elaborates relationships between the two professions, whose historical involvement is discussed in Mr. Spindler's overview.

1

In posing the question, Why Indians? Gearing is as much asking, Why anthropology? His response is uncompromisingly direct: whatever we know and can come to understand about others is in effect knowledge and understanding of ourselves, especially because we are ultimately defined by others. The anthropological experience, Gearing urges, informs at the same time as it sensitizes. Human behavior — however odd, bizarre, or dissimilar from our own — is at least meaningful to those whose behavior it is. The potential of anthropological study is that such behavior can become as meaningful to all who observe or otherwise engage it. The odd, bizarre, and dissimilar can become, as Gearing phrases it, the "humanly believable," no small accomplishment when, within the confines of our own society, fellow citizens are second-class, "disadvantaged," inadequately motivated — everything, in short, but "believable," everything but what we are. The meaning that emerges from "human believability" questions that definition. It raises a dignity to human difference. A sense of that dignity, Gearing suggests, is what humanizes us; thus we profit from the study of others — Indians or Pago Pago. Mr. Gearing's most recent book is The Face of the Fox. *He is currently Professor of Anthropology, State University of New York at Buffalo.*

FREDERICK O. GEARING

Why Indians?

I like American Indians, it happens, and that creates a certain handicap in pursuit of the current purpose. Liking something is a nice but rather trivial reason for suggesting that students study it, at least during the already crowded school day. The purpose here is to suggest that nontrivial, fully serious educational profit can be realized in the schools through the study of Indian communities, past and present. The case could perhaps be made more compellingly by an anthropologist who knows Indian life and finds that life personally unattractive. (Of which anthropologists there are, contrary to public myth, many; furthermore, to be such an anthropologist is quite respectable.)

Why Indians? I shall put the question in this form: What serious educational profits would accrue to a student who, after study, does not find Indian life especially attractive or fascinating or even interesting in and of itself?

From *Social Education*, vol. 32, no. 2 (February 1968), pp. 128–131; 146. Reprinted by permission of the author and publisher.

3

North American Indians form, of course, a highly varied array of communities. Southwestern groups are best known to most and include farmers settled in tightly knit villages, as the Zuni, and include other groups, nomadic and seminomadic, who once lived by hunting and gathering and by raiding. Along the northwest coast, from southern Alaska to northern California, is another array of Indian communities which, as the Kwakiutl, were blessed by bountiful nature (in the form of salmon, mainly) to the degree that they spent a good deal of their time gathering quite useless surplus wealth and giving it away in a stylized, often arrogant way. Southward from that area and into the desert interior lived the economic opposites of the northwestern groups, the very poor, as the Paiutes, whose lives often were an unceasing struggle for survival, so much so that their various cultures seemed to include virtually any practice that would help keep body and soul together. Through the entire eastern half of the continent, from Florida into the far northern interior of Canada, lived a very large array of groups — those of the Great Lakes were gardeners and hunters, and those north of there solely hunters. The Eskimos covered the entire northern fringe of the continent. Finally, after the coming of Europeans and the horse, there occurred a cultural explosion of sorts which resulted in the creation, overnight as it were, of the horse-and-buffalo cultures of the High Plains, as among the famous Dakotas (Sioux) and Cheyenne. All these peoples spoke over 150 mutually unintelligible languages which fall into five large language families. Among these peoples are found all the basic forms of human kinship organizations, a welter of forms of political organization, a wide variety of religious belief and ritual.

It of course follows: one does not in the schools "study Indians," but one may study some selected group of Indians. For serious educational purposes, it does not matter which, provided only that decent materials are available.

Such materials are becoming more readily available. For example, a recently published annotated bibliography gives as a sampler an outstanding group of books on North American Indians [1] — a survey book, a volume of illustrations and descriptions of two cultures within the area (respectively, *Red Man's America* by Ruth M. Underhill; *The American Indian* by Oliver LaFarge; *The Great Tree and the Longhouse* by Hazel W. Hertzberg; *The Ten Grandmothers* and *Kiowa Years*, both by Alice Marriott).

The serious educational profits to be gained from such study are, I judge, two. First, a proper study of an Indian community will permit a student to recognize that *any culturally patterned behavior, however bizarre it may at first appear, at bottom makes plausible sense, is believable*

---

[1] "Two Dozen Anthropology Books" by Kurt W. Johnson. Available from Anthropology Curriculum Study Project, 5632 Kimbark Avenue, Chicago, Illinois 60637.

and fully human (not personally attractive, necessarily, nor "good," necessarily, but humanly believable).

Educated men, perhaps misled by what they take anthropologists to have said, have become too much preoccupied as to whether one is sufficiently accepting or respectful of an alien culture he might encounter. There is some question as to what one can do about those things; good intent and will power go only so far. A better objective for the schools would seem to be firmly to implant in student minds the working assumption that culturally patterned behavior makes sense, and that any such behavior becomes believable to any man if he knows enough about it. Then, in some future real encounter across cultural boundaries, when an item of behavior is paraded which appears bizarre, or inscrutable (and this is inevitable), a bell should ring in the observer's head which means, quite simply: What don't I know? The first answers will be questions and these may be highly various; and no adequate final answer may be forthcoming, then or ever. But the mind-saving result follows in any case. The observer says, "The behavior appears to me bizarre, because there is something I don't know." He is at least, answer or not, set to looking. He will say to himself, "I wonder why those people are doing that," rather than saying, "Look at those crazy people." This shrunken world would perhaps be a bit less riskful were the concrete visceral recognition more widely spread that culturally patterned behavior at bottom makes human sense.

It is the overwhelming anthropological experience that culturally patterned bizarre behavior does in the end make sense. It is also the anthropological experience that, when men keep looking and look well, respect and the like tend to follow; in any event, it is then and not before that thinking men are able meaningfully to ask whether that behavior is "good."

The proper classroom study of any Indian community can provide serious educational profit. Given materials that are adequate, bizarre Indian behavior will inevitably be paraded and, as the study moves forward and additional facts come under scrutiny, some of that bizarre behavior will come to make sense, will be revealed to the student as humanly believable.

An example: Among many Eskimo groups (and among Paiutes as well), very old people are simply abandoned by their sons, or those old people voluntarily walk off into the cold and soon freeze or they ask their sons to strangle them. All these things are not rare but very common. At best such behavior seems to us so bizarre as to be beyond the pale of normal behavior. It perhaps helps one somewhat to take note of the extreme harshness of the Eskimo environment, of the very large demands made by that environment on sheer physical stamina, and thereby to note that Eskimos have, after all, little choice. It perhaps helps somewhat more to note that the question is not simply whether the old will live for a while longer. Rather, the question would concretely appear to a young adult, who is son to his aged parent but simultaneously father to his own young child, in this form: whether the old parent and the young child will live some short while, or whether the old parent will die now and the young child have a chance, at least, to live to maturity. Now, of course, the problem is recognizable as not merely a matter of necessity or utility, but also as a moral dilemma which demands a difficult and highly moral choice. Even so, the behavior — the killing or abandonment or suicide of the old people — seems at best, to an alien observer, hardly humanly tolerable; one cannot quite say, "Yes, knowing all these things I can imagine myself an Eskimo and can imagine myself, faced with that real choice, doing what I see Eskimos doing." However, the mind of the observer is additionally helped over this very difficult intellectual hurdle by still further information, by some brief glimpse into the mind of the old man himself. Humans unlike other animals, remember and anticipate; a human career is in some large measure memories and anticipations. Out of this can emerge a quietude, surprising perhaps but humanly compelling, in the face of the inevitable end. The Eskimo writer of the following poem knows he will quite soon walk off into the cold.

1.

Often I return
To my little song.
And patiently I hum it
Above the fishing hole
In the ice.
This simple little song
I can keep on humming.
I, who else too quickly
Tire when fishing —
Up the stream.

2.

Cold blows the wind
Where I stand on the ice,
I am not long in giving up!
When I get home
With a catch that does not suffice,
I usually say
It was the fish
That failed —
Up the stream.

3.

And yet, glorious is it
To roam

The river's snow-soft ice
As long as my legs care.
Alas! My life has now glided
Far from the wide views of the peaks
Deep down into the vale of age —
Up the stream.

4.

If I go hunting the land beasts,
Or if I try to fish,
Quickly I fall to my knees,
Stricken with faintness.
Never again shall I feel
The wildness of strength,
When on an errand I go over the land
From my house and those I provide for —
Up the stream.

5.

A worn-out man, that's all,
A fisher, who ever without luck
Makes holes in river or lake ice
Where no trout will bite.

6.

But life itself is still
So full of goading excitement!
I alone,
I have only my song,
Though it too is slipping from me.

7.

For I am merely
Quite an ordinary hunter,
Who never inherited song
From the twittering birds of the sky.[2]

I have cheaply tricked the reader, it is evident. I set out to show that serious educational profit accrues, as I said, "to a student who, after study, does not find Indian life especially attractive or fascinating or even interesting in and of itself." And to that purpose I have cited a bit of human drama which cannot but grip one.

I now move to more bland, even "academic," facets of Indian life. Two examples are drawn from earlier Cherokee life: A Cherokee addresses a dozen or so specified male kinsmen, including his father, by a single term roughly translatable as "father" and some of these "fathers" may be a generation younger than he, others his own age, others much older; he

---

2 Paul Radin, "The Literature of Primitive Peoples," in *Diogenes* (Number 12, Winter 1955).

addresses another dozen kinsmen, including some as old as his grandfather or others as young as his grandson, as "brother"; there are other such bizarre uses of kinship terms. These are, it should be noted, in no sense figurative extensions of kinship terms, but are the sole proper modes of address of these specified kinsmen. These facts do not come to make sense simply by learning that such are Cherokee customs; rather they make sense by putting those facts of customary usage together with other similar facts and by recognizing the systematic logic of the whole. The kinship usages at hand are transformed for the observer from the apparently bizarre to the eminently logical when it is recognized that Cherokee life is organized around an array of matrilineal kin groups. Every Cherokee automatically joins, at birth, the kin group of his or her mother; a man must marry outside his own (his mother's) kin group, and he usually resides, after marriage, with his wife's kin group; nevertheless he remains a member of his own kin group throughout his life. Most critically, all *these matrilineal kin groups act like corporations*: for example, land is owned by these corporate groups, and the rights to use land are passed from female to female within the kin group, thus a married man helps work gardens on his wife's land and lives off that produce; similarly, these kin groups act like corporate individuals in political life, thus when political decisions are to be made a married man leaves his wife's group for the moment and joins fellow males in his own kin group, and that group tries to arrive at a corporate opinion about the matter at hand. In general, in everyday life each Cherokee "sees" his community as a set of such "lines," matrilineal groups which in many critical realms act like corporate individuals; of course his welfare is variously affected by the actions of these groups, his own, his wife's, and others. The logic of those "fathers" is by these comments but dimly suggested.

Similarly, a second example: Cherokees once encouraged young men to go on the warpath and gave them formal honors for their noteworthy deeds at war; at the same time, they held the more successful warriors at arm's length and actively disliked many of them. This evident inconsistency similarly makes human sense, not merely because it was Cherokee custom. Rather, Cherokees placed very high moral value on extremely unaggressive behavior inside the group (for example, most kinds of political decisions were made unanimously or not at all), and, generally, the men who parcipitated out as the best warriors were temperamentally a bit "pushy" at home and so — by these severe Cherokee moral standards — were immoral men.

These Eskimo and Cherokee facts are of little or no importance in and of themselves, and it matters little whether the student finds them fascinating or whether he, for whatever reason, feels drawn to such a pattern of life. What matters is that the student repeatedly experience the transformation of the bizarre into the humanly believable. This is done by encountering bizarre behavior, then seeking additional information, and finally recognizing the ultimate sense of the no-longer-bizarre behavior first encountered. And what matters even more is the resulting visceral belief that, a priori, bizarre, culturally patterned behavior is, whether comprehended or not in any particular instance, humanly believable if and when knowledge is complete. Perhaps, with such a mental set, one can live in a profoundly heterogeneous nation and world in some measure of comfort and with some measure of effectiveness.

The proper study of an Indian community can yield a second serious profit. Such a study can powerfully *help a student to see well — accurately and in some measure of completeness — the social world immediately around him,* his own social world which is often too familiar to quite see. To study Indians is, through comparison, to see ourselves.

Other social science disciplines work in the classroom under a handicap; these other disciplines are in the position of trying, as the saying goes, to teach a fish about water. The anthropological impulse is to toss the fish onto the bank and there to instruct it some brief while about sand and dirt and dry leaves, and ultimately about oxygen. The anthropological faith is that a thinking fish, returned to the stream, would thereafter perceive water differently and better and would, indeed, be then better prepared for serious instruction, by anyone so inclined, about water, oxygen, gills.

The overriding purpose of the social sciences in the schools is to help students to see well. To this task, we are saying, anthropology brings especially the crucial heuristic device of comparison. It seems to be an unyielding and probably neurologically based fact that men perceive best through comparison and that the broader and more varied comparison, the more nearly adequate the perception becomes. Comparison assists powerfully in unclouding the senses. Thus, anthropologists do most literally insist that a student cannot adequately "see" pricing mechanisms in a market economy until he has looked also at pricing mechanisms in a non-market setting where the exchange price appears, superficially, to be firmly established by traditional usage; that a student cannot adequately see the flow of political influence through impersonal mass media and legislatures until he has also watched influence flow through a community-wide network established by some configuration of kinship relations; that a student cannot see status mobility until he also looked closely at communities where the sole "mobility" is to move from the status of infant to that of ancestor; that, generally, a student cannot see his own very big society until he has also viewed some array of very little societies.

Broad and varied comparison has hardly found its way into social sciences curricula in the schools. Curricular strategy could, to much profit, be exactly reversed and take the position that all junctures in curricula where broad comparison is not explicitly exploited would have to be specially justified.

The study of any Indian community provides just such dramatic comparison in the realm of economics, politics, social organization, subject only to the availability of adequate and appropriate materials. In several Plains groups a man gains stature by giving things to the point of rendering himself (and his family) virtually destitute; this could bring to a student a fresh perception of America's wealth-and-status system which might otherwise be too familiar and "natural" to see clearly. Many Indian communities, as we saw with Cherokees, make certain kinds of political decisions unanimously or not at all; perceiving this comparison acts to reduce, to some profit, the sense of contrast between modern liberal democracies and other more centralized systems, since both, in comparison, seem a bit "hard" on the dissenting few. And so on.

Two special applications of such comparison can be briefly named. First, where classrooms are markedly heterogeneous in respect to race and economic class and where there is, in the minds of the students, some anxiety about that heterogeneity: Indian studies, especially drawn so as to focus the student's attention on realms of experience which particularly "matter" to him (variously, according to his age, as the host of new "rules" in the classroom and on the playground must mystify and deeply bother a kindergarten or first-grade child), can be made to serve as a useful stimulus to cause the members of the class to look newly into their own diverse parallel experience (as to "rules" at home and in the neighborhood and now at school, for example) at first severally then perhaps collectively. Members of the class can frequently in such a context "triangulate," each with the alien culture and with his fellow's and with his own. This is especially useful in that, not only does the comparison cause students to see familiar things newly, in fresh perspective, but also the student is left to ponder privately or to discuss publicly, at his discretion, whatever he thinks he has seen in his own experience or in that of his fellows. In heterogeneous classes where heterogeneity itself seems to the students especially touchy, this "third culture" strategy is perhaps the only way to get the students to think afresh about themselves and each other.

A second application can be made in respect to realms of self-realization which are particularly bothersome to students. Materials which depict an array of diverse cultural handlings of such realms provide a measure of detachment which may in turn help the student resolve such a matter adequately for himself. Study of a variety of Indian patterns of restraint on sexuality would be an example; these range from great liberality to restraints of unusual severity. Adolescent students go into "sex education" classes with one over-riding question, and that question is the only one *not* answered. The question of course is, "Shall I? or shall I not?" A cross-cultural study doesn't answer the question, but it may help the student better to see in non-trivial terms the nature of the quesion and why he is asking it. Which is, at bottom, what a liberal education is about.

It should, finally, be noted: a class would not, as a rule, elect to pursue the first objective *or* the second, but both simultaneously. Time in the classroom is always at a premium. The study in some breadth and depth of one or two specific Indian communities gives the student much more than would some broad survey of equal duration of some single facet of the life of many Indian communities. The bizarre emerges frequently in in-depth studies and only in such studies is there chance that the bizarre will be transformed into the humanly believable. At the same time, in such in-depth studies, comparison will have a chance, in planned and unforeseen ways, to work its magic.

The thoughtful reader will have by now asked: Would not the Pago Pago serve as well? The answer is: Yes.

FURTHER READINGS

Gearing, Frederick O. *The face of the Fox.* Chicago: Aldine, 1970.
Gruber, Frederick C. (ed.) *Anthropology and education.* The Martin G. Brumbaugh Lectures, Fifth Series. Philadelphia: University of Pennsylvania Press, 1961.
Montagu, Ashley. *Education and human relations.* New York: Grove Press, 1958.
Opler, Morris. "Cultural alternatives and educational theory." *Harvard Educational Review,* vol. 17 (1947).
Sady, Rachel R. *Perspectives from anthropology.* New York: Teachers College Press, 1969.

2

Musgrove declares that the "teacher's first business is to be aware of the nature and assumptions of his own culture, and then to understand where and how it differs from that of his pupils." He is in essence arguing for the combined in-depth and comparative study of human behavior promoted as a classroom learning experience by Gearing, in the previous article. The patterned behavioral differences caught in detail by Musgrove may appear to be more extreme than those which ordinarily obtain in the classrooms and schools with which we are familiar. The differences he describes and analyzes do operate to some extent in all teaching and learning experiences.

The apparent extremity of those differences, here, does not distort and should not dissuade us from Musgrove's key points: that the "nature and assumptions" of one's culturally patterned behavior influence, directly or indirectly, one's instructional performance or administrative view or both, and that cultural difference affects learner response likewise. Mr. Musgrove was formerly associated with the (then-called) Colonial Education Service, Uganda, and is presently engaged in educational research and writing. He recently coauthored, with Philip H. Taylor, Society and the Teacher's Role *(New York: Humanities Press, 1969).*

FRANK MUSGROVE

Education and the Culture Concept

Two Cultures in Uganda

The culture concept carries many implications for the educationist which have still to be worked out. Perhaps its greatest value will prove to lie in providing a corrective to the intellectualist fallacy to which teachers and educationists are singularly prone. By taking into account the complex and largely non-intellectual processes of acculturation, the teacher in Africa will realize that he is unlikely to effect a direct transference of intellectual propositions and idea-systems; and he may be saved from disappointment when he sees the truths he has dealt in employed to subserve "illegitimate" ends.

Even when we attempt to maintain in our schools an "African bias" in the curriculum, inevitably we present our pupils with an alien culture. Regularity and punctuality are given a high valuation in the school: it is made clear that pupils are expected to reach lessons, games, and meals at the times laid down, and that compliance with these rules is an important virtue. In the school a boy is expected to behave with consideration to others who are not of his clan or tribe: if a Mutoro steals a shirt it is no excuse that it belonged to a Mukiga. Pupils are acquainted with the idea that they have a moral obligation towards all peoples irrespective of tribe and nationality, and that anti-social behaviour is not excusable because it benefited one's family: that there are loyalties wider even than the clan. (Most of my pupils in Uganda regard the work of the policeman as befitting only the most unscrupulous and unprincipled since, in the interests of the community as a whole, he may have to take to prison his mother, father,

From: *Africa*, vol. 23, no. 2 (London: International African Institute, April 1953), pp. 110–123. Reprinted by permission of the author and publisher.

or other close relative.) And further, except in our religious teaching, we assume that events in nature and society can be attributed adequately to "natural" causes. No matter how "African" we make our subjects, these three traits of an unfamiliar culture will normally confront the African at school.

Teaching in a Uganda secondary school, I have found that the intellectual demonstration of a proposition is not necessarily enough to convince my pupils if it is out of harmony with their culture. They can understand the explanation but they have not become persuaded of its truth. In an English school there is no need to teach the great majority of children that the earth is round; even the junior child already knows, and from an early age would have suffered ridicule from its elders by suggesting otherwise. But it does not know this truth in the sense that it has reached a logical conclusion from a consideration of the evidence. The teacher in England has no problem of convincing a child; he will merely give additional evidence to support what the child already accepts. In Uganda, the teacher's task has not been partially accomplished by social suggestion; his pupils, before coming to school, would probably have incurred the ridicule of parents and venerable village elders if they had maintained what the teacher is now trying to tell them. (Many of my boys have told me about arguments they have had during the holidays with uneducated relatives about the shape of the earth.) And when scientific evidence has been given to the child, because the new proposition does not receive general social approval, and because it is not in harmony with many other pre-school accounts of natural phenomena, it often remains unreal.

In England a teacher — at least below the Sixth Form — merely elaborates and explains an already accepted culture; but among the tribes of Uganda he is justifying the novel notions of a new one. He himself may not always be aware of the assumptions he is making: he has been stamped by what Leonard Woolf called (in *After the Deluge*) his "civilization," "the mould or matrix in which at any particular place or time a human community imposes upon individual lives an imprint or form." He has accepted, chiefly through social suggestion, the "communal psychology" (to use Mr. Woolf's phrase), and does not have to be convinced by logical argument of the validity of the major concepts which constitute that psychology.

Leonard Woolf distinguished three main elements in the communal psychology of the British people which were fashioned by the events and pronouncements of the American and French Revolutions — the ideas of liberty, democracy, and nationality. The peoples of Uganda have experienced nothing analogous to the American and French Revolutions; and I have found my pupils unable to understand these three ideas which, with their wealth of undertones, associations, and connotations, are part of the social inheritance of an English child. After making a study of their conception of liberty, I am struck by its similarity to that of Hobbes. Even with middle school and senior boys, who are acquainted with the main trends of British parliamentary history, with the American Revolution, and the extension of representative and responsible government in the Empire in the nineteenth century, the idea of liberty has not been engrafted with the need for the franchise. As with Hobbes, freedom is chiefly freedom from physical restraint, a condition of physical peace and repose. (It has, however, a second important element, freedom from the presence of the white man.) Senior boys preparing for the School Certificate have written for me as follows on the subject of liberty:

1. "Liberty is freedom from all kinds of work which keep our bodies busy."
2. "Liberty is the contrary of enslavement and imprisonment."
3. "Liberty is the absence of fighting and quarrelling. If you want liberty in your village you must send away quarrelsome people." (Over 80 per cent of the boys mention this aspect of liberty. Some draw the further conclusion that British rule serves true liberty by bringing protection and peace.)
4. "Liberty is freedom from rules." Cf. Hobbes: the greatest liberty depends upon the "silence of the law."
5. "Liberty is freedom from work under supervision." (When boys write: "Our liberty will come" they are referring not to the day of national self-government, but to the day of leaving school with its regulations and routine.)
6. "In England there is no liberty because England is so seldom at peace."
7. "Liberty is freedom from work and from prison." (I have been asked by a senior and highly intelligent boy: "Are there no free men in England?" meaning: "Are there no men not tied to regular employment?")

Like the peoples of central Africa today, the society of mid-seventeenth-century England had an immediate historical background of insecurity, fear, anarchy, and arbitrary rule. My pupils know, with a great wealth of circumstantial detail, of the capricious tyranny of Kabarega of Bunyoro and Mwanga of Buganda (one boy claims that his grandfather was mutilated and killed for the entertainment of Mwanga), of the anarchy caused by inter-tribal wars and by the Arab slave trade; just as young English Puritans were nurtured, in the 1650s, on stories of Stuart oppression and perfidy and civil strife. A Protectorate was appropriate to the England of the 1650s; and for substantially the same reasons my pupils see the benefits a Protectorate in Uganda today. They make a very sharp distinction between a Protectorate and other forms of imperial possession such as a Crown Colony; they are deeply conscious of their status as protected persons; and they see it as the only valid ground of their political obligation.

With historical backgrounds in many ways similar, my pupils are at one with Hobbes in regarding liberty as the opposite of anarchy, of "war of everyman against everyman," and as consisting in subjection to an authority which can ensure peace: "In the act of our submission consisteth both our obligation and our liberty" (*Leviathan*); and in the manner of Hobbes — who was able to argue that even liberty and fear are consistent — they do not extend the idea of liberty far beyond the idea of corporal freedom. Their view of rights and obligations is essentially contractual in the characteristic idiom of seventeenth-century political thought. For boys in Uganda, as for seventeenth-century philosophers, rights are not self-evident attributes of humanity, they are a function of contract. The Uganda Agreements, the bargain between ruler and ruled, are invoked in any justification of rights. The Uganda Agreement is generally held to be a fraud, the unscrupulous trickery of naïve by more sophisticated people (and thus a warning to Native peoples to reach a high standard of education so as to make impossible any such fraudulent dealings in the future); but it is still the basis of argument; they do not say: it is irrelevant, scrap it, we have inalienable rights anyway. They say: revise it.

It is the historical experience of their own peoples which shapes the ideas of my pupils, and the facts of the Arab slave trade are by far the most influential in shaping their idea of liberty. In argument they will always refer to these historical facts, but they regard the eighteenth-century American debate about representation, the programme of the Chartists and the activities of the twentieth-century Suffragettes as unnecessary fuss over a matter of little importance. The vote as an attribute of liberty has no place within their culture; but while they cannot enter into the Chartists' enthusiasm for the franchise, they can appreciate the agrarian programme of Feargus O'Connor as making a more effective provision for real freedom — the personal and corporal liberty of the individual.

Culture is a deposit of history, the values accepted without argument after the debates of earlier generations. Paine in the 1790s still had to argue about the worth of the franchise and to justify it against "pure democracy"; but by 1869, as Matthew Arnold complained, "the blessedness of the franchise" was undisputed and valued far above sweetness and light. For Mrs. Pankhurst and her followers it was self-evident that the vote was the prerequisite of liberty. My pupils have received the impress of no such historical deposit as that which reaches an English child; they need argument to convince them that the vote is valuable.

Similarly we present to students in Uganda an unfamiliar concept in nationality. Our teaching of modern history, our very terminology, presupposes an understanding of the nature of the nation-state. My pupils, who are Batoro, Banyoro, Baganda, Bakiga, Bamba, and Bakonjo (with small minorities of more distant foreigners such as Lugbara and Badama), are quite clear that the group which commands their over-riding loyalty is their tribe, and not the wider group from which the Government of Uganda claims allegiance. Two boys from the Belgian Ruanda are no more foreigners than two boys from the Uganda province of the West Nile. The fusion of the nation and the state, which has been the great European achievement of the past five centuries, has produced an institution whose coherence, whose "ethical idea," is largely incomprehensible to African boys. They are deeply puzzled over the unifying principle which embraces the linguistic differences of Switzerland, the racial differences of the U.S.A. and even the local differences of Great Britain. Their sympathies are always on the side of political fragmentation: they ask, Why should not Scotland and Wales be independent countries? They cannot appreciate, in the history lesson, the compulsions which drove Canada to unity in 1841 and to federation in 1867, and Australia to federation in 1901; they certainly feel no sentiment which calls for expression in a wider political unit in East Africa.

Nor has their indigenous history deposited upon them a belief in the equality of man. The Babito, the clan which supplies the Bakama of Toro and Bunyoro, are clearly, to my Batoro and Banyoro pupils, people of superior station, though economically and politically (they are not necessarily, or even frequently, chiefs) the majority have no basis of social power. My Banyankole students who are Bairu, descendants of the indigenous Bantu peasant cultivators, show a similar respect for the aristocratic, cattle-owning Bahima, even though the latter are not necessarily richer than themselves and are now failing to obtain the more important chieftainships in Ankole. My pupils are shocked to hear of modern British methods of redistributing national income, which they brand as "Communism." (The most reactionary western capitalist could not be more scornful than these boys of the British miner or docker, or of any British workmen who go on strike; yet this cannot be attributed to their reading only highly conservative newspapers and periodicals: their knowledge of contemporary Britain comes from a representative selection of journals in their library, from British Council publications and, occasionally, lectures and films.) They have a strong developed sense of status, of the type of work befitting rank and station. In their homes there is the sharp distinction between the work which befits a man and that which befits a woman, between the respect due to the old and mature and what is due to the young. In the school there is a sharp distinction between seniors and juniors, between school officials and non-officials; and they prize highly their status as schoolboys, educated men who will be insulted if asked to do the menial tasks of "porters" (labourers). Their "communal psychology" is very similar to that of eighteenth-century England: they accept a view of graded happiness in society, apportioned according to personal station. They reflect the contemporary upsurge of African feeling against the White, but they do not conduct their argument against the European on the grounds that they are his equals: while recognizing the superiority of the Englishman, they claim simply that he is a trespasser on their land. I have discussed the purpose of trade regulations and the competition offered to British goods by cheap and often inferior Japanese manufactures, and my pupils have replied: "Why cannot these cheap, even though inferior, goods, be allowed into Uganda? They are good enough for us Africans." The boys' outlook is that of the Englishman of the eighteenth century who accepted an unequal distribution of happiness in society, though affirming some compensation in the Hereafter.

In the natural as in the social sciences the English teacher in Uganda is presenting an alien culture. Within our own contemporary culture we readily accept the idea of "forces," gravitational and magnetic, as a sufficient explanation of natural phenomena. But it is an inherited culture concept rather than a scientific proposition recommending itself to all the members of our society on the strength of logical evidence and scientific demonstration. In an English school the existence of these forces does not have to be argued from first principles; in an African school it may. To English boys the idea is already acceptable, and the teacher simply illustrates its plausibility. Such explanations receive an unquestioning acceptance only within our own contemporary culture: we have accepted the conclusions of three centuries of debate. It was not self-evident to Descartes and many of his fellow scientists that Newton's forces provided an explanation of the movement of bodies in space or their state of rest; indeed, the former accused the latter of reintroducing occult powers which operated across space between bodies which did not touch. My African pupils, like Descartes, are sceptical about an explanation of the earth's suspension and movement in space under the influence of "forces": the majority frankly do not believe it. Like all pre-Newtonian scientists since the time of Aristotle, my pupils want the earth's movement and suspension explained in terms of physical agencies — if only air pressure — pushing and supporting. They want the proofs and evidence which Descartes demanded of Newton, but which no English schoolboy would think of demanding.

From being merely a statistical or mathematical description of events in the physical world, forces have also assumed, for people of Western society, the unquestioned validity of a culture concept in the realm of social science. The transposition of the concept of forces and the rule of natural laws into the field of social theory has probably been taken farther in American radical, than in British individualist, democracy.[1] The notion of the essential equality of individuals (each carrying an identical parcel of natural rights), of a society of qualitatively equal human atoms, has lent itself readily to a view of men behaving according to fixed and unalterable economic and psychological laws — responding, according to a set pattern, to the stimuli of advertising, broadcasting, etc. Newtonian natural science and the social philosophy of fundamental human equality are interdependent facets of our own culture, and it is unlikely that people of a different culture will feel the weight of the latter until they have accepted the former. The concepts of our natural and social sciences form a single cultural complex which probably cannot be exported in sections.

By people of our society, a man's economic circumstances are today accounted for in terms of economic forces: supply and demand, the trade cycle, terms of trade, etc. But as late as 1909 Beveridge was still on the defensive in arguing such a view of social causation, in singling out such factors, rather than individual failure and weakness, as the effective causes of poverty: "They (workers) are displaced by economic forces entirely beyond their control and taking but little or no account of personal merits" (see *Unemployment: A Problem of Industry*). Institutions were at last brought into line with the ideal element of our culture, which had been in the process of incorporating itself within the communal psychology since the age of Adam Smith and Malthus, by the National Insurance Act of 1911.[2]

My pupils are in the pre-Malthusian era of sociological thought: they have not inherited the deposit of a century and a half of economic speculation. They are not convinced of the fundamental assumption that events in nature and society happen in that way and for those reasons: they have not been persuaded of this pattern of causality. They will attribute a man's poverty either to his personal deficiencies, or, more probably, to the machinations of an enemy. But the effective causes of social circumstances are individual men, albeit, perhaps, exerting supernatural powers, operating through the essentially personal extension of magic. Malthusian forces

[1] See T. D. Weldon's analysis of American democracy in *Politics and Morals*, 1946, ch. 5.

[2] This form of cultural lag, in which appropriate institutions lag behind a change in ideas, is often as significant in the interpretation of social change as the process, given emphasis by Ogburn, in which ideas lag behind the changes in material culture and social organization. New ideas may cause tensions in, and bring about the modification of, social forms, just as changed social forms may cause a recasting of ideas — as the central thesis of Mr. Leonard Woolf amply illustrates. Ideas as causes rather than as consequences are similarly affirmed by Professor Gordon Childe: "An obsolete ideology can hamper an economy and impede its change for longer than Marxists admit" (*What Happened in History*).

do not convince them as an explanation of population trends in Uganda: they wish to explain human affairs in terms of individual human action: they maintain, against any show of evidence, a diminution of Native numbers, and the cause is held to be the conscious scheming by European men to this end.

But the culture which challenges the Uganda schoolboy is not wholly that of contemporary Britain. It is chiefly in the artificial circumstances of the History lesson that he meets the modern British ideals of liberty and equality: the European society of the territory as a whole is not necessarily stamped by the culture-traits of the parent society. Thus the social philosophy implied in the behaviour of the majority of the Europeans he knows — planters, businessmen, contractors, and even Government servants — approximates closely to his own: it is an eighteenth-century survival. Victor Murray in *The School in the Bush* (1929) drew a comparison between the social position of the British working man in the eighteenth century and that of the Bantu African today: Europeans in twentieth-century Africa fill the same social role as the upper classes of eighteenth-century England. The attitude of Bernard Mandeville, Wilberforce, and Hannah More to the poor, who, they were agreed, should receive education but not above their station, is not unlike that of even the more enlightened East African planter today. And the more articulate of the latter would probably share the eighteenth-century philosophy of Burke in regarding liberty as an "entailed inheritance."

East African pupils are confronted with the derelict items of a past culture which can survive in the colonial environment because the pressures which squeezed them out of existence in England are not felt there. No longer the dominant elements in our own communal psychology, the values of eighteenth century squirearchy can survive and thrive in the settler areas of East Africa. The professional soldier in retirement in England, maintaining a system of values profoundly out of consonance with twentieth-century social democracy, finds a congenial home in the East African highlands; even the economic individualist, the self-made man who has been fast disappearing from our own society in the past few decades, may flourish with something of his nineteenth-century splendour in the colonial world. An obsolete culture is ossified to confront the contemporary African.

Although the colony may thus tend to be the repository of a dead culture, the schools represent, with varying degrees of fidelity, the values of contemporary British society. Their most obvious cultural lag is in the sphere of religion. The historical deposit which has reached contemporary British society from the nineteenth-century mass-attack upon religion is religious scepticism and indifference. Yet my pupils in Uganda imagine that religion is as important in the lives of present-day Englishmen as it was in the lives of their nineteenth- or mid-seventeenth-century ancestors. The schoolboy in Uganda is unaware that the salvationist Balokole movement, inspired and led by European schoolmasters, is far from typical of contemporary British life, and would fit more easily into the pattern of Wesley's England. The challenge to the Uganda boy is often less severe because he is confronted with culture-survivals from a past which was nearer to his own level of development. He can understand the settler's social philosophy: it is near to his own; he is at home with a religion which draws its inspiration from a book which details the supersession of natural processes by occult forces, and which is as different from the liberal Christianity of contemporary advanced European thought as is the Christianity of Wesley (who publicly declared in 1768 that "the giving up of witchcraft is in effect giving up the Bible").

In the light of the culture concept it becomes clear that whereas in an English school a teacher illustrates truths, in Africa he must prove them. Our teaching must be in far greater depth and far more concerned with first principles. The teacher's first business is to be aware of the nature and assumptions of his own culture, and then to understand where and how it differs from that of his pupils. When talking about religion to pupils in an English school, I unconsciously made the assumption that what I had to demonstrate was the credibility of certain religious beliefs. The necessary attitude of the teacher of religion in England today is defensive, his concern to point out that some beliefs, e.g., in the resurrection, are worthy, perhaps, of the credence of an intelligent man. I have heard Englishmen address my African pupils in the same strain: they have made no allowance for the cultural difference; they have not realized that in the African situation it is probably necessary to begin from the very opposite position, and point out that there are limits to the credence we can give to the power and efficacy of spiritual and unseen forces.

When he has prepared his chart of cultural differences, the teacher is then in a position to control the contact situation. He will understand what elements in his culture are incomprehensible to his pupils, what are acceptable, and for what personal, social, and economic reasons they are acceptable.

PLAY AND IMITATION IN THE SCHOOL

The intellectual acceptance of new propositions on the strength of their logical force affords at best a partial explanation of the transfer of culture. Mimesis is probably the most important factor which the teacher in Africa must take into account. Whatever may be the estimate of the Bantu African's innate mental ability, of his high mimetic endowment there can be little doubt. It is this quality which accounts for the surprising educability of most East African peoples.[3] The tendency to imitate varies with the tribes of East Africa: the Masai of Kenya and the Bakonjo of Uganda, for example, have retained to a considerable extent their traditional habits, dress, and pursuits: they are relatively specialized to their environments, wandering pastoralists on the one hand, and mountain cultivators on the other. Cattle-keeping peoples generally, whose lives tend to be far more specialized than agriculturists', they show comparatively little interest in education. The cattle-owning Bahima of Ankole, the aristocrats and former conquerors, appear to be losing ground politically and economically to the peasant cultivators of the same district, the Bairu, who are more willing to turn from traditional pursuits in imitation of imported customs and to take advantage of educational opportunities. The peoples who have shown the greatest reluctance to imitate European ways are, significantly, comparatively little interested in schools, and in general appear to be less deeply influenced by education, when they do receive it, than, say, the Baganda or the Batoro.[4]

It is customary for Englishmen in East Africa to deride the African for aping European ways, and to charge the schools with producing "imitation-Europeans." Educationists themselves have often shared this view and have sought to keep school curricula and activities in some way "essentially African." They have failed to take advantage of the tendency in their pupils which makes them supremely educable; they have been inclined to deplore and discourage rather than to exploit the African's capacity for imitation. They have placed increasing emphasis on vernacular instruction without ascertaining whether pupils are interested in, and gain personal fulfilment from, learning the vernacular rather than English; they have revived Native legends and given the pupil old and familiar models in history and literature without attempting to discover whether his imagination in fact receives greater excitement, his outlook greater breadth and his sympathies greater depth from the study of the unfamiliar figures of a different culture; they have sought to confine geography to the African continent without considering whether Timbuktu has a greater relevance

---

[3] P. M. Synge observes: "The Baganda have shown a most unusual adaptability to modern European civilization, and a real seeking after knowledge, as I discovered at their Makerere College . . ." i.e. unusual in comparison with the peoples of Borneo and other Polynesians (*Mountains of the Moon*, 1937, p. xxiii).

[4] The Bakonjo are one of the biggest tribes in Uganda but send a very low proportion of their children to the schools (which are easily accessible to them in Toro and Bwamba). They will usually explain their indifference by saying: "We are too poor to pay school fees," but this is not convincing: the Bakonjo enjoy a high degree of prosperity, particularly those who are growing cash-crops — coffee, rice, and cotton — in Bwamba. Although four primary schools are taking an increasing number of Bakonjo, it is not clear that this reflects a genuine growth of interest in education, since the pressure brought to bear by Miruka chiefs on parents known to have money to send their children to school is considerable.

to the Mukiga of Uganda than Tientsin; they have, in some cases, introduced a tribal setting and duly expurgated tribal activities into the schools
without reflecting that their pupils might be thoroughly bored with what
was only too familiar.[5] They have failed to see that a truly "African" and
original character will emerge not by limiting the scope for imitation but
by enriching it as far as possible with a wide diversity of models.

I have endeavoured to estimate the extent, limits, and quality of mimesis among my pupils in Uganda. Although there is a considerable area of
European habit, thought, and custom which they reject, in the most fundamental aspects of education it is their tendency to imitation which makes
teaching possible. Alien western concepts in the natural and social sciences
are not necessarily accepted because of the weight of evidence which
supports them. Pupils accept novel and hitherto unsuspected truths when
they have become aware that they are the orthodoxies of the white man.
Junior boys can follow without difficulty the evidence which indicates the
earth's true shape, the account of the formation of mountains and lakes,
the explanation of lightning and thunder; but they may frankly admit
that they do not believe them. They remain convinced by the traditional
cosmology of their tribe. Senior boys in the School Certificate form have,
in general, accepted most of the new knowledge, but they have no greater
weight of evidence about these phenomena and no better intellectual
grasp of them than the juniors; they have been persuaded of their truth
or acceptability because they have become persuaded that loss of face and
falling below the standard of civilized men results from not accepting
them. What they have learnt is not the truth of propositions but more
about the characteristic idea-system of the "civilized man." They have
taken over at least part of this system, not by conscious calculation, but
through a process of thought mimesis. The essential though largely unconscious process of education lies, in fact, in revealing the ideal model
more clearly so that pupils may know what they ought to believe.

Although there is a copying of externals, particularly dress (a common
element in the dreams of my pupils is that they are resplendent at some
festivity in European-type clothes), there is little imitation of the personal
characteristics of their four English teachers. These have quite clearly
defined mannerisms of speech and gesture, but they never seem to be
"picked up" by the boys (as they are by some five- and six-year-old English
neighbours!). Mimicry [6] is at a more conscious level, and in a schoolboy

---

[5] This policy of "educational adaptations" to African conditions was the central
recommendation of the Phelps-Stokes Commission on East African Education (1924),
and has dominated the general trend of East African Education in the past quarter of a
century.

[6] Cf. L. P. Mair: "They (the Baganda) certainly love any kind of mimicry, whether
of notable village characters, animals or dramatic scenes such as a fight between two
warriors" (*An African People in the Twentieth Century*, 1934, p. 26).

concert these mannerisms will be reproduced to perfection in good-humoured ridicule. But they will be discarded afterwards. Day-to-day imitation, as opposed to stage mimicry, is not specific and detailed: even in dress it is sketchily impressionistic; and it is the most difficult problem of practical pedagogics to induce pupils to imitate precisely, to achieve accuracy and methodical layout in an exercise and to follow the model of neatness and arrangement with which the textbook and blackboard notes have made him familiar.

Imitation occurs when it is clear that the characteristics imitated are the necessary features of an ideal type of man — the educated man. Long hair has not, among the people of Uganda, become recognized as the hallmark of the intellectual, and my pupils remain close-cropped; they will ridicule an African with long hair by saying: "Your hair is like that of the *abaana bahaiguru*" (the "children of heaven" — the shaggy and generally evilly disposed inhabitants of an upper region in the religious beliefs of the Batoro). Even the cotton shirt is almost universally worn outside the trousers in the manner of the traditional robe or smock of bark cloth. It is only when they feel that they are in a situation which calls for educated manners — when paying formal visits or attending public functions — that a true imitation of the Englishman occurs and the shirt is tucked in.

In the relations between the sexes there is a similar partial adoption of western custom. Although boys will realize that they are expected to follow the rule of "ladies first," and will learn to make the most unusual gesture of offering a chair to a lady (even African), they still ridicule any display of affection between a man and a woman in public, even though they see daily the customary courtesies between Englishmen and their wives. A film in which an Englishman kisses his wife on the doorsteps of his house, in full view of the street, arouses from a schoolboy audience hoots of laughter and derision.

The view that Bantu Africans blindly and indiscriminately imitate things European needs considerable modification if my pupils may be regarded as a fairly representative sample. It is commonly believed that educated Africans are most eager to secure "European-type" employment — as clerks in offices or in the lower professional grades. This is untrue of most of my pupils. The traditional interests remain very strong: the Bahima retain a passionate interest in cattle, the Batoro remain deeply interested in cultivation, though they have no wish to follow agricultural pursuits in the school: that, they consider, is not the purpose of the school — experience of agriculture could be had far more easily and less expensively at home. The school garden is not popular. When I ask boys why they are going to take up European-type employment they answer: "In order to gain a money-income, save and get capital so that after a few years — five to ten — we can set up as farmers. It is no longer possible for us as it was for our forefathers, to do so without first enduring the slavery of office work: for our country has been made poor by Europeans who have killed our cattle with their innoculations."

Imitation of European habits has not led to an acceptance of the routine and regulated life which is accepted by our mechanized western society. The school timetable itself is a great burden — perhaps the greatest frustration which these boys feel in a school run on English lines; and the regularity of office work under the watchful authority of an Asian or European is not looked forward to with any pleasure. They wish primarily to be masterless men. They want an academic and literary education, but they want, eventually at least, to go back to the land. When they are asked "Why, then, do you want an academic education?" they find the question meaningless. It is self-evident to them that education is valuable to a person whatever may be his occupation after school.

Imitation is of a generalized, stereotyped Englishman — an historical model which has crystallized into an ideal. When boys prefer long trousers to shorts, even in the heat of the day, they are not imitating Europeans they have actually seen, for the latter predominantly wear shorts throughout the day. When they carry Bibles to church and look up and follow the lesson which is being read, they are not following the modern habits of Europeans known to them. They are imitating an historical figure whose traits have been transmitted through half a century to the present-day schoolboy — he always wore long trousers, he was essentially the literate man, he was a Christian, and he was polite and forgiving — a man known to them only through tradition, the missionary of the '80s and '90s. The schoolboy today is familiar with many Europeans, perhaps a majority, who have few or none of these characteristics. He is imitating a European he has never known, but whose ideal character is well known in his tribal society. The modern Englishman is often the exception which proves the rule for the African: "Of course he is not a true Englishman like the people in England; only the unwanted ones come to the colonies." [7]

[7] The boys have heard the great names in the history of the Mission — Hannington and Mackay — in the schools; but of missionaries such as Brewer at Hoima in Bunyoro, Miss Pike and Maddox at Kabarole in Toro, they have heard only from their parents and elders. Every Mutoro in the school knows, with a great wealth of circumstantial detail, of the work and personal characteristics of Miss Pike (whose name they cannot spell and whom they call "Miss Paker") and of Maddox. Boys from Bunyoro, Ankole, and Buganda are in full agreement that: "Unlike the modern merciless European, they were merciful men. They were not proud of their colour, like Europeans today, and did not despise us for ours. They lived with our people on equal terms, even eating the same food. They were kind and generous: they gave people clothes and taught them reading and writing without charging fees. They were learned men, and some, like Mr. Maddox, translated the Bible into the vernacular." The tradition insists on this unfavourable comparison of present-day Englishmen with the early missionaries. I have talked to no boy from Buganda, Toro, Bunyoro, and Ankole who could not recount intimate and detailed stories of the first missionaries (often ascribed to a period "a hundred years ago") in his district.

The schoolboy makes a sharp distinction between the educated and the uneducated Englishman. Schoolboys reflect the colour tensions and suspicions which are so widespread in modern Africa. They would wish to see the "Africanization" of all the services — except the teaching service. In particular they wish their country to be rid of the less educated, artisan type, of Englishman, whom the boys quickly assess and shrewdly perceive to be in a position of greater power and affluence than he could hope to secure in England. But they are unanimous in preferring white to black teachers and in insisting that more and not fewer teachers should come out from England. The teacher stands in the line of direct descent from Ashe and Mackay: he conforms most closely to the ideal stereotype.

An analysis of the play of my pupils both in pre-school and in school days seems to indicate a very narrow range of experimentation over possible lines of behaviour other than those customary in their tribes. Before they first attended school (at the average age of about eight), they played games which were mostly anticipatory of the traditional life of their people. Their games were marked by a strong utilitarian aspect, of which the boys themselves are fully conscious. They may even describe the play of their early years as "training." All my pupils spent three, four, or five years after the age of five or so in tending goats, sheep, and cattle, and during the long days of this passive occupation would play with other children similarly engaged. The most popular and universal game for these youngsters was throwing a stick fashioned like a spear at a wheel, made from a pliant plant stem, which would be rolled down a hill. Playing with bows and arrows, wrestling, and stick fighting were other games of almost equal popularity. My Bahima pupils reflected the traditional interests of their people by modelling cows and milk vessels in clay; my Batoro pupils by digging their own miniature gardens. All the boys showed, before the age of eight, the deep interest in mating, home-making, and begetting large numbers of children which remain the ambition of all the peoples of Uganda: all the boys spent perhaps the greater part of their leisure time in playing at families and being the fathers of numerous offspring. Play appears not to have been "recapitulatory" to any extent: few boys have been addicted to tree climbing (they are surprised to see that this, and swinging, are so popular with five-year-old English children); nor does their play seem to have had the strong element of fantasy and make-believe which may be observed in the play of most English children. It was closely geared to the life of hunting and cultivating which these boys would probably lead when they grew up — as one boy, writing for me about his childhood, said: "A boy or girl begins with simple games until he or she reaches the real game played by his or her parents"; and another: "The games played by our children soon become the real work of the tribe." Play was education, and even simple arithmetic was learnt, as it is still learnt, by a traditional game played and enjoyed by young and old throughout Uganda (and, I understand, over a much wider area of Africa): a game similar to our draughts, but requiring far more manipulation of numbers and, in some of its variations, calling for considerable skill in rapid addition and subtraction. This game seems to be universal in Uganda, played not only by Bantu but by Nilotic, Hamitic, and even Pygmy tribes.[8]

These games were the most popular in pre-school days, but a new range of interests is apparent in the games of pretence to which over 90 per cent devoted at least some of their leisure — the game of pretending to be an Englishman and wearing English-type clothes; and of writing with a stick in the soil. This make-believe included, with about 30 per cent of the boys, the pretence of being a clergyman or a teacher. The European ideal had been widened in 60 per cent [of the] instances to embrace not only the literate or educated man, but also the technical man — lorry drivers and mechanics and, in a few cases, airmen. More than 70 per cent had made a wooden bicycle (the most common and, indeed, almost the only toy, with the exception of a ball made from banana fibres).

In the secondary school spontaneous play ceases. This was an aspect of the school which struck me most forcibly after experience of English schoolboys and their playground games. The Phelps-Stokes Commission on East African Education, illustrating its account of school children's play, gave pictures which are not of spontaneous play at all: two are of organized games and the third is of a child doing a set exercise in modelling clay. *Children do not, of their own accord, bring traditional games into the school.*[9] Even the interest in cattle and cultivation does not appear in the school, nor, except very slightly, do the building crafts which were part of the home-making play of earlier years. There has been a tendency among European teachers to assume that anything with a tribal flavour must interest the African pupil, and this often leads to a form of bogus tribalism in the school. Lucy Mair observed: "I have never seen children

---

[8] The Baganda call it *Mweso*, the Lango *Coro*, the Etesot *Ailesit*, the Bakiga *Echisoro*, the Bamba *Kisoro*, and the Bakonko *Obwaso*.

[9] They practise surprisingly little traditional music, although on rare occasions a group will gather round the recreation-room piano and sing traditional songs. But a school concert party will choose predominantly Negro Spirituals or even hymn tunes. Yet these boys have been extremely interested in traditional music and musical instruments, as can quickly be discovered in a well-directed conversation; and most of them can play and even make the *endingidi*, a single-string violin, played with a sisal bow, popular in all the Bantu tribes in Uganda. The peoples of western Uganda — Batoro, Banyankole, Banyoro, and Bakonjo — make and enjoy a form of harp. I have never seen my pupils in possession of, or playing, either of these instruments (though I have seen boys making and playing a European-type banjo). Nor do they ever propose that they should obtain and play them at the frequent school concerts. The only traditional game played by the boys is *Mweso*.

spontaneously enacting the representations of folk-tales, or playing the singing games, which are encouraged in the school as traditional." In order to discourage imitation-Europeans, a school may be more tribal than the tribe itself: a dead and even an imaginary past may be fossilized in order to keep the African "truly African."

The boys explain their passivity by saying: "We have no time for play" or, "We don't want to play because we shall get dirty." Neither explanation carries much weight. The boys have, in fact, the usual breaks in the teaching timetable, and considerable freedom out of school hours and at the week-ends. But they will sit passively in the sun, pore over books, or lie on their beds with blankets pulled over their heads in cold or cloudy weather. Those boys — a majority — who remain at school during the three days of their half-term holiday because their homes are too distant for a brief visit, wear an air of boredom, walk round the villages, or read. There is no spontaneous attempt at more active amusements. They will play organized games — football, cricket, tennis — with enthusiasm; but it is the essence of these games that they are organized and run by the school staff. The same passivity is found in the classroom: the teacher has no problem of discipline: idle chatter, rolling and tapping pencils, playing with fashioned pieces of paper, surreptitious teasing of a neighbour, are not normal schoolboy antics with African pupils. A stolid and unmoving attention to the work in hand, suspicion or even open protest against any attempt to throw more of the responsibility of learning upon them or to introduce them to "activity" methods, are characteristic of the majority.

The absence of play even among the junior boys is not easy to explain with any certainty. The normal work and life of the school call for the maintenance of an elaborate new pattern of attitudes and behaviour and may, perhaps, be regarded as the equivalent of play in English society. Dress, daily habits, and routine, the school subjects themselves, are all unusual and, in relation to the familiar tribal life, are a form of play activity. This does not mean that they are treated frivolously, as of no real importance; on the contrary, they are taken with all the gravity and seriousness of purpose which are characteristic of the play of young (and old) in our society.

But the traditional play of the boys, as I have pointed out, anticipates the traditional life: for the minority who enter the secondary school and are thereby destined to lead a life very different from that of their fathers, this type of play ceases to have its former value. The boys realise how different their lives are likely to be: that even the unquestioned assumption of earlier years — that early marriage and rearing a large family constitute the main purpose of life — will be invalid in the urban life of an educated, professional man, for whom a money income is the sole income, and not merely a marginal income as it is for the peasant farmer; and that in these circumstances a wife (and certainly wives) and children will be not economic assets but crippling liabilities which may have to be forsworn. The boy on coming to school has entered a world to which the range of behaviour which he previously explored in play will have little relevance.

The schoolboy is deprived of many former certainties, and his passivity is probably in some measure a function of his uncertainty. He has been accustomed to attributing failure in all branches of life to the failure of the witchdoctor's "medicines" (though his faith in "medicines" is not therefore undermined: a good witchdoctor would not have been guilty of such faulty preparations). As his belief in this account of causality is slowly undermined at school, he himself is left unprotected, as a responsible agent. He is burdened by his responsibility: he slowly learns to say, when he makes a mistake, not "It happened" but, "I did it." A lack of self-confidence in most activities and, in particular, in their power to tackle successfully the usual school subjects unaided, their pathetic dependence upon the teacher, I have found to be one of the greatest obstacles to effective teaching. Boys who are quite capable of learning for themselves want the authoritative guidance and constant reassurance of the teacher. They worry abnormally, by English standards, about their work; their dreams reveal a deep state of anxiety about examinations — they see that no witchdoctor's charm will carry them through these crises. These boys are learning to face a personal responsibility which was rarely admitted by their fathers. The new school knowledge gives them an unfamiliar equipment for life; and while they are hesitantly testing its efficacy, the old armour is becoming increasingly vulnerable. . . .

Further Readings

Fortes, Meyer. *Social and psychological aspects of education in Taleland.* Oxford: Oxford University Press, 1938.

Gay, John, and Michael Cole. *The new mathematics and an old culture: a study of learning among the Kpelle of Liberia.* New York: Holt, Rinehart and Winston, 1967.

Raum, O. F. *Chagga childhood.* Oxford: Oxford University Press, 1940.

Read, Margaret. *Children of their fathers: growing up among the Ngoni of Malawi.* New York: Holt, Rinehart and Winston, 1968.

Shimahara, Nobuo. "Enculturation — a reconsideration," *Current Anthropology,* vol. 11 (April 1970).

3

Anthropology and education relate as practices. *Each informs and in other
ways contributes to the policies, performance, and substantive
accomplishments of the other. Anthropology and education are also* studies;
*each is an organization of knowledge, a field of intellectual interest. The
two relate as studies in that each concerns like, if not the same, phenomena:
the complex of learned, patterned behavior by which a being gains the
measure of social certainty and communicative skill necessary to group
(and, some add, intragroup) living. Herskovits explores that common ground
here. The late Mr. Herskovits was an experienced field researcher, and he
supported his contentions by exemplary use of ethnographic data.
Herskovits' distinctions between education, enculturation, and schooling
(see the selection by Wallace, Part Three), although not overdrawn, are
entirely subject to continuing argument. Theoretical discussions of the
multiple relationships between school and society seem terribly distant
from the real world of the classroom. Their outcomes, nonetheless,
powerfully influence the setting and maintenance of educational policies,
particularly those regarding educational change. Some command, if just
an appreciation, of them is thus advised, and Herskovits gives an insightful
introduction to the fundamental matter upon which such discussions are
based.*

MELVILLE J. HERSKOVITS

Education and the Sanctions of Custom

In its widest sense, education is to be thought of as that part of the
enculturative experience that, through the learning process, equips an
individual to take his place as an adult member of his society. The process, in most nonliterate communities, is carried on until the onset of
puberty for girls, and slightly later for boys. In Euroamerican groups, especially at upper socio-economic levels, the period is appreciably lengthened.
A much more restricted sense of the word "education" limits its use to
those processes of teaching and learning carried on at specific times, in
particular places outside the home, for definite periods, by persons especially prepared or trained for the task. This assigns to education the
meaning of *schooling*.

Despite the fact that, in the broadest sense, education can be regarded
as synonymous with the cycle of early enculturation, it is important for

From *Man and His Works*, by Melville J. Herskovits. Copyright 1947, 1948 by
Melville J. Herskovits. Reprinted by permission of Alfred A. Knopf, Inc.

purposes of analysis to differentiate the conceptual significance of enculturation from that we shall assign here to the word education; and equally
important to set off both these terms from the designation "schooling."
All three are to be regarded as expressions of a single process, whereby an
individual masters and manipulates his culture. But, as we have seen, enculturation continues throughout the entire life of an individual. It not
only includes the training he receives at the hands of others, but also the
assimilation of elements in his culture that he acquires without direction,
through his own powers of observation and by imitation. A new dance he
learns as an adult is a part of his enculturation, but hardly of his education; so is the manner in which, so to speak, he absorbs the motor and
speech habits of his group. Training in etiquette, however, is education,
as is instruction in some special technique such as pottery-making or
gardening, or the inculcation of moral values by the tales a boy or girl is
told for the purpose.

We must, therefore, be as cautious in evaluating definitions of education
that are too inclusive, such as that which holds this process to be "the
relationship between members of successive generations," [1] as in accepting
definitions that are drawn too narrowly. Just as enculturation is a term of
wider applicability than education, so education, in its ethnological sense
of directed learning, is of broader reference than schooling, that aspect of
education carried on by specialists. Enculturation and education are also
broader than schooling in another sense—enculturation and education
are universals in culture, schooling is not.

In any society, what the young may be taught is only limited by the
scope of the culture. Even where enculturation is achieved without any
formalized direction, a certain amount of guidance will be required. Communication can be achieved after a fashion by the use of baby talk, which
in turn is effortlessly transmuted into language. Yet there are always special
usages, such as honorific terms, or relationship designations, or even
plurals, that must be made explicit to the growing child if he is to use
them properly. Or, again, little attention may be paid motor habits, but
gesturing or modes of locomotion too far removed from the pattern will
call for correction.

In this sense, education may be thought of as the buffer that polishes
the rough surface of untutored behavior. It is a process whose function is
to bring individual behavior into line with the specific requirements of a
culture. In stating this, there is no need for us to take sides in the debate
over theories of learning. Controversies as to the role of imitation *versus*
conditioning, of reward and punishment *versus* association, have stimulated study and sharpened perceptions of the problems involved . . . when

---

[1] O. Raum, 1940, p. 62.

the nature of the enculturative process was discussed. Time and experience have so frequently demonstrated that no single explanation can account for any phenomenon of culture that, in principle, judgment must be withheld, with the expectation that the operation of each mechanism in the learning process will eventually be revealed and it function weighted.

Most persons of Euroamerican culture tend to regard education as synonymous with schooling. Few anthropologists who have discussed the training given boys and girls in nonliterate societies, and stressed the care taken by parents to make available to their children the cultural resources of their society, have not subsequently been confronted with statements such as "The X — tribe has no system of education." What is meant by such a statement is almost always revealed to be something quite different — that the people in question have no *schools*. The significance of the distinction between "schooling" and "education" is to be grasped when it is pointed out that while every people must train their young, the cultures in which any substantial part of this training is carried on outside the household are few indeed.

When we treat of education, we must again consider the important place specialization plays in machine cultures, as against its relative absence in nonliterate societies. What we call "vocational training" affords an excellent example. There is little need for specific training of this sort in nonliterate societies; no need for special buildings stocked with intricate machines that young men and women learn to operate so that they may function the more effectively in the economy of their society. Where the technology of a people is simple, every young person becomes proficient over its whole range. Within the limits of sex lines of division of labor, the child has from his early years been continuously engaged in learning the processes he must later employ in getting his living. He may be more effective in one activity than in another, but his opportunities to learn embrace all the techniques which in later life, as a grown man or woman, he will be called upon to handle.

The effectiveness of these systems has often been commented on, especially the sureness with which children are trained, early in life, to manipulate elements of their material culture that require no little skill. Among river-peoples, boys six and seven years old can be observed paddling canoes quite alone. In their villages even young children will be seen using long, sharp bush-knives to cut a branch off a dead limb. Little girls will tend a fire and see to it that the food in the cooking pots does not burn. Perhaps one reason for this seeming competence at an early age is that the material culture of nonliterate peoples, which is the aspect wherein it can best be observed, has less content than machine cultures and involves the use of less complicated implements. This permits children to be trained to do useful work at an earlier age. In linguistic proficiency, or in art or in a knowledge of the gods, however, most nonliterate children will be no more proficient, and indeed, no more concerned, than most children in literate societies who will eventually learn how to read and write.

An outstanding contrast between education in nonliterate cultures and in the Euroamerican scene is found in our attitude toward both learning and teaching.

Thus, in Wogeo, New Guinea, Hogbin reports that, "The children are in most cases even more eager to learn than the elders are able to teach." He illustrates this with an example:

> Sabwakai took up the adze on his own initiative [to help his father make a dugout] and on another occasion asked permission to come along with his father to one of our conferences at my house. "By listening to what I tell you," the father explained to me with a smile, "he thinks he'll find out about the things he'll have to do when he's a man." [2]

In nonliterate society, it is far more evident than among ourselves, for example, that all must master the techniques that provide a living. These techniques do not operate at a distance, as in more complex economies, where urban children can be found who have no idea that milk does not originate in a milk-bottling plant or a milk-wagon; or do not realize that a loaf of wrapped bread comes from a cereal called wheat. Where special skills are to be learned, the child in nonliterate societies is, as a rule, eager to acquire what its parent knows. The pride of workmanship and the prestige of the good craftsman carry over to him, and he needs only slight encouragement to seek these for himself.

Even where the esoteric enters, the emphasis is on learning. The priest is not eager to teach the novice; he must be convinced that the boy or girl who desires to serve the god is spiritually endowed for learning how to do this. This emphasis on learning as against teaching is to be correlated with the smallness of nonliterate groups, and the homogeneity of their cultures. Those from outside a society who wish to acquire a technique, a healing formula, a rite, or a knowledge of certain tales, must seek to learn it. Once learned, it is taken home, where it is made available for others either as a free good, with the reward for its transmission expressed in prestige, or for a price. Pressure is rarely laid on even at this point to convince fellow-tribesmen it should be accepted. Except where the new acquisition is sold for a price, those who wish to learn it, may; those who do not wish to, need not.

The urge to learn is basic in all children, and in nonliterate societies, this drive is pointed toward culturally sanctioned ends that are much

[2] H. I. Hogbin, 1946–47b, p. 282.

broader in relation to the cultural resources available than in a highly specialized culture such as our own. Here, where because of intense specialization choices are numerous, training must be along narrower lines — whether in terms of general behavior associated with one class as against another, or for a particular occupation, or even in chosen recreational pursuits. In nonliterate societies there are few square pegs in round holes. These are essentially the product of cultures wherein there are so many alternative possibilities that no individual can range at will over the entire body of traditions of his society, knowing the totality of his culture, being competent in most of it, and attaining special skill in such of its aspects as may appeal to him. To permit a child to explore as he wishes first one, then another compartment of a machine culture of Europe or America would make of him, in much more than the occupational sense, a "Jack of all trades and master of none."

It must not be supposed that because nonliterate peoples do not ordinarily educate their children in schools, educational devices are lacking. Knowledge must be acquired by learning, and it is not sufficient to lay it before even the most eager learner without organization and direction. Therefore, though schooling is not a factor in the education of the young of nonliterate peoples, there is no lack of educational techniques to encourage, to discipline, to punish. Punishment can be harsh indeed where consistent failure in some important aspect of life is continuous or incompetence is wilful. On the other hand, methods of arousing interest through rewards for the performance of duties laid on a child, or even by dramatizing the right to learn these duties, are frequently reported. Where a culture stresses competition, the play of competitive drives will be utilized to induce learning. Where competition is not important in ordering behavior, other methods of stimulating a child to want to be competent will be found. The process of educating the young, that is, like any other aspect of culture, is patterned and institutionalized.

Childhood is a carefree period of life for most human beings, despite the fact that they are continuously subjected to pressures and disciplines to shape them into functioning members of their society. The techniques of education used by nonliterate peoples vary as widely as any other aspect of their culture. They are expressed in overt training by elders, in emulating older children, in observation at ceremonies where only the mature are active participants, or sitting by while a parent or other elder relative goes about the daily tasks of a man or a woman, and watching what is done. They include the inculcation of moral values and proper conduct by direct instruction, the correction of an infringement of an accepted code by admonition, ridicule, or corporal punishment. Positive as well as negative measures are employed in bringing up a child. In many cultures, praise is lavished on the child who successfully performs an act, and various ways of encouraging him to attempt to do things he may be hesitant to try have been recorded, as where in West Africa bells are attached to the ankles of an infant who is learning to walk, so that he will increase his efforts.

It must be remembered that when we emphasize the primacy of the family in the education of children, we must accept this institution in a given culture in whatever form it may be defined. Within the family, education is principally carried on by the members of a household. Where family units are small, as among ourselves, this means that the father and mother, with perhaps a grandparent or uncle or aunt who is for a time a member of this grouping, discharge this obligation. In unilineal systems, where the classificatory relationship pattern prevails, the immediate contacts of the child will be far different from those of the individual brought up in a household whose members count their collaterals bilineally. Under a classificatory kinship structure, there will be several "fathers" or "mothers" to whom the upbringing of a child is of concern. All of these, by right, can admonish, encourage, punish, or reward in ways that even uncles and aunts in their own culture would rarely presume to do. Thus in a survey of the educational practices of American Indian tribes north of Mexico, Pettitt [3] names forty-three groups where the mother's brother plays a principal part in the education of the child.

In Zuñi, Li assigns this broad base of supervision an important place in the "working mechanism" of educational discipline the child is submitted to. "All the members of the family besides the parents coöperate to see that the child behaves well. In fact, any member of the community who happens to pass by will say something to correct some misbehavior of a child. Confronted with this united front of adults, so to speak, the child does not have much chance in trying to play one against the other. And if he is not unduly constrained, why should he make it unpleasant both for himself and for others? It is often observed that a very obstreperous child is easily hushed by a slight sound of any adult, in fact, by any facial expression which is seen by the child." [4] Here we have an extension of the function of correction from classificatory relatives to the other adults of the community. This, again, entails no difficulty. The homogeneity of the culture makes for a unity of teaching objectives that reflect unity of cultural aims and methods of inculcating them in the young, and thus leaves little room for conflict between the directives given by different preceptors.

[3] 1946, pp. 19–22.
[4] Li An-che, 1937, p. 70.

This conflict in directives is perhaps the source of the most serious difficulties in larger, less homogeneous societies, where the total educational process includes schooling as well as training in the home. Serious conflicts and deep-seated maladjustment may result from education received at the hands of persons whose cultural or sub-cultural frames of reference differ. The educational processes of nonliterate societies by no means make for perfect adjustment, or reflect complete cultural homogeneity. Such terms are always relative, and since culture is never static, continuous changes imply some measure of departure, everywhere, from the utter homogeneity that has mistakenly been held to characterize nonliterate societies. There are many sources of conflict and maladjustment other than imbalance in the educational system of a people, and many instances of these conflicts and maladjustments are reported in the ethnographic literature. Nonetheless, where a single agency — the family, however constituted, in most nonliterate communities — has for all practical purposes the sole responsibility for training a child, there is little opportunity to introduce the contradictions and confusions that can arise where multiple channels exist to teach the growing boy or girl.

Zuñi methods of "education for daily life," which, as Li puts it, "are in a sense more pervasive than formal school education," include three principal factors other than the one already mentioned, of supervision by a number of persons. He points out first, that though parental love is on occasion manifested in outward behavior, there is no excessive demonstrativeness. "Their children are allowed a much greater dependence in a free world of their own." They play in groups by themselves, so that the parents have no need to help in amusing or otherwise occupying their time. Parents are rather "taken for granted as the source of . . . well-being." In the next place, children are chastised if necessary. This, however, "is done deliberately and effectively. There is no fussing around on the part of the mother, nor is there endless talk among the adults so that the child is encouraged to be mischievous by giving him so much publicity and attention." Finally, as a fourth factor, religious beliefs lend appreciable weight to the educational system. Each religious group includes a functionary who, posing as one of the supernatural beings worshipped by the Zuñi, has the task of punishing children who misbehave.

Among the Chiricahua Apache Indians, says Opler, "the memory of training is synonymous with the consciousness of self." The following account by a native informant both documents this statement, and shows the injections one Apache remembers his elders to have given him in the process of inculcating in him the norms of sanctioned behavior:

> As far back as I can remember my father and mother directed me how to act. They used to tell me, "Do not use a bad word you wouldn't like

to be used to you. Do not feel that you are anyone's enemy. In playing with children remember this: do not take anything from another child. Don't take arrows away from another boy just because you are bigger than he is. Don't take his marbles away. Don't steal from your own friends. Don't be unkind to your playmates. If you are kind now, when you become a man you will love your fellow-men.

When you go to the creek and swim, don't duck anyone's children. Don't ever fight a girl when you're playing with other children. Girls are weaker than boys. If you fight them, that will cause us trouble with our neighbors.

Don't laugh at feeble old men and women. That's the worst thing you can do. Don't criticize them and make fun of them. Don't laugh at anybody or make fun of anybody.

This is your camp. What little we have here is for you to eat. Don't go to another camp with other children for a meal. Come back to your own camp when you are hungry and then go out and play again.

When you start to eat, act like a grown person. Just wait until things are served to you. Do not take bread or a drink or a piece of meat before the rest start to eat. Don't ask before the meal for things that are still cooking, as many children do. Don't try to eat more than you want. Try to be just as polite as you can; sit still while you eat. Do not step over another person, going around and reaching for something.

Don't run into another person's camp as though it was your own. Don't run around anyone's camp. When you go to another camp, don't stand at the door. Go right in and sit down like a grown person. Don't get into their drinking water. Don't go out and catch or hobble horses and ride them as if they belonged to you the way some boys do. Do not throw stones at anybody's animals.

When a visitor comes, do not go in front of him or step over him. Do not cut up while the visitor is here. If you want to play, get up quietly, go behind the visitor, and out the door."

Understandably, such a series of admonitions would not be given at one time. Yet the fact that parents were able to instill a code of proper behavior in an individual so that he could, when grown, tell it as consistently as it is given here demonstrates the effectiveness of the teaching. The Apache not only teach deportment and ethics; they point out to boys and girls the kind of work each will have to do, and see to it that they learn how to manipulate their technology:

The boys watch the men when they are making bows and arrows; the man calls them over, and they are forced to watch him. The women, on the other hand, take the girls out and show them what plants to use for baskets, what clay for pots. And at home the women weave the baskets, sew moccasins, and tan buckskin before the girls. While they are at work, they tell the students to watch closely so that when they reach womanhood nobody can say anything about their being lazy or ignorant. They teach the girls to cook and advise them about picking berries and other fruits and gathering food.[5]

Children in this culture are as a rule subjected to little corporal punishment: "We do not whip the child if we can help it." A blanket is thrown over the head of a child who persists in crying, until it stops, or a cup of cold water is poured slowly over its head. Enuresis is cured by putting a bird's nest in the bed. "Then the nest is thrown to the east, and the child won't wet the bed any more." Yet some men beat their sons. A girl who commits a breach of chastity is publicly flogged by her father, or if she is rude, may receive a "box on the ear" from her grandmother. More often children are disciplined by threats of punishment by fearsome creatures. The Gray One, a masked-clown dancer, figures most often as one of these. "The clown is going to put you into a basket and carry you off somewhere. Say this to a little child and he is going to mind right away." And when, as a child grows older, scepticism renders this threat no longer impressive, this being is made to "appear." The owl, associated with the dead, and as feared by adults as by children, is sometimes called on, or a child will be frightened by telling him that an old man "who looks fierce" will take him away. In one instance, an old man was called and did actually put a little boy in his sack whereupon a promise to obey came immediately.[6]

These varied techniques of teaching and disciplining the young make a point that controverts both of two stereotypes concerning the relationship between parents and children in "primitive society." One is that "primitive man" is savage and brutal towards children, regarding them as wealth and exploiting them to his advantage; the other is that because of his love of children, he permits them to grow up without correction, giving in to their every whim, until they metamorphose as full-fledged, responsible adult members of their group. Either view can be documented by examples from the literature, but not from the studies of those who in their field-work have been trained to record variation in custom even to the point of setting down practices that seem quite at odds. Here, in one culture, we find high-minded ethical precepts, and appeal to terror-inspiring beings. Among these Apache, a pattern of using the gentlest methods of correction and the heartiest encouragement does not preclude the use of corporal punishment when this is held to be necessary.

This wide range of educational procedures and methods of correction has been reported from every culture where careful studies of the training of children have been made. The South African Kgatla, for example, employ "exhortation and reprimand, as well as . . . chastisement, as the

[5] M. E. Opler, 1941, pp. 27–8.
[6] *Ibid.*, pp. 29–34.

occasion arises. Mistakes are corrected, ignorance is dispelled, good behaviour is applauded, and insolence or disobedience are immediately followed by punishment." This is generally a scolding or whipping, but sometimes a beating is administered: "The Kgatla say that thrashing makes a child wise, and helps it to remember what it has been taught." But they also say "A growing child is like a little dog," and even though it may annoy grown-ups, it must be taught proper conduct with patience and forbearance.[7]

The children of Lesu, a Melanesian village on New Ireland in the Bismarck Archipelago, are likewise exposed to various sorts of enculturative techniques. After the nursing period, a child receives the "careful attention" of adults and older children, though without the earlier petting and fondling. "Children from three to six are rarely left alone. They are either with their parents in the village, or, if the latter are away in the gardens or fishing, they are with their older brothers and sisters, classificatory ones if there are no real ones. . . . When the parents are in the village the little children follow them about. They are present at all adult activities — dance rehearsals, rites, communal preparations of food. . . . Occasionally they carry small, light articles, such as a basket for taro, from the house to the beach for their parents." Discipline begins at this time, too, and young children are spanked when they are disobedient. However, the hurt is mitigated by the fact that "if one parent quarrels with a child, the other will take the child's part," a pattern that "applies not only to parents but to other relatives." [8]

As the child grows older in Lesu, the process of learning by emulation and direction continues. The former is doubly important: "Respect for the wishes and commands of their elders is also impressed upon the children by their observation of adult behavior. They see their own parents meeting the wishes of the grandparents, and always it is the oldest people present who are the more important." [9] Knowledge of sexual behavior is likewise gained by observation, but this includes obtaining an understanding of the prohibited degrees of relationship as well as the techniques of the sex act. Thus in the sex play of early life, if a boy and girl of the same moiety are found together, they are scolded, beaten, and made to feel thoroughly ashamed of their acts. "The adults appear to be well aware of the laws of habit formation, and they take no chances on letting the children transgress an incest taboo even in play." [10] Girls, on the whole, are given more work than boys, but both sexes lend a relatively carefree pre-adolescent life. Formal teaching is at a minimum, being con-

[7] I. Schapera, 1940, p. 253.
[8] Powdermaker, 1933, pp. 81–2.
[9] *Ibid.*, p. 84.
[10] *Ibid.*, p. 85.

fined to the definite instruction provided by the telling of folk-tales, wherein, during a period of three or four weeks, the elders nightly recount the tales which explain the canons of proper behavior. On these occasions the code of etiquette and the accepted taboos are inculcated, and the punishment meted out to those who transgress them is made clear.

In a study of educational processes employed by the Kwoma, a New Guinea people of the Sepik River area, Whiting gives numerous instances to show that these people put to use all the customary teaching techniques. They motivate by punishing, scolding, threatening, warning, and inciting; they guide by leading, instructing, and demonstrating; they reward by giving gifts, helping and praising. These differing devices are not systematically used, but are rather to be abstracted from the day-to-day incidents observed in the field. A blow of a stick, the use of a word having associations of disgust or danger, will punish or scold. Showing a younger boy how to light a fire in a strong wind is instructing. Giving presents to young boys who participate in cooperative labor is training by rewarding them for meritorious behavior.[11]

We again see how in this region, as in the other parts of the nonliterate world, the education of the young is accomplished by the use of no single device. Rather each society calls on the resources of persuasion and compulsion to develop its young into the kind of individuals it holds desirable. In some cultures, it has been seen, more emphasis is laid on one method, or a particular group of methods, than on others; while still other devices, for all practical purposes, are excluded from the training repertory. They may be seldom employed, or may even be regarded with distaste, as in the case of corporal punishment among many American Indian tribes. But in no culture is education haphazard. Children nowhere "just grow" like Topsy. The elders watch, guide, supervise, correct. That all of them can perform this function is one of the reasons why, in nonliterate societies, education is so integral a part of day-to-day life that students could for many years have overlooked its existence as a ubiquitous aspect of culture.

Though the things any group may teach its young are limited only by the scope of its culture, education lays different emphases in different cultures. This must be so. No two cultures have similar orientations, and the transmission of cultural identity requires the continuation of the orientations that are the expressions of the differing interests people have in different aspects of their cultures. A complete catalog of what is taught a child would thus in the fullest sense constitute an ethnographic description of his culture. The order in which he is taught what he must

[11] J. W. M. Whiting, 1941, pp. 180 ff.

learn reveals the maturation patterns of his group and indicates what they hold important in their culture.

Certain aspects of education are universal. Every people conditions the infant to control his bodily functions. This is a phase of the educational process whose far-reaching effects on the personality structure of the adult are only beginning to be comprehended. All encourage linguistic communication, and see to it that the semantic values of the phonetic combinations in a language are properly used and understood. All instruct the young how to interpret the behavior of their fellows, and teach them how to act in specific situations and toward persons to whom they stand in particular kinds of relationships. There is none that does not teach ways of getting a living, and inculcate a sense of the economic values accepted by the group. Moral codes are everywhere emphasized, and those methods whereby an individual not only gets on with his fellows, but comes to be esteemed by them. Etiquette, in the widest sense of the term, is given continuous attention. As an extension of this, the meaning of the rituals of all kinds and a knowledge of how to conduct such of them as will fall to a given individual are taught, as well as the causes and cures of sickness, and the facts of birth and death.

In general, the practice of marking off literate from nonliterate societies as great categories is indefensible because of the variation in custom among "civilized" no less than "primitive" peoples. Nonetheless, certain widespread emphases are placed in the education of the young in a great many nonliterate cultures that, for historical reasons, are touched on with relative lightness by literate peoples, certainly in those societies that lie in the Euroamerican cultural stream. Two of these can be considered here. One is the importance of learning proper attitudes and behavior-patterns toward relatives; the other has to do with proper attitudes for accepted sexual behavior.

When we read of the complex order of kinship terminology that exists in most nonliterate societies, we must remember that the intricate system reflects certain sanctioned forms of polite conduct, certain emotionally toned affects, certain duties and obligations between individuals that have to be learned. "At every moment of the life of a member of an Australian tribe," writes Radcliffe-Brown, "his dealings with other individuals are regulated by the relationship in which he stands to them. His relatives, near and distant, are classified into certain large groups, and this classification is carried out by means of the terminology, and could apparently not be achieved in any other way. Thus in any part of the continent when a stranger comes to a camp the first thing to be done, before he can be admitted within the camp, is to determine his relationship to every man and woman in it, i.e., to determine what is the proper term of relationship for him to apply to each of them. As soon as he knows his relation to a given individual he knows how to behave towards him, what his duties are and what his rights." [12] These things, obviously, are not just absorbed. An Australian aborigine has to be taught the complicated kinship structure of his people, without which he would literally be unable to function as a member of his society. No sharper contrast could be cited to the way in which a man or woman in Euroamerican society may, without affecting his life, take only the closest relatives into account.

Kinship and sex may be intimately connected in the social structure of a people where institutionalized relationships of avoidance or preferential mating are found. The care with which the Trobriand child is taught to guard conduct where his *luguta*, his classificatory brother or sister is involved, is to the point here, for "the prohibition of any erotic or even of any tender dealings between brother and sister" is the "supreme taboo" of the Trobriander. "Round the word *luguta* a new order of ideas and moral rules begins to grow up at an early age of the individual's life history. The child, accustomed to little or no interference with most of its whims or wishes, receives a real shock when suddenly it is roughly handled, seriously reprimanded, and punished whenever it makes any friendly, affectionate, or even playful advances to the other small being constantly about in the same household. Above all, the child experiences an emotional shock when it becomes aware of the expression of horror and anguish on the faces of its elders when they correct it." [13]

The Chaga child, in East Africa, must first of all learn the difference between the use of his parents' personal names and the terms of address he must use in speaking to them. This is much the convention of our society, where the child is taught that though his mother addresses his father as "John," he must call him "father" or "daddy" or by some other appelation. The Chaga child, as he grows, must learn that terms are used in the singular for reference, and in the plural for address when speaking to those of the parental and grandparental generation to whom reverence must be shown. "From birth," we are told, "the child is taught the proper terms for addressing his relatives. He is told about paternal and maternal grandparents, uncles, and aunts before he understands one word of his language. It is the mother and nurse who teach the child to use the terms in appropriate situations. . . . Father, mother, elder siblings and nurse admonish the impolite child and advise it. . . . It is not to be wondered at that children are masters of kinship etiquette when they are six years old and that at fourteen they know most of the terminological subtleties." [14]

Similarly, "The Navaho child learns early that he can expect certain

[12] 1931, p. 95.
[13] B. Malinowski, 1929, vol. II, pp. 519–20.
[14] O. F. Raum, *op. cit.*, pp. 169–75.

relatives to follow a prescribed way of behaving toward him. He finds that his mother's brothers will scold him severely or punish him, but that he can get away with playing tricks upon them or making broad jokes about their sex life or disparaging their ability as hunters. He is taught, as he grows older, that toward all the persons whom he calls 'my sister' he must be respectful and practise certain avoidances. . . . He likewise notes that his elders preserve the same type of respect-avoidance relationship with their relatives by marriage and again follow different linguistic usages from those they employ with their blood relatives." But the manner in which he learns this, and the intensity of the experience, depends on many things — the size of the extended family to which he belongs, the number of playmates he has, the isolation of his immediate family. Whatever his situation, however, by the time he is grown, he has mastered the system of usage and behavior and functions effortlessly in it.[15]

In nonliterate societies, as we have seen, the knowledge and practice of sex is not left to chance. Some of the mechanisms that are employed demonstrate deep insight into the working of the human psyche. One instance of this is the practice in West Africa of requiring a newly circumcised youth to have sexual relations with an elderly woman, one who has passed the menopause, "to take off the burn of the knife." By her experience she not only aids him to perfect the technique of sex, but also helps to overcome any traumatic shock that may have resulted from the operation. The pre-marital experimentation that many nonliterate cultures sanction has a very definite role in inculcating skill and finesse in sex behavior. Those who enter on marriage are thus not exposed to the psychological hazards, manifest in the frequency of frigidity in women and impotence in men found by modern psychopathology in our own society, where matters of sex must be spoken of secretively, are often considered as partially evil, and for which the young person is prepared in a haphazard manner. Euroamerican culture, however, has no monopoly on puritanical attitudes toward sex. There are nonliterate groups where the conspiracy of silence is as strong where matters of sex are involved as was ever the case in Europe or America in mid-Victorian times. Yet these are in the minority. Most peoples, in numbering the facts of life, do not draw the line this side of the problems of reproduction.

Training in sexual habits can be formalized, or informally given, or both methods may be utilized even in the same culture. Much of the formal schooling given nonliterate boys and girls in the various "initiation" rites they undergo at puberty is concerned with the preparation for marriage. A mother, or more often a grandmother, may inform the nubile girl about the conduct of sexual relations, and the behavior expected of her as

[15] D. Leighton and C. Kluckhohn, 1947, pp. 44–5.

a married woman, just as later she will attend her on the first night of her marriage, and officiate at the birth of her child, and teach her how to care for it. The men of the family will teach the boy how to behave toward his female companions. In many societies, the maternal uncle is especially charged with imparting this information to his sister's sons. The attitude toward instruction in sex is generally marked by consciousness of a serious duty on the part of the older people, rarely by lasciviousness. Lasciviousness, like obscenity, is found among all people. Both the occasions permitting their expression, and the forms this may take are often institutionalized and channeled. Their universality documents the psychological release they afford, and their stimulus to sexual play. But situations where sex instruction is given differ in setting and tone from the lighter moods of the young folk as they go about the business of satisfying their sexual desires, before they eventually enter into an arrangement whereby they establish families and in turn take up the parental role.

Education carried on by means of schooling in the hands of specialists cannot be overlooked in considering the training of the young among nonliterate peoples, even though this is only a minor aspect of their educational systems. In the aggregate, the variety and number of these forms is greater than earlier studies have recorded. They vary from rather temporary groupings, meeting informally, as when a Plains warrior takes some boys with him to learn how to hunt, to the long periods of seclusion and intensive courses of instruction of some of the African "schools." In these schools, boys and girls who have attained puberty are initiated into the status of young men and women, stoically sustaining the ordeal of circumcision or excision of the clitoris, and thus demonstrating their right to be full-fledged members of their society, warriors, and mothers. Peristiany describes the purpose of these rites as practised by the East African Kipsigis as follows: "To sharpen the endurance of the initiate, to make good warriors out of men, and to teach women to love and care for their husband's cattle. To teach men that they are part of a complicated organization, family, clan, *puriet* [warrior group], and age-set, to each of which they must show obedience." [16]

Africa and Polynesia provide most instances of schooling, properly speaking, in nonliterate cultures. The East African example can be matched with similar institutionalized modes of instruction from all parts of the continent. They vary considerably in the period of seclusion, and in the rites they practise. But they differ little in their objectives, since all mark the transition from the status of child to that of adult, and demand the

[16] J. G. Peristiany, 1939, p. 26.

proofs of competence and endurance that set off the social life of the adult from that of the child. Junod's description of the formal educational processes among the Bathonga of Portuguese East Africa [17] has deservedly become classic, though this has been superseded by Stayt's more detailed study of the *thondo*, as the boys' school is often called among the Venda. These schools are attended by every boy of the eighteen districts where they are located. Attendance begins when the lad is but eight or nine years old, and continues until after he has attained puberty, when he completes his initiation and his age-set is recognized. The boys live at the *thondo*, undergoing the discipline that will make of them a military unit. Instruction is given in such techniques of warfare as ambush and night attack, and in spying. Such tasks as mat-making that are assigned them must be finished on time. The rules of tribal etiquette must be carefully observed, otherwise punishment, consisting of a severe beating with a stick, is inflicted. The youths also practise dancing while in school. They emerge from their training "hardened and disciplined, ready to shoulder the responsibilities as well as to share the privileges of a fighting man of the tribe."

The Venda girls' schooling is brief. It lasts only six days and nights. The *vhusha*, as the rite is called, marks the passage of girls from childhood to adolescence, and occurs shortly after initial menstruation. Tribal rules of etiquette and obedience, dancing instruction, and sexual behavior are the principal subjects taught. Still another occasion for formal instruction is in a mixed school called *domba*, described as "general preparation for marriage." Its intricate ceremonial, "by means of symbols and metaphors," teaches boys and girls "to understand the true significance of marriage and childbirth," and warns them "of the pitfalls and dangers that they are likely to encounter during the course of their lives." [18]

From the western part of Africa many examples of schools have been reported. We may cite Watkins' analysis of the *poro* and *sande* schools of Liberia and Sierra Leone. The first of these schools is for boys, the second for girls. As with the Venda, the boys' school involves protracted training; periods varying from eighteen months to eight years are mentioned for different tribes. How important these schools are is to be seen from the fact that despite growing European influence, they still function over periods varying from eighteen months among the Vai to three years among the Gola. Here circumcision precedes entry into the school, which is under the general supervision of a leader whose position in the community reflects the importance of his office.

The training the boys receive is outstanding in the nonliterate world.

---

[17] 1927, vol. I, pp. 71–94.
[18] H. A. Stayt, 1931, pp. 101 ff.

"The boys are divided into groups according to their ages and aptitudes," states this report, "and receive instruction . . . in all the arts, crafts and lore of native life. . . . It is by this means that the character is moulded and a youth is prepared to take his place among the generation of adults. . . . The first instruction involves a series of tests in order to determine individual differences, interests, and ambitions. . . . A youth who shows special aptitude for weaving, for example, is trained to become a master of the craft; while those who show distinctive skill and interest in carving, leatherwork, dancing, "medicine," folklore, etc., are developed along these specialized lines. This early training also includes work in the erection of the structures which are used while the session lasts. . . . All the laws and traditions of the tribe are taught, as well as duty to the tribal chief, tribe and elders, and the proper relations to women. Training is given in the recognition and use of various medicinal herbs, their curative powers, and various antidotes. Also, the secrets of wild animals are taught — how they live, how to recognize their spoor, and how to attack them." Finally, "all this training is tested out in the laboratory of 'bush'-school life," as when warfare is simulated, and the boys are called on to utilize, in planning and executing a campaign, what they have learned. The *sande* school, for girls, parallels in the organization of its staff, and other characteristics the *poro* training for boys. Its curriculum is directed toward training girls in their duties as grown women — wives and mothers — and thus with different content fulfils the same educational ends.[19]

In Polynesia, schools trained the young for the priesthood, and as specialists in entertainment. Luomala, in her useful summary of Polynesian literature, points out that, "New Zealand and the Society Islands had famous houses of learning, really primitive universities, at which the ancestral lore, genealogies, traditions, religion, magic, navigation, agriculture, literary composition, and all the arts and crafts were taught by learned priests." Schools in New Zealand were open for five months of the year, and the work was intensive, the pupils studying from sunrise until midnight in the special building dedicated to the holding of classes. Two branches of learning, the "Upper Jaw, having to do with the gods and cosmology, and the Lower Jaw, having to do with terrestrial matters," were taught. Emphasis was placed on repetition of religious formulae, and lay precepts, rather than on investigation; but "changes . . . to suit the current winds of political and religious schisms" were made when the occasion demanded.

Formal courses of higher learning have also been reported from other parts of Polynesia, such as the Hawaiian college of heraldry. In general, we are told, "the hallmark of any well-born and well-trained chief was his

---

[19] M. H. Watkins, 1943, pp. 670–1; 673–4.

ability to give orations with an abundance of religious and historical allusions, metaphors, similes, and proverbs" which obviously required special training; and such training was also required if a person was to qualify as a member of the companies of dancers, or as an entertainer of the kind found in Hawaii. For the most part, those who received training "in composition, narration and chanting were usually of noble birth . . ." though they "did not form a special, intellectual class except in Mangareva, Marquesas and Easter Island." On the other hand, Polynesians of all ranks and both sexes might cultivate the art of oral literature, and some became specialists in reciting the long and complicated narratives about "a single-favorite character." Furthermore, "daily life in Polynesia . . . required knowledge of many incantations, chants, traditions, proverbs, and fables. Every craft and occupation had its magical formulae, religious history, myths, and traditions. Besides their practical value in gaining the assistance of the gods, these gave dignity, prestige, and background to the worker and to those who used the results of his work." [20] These motivations would seem largely to explain why, here, the tradition of specialized training that marked the area developed and maintained itself as an important part of the culture.

Elsewhere, though initiation of boys and girls at puberty into the tribe is common, and is almost invariably employed as an instrument to point earlier instruction and extend its scope, the teaching function is somewhat more submerged in the ritualistic aspect of the "school," though these ritualistic elements are everywhere prominent, even in Africa and Polynesia. The initiation of young Australians into manhood has long been famous in anthropological literature. It lasts for several months, and is marked by both circumcision and subincision. The lad is beaten frequently, and is ceremonially tossed in the air by the older men. The educational aspect of these transition rites consists of imparting certain secret information concerning the supernatural beings who are held to rule the universe. Eventually they reveal to the youth his *churinga*, the object which symbolizes his totemic affiliation and is the place where the double of that portion of the ancestral soul believed to animate him is held to reside.[21] None of the teaching of practical matters of daily life, especially of sex, that is so important a part of the African curriculum is found here, however.

This Australian example brings into relief one further trait of education in nonliterate cultures that must be mentioned. It has been said that in nonliterate societies education continues until adolescence, or shortly after, but that the process is somewhat longer among literate peoples.

[20] K. Luomala, 1946, pp. 772–5.
[21] Cf. B. Spencer and F. J. Gillen, 1904, pp. 328–73.

Concerning the "everyday business of life" this is true. Yet when we touch the supernatural we come on a phase of the transmission of knowledge that is substantially confined to adults. The importance of religion as a force in the daily life of nonliterate peoples will become fully apparent when we discuss this aspect of culture. The control of the powers of the universe is conceived as an essential to the successful solution of most of their problems. But children, whose physical power is slight, are rarely conceded any greater amount of spiritual power. The religious training of children, therefore, is of a passive and very general nature. Not until they become older are they taught the theological concepts, the ritual practices of their tribe. For the most complete account of any religion we go to the elders, who, even though they are not specialists, are the ones versed in the supernatural sanctions of their society, and the accepted means of propitiation and expiation.

The education of nonliterate peoples, then, must not be thought of as reaching its completion with the assumption of adult status. Not even formal teaching ends then. But in the sense of education as *the process whereby the knowledge of a people is passed from one generation to the next*, a definition that refines the too inclusive one of Raum, a man or woman is fitted to carry on in his culture at an earlier age, and without the prolonged institutionalized training that exists where writing and the machine technology condition modes of living. In affairs of the spirit, however, this is but a beginning point. Those who are in charge with the direction of affairs continue to be taught by their elders, as long as there are those older than themselves. From them they eventually learn the means whereby they themselves, and those for whose existence they are responsible, may live in harmony with the forces of their world, supernatural no less than human.

Bibliography

Hogbin, H. I. "A New Guinea childhood: from weaning till the eighth year in Wogeo." *Oceania*, vol. xvi, pp. 275–96 (1946–1947b).

Junod, Henri A. *The life of a South African tribe*, 2nd ed. London, 2 vols., 1927.

Leighton, Dorothea and Kluckhohn, C. *Children of the people, the Navaho individual and his development*. Cambridge, Mass., 1947.

Li, An-che. "Zuni: some observations and queries," *American Anthropologist*, vol. xxxix (1937) pp. 62–76.

Luomala, Katherine. "Polynesian literature," *Encyclopedia of Literature* (J. T. Shipley, Ed), pp. 772–89 (1946).

Malinowski, B. *The sexual life of savages*. London, 1929.

Opler, M. E. *An Apache life-way*. Chicago, 1941.

Peristiany, J. G. *The social institutions of the Kipsigis*. London, 1939.

Pettitt, George A. "Primitive education in North America," *University of California Publications in American Archaeology and Ethnology*, vol. xliii (1946), pp. 1–182.

Powdermaker, Hortense. *Life in Lesu*. London, 1933.

Radcliffe-Brown, A. R. "The social organization of Australian tribes," *Oceania Monographs,* no. 1 (1931).

Raum, O. *Chaga childhood.* London, 1940.

Schapera, I. *Married life in an African tribe.* London, 1940.

Spencer, B., and Gillen, F. J. *The northern tribes of Central Australia.* London and New York, 1904.   ,

Stayt, H. A. *The Bavenda.* London, 1931.

Watkins, M. H. "The West African 'bush' school," *American Journal of Sociology,* vol. xlviii (1943), pp. 666–74.

Whiting, J. W. M. *Becoming a Kwoma.* New Haven, 1941.

Further Readings

Boas, Franz. "Education," in *Anthropology and modern life.* New York: W. W. Norton, 1928.

Ianni, Francis A. J. *Culture, system and behavior: the behavioral sciences and education.* Chicago: Science Research Associates, 1967.

Kneller, George F. *Educational anthropology: an introduction.* New York: Wiley, 1965.

Lee, Dorothy. "Cultural factors in the educational process," in *Perspectives on educational administration and the behavioral sciences.* Eugene: The Center for the Advanced Study of Educational Administration, University of Oregon, 1965.

Williams, Thomas R. *A Borneo childhood: enculturation in Dusun society.* New York: Holt, Rinehart and Winston, 1969.

4

Anthropology and education relate, as studies, by the coincidence of their subject matter. Cazden's review suggests another correspondence between the two fields, one that involves the character of research. Anthropological perspective emphasizes context. Behavior — any behavior or set of them — is seen in relationship to all other behaviors. Mrs. Cazden's stress on the concept "subcultural relativity," like Gearing's notion of "human believability" and Musgrove's concern with cultural integrity, respects this perspective. Though applied here to the study of language behavior, such perspective pertains equally to the research of all other teaching-learning behaviors (see Part Three). The conduct of anthropological study, its mode of inquiry, is local, intensive, and frequently prolonged. Speech activity — "who says what to whom, how, and in what situations" — by its nature demands a similar mode, if only because language is so easily mistaken out of context. Perspective and conduct refer mainly to descriptive phases of research. The task Mrs. Cazden considers is mostly analytic. Distinctions between what is language difference and what is language deficiency depend, finally, upon

whose terms *are in use, upon what is decided to be "standard," upon who is
"believable," and who is "odd, dissimilar, and bizarre." Making these distinctions is a matter of social policy, and Cazden provides a case to which
anthropological knowledge and attitude is clearly relevant. Presently Associate
Professor of Education, Harvard Graduate School of Education, Mrs. Cazden
is a regular contributor to the literature of educational research.*

COURTNEY B. CAZDEN

Subcultural Differences in Child Language:
An Inter-Disciplinary Review

The argument over whether children from Harlem or Appalachia
should be called "culturally different" or "culturally deprived" is more
than an empty terminological dispute. It reflects a basic and important
question: Is the concept of cultural relativity valid in this subcultural
context or not? More specifically, in what ways is the language used by
children in various subcultural groups simply different, and to what extent can the language of any group be considered deficient by some criteria? It is the purpose of this paper to explore a large body of literature
bearing on the basic question.

Necessarily, this review of the literature will be an inter-disciplinary one.
Linguists describe the nonstandard dialects of English in formal ways.
Developmental psychologists find variations in the rate of language acquisition by children that correlate with variations in status characteristics,
e.g., of social class or ethnic background. Anthropologists and sociologists
suggest that not only language, but speech, is structured. Under the heading
of ethnography of communication or socio-linguistics, they examine the
inter-individual functions that language serves in subcultural settings.
Lastly, experimental psychologists studying the intra-individual, or mediational, role of verbal behavior are becoming interested in the individual
and group difference among their subjects.

I will discuss these four strands of research in turn, not trying to list all
the studies and their findings but concentrating instead on an analysis of
significant issues. However, even though some of this work has been stimulated by pressing educational problems, the educational issues would re-

Originally published in *Merrill-Palmer Quarterly of Behavior and Development*, vol.
12, no. 3. Copyright by Merrill-Palmer Institute, 1966. Reprinted in Jerome Hellmuth
(ed.), *Disadvantaged Child*, vol. 2: *Head Start and Early Intervention*. New York:
Brunner/Mazel, 1968.

quire such a lengthy discussion in themselves that they must be considered as falling outside of the scope of the present paper.

Dr. Martin Luther King, speaking in Selma, Alabama, just before the civil-rights march to the state capital, said:

> Those of us who are Negroes don't have much. We have known the long night of poverty. Because of the system, we don't have much education and many of us don't know how to make our nouns and our verbs agree. But thank God we have bodies, our feet and our souls (*The New York Times*, March 22, 1965, p. 1).

As will be seen, Dr. King's example is pertinent in a discussion of standard and nonstandard English.

Standard English has been defined as "the particular type of English which is used in the conduct of the important affairs of our people. It is also the type of English used by the socially acceptable of most of our communities and, insofar as that is true, it has become a social or class dialect in the United States" (Fries, 1940, p. 13). Nonstandard English, by contrast, refers to dialects which deviate from the standard in pronunciation, vocabulary, or grammar. Social or class dialects are thus usually grouped into three main types: Standard English, common or popular English, and vulgar or illiterate English. However, the methods of distinguishing or describing the latter two types also vary in themselves.

Methods of Describing Nonstandard English

The differences between nonstandard dialects and Standard English have been described in three principal ways: in terms of frequency of errors, of contrastive analysis, or of transformational grammar. The oldest method, now discarded, is simply to count "errors" or deviations from Standard English and express the sum as a percentage of total use of a particular part of speech (e.g., pronouns), or as a percentage of total words used. Three studies of child language (Templin, 1957; D. R. Thomas, 1962; Loban, 1963) provide information on such deviations. All three find that verb usage is the most frequent source of errors: specifically, violation of subject-verb agreement; deviant use of the verb *to be*, "especially for Negro subjects whose parents have migrated from the rural South" (Loban, 1963, p. 52); use of present for past tense; and use of *got* for *have*.[1]

---

[1] This last instance deals primarily, of course, with *got* used as a transitive verb in a present-tense construction for *have* in the sense of "to possess, own, hold," etc., not with *got* as a past participle used with some form of *have* as an auxiliary verb. The writer recognizes that any discussion of *got*-versus-*have* is soon diverted into historic arguments on English usage, divergent British- and American-English practices, literary precedents

Other frequent errors are wrong forms of the pronoun, double negatives, and the use of *ain't*.

A second method is to describe nonstandard forms of English in terms of a contrastive analysis, a technique adapted from research on foreign language teaching. This defines the prints of maximum interference between the phonology, morphology or syntax of the speaker's native language and the "target language" which he is trying to learn. Thus a contrastive analysis would pinpoint, for example, the problems of learning English for a native speaker of Hindi. The same technique could be applied to the teaching of Standard English to speakers of nonstandard dialects.

However, this method entails making a separate analysis for each nonstandard dialect — regional, foreign-language background, or social class. Work is now in progress for Negro and Puerto Rican speech in New York City (Labov, 1965); for Negro and white middle- and lower-class speech in Chicago (Davis and McDavid, 1964; Pederson, 1964); for the speech of Negro students at Tougaloo College, in Mississippi (Beryl Bailey)[2]; and for the speech of school children in Washington, D.C. (Center for Applied Linguistics, 1965). These are particularly promising studies of language behavior and the psychological and sociological factors related to it. The Center for Applied Linguistics is also stimulating as well as coordinating activities in this field.

The third method uses the approach of "transformational grammar." Very briefly, each dialect is described in terms of the rules underlying it (descriptive, not prescriptive rules), and the rules for different dialects are then compared. A readable exposition of the basic theory is set forth by O. C. Thomas (1965). Rosenbaum (1964, p. 30) comments that the transformational approach "permits a precise and insightful characterization of the relatedness between grammatical systems" and notes some of the ways in which it seems to hold promise for dialect study. To date, the only example of this approach is Klima's (1964) analysis of the use of interrogative and personal pronouns in four "styles" — elegant or literary English, two intermediate styles, and vulgar English as found in the novels of Nelson Algren.

Nonstandard English as Deficient

There are both social and psychological criteria by which nonstandard speech might be considered deficient. The evidence on social grounds is

---

running from Shakespeare to Shaw, and so on and so on — all of which are beyond the scope of this review. Moreover, it is my impression that the use of *got* is increasing among speakers of Standard English; built into the definition of Standard English is the concept of the changing norm.

[2] Personal communcation from Beryl Bailey, 1964.

the more conclusive. There is little question that speaking a nonstandard dialect is a social liability, creating a barrier to the speaker's acceptance in the dominant culture. As Jespersen ([1946], 1964, pp. 70–71) has observed:

> [It is to the advantage of the children to speak Standard English] not only materially, because they can more easily obtain positions in society which now — whether one approves it or not in the abstract — are given by preference to people whose speech is free of dialect, but also because they thus escape being looked down on on account of their speech, and are therefore saved from many unpleasant humiliations. Apart from all this, merely by reason of their speaking they have a better chance of coming in contact with others and getting a fuller exchange of ideas.

Putnam and O'Hern (1955) provide recent evidence that features of nonstandard speech are indeed perceived and negatively evaluated by Standard speakers. Just which features elicit the most unfavorable reactions from teachers, employers, etc., is one of the points under study in several of the contrastive analyses referred to earlier.

Whether nonstandard English is, in addition, a cognitive liability to the speaker is much harder to determine. First, Standard English might be a more powerful means of communication. But all other things, such as vocabulary, being equal there is no evidence that this is so. "It is generally the very small points that are fixed upon as objectionable, often insignificant things that hardly affect the value of the language as a means of communication" (Jespersen [1946], 1964, p. 56 n.).

Second, the child who speaks a nonstandard dialect may have difficulty understanding his teacher and his schoolbooks. The evidence on this point is unclear. Cherry (1964) reports a pioneer attempt to use the Cloze technique "to evaluate the extent to which information is successfully communicated from teachers to pupils of various social backgrounds and the degree of effective communication among children from different social backgrounds" (p. 23). Words were deleted according to a pre-determined sequence from samples of teacher and peer-group speech, and the child's comprehension was measured by his ability to replace the exact word or suggest a substitute that made semantic or grammatical sense. Despite methodological problems in oral presentation of the speech samples and in the reliability of the scores, there were three major results: (1) social-class differences in understanding teacher speech were more apparent among fifth-graders than first-graders, but this effect was not maintained when intelligence was controlled statistically; (2) there were no social-class differences among fifth-graders in comprehending lower-class peer speech, but middle-class children were significantly superior to lower-class children in comprehending middle-class peer speech, and this effect was maintained even when intelligence was controlled; (3) Negro-white differences in these receptive language skills were virtually absent. In interpreting these results, we should note that while lower-class fifth-graders had more trouble understanding middle-class peer speech, the decreased comprehension across social-class lines was not reciprocal. The middle-class children understood lower-class peer speech as well as did the lower-class children. This finding suggests that dialect differences are confounded with other linguistic variables, such as vocabulary load and utterance complexity.

Here is a key problem. It is hard to determine whether nonstandard dialects are, "other things being equal," just as good a means of communication as Standard English. For such "other things" as the total repertoire of words and grammatical patterns are, in fact, rarely equal. Fries (1940, p. 287 ff.) reached the following conclusion:

> Over and over again . . . it appeared that the differences between the language of the educated and that of those with little education did not lie primarily in the fact that the former used one set of forms and the latter an entirely different set. In fact, in most cases, the actual deviation of the language of the uneducated from Standard English grammar seemed much less than is usually assumed. . . . The most striking difference between the language of the two groups lay in the fact that Vulgar English seems essentially poverty stricken. It uses less of the resources of the language, and a few forms are used very frequently.

Fries's language samples were taken from the correspondence of American citizens with agencies of the federal government, and it could be argued that the writers of Vulgar English were particularly impoverished in meeting the demands of that task. However, Loban obtained comparable results from an analysis of oral language of children in an informal interview. Thus it seems unlikely that the relative position of high and low social-class groups on a richness-impoverishment dimension can be explained wholly in terms of each given situation.

Loban (1963) used a two-level analytical scheme developed for his research. In the first level, utterances were classified into one of nine structural patterns — e.g., subject-verb-object (*George eats onions*), or subject-linking verb-predicate nominative (*Onions are roots*). In the second level, the component parts of these nine patterns were examined. From a comparison of the speech of a high group and a low group selected on the basis of language ability but contrasting on socio-economic status as well, Loban (1963, p. 46) concludes:

> All these subjects . . . use the relatively few structural patterns of the English language. Thus structural pattern reveals less remarkable differences than does dexterity of substitution *within* the patterns. The important differences show up in the substitution of word groups for single

words, in the choice and arrangement of movable syntactic elements, in the variety of nominals, and in strategies with prediction.

In other words, there is evidence that not only do nonstandard dialects use different rules once a particular construction has been selected (the so-called "errors") but, more importantly, people speaking these dialects tend to use fewer of the optional constructions in their native language and to fill all the slots in their constructions from a smaller set of words.

Sometimes a single utterance can be categorized in several ways. Take the case of verb usage and, specifically, this example heard from a five-year-old in a day-care center: *My Mommy help me*. It can be considered as containing an error at the morphological level of linguistic structure in the failure to observe subject-verb agreement in the third person singular. Such errors are common in nonstandard dialects, as has been seen above. But the same utterance can be considered evidence of impoverishment, in failing to encode a particular meaning in a unique way by taking advantage of the rich possibilities afforded by English verb auxiliaries. The weakness of *My Mommy help me* as a communication lies in the use of an unmodified lexical verb instead of one of many alternatives, such as *My Mommy did help me* or *My Mommy would have helped me*. (However, see Stewart, 1965, for evidence that nonstandard dialects make different, not simply fewer distinctions.) Further, since the use of unmodified lexical verbs like *help* precedes developmentally the emergence of more complex constructions, the same utterance can be considered an example of retardation. I will suggest later that such ambiguity in interpretation poses a serious problem in the attempts to establish dialect-free scales of language development.

The question of whether nonstandard dialects are deficient or just different is sometimes glossed over by the statement "you can say anything in any language." It may be true that any language has the resources available, in words and grammatical constructions, to encode any meaning in some way (although Hymes, 1961, offers an opposing view). What is meant by such "resources" is the contents of a complete dictionary. In this sense English is as good as, but not better than, French or Russian. However, when we shift from the difference between English and French to that between the speech of a middle-class child and a lower-class child, we aren't looking at the total of what is available in language as a set of symbols but only at what is actually used by certain individuals at the moment of framing and utterance. This is one distinction between language and speech, and it's a sign of confusion between the two to inject the idea that "one language is as good as another" into the controversy over the verbal inadequacies of children in some subcultural groups. In general, then, it is probably true, to quote Loban (1963, p. 85), "Subjects who are rated as most proficient in language are also those who manifest the most sensitivity to the conventions of language. The subject who, despite unconventional usage, exhibits verbal linguistic skill is the exception." But while a correlation between deviation from Standard English and impoverishment exists, it can't be explained on any intrinsic grounds. The causes must therefore lie in historical and sociological factors — such as isolation, discrimination, or distance from foreign-language background — and the degree of correlation will therefore vary from one subcultural group to another.

STAGES ON A DEVELOPMENT CONTINUUM

The findings of those studies of language development that make subcultural comparisons have become rather widely known. Therefore I will devote less space here to a summary of that work than to two related topics: an outline of the mediators by which such gross environmental variables as social class may affect language development, and an exploration of the problems which dialectal differences pose for the establishment of developmental scales.

Studies of Language Development

In addition to the work of Templin (1957), D. R. Thomas (1962), and Loban (1963) already touched on, the studies by Irwin (1948a, 1948b and Lesser, Fifer, and Clark (1965) should be mentioned. Research by various members of the Institution for Developmental Studies (e.g., Deutsch, 1963; John, 1963; Keller, 1963; Cherry, 1965; Deutsch and B. Brown, 1964; John and Goldstein, 1964) is cited elsewhere in this review. Except for the work by Lesser et al., these studies divide their subjects by social class only. They deal with three aspects of language development: phonology, vocabulary, and sentence structure (today more often termed grammar). The findings can be quickly summarized. On all the measures, in all the studies, children of upper socio-economic status, however defined, are more advanced than those of lower socio-economic status. Nevertheless, some points merit additional comment.

Phonology. Irwin's (1948a, 1948b) work is striking in that it pinpoints the early age at which environmental differences impinge on phonological development. Comparing the number of sound types and tokens produced by infants from birth to 30 months, he found that the infants from higher-status families had significantly higher scores for the last year of the period than did those from lower-status families. In other words, the developmental curves separated at 18 months of age.

Vocabulary. The study by Lesser et al. (1965) is included here because language development was measured with a vocabulary test, but the import of this research extends beyond that to intellectual development as a whole. The purpose was to examine the pattern of four mental abilities (verbal, reasoning, numerical, and space) among first-grade children in New York City from middle and lower social-class groups and four ethnic backgrounds — Chinese, Jewish, Negro, and Puerto Rican. Care was taken in preparing the test materials and in obtaining examiners from the child's own subcultural group to insure that "observed differences . . . reside in the respondents and not in the test materials themselves" (p. 13). Verbal ability was measured by a 60-item vocabulary test, one-half pictures and one-half words, administered in the child's native language, or English, or a combination of both.

Probably the most important finding is that ethnic background and social class have different effects. Ethnic background affects the pattern of mental abilities, while social-class status affects the level of scores across the mental-ability scales. Specifically, on *verbal ability* Jewish children ranked first (being significantly better than all other ethnic groups), Negroes second and Chinese third (both being significantly better than the Puerto Ricans), and Puerto Ricans fourth, On *space*, by contrast, the rank order was Chinese, Jewish, Puerto Rican, and Negro children. But in all four ethnic groups, on all scales and subtests, the middle-class children were significantly superior to the lower-class children. As Lesser and his co-workers (1965, p. 83) observe:

> Apparently, different mediators are associated with social-class and ethnic-group conditions. . . . The importance of the mediators associated with ethnicity is to provide differential impacts upon the development of mental abilities, while the importance of mediators associated with social class is to provide pervasive (and not differential) effects upon the various mental abilities. This conclusion allows selection among several explanations offered to interpret cultural influences upon intellect activity.

The same investigators also found that social-class position has more effect on mental abilities for the Negro children than for other groups, and that on each mental-ability test the scores of the middle-class children from the four ethnic groups resemble each other more than do the scores of the lower-class children. All the findings are discussed in the light of previous studies. For instance, the superior verbal ability of the Jewish children appears in many other studies. On the other hand, the verbal inferiority of the Puerto Rican children has been contradicted by other evidence (e.g., see Anastasi and de Jesus, 1953). Lesser et al. discount the possible effects of bilingualism.

Although measures of vocabulary consistently yield social-class differences in the scores, significant questions relevant to the difference-deficiency issue remain unanswered. Tyler says that "lower-class children use a great many words, and a number of them use these words with a high degree of precision, but facility with words commonly used by the lower classes is not correlated with success in school" (Eells, Davis, Havighurst, Herrick, and Tyler, 1951, p. 40). Does Tyler mean that children from different status groups know and use different words? If so, how can this be reconciled with Templin's (1957) results on the Seashore-Eckerson Test in which the sampling of words from an unabridged dictionary results in a bias in the direction of common, easier words (Lorge and Chall, 1963)? Or how can it be reconciled with the results obtained by Lesser et al. on the tests described above? Or does Tyler mean that lower-class children use "slang" from a different "dictionary"? How does this relate to Nida's (1958, p. 283) suggestion that "subcultures have proportionately more extensive vocabularies in the area of their distinctiveness"? Can one speak of the vocabulary of an idiolect or a dialect as structured? Is Tyler implying that, even for vocabularies similar in size, children from different groups may know fewer words in common than children from the same group? Conceivably, quantitative measures may conceal wide variation in overlap.

It has also been remarked that the language of the lower-class child is rich in something called "expressiveness." Cohn (1959, p. 439) speaks of "the great power of lower-class language to express emotions, a power ordinarily exploited with a clear conscience only by novelists." Is this just a romantic view in which the cliches of one subculture are perceived as creative expression by the listener from a different culture? Or does it mean that lower-class children use a small vocabulary in varied and novel ways, compensating by inventive encoding for what they lack in availability of single words? Or does it refer not to language as a code but to what it is used to say?

Sentence Structure. The most common measure of development in sentence structure, or grammar, is mean length of response (MLR), usually in words although it should be in morphemes. The validity of such a global and summary kind of measure rests on the widespread finding that it increases with age, and on more recent discoveries by Brown and Fraser (1964) and Bellugi (in press) of a close correspondence between mean length and the emergence of specific grammatical features in the speech of children under 4 years of age. We should not assume, however, that the correlation between length and complexity remains high at older ages. An average can include very short and very long. Thus, even if the MLR for two status groups were similar, the lower-status children might be speaking either in short sentences or connecting simple strings of words with "and" while the upper-status children utilize more complex syntactical patterns.

In a frequency distribution of the written sentences from Standard English and Vulgar English samples, Fries (1952, pp. 291–292) found that even though average lengths were similar, 23.46 and 23.16 respectively, the mode (most frequent length) in Standard English was 21 words, while Vulgar English had a mode of only 11 words but included more very long sentences. The same phenomenon can explain Templin's (1953, p. 79) finding in her study of children 3–8 years old, that while the MLR is the same or higher for upper-status children at all ages, the standard deviation of length-of-response scores is the same or higher for lower-status children above the age of 4 years.

Mediating Variables

In measuring aspects of the environment which correlate with the growth of intelligence and academic achievement, Wolf (1964) and Dave (1963) distinguish between *status* and *process* variables. Examples of status variables are the income of the family and educational level of the parents; examples of process variables are the nature of intellectual aspirations for the child and the academic guidance provided in the home. In short, the contrast is between what parents are and what they do. In a sample of all the fifth-grade children in a Midwestern community, Wolf obtained a multiple correlation of +.76 between the process variables and intelligence; Dave obtained a multiple correlation of +.80 between the process variables and achievement. These contrast with usual correlations of +.40 to +.50 between intelligence of achievement and usual measures of socio-economic status. (See Bloom, 1964, pp. 24 and 79, for summaries of these two studies.)

In this sense, the widespread finding of a significant positive correlation between social class (a cluster of status characteristics) and the rate of language development begs the important question of what mediating process variables may be operating. I have therefore adapted the categories used by Gray and Klaus (1964) and will outline the features of the environment that may be critical under three headings: context, or the non-verbal setting in which the language occurs; stimulation; and responses to the child's speech. Some of these may have a "differential" impact on language development, while others may have a more "pervasive" impact on cognitive development in general (Lesser et al., 1965). Unfortunately, we are not yet able to separate these two sets of variables.

Context. Five features of the non-verbal context may be important: the affective quality, whether the child talks to adults or other children, how varied the contexts are, the prevailing signal-to-noise ratio, and conversation versus television. These will be discussed in order.

Affective quality — There is widespread emphasis on the key role in language development of the mother-child relationship. It is difficult to test the specific influence of that relationship, however, because warm feeling and lots of talk tend to occur together. This confounding is present when home care is contrasted with institutional care (e.g., Provence and Lipton, 1962). It is also present when the home environments of high and low scores on reading readiness tests are compared (Milner, 1951).

Adults versus children — Children talk with adults and other children, and the relative amounts of such talk vary greatly among subcultural groups. Which has the greater influence on language development is still an unresolved question. On one side of the issue are those linguists who argue that children speak more like their peers than like their parents. This is the view of Jespersen (1922) and Hockett (1950). And more recently, Stewart (1964, p. 14 n.) has observed:

> It is easy to find cases involving second- or third-generation Washington [D.C.] Negro families in which the parents are speakers of a quite standard variety of English, but where the children's speech is much closer to that of the newer immigrants [from the South]. . . . This phenomenon, incidentally, seems to support the theory that children learn more language behavior from members of their own peer group than from their parents, and suggests that educator concern over the quality of "language in the home" may be misplaced.

On the other side are those psychologists who offer convincing evidence that the speech of children without siblings, who presumably have more opportunity for conversation with parents, is generally superior. Examples can be found in the studies of Koch (1954), Nisbet (1961), and most recently in Vera John's finding [3] of a birth-order effect on language development within a sample of lower-class Negro children.

No doubt, studies of conversation among children could help resolve the issue, but such studies are rare. One example is Smith's (1935) analysis of the mean length of utterance of 220 children, from 18 to 70 months in age, in two situations — at play with other children and at home with adults. The children used longer sentences in conversation with adults, probably because they answered fewer questions, gave fewer imperatives, and generally engaged in more connected discourse with active play and fewer interruptions.

Only a possible direction for resolution of these seemingly conflicting claims can be suggested. Extrapolating far beyond the present evidence,

[3] Personal communication from Vera P. John, 1965.

and using a computer analogy, I wonder if the opportunity to talk with adults may largely determine the complexity of the "programs" for constructing and understanding utterances which a child can handle, while conversation with peers has more effect on specific details of those "programs" such as features of phonology and morphology.

Contextual variety — A child's language develops within contexts of greater or less variety. Deutsch and Brown (1964) suggest that variety in family activities increases verbal interaction. Ausubel (1964) writes of the desirability of a wide range of objects which can serve as referents for speech. John and Goldstein (1964) report that a group of lower-class Negro four-year-olds had trouble on the Peabody Picture Vocabulary Test with such action words as *digging* and *tying*. They suggest that a word like *digging* differs from one like *Coca Cola* in the stability of the word-referent relationship: "Gerunds such as *tying* were failed, not because the children were deficient in experience with the referent, but rather because they had difficulty in fitting the label to the varying forms of action observed and experienced" (p. 269). They argue that the process of generalization and discrimination involved in learning the meanings of more abstract words does not come about simply through "receptive exposure" to many examples but through "active participation with a more verbally mature individual" (p. 273). The benefits of variety in non-verbal experience may depend on the availability of help in encoding that experience in words.

Varied surroundings can stimulate and reinforce different functions of language. Bernstein (1962a, p. 32) contrasts "restricted" and "elaborated" codes, and asserts that working-class speech is characterized by a restricted code which "is played out against a background of communal, self-consciously held interests which remove the need to verbalize subjective intent and make it explicit." It may be that during the period of language learning those children who are confronted with a narrow range of close personal contacts learn only the economical mode of communication that suffices within that small circle. A related hypothesis is suggested in Frake's (1961) study of folk taxonomies: ". . . the greater the number of distinct social contexts in which information about a particular phenomenon [e.g., skin disease] must be communicated, the greater the number of different levels of contrast into which that phenomenon is categorized" (p. 121).

Signal-to-noise ratio — Deutsch (1963) discusses the relevance to language learning of the overall signal-to-noise ratio prevailing in the daily environment. One characteristic of slum living which may contribute to language retardation is the high noise level, not only in the literal sense but in the minimum of non-instructional conversation directed toward the child. This situation is ideal for inducing habitual inattention. The child may learn to "tune out" both meaningless noise and the occasional meaningful stimuli, with the result of an absolute decrease in effective stimulation.

Conversation versus television — Lastly, what about television? Children from lower-status groups watch as much TV as higher-status groups, if not more (Keller, 1963; Wortis et al., 1963). Why isn't this extra language stimulation more beneficial? Is the critical difference passive listening to a monologue versus active participation in a dialogue? If so, then what of the supposed benefit of listening to stories? Is attention to language reduced when it is embedded in the context of constantly changing visual stimuli. There is evidence that TV has some positive effect on vocabulary (Schramm, Lyle, and Parker, 1961), but research is needed on what children attend to while watching TV and how they process the language heard in this context.

Stimulation. Language stimulation can vary both in quality and in quantity. The quality of the stimulus in turn can vary along lines of conformity to Standard English, variety, and sequence.

Conformity to Standard English — Ervin (1964, p. 163) states: "Children's grammar converges on the norm for the community in which they live." If that norm is not Standard English some of the effects may resemble retarded speech, as we have seen, and may be unfortunate from other standpoints. But when we study the rate of language development as such, a child's progress should be judged in terms of his approach toward the norm for his particular language community. Whether the nature of that norm can itself affect development is an open empirical question.

In studies cited earlier, Wolf (1964) and Dave (1963) found that a rating of opportunities provided in the home for enlarging vocabulary and using a variety of sentence patterns correlated highly with both intelligence and achievement, while a judgment by the interviewer of the quality of language usage of the mother did not. Dave (1963, p. 114) was thus led to observe, "This may imply that the quality of language usage of the parents, and the extent of verbal interaction among family members, are quite independent characteristics."

Linguistic variety — Variety in the non-verbal setting in which language occurs has already been discussed; here we are dealing with the variety in the words and grammatical patterns which the child hears. Razran (1961, p. 126) reports a Soviet experiment on the role of both kinds of variety in the development of lexical meanings. A group of nine children, 19 months old, were given 20 simultaneous exposures to a book and a sentence about a book. Three children received a single book and a single sentence; three received a single book and 20 different sentences; and three received 20 different books and a single sentence. Learning, as measured by the child's ability to select a book from a group of objects, was greatest for the varied language group, next best for the varied referent group, and practically nonexistent for the first group.

Another approach uses the "type-token" ratio. Briefly, the number of tokens — e.g., the total number of instances of plural nouns that a child hears — is an indication of the sheer quality of language stimulation. The number of types — e.g., the number of different nouns which the child hears pluralized — is a measure of variety. Miller and Ervin (1964) have asked whether greater variety, as measured by the type-token ratio, plays a role in the development of grammatical meanings, specifically in the child's developing use of the plural inflection. Starting from non-contrast (e.g., using *boy* for both singular and plural), the child occasionally uses contrasted forms, then correctly contrasts all familiar words, and finally generalizes to irregular nouns (*foots*) and, in an experimental situation, to nonsense words (*biks*). Contrast with familiar forms always precedes generalization to nonsense forms, but the time lapse between the two stages varies. Miller and Ervin (1964, p. 33) therefore point out, "We do not know whether it is the variety of types or the frequency of tokens showing contrast which is crucial in determining the length of time before generalization occurs." The question at issue is whether increased variety, often termed "richness," adds anything to increased quantity alone. It is at least a hypothesis to be explored that variety does aid the child, in and of itself; and, conversely, that language that is impoverished is harder to learn, not easier.

Three arguments can be suggested for this hypothesis. First, if as Cofer has commented, "learning of inflectional and syntactical skills is akin to concept formation" (Cofer and Musgrave, 1963, p. 198), then variation in irrelevant features (e.g., particular count nouns) may aid learning of the concept of inflectional marking of plurality. Second, increased variety of language stimulation may enhance attentional processes in the child (Fiske and Maddi, 1961). Third and purely theoretical, if the process of first language acquisition is akin to scientific theory construction in which hypotheses are tested against available data, as the transformational grammarians argue, then a meager set of data could be a hindrance. Fodor (ms.) makes this argument explicit:

> If parents do simplify the syntax of their speech when they address children they may make it *harder* for the child to learn the correct syntactic analysis of his language. Rules that hold for selected sets of simple sentences may have to be abandoned in the light of examples of sentences of more complicated types.

In contrast to variety are well-learned routines. These may include sentences such as *I don't know;* they may also include bits of nursery rhymes and songs and, perhaps most important of all, phrases from books read to the child many times. It has been a long time since Carroll (1939, p. 222) suggested, "An interesting investigation could be set upon the hypothesis that learning of rote material is an important factor in speech development." That investigation still remains to be done.

Sequence — In analyzing the detrimental effects of the slum environment, Deutsch (1963, p. 168) suggests that "in addition to the restriction in variety . . . it might be postulated that the segments made available to these children tend to have poorer and less systematic ordering of stimulation sequences, and would thereby be less useful to the growth and motivation of cognitive potential." Variety can be described in absolute terms, e.g., by the type-token ratio, but sequence cannot. For while an optimal sequence may incorporate some absolute dimension of complexity, there remains as a relative component the "match" between the stimuli the child encounters in his environment and the cognitive structures which determines his readiness to respond to them (Hunt, 1961).

This match can be improved in two ways. The adult might provide a rich and varied supply of stimuli and let the child find what he needs. This was the principle involved in the self-selection feeding practices of some years ago; it is also the principle recommended by the Montessori method (Hunt, 1964). Applied to language development, this principle would predict that if a child has the chance to hear a sufficiently varied and large sample of well-formed sentences, he will take from it what he needs for the acquisition of his own language system. Alternatively, the adult might preselect certain stimuli for the child. Such preselection could be either purposeful or fortuitous. For first language learning it would have to be fortuitous, since no one knows enough about what the child is doing to plan his curriculum.

Quantity — Finally, the language stimulation available to a child can and does vary in quantity. It seems intuitively obvious that differences in quantity should affect language development, although frequency of exposure may matter only up to some threshold, beyond which no additional benefits may accrue. But severe problems face any attempt to separate the effects of frequency of stimulation from the effects of responses to the child's speech.

Response to the Child's Speech. It is still an open question whether some category of response, such as reinforcement or feedback, is necessary or at least very helpful to language development, or whether rich stimulation or exposure is sufficient. For the most part, the theoretical controversy is carried on between experimental psychologists who attempt to substantiate their theories of human learning by fitting them to the child's strikingly successful acquisition of language (e.g., Staats and Staats, 1963), and linguists and their cognitive psychology associates who derive implications for the process of acquisition from the transformational model of language structure (e.g., Fodor, ms.; Lenneberg, 1964; Katz, 1969; McNeill, 1968). A review of the arguments is outside the scope of this paper. I will only suggest one way in which reinforcement may apply, then review several empirical studies.

Whether reinforcement applies to any of the actual content of the language learning process — to any aspect of phonology, vocabulary, or grammar — it may apply to the child's interest in, valuing of, and motivation toward language. It may affect his attentiveness, regardless of what is happening while he is attending. It seems to me that some global effect such as this, ill-defined as it is, is necessary to explain the role of the Jewish tradition in consistently producing an impact in the direction of superiority in verbal development. (See Lee, 1960, for a description of this subculture.) At the opposite extreme is the isolated and hopeless situation of many mothers on Aid to Dependent Children, where "the reduction of absolute power undercuts the motivation for protracted verbal exploration of action possibilities" (Strodtbeck, 1965, p. 108).

Studies of infant vocal behavior have been widely cited in support of reinforcement theories of language learning. Detailed comparisons have been made of caretaking activities of parents in homes and of adults in institutions (Rheingold, 1960, 1961; Provence and Lipton, 1962). There is notably more talking to the infants at home — five to nine times as much, according to Rheingold's time-sampling data. There is likewise more vocalizing by the infants themselves. Experimental studies with infants — such as those of Rheingold, Gewirtz, and Ross (1959) and Weissberg's (1963) carefully controlled follow-up study — offer convincing evidence that reinforcement rather than stimulation is operating. But it is questionable whether any results should be generalized across the discontinuity which separates pre-linguistic babbling from true verbal behavior.

Irwin's (1960) experimental study with slightly older children has been widely cited in support of the value of added stimulation. He induced working-class mothers to read to their children for 20 minutes a day from the time the children were 12 months until they were 30 months old. The result was a significant increase in production of speech sounds, both in tokens and in types. Irwin interpreted this result as a response to the systematic increase in the "speech sound stimulation" (1960, p. 189). While reading could indeed have provoked an increased quantity of stimulation alone, it is possible and even likely that in the course of reading the mothers also responded to the vocalizations of the child which the reading may have prompted. Moreover, we do not know how this induced attention to the behavior of her child may have affected the mother's response to him during all the non-reading parts of the day. Once a child has started to speak, it is not feasible to withhold response even for experimental purposes. Consequently, the effects of exposing a child to language and of responding to his language become confounded.

It is commonly assumed (e.g., Ausubel, 1964; Bloom, Davis, and Hess, 1965) that where language has developed well something termed "corrective feedback" has been in ample supply. For this to exist, the child must make errors and the adults must recognize those errors. Parents do seem to correct errors in naming, e.g., of *cat* for *dog*, and feedback may be very important for the learning of vocabulary. But errors of a non-referential nature seem to be largely ignored.

Miller and Ervin (1964, p. 26) give this summary of errors in the speech of two-year-old and three-year-old children:

> Most of the mistakes or deviations from the model can be classified as omissions (*I'll turn water off* for *I'll turn the water off*), overgeneralization of morphophonemic combination (*foots* for *feet*, *a owl* for *an owl*, *breaked* for *broke*), the incorrect use of a function word with a subclass of a lexical class (using *a* with mass nouns and proper nouns), or doubly marked forms (adding the possessive suffix to possessive pronoun, *mine's*).

While no frequency counts are yet available, it is safe to say that except for the category of omissions the proportion of errors in the young child's speech is remarkably small. Furthermore, it is my impression that adults without special training do not "hear" such errors even when they are made. Persons trained to be attentive often cannot catch them except under special conditions, such as repeating tape recordings at half-speed. Ordinarily, we hear what we expect to hear — normal English speech. Not surprisingly, R. Brown and his colleagues (conference discussion in Cofer and Musgrave, 1963, p. 203) found "little correction of children's speech by their parents." Furthermore, there is no evidence that the non-verbal responses of adults match in any way the degree of the child's approximation to the adult model.

Sentences containing errors of omission are one exception to the generalization that errors of a non-referential nature are largely ignored. Such sentences constitute the typical "telegraphic speech" of the young child (Brown and Bellugi, 1964; Brown and Fraser, 1964), and a gradual filling in of the omitted morphemes is the most prominent change characterizing the child's acquisition of grammar. From transcriptions of the speech of two children with their respective graduate student parents, Brown and his colleagues discovered that to the child's telegraphic utterance, e.g., *Mommy lunch*, the parent often responds with the nearest complete sentence appropriate to the particular situation, e.g., *Mommy is having her lunch*. To the content words of nouns, verbs or adjectives in the child's speech, the parent adds mainly the functors: auxiliaries, prepositions, articles, pronouns, and inflections.

Expansions seem to constitute perfect examples of feedback. In fact, they constitute the one category of adult responses where the nature of the assistance to the child can be specified. Again, to quote Brown and Bellugi (1964, p. 143):

> By adding something to the words the child has just produced one confirms his response insofar as it is appropriate. In addition, one takes him somewhat beyond that response but not greatly beyond it. One encodes additional meanings at a moment when he is most likely to be attending to the cues that can teach that meaning.

In discussing the optimal sequencing of stimuli, I suggested that if it does occur in the language learning process it must occur fortuitously. Expansions, by their very nature, provide such sequencing. No one has suggested that parents expand with any conscious tutorial intention. It seems simply to be one spontaneous way of keeping the conversation with a young child going.

Discovery of the category of expansions made possible a new attempt to separate the effects of exposure and contingent responses. At first it seemed this might be possible even in natural observations, and that it would therefore be informative to compare the emergence in the child of grammatical construction heard in the adult's non-expanding speech with those appearing in the adult's expansion of the child's telegraphic utterances. Brown [4] found that for his two subjects the order of emergence of some 40 different grammatical constructions can be well predicted (rank order correlation near .80) by the frequency with which the same constructions are used by the mothers. But the constructions more often used in the parents' non-expanding speech were also the ones more often expanded. The confounding of the two variables was still present.

Part of the present writer's own research (Cazden, 1965) was an experiment designed to separate adult expansions from adult modeling of well-formed sentences. The subjects were 12 Negro children, 28–38 months old, attending an urban day-care center. One group (expansion) received 40 minutes a day of intensive and deliberate expansions; another group (modeling) received 30 minutes a day of exposure to an equal number of well-formed sentences which deliberately were not expansions. One of two tutors, trained for the research, talked with each child in these two groups in an individual play session every school day for three months. A third group (control) received no special treatment. Six measures of language development were used, one being a structured sentence imitation test. The other five were measures of spontaneous speech — mean length of utterance, complexity measures of noun and verb phrases, percentage

[4] R. Brown, unpublished memorandum, 1964.

of copulas supplied, and percentage of sentences which included both subject and predicate.

Contrary to predictions, the children who received the non-expanding language simulation gained the most. One possible explanation is that as the concentration of expansion goes up, in this case far above that occurring in natural conversation, the richness of the verbal stimulation goes down. By definition, expansions are contingent on the child's speech, in content as well as in timing. To the extent that they are pure expansions, just filling in the child's telegraphic utterance to make it a complete one, they will have less variety of vocabulary and grammatical patterns than the adult's non-expanding speech normally contains.

In summary, a tentative resolution of the stimulation-reinforcement controversy can be suggested. Reinforcement, in the classical sense, probably operates to increase vocalizations at the babbling stage of infancy. But once true language begins to develop there is no clear evidence that any specific kind of adult response, verbal or non-verbal, aids the child's progress. Natural observations and the few existing manipulative studies are consistent with the hypothesis that it is the amount and richness of language stimulation available in the context of face-to-face interaction which is most important. Differential access to such stimulation by children from different subcultural groups can be explained by differences in the conditions of their lives, as outlined above under "Context."

Developmental Scales

There is general hope that current research on the acquisition of language [5] will eventually make possible developmental scales which will be more valid measures than mean sentence length (Carroll, 1961). Little consideration has thus far been given to problems which dialect differences pose in establishing such scales. Ervin and Miller (1963, p. 126) recognize the problem: "Adult usage differs in the various subcultures of any community. A good developmental measure for general use should include only those features common to all adult speech in the presence of children." The author faced this problem in the research reported above (Cazden, 1965). I needed to measure the grammatical development of working-class Negro children, but had to devise scales from data on the language of two children from graduate-student families. Because that experience suggests that the problems posed by dialect differences will not be easily solved, it will be recounted in some detail.

The grammatical structure of child speech can be scaled along at least three dimensions — developmental sequence, structural complexity, and conformity to Standard English. Complexity undoubtedly influences the

---

[5] See Bellugi and Brown (1964) for a report on current research in this area.

sequence of emergence but is not in any one-to-one correspondence with it.

Two examples may clarify this point. Brown and Bellugi (1964) have studied the development of the noun phrase. They found that in the first stage any modifier was used with any noun. When the differentiation process began, articles were separated out of the class of modifiers. The children said *A blue flower* but not *Blue a flower*. Only later did they use two modifiers other than articles before a noun (*My blue flower*). Therefore, on a weighted index, *Flower, Nice flower, A blue flower,* and *My blue flower* may be scored from 1 to 4, respectively. There is no objective difference in complexity which dictates this separation of articles from other modifiers. *A blue flower* and *My blue flower* each contain three units in a common pattern. Yet the developmental sequence is clear.

Verb forms present a contrasting case. The sequence of *I drop, I dropping,* and *I'm dropping* represents both increasing complexity and sequence of emergence, and the forms may be accordingly scored 1, 2 and 3, respectively. But what of the past tense *dropped?* On the basis of complexity it should be grouped with *dropping,* as a verb plus one additional element, but its period of emergence is definitely later. If we knew exactly when it appeared in relation to other forms, it could be scored accordingly. Since we don't know, the decision has to be made on grounds of complexity: *dropped* thus receives 2 points.

Conformity to Standard English is another possible criterion — one I deliberately did not apply. Thus *a trees* and *a coffee* were each given full credit on the noun-phrase index. But conformity did intrude. Sometimes deviations from Standard English left the meaning ambiguous. If the child said *Her go upstairs,* clearly *her* was being used in the subject position. But if the child said *He wet him bed,* it was not equally clear whether *him* was being used as a possessive pronoun. Sometimes non-standard forms raised problems in scoring even when the meaning was clear. The children in my sample often used an auxiliary with an unmodified verb, such as *He's go* or *I'm put.* These patterns hadn't been anticipated, since they had not appeared in Brown and Bellugi's data. Strictly on a criterion of complexity, *I'm put* would be counted as two verb elements, along with the more familiar *He going* or *I putting.* Dialect differences also made it impossible to measure the use of negation. Basis for such an analysis has been provided by Bellugi's (in press) study of the sequence of emergence of particular negative forms, but many of the utterances of the subjects in my study could not be placed on Bellugi's scale. First, the frequent use of *got* and *ain't got* produced a construction where the negation appeared after the verb, as in *I got no crayons.* Second, multiple negatives (*I not kiss no people*) were more frequent and seemed to appear at earlier stages than in Bellugi's data. In the end, I gave up the attempt to do this analysis.

I have already suggested that, ideally, a child's language development should be evaluated in terms of his progress toward the norms for his particular speech community. My reliance on complexity more than on developmental sequence as a criterion for evaluation helped make possible the transfer from one dialect to another. A scale which accepts alternate forms of the complexity on which it is based can be applied cross-culturally more appropriately than one based on sequence of emergence. Though the latter is otherwise the superior criterion, it is more likely to penalize departures from a preconceived norm. This issue of "dialect-fair" scales of language development may become as significant in the future as that of "culture-fair" tests of intelligence has been in the past.

DIFFERENT MODES OF COMMUNICATION

To view the language of subcultural groups as different modes of communication, it is necessary to go beyond the structured system of symbols and the rate at which parts of that system are learned to the functions the language serves in actual verbal behavior. This requirement is one version of the contrast between language and speech, which is at once so important and subject to many interpretations.

The two main categories of language functions are, as Carroll (1964, p. 4) has stated them, "(1) as a system of responses by which individuals communicate with each other (inter-individual communication); and (2) as a system of responses that facilitates thinking and action for the individual (intra-individual communication)." In this paper I use the term "mode of communication" to refer to both subsystems of language functioning, which are somehow intimately related. I say "somehow related" because we do not know how overt speech becomes internalized into covert thought, particularly in the case of the growing child (John, 1964). Of great importance for the study of subcultural differences in child language, we don't know how variation in the use of language for inter-individual communication affects its use as an intra-individual cognitive tool. For reasons that have to do with the intellectual history of the behavioral sciences,[6] the two functions of language have been studied in separation. One reason for subsuming my discussion under one term, "different modes of communication," is to emphasize the importance of their relationship.

[6] In this regard, see Hymes (1963) for the viewpoint of those in the field of linguistics, and Cronbach (1957) for those in psychology.

Inter-individual Communication

A statement by Hymes (1961, p. 57) is immediately pertinent here:

> In a society, speech as an activity is not a simple function of the structure and meanings of the language or language involved. Nor is speech activity random. Like the languages, it is patterned, governed by rules; and this patterning also must be learned by linguistically normal participants in the society. Moreover, the patterning of speech activity is not the same from society to society, or from group to group within societies such as our own.

How speech activity is patterned is the focus of a new inter-disciplinary study, the ethnography of communication. More recent publications by Hymes offer both an overview of the field (Hymes, 1964b) and a provocative discussion of the inadequacies of the description given by the transformational linguists of the capabilities of language users (Hymes, 1964a). Overlapping with an ethnography of communication, but not confined to naturalistic observations, is another inter-disciplinary field, socio-linguistics (see Ervin-Tripp, 1964). Both deal with the questions who says what to whom, how, and in what situations.

Studies of subcultural differences in inter-individual communication have been carried out by Bossard (1954), Schatzman and Strauss (1955), Bernstein (1959, 1960, 1961, 1962a, 1962b), Loban (1963), and Lawton (1964). (The work of Hess and his colleagues will be considered in the next section.) These studies are quite different, and the story of their work will not be a connected one. But each raises interesting issues for further exploration.

Bossard (1954) was a pioneer in what used to be called "the sociology of language." He analyzed the mealtime conversations of 35 families and found differences in amount of talk per unit of time, in range of vocabulary, in the use of imagery, in the extent to which children were interrupted, and in whether the talk was child- or adult-centered — with social class "the most important line of cleavage in our language records" (pp. 190–191). Studies by Milner (1951) and Keller (1963), previously cited, found that lower-class children are more apt to eat alone or with siblings, and less apt to eat with adults, than middle-class children. What Bossard's work indicates is that children not only participate in different speech situations, but that even where the situation is a common one, family mealtime conversations, the patterns of speech activity vary along social-class lines.

The study by Schatzman and Strauss (1955) is included here even though the subjects were adults, because it raised important questions about inter-group versus intra-group communication. Twenty subjects, 10 upper-status and 10 low-status individuals selected from the extremes

of income and education, were interviewed in a small Arkansas town after
a tornado. The authors summarize the difference in the resulting narratives of members of the two groups:

> The difference is a considerable disparity in (a) the number and kinds
> of perspectives utilized in communication; (b) the ability to take the
> listener's role; (c) the handling of classification; and (d) the framework
> and stylistic devices which order and implement the communication
> (p. 329).

In analyzing these differences, Schatzman and Strauss express two different ideas. On the one hand, they say that the upper-status subject is
better able to make his meaning explicit because he has been more
often in situations where this is necessary, whereas the lower-status subject
is accustomed to talking about his experiences only with people with
whom he shares a great deal of previous experience and symbolism. By this
view, the experience of the upper-status speakers has taught him how to
encode more information. Yet, on the other hand, the authors also seem to
assert that the important variable is not how much information the speaker
has encoded, but the extent to which communication of it from speaker to
listener may be impeded by "differential rules for the ordering of speech
and thought" (p. 329). These rules, describing the structure of speech, are
independent of those describing the structure of language, referred to earlier in the discussion of dialects. Subcultural differences in both kinds of
rules may have been tapped in Cherry's (1965) study of communication
in the classroom.

Bernstein's work in Great Britain is cited in virtually every discussion of
the influence of subcultural differences — in this case, social class — on
language and cognition. It is cited, but rarely is it subjected to the analysis
it deserves. He set out "to find a way of analyzing some of the interrelationships between social structure, language use, and subsequent behavior"
(Bernstein, 1962a, p. 31). He postulated the existence of two codes,
restricted and elaborated. These are defined in terms "of the probability
of predicting which structural elements will be selected for the organization of meaning" — highly predictable in the first case, much less so in
the second. Further, the first is considered to facilitate "verbal elaboration
of intent," the second to limit "verbal explication of intent" (Bernstein,
1962b, p. 233).

So far, he has reported one experiment testing three hypotheses related
to these codes: that they can be distinguished, that their use is associated
with social class, and that their use is independent of measured intelligence. For a non-linguistic measure of the verbal planning functions associated with speech, he drew on Goldman-Eisler's (1958) research on the
nature of hesitation phenomena. Goldman-Eisler differentiates between

two kinds of gaps in the continuity of speech-production: breathing, related to the motor dimension; and hesitations or pauses, related to the symbolic dimension. Measuring the frequency and duration of pauses, she found that they anticipated a sudden increase in information as measured by transitional probabilities:

> Fluent speech was shown to consist of habitual combinations of words such as were shared by the language community and such as had become more or less automatic. Where a sequence ceased to be a matter of common conditioning or learning, where a speaker's choice was highly individual and unexpected, on the other hand, speech was hesitant (1958, p. 67).

Using Goldman-Eisler's procedures, Bernstein analyzed the verbal behavior of a group of 16-year-old boys. From 61 lower-status messenger boys and 45 (British) "public school" boys he selected five subgroups of 4 or 5 boys each, arranged so that their speech patterns could be compared while holding social class or verbal and non-verbal intelligence constant. An unstructured discussion of capital punishment was held with each subgroup, with only one special provision: "It was thought the working-class group would find the test situation threatening and that this would interfere with the speech and consequently all working-class groups had two practice sessions (one a week) before the test discussion" (1962a, p. 37). Analysis of the recorded group discussions confirmed all three of his hypotheses in regard to the "codes."

Bernstein (1962b) acknowledges the limitations of a small sample and a discussion topic which may not have had the same significance for the two social-class groups. But he has not raised the question of the possible effect of the two practice sessions on the fluency of the working-class speech. Fluency, as measured by the hesitation phenomena, was taken as the operational definition of predictability, and that in turn was the defining attribute of the restricted code. Any influence of the practice sessions would have been in the direction of greater fluency. But sound research procedures requires that bias, if unavoidable, should work against one's hypothesis, not for it. The experiment has since been replicated by Lawton (1964) — but the analysis of the hesitation phenomena is not yet available and he does not indicate whether he repeated the practice sessions for the working-class group.

Of greater importance is that Bernstein's theory reaches beyond verbal behavior to cognitive functioning in general. He believes that differences in the habitual modes of speech arise out of "a different way of organizing and responding to experience" (1959, p. 312), and that they accordingly "create and reinforce in the user different dimensions of significance" (1960, p. 276). In other words, speech is seen as both effect and cause:

"In some way the form of the social relationship acts selectively on the speech possibilities of the individual, and again in some way these possibilities constrain behavior" (1962a, p. 31). Further, he believes that the nature of the restricted code has far-reaching implications for the behavior of its speakers: a low level of conceptualization, a disinterest in process, a preference for inclusive social relationships and group solidarity, and socially induced conservatism and acceptance of authority (1961, pp. 300–303).

With these last assertions we are right in the middle of the well-argued controversy over the Whorf hypothesis that language conditions our perceptions of and responses to the environment. Bernstein's version of that hypothesis may be a particularly interesting one. Whorf was interested in the influence of the structure of language, whereas Bernstein was interested in the influence of the structure of speech activity. Hymes (1964b, p. 20) suggests that the latter is the more fundamental question: "What chance the language has to make an impress upon individuals and behavior will depend upon the degree and pattern of its admission into communicative events." But Bernstein's formulation is a hypothesis, nonetheless.

It is not possible to review here the arguments for and against the strong ("language determines") and the weak ("language predisposes") versions of the Whorf hypothesis. It is sufficient to report the widespread agreement that evidence of differences in language, no matter how extreme, cannot be used both to suggest and to prove differences in feeling, thought, or other non-verbal behavior. The claimed effects of language or speech differences on ways of perceiving or responding must be demonstrated and not merely assumed, and their proof must involve independent measures of linguistic and non-linguistic behavior (Carroll, 1958). Since all of Bernstein's data deal with speech, there is so far no supporting evidence for the broader implications of the differences he reports.

Bernstein is dealing with a topic of great interest today, and he has engaged in theory construction in a field where theory is sorely needed. The danger is that those reading the widespread references to his work may take his assertions as proven fact, rather than as hypotheses to be tested. The result could be a stereotype of working-class children and adults as unfortunate as the now-discredited stereotype of limited genetic potential. Schorr (1964, p. 911) retells a poignant admission by sociologists that, "according to all that they knew of it, the [civil rights] sit-in movement should never have happened." At least sociologists were in no position to make their erroneous prediction come true. But educators are among the readers of the frequent references to Bernstein's work, and through them the danger of a self-fulfilling prophecy is a real one.

One other point merits examination before leaving Bernstein's work. Earlier, I mentioned that he found a social-class difference in the use of what he calls "egocentric" and "sociocentric" sequences. The former refers to the sequence *I think*, which is more used by middle-class speakers. The latter refers to terminal sequences such as *isn't it, you know, ain't it, wouldn't he* — "sympathy circularity sequences" (1962b, p. 223) — used more by lower-class speakers. Bernstein considers both egocentric and sociocentric sequences to be ways of dealing with uncertainty, with quite different results. For example, he has stated (1962b, p. 237):

> Inasmuch as the S.C. [Sociocentric] sequences . . . invite implicit affirmation of the previous sequence, then they tend to close communication in a particular area rather than to facilitate its development and elaboration. . . . The "I think" sequence, on the other hand, allows the listener far more degrees of freedom and may be regarded as an invitation . . . to develop the communication on his own terms.

His interpretation of the function of these two modes of communication contrasts with one of Loban's findings. Loban (1963, pp. 53–54) has reported:

> Those subjects who proved to have the greatest power over language by every measure that could be applied . . . were *the subjects who most frequently used language to express tentativeness* . . . These most capable speakers often use such expressions as the following:
>
> > It might be a gopher, but I'm not sure.
> > That, I think, is in Africa.
> > I'm not exactly sure where that is.
>
> The child with less power over language appears to be less flexible in his thinking, is not often capable of seeing more than one alternative, and apparently summons up all his linguistic resources merely to make a flat dogmatic statement.

Remembering that his high language group was also higher in socioeconomic status, we see that Loban, in a study of elementary school children in California, and Bernstein, in a study of adolescents in England, both found that higher-status subjects say *I think* more than lower-status subjects do. What is striking is the ease with which two interpretations are placed on the common finding. Bernstein contrasts *I think* with *ain't it*, and finds an egocentric-sociocentric contrast. Loban groups *I think* with *I'm not exactly sure* as examples of cognitive flexibility.

Intra-individual Communication

The use of language as a cognitive tool for intra-individual communication places its own demands on some special set of inner resources. Jensen (1968) sees it as depending on the existence within the individual of a hierarchical verbal network "which environmental stimuli, both verbal and non-verbal, enter [into] and ramify. . . . A great deal of what we think of as intelligence, or as verbal ability, or learning ability, can be thought of in terms of the extensiveness and complexity of this verbal network and of the strength of the interconnections between its elements." There are at least two variables here: the number of elements and the quality (which could be further subdivided at least into complexity and strength) of their connections. In discussing measures of vocabulary, I reported studies which found subcultural differences in the repertoire of words or grammatical patterns available or used. A repertoire can be defined by a list and is synonymous with the number of elements in the network. But network has a second attribute which repertoire does not — the structure or relations of its parts. We know little about subcultural differences in the use of this verbal network in purely mediational, covert ways, because few experimental psychologists have been interested in individual differences, much less group differences, among their subjects.

The work of Jensen (1963a, 1963b, 1968) indicates important directions for such research. He reports an experiment (Jensen, 1963a) in which gifted, average, and retarded junior high school students, predominantly middle-class, were presented with a multiple stimulus-response problem. On the first presentation of 200 trials, only students in the gifted and average groups gave evidence of learning. Students in the retarded group were given additional trials on subsequent days until their performance also rose above the chance level of correct response. Each day a new procedure was used: first verbal reinforcement by the experimenter, then stimulus naming by subject prior to responding, stimulus naming while learning, and last, enforced delay of response following reinforcement. All three groups were then tested on a similar but harder task. Here the groups still differed significantly, but the retarded group showed marked improvement. An unusual feature of the data was that the retarded group, while as homogeneous in I.Q. as the other two groups, was far more heterogeneous in learning ability. The Mexican-American children, who constituted one-third of the retarded group, were significantly lower than the rest of that group on the first test but then improved markedly.

In discussing these results, Jensen (1963a, p. 138) suggests:

> The normal and fast learners in the retarded group are not really retarded in a primary sense, but are children who, at some crucial period in their development, have failed to learn the kinds of behavior which are necessary as a basis for school learning. . . . The habit of making verbal responses, either overtly or covertly, to events in the environment seems to be one of the major ingredients of the kind of intelligence that shows itself in school achievement and on performance tests. Without this habit, even a child with a perfectly normal nervous system in terms of fundamental learning ability will appear to be retarded, and indeed

is retarded so long as he does not use verbal mediators in learning. Some of the fastest learners among our retarded group, for example, were those who showed no appreciable learning until they were required to make verbal responses to the stimuli.

Jensen (1963b) also reports an experiment by Jacqueline Rapier in which Mexican-American children who were taught verbal mediating links spontaneously used them to form new associations. He suggests that comparisons of the amount of gain in learning ability from such instruction can be used to separate retardation due to neurological causes from retardation due to a verbally impoverished environment. In addition, he gives (Jensen, 1968) extensive proposals for further research.

We do, however, know something about group differences in characteristics of the verbal network. Three studies are available on subcultural differences in word-association responses. In one dating back almost half a century, Mitchell, Rosanoff, and Rosanoff (1919) found that Negro children, ages 4–15, from New York City were less apt to give a common specific reaction (e.g., *chair* to the stimulus *table*) than white children of the same age, and correspondingly more apt to give idiosyncratic reactions. Since commonality of response increases with age, the authors concluded that the Negro children were developmentally immature. The other two studies, both current, deal with another trend in word-association responses. This developmental trend, related to increasing commonality, is the shift from syntagmatic responses (*deep . . . hole*) to paradigmatic responses (*deep . . . shallow*). In an all-Negro sample of first- and fifth-grade children, John (1963) found significant social-class differences only in the first-grade latency scores. Entwisle (1966) also found very slight social-class differences between high-status urban Maryland elementary school children, matched for I.Q., but some retardation for rural Maryland children at the lower I.Q. levels, and further retardation in an Amish group. Recent evidence thus shows that status differences are less dramatic for word-association measures than for other measures of verbal ability, and that those differences decrease, rather than increase, with age. The tendency to give common and paradigmatic responses reaches an asymptote during the age range being studied, and the initially retarded children do catch up.

Vocabulary tests indicate whether certain items are part of a person's verbal network and thereby provide estimates of its total size. They can, if the definitions are scaled, provide additional information on network structure. Carson and Rabin (1960) matched three groups of fourth- to sixth-graders — Northern White, Northern Negro, and Southern Negro (recent in-migrants) — on the Full Range Picture Vocabulary Test. They then administered the same test as a word vocabulary test and grouped the definition into six levels. For example, the six levels for *wagon* could be: (1) a *vehicle* — categorization; (2) *a cart* — synonym; (3) *a wooden thing with four wheels* — essential description; (4) *you ride in it out West* — essential function; (5) *it bumps into people* — vague description or function; and (6) complete error. Even though the groups were matched when the task required only finding a picture to match a word, the Northern White children gave significantly more definitions from levels 1–3 and the Southern Negro children least.

Spain (1962) analyzed definitions given by "deprived" and "non-deprived" elementary school children in central Tennessee. Ten stimulus words were carefully selected to insure that both the word and its superordinate (e.g., *bread* and *food*) were of high frequency and familiar to local first-graders. Definitions were categorized as generic (superordinate), descriptive, and functional. He found that functional definitions remained the predominant response for the deprived children at all age levels; descriptive definitions increased with age at a rate similar for both groups; and that generic definitions increased most sharply for the non-deprived, while the deprived group showed a 4-year lag in this mode of response by the end of elementary school.

The use of language in relation to cognition can also be tapped by categorizing tasks. In general, status differences on such measures increase with age (e.g., see John, 1962). But here the line between studies of language and studies of concept formation disappears, and the limitations of this paper preclude a proper review of such research.

Nevertheless, mention must be made of the large-scale project of Hess and his associates at the University of Chicago, reports of which are now beginning to appear in the published literature (Hess and Shipman, 1965a, 1965b). This is a particularly important study because it relates intra-individual and inter-individual modes of communication. It has been planned as a test of the Bernstein hypothesis of a relation between the child's cognitive development and the mother's verbal ability, maternal teaching style, and characteristic mode of family control. In all, 160 Negro mothers from four socio-economic levels were interviewed, tested, and brought to the university for a structured session of mother-child interaction. Each mother was taught three tasks — two sorting tasks and the use of an Etch-a-Sketch board — and then asked to teach those tasks to her four-year-old child. Her maternal teaching style was monitored and analyzed. The children were subsequently tested by being asked to sort new material and give a verbal explanation. (See Bing, 1963, for similar use of an experimental teaching situation to study mother-child interaction.)

Preliminary results indicate that, while there were no social-class differences in affective elements of the interaction or in persistence of the mothers or in cooperation of the children, on at least some of the performance measures social-class differences were in the direction expected. Hess and Shipman (1965a, p. 192) have reported:

> Children from middle-class homes ranked above children from the lower socio-economic levels in performance on these sorting tasks, particularly in offering verbal explanations as to the basis of sorting. These differences clearly paralleled the relative abilities and teaching skills of the mothers from the different groups.

Additional information on a subset of this sample is available in Stodolsky's (1965) doctoral research. One year after the original data had been collected, she administered the Peabody Picture Vocabulary Test and Kohlberg's Concept Sorting Test to 56 of the original 160 children from three of the four socio-economic groups. The children's scores were then correlated with a selected set of maternal variables from the previous year to find the best predictors. She found that there were significant social-class differences in the vocabulary scores of the children, and that a set of maternal variables predicted those scores with a multiple correlation of .68. The best single pair of maternal variables, in this respect, proved to be the mother's score on the vocabulary part of the WAIS and one of the indices of teaching style. The latter was the "discrimination index" that measures the extent to which the mother isolates task-specific qualities of the environment. While scores on the WAIS differentiated among the mothers on social-class lines, scores on the discrimination index did not. In other words, there is an interaction between characteristics that are class-linked and those that are not.

The entire Hess project is planned to continue until the children have completed four grades of school, with further data being collected on both the mothers and children. Hopefully, analysis of all the data will proceed beyond a test of the Bernstein hypothesis to provide a differentiated picture of how the maternal variables interact in affecting the verbal and cognitive behaviors of the child.

SUMMING UP

In conclusion, the relative space devoted to the three main divisions of this paper is a rough guide to the extent of our present knowledge. We know little about dialect differences as yet; but we should learn much, about urban Negro speech in particular, from the contrastive studies in progress. Relatively, we know the most about language development. Here the evidence of retardation among lower-class children is extensive, and future work will probably concentrate on more precise analysis of the process variables that mediate this relationship. We know very little about differences in language function. Basic research is needed in this area on ways of categorizing the functions that language serves in natural speech communities, and on ways of analyzing the mediational use of language as well.

At the present time, we cannot completely resolve the difference-deficiency issue on which this review has focused. Children who are socially disadvantaged on such objective criteria as income and educational level of their parents do tend to be deficient on many measures of verbal skills. But the concept of subcultural relativity is nevertheless relevant. We must be sure that developmental scales of language development do not distort our assessment of children who speak a nonstandard dialect. We must be equally sure that studies of language function do not simply reflect the predilection of the investigators. In short, subcultural relativity provides an essential perspective for objective analysis and for any program of planned change. Unfortunately, when pressure for change is great, the danger exists that such perspective may be discarded just when we need it most.

References

Anastasi, Anne, and De Jesus, Cruz. Language development and non verbal I.Q. of Puerto Rican children in New York City. *J. Abnorm. Soc. Psychol.*, 48:357–366, 1953.

Ausubel, D. P. How reversible are the cognitive and motivated effects of cultural deprivation? Implications for teaching the culturally deprived child. *Urban Educ.*, 1:16–38, 1964.

Bellugi, Ursula. A transformational analysis of the development of negation. In T. Bever and W. Weksel (eds.), *Psycholinguistic Studies: Experimental Investigations of Syntax.* New York: Holt, Rinehart and Winston, in press.

Bellugi, Ursula, and Brown, R. (eds.) The acquisition of language. *Monogr. Soc. Res. Child Develpm.*, 29:No. 1 (Serial No. 92), 1964.

Bernstein, B. A public language: some sociological implications of a linguistic form. *Brit. J. Sociol.*, 10:311–326, 1959.

Bernstein, B. Language and social class. *Brit. J. Sociol.*, 11:271–276, 1960.

Bernstein, B. Social class and linguistic development: a theory of social learning. In A. H. Halsey, Jean Floud, and C. A. Anderson (eds.), *Education, Economy and Society.* Glencoe, Ill.: Free Press, pp. 288–314, 1961.

Bernstein, B. Linguistic codes, hesitation phenomena and intelligence. *Lang. & Speech*, 5:31–46, 1962a.

Bernstein, B. Social class, linguistic codes and grammatical elements. *Lang. & Speech*, 5:221–240, 1962b.

Bing, Elizabeth. Effect of child-rearing practices on the development of differential cognitive abilities. *Child Develpm.*, 34:631–648, 1963.

Bloom, B. S. *Stability and Change in Human Characteristics.* New York: Wiley, 1964.

Bloom, B. S., Davis, A., and Hess, R. *Compensatory Education for Cultural Deprivation.* New York: Holt, Rinehart and Winston, 1965.

Bossard, J. H. S. *The Sociology of Child Development.* (2nd ed.) New York: Harper, 1954.

Brown, R., and Bellugi, Ursula. Three processes in the child's acquistion of syntax. *Harvard Educ. Rev.*, 34:133–151, 1964.

Brown, R., and Fraser, C. The acquisition of syntax. In Ursula Bellugi and R. Brown, (eds.), The acquisition of language. *Monogr. Soc. Res. Child Develpm.*, 29, No. 1 (Serial No. 92):43–79, 1964.

Carroll, J. B. Determining and numerating adjectives in children's speech. *Child Develpm.*, 10:215–229, 1939.

Carroll, J. B. *Some psychological effects of language structure.* In P. Jock and J. Zubin (eds.), *Psychopathology of Communication.* New York: Ginn & Stratton, pp. 28–36, 1958.

Carroll, J. B. Language development in children. In S. Saporta (ed.), *Psycholinguistics: A Book of Readings.* New York: Holt, Rinehart and Winston, pp. 331–345, 1961.

Carroll, J. B. *Language and Thought.* Englewood Cliffs, N.J.: Prentice-Hall, 1964.

Carson, A. S., and Rabin, A. I. Verbal comprehension and communication in Negro and white children. *J. Educ. Psychol.*, 51:47–51, 1960.

Cazden, Courtney B. Environmental assistance to the child's acquisition of grammar. Unpublished doctoral dissertation, Harvard Univer., 1965.

Center for Applied Linguistics. *Urban Language Study: District of Columbia Proposal.* Washington, D.C.: Author, 1965.

Cherry, Estelle. Children's comprehension of teacher and peer speech. *Child Develpm.*, 36:467–480, 1965.

Cofer, C. N., and Musgrave, Barbara (eds.). *Verbal Behavior and Learning.* New York: McGraw-Hill, 1963.

Cohn, W. On the language of lower-class children. *School Rev.*, 67:435–440, 1959.

Cronbach, L. J. The two disciplines of scientific psychology. *Amer. Psychologist*, 12:671–684, 1957.

Dave, R. H. The identification and measurement of environmental process variables that are related to educational achievement. Unpublished doctoral dissertation, Univer. of Chicago, 1963.

Davis, A. L., and McDavid, R. I., Jr. A description of the Chicago speech survey: communication barriers to the culturally deprived. Ithaca, N.Y.: Cornell Univer., *Project Literacy Reports*, 2:23–25, 1964.

Deutsch, M. The disadvantaged child and the learning process. In A. H. Passow (ed.), *Education in Depressed Areas.* New York: Teachers College, Columbia Univer., pp. 163–179, 1963.

Deutsch, M., and Brown, B. Social influences in Negro-white intelligence differences. *J. Soc. Issues*, 20:24–35, 1964.

Eells, K., Davis, A., Havighurst, R. J., Herrick, V. E., and Tyler, R. W. *Intelligence and Cultural Differences.* Chicago: Univer. Chicago Press, 1951.

Entwisle, Doris R. Developmental socio-linguistics: a comparative study in four sub-cultural settings. *Sociometry*, 29:67–84, 1966.

Ervin, Susan M. Imitation and structural change in children's language. In E. Lenneberg (ed.), *New Directions in the Study of Language.* Cambridge: MIT Press, pp. 163–189, 1964.

Ervin-Tripp, Susan M. An analysis of the interaction of language, topic and listener. In J. J. Gumperz and D. Hymes (eds.), The ethnography of communication. *Amer. Anthrop.*, 66, No. 6, Part 2:86–102, 1964.

Ervin, Susan M., and Miller, W. R. Language development. In H. W. Stevenson (ed.), Child psychology. *Yearb. Nat. Soc. Stud. Educ.*, 62, Part 1:108–143, 1963.

Fiske, D. W., and Maddi, S. R. *Functions of Varied Experience.* Homewood, Ill.: Dorsey Press, 1961.

Fodor, J. A. How to learn to talk: some simple ways. Unpublished ms., undated.

Frake, C. O. The diagnosis of disease among the Subanun of Mindanao, *Amer. Anthrop.*, 53:113–132, 1961. Reprinted in D. Hymes (ed.), *Language in Culture and Society.* New York: Harper & Row, pp. 193–211, 1964.

Fries, C. C. *American English Grammar.* New York: Appleton-Century, 1940.

Fries, C. C. *The Structure of English.* New York: Harcourt, Brace, 1952.

Goldman-Eisler, Frieda. Speech analysis and mental processes. *Lang. & Speech*, 1:59–75, 1958.

Gray, Susan W., and Klaus, R. A. An experimental preschool program for culturally deprived children. Paper read at Amer. Assn. Advancement Sci., Montreal, December, 1964.

Hess, R. D., and Shipman, Virginia. Early blocks to children's learning. *Children*, 12:189–194, 1965a.

Hess, R. D., and Shipman, Virginia. Early experience and socialization of cognitive modes in children. *Child Develpm.*, 36:869–886, 1965b.

Hockett, C. F. Age-grading and linguistic continuity. *Language*, 26:449–457, 1950.

Hunt, J. McV. *Intelligence and Experience*. New York: Ronald Press, 1961.

Hunt, J. McV. The psychological basis for using pre-school enrichment as an antidote for cultural deprivation. *Merrill-Palmer Quart.*, 10:209–248, 1964.

Hymes, D. Functions of speech: an evolutionary approach. In F. C. Gruber (ed.), *Anthropology and Education*. Philadelphia: Univer. Pennsylvania Press, pp. 55–83, 1961.

Hymes, D. Notes toward a history of linguistic anthropology. *Anthrop. Linguistics*, 5:59–103, 1963.

Hymes, D. Directions in (ethno-) linguistic theory. In A. K. Romney & R. G. D'Andrade (eds.), Transcultural studies in cognition. *Amer. Anthrop.*, 66, No. 3, Part 2:6–56, 1964a.

Hymes, D. Introduction: toward ethnographies of communication. In J. J. Gumperz and D. Hymes (eds.), The ethnography of communication. *Amer. Anthrop.*, 66, No. 6, Part 2:1–34, 1964b.

Irwin, O. C. Infant speech: the effect of family occupational status and of age on use of sound types. *J. Speech Hearing Disorders*, 13:224–226, 1948a.

Irwin, O. C. Infant speech: the effect of family occupational status and of age on sound frequency. *J. Speech Hearing Disorders*, 13:320–323, 1948b.

Irwin, O. C. Infant speech: the effect of systematic reading of stories. *J. Speech Hearing Res.*, 3:187–190, 1960.

Jensen, A. R. Learning ability in retarded, average, and gifted children. *Merrill-Palmer Quart.*, 9:123–140, 1963a.

Jensen, A. R. Learning in the preschool years. *J. Nursery Educ.*, 18:133–139, 1963b.

Jensen, A. R. Social class and verbal learning. In M. Deutsch, I. Katz, and A. R. Jensen, (eds.), *Social Class, Race and Psychological Development*. New York: Holt, Rinehart and Winston, 1968.

Jespersen, O. *Language: Its Nature, Development and Origin*. London: George Allen & Unwin, 1922.

Jespersen, O. *Mankind, Nation and Individual From a Linguistic Point of View*. (Originally published, 1946) Bloomington: Indiana Univer. Press, 1964.

John, Vera P. The intellectual development of slum children. *Amer. J. Orthopsychiat.*, 33:813–822, 1963.

John, Vera P. Position paper on pre-school programs. Unpublished manuscript prepared for Commissioner Keppel. Yeshiva Univer., 1964.

John, Vera P., and Goldstein, L. S. The social context of language acquisition. *Merrill-Palmer Quart.*, 10:265–275, 1964.

Katz, J. *The Philosophy of Language*. New York: Harper & Row, 1969.

Keller, Suzanne. The social word of the urban slum child: some early findings. *Amer. J. Orthopsychiat.*, 33:823–831, 1963.

Klima, E. S. Relatedness between grammatical systems. *Language*, 40:1–20, 1964.

Koch, Helen. The relation of "primary mental abilities" in five- and six-year-olds to sex of child and characteristics of his siblings. *Child Develpm.*, 25:209–223, 1954.

Labov, W. Stages in the acquisition of Standard English. In R. W. Shuy (ed.), *Social Dialects and Language Learning*. Champaign, Ill.: National Council of Teachers of English, pp. 77–103, 1965.

Lawton, D. Social class language differences in group discussions. *Lang. & Speech*, 7:183–204, 1964.

Lee, Dorothy. Developing the drive to learn and the questioning mind. In A. Frazier (ed.), *Freeing Capacity To Learn*. Washington, D.C.: Association for Supervision and Curriculum Development, pp. 10–21, 1960.

Lenneberg, E. H. The capacity for language acquisition. In J. A. Fodor and J. J. Katz (eds.), *The Structure of Language: Readings in the Philosophy of Language.* Englewood Cliffs, N.J.: Prentice-Hall, pp. 579–603, 1964.

Lesser, G. S., Fifer, G., and Clark, D. H. Mental abilities of children in different social and cultural groups. *Monogr. Soc. Res. Child Develpm.,* 30, no. 4 (serial no. 102), 1965.

Loban, W. D. *The Language of Elementary School Children.* Champaign, Ill.: National Council of Teachers of English, 1963.

Lorge, I., and Chall, Jeanne. Estimating the size of vocabularies of children and adults: an analysis of methodological issues. *J. Exp. Educ.,* 32:147–157, 1963.

McNeill, D. Developmental psycholinguistics. In G. Lindzey (ed.), *Handbook of Social Psychology* (2nd ed.). Reading, Mass.: Allison-Wesley, (1968).

Miller, W., and Ervin, Susan. The development of grammar in child language. In Ursula Bellugi and R. Brown (eds.), The acquisition of language. *Monogr. Soc. Res. Child Develpm.,* 29, 1 (serial no. 92):9–34, 1964.

Milner, Esther. A study of the relationship between reading readiness in grade one school children and patterns of parent-child interaction. *Child Develpm.,* 22:95–112, 1951.

Mitchell, I., Rosanoff, Isabel R., and Rosanoff, A. J. A study of association in Negro children. *Psychol. Rev.,* 26:354–359, 1919.

Nida, E. A. Analysis of meaning and dictionary making. *Internat. J. Amer. Linguistics,* 24:279–292, 1958.

Nisbet, J. Family environment and intelligence. In A. H. Halsey, Jean Floud, and C. A. Anderson (eds.), *Educational, Economy and Society.* Glencoe, Ill.: Free Press, pp. 273–287, 1961.

Pederson, L. A. Non-standard Negro speech in Chicago. In W. A. Stewart (ed.), *Non-standard Speech and the Teaching of English.* Washington, D.C.: Center for Applied Linguistics, pp. 16–23, 1964.

Provence, Sally, and Lipton, Rose C. *Infants in Institutions.* New York: Internat. Univer. Press, 1962.

Putnam, G. N., and O'Hern, Edna M. The status significance of an isolated urban dialect. Language dissertation No. 53, *Language,* 31, no. 4, Whole part 2, 1955.

Razran, G. The observable unconscious and the inferable conscious in current Soviet psychophysiology: Interceptive conditioning, semantic conditioning, and the orienting reflex. *Psychol. Rev.,* 68:81–147, 1961.

Rheingold, Harriet L. The measurement of maternal care. *Child Develpm.,* 31:565–575, 1960.

Rheingold, Harriet L. The effect of environmental stimulation upon social and exploratory behavior in the human infant. In B. M. Foss (ed.), *Determinants of Infant Behavior.* London: Methuen, pp. 143–170, 1961.

Rheingold, Harriet L., Gewirtz, J. L., & Ross, Helen W. Social conditioning of vocalizations in the infant. *J. Comp. Physiol. Psychol.,* 52:68–73, 1959.

Rosenbaum, P. S. Prerequisites for linguistic studies on the effects of dialect differences on learning to read. Ithaca, N.Y.: Cornell Univer., *Project Literacy Reports,* no. 2:26–30, 1964.

Schatzman, L., and Strauss, A. Social class and modes of communication. *Amer. J. Sociol.,* 60:329–338, 1955.

Schorr, A. L. The nonculture of poverty. *Amer. J. Orthopsychiat.,* 34:907–912, 1964.

Schramm, W., Lyle, J., and Parker, E. B. *Television in the Lives of Our Children.* Stanford, Calif.: Stanford Univer. Press, 1961.

Smith, Madora E. A study of some factors influencing the development of the sentence in preschool children. *J. Genet. Psychol.,* 46:182–212, 1935.

Spain, C. J. Definition of familiar nouns by culturally deprived and non-deprived children of varying ages. Unpublished doctoral dissertation, George Peabody College for Teachers, 1962.

Staats, A. W., and Staats, Carolyn K. *Complex Human Behavior.* New York: Holt, Rinehart and Winston, 1964.

Stewart, W. A. Foreign language teaching methods in quasi-foreign language situations. In W. A. Stewart (ed.), *Non-standard Speech and the Teaching of English.* Washington, D.C.: Center for Applied Linguistics, pp. 1–15, 1964.

Stewart, W. A. Urban Negro speech: socio-linguistic factors affecting English teaching. In R. W. Shuy (ed.), *Social Dialects and Language Learning.* Champaign, Ill.: National Council of Teachers of English, pp. 10–18, 1965.

Stodolsky, Susan. Maternal behavior and language and concept formation in Negro preschool children: an inquiry into process. Unpublished doctoral dissertation, Univer. of Chicago, 1965.

Strodtbeck, F. L. The hidden curriculum in the middle-class home. In J. D. Krumboltz (ed.), *Learning and the Educational Process.* Chicago: Rand McNally, pp. 91–112, 1965.

Templin, Mildred C. *Certain Language Skills in Children: Their Development and Interrelationships.* Minneapolis: Univer. Minnesota Press, 1957.

Thomas, D. R. Oral language, sentence structure, and vocabulary of kindergarten children living in low socio-economic urban areas. Unpublished doctoral dissertation, Wayne State Univer., 1962.

Thomas, O. C. *Transformational Grammar and the Teacher of English.* New York: Holt, Rinehart and Winston, 1965.

Weissberg, P. Social and non-social conditioning of infant vocalizations. *Child Develpm.,* 34:377–388, 1963.

Wolf, R. M. The identification and measurement of environmental process variables related to intelligence. Unpublished doctoral dissertation, Univer. of Chicago, 1964.

Wortis, H., Bardach, J. L., Cutler, R., Rue, R., and Freedman, A. Child-rearing practices in a low socio-economic group. *Pediatrics,* 32:298–307, 1963.

FURTHER READINGS

Aarons, Alfred C., Barbara Y. Gordon, and William A. Stewart (eds.) *Linguistic-cultural differences and American education.* Special anthology issue, *The Florida FL Reporter,* vol. 7 (Spring–Summer 1969).

Cazden, Courtney B., Vera P. John, and Dell Hymes. *Functions of language in the classroom.* New York: Teachers College Press, in press.

Hymes, Dell (ed.) *Language in culture and society: a reader in linguistics and anthropology.* New York: Harper and Row, 1964.

Miller, Wick R. "Language," in Bernard J. Siegel (ed.), *Biennial review of anthropology 1969.* Stanford: Stanford University Press, 1970.

Slobin, Dan I. (ed.) *A field manual for cross-cultural study of the acquisition of communicative competence.* Berkeley: University of California Press, 1967.

Tax, Sol. "Group identity and educating the disadvantaged," in *Language programs for the disadvantaged.* Report of the NCTE Task Force on Teaching English to the Disadvantaged. Champaign, Ill.: National Council of Teachers of English, 1965.

5

Anthropology is commonly referred to as the "science of man." If indeed a "science," anthropology typically looks toward the human future with less confidence and enthusiasm than it evidences in dealing with the past or passing. The most definite science in anthropology is retrodictive, *as opposed to* predictive. *Anthropologists are more skilled in and thus disposed to "predicting backward." Their recognized expertise is in explicating what came or occurred before by what is now. The reluctance of anthropology to infer or seriously imagine the human future in any detail derives as much from the logic and method of the profession as from the occasionally punitive sense of "scientific" responsibility attached by some anthropologists to their efforts. Mead for many years has questioned the tendency of anthropologists not to practically engage the human future. She has persistently argued for the various and significant uses of anthropological perspective, inquiry, and knowledge in the daily affairs of contemporary man. Mead's challenging analysis of future directions in American secondary education is indicative of her (sometimes special) insight and of her commitment to a relevant anthropology. She "sees" people, instead of institutions. Her commentary centers primarily on human needs and potential, less so on institutional reform or revision. The high school serves us; its future is predictable in terms of how humane and socially effective that service is and not in terms of what may revive or preserve the institution. Miss Mead is Curator Emeritus of Ethnology, American Museum of Natural History, and Adjunct Professor of Anthropology, Columbia University. The most recent of her many books is* Culture and Commitment: A Study of the Generation Gap *(New York: Doubleday, 1970).*

MARGARET MEAD

The High School of the Future

In today's world, when we consider the fate, educational or otherwise, of any one group, we must also consider, with equal responsibility if not equal intensity, the fate of all other groups. We must remember that not only is the whole world watching outside our windows, but the whole world is vulnerable to every step we take into the future, not only to the missiles we build, but to the models we set, to the kind of schools and hospitals and social security systems, architecture and television networks, kinds of manufacture and planned obsolescence, to the poems we write and the satellites we send into space.

We cannot afford to plan some special kind of education for those who

From *California Journal of Secondary Education*, vol. 35, no. 6 (October 1960), pp. 360–369. Reprinted by permission of the author and publisher.

are best fitted to use the only kind of education we can take the trouble to invent and implement and leave the rest to get on somehow with some sort of secondary education which won't do any more harm than can be helped and which isn't expected to do much good. The use that the most gifted child makes of the most perfect educational resources is a function of how we succeed in helping the least gifted child.

It is now necessary to answer a few fundamental questions which are currently being dodged as we limit our discussions of education to how to get ahead of, or at least keep up with, the Russians.

Do we mean by *high school* simply a stage of education which is possible for any individual, child or adult, who has an elementary school education?

Do we mean by *high school* a stage of education which is the appropriate precursor of some other stage of education without which the latter or further stage cannot be undertaken?

Do we mean by *high school* a kind of schooling which opens many doors, even though they lead to paths not taken at once, not taken for years, or not taken at all, or do we mean a kind of schooling which — like a hospital for incurable cancer patients or the senile — is supposed to be "terminal"?

Do we mean by *high school* not really a school at all in these three rather limited, specialized and archaic senses, but instead a setting for the life of our adolescents with the emphasis upon a phase of growth rather than upon a stage of schooling?

Without answers to these questions, a great deal of contemporary educational discussion loses all focus. If we ask instead: What is there about young people between the ages of twelve and twenty that requires special measures by society, different from the social measures devised for the protection, the education, and the underwriting of achievement in human beings under twelve and over twenty? And is twelve-to-twenty — so unfortunately pickled in the phrase "teenage" — a group in any sense? Is, in fact, chronological age a meaningful form of classification at adolescence, or does its use reflect a laziness that permits us to ignore all the problems of individual difference on which our ideas of freedom, democracy, and human dignity are built?

Don't we need instead some wholly new concept of the period when young are old enough to take part in society at differing rates of learning, maturation, and responsibility? Shouldn't there be some new sort of division among our population into phases of growth like these:

Phase I — Those who are so young or vulnerable or slow growing that continuous contact with a familiar place or a familiar person is needed if learning is to take place. (This phase includes *all infants*, some otherwise ordinary children of five or six who are very slow learners, and children with some kind of mental defect, emotional disturbance, or sensory handicap — as, for example, Helen Keller — and some individuals who must always learn by apprenticeship.) It also includes some individuals who are recovering from situations of extreme destructiveness: from severe operations which require relearning the ability to walk, or talk, or read, or from an experience like concentration camp torture. When individuals are in this vulnerable phase, the learnings are basic to being a human being — learning to recognize and trust, to conceptualize accurately, to speak and to understand language, to control bodily behavior and impulses within the limits set by social propriety, to sleep at the times set for sleep and eat food when food is set before one, to respond with modulation to frustration, and to know the difference between good and bad behavior. These are the learnings that make human beings, born to be human, really human in the ways that human societies have developed through half a million years. These are the things that *all* infants have to learn, that some children can learn only very slowly, and that some older people have to relearn. Effective learning in this phase depends upon the existence of a close personal relationship to an identified person. In group situations, without some strong individual supporting relationship, babies die in the best regulated orphanages, patients in the chronic wards of hospitals deteriorate and even cease to speak, and the old become senile long before their time. For the same reason emotionally disturbed children must have individual educational and therapeutic care.

We may call this first phase *the period when individual personal relationships are essential to the learnings basic to being human.* As our definition of what constitutes being human becomes more complex, more persons will need such individualized care oftener and for a longer time.

Phase II — Those who are ready to learn in groups skills which are the products of higher civilization and for which it has seemed more economical to be wasteful of the pupil's time rather than burden each adult with the teaching of a few children, or apprentices, or college freshmen, or members of a new UN team, or young space engineers. Careful consideration will show that in all schools large groups are taught by the same methods things that each individual, working at his own pace and in his own style could have learned faster with an individual tutor. By developing such schools we have made primarily a differential choice between wasting the time of the learners and wasting the time of those who already know how to write, or mend motor engines, or march, or negotiate with the Iranians, or take account of gravitational differences. The more the results of years of specialized experience have been reduced to forms that could be taught by someone who knew how to teach but had not spent time on the behavior itself, the greater the saving society has been felt to make — especially in those periods of history in which the number of specialists in each new skill has been too small for the number of jobs that needed to be done. The more the teaching could be downgraded, the more teaching aids we would substitute for teacher knowledge, the more economical it was. This was equally true of the dame school in England, where the dame knew little more than her pupils, and the Little Red School House whose most recent graduate became next year's teacher with the help of McGuffey readers and arithmetic books with a separate "answer book" for the teacher.

A secondary purpose of the group learning phase is to keep track of children who have learned enough to be managed easily in groups but are not yet experienced enough to be left without supervision. This need for supervision is strictly a function of immaturity or ignorance of some sort which children from six to twelve display and which also characterizes immigrants to a new country who have not yet learned the language, recently discharged patients from a mental hospital, rural-born workers trying to learn urban skills. Such supervision should not be confused with education.

In this phase of group learning, the group itself may be utilized to standardize the learning. In every civilization there is some need for highly standardized behavior, and just those things for which we want high standardization — spelling, military drill and habits of obedience to command, attention to the dangers of a factory environment, habits of courtesy, honesty, and public cleanliness — are best taught in groups. The group tends to iron out individual differences, is intolerant of deviation, and contributes to the multi-sensory quality of the learning so that what is learned stays closer to a cultural mean appropriate for a wide range of intelligence and ability.

It should also be recognized that this conformity-breeding aspect of a "school" — defined as a group of individuals who are at about the same stage of ignorance and are willing to treat each other as contemporaries worthy of respect, a situation necessary for the standardizing and conforming aspects of group learning — is all too often carried over into inappropriate situations. Where the cultivation of individuality and compensation for special idiosyncrasy in knowledge or skill or experience are desirable, an emphasis upon conformity is misplaced. Very often the all too convenient supervision is also carried along, like so much accidental cultural baggage, into "schools" for adults where such supervision is irrelevant, time consuming, and demeaning to the learning group.

Phase III — Those who are growing so unevenly that they require protection in some sectors of life if learning, growth, and achievement are to be possible in other sectors of life.

This phase includes all children who have come out of Phase I, all adolescents, whether adolescence ends at fifteen or sixteen, as it does for some girls, or extends to old age, as it does for some gifted and one-sided artists, scientists, and statesmen. The unevenness of growth may be of many sorts — physical maturation with a poor development of judgment or extreme intellectual or artistic precocity combined with slow or poor physical or social development. This unevenness is characteristic of most, but not all, adolescents. Yet our present way of treating "teenagers" is based on exactly the opposite set of premises (premises, incidentally, that are completely denied by behavioral science research) — namely, that growth, physical, mental and moral, is an orderly and homogeneous process, tightly bound to chronological age. So we regard twelve year olds as *not* ready, but thirteen year olds as ready for a certain set of experiences, which the state then arbitrarily and coercively provides for all thirteen year olds. So many hours in school, so many hours of transportation in school buses, such and such exposures to ideas about atoms, human physiology, Shakespeare, the binomial theorem, and the Constitution of the United States, so many hours sitting still — without recess — so much physical education, so much social life — dating, dances, etc., with individuals of some specified chronological age range — so much summer reading — governed also by libraries who define those over thirteen as "young adults." This suddenly comes to an abrupt halt, however, with the legal age of school leaving when, in whatever state of incompleteness, immaturity, or infinite, unfulfilled promise, the fourteen, sixteen, or eighteen year old ceases to be a "student." It is small wonder that, as recent studies have shown, the major "loss" of that unfortunately phrased group, "college material" — as if human minds were raw materials for the assembly line — occurs. All through school, the assumption of homogeneous growth exaggerates the unreadiness of some at each step; legal school-leaving age suddenly highlights the inappropriateness of the system.

Phase IV — Those who are mature — and I mean *mature*, not just adult — whose need for special protection from the community is minimal, and who are most able to carry the major economic, political, and ethical responsibilities of our society. At present we variously assume that membership in this group is attained by graduating from high school at unknown age, by entering the Armed Services, by marriage, by reaching the age when it is legal to leave school and get a work permit.

None of these criteria has anything to do with maturity; they are actually all artificial constructs which are based partly on chronological age and partly on our ideas of adulthood which include *not* going to school, *not* being subject to parental consent for any type of activity, *not* being protected against certain kinds of gainful employment, or physical or moral dangers open to adults — such as smoking, cigarettes, drinking beer, or electing the risks of sexual promiscuity. A good look at these criteria — as opposed to such criteria as readiness to stop formal learning, readiness to hold a job and to assume the responsibilities of marriage and of full political citizenship — is enough to show how grossly inadequate our current definitions are.

What would be the consequences of our abandoning our contemporary treatment of adolescents, based as it is on a mixture of the planting and harvesting practices of an agrarian society, a long outmoded class structure, a nineteenth century type of exploitive industrialism, a type of restrictive trade unionism that retained medieval features, and an expectation of much slower change? If, instead, we were to say that there is a very large group of adolescents in our society who need special social measures (whether they are precocious physically and mature at ten or eleven, or are in some way slow growers so that they need special treatment at fifty), we could then ask what these measures should be? We would have to add, of course, that in spite of the great range, adolescence occurs for most people in association with physical puberty, so that the *peak* of adolescent needs occurs somewhere within the period now called the "high school years," somewhere within "the 'teens." Public provision for the "high school years" when we place little children and expectant mothers together in the same room is inevitably provision for physical puberty — for the period when young people of the same age may in some respects look and act ten years apart but just alike in others.

Which would be the effect of taking a long look at our *adolescents*, a word which emphasizes a phase of development, instead of at the *high school*, which is historically limited by the history of our educational system? . . .

If we are to plan for adolescence, and recognize that this is a condition that while clustering for most people in the 'teens, for many of the most and least gifted stretches far beyond the end of the 'teens, and sometimes begins before, it is necessary to think of this as a part of life and include the specifics of schooling and learning within that much wider context.

So we may ask what are the protections that adolescents need? Adolescents need protection from discrepancies in their own growth — from the consequences of feeling at one minute like children and in the next like adults; from attempting to cope with newly aroused impulses by psychological mechanisms appropriate to an earlier phase of development; from demanding privileges that go with the status of their dreams rather than with their real capabilities. They need protection from group pressures which deny the different rates and different ways in which they are developing, pressures that force on them too early sexual behavior or too late, too much independence or too little, too little new learning or too much, too much expenditure of energy or so little that hot rods and the games of "chicken" are the answer, too little contact with experienced adults who can serve as models and too much contact with parents who find their children's adolescence more than they can bear, too much freedom from supervision or oversight, so that their health and safety are endangered, and too little chance to experiment.

This may sound like a counsel of perfection, but it can be reduced to some very simple questions: Where should adolescents live; if not at home, in what sort of protected environment? What kind of schools should they attend, and how should classifications be made within the school to correct for our present tendency to substitute chronological age for real indices of maturity? Where should adolescents work, if for particular adolescents working most of the time rather than going to school most of the time seems to be the better solution? It boils down to our accepting responsibility for all adolescents, not just for those in school or those in institutions, or just negative responsibility for those who want to work where they might be exploited, or who might be exposed to moral hazards.

At present, the narrowness of our social responsibility is frightening. Consider a gifted boy of sixteen, who is finishing high school and has given every promise of making some magnificent contribution. The school authorities who registered him know that he lives at home with a father and a mother. If his parents should be killed in an accident while he is still in school, most first-class schools today would ask: Where will he live now? Who will take responsibility for him? Who will see that he is fed and clothed, nursed when he is ill, counseled and cared for? But suppose that on the day after he graduates, the family moves to a new city, where, as they arrive, both parents die in an accident. He is alone in a strange city. Since he has graduated from high school, he is of no concern to the school system. By law he is allowed to work, but no one will be concerned about his occupation unless he works in some industry in which minors are protected, or unless he tries to enter a unionized industry that limits apprenticeship or charges high entrance fees — then someone will bother to keep him out. Only if he breaks the law, will he come to the attention of the court; then possibly the full apparatus of social work and parole will be set in motion to deal with him. If he tries to enlist, the Armed Services may verify his age and turn him away. If he tries to marry and tells the truth about his age, he will be turned down. But as long as he does not get involved with any of the laws which have specified what a boy of sixteen can *not* do, no one in the world has any responsibility for what he does do. Normally he should have had several years of protection while he was helped — his eyes examined, his temperature taken, his clothes checked, his worries listened to and attended to — and guided toward more education or a meaningful job. But because he is *through* high school, is *not on relief*, is *not on probation*, he is just a gifted, immature human being who is left to his own devices.

I have purposely made this a gifted boy who finished high school early and who was suddenly deprived of his only relatives, and this at a time when the family had moved as strangers to a new city. True, this is an extreme case. But none of this essentially changes the picture of how very narrow our social responsibilities are or how differently we worry about those who are in school and those who are out, about those who have passed the tests of acceptability for the Army and those who are rejected, about those who, living in an impoverished and degraded environment, get into trouble and those who don't. There are, in fact, two roads to some sort of guaranteed protection during adolescence. One way involves staying in school, or in the Army, or in some sort of supervised industrial training program, where someone always knows if one is ill or in gross trouble; the other involves *getting into trouble*. In between, there is great wastage of another kind that affects those who leave school, are partly unemployed, take the wrong jobs, marry the wrong girl just to have some feeling of being adult, of being valued as people, in a society in which they can't vote and can't serve in the Armed Services, but must pay taxes, obey laws, and somehow find enough money to pay for a place to lay their heads and for food to stay their hunger and to buy whatever else they crave — a car, a record player, a sharp suit, books.

Out of this unevenness of concern, our adolescents have been building a picture of a society that wants things *from* them but has very little concern for them. If they want to get on, they must finish school, this course or that, with marks good enough at least to open the next door. If they want to stay out of jail, they must be — not law abiding, but — careful. If they want to have some stature in their own eyes, there is little left except the simplest form of adulthood, often lacking in any maturity, premature and dead-end work, marriage, parenthood, bills, and taxes. Everything from them; nothing for them.

So a first step in planning the high school of the future is either to broaden or narrow its functions. If broadened it should be a community center where all adolescents are given a focus and some sort of protection. In this case the high school should no longer be called a "school" both because it would now be dealing with individuals, not with groups gathered together to learn easily transmissible skills, and because it would be dealing with these individuals not in terms of their age and the academic grade they had managed to "pass" or "fail" but as young people some of whom were studying part time, some working, some preparing for national service, some in between any of these. Within this whole youth world, those who happened to be the physicists or poets or statesmen of the future would be given the special facilities they needed, and those who were handicapped — by poor environment, physical defect, emotional disturbance, and mediocre abilities — would be given the facilities they needed. It would be as unthinkable to hold a brilliant boy back in his mathematics as to force a boy who found all school work dull into staying in school when he wanted to go to work. It would be as unthinkable to force a little undersized boy, who hadn't yet started to grow, into unprotected contact with larger boys or forced social relations with girls mature enough for physical motherhood as to insist that these mature girls should date only junior high school boys. It would be as unthinkable to force a boy into science instead of art because he was a boy as to force a girl brilliant in mathematics into typing because she was a girl. No one would have to held back so that other members of the class would learn a little or forced forward so that other members of the class could learn a little bit more. The smaller in size would play games with the smaller in size and study with those at the same stage and with the same degree of intellectual maturity as their own — as has been done for generations in English boys' boarding schools. Good musicians would meet as musicians, those good at sports would meet in sports, and the development of those special forms of intellectualism that now take young people forward to college and graduate school would be protected also. There would be parts of the "school" where the desperate economies of mass teaching would be rigorously eschewed, where the most idiosyncratic and capriciously gifted would be protected.

All of these things could, of course, only be done for large groups of adolescents. But we are moving into a period of large, consolidated schools at such a distance from the pupils' homes that they become their whole world. Such an adolescent center would have many new functions if work and interim periods were also to receive some support and supervision. But decentralization and reclassification would be possible. There might still be neighborhood centers, but young people could be gathered for academic work of different sorts in various parts of a city and they would go to work in many places without introducing the invidious distinctions that still exist, even in the same high school, between those who take an "academic" and those who take a "commercial" course. If the intellectual and gifted students were permitted to go fast enough, there would be plenty of time for those courses against which President Griswold of Yale and Admiral Rickover thunder and fulminate. The good student does not waste nearly so much time learning how to be a responsible driver or something about human relationships, as he does as he sits all day in a class where 75 per cent of the students cannot go as quickly as he can. The grueling schools of European schools — where languages and mathematics are forced on all students — are as wasteful of talent as our schools, destroy children whom we save, and are farther from any real solution for a changing society than we are.

The other solution, a meagre one, is to narrow the school to what it once was — a little academic enclave for the children with the economic resources and the intellectual ability to go on to higher education. We could then undoubtedly return to teaching more mathematics by out-moded methods. Those who did attend would be more firmly prepared to stand outmoded methods of work in college and graduate school. But we would have gone back, not forward, we would have accepted our economic niggardliness, our fear of experimentation, our unwillingness to carry experimentation *far enough,* our fixation on the kind of competition that in the end is certain to give one the defects if not the virtues of one's competitor — as we become made more and more in our rival's image. We would have let competition force us back from the dream that has been so consistently American of some new universal form of responsibility for our children, for all our children, that would provide equality of opportunity, first for all those on our own soil and then hopefully contribute, by example and help, to the children of all the other peoples on this earth. Following this dream would not only protect our children and those of our allies and our possible allies, but the children of our enemies also, *while they are our enemies.* Our image of Russian education, of ruthlessly forcing children to learn science for a devouring state machine endangers our children; echoes of how we react to this image in turn endangers their children, in a rat race of exploitive competition, in which the reason for a community existence is lost sight of and the end becomes not the individual, but the state. The opportunity to learn to be a full human being — which is education in its widest sense — is as indivisible as freedom itself.

FURTHER READINGS

Henry, Jules. "A cross-cultural outline of education," *Current anthropology,* vol. 1 (July 1960).

Mercer, Blaine E., and Edwin R. Carr (eds.) *Education and the social order.* New York: Rinehart and Company, 1957.

Newmann, Fred M., and Donald W. Oliver. *Clarifying public controversy: an approach to teaching social studies.* Boston: Little, Brown, 1970.

Paulsen, F. Robert "Cultural anthropology and education," *Journal of educational sociology,* vol. 34 (March 1961).

Spindler, George D. "Education in a transforming American culture," in George D. Splinder (ed.), *Education and culture: anthropological approaches.* New York: Holt, Rinehart and Winston, 1963.

6

The mutual influences of anthropology and education have an extensive, if irregular, history. Spindler's treatment of their historical involvement is among the most comprehensive. An additional benefit of the overview is his discussion of "roles the anthropologist may assume in the context of professional education." Mr. Spindler, who is jointly appointed as Professor in the Department of Anthropology and in the School of Education, Stanford University, has long advocated closer working relationships among anthropologists and educators, often by his own example. His approach to the potential, real and imagined, of professional interaction tends to maximize disciplinary differences between the two professions. Other approaches argue that the interaction of anthropologists and educators does not need always to contend with structuring by roles, academic imperialisms, the brands of "show and tell" behavior characteristic of "outside" expertise (invited or voluntary), or restricted concerns with research "method." There is an interaction based on shared commitments to improved public education. In the way that Mead "sees" people, so are there those who "see" anthropology and education as a primer of policy decisions that ultimately affect children rather than as a special allocation of work-study among two, presumably expert bodies. Education is the public domain. Alternatives to the way things are in public education demand a sense of what is truly alternate as well as cultural insight. If Spindler edges up to questions of social commitment, he does not fail in stating the relevance of anthropology to those educational problems that prompt commitment.

GEORGE D. SPINDLER

Anthropology and Education: An Overview

INTRODUCTION

Some educational theorists cite the concept of culture as most crucial in their systematic thinking. Text books used in the training of teachers contain references to anthropological literature. Elementary school teachers include projects on "Peoples in Other Lands" or "Our Indian Friends" in social studies units. A growing number of departments of anthropology are offering courses with the specific needs of teachers-in-training in mind. Anthropology has been applied to educational problems since at least 1904, when Hewett wrote his first pieces on education for the *American Anthropologist* (1904, 1905). The *Yearbook of Anthropology* contains a

Reprinted with revisions from *Education and Anthropology* edited by George D. Spindler with permission of the publishers, Stanford University Press. Copyright 1955 by the Board of Trustees of the Leland Stanford Junior University.

substantial review of the work by anthropologists on education (Hoebel, 1955). An important lecture series in 1961, the Martin G. Brumbaugh lectures on education, is devoted exclusively to anthropology and education (Gruber, 1961).

But education was not even listed as an area of application for anthropology in the encyclopedic inventory, *Anthropology Today* (Kroeber, 1953). Education is not in the subject index of the *Decennial Index: 1949–1958* to the *American Anthropologist* and *Memoirs* of the American Anthropological Association. Only a handful of joint appointments in education and anthropology exist in American colleges and universities. Very few anthropologists have attempted to study the educational process in our society. Despite the steady increase of interest, anthropology and education still maintain a tenuous relationship as Brameld has pointed out (1961). It is a frontier area.

The purpose of this overview paper is to survey this frontier area — to outline the parts of both anthropology and education as they relate to mutual interests, to indicate those points where the anthropologist can help formulate meaningful educational research and theory, mention what anthropologists have written about education and what educators have used of what anthropologists have written, describe some special problems that exist in the relationships between the two fields, and provide useful bibliographic citations for those who may wish to read further. . . .

Relevant Fields and Interests in Anthropology

Anthropology as a Resource for General Education

Anthropology as the "study of man and his works," with its traditional interests in cultural process and in language, race, and human evolution, is a potential contributor to a good general education at all levels of educational experience. This potential contribution of anthropology as a source of data and of concepts to be used in the development of curricula will be discussed first. . . . While no claim is made here that anthropology should become the core of a complete social studies program in the secondary school, or in the liberal arts (or "general studies") program at the college level, it seems clear . . . that no other existing discipline provides an integration, however loose, of so much that is so important concerning man and his behavior. The study of man thus broadly conceived makes it possible to bridge the gap between the animal and the human being, to conceive of both the relativity and universality of human behavior and propositions about it, to project human affairs upon a time plane that stretches far into the past and future, and turns the focus upon the basic round of life and man's relation to nature.

The implication is clear that anthropology should be used as a contribution to general education more widely than it is. It should not be taught as it must be to graduate students training to become professional anthropologists. Nor should it be taught as an introduction to a scholarly discipline, as it often is at the college level, even in the beginning course. It should be taught as an introduction to a new perspective on human life, as a way of thinking that we might call "humanistic objectivity." This is not merely a personal opinion. It is a value judgment, but one shared widely by professional anthropologists who are teaching introductory courses in colleges and universities. The overwhelming majority of anthropologist respondents from thirty-seven colleges and universities placed humanistic purposes first and training in the "science" of anthropology second (Bruner and Spindler, 1961). The anthropologist has a point of view and wants to communicate it.

Anthropology should probably also be taught in the secondary school (Lee, 1960; Mandelbaum, 1961), possibly under some already existing rubric (Spindler, 1946). As Mandelbaum has pointed out, most American anthropologists would agree that ". . . modern concepts of culture, cultural similarities and differences, race, and evolution should properly be a part of the high school curriculum," (Mandelbaum, 1961b). But at the same time anthropologists will agree that these concepts are easily misinterpreted. Uninformed teachers will make serious errors that are all the more serious because the concepts are so powerful. It is crucial that teachers who are going to use anthropological concepts and data get good training in anthropology. . . .

Anthropology is being taught at the elementary school level when teachers develop lesson units or activities centering on American Indian tribes or peoples in other lands — but sometimes badly because the teachers have had little or no exposure to anthropology as such and consequently contravene their primary goals. A teacher who has had no direct exposure to another way of life, particularly a primitive way of life, and who has had no instruction in how to objectify perceptions of other cultures or how to control value judgments, is very likely to communicate prejudicial views when he or she teaches a unit on the Hopi, or Navaho, or the village peoples of India. It is hoped that teachers in elementary schools will be able to obtain training in anthropology as a part of their preparation in social studies.

Anthropologists have been aware of the potential contributions of their field to general education and have written about it (Ehrich, 1947; Howells, 1952), but they have until recently rarely done anything about it. . . . We can expect these efforts to have an important direct effect on the teaching of anthropology in colleges and universities, and an equally important, but less direct effect, on the use of anthropological resources in the secondary school. The *Teaching of Anthropology*, to be published as a Memoir of the American Anthropological Association, edited by David Mandelbaum, Gabriel Lasker, and Ethel Albert, out of the many conferences held, will include papers on most phases of the use of anthropology as an educational resource for higher education, and supplements on teaching aids and recommended bibliography will either be included or published separately (Mandelbaum, 1961a).

As a source of materials to be used in general education all of anthropology is relevant. Selections need not be made only from the sociocultural side of the discipline. The most important contribution of physical anthropology to education has been on the subject of race and the relationships — or rather lack of them — between race, culture, and intelligence. Anthropological perspectives on the meaning of race and the myth of racial superiority have been popularized by Ethel Alpenfels in her capacity as staff anthropologist for the Bureau for Intercultural Education, and have become familiar to many social studies teachers through this and other agencies. Otto Klineberg has given us the classic treatment on relationships beween race, culture, and I.Q. (1935), that has had wide circulation in an encapsulated form in a UNESCO pamphlet (1951) and in a symposium edited by Linton (1947). Teachers will find G. Lasker's introduction to physical anthropology (1961) and the articles by Washburn, Deevey, Dobzhansky, Howells from the September, 1960, *Scientific American*, useful for information on various aspects of physical anthropology and human evolution.

Anthropology as a Resource in the Analysis of Educational Process

So far the relevance for anthropology as a body of knowledge and way of thinking to the development of curricula and programs in general education has been discussed. Now attention shifts to the contributions of anthropology as a frame of reference for analysis of the educative process. This is a different kind of utilization of the resources of anthropology. It is not, however, an attempt to create an "educational anthropology." Though they demonstrate some unique properties, the processes and structures of education are not fundamentally different in kind from the processes and structures involved in other areas of human life. Anthropology can help shed light on human behavior in educational situations just as it has on behavior in factories, hospitals, peasant communities, air force installations, Indian reservations, New England towns, and various primitive societies. . . .

Directly relevant are the concepts and data of specialized and relatively new fields in anthropology, such as personality and culture ("psychological anthropology"), and cultural dynamics (culture change and acculturation). In fact, when use of anthropology as an analytic frame of reference in education is considered, this is usually where people in both fields begin to look first (Kimball, 1956; Taba, 1957; Rosenstiel, 1959). . . .

For certain purposes it is useful to view education of the child to human, group-accepted status as a total process of growth and adaptation. The center of the process is the child — adapting to an environment structured by culture, as well as by group size, climate, terrain, ecology, and the personalities of his always unique parents or parental surrogates. Education may also be thought of as a more limited process — what is to and for a child, by whom, in what roles, under what conditions, and to what purpose. Jules Henry has given us the first substantial cross-cultural outline for the study of education from this point of view (Henry, 1960). Education in this focus is the process of transmitting culture — including skills, knowledge, attitudes, and values, as well as specific behavioral patterns. It is the culture of the human being — where culture is used as a verb.

There are many books, monographs, and articles by anthropologists on socialization of the child — education in the total sense — in different cultures. One of the most significant problem-oriented comparative researches is Whiting and Child's *Child Training and Personality* (1953). Spiro provides us with a very interesting analysis of socialization and education in Israel, in his *Children of the Kibbutz* (1958). . . . A recent survey by the Whitings provides reference to many of the relevant publications (Whiting, 1960). There are relatively few studies on education in the more strict sense of the word. British anthropologists, with their functionalistic predilections, have provided relevant analyses (e.g., Read, 1960). Pettit has provided one of the most useful studies by an American anthropologist on the who, what, when, and where questions of educational process seen cross-culturally, as he summarizes education in North American Indian cultures (Pettit, 1946). . . .

The data used by Whiting and Pettit were provided by ethnographies written by others. The fact that such analyses could be carried out despite the fact that the people who did the actual studies in the field could not have anticipated their use is a tribute to the inclusiveness of a good ethnography. But only too often, Whiting, Pettit, and others who have attempted similar analyses, have looked for the pertinent facts in ethnographies and have not been able to find them, or find them partially or ambiguously stated. Most often anthropologists will describe the *results* of education but not the *process*. There is a great deal more to be done with the materials furnished by ethnographies and other field studies already completed, but it is crucial that future studies in the field be done with a good cross-cultural outline of education in mind. Henry's (1960) outline will doubtless prove very useful in this respect. What is lacking, however, even in Henry's excellent attempt, is a consistent, underlying theory that can give coherence and organization to the categories of behavior to be observed and their interpretation. Culture theory, personality theory, and social interaction theory must be joined. When such an "outline" for the cross-cultural study of education is developed, with a comprehensive and consistent theoretical structure behind it, we will be on our way towards a truly *comparative* education. The indispensable, basic requirement for the development of a comparative education is that there be a systematic frame of reference, with consistent theoretical underpinnings, to guide the collection and interpretation of relevant data cross-culturally, so that meaningful processual comparisons can be made. Anthropology can provide a significant part of the frame of reference needed. . . .

Anthropological work in cultural dynamics is concerned primarily with those processes of cultural change and stability that are frequently included under the heading "acculturation." For our purposes we can define acculturation as subsuming those processes that occur as a society (or a group of people) with a distinctive culture adapts to changes in the conditions of life brought about by the impact of another population and its culture. Much of the work done so far on acculturation has been characterized by a lack of penetrating interpretation — most of the issues are left at the descriptive level — and very little attention has been paid to the role of cultural transmission and education in culture change. Cultural change as well as stability must be mediated by what is transmitted from parents and teachers to children. Unless these variables intervening between changes in the conditions of life and the adaptations of people to them are understood, much of the "dynamic" part of cultural dynamics is left unilluminated. Anthropologists have done little here. All of the studies by anthropologists of the socialization and enculturation of children in different cultural settings are contributions to our knowledge of how education functions to preserve cultural continuity, but few of them have focused on cultural transmission or have been explicitly concerned with the problems of cultural change. Herskovits has supplied one of the few explicit statements of some relationships between education and cultural change in his "Education and Cultural Dynamics" (1943). Dorothy Eggan's analysis of education and cultural continuity among the Hopi Indians and the author's analysis of the Menomini . . . give us insight into the stability-maintaining functions of education in situations where external pressure for change is great. In her . . . "Our Educational Emphases in the Perspective of Primitive Societies," Margaret Mead shows us how our educational process is geared to change — to the creating of discontinuities in experience for the child. She provides an illuminating analysis of the role of education in induced cultural change in . . . "Cultural Factors in

Community Education," . . . and Jack Fischer . . . shows us that many of the same processes are activated even when the inducing or "donor" culture is nonwestern. Bruner (1956a, 1956b) has provided pertinent analyses of the influence of experience in the primary group on cultural transmission in culture change situations. Fred Warner has analyzed a culture conflict situation in college experience. . . . Other relevant writings include Frank (1959) and Mead (1959, 1960), which are less explicit in their use of concepts and data from the field of cultural dynamics but illuminating in their attention to cultural change as the context of modern education.

One field of interest in anthropology that has realized relatively more of its potential in relation to educational problems is that of social structure. If the interests here are conceived as broadly relating to group alignments, prestige ranking, status and role interrelationships, and social control in the community context, all of the very useful work of the Warner group and other closely related efforts may be regarded as a contribution from this area. The contributors include, besides Warner, such workers as Davis, Gardner, Dollard, Loeb, Withers, Useem, and many nonanthropologists who have been strongly influenced therein, such as Havighurst, Hollingshead, the Lynds, Taba, and so on. The relevance of this field to education, particularly with respect to a concept of social class that has been regularized by Warner and his associates, is indicated by two special issues of the *Harvard Educational Review* on the subject (1953). Recent textbooks on the social foundations of education, such as Mercer (1957), Cox and Mercer (1961) use these materials extensively. No claim is made that this is exclusively an anthropological domain or contribution, but one of the mainsprings driving the interest and its application is fastened to an anthropological pivot.

In this instance the situation as it exists otherwise in the various potential or emergent articulations with education is reversed. More is known about how the educative process is affected by social class and community structure in Jonesville and Elmtown than in the nonliterate societies that are the accustomed habitat of the anthropologists. To be sure, nonliterate societies rarely have social classes in the same sense that Jonesville has, but some do, and all have groups structured into a social organization. Whether a social structure is formalized by a widely ramifying kinship system, or by inherited statuses, or by a complex political-social power system, or is atomistic and individuated — the who, what, when, and why of education — will reflect this structure at every turn, since education must produce the men and women to function in the structure. For the sake of a clearer concept of education as a sociocultural process something more should be known about these functional interrelationships between educational goals, educative process, and social structure in nonwestern societies. . . .

Other uses for the anthropological frame of reference in analyses of educational process will be discussed below, as fields and interests in education are surveyed.

RELEVANT FIELDS AND INTERESTS IN EDUCATION

When we view education as a field with its own problems and institutional structure, it becomes clear that there are more relevant problems and interests than anthropologists could begin to bear appropriate gifts to — even if they were so motivated. Some of the particularly significant problems have been succinctly described by James Quillen. The discussion below will approach some of these same problems from a different perspective and describe certain interests and fields in education in which these problems occur.

The Foundation Fields and Professional Education

The first part of the discussion will be concerned with the institutional context called "Professional Education" — programs where teachers, administrators, counseling and guidance personnel, educational psychologists, and others are trained, usually in schools of education or teachers colleges. That part of these programs that most clearly provides a suitable context for anthropology is that of the "foundation" fields. The general rubrics are social, psychological, philosophical, historical, comparative, and biological. They represent what is drawn into education as a professional field from the behavioral and social sciences, the humanities, and natural sciences, as their data and concepts are used in educational research, the building of educational theory and philosophy, and in the training of teachers. It is important to understand how anthropology as a contributing discipline and the anthropologist as a contributing professional can function appropriately in this context. The fact that few anthropologists hold positions in Schools of Education and that there are few joint appointments in education and anthropology despite a professed interest on both sides suggests that the institutional arrangements do not function satisfactorily in some cases. The organization of courses and their purposes will be discussed now. Later on, the role of the anthropologist in the milieu of professional education will be described.

Anthropology has only recently begun to make a significant contribution to the social foundations of education. Educational psychology has clearly dominated the scene, partly because of a historical accident that institutionally wedded psychology and education rather early in America and partly because the need for tests and measurements and applied principles of learning have been particularly obvious in the educational milieu of American schools and have been appropriate for psychological applications.

In many teacher-training institutions psychology is still the only behavioral science explicitly recognized in the organization of professional education courses.

Education as a professional field has also drawn from political science, economics, and jurisprudence, but particularly from sociology. Educational sociology has its own house organ, numerous texts bearing its name, and an impressive pile of research to its credit. Most foundation courses in professional education in the social area are called "educational sociology"....

At Stanford University, as an illustration of the ways in which anthropology can contribute to the foundation fields in education, relevant materials are presented in two courses: "Social Foundations in Education"; "Cultural Transmission"; and one seminar, "Social Anthropology in Education." They are given under the aegis of a joint appointment in the School of Education and the Department of Anthropology. Credit is given to students in both fields in their respective undergraduate majors or advanced degree program and the courses are cross-listed in the course announcements of both the School of Education and Department of Anthropology.

"Social Foundations in Education" is required of all upper division education students and all candidates for the Master of Arts degree in education, as well as for the various professional credentials. It combines selected materials from sociology, anthropology, and social psychology. The anthropological contribution lies mainly in a systematic analysis of American cultural patterns and values as they bear directly upon the role and functions of the teacher and public school system. Cross-cultural data are used here for illustrative purposes. Other topical areas covered include social class and education, problems in student-teacher communication, group stereotypes and prejudice in schools, the community context of the school, and the school as a social system.

"Cultural Transmission" is offered as a course at Stanford for advanced degree candidates and is presented jointly within the advanced social foundations sequence in education and the advanced offerings in the Department of Anthropology. In this course a frame of reference for viewing transmission and enculturation processes is constructed. This frame of reference is then used in the analysis of these processes in nonliterate societies, European societies, and American society. The course ends with case studies of selected types of teachers in their classrooms and schools in our society. Sociometric, autobiographic, socioeconomic, observational, and community "social base" data are included in the case study materials.

"Social Anthropology in Education" at Stanford is a seminar taken by advanced graduate students in education, anthropology, and psychology. It is likewise listed as part of the advanced course offerings in both the school of Education and the Department of Anthropology. It has been devoted so far to an analysis of the educative process in nonliterate societies, using ethnographic references and the Human Relations Area Files. Special problems in cultural transmission are explored, such as explicit and implicit transmission of values in the education of adolescents, and the application of learning theory to the analysis of educational situations and events reported for other cultures by ethnographers.

These courses accomplish different things in different ways. An important point in relation to the problem of an education-anthropology articulation is that the frame of reference is not exclusively anthropological; in all of the courses it seems essential to include selected aspects of sociology and psychology. When the educative process is the focus, and particularly in our own society, the anthropological frame of reference is not sufficient by itself. But it is essential. The core of the contribution is in the attention to culture as an influence on behavior, as a perception-mediating set of patterns, and in the attention to the variable forms these patterns take. *Cultural awareness* is one vital aim of each course, but not merely generalized cultural awareness; the aim is to create in the teacher an awareness of how his own culture influences specifically what he does as a teacher and how his students' cultures influence what they do, and how to think about, observe, and analyze these influences. Cultural awareness as one goal in professional preparation with which the anthropologist can help is also particularly important for the administrator, since he manipulates the setting in which the teacher interacts with students and parents. He must not only display cultural awareness but must also understand the mechanics of culture change, the cultural expectations affecting the leader's role, the concrete as well as idealistic meaning of cultural values, and the social system of the school in the setting of the encompassing community and national social structure. . . .

Courses in conventional anthropology do not serve this same purpose directly, even though they are necessary as a phase of professional educational training. By the time the student is preparing to be a professional educator, or is improving his already established proficiency, he should have had an introduction to the materials of at least cultural anthropology as a part of his general education, though he should also have some experience in intermediate and advanced course work in anthropology as a graduate student. Many graduate students majoring in the social foundations of education, comparative education, educational administration, and elementary education at Stanford take advanced degree minors in anthropology. The anthropology a student gets in his *professional* education within the college or school of education should be integrated with the other foundational offerings and applied to analysis of educative process.

Otherwise we are asking him to provide this integration and make this application; and most students — in education or otherwise — simply cannot do it without expert help. . . .

Educational Research

Education as a professional field is not only concerned with teacher training, teaching, curriculum design, and administration of schools; it has a research base. Probably no social or behavioral science has as great a backlog of research nor encompasses such a high degree of variability of quality of research. The reason for the first fact is obvious. The reason for the second one is partly that education cuts across every phase of human activity, and it is impossible to do good research without specialization in the science or discipline treating with selected dimensions within this range. This is very difficult when so much has to be done all at once.

There are many phases of research within the framework of education that call for anthropological attention. There has been an incorporation of anthropologically based concepts and methods in the studies of social class influences on learning (Davis, 1952), social class and community structures in relation to the social organization of the school and educational opportunities (Warner, Loeb, et al., 1944), and problems of adolescence (Havighurst and Taba, 1949), in the extensive study of the relationships between intelligence and cultural differences by the Chicago group (Eells, et al., 1951), and in the studies of social class differences in socialization with their implication for education (Davis and Havighurst, 1947). This interest in social class and learning, and social class and school organization, has been the main stream of influence on research directly relevant to education and stemming from anything that can be regarded as an anthropological source. The main contribution of anthropology, other than in the form of some of the personnel involved, has been in the notion of cultural relativity and in a functional total-community approach.

Thus a definite and extensive contribution to research on educational problems, in American society at least, has yet to be made by anthropology. This reflects the fact that until quite recently anthropologists have not been very interested in our own society. Their proper object of study has been the nonliterate peoples, in their pure or reconstructed form, or as these peoples have struggled to adapt to the impact of the industrial-based civilizations.

Anthropologists have been interested in and involved with the problem of education in dependent, trust and colonial territories, and Indian reservations, where nonliterate or recently nonliterate indigenes have been exposed to a Western-mediated education. But the involvement has been largely in terms of an applied anthropology in various administrative and consultative capacities, and actual research reports on the processes involved are quite scarce. Felix Keesing has described some of the interesting problems that arise in these contexts in a summary of a seminar conference, including educators, anthropologists, sociologists, and government officials, on the problems of education in Pacific countries (Keesing, 1937). . . .

There are many areas of potential application of anthropologically based concepts and methods in educational research in our own society to which more attention should be directed. The roles of teacher and school administrator in American society call for treatment from a cultural point of view that will focus on some of the paradoxes projected in the role expectations. . . . New approaches to the study of the school as a social system need to be devised — perhaps in the manner of the factory system studies that were in part anthropologically inspired. James Coleman (1961) has provided a most significant analysis of the social climates in high schools and the development of a separate teen-age culture. American culture as a specific context of the goals, expectations, and functions of education needs exploration — possibly in the vein of national character approaches. . . .

Particularly appropriate to anthropological interests is the need for cross-cultural research in education. Culture is idealized in. the educative process. Every teacher, whether mother's brother or Miss Humboldt of Peavey Falls, re-enacts and defends the cultural drama. As the culture is passed on from one generation to the next in the hands of the teacher, it assumes a patent and rationalized shape. The world view is somehow encapsulated in each gesture, admonition, indoctrination, or explanation. And this seems true whether physics or sacred origin myths are being taught. Cross-cultural research on education puts our own educational process in new perspective. Education is a pan-human process, but one that varies sharply from culture to culture. . . .

THE ROUTES OF DIFFUSION

Anthropological Routes

The institutional and research routes of diffusion of knowledge between education and anthropology have been described. The routes of diffusion through anthropological and educational literature exhibit certain characteristics that have affected the articulation of the two fields and will be analyzed briefly.

Maria Montessori's influence is of particularly long standing (1913). Her principal assumptions have been integrated into the framework of modern education through the progressive "school." She saw clearly the need for stressing the "organic" relation of the whole child to the environment; emphasized the developmental process so that the child was not seen as a "diminutive adult"; anticipated the problem of the differential meaning of school experience to children from various social classes and ethnic groups in her concept of a "regional ethnology" and study of local conditions; called for respect for individual differences in growth and function; demanded that a "scientific pedagogy" concern itself with normal individuals primarily; and developed a "biographical chart" that took the place of the report card and included "antecedents" — vocation of parents, their aesthetic culture, their morality and sentiments and care of children — as well as reports of physical and psychological examinations and ongoing observations in the form of "diaries."

Educators may contest the characterization of this work as an anthropological influence, since Montessori is so clearly a part of the educationist's heritage, but she called her approach a "Pedagogical Anthropology," and used what were regarded as anthropological concepts, methods, techniques, and data. Though her cultural anthropology is guilty of what today would be regarded as certain racist errors, and her physical anthropology is now outmoded, her farsighted anticipation of much of the best of the contemporary art and science of education is impressive. Whether this is true because she had genius or because she had an anthropological orientation cannot be divined. She had both.

A history of anthropology-to-education diffusion cannot omit the early contributions of Edgar L. Hewett (1904, 1905). His articles "Anthropology and Education" (1904) and "Ethnic Factors in Education" (1905) in the *American Anthropologist* were the first and almost the last contribution of their kind in that journal. He argued for an "enrichment of the course study of every public school in the land" through the incorporation of ethnological materials, particularly on culture history not confined to the Western world; called for joint meetings of the national education and anthropology societies to discuss mutual problems; scored culture historians for misuse and lack of use of ethnological data; claimed the clear relevance of an "ethnic psychology" that would contribute to the teacher's understanding of the fact that ". . . Italian and Bohemian, Celt and Hebrew, Anglo-Saxon and African look upon questions of honor, morality, and decency out of separate ethnic minds. . . ."; asked educators to realize that "a civilization imposed from without is usually harmful, often destructive, always undesirable," because the "development of a race must be from within"; and suggested that for all these reasons "normal schools and other institutions for the training of teachers should give a prominent place to the anthropological sciences." The fact that none of his calls was implemented reflects partly an ethnocentrism of American culture, partly the peculiar conservatism of American public education, and particularly the fact that American anthropologists did not have time for much of anything but ethnographic and culture history salvage until the 1930's.

Franz Boas, the dean of American anthropology, clearly saw the relevance of anthropological and educational interests. In his *Anthropology and Modern Life* (1928) he devotes one whole chapter to these interests. He points out that "anthropological research offers, therefore, a means of determining what may be expected of children of different ages, and this knowledge is of considerable value for regulating educational methods." He talks of "normative data for development," sex differences, ethnic differences, and differences in environmental conditions that should be taken into account. He treats of some of the problems of cultural transmission, and points out that "our public schools are hardly conscious of the conflict" between democratic ideas of freedom and flexibility, and coercion; "they instill automatic reactions to symbols by means of patriotic ceremonial, in many cases by indirect religious appeal, and too often through the automatic reactions to the behavior of the teacher that is imitated." He suggests that tradition-based transmission of values and ethics is particularly strong among intellectuals and that the "masses" respond "more quickly and energetically to the demands of the hour than the educated classes. . . ."

Articles by anthropologists on education have turned up persistently in educational journals and elsewhere for the past twenty-five years. The place of anthropology in a college education, the contributions of anthropology to the training of teachers, the place of primitive education in the history of education are the favorite themes. The articles add to what Montessori, Hewett, and Boas spelled out, but few of them produce clear innovations. Exceptions to this general rule include Mead's suggestive article on education in the perspective of primitive cultures (1943) and her Inglis Lecture, under the title, *The School in American Culture* (1950); Kluckhohn's comments in *Mirror for Man* (1949); Opler's "Cultural Alternatives and Educational Theory" (1947); Goldenweiser's "Culture and Education" (1939); and Herskovits' stimulating discussion in his text, *Man and His Works* (1950). The whole issue of the *American Journal of Sociology* (1943) devoted to "Education and Cultural Dynamics," including articles by Johnson, Redfield, Malinowski, Mekeel, Benedict, Herskovits, Powdermaker, and Embree is an especially outstanding contribution. Fred Eggan (1957, 1959) and Dorothy Lee (1957) provide useful perspectives on the relevance of anthropology to education. T. Brameld (1961) reviews recent contributions.

It seems clear, upon examination of what has been done, that anthropologists have not been able to say much more than was said fifty years ago by Hewett when they talk about the general relevance of anthropology to general education. This is primarily because there is not much else to say.

When the anthropologists have either analyzed their own intimately understood cross-cultural data or have analyzed the educative process in our society, using empirical data, they have made a definite contribution.

Educational Routes

Irrespective of the attentions by anthropologists to education, the educators have gone ahead on their own to search out and utilize what seemed relevant to them of the anthropological products. An examination of representative and substantial texts in the psychological, sociocultural, philosophical, and comparative historical foundations of education used in professional teacher-training institutions about the country reveals a clear shift toward appropriation of social and cultural concepts and data produced by anthropologists.

In educational psychology, for example, the text by Pressey and Robinson (1944) mentions no anthropological references, and uses no cross-cultural data for illustrative purposes. Cronbach, in his model for educational psychology texts (1954) draws upon Mead, Davis, Warner, Benedict, and Kluckhohn, among others, and makes considerable reference to cultural pressures, different cultural settings influencing personality development and learning, and formation of social attitudes and values. Martin and Stendler's text, *Child Development,* intended for use by educators and noneducators both, and already used widely in elementary education and other professional education courses, places a very heavy emphasis on culture-personality relationships. Culture case data are cited for the Alorese, Balinese, Comanche, Japanese, Kwoma, Mentowie, Navaho, Samoans, Sioux, Tanala, Tepoztecans, Yurok, Zuñi, and others. Cultural relativism has found its way into the heart of this book. McDonald in his popular text (1959) depends less heavily upon cultural concepts but does cite numerous works by anthropologists. Of the seven textbooks in educational psychology examined, published between 1958 and 1961, five cite anthropological works, but mostly the same works by Mead, Benedict, and Linton.

In educational sociology — a field that is rapidly being expanded into a sociocultural foundation of education — a like trend is occurring. The Cooks' book (1950, revised edition), a text of long standing and wide use in educational sociology and social foundations, cites cross-cultural materials infrequently but draws much from the anthropologically influenced community studies on Middletown, St. Denis, Yankee City, and Plainsville. Robbins' *Educational Sociology* (1953) uses many of the same references and refers to writings by Mead, Benedict, Murdock, and Linton for the notion of cultural relativity. Brown's 1954 edition of *Educational Sociology* uses extensive references to cultural data on the Navaho, Australian tribes, Zuñi, and the Acoma Pueblo, and cites anthropological pieces — by

Gillin, Kluckhohn, Wagley, Herskovits, Goldfrank, Redfield, Tylor, Stirling, Warner, Rivers, Linton, Hewett, Mead, Powdermaker, Benedict, and Montague — approximately twice as often as in the 1947 edition. Twelve textbooks in the social foundations of education published between 1956 and 1961 were examined. All but one cited anthropological works.

The trend is not as noticeable in the philosophical and comparative foundations of education — in so far as the limits of the sample of texts permit generalizations. The tendency in these fields has apparently been to utilize highly generalized and Western-limited concepts of culture as an important part of the frame of reference, but to draw relatively little from any of the work by anthropologists in cross-cultural contexts. Brameld has made one of the strongest arguments for a culture base for educational philosophy, but even he cites only a few anthropological works — namely, some by Davis, Kluckhohn, Benedict, Warner, and Herskovits in his earlier text (1950). But he has made the most consistent and substantial contribution to a thorough articulation of educational and anthropological theory (1957) since then, and he has tested out this integrated theory in a field situation (1959). These recent important works have been reviewed by Siegel (1959) and Spindler (1961), and the gist of his point of view is expressed in his paper "The Meeting of Educational and Anthropological Theory". . . .

An over-all summation of the anthropological concepts and data utilized in the contemporary texts in the foundations of education reveals certain general trends. It is clear that educators interested in childhood education, elementary curriculum, school-community interrelations, and all of the social and behavioral foundations of education have arrived at the point where an anthropological point of view and, particularly, cross-cultural materials have a positive value for them. They indicate an awareness of culture concepts and cultural data produced by anthropologists by fairly extensive documentations with appropriate literature. They include anthropological references in their recommended reading lists. They consider it desirable to qualify generalizations about learning, cultural transmission, human nature, the functions of education, child growth and development, by invoking the notion of cultural relativity. Some of them incorporate a cultural perspective into their thinking — beyond using cultural relativity as a valued check.

The number of concepts used by educators relating to the cultural process is impressive. Anthropologists have no copyright but certainly some possessory rights over these concepts. To the anthropologist the terms values, acculturation, cultural normalcy, cultural diffusion, cultural change, cultural transmission, subcultures, peer culture, folk culture, enculturation ring with authentic familiarity as they are used by educationist authors.

But it is also clear that the range of materials being diffused through educationist channels from anthropological sources is in actuality quite limited. The same names and same references keep turning up constantly. Kluckhohn, Mead, Benedict, Davis, West (Carl Withers), and Warner are cited in great disproportion to all others. This suggests that the purveyance of anthropological thinking to education has at most two main disciplinary vehicles — personality and culture, and community studies — and that the mediation of data and concepts is inevitably given an indelible impress by these particular workers. Particularly significant is the fact that it is the relatively most popularized works of these contributors that are cited most frequently. These two tendencies indicate that however useful the contributions and however able the contributors, the educators are not getting a fair and substantial diet of anthropological materials. It is up to them to actively search out, with anthropological help, the richly relevant materials that await them.

THE ROLES OF THE ANTHROPOLOGIST IN THE EDUCATION CONTEXT

One clear implication in this overview has been that if anthropology is actually going to contribute to education, the anthropologists will have to act at times within the setting of professional education. This is no argument that all anthropologists should. Anthropology has many dimensions and interests, and nothing should be permitted to happen in relations with other fields that draws many anthropologists away from its central purposes. But anthropologists have always been marked with a certain versatility. If there is a job to do in education some anthropologists will, for one reason or another, be bound to do it. Therefore an explication of some of the roles possible in the context of professional education is in order.

The anthropologist may act as a consultant. Ideally, he should be able to contribute ideas to every division of educational specialization — elementary, secondary, higher education, health, guidance, administration. He contributes, ideally, a widened perspective on human behavior. He sees the educative process as a cultural process, and thus not bounded by formalized, or ritualized, lines of specialization or conceptual compartmentalization. He devotes some of his attention to breaking down ethnocentric biases. He is, ideally, not time-bound. He provides objectification of cultural values and, if he is successful, brings educational objectives into appropriate congruence with them. He contributes some useful analytic-descriptive categories, the foremost of which is culture, followed by a train of constructs like cultural transmission, enculturation, role and status, and social organization. To do these things he has to act as a participating member of the groups for which he acts as a consultant, for it is necessary for him to grasp the point of view and problems of those with whom he is consulting. He has already had experience in doing this in his field research.

The anthropologist may do research in education or act as a consulting member of a team that is doing research. He does so with the same perspectives and capabilities that have been outlined above and in attacks upon problems that fall into areas described previously in this chapter. His major contribution lies in the molar approach that characterizes anthropological method. His greatest problem is one of relevance. His problems, definitions, and research values cannot remain exactly the same as they would if he were doing anthropological field research in a nonliterate, or even an acculturating community. He must understand what it is that educators need to know in order both to build better educational theory and to solve problems of immediate applied relevance. In the research team developed at Stanford under the direction of Robert Bush and known as the Stanford Consultation Service, it was found that a good *modus operandi* was achieved when the educator, psychiatrist, and anthropologist exchanged roles for a time so that each could achieve insight into the other's problems. In this project, also, a unique combination of ameliorative case consultation goals and pure research goals has been achieved, so that neither end-point of the value pendulum in educational research is lost. There are frustrations inherent in this procedure, to be sure.

The anthropologist need not work within the framework of immediate education interests in his research. He may confine himself to his own cross-cultural field, chasing down questions on educative process in non-Western societies, as John Whiting has done in his Laboratory of Human Development in the graduate school of education at Harvard University. Possibly the most significant contributions of anthropology to education through research channels actually lie here.

The anthropologist may also act as a teacher in the setting of professional education. Certain propositions concerning this role have already been explicated. His obligation lies mainly in making explicit the cultural assumptions and values that are a substratum of every move in educational action or theorizing. His contribution is particularly critical because education is a sensitive part of the total cultural process, and because in its very nature as an art and science of human cultivation it is loaded with a heavy burden of values. To achieve this contribution he goes to cross-cultural variability first, then turns to our own cultural modes as they bear directly upon the educative process — from the viewpoint of both the learner and the teacher. His aim is to create cultural awareness, which is even more important than self-awareness in the teacher's sphere of activity and which is pedagogically much more attainable.

LIMITATIONS AND RESERVATIONS

The list of particulars for the roles the anthropologist may assume in the context of professional education is stated in ideal terms. No one anthropologist could do all of these things equally well. Choices have to be made on the basis of personal inclination and unique situations.

But other limitations on his functions call for statement. One danger is that the "study of man" can sometimes seem so total that it becomes *the* study of man. One ethnocentrism is substituted for another. The anthropologist's comments seem to glitter like gold — to him at least — because for a time they are new and fresh. He becomes a kind of cultural oracle. But when his stock of illuminating asides on the Upper Pukapuka or the Lower Zambesi runs low he will be forced to take another stance. Then he may be reduced to making broad, conjectural statements that he may confuse as final judgments or substantial generalizations rather than a potential source of hypotheses. He may fool some of the educators some of the time, but he can't fool them all.

Further, the anthropologist's experience with small and relatively integrated societies sometimes gives him an extraordinary naïveté about the complex relations in our own society — a society that he himself may have escaped from — into anthropology. He fails to see complications and looks for integrating features, consistencies, and values where there are none. And as a consequence he may make outlandish pronouncements as to what educators should or should not do.

Beyond this, the anthropologist is not always particularly sophisticated intellectually. He is often not sufficiently familiar with the social and intellectual histories of the great civilizations — including his own. He may have become an anthropologist in order to become an explorer (subconsciously, of course), or buried himself so thoroughly in ethnographies that he has no room in his head for other thoughts. If so, his suggestions to educators would fall short of the mark when he talks about cultural transmission, since he would not know the culture to be transmitted.

And there are limitations inherent in the culture concept. Though no anthropologist would limit his conceptual repertoire to it exclusively, most are heavily influenced by it. Though the great utility of this construct cannot be denied, it is not a theory in itself. It is not sufficiently dynamic, or field-oriented, but tends to contain itself around patterning phenomena that provide form but not function as variables for analysis. The anthropologist will usually find in the educational context that he has to turn to other disciplines, along with his anthropological armamentarium, for concepts and methods.

Despite these reservations, it does appear that anthropology has a new and needed perspective on education. . . .

REFERENCES

Boas, Franz, 1928, *Anthropology and Modern Life*. New York: W. W. Norton.
Brameld, Theodore, 1950, *Patterns of Educational Philosophy*. New York: Harcourt, Brace & World.
———, 1957, *Cultural Foundations of Education: An Interdisciplinary Exploration*. New York: Harper & Row.
———, 1959, *The Remaking of a Culture — Life and Education in Puerto Rico*. New York: Harper & Row.
———, and E. B. Sullivan, 1961, Anthropology and Education. *Review of Educational Research*, 70–79.
Brown, Francis J., 1954, *Educational Sociology*, 2d ed. Englewood Cliffs, N.J.: Prentice-Hall.
Bruner, Edward M., 1956a, "Cultural Transmission and Cultural Change." *Southwestern Journal of Anthropology*, 12:191–199.
———, 1956b, "Primary Group Experience and the Process of Acculturation." *American Anthropologist*, 58:605–623.
———, and George D. Spindler, with the assistance of Fred H. Warner, 1963, "An Introductory Course in Cultural Anthropology." *The Teaching of Anthropology*, edited by David G. Mandelbaum, Gabriel W. Lasker, Ethel M. Albert as Memoir 94, American Anthropological Association.
Bryson, Lyman, 1939, "Anthropology and Education," in D. D. Brand and Fred Harvey, eds., *So Live the Works of Men*. Albuquerque.: University of New Mexico Press.
Coleman, James S., 1961, *Social Climates in High Schools*. Cooperative Research Monograph No. 4, U.S. Dept. of Health, Education and Welfare.
———, 1961, *Adolescent Society*. New York: The Free Press of Glencoe.
Cook, L. A., and Elaine F. Cook, 1950, *A Sociological Approach to Education*. New York: McGraw-Hill.
Cox, P. W., and B. E. Mercer, 1961, *Education in Democracy*. New York: McGraw-Hill.
Cronbach, Lee J., 1954, *Educational Psychology*. New York: Harcourt, Brace & World.
Davis, Allison, 1952, *Social Class Influences on Learning*. Cambridge: Harvard University Press.
Davis, A., and R. J. Havighurst, 1947, *Father of the Man*. Boston: Houghton Mifflin.
Deevey, E. Jr., 1960, "The Human Population." *Scientific American* 203, No. 3, 194–204.
Dobzhansky, Theodore, 1960, "The Present Evolution of Man." *Scientific American Reprints*, 203, No. 3, 206–217.
Eells, Kenneth, Allison Davis, Robert J. Havighurst, Virgil E. Herrick, and Ralph W. Tyler, 1951, *Intelligence and Cultural Differences*. Chicago: University of Chicago Press.
Eggan, Fred, 1957, Social Anthropology and the Educational System. *School Review*, 65:247–259.
———, 1959, "An Anthropologist Looks at Discipline." *Grade Teacher*, 76:93–95.
Ehrich, Robert W., 1947, "The Place of Anthropology in a College Education." *Harvard Educational Review*, XVII:57–61.
Frank, Lawrence K., 1959, *The School as Agent for Cultural Renewal*. Cambridge, Harvard University Press.
Gruber, Fred C., ed., 1961, *Anthropology and Education*, The Martin G. Brumbaugh Lectures in Education. Philadelphia: University of Pennsylvania Press.
Harvard Educational Review, 1953, "Social Class Structure and American Education." Parts I and II, XXIII, 149–338.
Havighurst, Robert J., and Hilda Taba, 1949, *Adolescent Character and Personality*. New York: John Wiley & Sons, Inc.
Henry, Jules, 1960, "A Cross-cultural Outline of Education." *Current Anthropology*, 1:267–305.
Herskovits, Melville J., 1943, "Education and Cultural Dynamics." *American Journal of Sociology*, XLVIII:109–21.

————, 1950, *Man and His Works.* New York: Alfred A. Knopf.

Hewett, Edgar L., 1904, "Anthropology and Education." *American Anthropologist,* VI:574–75.

————, 1905, "Ethnic Factors in Education." *American Anthropologist,* VII:1–16.

Hoebel, E. Adamson, 1955, "Anthropology in Education," in W. L. Thomas, Jr., ed., *Yearbook of Anthropology.* New York: Wenner-Gren Foundation for Anthropological Research.

Howells, W. W., 1952, "The Study of Anthropology." *American Anthropologist,* 54:1–7.

————, 1960, "The Distribution of Man." *Scientific American,* 203, No. 3, 113–130.

Johnson, Charles S., ed., 1943, "Education and the Cultural Process." *American Journal of Sociology,* XLVIII, 1–136.

Keesing, Felix M., 1937, *Education in Pacific Countries.* Shanghai, China: Kelly and Walsh.

Kimball, Solon T., 1956, "Anthropology and Education." *Educational Leadership,* 13:480–483.

Klineberg, Otto, 1935, *Racial Differences.* New York: Harper & Row.

————, 1947, "Racial Psychology," in Ralph Linton, ed., *The Science of Man in the World Crisis.* New York: Columbia University Press.

————, 1951, *Race and Psychology.* New York: UNESCO.

Kluckhohn, Clyde, 1949, *Mirror for Man.* New York: McGraw-Hill.

Kroeber, A. L., ed., 1953, *Anthropology Today.* Chicago: University of Chicago Press.

Landes, Ruth, 1960, *Tools of Desegregation.* Paper read before the American Association for the Advancement of Science, Section H (Anthropology), in December, New York City (mimeographed).

Lasker, Gabriel, 1961, *The Evolution of Man, A Brief Introduction to Physical Anthropology.* New York: Holt, Rinehart and Winston.

Lee, Dorothy, 1957, "Anthropology and American Secondary Education," in P. M. Halverson, ed., *Frontiers of Secondary Education.* Syracuse: University of Syracuse Press.

Mandelbaum, David, 1960, *The Teaching of Anthropology in the U.S.A., A Review of the Symposia of the Project in Educational Resources in Anthropology.* New York: Wenner-Gren Foundation for Anthropological Research (mimeographed).

————, 1961a, "Progress Report on Educational Resources in Anthropology Project." *Fellow Newsletter,* American Anthropological Association, 2:2–3.

————, 1961b, "Anthropology in the High Schools." *Fellow Newsletter,* American Anthropological Association, 2:2–3.

Martin, William E., and Celia Stendler, 1953, *Child Development.* New York: Harcourt, Brace & World.

McDonald, Fred, 1959, *Educational Psychology.* San Francisco: Wadsworth.

Mead, Margaret, 1943, "Our Educational Emphasis in Primitive Perspective." *American Journal of Sociology,* XLVIII:633–39.

————, 1946, "Professional Problems of Education in Dependent Countries." *The Journal of Negro Education,* XV:346–57.

————, 1950, *The School in American Culture.* Cambridge: Harvard University Press.

————, 1959, "A Redefinition of Education." *NEA Journal,* 48: 15–17.

————, 1960a, "Anthropology as Part of a Liberal Education." Paper prepared for symposium No. 5, Summer 1960, Burg Wartenstein, Austria, sponsored by Wenner-Gren Foundation for Anthropological Research.

————, 1960b, "The High School of the Future." *California Journal of Secondary Education,* 35:360–69.

Mercer, B. E., E. R. Carr, 1957, *Education and the Social Order.* New York: Holt, Rinehart and Winston.

Montessori, Marie, 1913, *Pedagogical Anthropology.* New York: J. B. Lippincott Company.

Opler, Morris, 1947, "Cultural Alternatives and Educational Theory." *Harvard Educational Review,* XVII:28–44.

Pettit, George A., 1946, "Primitive Education in North America." *University of California Publications in American Archeology and Ethnology*, XLIII:1–182.

Pressey, Sidney, and Francis Robinson, 1944, *Psychology and the New Education*. New York: Harper & Row.

Read, Margaret, 1960, *Children of Their Fathers: Growing Up among the Ngoni of Nyasaland*. New Haven: Yale University Press.

Robbins, Florence G., 1953, *Educational Sociology*. New York: Holt, Rinehart and Winston.

Rosenstiel, Annette, 1954, "Educational Anthropology: A New Approach to Cultural Analysis." *Harvard Educational Review*. XXIV:28:36.

———, 1959, "Anthropology and Childhood Education." *School and Society*, 87:482–83.

Siegel, Bernard, 1959, Review of *Cultural Foundations of Education* by T. Brameld. *American Anthropologist*, 61:118–120.

Spindler, G. D., 1946, "Anthropology May Be an Answer." *Journal of Education*, CXXIX: 130–31.

———, 1959, *The Transmission of American Culture*, Third Burton Lecture. Cambridge: Harvard University Press.

———, 1961, Review of T. Brameld, *Remaking of a Culture*, with reply by T. Brameld. *Harvard Educational Review*, 31:345–353.

Spiro, Melford, 1958, *Children of the Kibbutz*. Cambridge: Harvard University Press.

Stanley, William O., et al., 1956, *Social Foundations of Education*. New York: Holt Rinehart and Winston.

Taba, Hilda, 1957, "Educational Implications in the Concepts of Culture and Personality." *Educational Leadership*, 15:183–86.

Warner, W. Lloyd, et al., 1949, *Democracy in Jonesville*. New York: Harper & Row.

———, Robert J. Havighurst, and Martin B. Loeb, 1944, *Who Shall Be Educated?* New York: Harper & Row.

Washburn, Sherwood, 1960, "Tools and Human Evolution." *Scientific American Reprints*, Vol. 203, No. 3, 12 pp.

Whiteford, Andrew H., ed., 1960, *Teaching Anthropology*. Logan Museum Publications in Anthropology, No. 8, Beloit, Wisconsin: Beloit College Press.

Whiting, John, and Irvin L. Child, 1953, *Child Training and Personality*. New Haven: Yale University Press.

Whiting, John, and B. B. Whiting 1960, "Contributions of Anthropology to the Methods of Studying Child Rearing," in Paul H. Mussen, ed., *Handbook of Research Methods in Child Development*. New York: John Wiley.

Further Readings

Brameld, Theodore, and Edward B. Sullivan. "Anthropology and education," *Review of Educational Research*, vol. 31 (February 1961).

Shunk, William R., and Bernice Z. Goldstein. "Anthropology and education," *Review of Educational Research*, vol. 34 (February 1964).

Sindell, Peter S. "Anthropological approaches to the study of education," *Review of Educational Research*, vol. 39 (December 1969).

Spindler, George D. (ed.) *Education and anthropology*. Stanford: Stanford University Press, 1955.

———, *Education and Culture: Anthropological Approaches*. New York: Holt, Rinehart and Winston, 1963.

Wolcott, Harry F. "Anthropology and education," *Review of Educational Research*, vol. 37 (February 1967).

ANTHROPOLOGY IN EDUCATION

Anthropology is content. It is something that is taught. It is also a perspective on the teaching and learning experience. And, finally, anthropology is a way of teaching; it is a form of pedagogy.

The two groups of writings that comprise Part Two consider anthropology *in* education, the effects and uses of anthropological data, inquiry, and perspective in educational encounters — formal and informal. The articles deal variously with anthropology as an instructional substance or additive; with anthropology as an integrated, whole instructional system; with anthropology as affect; and with anthropology as a mode, or design, for the preparation of teachers, administrators, and other school specialists.

The emergence of anthropology as a discrete component of instructional programs — or as a course of instruction itself — is relatively recent. The cause for its inclusion in precollege curriculum is unclear. It is due in part to the increased sensitivity of educators and educational leadership to the relevance of anthropology to general education. It is in part an outcome of expanding interest in social science, at large and specific to schools. It is also due, and in no small way, to the continuing efforts of a committed (and hardy) band of anthropologists and anthropological-minded educators to introduce anthropology *into* the schools.

Revisionary trends in the social studies, coupled with the redevelopment of methods and materials for social *study*, are as much responsible for the somehow sudden appearance of anthropology in precollege classrooms. The "strange lands and friendly people" syndrome that affected the social studies for educational generations has, of late and at last, begun to recede. The influence of unilinear schemes that explain the "growth of civilization" has similarly diminished. Replacing traditional attitudes toward other peoples are more realistic approaches to social study, which view other human groups as being no less exotic to us than are we to them; stress similarities among human peoples, as well as factual differences; emphasize sociocultural processes, as well as events of them and their structure; and rely upon multilinear schemes for comprehending the developmental variety of human societies.

Such approaches (which tend to associate with innovative instructional modes: "discovery" learning, simulation, hypothesis-testing, etc.) devastate the ethnocentric, Westernized notion of an inexorable advance of mankind to what *we* are. This idea is so conventional as to be fixed, even, in the frontispieces of typical social studies texts, where human progress is portrayed (from left to right!) in a series of sketches, beginning with a "cave man" and concluding with a stylized, white businessman who, if nothing else, resembles a hometown Rotarian. This repugnant idea, less graphically but no less effectively, masquerades as mature understanding of who and what we are in the chapters of those texts.

We are ultimately defined by others; we are what *we* are mostly because *we* are not *them*. If our social study is organized about the idea that *we* are what Man is, that what *we* are doing is most worthy, and that what remains essentially is to detail the distributions of other unmanly and unworthy peoples — like so much tin, quaint customs, or zones of heavy rainfall — then such an idea is not only biased in the extreme but is also disadvantaging. Through its insinuation we produce social cripples, whom we further deprive by encouraging them to perceive the variety of human groups within our *own* society as so many *others*, as *not* us.

Traditional approaches to human progress, the "rise" of civilization, and to the human potential therefore, together with attitudes toward "primitives," the "inscrutable Orient," "darkest Africa," and the sombrero-shaded, dozing, dusty "Mexican," which are associated with them, have terribly misread human advance, if it really be that. These simply ignore or repudiate the critical involvement of the female as well as of the male, of black and red as well as of the white, of adaptation as well as of invention, and of material conditions as well of the ideal in shaping the human past and in deciding the human future. Their strong suggestion, if not bald claim, of white and West superiority is racist, however benign. A conception of unilineal, manifest progress suffers empirical evidence to the contrary. It accounts neither for the enormously complex and imaginative societies that predate the West nor for the clear barbarisms that have been enacted in the names of Western societies.

In transforming the social studies — a process by no means complete — anthropology is a constant ally. Anthropology, first, has itself undergone serious revision, from "armchair," speculative folklorist studies to field-based, empirical behavioral science. That (continuing) experience equips it with the special antennae of a combined humanism and science, which duality is never an either/or proposition, but a balance of perspective, the same that social study intends. Second, anthropology has been and continues to be used and, by some, abused as the primary source of information about man and groups of men. Third, anthropology is a way of seeing human difference, not inferiority; variation, not hierarchy; true alternatives, not lesser choices; and the implication of others in us and of ourselves in others, not we and, forever, them.

The anthropological *way* is sensitively phrased, here, by Mr. Rosenfeld, whose elaboration of anthropology as pedagogy compares with the intense teaching and learning experience recalled by Mr. Leeds. The accounts of Misses Emmons and Cobia and of Mr. Stong directly illustrate the uses of anthropological data and inquiry in social study, whereas the assertion of anthropological relevance to issues and topical matter of the social studies is given substance by Mrs. Collier and Mr. Dethlefsen.

The anthropological presence in teacher training and in other activities that prepare educators usually takes the form of academic courses or workshop sessions. The articles of the second section of Part Two describe the contributions of anthropology, actual and possible, to teacher training and other situations of educator preparation.

Though remarkably little effort has so far been made to enlighten the teaching of *anthropology*,[1] in most undergraduate and graduate education degree programs anthropology is available, and in some cases required, as an academic experience. Mr. Bohannan relates such an experience. Typically, it concerns minority education; much of current anthropological involvement in the preparation of teachers, administrators, and school specialists does.

Anthropological contributions to teacher education characteristically emphasize the "wholism" of anthropological perspective, particularly of educative processes and their articulation and certain educational structures to other behavioral institutions. Mr. Redfield

---

[1] The most exhaustive (but now seriously dated) treatment of anthropology as a field of instruction is *The Teaching of Anthropology*, edited by David G. Mandelbaum, Gabriel W. Lasker, and Ethel M. Albert, and published as Memoir 94 by the American Anthropological Association (Washington, D.C.: The Association, 1963). An abridged, paperback version was published by the University of California Press in 1967.

dwells on these relationships in a plainspoken statement of what else we need to understand in coming to "know" education. Mr. Khlief, too, stresses the pertinence of "wholistic" approaches to teaching and learning, an outlook fundamental to Mrs. Leacock's discussion of the uses and abuses of the concept culture, as intended for school counselors.

Atypically, Mr. Bohannan suggests that teaching, especially when it is committed to *engage* learners meaningfully and not merely to caretake them, corresponds closely to the "doing" of anthropology. Anthropological fieldwork, he observes, has much the same sensitivity to deepset meanings that are easily misinterpreted and to which we may react carelessly, if not insecurely. The suggestion is of anthropology as pedagogy, as a way of teaching and learning altogether, and it deserves more exposition than the confines of this book permit. Lack of space has meant the exclusion, also, of writings that treat anthropological involvement in such areas of teacher preparation as bilingual programming, practicum or pre-service, and techniques of classroom observation.

The insights evident in both groups of selections here raise hopes for the continued development of anthropology in education, of a more pronounced anthropological presence. At the same time, the understandings generated here hold an immediate promise for more effective education and better teaching — trite, but earnest claims.

A. ANTHROPOLOGY AS CONTENT AND PERSPECTIVE

7

The deliberate involvement of young children in the study of human groups other than their own has long taken on the character of "Dutch days" and endless series of "Peter goes to Peru" stories. In falsely portraying the existence of various human groups as so much us — excepting color of faces, dress, and the funny names — such an approach obfuscated or, worse, ignored real sociocultural differences and similarities among peoples of the world. The emergence of a new order in the social studies exposed both the extreme bias and questionable learning strategy of this traditional approach. It also served to expose anthropology. The uses of anthropology in the elementary school instructional regimen was no doubt retarded, as Emmons and Cobia observe, by its reputation as a "college" subject. Its application also suffered an almost total lack of working experience on the part of anthropologists in curriculum development. Misses Emmons and Cobia, teachers at the Juliette Low School, Savannah, Georgia, report some outcomes of a programmatic effort to teach anthropology in early grades.

FRANCES EMMONS AND JACQUELINE COBIA

Introducing Anthropological Concepts in the Primary Grades

The initial reaction of a primary grade teacher to the idea of teaching anthropological concepts is often negative. One obstacle is the teacher's lack of knowledge of anthropology. Another is the idea that anthropology is just too hard for primary children: it's a college subject.

From *Social Education*, vol. 32, no. 3 (March 1968), pp. 248–250. Reprinted by permission of the authors and publisher.

121

However, once a teacher is willing to teach anthropology, he is likely to discover that children react enthusiastically. They do not find the subject matter too hard. The teacher is also likely to see that behind the concepts of anthropology are many facts and ideas that he has been transmitting all along. His fear of personal inadequacy will probably give way to interest in anthropology and self-confidence in teaching it. All of the teachers in Juliette Low School who have taught anthropology have been impressed with the high degree of pupil interest.

This article tells how a first and a second grade teacher introduced anthropological concepts in the primary grades.[1] An elementary teacher who reviews this account of their experiences will quickly realize two things. The activities these two teachers used to reinforce conceptual learning are similar to devices used in regular elementary teaching, adapted to the content of anthropology. The language of anthropology, however, is more abstract than words that appear in much social studies teaching.

One of the main concepts in anthropology is the concept of culture. To make this concept meaningful, we first tried to build up the idea of what an anthropologist does. We focused on the role of the anthropologist as a participant observer and asked each child to report on something that his family did. For first grade children reporting on family activities is exciting.

We used part of our daily sharing time for reports of the participant observers, and we used some of our language arts time to write experience stories based on these reports. To emphasize the need for accuracy in reporting, we asked children to write one sentence statements about what they saw. This helped demonstrate to the children the variety of ways that ordinary activities are carried out and the need for exact reporting.

The participant-observer experience stimulated offshoots in many directions. Children began to ask questions about how the anthropologist would really understand what was going on if he were to study other people. We were able to establish the idea of people having different languages and the need of the anthropologist to speak the language of the people he is observing. Language differences automatically led to the idea of differences in groups in various parts of the world, and the globe was used to help children locate areas of the earth occupied by the people they were to study.

Use of the participant-observer technique in the context of the family can be more than the study of an anthropological method for data collection. It can help to develop the concept of the family in American culture and lay a basis for asking questions about families in other cultures.

[1] The units prepared by the Anthropology Curriculum Project, University of Georgia, gave a common core for teaching that made it easier to introduce anthropological concepts.

For example, to ask and answer the question "What does your daddy do to make a living?" or "What kind of work is your daddy in?" sets the stage for asking a parallel question, "What kind of work does an Arunta daddy do?" The technique of participant observation related to a particular cultural trait leads very naturally to the method of cross-cultural comparison. This is the method by which the anthropologist looks at behavior in one culture in contrast to behavior in another culture. Primary grade children find such comparisons fascinating.

In the primary grades we are not concerned with the formal introduction of the concepts of trait variability, trait universals, and cultural patterning. What we try to communicate is the idea that people have common needs. Because they have learned to meet these needs in different ways, there are differences in the way people do things. Formal concepts may be introduced to the students later. The teacher, however, must know the concepts. Otherwise he is likely to present cultural patterns as so many discrete and bizarre ways of behaving rather than as understandable, functional variations in human behavior.

We do not merely talk about differences in behavior; we try to involve the children to such an extent that they identify with behavior in a culture. Role-playing, dramatization, and the stimulation of cross-cultural comparison appeals strongly to the primary grade child. "Let's pretend" is equally attractive to boys and girls, but it is strictly sex-typed, boys imitating males and girls imitating females.

To enact the role of a Paleo-Indian, Arunta hunter, Kazak herdsman, Mayan priest, or Hopi gardener is more than play. This requires the child to ask himself questions as to what he would do in a particular environment with the tools that a people have. He therefore has to know something about tools and how they are used. Knowledge of tools leads the child to ask questions about what people in another culture have to know about their environment in order to survive. The idea that people we think of as primitive have an organized knowledge system is a striking one to young children. How a group can go about applying this knowledge in the best way leads into the concept of social organization, a base for which is laid in the consideration of family activities.

"Let's pretend," when done honestly in terms of the behavior in a culture, helps transmit the idea that people we think of as being very primitive have many skills that advanced people do not have. In practicing cross-cultural comparison, children become aware of the need for specialized skills in technological cultures. Here is a base for the investigation of division of labor and interdependence in different cultures. Such investigations will give added meaning to a subsequent study of interdependence and cooperation in American culture.

Sometimes activities that fail technically turn out to be the most meaningful. We always try to engage in activities that duplicate those in a given culture. A favorite one for boys is tool making. They are often unsuccessful at this. Trying to attach a stone point to a spear or an ax head to a handle can be a difficult task. Therefore the activity conveys an idea of technical skill better than a picture or films could.

One day we attempted to make an Arunta house, not a small model but a large one that the children could enter. We went out to a nearby wooded area and collected a large supply of limbs and small branches. After we had managed to get it up, it fell down on the children. We thought at first that this activity was a failure, but then we heard the children saying that the Arunta must be smart to build their own houses. We then realized that they had learned something more important — that even the Arunta had skills that made it possible for them to survive in their own environment.

Many of our activities are selected to convey the idea that differences in human behavior are related to differences in the artifacts in a culture. One of the favorite activities was to have a Kazak meal. We sat on the floor and tried to eat in the Kazak manner using only a few utensils. We found this very awkward, but when we asked ourselves "How could the Kazak follow their herds if they had to carry around tables and chairs?" we were able to understand better the idea of cultural patterning — that things in a culture have to fit together in a certain way in order for people to live.

One of the questions we asked was whether children could see any similarities in the way the Kazak lived and the way American cowboys lived. This simple question led us to ask more questions about the Kazak environment and the cattle and sheep country of the West. The children were able to see how similarities in environment led to similarities in using that environment, even when there is a great difference in the technology of the people.

In addition to role playing, another way that children enjoy learning anthropology is through art and craft activities. During the anthropology unit, the "art" time is devoted to anthropologically related activities. Making houses from clay, sticks, straw, mud, papier-mâché, and grass sod is interesting for children, both inside and outside class. The Kazak winter house is one appropriate subject for this activity. Another art activity especially useful in the study of American culture is the construction of picture books. All kinds of flat pictures may be used to make both individual and class books.

The study of a group can also be enriched by playing its music. This activity helps children to learn differences in musical sounds and to perceive that all people do not have the same kind of music. It also seems to stimulate children to attempt to create art like that of the culture they are studying.

There are many opportunities during the school day to introduce anthropological concepts incidentally rather than as a lesson. For example, primary grade children find the subject of food very interesting. In talking about what they have for a meal at the school cafeteria, and why they eat certain things, the class can also discuss what children in other cultures eat. The fact that a Hopi child eats *piki*, or an Arunta child eats a *witchetty* grub can be related to the economic system of the culture. Such illustrations will give the concept of division of labor a dimension that is not merely definitional: food is an end product necessary for survival, and all people have different ways of dividing up the responsibility for obtaining it.

In studying about a culture, young children prefer topics that have some kind of concrete referent, such as tools, ways of making a living, or house types. Partly for this reason, archeology has great appeal. Primary grade children know only a little about religion and government and seem to find these more abstract subjects less interesting. It is usually difficult, within the short time allotted to the anthropology unit, to develop reference points for such topics.

The lack of interest in abstract ideas, however, needs to be qualified. Sometimes, depending on the way a unit develops and the interests of the children in the class, even the idea of social organization can be a very exciting one. One year there were a few boys in a second grade class who became very interested in the concept of Aztec military government. One of the boys had a father who was an army officer, and he just knew that the army didn't run the United States. This served as a point of departure from which looking at a headman in a tribe, a priest king, a military ruler, and a democratic government took on a different meaning.

Young children are fascinated with archeology. This has in part to do with the use of tools — our children love to bring in tools and make displays of tools used by archeologists. Another reason is that archeology tells about how man uncovers artifacts. For the children, excavating artifacts is like hunting for buried treasure. Just as there are clues to find treasure, there are clues to find a site. Before you excavate, you must make a map to show where the treasure is located. All of these things make finding out about archeological methods very appealing to children.

Another reason for its appeal is that in Savannah somebody is always digging up something old from a house or a road bed. One year a lot of old bottles were found when a roadway was cleared. Some of the parents of our children had gone out to hunt for these bottles that took on a nice color with age. We used this as a starting point. First we asked what people would think about our culture if they dug up things we have today. Then we raised questions about what kind of artifacts endure and how the archeologist goes about reconstructing the life of people from only a small part of the evidence they leave. The idea of the archeologist as a scientific detective of the past has strong appeal for children.

In Savannah there is a children's museum, which helps youngsters to visualize some of the work of archeologists. Our area also has a number of reconstructed fort sites that display principles of archeological methodology. Ocmulgee National Park at Macon gives an opportunity for an extended field trip to an impressive Indian site. Field trips to sites and museums help children understand the idea of archeology as a science because they can see excavations and the interpretations and reconstructions based on excavation.

But we believe that a teacher can find opportunities to make anthropology meaningful in many ordinary things. When we were talking about dendrochronology, or tree-ring dating, it was easy to ask a child to bring in a cut from a tree. When we were talking about stratigraphy, it was simple to dig a hole in the playground and see the various strata of earth. The sandy loam was easy to dig, and the earth shaded off even at a shallow level from the thin black top soil into several different colored layers. A terrarium in the classroom, with objects placed at different depths, was a convenient way of illustrating the principle of stratigraphic dating.

In communicating the idea of how man entered the New World, we made use of map work; in fact, we found maps just as useful in anthropology as in geography. Children need to know where people and things are in space. We used the globe and wall maps as well as desk maps to help children get an idea of the location of people and things. Most of the time we drew the maps freely from a model; the idea was not to produce an accurate map but to give children an idea of relative location.

Pictures and three-dimensional models were useful ways to teach that the Indians in pre-Columbian America developed in different stages. We have not always been successful in teaching the idea that some Indians did not go beyond the archaic stage of hunting and gathering. However, the various activities — from cooking with heated stones dropped in water to building models of Mayan religious centers — helped children to understand that Indians had a more complicated way of life than just hunting.

In addition to class discussion and explanation, we try to engage the pupils in activities that add meaning to the concepts. Art work, modeling, role playing, listening to records of native music, seeing pictures and films, making scrapbooks, murals, and dioramas, putting on puppet shows, writing class plays and experience charts, making tools and artifacts, bringing in things from other countries and telling about them, learning songs and dances from other cultures, and reading stories about other people are all methods that primary grade teachers use to convey ideas to young children.

These methods, adapted to the content of anthropology, give meaning to anthropological concepts.

The use of the language of anthropology is a challenge to the primary grade child. He loves to master new ideas and words and to learn something that even his parents do not know. His success in seeing the new conceptual world that anthropology opens up to him is self-motivational.

At the present time our children are asking, "When are we going to study anthropology?" Their eagerness to study a new subject and to master difficult material reflects the success we have had in introducing anthropology in the primary grades.

Further Readings

John, Vera P. "Analysis of story retelling as a measure of the effects of ethnic content in stories," in Jerome Hellmuth (ed.), *Disadvantaged child*, vol. 2. New York: Brunner/Mazel Publishers, 1968.

Potterfield, J. E. "An analysis of elementary children's ability to learn anthropological content at grades four, five, and six," *Journal of Educational Research*, vol. 61 (March, 1968).

Teaching anthropology in the elementary school: a symposium. General Information Series No. 5, Anthropology Curriculum Project. Athens: University of Georgia, 1967.

Warren, Richard L. "The role of anthropology in elementary social studies," *Social Education*, vol. 32 (March 1968).

8

Emmons and Cobia, in the previous selection, were intent on establishing selected anthropological ideas in the repertoire of children in the early grades. Rosenfeld here establishes the idea of anthropology as a pivotal learning experience in the whole instructional environment of elementary school. He urges us to consider the total affect that might be realized by purposely engaging young children in, as he puts it, "a simultaneous sense of their own behavior and the means by which to assess it." Mr. Rosenfeld, like Gearing, responds emphatically to the question, Why Indians? And, like Musgrove and Spindler he is convinced of the important insights into teaching behavior that are made available through anthropological perspective and inquiry. Formerly an elementary school teacher, Rosenfeld is persuasive in his special commitment to the integrity of children. There is a way of viewing kids as nothing but intending adults, as thus understandable imperfections, as — again — "odd" and "dissimilar" persons who are "humanly believable" perhaps only to an Art Linkletter or in displays of scrub paintings. Children are different; that they are deficient in not being adults is another matter. Children are not without an essential dignity in being different; that they deserve a schooling that, although it presumes their adulthood, effectively deprives them of more than an occasional chance to evaluate their "becoming" is indeed dubious. Rosenfeld's lucid, frank commentary remarkably presages much of current concern with curricula of affect and "inquiry" social sudies. He is presently Associate Professor of Anthropology, Hofstra University.

GERARD L. ROSENFELD

Anthropology as Social Studies in the Elementary School

As newcomers to an emerging, more intimate world community, new nations have an imperative sense of the need for deliberate education. "It is important that native manpower be developed," said a visitor from Israel recently, "but educate a *woman* and you educate a whole family." If this idea has import for the "Third World," it may also be relevant to a consideration of social studies programs for elementary school children. Our investment in the education of those children, the newcomers to our own culture, is an investment in future parental generations.

History and geography have traditionally composed the subject matter of elementary social studies; and students have only encountered the wider constellation of behavioral science when they reached the university. The implication is that many social sciences are not considered relevant in the training of children. Thus, anthropology — along with philosophy, psychology, economics, sociology, and political science — is omitted from public school curricula. Anthropology is still a strange subject to most people.

It should be noted that anthropologists, likewise, have seemed content to remain unnoticed in public school settings. Few feel an urgent desire to foster the inclusion of their particular passion in the learnings of children. One might conclude, in any case, that anthropology would clutter the curriculum. Schoolmen seem to see no need for it; and the anthropologist feels he had best remain aloof.

Yet one is prompted to grosser concerns. Most of the world lives in dis-

From *Teachers College Record*, vol. 69, no. 8 (May 1968), pp. 767–770. Reprinted by permission of the author and publisher.

advantage; and pockets of poverty dot our own countrysides. War has become as formidable a human creation as the wheel and the tinderbox. Has it not, in fact, been easier to exploit the technological than to ameliorate the social? Life is both prolonged and undermined, as it were, in the same culture. Commitments seem easily won and lost within the same person.

WHAT CHILDREN LEARN

What is it, then, that our children must know? After all, they learn many things in the elementary school. Initial steps in reading are taken; there is use of maps, and there is getting on with peers. Value patterns are formed; belief systems, fostered. Children learn to be quiet during fire drills; they learn to excuse their absences; and they eat their lunches because children in other lands "are starving."

Where, however, are commitments grounded? Which disciplines and classroom activities are expressive of the human condition? For example, a two place multiplier does not of itself predispose the child to a knowledge of pattern and process in culture (nor, perhaps, to an understanding of the functional role of mathematics in American culture), just as the teaching of reading need not give a sense of the writer. Obviously, the "felt need" for anthropology is present. If children, as seedlings, are to ripen, they must be given a simultaneous sense of their own behavior *and* the means by which to assess it.

The Bushman child carries with him, in the trek across the African Kalahari, a more inclusive inventory of his culture. He moves within a total group, seeing before him the fullest range of models spanning past and present. Even his material goods are in his company. What he will become is in his consciousness. For the American school child, becoming is not so clear, nor so personal. Further, what occurs in his behalf during school years will have its most critical manifestation in later generations. And the tools afforded him by which to characterize his existence will either smoothe or roughen the way.

So it is that omens of future difficulty are discernible in our early education programs. Although we would think it absurd to graduate children who couldn't add or subtract, who couldn't read or write, we do not find it absurd to pass children through our schools who lack the tools of social science: survey, observation, interview, case study, and the like. Perhaps what the child doesn't know, however, is really what the teacher doesn't know. Yet, how does one commit a child to social systems in which he must move when he is not given the tools and skills by which to analyse them?

One hopes that information is not intentionally withheld, for one is otherwise forced to a fearful analogy. Colin Turnbull suggests in *The Lonely African* that the European's most notable contribution to the

African was, perhaps, the cure for the syphilis he initiated to begin with. Is, in kind, the major advantage of elementary school social studies programs the guarded insularity which shields the child from his own unawareness? How else, then, could the "proper study of mankind" (social studies) proceed without "the science of man" (anthropology)?

The Relevance of Anthropology

There appears to be a basic dishonesty in many social studies programs, if dishonesty is akin to faulty and fragmented knowledge of subject matter. Thus, we teach geography without revealing how the geographer works; and we teach history without a sense of the historian. While mathematics reveals the circle, the square, and the graph, the social science analogues of settlement pattern, clique, rites of passage, and the like, are nowhere present. Yet the teacher might perform an appropriate service in allowing the child those tools and insights by which the things he does not know are discerned and made comprehensible. If every man is a record of man's past, every child ought, in kind, be a researcher of himself; a participant — observer, as it were, on his own condition.

Content in social studies is derived from interacting parallel systems: man's bio-social nature and his cultural responses to life's demands. This, traditionally, has been the preoccupation of anthropologists, who in their study of culture and cultures have sought meaning in the pedestrian and pattern in the idiosyncratic. The passion for diversity in human behavior has revealed the spirit and images of man, while comparative perspectives move toward fundamental understandings of cultural life. These accomplishments have been won, most often, in the remote group, where anthropologists have been foreigners proving their own humanity while probing the humanity of those studied. The elementary school child, as well, is a newcomer to culture. He learns, too, that people live in families, that environment prompts and limits human reaction, that common orientations bind, that humans talk. Thus, a prolonged dialogue is initiated for every child, between himself and his world, with the social sciences as intermediaries.

If, then, the world is the anthropologist's playground, the school can well be the child's proving ground. It is here that Philip Phenix's "representative ideas" and Jerome Bruner's "organizing concepts" in the disciplines are revealed. And, if L. S. B. Leakey, as reported, tried to skin an antelope with his teeth to see if man's precursors could have accomplished this, the child can "cut his teeth" in other daring endeavors as well. Do all children play games? Must the hunter be invested with a particular temperament? Can inquiries be made into the division of labor in society, rites of passage, family structures, ecological alignments, cultural use of time, age gradings, etc.? Why not?

There are, to be sure, many who feel the teacher is not prepared to foster such learnings; that the child is not *ready* for these undertakings. Yet, the teacher is not mathematician, historian, or scientist, although he is charged with representing these. And if the child is not ready for new learnings, he can be made ready by his very involvement in those subjects it is feared he cannot handle. A fundamental insight may emerge here. We judge children's abilities by past conditions, just as some describe race in a present sense, discounting the fact that manifestations of race are the results of adaptations to past conditions no longer extant. Therefore, the absence of anthropology from certain teacher training institutions and from elementary schools is not, itself, testimony to the soundness of this practice. In fact, in the scientific spirit of anthropology, anthropologists ought to test the hypothesis implied here: Does the exclusion of anthropology in public schools inhere, in any way, in anthropology's own "shortcomings"?

A good social studies program would include biological science and the humanities, as well as the social sciences. Anthropology would be the mortar in its construction, for anthropology is the starting point; it is method for inquiry, as well as frame of reference. If it does not always yield simplicity, it does offer an alternative. It illuminates culture and is a "tool for cultural criticism" at the same time. And, if anthropology makes no absolute judgments, it would be false to conclude that anthropology has no place in the education of children and teachers. Children who are caught up solely in their own life-ways have been rendered no service in our public schools.

FURTHER READINGS

Dow, Peter B. "*Man: A Course of Study:* an experimental social science course for elementary schools," *Man: A Course of Study, One: Talks to Teachers.* Cambridge: Education Development Center, Inc., 1968, 1969.

Gearing, Frederick O. "Toward a mankind curriculum: from kindergarten through twelfth grade," *Today's Education*, vol. 59 (March 1970).

Kimball, Solon T., and James E. McClellan, Jr. *Education and the new America.* New York: Random House, 1962, 1966.

Laliberté, Cécile, and Maleleine Lefebvre. "*Teaching social sciences at the elementary level.*" Paper read at the Annual Meeting of the American Anthropological Association, New Orleans, La., 1968.

9

"Teaching" anthropology at other than graduate or undergraduate levels is, it is fair to say, hazardous. First, anthropology itself is anathema to segments of the population to whom is conjured up the troubling idea of evolution and other social threats. Second, professional anthropology is quick to flag or, in some instances, repudiate "amateur" efforts at substantive treatments of the discipline. Third, anthropology is not easily "taught." Its structure is frail compared to that of most social sciences. It is, possibly, as much of an attitude as it is a logical set of behavioral propositions. Above all, it is something that is done, and the actual doing of it emerges as a critical event in teaching it. Leeds recounts his personal experience in conducting a high school course in anthropology as having dealt in another hazard — that of so liberating students from the confines of their own cultural context as to either dissuade them from identifying with that context or dislocate them entirely. The extraordinary situation of his experience may have led Mr. Leeds to devote more than usual attention to this phenomenon. Yet, even in ordinary secondary school instruction, a sensitive, engaged rendering of anthropology runs a similar risk. It can be suggested that, where there are hazards, there are opportunities. Leeds shows some of these hazards and opportunities, which are given detailed consideration in the two articles that follow his. Mr. Leeds is currently Professor of Anthropology, University of Texas at Austin, and is a much published scholar in Latin American anthropology.

ANTHONY LEEDS

Considerations Regarding Anthropology in High School Curricula

Few courses in anthropology have been taught as such at the high school level in the United States.[1] Nevertheless, both in high schools and in elementary schools, and more particularly in the private schools, information which the anthropologists consider their own special interest has been used. Thus, children may be taught information about the Eskimo,

---

From *Human Organization*, vol. 20, no. 3 (Fall 1961), pp. 134–140. Reprinted by permission of the author and publisher.

[1] Alexander Goldenweiser is reported to have taught a course in anthropology at the Walden School, New York, some 30 years or so ago. Jack Ellison has been teaching anthropology for 11 or 12 years at the Frances Parker High School in Chicago. In 1959–1960, high school students, invited to Columbia University in an experiment aimed at exposing these students to more advanced teaching in various branches of knowledge, heard lectures on anthropology given by Charles Wagley and Morton H. Fried, both of the Columbia University Anthropology Department.

apparently the favorite culture to represent the non-Western world and almost undoubtedly the only primitive one existing in the curriculum-makers' Baedeker, although an occasional bow is made to the American plains or Southwest. Now and then, studies of the major Asian countries are made whose focus is cultural rather than properly geographical.[2] Other cultures, ranging up to the most complex, ordinarily appear to be brought into a curriculum more as functions of the description of the locations inhabited by humans than as descriptions, informed by some conception as to the nature of culture, of the specific cultures themselves. In short, one may safely assert, I believe, that the students get some sense of the variations exhibited by societies but mostly as curiosa and oddities of peculiar peoples. They do not get a sense of the cultural necessities of variation and differences as these derive from the technological articulations with environment. Rather, variation and differences are presented as if they were more or less accidentally associated with particular kinds of geographic features. Children appear rarely to be taught that there is such a class of events as technologies which can systematically be studied like geography or economics. Rather, they become familiar only with technical activities which they see as scattered hither and yon rather planlessly on the earth's far-away surfaces, activities such as camel-herding here, rice-paddy planting there. Certainly they get no sense of the effects of technology as a formal determinant of social structure and as conditioners of ideologies; far less are they presented, or do they achieve, a notion of culture as a total system. Much less are they led to see culture as a system which operates by its own laws, which has its own distinguishing characteristics and process, and whose variants cannot be reduced to any known ultimate value hierarchy. Thus, by learning mere esoterica, they are prevented from learning the fundamental first step required of all anthropologists, the scientific and ethical principle of cultural relativism. Consequently, too, they are prevented from learning the kind of perspective on world, culture, and self which anthropology can afford.

Whether a developed and sophisticated notion of these things can be taught at a high school level is not the question here. One might question whether the indoctrinated and simplistic, overly patterned view of life brought by high school students to college today permits them sufficient freedom to be open to these notions even at the college level. For the present, it must suffice to assert that both some substantive experiential awareness and abstract conceptualization of the cultural point of view can be achieved with high school students, and that this learning can expand

---

[2] E.g., *The New York Sunday Times*, March 27, 1960, p. E 9, illustrating exhibitions sponsored by the Board of Education "designed to make geography come to life and to offer both students and teachers new ways to give meaning to the social studies."

their educational perspective both in high school and subsequently in their college careers. The present paper describes an experiment in teaching a course in anthropology at the high school level and tries to assess some of its results.

THE VALUE COMMITMENT OF THE ANTHROPOLOGIST

Before turning to the experimental course, however, it is necessary to say something regarding the value commitment of the anthropologist who would be teaching such courses. Let us grant for the moment that the practicing anthropologist, when dealing with anthropological data, as such, is able to achieve the non-evaluating objectivity of the astronomer looking at cosmic events and objects. Value notions are not intrinsically relevant to the cosmographer's data. I doubt, further, whether most cosmographers would claim that a closer knowledge of the intimacies of the universe would be of import to the greater mass of humanity. The cosmos is remote from the sources of man's action and from those matters which men most urgently consider impelling problems. No doubt, however, the astronomer would make the assumption, common to all knowers of things, that knowledge itself is a Good, even if it leads to no foreseeable end. Because some intimation of an inscrutable mystery is imminent in this fundamental axiom, since we can give no ultimate rationale for it, the state of knowledge is the nearest thing to a state of grace which the scientist achieves. In contrast to the cosmographer, the anthropologist feels that his subject-matter approaches the very heart of man's action and is directly relevant to those matters which are of greatest moment in his daily life or the long span of his existence. Anthropologists are directly involved in whatever are considered major problems by men, whether problems of individuals, societies, or cultures. We have assumed that the anthropologist can look at the data of such problems with supernal objectivity, removing all value commitments from his descriptions and inferences. We may grant further that he can, with equal objectivity, present his cultural theory and descriptions in a situation where anthropology has been included in a curriculum as a discipline which must be known if one is to deal *scientifically* with social phenomena. Under these conditions, the effect on students, especially if, out of their own prior orientations, they have *voluntarily* exposed themselves to the discipline, is generally determined largely by the state of the science itself as a value-free descriptive and theoretical discipline, but not as an ethical one. If within its scope, such students make ethical choices, that is their private affair, not a disciplinary one.

The situation is different, however, where the decision is made to intrude anthropology into a liberal arts or general education curriculum. Here, at least implicitly, the assumption is made that the subject matter of anthropology is, in itself, a good thing to know, and further that it is a good thing to be known by all who are subjected to the curriculum. Here it appears to me that we find operating several values which are essentially outside the range of science, constituting basic ethical commitments on the part of the anthropologist regardless of his experience with cultural variability. Briefly, these largely unconscious value axioms may metaphorically be summarized in an argument somewhat like this:

> Happiness is an ontological phenomenon. Happiness, whether defined as material or spiritual comfort or fulfillment, is a good thing for all individuals and all individuals should have a chance to strive for their happiness. Because of various impediments, not all individuals or groups are achieving happiness. Such impediments are undesirable because they interfere with happiness. Increased knowledge is not only good in itself but is good, too, because it can be used to decrease or remove the interferences against happiness, or at least to reduce the forces for unhappiness, which is an evil. The application of anthropological knowledge towards the goal of alleviation or improvement is a good, it being assumed that alleviation and improvement (itself a value judgment) are in fact achievable without compensating ill effects elsewhere in the system.

Plainly, such values and assumptions need intensive philosophical and scientific discussion but clarification, if possible at all, will be long in coming. Meanwhile, life goes on for the subjective citizen, anthropologist or otherwise. Feelings and action-requiring situations must be accounted to, decisions must be made. Under these circumstances, the anthropologist appears to feel that, at any given point in the evolution of knowledge, a best use of his anthropological knowledge can be made, even if he be groping in a misty twilight.

In a general sort of way, values and only partially analyzed assumptions about the nature of things such as these underlay the experimental course in high school anthropology which I undertook at the B. School in New York in the spring of 1956.

THE SCHOOL SETTING

At that time, the B. School was devoted to dealing with students who had, for social or psychological reasons, failed to operate in ordinary school environments, public or private, progressive or conservative. It is difficult to characterize the students as a group for those who did not experience them, not so much because of the range of types but because the words we use tend to raise connotative images in our minds which are misleading for the students in question. Many were "disturbed" in the everyday sense of the word. Others were "psychoneurotic" in the clinical sense of the word, but, at the same time, this word is much too strong for many who had problems of a neurotic order without being severely or permanently disabled. Students of most of these types are known to all of us from our college classes, one might say almost in profusion, a fact reflected in the not infrequent reports of breakdown and even suicide among college and university students. Similarly, a large proportion of the students at the B. School had arrived, in the course of their high school academic careers, at a point of crisis which reflected itself in failure, often accompanied by the inability to socialize adequately in the school or by severe psychological symptoms, as of sudden extreme work blockage, or by both. At the B. School, these students encountered an atmosphere in which rehabilitation was at least partially possible, first, through the removal of the rigors of institutional pressures especially prevalent, although differing somewhat, in the public and genteel private schools; second, the personal supervision of students in small classes, or sometimes, for a preliminary period, as individuals, by interested and sophisticated teachers who, for the most part, possessed superior training; third, the introduction into the school, directly or indirectly, of a therapeutic atmosphere. All these things occurred within the framework of an academic program for the greater majority of the students. According to the severity or benignancy of their disorder, they were able to cope with a regular academic program with more or less success. A large percentage of the high school group I knew went to college, and several have since graduated. Some who left college have made other more or less successful adjustments. At the very least, one may say that a number of children were able to find a degree of pleasure and profit in their schooling where before they had been experiencing sheer personal torment and waste such as few of us are able to envision.

These were the value commitments and the setting within which the experimental anthropology course was taught. In addition, I was (and am) possessed of that general sub-stratum feeling that anthropological knowledge is a good thing in itself, and, further, that it is a good thing because it can contribute to a desirable personal liberation. Hence, it has profound relevance to what we call a liberal arts and possibly also a "general education" curriculum. The term "general education" is a difficult one since its meanings seem to be as numerous as the disparate interest groups active in education today. On one hand, writers identify it with an almost scholastic view of "liberal arts," while, at the other end, we find it viewed as contentless methodology, which, through some inarticulate experience on the part of the student, is supposed to create in him something which may be designated as learning.[3] Almost universally, however, it seems to

[3] Cf. T. R. McConnell, "General Education: An Analysis," in N. B. Henry (ed.), *General Education*, 51st Yearbook of the National Society for the Study of Education,

imply an education for "citizenship," according to standards called "democratic," the fundamental issues of whose definitions are ever so skillfully avoided. In effect, the student is to be trained to accommodate to the here and now, to accept his present condition as a given in life, to be a patriot.[4] If these are the primary aims of "general education," then, it seems to me anthropology has no place in its curricula. My own concern was more with anthropology as a "liberal art," understood as a way of thought which liberates, an understanding which seems to me opposed to many of the notions prevalent under the term "general education" today. In the liberating sense, knowledge can contribute to raising students, or persons in general, out of a morass of trivial responses to those immediate and local cultural cues which occur as a superstructure upon the fundamental inescapable determining effects of cultures on persons.[5] The less knowledge a person has of cultural possibilities or alternatives, the smaller the range of possible cultural choices which can be conceived of as responses to social and cultural situations, and consequently the less the range of the individual's freedom of self-determining choice, *with respect to the cultural*

Chicago, 1952; also A. Naftalin, "Social Science in General Education," *ibid.*, pp. 111–135, and H. E. Wilson and M. R. Collings, "Education for International Understanding" in *Social Studies in the Elementary School*, 57th Yearbook, Part II, 1957.

[4] Wilson and Collings, *op. cit.*, pp. 247–248.

[5] Implied here is a theory of the relationship between persons and culture, which may briefly be stated as follows: The individual and the culture are partially autonomous systems, that is, the form, characteristics, and dynamics of one system, are, at most, only partially causal of the form, characteristics, and dynamics of the other system. This implies that, with respect to each other, there is a considerable degree of freedom, although this fact does not entail any conception of indeterminacy or non-determinacy of each system within itself (cf. in this connection, D. M. McKay, "Man as Observer-Predictor" in H. Westmann (ed.), *Man in His Relationships*, Routledge and Kegan Paul, London, 1955). The degree of freedom increases with the increased recognition and discrimination of the laws of culture or culture-personality relationships and the levels of generality of these laws. The more limited a person's knowledge of laws and the variations of culture content, the fewer are his thinkable choices, while the greater, the greater his ability to choose among varying lines of thought or action and the greater his adaptive flexibility. Thus a person can increasingly confront his own culture, in some measure independent of its specific content and form, although of course not of culture as such, since the class personality, possessed by all persons, derives sustenance for certain of its parts from the class, culture (whatever the unique content absorbed and however any particular personality integrates this material). It seems to me that this conception of the relation between persons and cultures is to some extent the experience of all anthropologists who have been to the field and undergone culture shock — usually on their return to their *own* culture. It seems to me to be the experience of all anthropologists, as well as others, who, exposed to foreign cultures, have felt a sense of identity and empathy, no matter how different the culture may have been from anything with which they were customarily familiar. What has happened is that they have seen more fundamental human conditions — human relations to cosmos, man, and self — than they had known from the immediate vicissitudes of their everyday existence in their own culture — in their jobs, their families, their work. The same conception seems to me necessarily also a fundamental assumption, even where it is not usually explicit, in all psychotherapeutic techniques. Both in its therapeutic and its purely anthropological aspects, the course described operated with this assumption.

system or regarding action which might contribute toward transforming that system: Also, the fewer the chances, the smaller are his adaptability and his opportunities for that fulfillment which we have already established as a sought-for value. Thus, if the individual has learned to respond mainly to the minutiae of his local culture, and his own culture only, the range of alternatives his person might use is necessarily minimized. The more inhibited the availability of knowledge of the alternatives and possibilities, the greater is this limitation. Conversely, as knowledge increases, the individual, although having to account to fundamental cultural relations without which persons cannot operate is, at the same time, liberated from the trammels of this time and that place, and can, presumably, maximize his own individual worth and that of his society as he sees them.

His augmented worth may be a purely internal phenomenon, a truer awareness of self and of the unique interest and intrinsic value of his own being, regardless of the superficial judgments of the conforming mass about him. It may also, however, flow outward in actions, derived from discriminations based on knowledge, directed toward reinforcing or repudiating aspects of his own culture, whether systems of ideas or of social organization.

In short, he has to some extent been "liberated." Implicitly, at least, he has moved toward discovering some universal human values, in the broadest sense of that word. In fact, the anthropologist's discipline is inherently directed toward that aim when it pursues cross-cultural and comparative methods. Even if he must, as a person, carry on action and make decisions which necessarily confront him in a particular situation, he is freer to choose alternative means if he knows of other possibilities, and, above all, he is almost infinitely freer to pour in or withhold affect, thus being, in his person of persons, less at the mercies of cultural vagaries and vicissitudes. In this sense he is a freer being.

These considerations were vital in planning the anthropology courses at the B. School. We are here concerned mainly with the general educational aspects of the course, although in the plan as organized specifically for the B. School, the liberating, or let us say therapeutic, aspect was quite as important. I shall not discuss this aspect here, except in passing. Had it been less important, a more integral connection between the anthropology course and the rest of the curriculum could easily have been achieved.

THE COURSE

First, I assumed that a cross-cultural, yet fully relativist, view of culture systems has applicability to "general education." I wished to select a range of culture types which would show both the plasticity of human behavior under different environmental-technological conditions and, at the same time, emphasize the *necessities* for cultural variation and difference. Further, I wished to show the *range* of possible responses, even with a single culture type. To some extent, cultures were selected with this in mind. Second, I assumed that the understanding of the concept of culture itself, with special emphasis on the structure and functions of culture and its changes through time — even if only vaguely formulated in their minds — would generally serve to illuminate the students' views of the human landscape in other courses, particularly world, European, and American history, economics, literature, and language courses. Third, I assumed that the children at the B. School were what they were because of what they had experienced in the sociocultural and psychological structure of their families. Observation of these families generally confirmed this assumption. I felt that, if these students could see themselves as persons in some sense independent of the structure and private cultures of their families, or, at least, as *potentially* independent of them, a long liberating step forward would have been accomplished. Such insight could be achieved by constantly having to measure themselves as products of American family situations against products of other systems. Within these varying situations, they would discover a range of alternatives which, for any one individual, might present differing value systems and possibilities of action among which to choose. The final consideration in planning the course was the availability of literature. I needed cultures which were well described in book form and in accessible, but not diluted and over-simplified sources. As it turned out, many of these came from my own library.

The following cultures were chosen: Eskimo, Iroquois, Polynesia, and China, as well as the United States. The Eskimo were chosen because of the intense importance of, and dependence on, cooperation within the nuclear family and the possibilities of achieving this, as well as because of their extreme form of ecological adaptation with its concomitant sociocultural organization. The Iroquois were chosen because of the importance of women in the family and larger social organization, a situation so different from our own in many ways. They also represent a stage of technological development far more advanced than the Eskimo and less developed than the irrigation horticulture of the Polynesians. Polynesia appeared to present a situation in which youth had a degree of relaxed freedom in and out of the family structure. It also presented a situation in which the family exercised maximal functions, permeating the economic, political, and religious orders, by being extended to the entire body politic. Also the presence of certain associations showed ways in which individuals in other cultures could exercise a limited choice in the pursuit of personal satisfaction. Pre-revolutionary China presented, at least ideally, a patripotestal family — a sort of counterpoise to the Iroquois situation. Furthermore, it was the only state-organized society, other than the students' own culture, in the sample, and the only other culture possessed of advanced agriculture, manufacturing, and commerce. At the same time, it differed from the United States in being largely non-industrialized.

At some point during the discussion of each culture, except the Iroquois, a film was presented. The first, accompanying our discussion of the American family, dealt with the upbringing of an American child.[6] *Nanook of the North* illustrated the Eskimo; *Moana* and *Pacific Island* accompanied the Polynesians, and a movie describing the life of an urban Chinese family introduced our study of the Chinese.

Since considerable time was spent in describing the fundamental characteristics of the technology and economy and their effects on the social order, visits were made to the Museum of Natural History, sometimes to the exhibition halls, sometimes to the collection rooms, to see items from the three simpler cultures. Chinese cultural materials were seen in a trip to the Metropolitan Museum of Art. The study of the Chinese was illuminated by a lecture by Morton A. Fried, who elaborated on the organization of the Chinese family and its relations to Chinese society.

As a further aid, I decided to use the recorded series called *The Ways of Mankind*, which I had previously heard and enjoyed on the radio. Volume I, containing dramatized accounts of the Eskimo and Chinese and several other cultures, was rented. Unfortunately, it was anything but a success. It is possible that this group of students was particularly sophisticated, and not a little critical. However this may be, they found the manner of presentation, as they put it, "corny," and a subject for hilarity. The records served better as material for satire than for instruction.

Finally, we must speak of the literature used. The course, as we noted, was not part of the general curriculum, nor was it open to anyone who chose to take it. Rather, in this instance, I was able to select the students I wanted. The eight students selected were undoubtedly the best in the school, probably comparable to students in the upper half of the entering freshman class of an average college.[7] None had any problems in reading, little as one or two of them cared to read. Under these circumstances, I was able to require them to read the best that could be gotten from them, rather than to ask them to use watered-down tertiary sources. A number of standard sources were used.[8]

---

[6] One of the students objected, quite rightly, that this somewhat saccharine film showed no family conflict. All was honey and harmony. The Chinese film was called *Peiping Family*, and was also somewhat saccharine.

[7] The students in this class were accepted upon graduation into the following colleges: Universities of Michigan, Denver, and New Mexico; Long Island and New York Universities; and Antioch, Oberlin, and American International Colleges.

[8] Among the sources used were the following: R. Bunzel, *Leads for Field Workers*,

During the first weeks of the course, while the students were reading on their cultures, we discussed the American family, starting with their own observations and, to a considerable extent, with their subjective experiences of it. I hoped to elicit their conception of what the family is and to show them that there are standard American patterns, at least within their class, of family organization as well as standard American family stereotypes. To a considerable extent, this was successful, although the variation of the families of these eight young people was considerable. In order to get material to use for contrast with the cultures which we were to study later, I had asked the most literate of the students to keep notes on the expressions of value and fact uttered by each of her classmates about their families. These comments were systematized in order to make some generalizations about the forms and functions of the family in the United States, and a general outline of points to be compared in other cultures was arranged. This included such questions as how are marriages contracted; religious, civil, public, and private aspects of marriage; the obligations between the families of the marrying couple; the positions of men, women, and children within the family; authority and decision-making; sexual relations in and out of marriage; fidelity; divorce and widowing; multiple marriages; adoption; relationship of the living to the dead of the family; institutions of family continuity; relationship with units, especially associations, outside the family unit; life cycle and the concepts of childhood, adolescence, and the nature of the transition to adulthood and maturity. The discussion of some of these aspects raised the question of what happens when standard patterns are not followed. This was of particular interest in view of the then-beginning publicity about delinquency, whose causal factor daily is heralded to us all in poster and public-service billboard as being the family whose life stops. This led to an extensive discussion of the gang as an associational group having a number of vital social functions which are not fulfilled in the families of its members. It also led to a discussion of the rather anomalous position of "the adolescent" in our society, or

mimeographed, n.d.; R. Firth, *We the Tikopia*, American Book Co., New York, 1936; M. H. Fried, *Fabric of Chinese Society*, Praeger, New York, 1953; O. Lang, *Chinese Family and Society*, Yale University Press, New Haven, Conn., 1946; M. Mead (ed.), *Cooperation and Competition in Primitive Societies*, McGraw-Hill, New York, 1937; L. H. Horgan, *League of the Ho-De-No Sau-Nee or Iroquois*, Human Relations Area Files, New Haven, Conn., 1954; G. P. Murdock, *Our Primitive Contemporaries*, Macmillan, New York, 1934; I. Pruitt, *A Daughter of Han*, Yale University Press, New Haven, Conn., 1945; F. G. Rainey, *The Whale Hunters of Tigara*, Amer. Mus. of Nat. Hist. Anthropological Papers, XLI, Part 2, 1947; F. G. Speck, *The Iroquois*, Cranbook Inst. of Science, Bulletin 23, Bloomfield Hills, Mich., 1955; R. Williamson, *Religion and Social Organization in Central Polynesia*, Cambridge University Press, Cambridge, Eng., 1939, and *Essays in Polynesian Ethnology*, Cambridge University Press, Cambridge, Eng., 1939; M. Yang, *A Chinese Village*, Columbia University Press, New York, 1945.

rather his lack of position since he is neither child nor member of an adult world, nor has he any immediate prospects of entering one. The theme of associational ties as alternatives to familial ties was raised again and again, both in terms of these students' observations of themselves and their parents and in cross-cultural terms, as, for example, in the Chinese family mutual aid societies, the Polynesian *arioi* and the Iroquoian secret societies.

After our initial examination of the American family, accompanied by a much less intensive examination of its place in American society at large and its relation to associations, the class proceeded to examine the Eskimo, Iroquois, Polynesian, and Chinese family systems, again in their larger social contexts, especially of class and associational ties.

TEACHING METHOD

For pedagogic purposes, an inductive approach was, at first, intensively used in order to lead students, almost surreptitiously, into insights about the principles underlying cultural relativism, cultural organizations, and cultural regularities. As each culture was introduced, and, where possible, as each topic was begun, purely descriptive data were presented from which the students were gradually to generalize in order to abstract some principle. Using the family data of the students themselves is the best example of this procedure. It seems to me that this is a useful procedure in any type of introductory anthropology course. A shift in the procedures of teaching takes place, as it did in this case, once these inductively derived principles have been established, although additional inductions may be made throughout the course. The structure of thought, in the classroom as in the profession at large, becomes increasingly deductive. Students must increasingly deal with *logical* inferences from previously established principles, generalizations, and facts; with the construction of hypotheses; and must learn to understand the relationship between deductively arrived-at hypotheses and the accumulation of data by observation. In passing, it might be remarked that this understanding of the relationship between induction and deduction might well be more prevalent in the profession, which, as a whole, still tends to regard itself as practicing a largely, if not exclusively, inductive science. I think it is just to say that, in fact, no such science exists.[9]

About a year after the course ended, I was able to administer a ques-

---

[9] J. K. Feibleman, "The Role of Hypotheses in the Scientific Method," *Perspectives in Biology and Medicine*, II, No. 3 (1959), 335–346; S. T. Kimball, "Anthropology versus Sociology: A Contrast in Method," paper read at the 59th Annual Meeting of the American Anthropological Association, Minneapolis, Minn., 1960.

tionnaire to all but one of the students. In general, the responses confirm my own impressions as to the results of the course. Although a full analysis is not presented here, some of the comments written in the questionnaires were illuminating, especially from the point of view of the students' personal sense of the "liberating" experience. From a general education point of view, however, assessing the effects of the course is somewhat more difficult. I was able to arrange with the English teachers that they ask their students to write compositions revolving around materials derived from the cultures they were studying. Several of the essays displayed a keen understanding of, and empathy with, the culture studied. The students seemed quite able to understand the relativity of values involved, and also to see that the cultures they had read about were neither peculiar aberrations of humanity nor so esoteric as to be merely some faraway unreal things. They seem to have acquired some concept of the structure of culture and culture's determinate relationship to environments. How much this carried over into their other studies, especially history or literature, I am unable to assess. Other teachers reported that they felt the students got a good deal out of the course which in some way was projected into their other course work but they were not able to specify just how. Several of the students reported that they felt the course helped them somewhat in their academic functioning. My own general feeling is that the students expanded in their critical faculties considerably. This was a function partly of their increased personal insight, but also of the mental stretching which came from a reasonably well-understood cross-cultural exposure. I feel that, for the same reasons, there was a marked increase, not always consciously realized, in the appreciation of the values and differences of others and an ability to live with them with greater appreciation or less derogation and even, at times, to enjoy and learn from them.

A final word about the more strictly anthropological aspects themselves. Almost without exception, the students felt the literature used to be quite understandable, as were, also, the other teaching materials such as the movies and even the recordings, and the talk of the visiting lecturer. Similarly, they felt that the concepts presented, such as culture, structure, function, and so on, were quite comprehensible. To the question whether they wanted to find out more about anthropology as a result of having taken the course, three said yes, three said maybe, one said no. The eighth went to the University of New Mexico, ostensibly to major in archaeology, but he had already been interested in so doing before the course. Most of the students felt that the kind of literature used, as compared with ordinary high school texts, made it easier to maintain interest and was, in itself, more interesting than the usual school texts. They also found the seminar-like manner of holding the course more profitable than the usual classroom procedures.

Psychologically, almost all the students benefited in one way or another, although in very different degrees. Interaction within the group increased notably, and, in some cases, overflowed into their other relationships. Various aspects of the course contributed to this. First, each student's gradually developed exposition of his or her own family made the others generally more sympathetic to, and understanding of, the nature of the effects of family structure and values on the person. Second, in the act of talking, each student exposed himself as a matter of course, and the more so when disagreements forced each to take positions, for example, on the social significance of friendship as an institution or on the nature of authority in the family. Third, in several cases, having read the same material as another student, and interpreted it differently, led to insightful discussions not only about the material, but also about the interpreters and their relations to their life contexts.

CONCLUSIONS

In conclusion, it seems to me safe to assert, if somewhat tentatively, on the basis of this experience, that anthropology can make a contribution to general education at the high school level. I feel that it could be made to do so much more if the course were to last a year instead of one semester as in the present instance. This would give time to develop in the students a sense of the relevance of these materials to other parts of the curriculum, particularly the understanding of history, geography in its human implications, and literature. This did not happen to be the main focus of the course as I gave it, so that the sense of relevance achieved was probably less than might have been elicited even with the amount of time at my disposal. With more time and a stronger focusing on the general curriculum, I think that a thorough grounding in cultural differences and cultural structure achieved in a semester's work could then serve as a foundation to move on into the analysis of current events in the world and to achieve a level of international understanding [10] rarely achieved otherwise. For example, had I just finished a course such as I have described, although with slightly less emphasis on the personal interactions, I could go on to demonstrate to the students how one might apply the anthropological approach to the understanding of the current Cuban, South African, Korean, and southern United States upheavals as results of the internal dynamics of cultural systems affected by different geographies, histories, and external cultural systems.

[10] Wilson and Collings, *op. cit.*

Finally, I feel that anthropology would be desirable only for certain students as a general curriculum requirement. Hence, some sort of selection procedure would be needed. A certain degree of sophistication, combined with a prior element of inquisitive dissociation from the world, allowing the students to look *at* their own and other cultures as objects rather than as subjective parts of themselves, is almost a prerequisite. It would be a grave mistake to force all students to take an anthropology course. For those whose identity is associated most closely with the cultural cues and patterns, the results, at best, would be relatively sterile and boring. At worst, a wedge might be driven between them and their self-identification by use of such cues, leaving them with less identity than they had at first, but with nothing in place of what they had lost to use in their own further growth.

A word needs also to be said about those who are to teach anthropology in high schools. I do not believe that *any* teacher should teach anthropology; neither do I think it desirable that it be taught by any special science or humanities teacher who has chanced to take a course in anthropology during his college career. Adequate teaching of anthropology requires of the teacher, just as it does of students, the ability to look *at* his own or another culture, and, more, requires teachers to have experienced some other culture, even if only by intelligent travel in a foreign land or in a sub-culture in their own society distinctly different from their own. Furthermore, adequate teaching of anthropology in high schools requires a substantial training in that field, accompanied by professional authorization to give instruction in that subject matter.

If one makes a distinction between liberal arts and general education, which I believe is justifiable in view of the common emphasis in the general education literature [11] on the immediate applicability of education to life problems, or, even more narrowly, to adjustment, then I believe that anthropology at the high school level can be a liberating experience for qualified students and can subtly make more profound their preparation for the wrenching first year of college with its suddenly expanding horizons. While, on one hand, giving the students more perspective on their own culture by helping them to remove themselves from its immediate trammels, and thus, to some extent, separating them still further from it (a result, incidentally, which thoroughly opposes liberal arts to general education), the study of anthropology brings them closer to discovering a universal humanity and an aesthetic common to all men, regardless of time and place, a discovery which can be the most satisfactory of all.

---

[11] See footnote 2. Also E. J. McGrath (ed.) *Social Science in General Education,* Wm. C. Brown, Dubuque, Ia., 1948; A. W. Levi, *General Education in the Social Studies,* American Council on Education, Washington, D.C., 1947.

FURTHER READINGS

Bohannan, Paul, Merwyn S. Garbarino, and Earle W. Carson. "An experimental ninth-grade anthropology course," *American Anthropologist*, vol. 71 (June 1969).

Hanvey, Robert. "Anthropology in the high schools: The representation of a discipline," in Irving Morrissett (ed.), *Concepts and structure in the new social science curricula*. West Lafayette, Ind.: Social Science Education Consortium, Inc., 1966.

Mandelbaum, David G. "Anthropology in the high schools," *Fellow Newsletter*, American Anthropological Association, vol. 2 (1961).

Mead, Margaret. *The school in American culture*. Cambridge: Harvard University Press, 1951.

Steubing, Carl M. "Some role conflicts as seen by a high school teacher," *Human Organization*, vol. 27 (Spring 1968).

10

Stong's article is in the form of a project report by a member of the Novato (California) Senior High School Archaeology Club. It is an extraordinary account, not only for the actual accomplishments of the group but also for the understandings of human process that are shown, here, to have been gained from their activity. The report prevails, too, as a record of the kinds of opportunities that attend guided archaeological studies in secondary school. In addition to having acquired substantive knowledge about a Miwok site and thus of a human settlement appreciably different from those with which the students were familiar, the Novato group experienced the known satisfaction of recovering centuries-old artifacts from the blades of bulldozers. The students "did" archaeological inquiry, during which specific cognitive operations, e.g., inference, no doubt came "alive." And, considering current emphases on environmental quality, which promote, in part, individual awareness of man-land relationships, the Marin County dig served to draw meaningful connections between past solutions, such as that of the Miwok, and present-day needs to rethink our arrangement with — and in — the natural world. Mr. Stong regularly contributes a column to Scientific American.

C. L. STONG

An Indian Mound Is Excavated by High School Archaeologists

In 1961 members of the Northwestern California Archaeological Society surveyed an area of the San Antonio Valley in Marin County, just north of San Francisco, where they hoped to discover the remains of Indian dwellings and related artifacts. The survey was conventional in all respects but one: high school students were among those recruited to help in the work. Most archaeologists stay clear of amateurs, and for good reason. Young or old, untrained laymen tend to develop unbridled enthusiasm for the work, to strike out on their own, stumble over a site and dig up buried treasures for collections of curios. Irreplaceable information can be — and has been — so lost. If, on the other hand, one can harness the amateur's enthusiasm and direct his efforts, there may be a nice profit in terms both of recovered lore and of instruction in the potential value of undisturbed antiquities. That is what happened in Marin County.

In the course of the survey the group located a number of promising sites. One, in the form of a roughly circular mound a foot high and 100 feet in diameter located 10 miles northwest of the town of Novato, was designated Marin-374. Two test excavations were promptly made: a circular pit approximately 20 feet in diameter, where a shelter had once stood, and a rectangular pit three feet wide and six feet long just south of the circular pit. A student, Peter Moore, was made responsible for digging the rectangular pit. Although these pits produced a number of artifacts, the archaeologists decided to move on to more productive sites. By this time, however, Moore had become deeply engrossed in the work; he sought and obtained the permission of the archaeologists and the owners of the land to continue the dig. With the help of John MacBeath, a social studies teacher at the Novato Senior High School, he recruited several small teams to assist in the work and eventually helped to organize the Novato Senior High School Archaeology Club. The club, with Moore as president and in close cooperation with the archaeologists, completed a detailed analysis of Marin-374 early this year. The results of the project are reported by Terrence Jay O'Neil, who joined the club in 1966.

"I was not allowed to do any digging at Marin-374 until I had been exposed to a series of informal lectures on technical procedures," he writes. "In time I became responsible for mapping the site, preparing drawings of artifacts, analyzing materials and editing the final report. Approximately 40 club members had participated in the excavation by the time the work was finished.

"Marin-374 is a so-called single component site: a deposit made by people who set up a complex of dwellings, remained for a time and then disappeared. Our findings indicate that Marin-374 became a dwelling place between 2,000 and 3,000 years ago. The Indians who made and used the objects were the coastal Miwoks, who spoke the language of the Hokan group of California Indians and were descended from early settlers who established small camps in the San Francisco Bay area at least 5,000 years ago. The relative richness of the area encouraged loose tribal organization. Groups of one or two families could maintain themselves on small sites, and Marin-374 marks a site of this kind.

"The soil of the site is fine-grained, with a large amount of black organic material that contrasts with the light-colored soil nearby. In dry weather this 'midden,' when disturbed, turns into a powdery gray dust that makes excavation unpleasant in summer. The area supports foot-high field grasses, including Russian thistle, and about 25 buckeye trees, two of which stand within the boundary of the site. These trees are very old; their immediate ancestors doubtless predated historic times. San Antonio Creek, which forms the northern and western limits of Marin-374, tends to reach flood stage in early spring, but it seems not to have eroded the midden. Examination of sediments in the first four inches of the site material indicated that the topmost layer of soil had probably never been disturbed. Leaching by rain had not significantly altered the location of artifacts, as far as we could tell, nor did we find large numbers of rodent burrows — all of which led us to believe Marin-374 was an undisturbed site.

"Archaeologists have developed two approaches by excavation. In either case one begins by driving a stake that serves as a reference mark from which measurements are made, and outlining rectangular areas, usually in the pattern of a numbered grid. In the case of 'micro-methodology,' the rectangular areas are then excavated one layer (about four inches thick) at a time, and the location of each artifact is recorded by exact measurements on a three-dimensional grid. In the case of 'macromethodology,' pits that measure 10 feet square are dug out in foot-thick layers and artifacts are located and recorded only by pit and layer [see Fig. 1]. Scrupulous controls are maintained in all phases of excavation and record-keeping. Undisturbed soil is closely examined for any texture and discoloration that might suggest a disintegrated artifact. All soil is screened and from the screenings materials are sorted according to type (shell, bone and so on). Artifacts are inspected, described, logged and labeled for storage. In micromethodology the ratio of area processed to man-hours is low; macro-

FIGURE 1
Plan and elevation diagrams of artifacts uncovered in house pit.

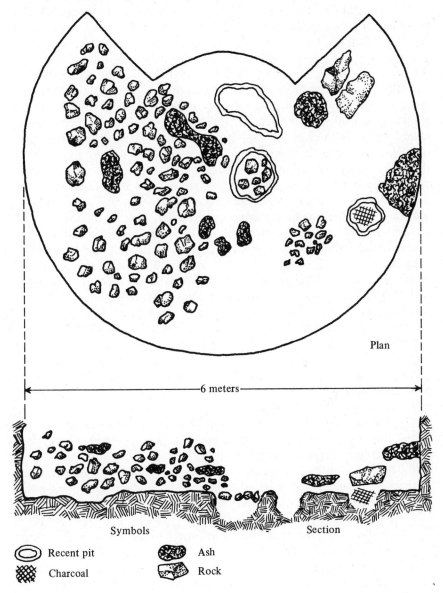

Plan

←————————6 meters————————→

Symbols   Section

Recent pit   Ash

Charcoal   Rock

methodology stresses examination of the largest possible amount of material per man-hour.

"We learned that the area of the site was scheduled to become a trailer park but that the bulldozers would not move in for some months. At the suggestion of the supervising archaeologists we laid out a grid of intermediate size that could be worked within the scheduled time. After the boundary of the site had been determined through an examination of the soil, trench lines were laid out with broad undisturbed strips between them so that representative samples of the entire site would be dug for study. In general the pits were six feet square. In one case they were arranged in the form of an L [see Fig. 2]. The soil was removed, in 10-inch horizontal layers, with trowels and shovels. All measurements were made in metric units to within a tolerance of 10 centimeters. Two people were assigned to each pit, one digging a shovelful at a time while the other screened and examined the material. (There are advantages to washing the soil through the screen with water, but San Antonio Creek was almost dry, and so our materials were sifted dry.) Bits of bone and other animal remains, together with fragments of rock, were collected in bags labeled according to level. Each artifact of value was labeled and listed: its pit and level number, its location and its description. Club members had been trained to recognize projectile points, scrapers, pottery and modified stone.

"Hundreds of objects were uncovered. As we subsequently learned, the collection includes most of the types of implements that were used by the coastal Miwoks during the final stage of their cultural development. Represented in it, by class, are hunting implements, tools for preparing food and making clothes, adornments, trading goods, ceremonial items and at least one house floor.

"Blades of chipped stone that were used for scraping constitute the largest single group of artifacts. A very few display remarkable craftsmanship but most are nonsymmetrical and otherwise carelessly made — generally by chipping one or more fragments from the edge of a natural fracture in obsidian, chert or other local rock. Others were improvised from broken projectile points, and one blade was made from a fragment of pottery.

"Projectile points make up the second most numerous type of artifact, and their workmanship is somewhat better than that of similar points found in other Marin County sites. Some, which appear to be unique to this site, have sawtooth edges, a notch at one corner and a concavity in the base. The points range from about two inches in length down to less than an inch. Many spearpoints were recovered. . . .

"The collection includes 16 mortars and fragments of mortars, the largest of which is 32 inches in diameter. They were excavated at an

FIGURE 2
Map of pit pattern at site, Marin-374

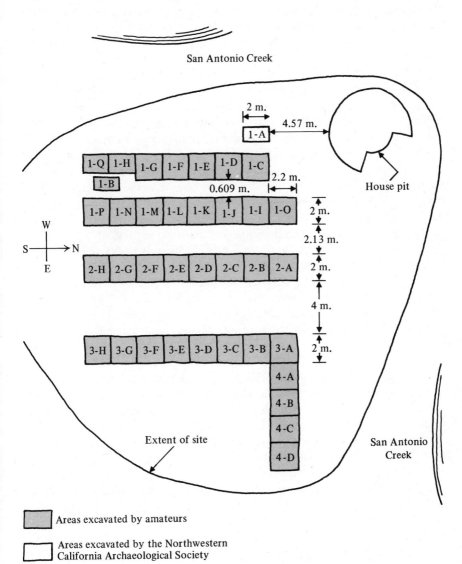

Areas excavated by amateurs

Areas excavated by the Northwestern
California Archaeological Society

average depth of about 18 inches. Two have round bottoms and round rims. Three have flat bottoms and flat rims and range in weight from 2½ to 45 pounds. Nineteen pestles were recovered, 13 of which were conical in form, five cylindrical and one globular. They were made of various native rocks, including basalt, sandstone, diorite and andesite. One bore asphaltum stains.

"A total of nine charmstones were excavated at an average depth of about 15 inches. Most were phallic types, and several had partial coatings of asphaltum. Ornamental artifacts included pennants made of shell and an earplug of steatite. Fragments of nine pipes were also found. One, of white serpentine, is excellently made and bears attractive ornamentation.

"Beads of various kinds and sizes were common. Some were made from the bones of birds; the largest was 1.5 inch in length and .4 inch in diameter. (The smallest complete bead measures a mere .06 inch in diameter — indicating the care with which the soil must be screened to ensure the recovery of interesting materials.) The collection includes various beads made from the shells of marine animals, particularly clams and olivellas; perforated disks of clamshell make up the majority. Eight stone beads made of black steatite, marl limestone and slate were found. The largest, of carved steatite, was found at a depth of 20 inches. Three beads turned up that could not have been manufactured by the limited technology of the Miwok culture. One is made of a translucent, iridescent blue glass and is oblong in shape. Another, of the same general shape but more crudely formed, is of a red glassy material that has been glazed. Both of these beads were found at a depth of eight inches. The third is of a porous, translucent yellow glass and is almost perfectly spherical; it was found at a depth of 28 inches. Obviously these beads are trade items from Spaniards or other white pioneers. Other 'foreign' objects, found near the surface, were a piece of iron in the form of a slender U, thickened in the curved portion, and two forged nails of the type commonly used during the first half of the 19th century.

"Contact between the Miwoks and the white pioneers is also indicated by a profusion of porcelain fragments in light blue, dark blue, yellow and white. Some fragments are well glazed and carry designs of thin lines in dark blue. They were found mostly on the surface and to a depth of a few inches. They have been tentatively identified as parts of 19th-century Spanish cups, bowls and plates. One white fragment had been modified by secondary chipping to serve as a scraper.

"Perhaps the most interesting evidence of foreign technology was a Minié ball found at a depth of 10 inches in pit 3-C. The somewhat dented end and the rifling marks indicate that the bullet was fired from a gun and either hit a soft, resilient surface or fell at low velocity at the end of a long flight. . . . We were tempted to use this artifact as a method of dating material at the 10-inch level. The Minié ball was developed by Captain Claude Étienne Minié of the French army in 1849 and quickly circled the globe. It marked a distinct advance in arms technology, since the force of the exploding charge expanded the bullet to form a gastight seal against the bore of the gun, conserving the compressed gases and increasing the bullet's muzzle velocity and killing power. Bullets of this type were in wide use in the U.S. from about 1860 to 1880. Other evidence, however, suggested a much older date for the layer in which the Minié ball was found, and it may have buried itself to this depth on impact.

"One of the most interesting artifacts turned out to be a small slab of clay that bore the impression of a woven basket. This fragment was examined by Lawrence E. Dawson at the Robert H. Lowie Museum of Anthropology of the University of California at Berkeley, who made a positive reproduction of the depressions by pressing potter's clay against the slab. The weave is much finer than the weave in similar baskets found elsewhere in California: 10 weft courses per inch and 7.6 warps per inch. In Dawson's opinion the basket was made of the split roots of a local grassy plant that resembles sedge and was so tightly woven that it must have been watertight.

"No human burials had been made at Marin-374, although one group of bones was found that appears to be human. Four human burials were uncovered by archaeologists at a neighboring site 500 yards away.

"The matter of dating site materials turns out to be difficult for amateurs and is relatively uncertain. It is reasonable to suppose that artifacts found at or near the surface were deposited more recently than those below. For example, one would expect to find fragments of porcelain above artifacts that were deposited before porcelain became available. On the other hand, sites can be disturbed and the materials mixed, particularly to a depth of a foot or so in small local areas. Examination might easily fail to disclose traces of a hole that was made 50 years ago by driving a stake into the ground. Yet a piece of porcelain that accidentally dropped into the hole would come to rest in a layer of materials that had accumulated centuries before porcelain could have found its way to the site. That is why sites are excavated layer by layer and a statistical evaluation is made of the contents of each layer.

"When a site contains charcoal, the possibility exists of dating the layer by the carbon-14 technique. . . . Our site contained no usable charcoal, however. Only one modern technique of dating was available to us: the hydration method, which is based on the slow corrosion of glassy materials by water. Obsidian and other glassy materials that are moist tend to corrode very slowly through the centuries at a constant rate. Water that is naturally present in the soil diffuses into the noncrystalline structure of the glass and leaches out soda, lime and other substances, thus creating a surface skeleton of silicon. The action is retarded during dry weather. The result of prolonged exposure to varying wet and dry seasons is the growth inward of alternating dark (unleached) and clear (leached) bands roughly analogous to the annual growth rings in trees. The partial reflection of light by the layers sets up optical interference between reflected light waves with the result that the corrosion appears in the iridescent colors observed occasionally in old glass. . . . The fragile layers tend to flake away when the glass is touched, particularly in man-made glass, and so artifacts to be dated by the hydration method must be handled gently. Technicians select specimens that show little wear and remove slices from facets that appear to be fashioned by man — not from surfaces of natural origin. The slices are ground to thin sections and treated chemically to emphasize the bands. The bands, which vary in thickness from about 20 to 120 millionths of an inch, are then examined under a microscope.

"Amateurs who are skilled in lapidary techniques could doubtless master the hydration method of dating, but we did not attempt it. Instead we submitted 18 specimens of worked obsidian to Harvey Crew of the University of California at Davis for analysis. Two of the specimens were unsuitable for analysis; the remainder indicated ages ranging from 680 to 1,800 years, with the exception of one that indicated 2,900 years.

"A lot of work went into the excavation of Marin-374. At the conclusion of the dig we spent three months compiling data and writing a report that has been distributed to interested archaeologists. Some of the recovered artifacts are now in storage. Others are on display at the Boyd Natural History Museum in San Rafael, Calif., or in the files of the University of California at Berkeley and San Francisco State College, along with copies of our report. . . .

"About 60 percent of Marin-374 was left undisturbed; doubtless it contains more material than we removed. Soon the site will be obliterated by earth-moving machinery, as was a neighboring site, Marin-196. We have recently participated with local archaeologists in a successful campaign for an ordinance forbidding the destruction of sites in Marin County by commercial agencies until a representative sample of artifacts has been unearthed.

"The dig at Marin-374 was a fascinating (if sometimes exhausting) experience, and our club members enjoyed it thoroughly. We feel that our work helped, if only a little, to reconstruct the story of how the Miwok Indians lived during their last 1,500 to 2,000 years.

"There are records of contacts between these Indians and Spanish settlers, but no substantial intermarriage with the Spaniards took place and the line seems to have died out. We have heard, however, that one mixed-blood coastal Miwok still lives in Marin County. We are trying to locate him — or her."

Further Readings

King, Thomas. "Archaeological materials in secondary education." Paper read at the Annual Meeting of the American Anthropological Association, New Orleans, Louisiana, 1969.
Mandelbaum, David G., Gabriel W. Lasker, and Ethel M. Albert (eds.). *The teaching of anthropology.* Washington, D.C.: American Anthropological Association, Memoir 94, 1963.
Whiteford, Andrew H. (ed.). *Teaching anthropology.* Logan Museum Publications in Anthropology, no. 8. Beloit, Wisc.: Beloit College Press, 1960.
Zahniser, Jack L. "A new science for secondary schools," (originally titled "A didactic postscript"), *The Kiva*, vol. 31 (February 1966).

11

The presence of anthropology as instructional content in secondary schools is, as yet, sporadic and colloquial. Several programmatic efforts at the presentation of anthropology in secondary education are now available, however. One is the Anthropology Curriculum Study Project, which Mrs. Collier and Mr. Dethlefsen report in part here. The approach to "race" they describe and discuss is conspicuous, first, by its emphasis upon the criteria by which human groups are socially differentiated; second, by its deliberate integration of materials and instructional strategy. Content, in the sample introduced here, is implicit in strategy and vice versa. This is not so much a unique curriculum development as it is tangible use of anthropology, in which the simultaneity of "view" and assessment of what is "seen" referred to by Rosenfeld translates to, in effect, a kind of pedagogy. The reports of Stong and Collier and Dethlefsen evidence the diverse (and durable) teaching and learning opportunities that are possible in anthropology, the experience of Leeds notwithstanding. Mrs. Collier is Director of the Anthropology Curriculum Study Project. Mr. Dethlefsen, formerly a writer and a unit director for that Project, is presently engaged in independent curriculum development.

MALCOLM COLLIER AND EDWIN S. DETHLEFSEN

Anthropology in the Pre-Collegiate Curriculum

College and university people often think of secondary curricula as watered-down college courses. Some express a related concern that studying a subject in high school somehow takes the edge off the "real thing," which the student should first encounter in college. According to this view, economics taught in high school would satiate rather than whet a student's interest in that discipline. There are certainly shortcomings in secondary school studies, but these are not among them. The real threat is that traditional secondary school social studies courses may blunt forever the student's interest in social data through sheer boredom produced by inept and inadequate exposure to the social sciences rather than too little or too much.

It is our observation that high school students consistently rate social studies low on their scale of interests. Among the factors responsible for low interest are the remoteness and unreality of the social data presented, the passiveness and noninvolvement of the students with the data, and the methods used in covering the data. Conventional social studies courses present masses of facts with few glimpses of the theoretical principles needed to understand them. We believe the social sciences can and should provide secondary social studies curricula with the needed conceptual framework.

Whether or not the social sciences can indeed bring enduring light and interest to the high school curriculum remains to be seen, but present attempts in this direction show promise. Curriculum improvement projects in geography, sociology, economics, political science, and anthropology have been under way for several years. In varying degrees these efforts are made on the assumption that there are disciplined ways of looking at social data and that high school students are capable of comprehending and using them profitably in studies of human history and human behavior. Certainly the Anthropology Curriculum Study Project has assumed that Anthropology can contribute to high school studies both in content and in pedagogy. It has further assumed that:

> If high school education marks, for the moment, the minimal education we expect of all citizens, then it must be said that the capacity to think systematically about man's nature, his many societies, the whole career of his species, has not been included in our definition of the educated

From *Human Organization*, vol. 27, no. 1 (Spring 1968), pp. 11–16. Reprinted with the permission of the authors.

citizen. Knowledge of man produced by the disciplined researches of social scientists has not been generally available to public school students. The high school graduate who has been taught to expect regularities in in the affairs of the physical universe will never have heard of the search for regularities in the affairs of men. But the schools seems to be on the threshold of offering access to such understandings, ready in effect to *democratize a social scientific comprehension of man.* It will be in the context of such a development that Anthropology may find a role in the schools.[1]

The development of this contribution involves four steps: (1) Selection of some of the most significant topics from the rich mass of anthropological information and understanding; (2) Identification of the specific relevance of each topic to the high school student's own experience with the world; (3) Isolation of the essential aspects of each topic; and (4) Development of methods for helping the student grasp and use the data and concepts needed to understand the selected topic.

The materials which follow illustrate the four points. They are taken from the 1965 version of "The Study of Early Man" teaching materials developed by the Project. The total unit, which is about eight weeks long, is designed for ninth or tenth grade students. It includes readings and activities regarding race that occupy several days within the larger sequence.

It can be argued that adults should know something about race formation and classification. The criteria by which most adults identify the peoples of the world and classify them into national or racial groups are unclear and implicit where it is most important that they be clear and explicit. Development of this topic begins with an effort to have the students make explicit what they already know or believe about race. This is done in order to establish a baseline of present knowledge (or lack of it) from which they can work toward new understandings. The teacher is given specially prepared materials to supplement his own information and to help him guide students through the related lessons. We present the following excerpts from the experimental teacher's guide as an example of the level and depth at which an anthropological topic may be approached in a high school social studies class.

SAMPLE PAGES FROM THE "STUDY OF EARLY MAN" UNIT [2]

[The example begins with a brief exposition on race to provide a frame of reference to the teacher.]

[1] Robert G. Hanvey, "Anthropology in the schools," *Educational Leadership*, vol. 22, no. 5, February 1965, p. 313.
[2] Teaching Plan, "Study of early man," ACSP 1965 Experimental Version, pp. 68–74.

Race is not an easy term to define, particularly in the case of our own species. Biologists use it more or less interchangeably with subspecies when they are talking about other animals or plants. There may be some plausibility in referring to Hottentots, Eskimos, Pygmies, Ainu, or a few other more or less reproductively isolated human populations as races in the biological sense of the term. They may indeed have considerable with-group uniformity with respect to the physical characteristics by which we may attempt to distinguish them.

But the great numbers of men and their mobility render the present concept of the human group as divisible into races as useless except for the specialist interested in studying human adaptations and evolutionary prehistory. The specialist knows that wherever large human populations occur there has been so much genetic mixture that variation is too great for racial descriptions to have any real meaning, except in a purely statistical sense. What are observed are the tag ends of environmental adaptations, many of which may be shared by quite unrelated peoples who simply have existed in similar environments for very long periods of time.

In the last few thousands of years men have so learned to control their environments that at present almost anyone can live almost anywhere with little or no naturally selective disadvantage. The result is that the greater proportion of the world's peoples have so mingled their genes that populations can be differentiated only by gene frequencies that compare proportions of populations exhibiting a given trait. . . . The concept of race, under such circumstances, cannot intelligently be applied to individuals. . . . One need remember . . . that not only is it practically impossible to describe a "typical" member of a race but that there are untold numbers of people who defy such categorization.

Furthermore, one can easily become too arbitrary about his bases for racial classification of individuals. It is easy to say that a man with "slanty eyes" is a "Mongoloid." But if three of his four grandparents were, in fact, "Caucasoid," and "slanty eyes" happened to be one of the few traits inherited from the fourth, such a categorization is scientifically ridiculous and philosophically without rationale. . . . Defining a race socially is, of course, a different and much simpler matter. The membership of any "race" is defined by those people who claim membership in it.

Human races are hardly valid as biological units, being so arbitrarily based, but the term is probably with us to stay, despite the protestations of scientists and humanitarians, so it behooves us to develop sufficient understanding of its "meaning" (and the problems of its definition) to talk about it intelligently. This is an area of knowledge/folklore where, for the moment at least, a lack of assurance may be a good thing; so one of the main purposes of the following suggestions is to make students a little more conscious of the difficulties involved in defining the term.

Although the following suggestions are given by "days," there is more than can be done in the time allowed. What to condense or leave out must be a matter of judgment in context — what do you want to emphasize that ties in with later sections of the unit or ties up earlier ones? As a last resort some exercises can be described rather than transformed. Discussion of some readings can be handled more speedily by means of worksheets, and you will no doubt see a number of instances where points can be made with less ado.

Before the first session, give the students the following list of questions. Answers may be written and handed in the next day (Day 1):

How many races are there?
How can you tell them apart?
What is a race?
Of what race are you? How do you know?

Day 1. [Assignments are collected and the class listens to a tape in which other youngsters attempt to answer the first three questions above and to identify by race the photographs of four people. The class looks at the photos while listening. The class attempts to identify the people in the photos after hearing the variety of identifications on the tape, and are asked what criteria they are using. They then are asked to differentiate between physical and cultural criteria.]

Work with the class to construct a chart of the "major races" on the blackboard. Elicit agreement as to ". . . what we shall consider for the time being to be the major races," and list them down one side. Across the top list the physical traits which will be referred to for "distinguishing characteristics," calling upon the class for the terms, but making sure some continuous variables are included, such as skin color, eyes, lips, nose, etc. Draw lines to make boxes in which will be placed the appropriate objectives. When the chart is finished, it should bear some resemblance to this:

	Skin	*Lips*	*Hair*	*Nose*	"X"	"Y"
"White"	white			straight		
"Oriental"	yellow	thin	straight			
"Negroid"	brown	thick	kinky	flat		
. . . . .	etc.	etc.	etc.			

In helping to construct the chart be relatively uncritical of students' choices, but demand that the adjectives be reasonably specific. Sooner or later, the students should themselves remark, "But some 'whites' have kinky hair," or make similar comments. At this point you should begin to ask for other exceptions, e.g., "Do all Negroes have thick lips?" and so on. After a while it will be clear that the chart needs revision. Some of the

adjectives will need to be changed from specific to more inclusive. . . .
Don't be dismayed if the whole activity begins to bog down in disagreement — this is what should happen. If the class is too agreeable, press them
with questions using combinations of characteristics — "Do all 'whites'
have white skin, thin lips, wavy hair, straight noses . . . ?" "What about
the 'new race' of Hawaiians?" (This is a cross among Japanese, Chinese,
occidentals, and natives.) "How long have races been mixing?" "American
Negro different?" But it is not yet time for conclusions.

Having students prepared with pencils and paper, begin to show the
set of slides of peoples of the world.[3] Refer to the slides only by number,
asking that the students name from the chart the race of each person
shown. (If there are no more than three races on the chart, let students
locate the people geographically, rather than "race" them.) They should
write their conclusions beside the corresponding slide number. Show the
23 full-face views only. When the slides have been shown, discuss what
the students have written to see the extent of disagreement. Show the
pictures (slides) again, this time the 23 profile views. See how many
instances of mind-changing have occurred and how much disagreement
there is now.

Now tell the class where each of the slide people came from, emphasizing that the examples were chosen at random, not for the purpose of
fooling students. Exhibit the "tape" photos again and tell where these
people live.

Discussion: Egypt is part of the UAR. Are Egyptians "Whites," "Negroes," or what? If "Negroes" (or whatever), do they fit all the adjectives
in the chart? Apply similar questions to other people shown, reviewing
slides as necessary.

For homework, read "Genetic and Environmental Influences on Body
Measurements," from *The Human Species,* by F. S. Hulse.

Day 2. Discuss the homework reading from the standpoint of the influence of environment and genetics on some of the factors listed on the
chart. Nose shape is, for example, illustrated and discussed in the reading,
as are body form, stature and weight. Get the class to try to elaborate on
the environmental reasons for these "racial" differences, and to speculate
on some of the others.

Referring again to the homemade race chart, you should begin to bring
out the point that many of the characteristics listed, such as skin color,

[3] The complete set includes 23 full-face and 23 profile views of young adults from all
continents, from all over the world. The pictures cannot be reproduced here but are easy
to imagine — standard "peoples of the world" but wearing modern "Western" clothes.

represent continuous variables — that is why it is so difficult to draw a line between two races, if a single characteristic of this sort is used. A light "Negro" may be considerably lighter than a dark "white."

Let the class think of themselves as a population, and measure the frequency and range of some continuously variable characteristic. Height is probably easiest to measure though skin color may be more interesting and fun to chart, provided there are not individual students whose extreme position in the range might embarrass them too much. The latter can be measured by means of a good photographic light meter held no more than three inches from the inside (lightest part) of the forearm, about three inches below the point of the ulna (inside point of the elbow). Be careful that the light source is always the same distance from the spot measured and that its angle and that of the light meter are constant with respect to each skin surface measured. Using an arbitrarily chosen meter range, chart the distribution of skin shades in the class. (See below for the "point.")

If a good meter cannot be obtained, or if for any reason the measurement of skin shade is impracticable, measure stature instead. This is best done with the student standing against a smooth, vertical surface to which a yardstick has been attached vertically, its lower end forty inches from the floor. If possible, have the students remove shoes and stand with back to wall, straining erect but on flat feet with shoulders back and chin tucked in. Using a cigar box or small pasteboard box hold it flush against wall and ruler, and bring it down to top of student's head for a reading. This should be done firmly so as to eliminate the effect of high hairdos. Then add forty inches to the reading on the yardstick and write each height on a 3 x 5 card. Boys' cards should be a different color from girls'.

In a vertical column on the bulletin board list intervals of two inches (or three, if you have less than twenty students) from the lowest to the highest heights recorded. Attach the cards in horizontal rows by the interval in which each card falls. Rows near center of range will be longest and, if class is large enough, there will be a fairly even distribution of cards above and below this mode. (If the boys are of an age to be well into their adolescent growth spurt, the distribution may be bimodal, with a different distribution for girls. If not, or if there are very tall girls or very short boys, it may be best not to use separately colored cards to avoid embarrassment for them). There will be relatively few cards near the extremes of the height range.

Conclusions to be reached:

1. In any population there is a range of variation with respect to any variable characteristic.

2. Most individuals are more or less "average," but a description of the "average" does not truly describe the whole population.

Discuss height and hair color as a combination, or if you charted skin shade, combine this with height. Do these variables vary together?

Conclusion: Persons who are "average" in one respect may be quite extreme in another. Refer back to the race chart and discuss it critically in the light of the above conclusions.

For homework, read "Biological Adaptations to Culture," from *The Human Species,* by F. S. Hulse.

Day 3. Using the Population OHT #11 (see Fig. 1) Overhead Trans-

FIGURE 1
Overhead transparency #11

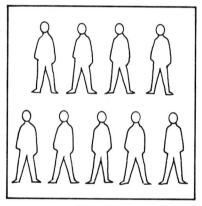

Basic chart

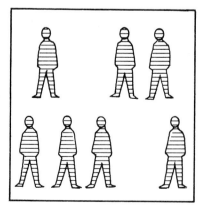

Overlay 1

Overlay 2

parency #11 consists of a basic chart and two overlays. In the original, the basic chart shows four rows of six figures each. Each overlay represents a particular characteristic, and when superimposed on the basic chart, the proportion of that characteristic in the total population appears.] pound home the point made that traits in a population vary independently of one another. . . . If horizontal lining (Overlay 1) is "typical" of this population, that does not signify that all members in good standing have horizontal lines. If vertical lines (Overlay 2) are also "typical" this means neither that those with horizontal lines also have vertical lines nor that those without horizontal lines lack vertical lines.

Conclusion: While it may be possible to describe particular races for

FIGURE 2
Matrimonial ads

MATRIMONIAL CORRESPONDANCE invited for Matriculate Punjabl Khatri girl, 21, beautiful, slim, well-versed in household. Decent marriage. Apply Box 23032 The Times of India, Bombay 1.   A38144(X)
MATRIMONIAL CORRESPONDENCE is invited from well settled boys for a fair Kerala Brahmin girl of 21, studied up to Matric. Please reply to Box 23948 The Times of India, Bombay 1.   A39072(X)
PARENTS OF EDUCATED AND DO-mestically trained Parsee girl, aged 22, invite matrimonial correspondence from well placed Parsee bachelors of respectable family. Write in details Box 23376, The Times of India, Bombay 1.   A38466(X)
PARENTS OF CUTCHI SWETAMBER Murtipujak Jain civil engineer, aged 26, invite matrimonial proposals from parents of healthy educated Gujarati girl, Jan Bania preferred. Early marriage. Please reply with particulars. Box 2292 The Times of India, Bombay 1.   A38036(X)
RESPECTABLE, W E L L PLACED Christian gentlemen, 40, employed in reputed foreign firm, seeks suitable match. Apply Box 23944, The Times of India, Bombay 1.
SUITABLE MATCH FOR GUJARATI Kapol Bania homeloving girl, age 22, passed SSC. Well settled Gujarati preferred. Write full particulars Box 23630, The Times of India, Bombay 1.   A38715(X)
SUITABLE MATCH WANTED: (a) Kerala Bramin girl 26, very fair, employed, only daughter Pooram, Atreya Gotram (b) Boy 28, Cost Accountant earning 300 monthly in reputed firm Bharadwaja Gotram Pooratem. Reply Box 23860, The Times of India, Bombay 1. A38979(X)
WANTED IMPRESSIVE, TALL, FAIR, preferably Medical Graduate Maharashtrian Brahmin bride from respectable family, prepared to go abroad, for healthy, handsome, Maharashtrian, 28, foreign qualified, Government of India Service. Apply with horoscope, to Box 23856, The Times of India, Bombay 1.   A38946(X)

some purposes, the descriptions must be understood to apply only to populations, not to their members as individuals.

While the Amerind "race" is indeed "typified" by presence of Diego antigen, it is nevertheless a fact that many Amerinds lack this trait. Similarly, while the "Alpine race" is characterizable as blond, it contains a great many brunettes . . . and so on.

Use OHT #2 [Overhead Transparency #2 is a map of Europe zoned and colorcoded to show percentage of light eyes in the population: (100–90), (90–80), (80–70), etc.] to make the point that races, if they must be defined, are best defined on the basis of *trait frequency*. This eliminates the problem of racial categorization of individuals. We can characterize the Northern European "race" as having 50 percent or more light eyes, and the African "race" as having 49 percent or less of light eyes. With respect to this one trait any individual could be either a Northern European or an African, for there would be no way of telling which; but any given population is immediately distinguishable as not Northern European or not African. (One might add parenthetically that it is usually a good deal easier to say who is not of a given race than it is to say who is.)

Discussion: What are some of the causes of these "racial" differences? It should be brought out here that, as seen in the homework reading, cultural factors are very much involved.

Distribute the matrimonial ads of the *Bombay Times* (Fig. 2) and have the students discover some of these cultural influences. It might be fun to discuss mating preference in our own society.

Is natural selection also involved? Allow further speculation on this, then assign (for homework) reading of "Historical Distribution of Racial Varieties." Distribute also the following worksheet to be filled out in conjunction with the reading:

Characterize, if you can, each of the following human groups:

1. American Indians
2. Arctic peoples
3. Eastern Asians
4. Pacific Islanders
5. East Indians
6. Africans
7. Caucasoids
8. Central Asians

For each of ten subgroups (subheadings in article) of your choice, decide on one characteristic that may be adaptive, and explain why you think so.

Day 4. Discussion: How may natural selection have been influential in the formation of races? Review the characteristics of some of the varieties Hulse describes and their possible adaptive value:

Eskimos — built for least heat loss
Melanesian and Africans — built for most heat loss (dark skin for protection from U-V radiation of equatorial sun)
Why are Pygmies small?
Why are Plains Indians, and some other savanna hunters, tall?
Why do temperate zone dwellers tan readily but have relatively light skins?
Why do very fair-skinned northerners tan not quite so readily?
And so on.

Discussion: Race and Intelligence

Why are humans more "intelligent" than other animals?
What is intelligence?
Why should any group of humans be more or less "intelligent" than another? (This is a very good argument for intellectual "equality.")

It should be pointed out that every human trait is ultimately a product of natural selection. This certainly applies to "intelligence." It is probably true that, generally speaking, there has occurred selection for particular kinds of specific intellectual abilities (perhaps in our society for mathematical reasoning), but there are as yet no valid criteria or methods for evaluating the innate learning capacity of any group of people in contrast to another. To say that all groups are equal in this respect because evidence to the contrary is lacking is, however, as logically fallacious as to assume the opposite. But a couple of points are worth making:

1. Since all human groups are capable of communicating clearly with one another, and with no other species of animal, they can't differ so very much in intellectual capacity.
2. For a Bushman to learn to stalk a kudu is easily as difficult as for a French cab driver to learn his way about Paris.
3. "Intelligence," if and when it is definable, is a continuous variable and cannot, therefore, ever be applied as a racial characteristic to individuals.

Assignment: Read "Technological Advances and Population Change." Review and revise the first homework paper — questions on race. What is the difference between an Englishman and a Caucasoid? (Can a Negro be an Englishman?)

DISCUSSION AND CONCLUSION

The aim of these lessons is to convey more than just information about race formation and classification. The hope is, first of all, to involve the student by starting him with his own experience of the topic and then to help him place that experience in a context that provides new perspectives which may also be applicable to other areas of knowledge. In the case of the materials presented above, the problem is to make the student aware of the confusion of criteria in the conventional classification of peoples into "racial" groups. He may realize — by becoming aware of the criteria he himself customarily uses, and by trying to apply them systematically — that there can be no definitive grouping. He finds that he cannot assign the accepted "facts" into categories of similar and dissimilar objects.

In constructing the "race chart" and tabulating the variations among his classmates in height, skin color, nose shape and so on, he may come to see that the criteria chosen to describe a race are not mutually supportive; that they are often, in fact, continuous variables. This understanding will, hopefully, lead him to the realization that it is population and not individuals that determines the pattern of transmitted genetic traits. This is a basic and far from watered-down lesson in anthropology.

Because these ways of thinking have become clearer to him, the student has something more than mere data (which may become obsolete) with which to work. He may be able to apply such thought processes to other kinds of data and even, perhaps, to improve upon them.

It is difficult to evaluate the effect of such lessons because the results desired most are behavioral objectives which elude most testing procedures. Interviews with students and teachers do not suggest that sweeping reforms have been initiated. They do demonstrate that students and teachers have become aware of certain qualities of teaching and learning. Teachers realize, some for the first time, that students can think. One teacher who had literally considered his students to be sponges, reported this realization with enthusiasm. Another teacher commented, "For the first time the students themselves were aware that they knew how to discuss something and realized that they were not just exchanging opinions." Another effect reported by one teacher was that ACSP materials had led (forced?) him to do more reading than he usually did in preparing for class.

Some students respond that they are relieved to be "allowed" to think. One said, "It made me have a good feeling — like I had done something worth doing and not just read it out of a book."

There are no panaceas in a situation as vast and differentiated as secondary education. But there is evidence that ACSP materials can help students and teachers who know what they need and can move others towards goals they otherwise might not have perceived.

FURTHER READINGS

Hertzberg, Hazel. "Using anthropology to teach New York State history," in Martin Feldman and Eli Seifman (eds.), *The social studies: structure, models, and strategies*. Englewood Cliffs, N.J.: Prentice-Hall, 1969.
History as culture change: an overview. Anthropology Curriculum Study Project. New York: Macmillan, 1968.
Lee, Dorothy. "Anthropology and American secondary education," in P. M. Halverson (ed.), *Frontiers of secondary education*. Syracuse, N.Y.: University of Syracuse Press, 1957.
Sady, Rachel R. "Anthropology and world history texts," *Phi Delta Kappan*, vol. 45 (February 1964).

B. ANTHROPOLOGY IN THE PREPARATION OF EDUCATORS

12

Using anthropology as a part-framework for a training program, Mr. Khleif notes, makes it possible to view the classroom "through the eyes of its natives. . . ." It prompts a working perspective of teachers and learners as thinking, feeling participants in — and not merely as ciphers of — the system of behaviors we call the school. The school and its classrooms articulate in real ways to the worlds of people, events, and expectations "outside." That much is plain; what is not so clear is the extent to which this is so, the mechanisms by which such articulation occurs, and the social sense it appears to be making, in its present and usual form. The program described here sought to "impart the viewpoints of anthropology and sociology [in training teachers] to see interaction and to relate behavioral problems to the general value system (culture) and social structure." Seeing the classroom "through the eyes of its natives" promises not only some clarity in understanding the various and sometimes equivocal relationships between it and the real world, but also provides critical insights into the experience of those being schooled. Mr. Khleif is Associate Professor of Anthropology, University of New Hampshire.

B. B. KHLEIF

A Sociocultural Framework for Training Teachers in a School Mental-Health Program[1]

Through their professional associations, anthropologists and sociologists are becoming increasingly interested in the application of their fields to education. The American Anthropological Association, for example, has

From *School Review*, vol. 73, no. 2 (Summer 1965), published by The University of Chicago Press. © 1965 by the University of Chicago.

[1] Revision of a paper read at the annual meeting of the Central States Anthropological Society, St. Louis, Missouri, May, 1962. This paper is part of work done on the Kansas City, Missouri Youth Development Project, a joint endeavor between the Kansas City,

168

a project under way to study the utilization of anthropology in high schools.[2] More recently, the American Sociological Association has established a committee to look into potentialities for the use of sociology in the high-school curriculum.[3] This paper is concerned with adaptation of some concepts and materials from social anthropology and sociology to an applied school program. The paper reports the contribution of the two fields to the planning of a program for training sixth-grade teachers to deal with mild and moderate behavioral disturbances of children in the regular classroom.

In a conventional subject-and-control design, two matched groups of volunteers, thirty teachers in each group, will be trained in consecutive years. The training program consists of a three-week summer institute followed by thirty-two, two-hour weekly meetings during the school year. The thirty subject teachers are trained together, as well as in five small groups. Each small group is of permanent membership and represents a cross-section of school neighborhoods of various socioeconomic levels. Every fourth meeting during the school year is a total-group meeting of the five small groups.

The program includes subject matter and practical techniques. The subject matter is derived mainly from sociology and anthropology and is intended to increase teachers' understanding of behavioral problems in terms of their work-setting, the classroom, in its relation to two other settings: (1) the cultural hinterland of the school, the neighborhood, and (2) the national cultural context, the larger community. The techniques, such as role-playing, are intended to help teachers deal with three varieties of problem children: the disruptive, the withdrawn, and the "culturally deprived." Neither the practical techniques nor the non-socioanthropological subject matter will be discussed here.

Specifically, social anthropology and sociology have provided the unifying point of view, the basic framework for training. Obviously, the theoretical framework not only determines the selection of subject matter to

---

Missouri Public Schools and the Greater Kansas City Mental Health Foundation. The project is concerned with research and action for dealing with behavioral disturbances of school children. Initially, the project was financed by the Kansas City Association of Trusts and Foundations; now it is supported by a grant from the National Institute of Mental Health (OM-535). The teacher-training program is sponsored by the University of Missouri, which grants participant teachers six graduate credits. The author wishes to express his appreciation to Dr. Weston LaBarre for a stimulating discussion that led to this paper, to Mr. Robert W. MacNeven for helpful reading of an initial draft, and to Dr. Blanche Geer for critical comments.

[2] Malcolm Collier, "Report on the Anthropology Curriculum Study Project," *Fellow Newsletter of the American Anthropological Association*, IV (November, 1962), 2–4.

[3] B. R. Clark, "Report of the Section on Sociology of Education," *American Sociological Review*, XXVII (December, 1962), 937.

be adapted to teachers but also influences the method of training and the evaluation of the program.

What is the rationale for the theoretical framework of this teacher-training program? What emphases, concepts, and materials are to be used? What kind of training experience is contemplated for teachers? Are there any practical issues in adopting a certain framework and a certain training approach? Are there any precautions to be taken? How is the program to be evaluated? These will be the questions for exploration here.

Framework for the Training Program

Traditional teacher-training has perhaps overemphasized a psychological frame of reference, viewing the individual pupil as a separate entity, an island. Herein lies the preoccupation of teachers with such clinically flavored concepts as the "whole child" and "meeting the individual's needs." The conceptual framework of the present training program stresses viewing the individual as a social product and as a process, with "rites of passage" and "significant others" at different stages of his life.[4] The pupil is considered as a social participant, the emphasis of the program being on the classroom as a group rather than as a loose aggregate of "whole" children standing apart from the teacher. The program thus seeks to impart the viewpoints of anthropology and sociology, that is, to train teachers to see interaction and to relate behavioral problems to the general value system (culture) and social structure. Such a sociocultural framework is prompted by a number of considerations that are known to anthropologists and sociologists but not well known to teachers. It would be helpful, for instance, to point out to teachers the following assumptions, and to discuss these assumptions with them as hypotheses:

1. In the classroom situation, teachers are group workers, not individual caseworkers; they meet their clients, not one at a time, but all at once. The child's classroom peer group not only exerts considerable influence on individual learning but also sets limits to the teacher's efforts.

2. Teachers only vaguely realize that pupils from school neighborhoods of different socioeconomic levels have different assumptions about co-operation, competition, and the worth of school work and that a pupil's failure in school may be a badge of achievement in his neighborhood.

3. Lack of teachers' understanding of the behavior motivations of children whose cultural norms are different from their own leads to selective communication with such children and influences their learning.[5] Allison

---

[4] Arnold Van Gennep, *The Rites of Passage* (Chicago: University of Chicago Press, 1960).

[5] George D. Spindler, "Learning in Culture: An Anthropological Perspective," *Educational Leadership*, XVI (April, 1959), 394–97.

Davis, for example, has shown that teachers, who come mainly from middle socioeconomic backgrounds, often fail to offer rewards that seem reasonable to children of a lower socioeconomic level.[6]

4. Teachers seem not to realize that quite often there is contradiction between declared educational goals and operating goals in the classroom. Anthropological observation of the classroom indicates that teachers sometimes unintentionally encourage destructive impulses in their pupils and increase anxiety and dependency.[7]

5. Teachers only vaguely recognize society's shifting value system and its effect on the classroom, for example, the change from such traditional values as self-denial and hard work to such emergent values as sociability.[8] Of particular relevance, perhaps, is the emergent concept of authority, which, according to Eggan, has shifted from parental figures to approval by contemporaries or peers and has resulted in the maintenance of artificial childhood in some classrooms.[9] (One is tempted to add that such emergence puts the teacher, not *in loco parentis* as is usually supposed, but *in loco* baby-sitter.) Moreover, a recent high-school study by Coleman seems to indicate that a possible effect of the emergent value system of teen-agers on education is the removal of highly intelligent students from an academic-achievement orientation to that of greater prestige among peers.[10]

TOPICS AND MATERIALS

The previously mentioned considerations suggest a number of topics for teacher-training, presented here with some illustrative references:

I. Education as a cultural process:
   A. Emile Durkheim, *Education and Sociology* (Glencoe, Ill.: Free Press, 1956).
   B. George D. Spindler (ed.), *Education and Culture: Anthropological Approaches* (New York: Holt, Rinehart & Winston, 1963).
   C. Jules Henry, "A Cross-Cultural Outline of Education," *Current Anthropology*, I (July, 1960), 267–304.

II. The classroom as an agency of socialization:
   A. Talcott Parsons, "The School Class as a Social System: Some of

[6] Allison Davis, *Father of Man: How Your Child Gets His Personality* (Boston: Houghton Mifflin Co., 1961).

[7] Jules Henry, "Attitude Organization in Elementary School Classrooms," *American Journal of Orthopsychiatry*, XXVII (January, 1957), 117–33.

[8] George D. Spindler, *Transmission of American Culture* (Cambridge, Mass.: Harvard University Press, 1959).

[9] Fred Eggan, "An Anthropologist Looks at Discipline," *Grade Teacher*, LXXVI (April, 1959), 55, 93–95.

[10] James S. Coleman, *The Adolescent Society* (Glencoe, Ill.: Free Press, 1961).

Its Functions in American Society," *Harvard Educational Review,* XXIX (Fall, 1959), 297–318.
III. The dichotomy between the world of adults and that of children:
   A. Francis L. K. Hsu, "Structure, Function, Content, and Process," *American Anthropologist,* LXI (October, 1959), 790–805.
IV. Culture and personality:
   A. Francis L. K. Hsu (ed.), *Psychological Anthropology: Approaches to Culture and Personality* (Homewood, Ill.: Dorsey Press, 1961).
   B. Y. A. Cohen, *Social Structure and Personality: A Casebook* (New York: Holt, Rinehart & Winston, 1961).
   C. Marvin K. Opler (ed.), *Culture and Mental Health: Cross-cultural Studies* (New York: Macmillan Co., 1959).
 V. The changing forms of the family:
   A. S. A. Queen, J. B. Adams, and R. W. Habenstein, *The Family in Various Cultures* (Chicago: J. B. Lippincott Co., 1961).
   B. Talcott Parsons and Robert F. Bales, *Family, Socialization and Interaction Process* (Glencoe, Ill.: Free Press, 1955).
   C. Oscar Lewis, *Five Families: Mexican Case Studies in the Culture of Poverty* (New York: John Wiley & Sons, 1962).
VI. The effect of social background on educational achievement and motivation:
   A. Allison Davis, *Social-Class Influences upon Learning* (Cambridge, Mass.: Harvard University Press, 1961).
   B. A. B. Hollingshead, *Elmtown's Youth: The Impact of Social Classes on Adolescents* (New York: John Wiley & Sons, 1961).
   C. W. Lloyd Warner, R. J. Havighurst, and M. B. Loeb, *Who Shall Be Educated?* (New York: Harper & Bros., 1944).

TRAINING METHOD

We have selected materials from sociology and anthropology in order to anchor discussion of disturbed as well as normative behavior. We think that the comparative approach inherent in anthropology contributes to the understanding of complex problems and their interconnections by increasing awareness of differences and similarities both across cultures and within cultures. The approach would be useful in training teachers, for example, in discussing disturbed behavior as not only deviance from generally prevalent norms but also deviance within a particular group. By providing a set of contrasts, the approach contributes to teachers' perspective, to perception of a number of unobvious things that lie behind the obvious. Moreover, the approach promotes a nonethnocentric outlook by pointing to the wide range of human adaptation.

For encouragement of the comparative viewpoint and development of an anthropological perspective among teachers, we have selected some problems for discussion. These problems are to be presented as assumptions, meant to be explored and criticized by teachers:

1. "If men define situations as real, they are real in their consequences." [11]

2. We might see the familiar in the unfamiliar if we consider that in certain respects every man is like all other men, like some other men, and like no other man.[12]

3. The school cannot but assume new functions: In neighborhoods where the traditional influence of the home and the church is not strong and in cases of rapid physical or social mobility the school has become a major stabilizing force in the life of the child.

4. Generational disarticulation may be forcing teen-agers to take the mores in their hands.

5. Sanity, perhaps, is directly proportional to awareness; it is the unexamined things that we are victims of. "We have nothing to fear but fear itself."

6. It may be maladaptive to be an individual nowadays, adaptive to live in "togetherness." The classroom, where the teacher has a legal mandate, need not be a palship system.

These assumptions, which are used as a training device for making teachers understand their work in relation to the general sociocultural matrix, necessitate a certain training approach and certain precautions. For one thing, the socioanthropological subject matter to be presented to teachers may be novel to most of them. Hence training may be best approached by moving gradually from a didactic presentation to more supportive discussion. Such an approach may be illustrated as follows.

1. The study of cultural values, for example, could proceed from exotic and faraway people to those familiar and close at hand, for example, from Pitt-Rivers' *People of the Sierra* [13] and Margaret Mead's *Cooperation and Competition among Primitive Peoples* [14] to Warner's *American Life: Dream and Reality*;[15] from Lewis' *Tepoztlán* [16] to Vidich and Bensman's *Small Town in Mass Society*.[17]

[11] W. I. Thomas, *The Unadjusted Girl* (Boston: Little, Brown & Co., 1923).

[12] Clyde Kluckhohn, H. A. Murray, and D. M. Schneider (eds.), *Personality in Nature, Society, and Culture* (2d ed.; New York: A. A. Knopf, 1953).

[13] J. A. Pitt-Rivers, *The People of the Sierra* (Chicago: University of Chicago Press, 1961).

[14] Boston: Beacon Press, 1961.

[15] W. Lloyd Warner, *American Life: Dream and Reality* (Chicago: University of Chicago Press, 1962).

[16] Oscar Lewis, *Tepoztlán: Village in Mexico* (New York: Holt, Rinehart & Winston, 1960).

[17] A. J. Vidich and J. Bensman, *Small Town in Mass Society: Class, Power, and Religion in a Rural Community* (Garden City, N.Y.: Anchor Books, 1958).

2. Such topics as family disorganization have to be discussed in a detached and dispassionate manner.

3. Concepts will be clarified in their intradisciplinary usage so that teachers can understand their full meaning, for example, "culture" according to Benedict, Opler, Kroeber, Kluckhohn and Mowrer, and White.[18] The sociocultural meaning of psychologically derived concepts will be explored, for example, "personality" according to Whiting and Child's formulation and "displacement" [19] according to Ingram's formulation.[20]

4. Community case studies that contain adequate specification of the total social context for the educational system will be used, for example, the Lynds' *Middletown* and *Middletown in Transition*,[21] and Wood's *Hamtramck*.[22]

5. The experience of teachers will be drawn upon, for example, when discussing the school neighborhood's cultural norms in relation to the learning situation in the classroom. This would be done in part through written cases that the teachers themselves would prepare about varieties of pupils, for example, "culturally deprived" and "culturally endowed" children. The case presentations would incorporate the pupils' point of view in addition to the teachers', and would examine behavioral problems in relation to cultural assumptions.

Implicit in the preceding account are some elements of the socio-anthropological method used as foci for training. One is a detached interest in phenomena, a preference for the "is" of analysis in contrast, perhaps, to the more prevalent "should" of educational literature. Another is an attention to concepts as analytic tools and determinants of vision — as lenses for discovering facts and hauling them into focus.[23] (There is perhaps a sort of Gresham's Law for conceptual currency, particularly in interdisciplinary transactions; hence this deliberate attention.) A third is

---

[18] Ruth Benedict, *Patterns of Culture* (New York: New American Library, 1960); Morris Edward Opler, "Themes as Dynamic Forces in Culture," *American Journal of Sociology*, LI (1945), 198–206; A. L. Kroeber, *The Nature of Culture* (Chicago: University of Chicago Press, 1952); Clyde Kluckhohn and O. H. Mowrer, "Culture and Personality: A Conceptual Scheme," *American Anthropologist*, XLVI (1944), 1–29; Leslie White, "The Concept of Culture," *American Anthropologist*, LXI (April, 1959), 227–51.

[19] J. W. M. Whiting and I. L. Child, *Child Training and Personality: A Cross-cultural Study* (New Haven, Conn.: Yale University Press, 1953).

[20] G. I. C. Ingram, "Displacement Activity in Human Behavior," *American Anthropologist*, LXII (December, 1960), 994–1003.

[21] R. S. Lynd and H. M. Lynd, *Middletown: A Study in American Culture* (New York: Harcourt, Brace & Co., 1929); and their *Middletown in Transition* (New York: Harcourt, Brace & Co., 1937).

[22] A. E. Wood, *Hamtramck: A Sociological Study of a Polish-American Community* (New Haven, Conn.: College and University Press, 1955).

[23] Everett Cherrington Hughes, "The Study of Institutions," *Social Forces*, Vol. XX (March, 1942).

the anthropological perspective of looking at the classroom through the eyes of its natives, of giving teachers and pupils their voice. Finally, there is the Ogburn emphasis on sequence: in the analysis of social phenomena, cultural explanations precede psychological ones.[24] To put it somewhat differently, there is no psychology without a sociology.

The climate to be established in the training sessions is that of therapy, not in its psychoanalytic connotation but in its ancient sense of clarifying one's knowledge of oneself, which includes those skills of controversy with oneself, which can be called thinking, and of controversy with others, which can be called debate.[25] Hence teachers are to be encouraged to get in touch with the realities of their cultural function and of their world and to explore problems in terms of human meaning. In this connection we would like to advance one more precaution: in this training program we assert the freedom of the individual, the teacher, to reject whatever is presented or discussed.

EVALUATION OF TRAINING

It is assumed that the effect of training on teachers may manifest itself in changes in their attitude toward others, in their receptivity to new ideas, and in the way they view their work. In addition, there may be changes in the interaction of teachers with their pupils in the classroom. Obviously, we have no assurance that any changes at the end of the training period would not have occurred without, or in spite of, training. Hence, comparisons will be made between the group of teachers that has received training (the subject group) and the one that has not (the control group). Not only will the differences between the two groups at the end of the training period be looked at but the situation of each group immediately prior to training will be taken as a base line to compare the group with itself and to determine the direction and type of any change it may have at the end of the school year.

It can be said that we are interested in finding out whether or not there is an over-all change in the attitude and classroom interaction of teachers that may be associated with the training program. We will not be able to relate any particular aspect of change to any particular content of the training program. For one thing, our independent variable, the training program, is too gross to lend itself to the testing of hypotheses in the experimental sense. Besides, even with a set of precise hypotheses there are many intervening variables in the everyday work of teachers that

[24] Thomas Gladwin and W. C. Sturtevant (eds.), *Anthropology and Human Behavior* (Washington, D.C.: Anthropological Society of Washington, 1962).

[25] C. W. Mills, *Mass Society and Liberal Education* (Chicago: Center for the Study of Liberal Education for Adults, 1954).

cannot be rigorously controlled. Moreover, we assume that the sociocultural segment of the training program as well as the not-so-sociocultural — for example, role-playing — interact in such a manner as to produce different as well as unforeseeable patterns in their effect on teachers. These patterns can be more meaningfully discovered and accounted for through observation than through a priori instrumentation. At any rate, we think of our dependent variable as an over-all outcome that may be associated with the over-all program.

The following is our attempt at gathering evaluation devices that may point to and qualify differences between the subject and control teachers. The evaluation devices are centered around teacher attitude and classroom interaction.

A. Standardized instruments:
1. The FIRO-B (Fundamental Interpersonal Relations Orientation Behavior),[26] a set of Guttman scales that deal with three categories of interpersonal responses: affection, inclusion, and control.
2. The Rokeach Scale,[27] an attitude scale that deals with open-mindedness and dogmatism in interpersonal relations.
3. The MTAI (Minnesota Teacher Attitude Inventory),[28] which deals with the attitude of teachers toward teaching.
4. The Flanders Classroom Interaction Categories,[29] which deal with supportive and dominative teacher actions in the classroom.

B. Structured questionnaires:
These deal with (1) concepts and materials discussed with teachers, (2) hypothetical problem situations in their classroom work, and (3) satisfaction and dissatisfaction with the training program. Obviously, only part (2) is given to the control teachers.

C. Open-ended interviews:
These are end-of-year interviews of about an hour's duration. They deal with (1) teaching career, movement through varieties of school systems and school neighborhoods, (2) the teacher's own characterization of her present school neighborhood, (3) cultural differences between the teacher and her present group of pupils, (4) influence structure and behavioral characteristics of her pupils, (5) relations with principal, parents, colleagues, substitute and special-service teachers, and (6) reactions to the training program. Part (6) is not used with the control group.

26 W. C. Schutz, *FIRO: A Three Dimensional Theory of Interpersonal Behavior* (New York: Rinehart & Co., 1958).

27 Milton Rokeach, *The Open and Closed Mind: Investigations into the Nature of Belief Systems and Personality Systems* (New York: Basic Books, 1960).

28 W. W. Cook, C. H. Leeds, and R. Callis, *Minnesota Teacher Attitude Inventory: Form BX* (New York: The Psychological Corporation, 1953).

29 N. A. Flanders, "Teacher Influence, Pupil Attitudes and Achievement" (Ann Arbor: University of Michigan, 1962). (Dittoed.)

D. Observational protocols:

These consist of unstructured data, gathered in an ethnographic manner. Each subject and control classroom is observed ten times during the school year, an hour to an hour and a half each time. In matters of method, our orientation stems primarily from the work of Jules Henry, who has been the project's consultant on classroom observation.

It is also assumed that the training program may produce changes in the academic achievement of the subject pupils, in their attitude toward school, and in their sociometric choices. In addition to collecting observational protocols, hence, standardized achievement tests, Guttman-type attitude scales, and sociometric tests will be administered to pupils before and after the program. A sample of pupils will also be interviewed; the interview schedule will be similar to the one used with teachers. Moreover, there will be a follow-up of pupils during their schooling careers. The subject and the control pupils will be compared.

We have formulated some questions that cannot be answered at this stage of the training program:

1. Can teachers acquire an anthropological perspective without being overburdened? What are the limits of their trainability: age? sex? length of teaching experience? character types?

2. If training is regarded as a problem in cultural change, how best can we use participant observation to evaluate teachers' reaction to the training experience — to the staff, orientation, method and content of training? Would Spicer's five processes of contact change (incorporative integration, assimilation, fusion, compartmentalization, and bicultural behavior) be useful for studying change in teachers' outlook? [30]

3. Can a system of empirical categories, flowing out of the unstructured data themselves, be so constructed as to account for all the interactive events in the observational protocols? Among other approaches to the observational data, would scalogram analysis (the Guttman scalogram technique) [31] lead to a crucial core of content that would differentiate the interactive patterns in the subject and control classrooms?

Social anthropology and sociology not only have contributed a theoretical framework and content to the training program but have also been of value in planning its evaluation.

---

[30] Edward H. Spicer (ed.), *Perspectives in American Indian Cultural Change* (Chicago: University of Chicago Press, 1961).

[31] A. L. Edwards, *Techniques of Attitude Scale Construction* (New York: Appleton-Century-Crofts, 1957); M. W. Riley, J. W. Riley, Jr., and Jackson Toby, *Sociological Studies in Scale Analysis: Applications, Theory, Procedures* (New Brunswick, N.J.: Rutgers University Press, 1954); S. A. Stouffer, Louis Guttman, E. A. Suchman, P. F. Lazarsfeld, S. A. Star, and J. A. Clausen, *Measurement and Prediction* (Princeton, N.J.: Princeton University Press, 1950).

Further Readings

Burger, Henry G. *"Ethno-pedagogy": a manual in cultural sensitivity, with techniques for improving cross-cultural teaching by fitting ethnic patterns.* Albuquerque, N.M.: Southwestern Cooperative Educational Laboratory, Inc., 1968.

Forbes, Jack D. *The education of the culturally different: a multi-cultural approach* Berkeley: Far West Laboratory for Educational Research and Development, 1969.

Landes, Ruth. *Culture in American education: anthropological approaches to minority and dominant groups in the schools.* New York: Wiley, 1965.

Parsons, Theodore W. "Psycho-cultural determinants of teaching behavior: a southwestern example," in Frederick O. Gearing (ed.), *Proceedings: the National Conference on Anthropology and Education.* Miami Beach, Florida, 1968.

Waller, Willard. *The sociology of teaching.* New York: Russell and Russell, 1932. (Reprinted, Wiley, 1961.)

13

In Bohannan's view, much of classroom process is a function of communication across cultural barriers. His view is persuasive on two accounts. First, teaching and learning involve shared understandings. These transactions are as broadly behavioral as they are strictly "factual," and in either case are eventually subject to cultural definition. Second, the sets of patterned behaviors that in part distinguish students from teachers, adults from youth, the context of the school from that of home and neighborhood, and ethnic groups from one another, are often cited as obstacles to effective classroom process. Mr. Bohannan's comparison of field anthropologists and front-line teachers is also persuasive, especially in what it implies to the professional development of educators. Less convincing, perhaps, is Bohannan's assumption of "middle-class" culture as standard school fare and of teachers as its inevitable accomplices. The contrasting of two cultures, here — the middle-class of the intending teachers and the "difference" of those students for whom they are being prepared — is an exemplary illustration. As with Musgrove, however, such a contrast may fail to show the subtle, complex patterned behavioral differences that attend any classroom, including those where both teachers and students are middle class. Mr. Bohannan, Professor of Anthropology and of Education, Northwestern University, asserts that it is the business of educators to adjust or adapt to the realities of students as they are. This presupposes that every teacher has an anthropological "sense" of himself as well as of others and that communication is less a method to be learned than the art of oneself to be performed. Bohannan recently edited Divorce and After *(New York: Doubleday 1970); his multiple contributions to anthropological literature include outstanding works on the Tiv of Nigeria and the Wanga of Kenya.*

PAUL J. BOHANNAN

Field Anthropologists and Classroom Teachers

There are three major areas in which anthropology is relevant in primary and secondary schools. First, of course, it is important as a subject matter. A great deal of anthropology is already taught in the schools. Often it is not called by its name, but Eskimos and Bushmen and Pygmies are standard fare in the primary grades. L. S. B. Leakey is a national hero in our junior high schools, and non-Western and world history courses are laced with anthropology. Much of this anthropology seriously needs upgrading to meet professional standards of relevance and accuracy and (ironically enough) to remove from it inaccuracies and romanticism such as those that have been introduced into American Indian studies by the Boy Scouts. But, on the other hand, some of it is already of pretty good quality — particularly the anthropology of early man and evolution.

Second, anthropology, better than any of the other social sciences, provides a method of investigation that is suitable for the study and evaluation of classroom procedures and cultures. Anthropologists, over the decades, have evolved a way of analyzing and presenting small communities that can almost without alteration be switched to the study of schools and the cultural associations among classroom, community cultures, and the educational systems of our nation. It is, at the moment, becoming stylish for anthropologists to study schools. People from other disciplines are also studying classrooms and schools in the community, and are borrowing extensively from anthropological techniques when they do it. It is becoming obvious — and heartening — that we shall within the next few years see the efflorescence of a large body of data and no inconsiderable insight about the educational process in our own society, with a good bit of interesting comparative material. The school is, after all, one of the main "institutions of cultural transmission" in modern societies; education is one of the most vital activities that any society must carry out. Finally we are getting around to investigating it directly.

The third point, however, is the one to which this article is devoted: the technique of anthropological field work offers great insight into some of the problems of teachers, both during their training and in their classrooms. I have found, to my great astonishment and delight, that teachers take to these ideas and techniques with almost no adaptation at all. It is very

From *Social Education*, vol. 32, no. 2 (February 1968), pp. 161–166. Reprinted by permission of the author and publisher.

soon possible to develop in the teacher an awareness of social and cultural dynamics, as well as a mode of action which enables him to participate fully and vitally and at the same time to stand back far enough to see what is going on. It offers a proven device to control his emotions and his actions so that he stays in touch with the real world — with what is going on out there in the classroom. . . .

The Cultural Anthropologist in the Field

Like the teacher, the field anthropologist does his job with his entire personality. His acceptance into the community, and his ultimate success or failure, depends almost as much on what he is as a person as on what he does as a trained professional. It is well to keep this idea in mind as we explore the job of the anthropologist.

The anthropologist, as ethnographer, is faced with the task of going into another culture and adjusting to it as he learns it. This learning is no mere question mongering — it means getting the other culture into his mind and his muscles, learning to speak its language as well as he can, and participating in the life of "his community" to whatever degree his people and his own personality will allow. Then, even more difficult, he must return to his own culture and must devise ways of communicating in English, what he has learned in a foreign tongue and alien culture. And he must do it so that there is as little warping as possible of the values and ideas current in the culture he has studied — no mean task when all of the technical terms in English have themselves been developed to explain and adjust American and British cultures.

The first task for the field anthropologist is to learn the language. In the process, of course, he must learn new facts about his own language — about the strange ways in which he is accustomed to putting things to himself, and about the particular limitations and elasticities of English. Even more important than learning the words, he must learn to "hear," in the sense of understand in *their* terms, what it is that his informants are trying to tell him. If they do not answer his questions straight, it's three to one that the difficulty lies in the question and the way the ethnographer is asking it. In the course of learning the language, he must also learn new sets of gestures (and hence the literal "feel" of that language may be much different) and new ways of evasions and new ways of hiding things from one's self. In short, he must learn new aspects and new deep meanings of his own "body English" as well as of his own spoken English.

In this process, the anthropologist is constantly discovering himself as he investigates and records the data concerning the people he studies. It is no easy matter to get over *assuming* you know what is being said out there in the "real world." But you cannot really look at the real world of a foreign culture until you can see it in its own terms the very while you look at yourself looking at it.

Thus, both teachers and field anthropologists are in unparalleled situations for getting their own cultures straight in their own minds. They will discover, in the course of doing their work, that much of what had seemed common sense — ordinary background of ordinary social life, about which it had never before been necessary to think — is suddenly thrust into prominence and awareness.

In short, the teacher (like the anthropologist) must be made aware of his own values, his own unstated assumptions, his very bodily movements, if he is to learn the culture of his students. And the greater the difference between his own background and that of his students, the more aware of it he becomes — and hence, ironically, the clearer his job will be.

In short, if you are going to use your personality as the primary tool in your work, you have to learn something about your own personality and the cultural idiom in which it is accustomed to express itself. Only then are you in a position to modify or utilize your own techniques of learning and hence of teaching so that they do indeed serve the ends that you intend them to serve.

An anthropologist selects a people he is to study on the basis of two major considerations: his own capacity to live the kind of life these people live, and the problems which are currently paramount in his discipline. In this way, he will know that such-and-such a person or institution or situation is "ready" to be studied, and that he can likely make a significant contribution to the knowledge in the field. Both these considerations are important.

It is necessary first to have an overt and intellectual goal in mind — that is, for the field anthropologist to learn something about the way a specific human group, whatever it may be, faces some of the fundamental problems of human living. It may be a problem in law and the way in which conflict is either settled or handled in the absence of settlement. It may be a problem in economy, and the way in which provisioning is taken care of in the absence of familiar institutions such as markets. It may, indeed, be a problem in cultural transmission, and the way in which present-day schools drive a wedge between generations and turn some of the children into near schizophrenics because of the double messages that they receive at home and at school. The consideration is always that the discipline has the conceptual equipment to confront a problem, but needs more facts and ideas to solve it, and that the individual practitioner has the requisite imagination and nerve to turn new ideas and new data to the benefit of the discipline.

However, there is another matter here: every individual field worker goes to the field with a developed and entire personality and mode of life. He obviously cannot make himself entirely over. Therefore, he must select a people whose temperament and mode of life he finds bearable. Not admirable, necessarily; not even pleasant. But bearable. After all, a field worker is going to be living with these people for a period of from one to three years, and if he did not find them at least minimally congenial, it would be absolutely impossible for him to do his job. Yet, if the anthropologist works among his own people, he is not going to have to alter the frame of reference of his very life — and it is this very alteration that leads to anthropological insight.

Therefore, the first requirement for an anthropologist is to find a place to work in which he is not grossly uncomfortable, but with which he is not overly familiar either. Now, this seems to me to be precisely the situation of any neophyte teacher — particularly those who have chosen to work among the various ethnic groups in our country that are different from the one in which they have grown up. It is especially true of American middle-class teachers who, in line with the commitment to middle class values of helping others, have chosen to face the ethnic groups of the inner cities.

An anthropologist cannot use interpreters as a short cut for learning the language. If he does, he is not going to get to the heart of the meaning that these people attach to their institutions for living. He cannot both understand what they are about and allow himself the luxury of somebody else's doing his analysis and telling him how to behave (although if other people have been there before him, some of their hints may be useful — but they may be also worse than useless).

Again, I think the parallel is evident: the teacher cannot depend on somebody else, either his own teachers, or his principal, or anybody else, to tell him how to do this job. He must himself learn to communicate with his charges. The problem of communication may stem from no more than a difference in age. (I was acutely aware when I first faced a ninth grade of middle-class Americans that I, a middle-class American, had not dealt with 14-year-olds since I was 14, and that the world had changed a lot since then.) However, in the present day in which we are trying to upgrade the schools of our inner cities and to educate a greater range of Americans to ever more demanding social roles, I venture that a large proportion of teachers find themselves face to face with people whose language they do not understand — in some cases because it may not be English, in others because it may not be the standard dialect of English, in still others because there may be secret languages or other secret modes of communication among students who zealously keep the teacher from understanding their private means of communicating.

The anthropologist — and the teacher — must also discover the degree to which he or she can be taken into the community that is the subject of study. In some African communities every anthropologist is required to live as a chief because the people will not accept him on any other basis. In some American communities every teacher is required to present himself as a middle-class arbiter of morality because the students and the community will not accept him on any other basis. You must learn to work within an ascribed status, perhaps trying to change it a little, but more importantly, understanding the constrictions that it puts on your activities and your opportunity to learn.

In some African communities, the people are delighted when an anthropologist wants to live among them, in superficial ways at least, as they themselves live. In the same way, in some American communities some teachers will be welcomed into strange ethnic groups, but this experience, I judge, is exceptional. I think it is unlikely that most teachers will find themselves allowed to speak the local dialect, even if they learn to understand it. Middle-class teachers in lower-class Negro schools are faced with having to learn to understand a kind of English which they are never allowed, by their students, to use. They have to be circumspect enough to discover the limitations (either from self or from community) in living with and utilizing the culture of the people they teach or study.

Learning a language can be a tricky matter because no two languages structure the sense world in precisely the same way. When, as children, our five senses are culturally educated, we also learn that language in terms of which we shall for the rest of our lives cut up our perceptions in order to communicate about them. When we learn only one language, the result is necessarily a monoglot's view of culture and the whole world.

Therefore, in the process of learning a new language, an anthropologist begins to know overtly what he has formerly perceived only covertly: a specific organization to his cultural and social world, a palette of color, as it were, with which life in his particular latitudes is always presented and perceived. This kind of self-knowledge is the essence of field anthropology — and, I suggest, of successful teaching.

Something else happens too: we discover not just the way we see the world, but we also discover some of our feelings about it — about morality, about cleanliness and godliness, about money, and about ambition. We may thereupon become indignant, angry, frightened. The "way out" of these feelings is, for the untrained, to blame the other guy, and belittle his culture and his values. This is one way — but a naive way — of saving your own value system, making it unnecessary for you to question your own assumptions and your own feelings.

This set of threats to the individual is usually called "culture shock," especially in its more acute form. Culture shock may occur to anyone when he finds his feelings threatened by matters he does not understand, and his actions made insecure by social situations in which he cannot make accurate predictions. Culture shock is a result of having to face situations in which you do not know what you are expected to do next, and hence any action you take may lead to misfortune or disaster. It is a kind of psychic deprivation, and can lead to serious consequences if you do not know how to deal with it, and yet cannot run away.

Let me give two examples of culture shock — both from my own life. One of these occurred in the Ivory Coast, long after I knew about culture shock — and indeed, only a few days after I gave a series of lectures on it. I proceeded immediately from an Eastern university in the United States, where I had been giving my lectures to a group of students who were proceeding overseas, to a conference in Abidjan. Everything went swimmingly until the weekend. I had accepted an invitation from an African colleague in the conference for Sunday, an invitation that I thought I ought for my own edification to accept, but which I was quite unenthusiastic about. A few hours later I felt I had to turn down another invitation from a group of French participants to spend Sunday with them at the beach swimming and picnicking. Then, on Sunday, I was stood up by the African. Now, I know perfectly well that such behavior on the part of the African was not, by his standards, anywhere nearly as rude — indeed, insufferable — as it was by mine. Something else had come up, and it would have been extremely awkward for him to have notified me. However, when I realized what had happened, I went to my hotel room, pulled the blinds, and went to bed. I was emancipated enough not to blame him — I blamed his "lousy culture."

Within a few minutes, fortunately for me, I realized what I was doing — and recalled that I had only a few days before told my audience that if you are lonely or angry or home-sick or feel ill-used, you had better ask yourself, "Buddy, what's biting you? What are you trying to get by with?" I had, to cover my own disappointment and to keep from being annoyed at my own "virtue" in keeping the standards of my own culture about invitations, labeled *his* culture inferior. I dressed again, pulled up the shades, went out and found some people, and had a good day.

The other example is not so trivial. When I had been among the Tiv of Nigeria for about ten months, I hired a young man Tiv as my servant — what was called a "steward" in Nigerian English. He was not a good steward. However, he could read and write in Tiv, and he took an immense interest in my work. I subsequently learned that the interest arose because he had been brought up by white missionaries and needed, like me, to learn his own culture intellectually and as an adult rather than as a by-product of being a child. He began to write text for me in the Tiv language and to help me with my ethnographic investigations in many other ways. I soon realized that I had a very important assistant here. I turned him into my "scribe" and hired another steward. He and I became good friends, and we worked together several hours almost every day.

One evening, he came back from the river where he had been bathing and swimming. I asked him casually if anything was going on, and in a casual way he replied that a man had drowned in the river. I discovered through questioning that the man was a stranger who could not swim, and had stepped off a drop-off a few feet from the bank. Nobody had tried to save him. I knew my scribe to be a strong swimmer. "Didn't *you* go after him?" I demanded. "He wasn't mine," was the laconic answer.

This incident upset me. I found that one of my most basic values had been flouted: the worth of individual human life. It took me several days to realize that this was not one of *his* basic values, and that in fact I had shocked *him* a few weeks before when he had learned that I had not seen my parents for four years, or my brother for seven, which to him showed absolutely appalling neglect. It took me several days to learn to like him again.

It is out of just such events that culture shock is made, and it is out of just such experiences that one comes upon the "cure" for it: learning what one's own values are, then either abandoning them or else making an intellectual commitment as well as an emotional commitment to them, so that they need never turn up again merely as raw feelings. I do not mean that you cease to feel strongly about such things. I only suggest that you know which things you feel strongly about and then govern yourself sensibly when you are in some other ethnic group.

Thus, it is out of culture shock that the anthropologist gets the most important part of his understanding of his data, and learns to do his job better.

In fact, the anthropologist becomes the medium in which the two sets of cultural values, those of his mother culture and those of the subject culture, are brought into focus. The next few years of his life are to be spent in trying to translate into English, for communication to his colleagues, the very values that he learned in order to get along with and to understand the culture and the communications of his informants.

It seems to me that many middle-class American teachers are in a "field situation."

A Seminar for Teachers in Anthropological Method

In the spring of 1967, I ran a seminar at Northwestern for 18 M.A.T. candidates, all of whom were teaching in ethnic groups other than their own. One of the candidates was a young man from middle-class small-town

New England who had chosen to go into lower-class Negro schools of Chicago, another was a Wisconsin Lutheran girl who was teaching in a school made up almost entirely of second- and third-generation Eastern European Jews. Some of the other candidates were teaching Puerto Ricans, others were teaching new arrivals from southern Europe. Some were teaching in Chicago communities made up of a combination of Appalachian whites and American Indians; still others in schools that were operated especially for delinquent rejects from the public schools; two were teaching in the psychiatric ward of a city hospital. All of them had in common that they could not merely call upon the culture of their youth and of their college days to see them through their present situations.

After a short introduction to the basic concepts of cultural anthropology — the way in which social relationships structure themselves, and the way in which any people in communication need, and daily re-create, a culture for their interaction — we began a series of reports about the kind of problems that they faced in their daily work. Some rather astonishing results were soon apparent.

Whereas they had formerly been asking such remote and philosophical questions as whether their task was to change the culture of the groups they were teaching to some sort of middle-class WASP amalgam, they began to realize that this was not the immediate point. Except for the new arrivals, almost all of the various ethnic groups in the United States already knew middle-class WASP culture. They learn it on television, in magazine ads and comic books, on the city streets. Some of them actively — hostilely — reject it. Some of them are uncomfortable because they do not know what unimagined doom their trying to emulate it might bring about. The point is not whether you are going to teach them middle-class culture — obviously, you are. It is one of the cultures — and the dominant one — that is here to be dealt with.

The question is not whether you are going to teach it to them, but rather how you understand what their difficulties with it are, and the fact that two cultures are seldom an either/or proposition. When you discover this, you and they can decide in concert whether you are actively engaged in teaching it to them or whether they are going to reject it. You know where you stand — and you have not only communicated across a cultural barrier, you have gone a long way toward explaining that cultural barrier to them.

The seminar considered ways and means that mathematics can be taught to youngsters who do not see its function in their daily lives; we talked about how to teach literature in such a way that cultural differences become the essential point rather than the block to understanding. We talked about problems in teaching history and science and social studies — and in every case we discovered that the secret was an additive element: the inclusion of cultural differences in understanding and using such subjects. We even began doing a comparative study of roadblocks that different ethnic groups put up against good study habits. There are vast pressures in some lower-class groups against studying, and if a child studies, he may have to do it on the sly. In upper-middle-class third-generation European-Jewish children, the problem was how to make them behave in study hall — until it was discovered that they refused to study in study hall for good reason: if they did not do their studying at home, their parents called the teachers demanding larger homework assignments.

What we really accomplished in this seminar was that, for these teachers at least, there came to be an awareness that communication is affected by culture, and that *it is the teacher* (just as it is the field anthropologist) *who must make the major adjustment*. Only in that way can any real appreciation of the overt situation be learned. And only then can any real program of change and upgrading be instituted: on the basis of knowledge not only of facts but of the internal attitudes of the students. And, most important of all, of the teacher.

We also discussed the attitude of middle-class Americans to the problem of power. We discovered that most of the neophyte teachers had never before in their lives been in a position of power, and as a consequence they were not only worried about the way in which their exercise of authority would be received in their student's ethnic groups, but they had never adjusted to an image of themselves as powerful people in terms of their own values. They began to realize that the power of every authority figure must be limited. We began to ask, "What is worth enforcing in this particular situation?" Discipline? This problem turned out not to be especially difficult for most of these student teachers. Their problems of discipline were reduced vastly when they understood that listening behavior and attention are shown in different ways in our different sub-cultural groups. Quiet in the classroom? In most cases, it was necessary to placate the principal, but not necessary in the teaching process. Picking up scrap paper off the floor? Except for one young lady who decided she would demand it as an eccentricity of her own, we decided that we would not spend any of our authority on *that*.

In short, what matters? What is worth making a fuss about if you are to do the teaching job? I know that many school administrators take quite a different view of this — but I ask them, too, to get in the act. What is worrying *you* about this situation? What is really worth taking a stand on? Is it important in the educational process, or is it just your middle-class background showing?

TEACHERS IN THE CLASS ROOM

I decided as a result of this seminar that such training is almost essential to the training of teachers who will be working "cross-culturally."

I have no doubt that it will allow them more profitably to work in and live in the communities of their students. Such teachers can, I trust and hope, avoid in large measure that greatest of personal and social tragedies in our schools — the teacher who, under constant threat of cultural strangeness, either becomes so authoritarian that education is impossible, or so apathetic that education seems scarcely desirable, or so angry that education seems "too good for them." It is teachers in this situation who have, quite understandably, led educational critics and civil rights leaders to believe that lower-class schools are the worst staffed (when, in fact, many people in them began as hand-picked experts and even volunteers). Apathy and anger are the great protectors of the self. When all else fails, they still protect.

There are a few simple questions that must consciously and repeatedly be asked: Why am I angry? Why am I homesick? Why am I discouraged? Why am I hostile? Why am I afraid?

The answers to these questions can almost always be found in the fact that your expectations have not been fulfilled, that you are left high and dry, not knowing where to turn or how to behave, that you have "failed."

And, of necessity, that leads to the next set of questions: What are these people doing and saying *in their terms?* What are their purposes, their underlying and unstated value positions? What do they want? And finally: Why are *they* angry and afraid?

From the answers to these questions can come, in many cases at least, and by some teachers, a firm basis for achieving the cross-cultural communication whose absence is one of the primary plagues in our schools today.

Teachers are, to repeat, in some ways like field anthropologists: since they work with their entire personalities, and since their fundamental problem is one of cross-cultural communication, and since their feelings are as important a cue as their intellects to discovery of hidden cultural differences, some training is necessary if they are to avoid the destructive emotions which make impossible the very job they set out to do. Field anthropologists have faced these problems; some have found solutions to some of them from which, it is apparent, teachers can profit.

Further Readings

Dumont, Robert V., Jr., and Murray L. Wax. "Cherokee school society and the inter-cultural classroom," *Human Organization*, vol. 28 (Fall 1969).
Eddy, Elizabeth M. *Becoming a teacher: the passage to professional status.* New York: Teachers College Press, 1969.
Mair, Lucy P. *Studies in applied anthropology.* London: University of London, Athlone

Press, 1957. (See especially chap. 4: "The anthropologist's approach to native education.")

Willower, Donald J. "The teacher subculture and rites of passage." Paper read at the Annual Meeting of the American Educational Research Association, Los Angeles, 1969.

Zintz, Miles V. *Education across cultures.* Dubuque, Iowa: William C. Brown Book Company, 1963.

14

Anthropological influences upon and practical contributions to the preparation of educators occur in various programs and practices. Khleif and Bohannan previously described formal involvements. Leacock explores the informal, although not less significant, involvements. Her interest is in the utility of the concept of "culture" to working teachers, administrators, and school specialists; it is also in the frequent misuse of the idea of culture. Leacock argues that perceived behavioral differences are sometimes simply the product of distorted social outlook and, further, that behaviors we willingly attribute to "other" human groups often reflect our expectations of how such groups (and everyone in them) ought to behave. Professor of Anthropology, Polytechnic Institute of Brooklyn, Mrs. Leacock wrote Teaching and Learning in City Schools (New York: Basic Books, 1969), in which her argument here takes more comprehensive form. "Cultural disadvantage" and "culture of poverty" are disposable terms. In labeling a problem, some professionals — and not a few anthropologists among them — are ready to believe it explained. Leacock examines routinized assumptions of the "middle class" as sufficient measure of what is advantaged and what is disadvantaged, and finds children hidden among the labels; children, she urges us, are not only more worthy than labels, but also deserve the most objective insight possible from those whose business understanding children is.

ELEANOR LEACOCK

The Concept of Culture and Its Significance for School Counselors

The culture concept, central to the field of anthropology, is becoming increasingly familiar in the social service fields. When properly applied, the idea of "culture" can be extremely useful for the understanding of behavior

From *Personnel and Guidance Journal*, vol. 46, no. 9 (May 1968). © 1968 by the American Personnel and Guidance Association.

and the breaking down of many barriers to effective communication. However, like most ideas, it can also be distorted, and defeat the very purpose it should serve. This paper will discuss the appropriate use of the culture concept, and indicate the way it can be distorted when incorrectly applied to differences between children from "middle class," economically well-off homes, and children from economically marginal or insecure homes.

True cultural insight enables us to see behind superficial, socially patterned differences to the full integrity of an individual. It prevents us from misinterpreting behavior different from that to which we are accustomed. To take an example from American Indian culture, people working with Indian children have found that they often do not respond well to teaching techniques that depend on the desire to do better than one's peers on a test, to answer a question more capably, in short to compete successfully. Where Indian societies have retained roots with the past they are still pervaded by a cooperative spirit, and children feel uncomfortable in competitively structured situations, at least insofar as learning is concerned. This is often misinterpreted as a lack of desire to learn, but an awareness of cultural differences reveals that the motivation for learning is present, but that it is being inhibited rather than encouraged by teaching practices foreign to Indian culture.

The persistence of such responses was brought home sharply to me when I assigned oral reports, seminar style, to a college class of bright, argumentative students. One of the girls, who had seldom spoken up in class, asked for permission to write rather than deliver her paper. I was unsuccessful in my attempt to persuade her to try the experience of oral delivery. She later told me that the course had given her insight into her reason for declining, and to the discomfort she had always felt in school. Her father was Indian, she said, and though there was little of an ongoing Indian community in Connecticut where she was raised, nonetheless the style of American Indian discourse had persisted in her family. For her, discussion should not involve the rapid-fire, essentially competitive argument to which we are accustomed. Instead, it should involve measured, considered statements, and — so difficult for us — attentive listening. Each person should listen patiently to everyone else, and the attempt should be at reaching consensus rather than winning an argument. Therefore, this student had always felt uncomfortable in classrooms, with their built-in competitive atmosphere.

Thus, learning and exchanging knowledge are conceived differently in different cultures. So, too, are traditional styles of behavior between adults and children. Teachers working with Puerto Rican students often find that a child being reprimanded does not look at them or respond to their statements. They may think the child sullen, rebellious, or rude. In the cultural terms of the child, however, he is expressing acquiescence and respect. Understanding this culture difference enables a teacher to see behind socially patterned behavior to a child's actual feelings, and to relate to him as an individual.

MISAPPLICATION OF THE CULTURE CONCEPT

However, the awareness that such differences exist can lead to their exaggeration and misapplication. Such is often the case with the "culture of poverty" described for economically underprivileged and minority communities. Unfortunately, "lower class culture" is fast becoming a new stereotype behind which the individual is not revealed more fully, but instead is lost. Indeed, the "old fashioned" but sympathetic and insightful person, who is skeptical of "all this talk about culture," and asserts that what really counts is the individual child, is more correct than those who have gone overboard with distorted expectations for "cultural" differences. Such a person knows intuitively that, although people act and react in terms of learned patterns for behavior, which may differ, nonetheless *all people respond positively to respect and real interest.* The study of man's many and varied cultures indicates that in this regard all human beings are alike. Further, while there are differences among class, religious, national, and racial groups in this country, all are part of a total "American culture."

An example of what can happen when the concept "culture of poverty" is carried too far is described in Estelle Fuch's *Pickets at the Gates* (1966). A principal in a school that had shifted from predominantly white to Negro in the course of several years, wanted to prepare his new teachers, fresh from college, for the children they would be teaching. Drawing from the literature on the "deprived child," he wrote a letter stating that, compared with children from middle class homes, the school children would be poor financially, academically, and socially. Many would be on welfare; the school lunch would be the best meal they would get. Their mothers would be so busy with their "broods" that the individual child would be lonely. Often there would be no fathers in the home, and there would be no organized family activities. The children, he continued, would come from noisy atmospheres, and would not hear the quiet voice of the teacher until trained to give attention. They would have received no encouragement to achieve, and socially, economically, and culturally would be poor and not ready for school. This was true, he stated, of poor groups generally; the same characteristics found among our Negro and Puerto Rican families are found in Appalachia, among the hillbillies of the Ozarks, and among Mexican-Americans.

The unfortunate principal continued the letter with specific directives for handling these children and, proud of his efforts, sent a copy to each new teacher and also to the president of the PTA. He was shocked, hurt, and puzzled when irate Negro parents, active PTA'ers working hard to see that their children got the best education possible, promptly organized a picket line in front of the school, distributed a leaflet describing the principal's insulting attitude toward their children, and demanded his ouster.

The principal had utterly ignored wide variations within the Negro community. Further, by taking all the negative aspects of poverty and grouping them into a composite picture of all the children, he had drawn a picture that could only be false and damaging. It is one thing to say that in a poor community one would expect to find more bitter, angry, and withdrawn children, and greater difficulty mastering school lessons because of the tremendous objective difficulties with which many children are coping. It is quite another to say that children from poor families generally are uninterested in learning — an inference that unfortunately can so easily become a convenient rationale to excuse inadequate teaching and unequal school facilities in low income areas. Many are the working class families who aspire to a college education for their children (Purcell, 1964). Many also are the hard-working mothers without men at home, facing combined difficulties of bad housing, long hours, low pay, and inadequate community facilities for their children, who nonetheless give them a great deal of love, respect, and encouragement.

Wrenn (1962, pp. 31–32) warns against making premature judgments about family atmosphere based on demographic features alone. He writes:

> . . . Whatever the facts about birth rate, family size, and divorce, there are widely varying and deeply held opinions on these topics in any community. . . . There is little evidence that a small family or large one per se provides the "best" climate for child growth. Economic capacity to support the children's social and educational needs is a factor, but so also is the love support the child receives, the integrity of the family unit, and the general psychological climate of the home.
>
> Counselors should be knowledgeable about the interrelationship of such family factors and be slow to prejudge the home. . . . A counselor . . . needs to be wary of coming to conclusions about a family which may deviate from his stereotype of a "good" family.

Some literature on "disadvantaged children" begins to sound as if broken homes are the exclusive property of the poor. I have to comment here on the fact that in a parochial nursery school one of my children attended, half of the "white, middle class, Protestant" children in one grade were from broken homes, several were quite emotionally disturbed, and the mother of one was dying of acute alcoholism. Yet expectations for the children's performance were high, and the children were on the whole living up to them.

CULTURE CONCEPT AS A TOOL

Does this mean the "cultural" dimension should be abandoned entirely by the school counselor who is trying to help children from working class homes? The answer is no, *if it is used as a tool for reaching and understanding the individual as an individual, not for burying him behind generalizations about a group.* "Culture" refers in part to the general style of interpersonal relations and related attitudes that are traditional in a given society. It does not refer to the infinite variety of ways each individual feels and responds in dealing with his own life circumstances. In addition, the notion of cultural consistency becomes fuzzy when it is applied to class differences in our society. True, any definable group has what can be called a "culture." One can speak of the "culture" of different institutions — hospitals have different "cultures" on the whole from schools, and both from business houses. Within certain general patterns of "school culture," each school develops its own traditions. One can even speak of a certain "classroom culture," developed during the short lifetime of a common experience shared by a teacher and a group of children.

However, when one talks of anything as general as "working class culture" or "lower class culture," one must do so warily, and define what one means. On the one hand, it is part of American "culture" as a whole; on the other, the "working" or "lower" class includes many national, regional, religious, rural-urban, and income variations. Finally, as stated above, one is only referring to certain very general expectations for attitudes and behavior — one is not talking about how the individual incorporates these into his total self.

At present we know more about these general expectations for attitudes and behavior within the so-called "middle class" than we do for the "working class." Therefore, the best use that can be made of the culture concept is as a tool enabling the counselor to understand his own "values" — or, as others may see them, biases. He needs as open a mind as possible when attempting to develop rapport with children who are bitter, angry, or withdrawn, and with their families. Conrad Arensberg and Arthur Niehoff (1964), writing a manual for Americans overseas, felt that the basis for giving people insight into other cultures was to give them some understanding of their own unquestioned assumptions about how people should be motivated and how things should be done. They discuss the cluster of attitudes involving time, work, and money, historically based in the Protestant Reformation, and changing with time, but still functioning. Time as a commodity to be apportioned and either "spent well" or "wasted"; work as an activity important for its own sake, as well as a means to an end; money as a measure of personal worth (hence people's embarrassment about revealing their salary) — these tie together in a specifically

American pattern based on the assumption that effort leads to success. This pattern was well suited to a frontier country where hard work did indeed lead to financial success for many, and where the many more for whom it did not are forgotten. That effort will succeed is one of the most treasured of American beliefs. For "middle class" Americans, where it is more or less true, and for those from working class homes who have moved into a higher social status, it is so central a belief that they cannot empathize with those whose experiences have rendered it meaningless. On the whole, they are unable to see life in any other terms and hence are unable to communicate with children to whom the notion that effort will be rewarded has become an empty platitude.

Sensitivity with regard to his own attitudes enables the counselor to put himself in another's place — to *understand* rather than jump to a conclusion. On this basis, he is better able to assess materials he will be using, to evaluate forms of discourse he is employing. Do the filmstrips he is planning to use with a parent group deal realistically with the problems they are facing, or do they take a naïve and superficial approach that will only be a slap in the face? (This would be true of many psychologically oriented films geared to families living in quite comfortable circumstances.) How does the counselor introduce and evaluate test materials? What kinds of questions does he ask children who are in trouble? How meaningful is their experience to the counselor? How are children's problems reinforced by the role defined for them in the classroom? When the world is seen in their terms, do the children who appear unreachable reveal themselves as actually waging a desperate struggle for a sense of identity and self-respect?

Counselors already know the limits of testing and the fact that a child should not be assessed on the basis of test information alone. They also know that children from low income homes will generally do less well than those from middle income homes, even on the Rorschach and other projective tests of personality. Differences in previous educational experience of children, including familiarity with tests, and a bias in constructing and interpreting tests (a matter presently of concern to testing services) are partly responsible.

The problem of motivation is also important, as indicated by a study of the effect upon test scores of money incentives as compared with praise. Klugman (1944) tested a heterogeneous group of children twice, using the revised Stanford-Binet, and the second time offered some of the children money rewards for good scores. Whereas scores on a second testing generally rose somewhat, there was no demonstrable difference between the scores of those white children who were offered a money reward and those who were not. However, the Negro children given money rewards showed definitely better performances than those to whom praise was the only incentive. Now they had something real to work for!

How Not to Win Friends

An example of how a "middle class" cultural bias can hinder communication is afforded unfortunately by an "Inventory" of a "Child's Background of Experience and Interest" in an otherwise fine New York City guide for counseling (Board of Education of New York City, 1955–56). The first heading is "Fun at Home," the second, "Reading Fun." The child is asked about favorite activities at home, according to the sample questionnaire, and then, "Do you read aloud? To whom? Does anyone ever read to you? How much of your free time do you spend reading for fun? What kinds of books do you like best? What books have you read this term? How many books do you own?" Anyone who has worked in a low income neighborhood will recognize that this is hardly the way to establish rapport with a hurt and angry child.

The next topic is "Your Pet," with questions like, "Have you a pet? Who takes care of it?" Then, "Do you take lessons outside of school?" and, "Making and Collecting Things: What things did you make? What things do you want to make soon? What collections have you started?" Only then does the schedule come to less biased topics — helping around the house, friends, radio, TV, movies. The sensitive counselor would know that such questions could only further alienate a child from poor circumstances who is embittered and confused, and has been referred for help.

The consistent bias of school readers with their blond, suburban world that completely negates the existence of urban workers, and especially dark-skinned workers, has become a matter of concern. The presentation of life as a series of amiable and quite vapid incidents where all is "sweetness and light" is unhealthy not only for middle class children; it has become clear that it is especially hard on underprivileged and minority group children. Fortunately there are attempts to redress the situation. Illinois has a broad enough guidance program to plan improvements in texts and materials along these lines; Detroit has for some time been addressing itself to this problem; and the Bank Street readers picture urban scenes that include Negroes and Puerto Ricans as well as whites engaged in all manner of activities. However, it takes a long time to change a whole system of textbooks, and it is important for counselors, where it is part of their responsibility, to help introduce more varied materials into classroom libraries. This can be particularly helpful where there is an individualized reading program.

Another instance where the very existence of working class and minority group children is denied — but one that lends itself easily to improvements — involves the use of classroom walls. One can still enter classroom after classroom in our public schools without seeing a Negro adult or child pictured on the walls, and this extends to Puerto Ricans, Oriental people, Mexican-Americans. Classroom walls carry a clear message to the children as to what is and is not of value, and here an unhealthy message is being conveyed to children, white as well as nonwhite. Nor is this message fundamentally altered by posting a picture of Frederick Douglass during Brotherhood Month, along with a painting of a Negro and white child happily running hand in hand. A subsidiary message is only being added: pay lip service to the family of man at the appropriate times.

CREATIVE CHILDREN

A final point to develop in relation to cultural bias concerns the question of lost talent and creative children. Sometimes the more creative children are withdrawn, concentrating on their private thoughts, but often they are "difficult" or "rebellious" from a teacher's point-of-view (Wrenn, 1962, pp. 55–56). Generally, in handling too large a group it is a temptation for a teacher to value and lean heavily on the more conforming children. Unless she knows how to use the questions raised by more creative children, and feed them into discussions that are meaningful for the class as a whole, creative children become a problem to her.

When a creative child is from a low income home his difficulties are compounded, and his creativity is more likely to be channelled into unproductive rebellion. We have already mentioned the denial of his very being by classroom materials and exhibits. He is also likely to receive more punishment for transgressions in behavior than is a middle class child. First discussed by Davis and Dollard in their *Children of Bondage* (1940), this aspect of school life for children was further documented by Hollingshead in his *Elmtown's Youth* (1949). He gives in detail one incident in which a working-class youth was literally driven out of school in the course of an episode stemming from initial lateness, although a worse record of lateness had been ignored in the case of a wealthy boy (Hollingshead, 1949, pp. 185–198). In *Education and Income* (1961), Patricia Sexton carries the point further, and shows the extent to which differential punishment and other inequities for middle and low income children permeate an entire urban school system, and in *The American School* (Sexton, 1967) she summarizes more recent studies of these inequities.

The study of classroom life carried on by the present author under the auspices of the Bank Street College of Education revealed another type of punishment disadvantaged children experience to a greater extent than middle income children. This is the subtle but pervasive derogation of their personal experiences, which, unfortunately, can be conveyed even by kind and well-meaning teachers. For example, in one classroom an eight-year-old Negro boy talked eagerly and at length about the planes he had seen at the airport. The lesson was on transportation, and one would expect the teacher either to open up the child's account for class discussion, or to question him further. Or she might simply have said, as observed in other classrooms, "How wonderful," or "Good," and asked another question — unimaginative, perhaps, but at least approving. Instead, the teacher asked, "Who took you?" She was clearly puzzled, since children in this neighborhood presumably did not go on trips. Deflated, the child answered, "Day Care," and the incident was closed. A little enough episode, but when repeated many times in the course of a week, the result would well be what was witnessed in a higher grade in the same school — children listlessly sitting through the day.

When interviewed, the teacher said she felt the "middle class" content of school readers was desirable since there was nothing in the children's lives on which learning could be built. At least, she said, the readers held up an image of something better (a professional and suburban life) to which the children could aspire. It never occurred to her — nor does it to most teachers — how undermining this would be to Negro children for whom the "something better" was not only largely unobtainable, but also totally white. Given this, plus the other kinds of denial mentioned, one could only expect a self-respecting Negro child from a low income environment to meet school personnel with suspicion and growing anger. Many children express this passively through resistance of learning; others, especially those who have been deeply hurt at home as well, are moved to active rebellion.

The Counselor's Responsibility

It becomes the counselor's responsibility to help reach these children and, whereas one can be depressed at the difficulties of the task, one can, on the other hand, be impressed by how many of them appreciate and respond to the honest concern of a sincere and emphatic counselor. However, to return to the question of creativity, it is sometimes the potentially more creative children, those who in the long run might have more to offer, who give the counselor the hardest time, more consciously challenging him, putting him to the test. Thus a counselor, overburdened though he may be, must be wary of giving up too soon with a very difficult child. But he must deal with the reality of the child's total life situation, and not gloss over problems of inequality and discrimination with a wishful belief that individual effort will necessarily win success. One cannot expect to help a socially disadvantaged child simply to "conform," and this is even more true of a deeply thoughtful and sensitive child. The counselor must instead help him learn that certain forms of rebellion are pointless and self-destructive, whereas other forms are meaningful.

Wrenn writes that the school counselor must be " 'radical' in encouraging individualism . . . while at the same time he helps the student see the need for living within present societal expectations. . . ." He goes on to say that counselors are often accused of encouraging conformity, and it is indeed their responsibility to help students "learn systematically what is now known, to build a solid foundation of understanding the present." This is not an end in itself, however, but "the *means to the end* [italics his] of creating the new and of being oneself. To understand the present and be dissatisfied with it enough to change it . . . *is to complete the process* [italics his] of which present knowledge and socialization are but introductory steps" (Wrenn, 1962, p. 79). Marie Jahoda touches on the same point when she writes of positive mental health as involving "environmental mastery," in the sense that "hard reality" is not seen as "unchangeable and only the individual as modifiable" (Jahoda, 1958, p. 60). The individual must see himself as capable (along with others) of modifying environmental factors. In the last analysis, it is only on the basis of such an understanding that socially disadvantaged children really can be reached — precisely because they are *socially* disadvantaged — and this is not only for psychological reasons, but for ethical ones as well.

The School as a Social System

The concept of culture also has relevance for a totally different aspect of the guidance counselor's functioning, i.e., his role in the school as a social system. Here he has much in common with the applied anthropologist, for both are faced with an impossible task. Both must relate positively and constructively to virtually all members of a social system in order to enable the system to fulfill its functions more adequately. The counselor's role involves helping teachers and children communicate more effectively with each other, likewise teachers and parents, and even parents and children. It also involves smoothing the channels of communication throughout the administrative structure in relation to myriad special services. Above all, his responsibility is to help children relate to schooling more positively, and to encourage their willingness to be taught as the school sees teaching them. Inherent in his role is the implication that he must do this without stepping on any toes, taking his lead from the principal's and teachers' ideas and desires, always being helpful, not threatening or irritating anyone. Nor should he overstep his position with regard to teaching, which is the teacher's responsibility, or individual therapy, which is the school psychologist's province (if there is one), or administration, the task of the principal and his assistants. Yet his contribution to the school as a whole should be substantial.

As to what the science of anthropology has to offer, it is in part to generalize about what the good counselor has already learned from his own experience. As an innovator, he will have learned that many other things besides the intrinsic desirability of an innovation will determine whether or not it will be accepted. He will also have learned not to be unduly discouraged if he meets what seems to him totally unreasonable resistance to an innovation he feels essential. And he will have experienced the fact that success does not automatically lead to encouragement and praise. Insofar as he is socially wise, the counselor — like anyone working in an institution — will know that, while irrationalities vary from school to school, they are characteristic of "bureaucracy" in general. He will know that the better he understands his own institution, and the clearer he is in his own mind about what he wants to accomplish, the readier he will be to develop the most favorable avenues for broadening his program. He will have sized up the "decision-making structure" of his school — the role played by the principal in relation to the older group of teachers, and the influence of the senior teachers as compared with that of new appointees. He will be wary of being caught between diverse interest groups in the school, and of being forced to decide which to please or displease.

The anthropologist and sociologist rephrase this everyday experience of the counselor in terms of recurrent patterns in the operation of bureaucratized structures. Merton (1964) developed the point that the "manifest" functions of an institution — in this case the education of children — are not the same as the "latent" functions, or the various social and cultural pressures that operate as an institution perpetuates itself and attempts to expand its area of influence and control. For example, the concerns with job security, with promotion, with status and prestige, result in sometimes more hidden, sometimes more open jockeying for position in all institutions.

Furthermore, from a teacher's point-of-view, record keeping, management problems, and other "custodial" duties are constantly competing with the task of *teaching*, and each day presents the problem of trying to accomplish more than can be done. Any change in routine is thus a burden unless it clearly and immediately reduces the tasks to be carried out. However, innovation usually involves a greater expenditure of time and energy *now*, with, it is to be hoped, reduced time and energy — or at least increased success — later. Further, teachers have all too often had a backlog of experience with unsuccessful innovations. Thus, they are often "unreasonable" from the counselor's point-of-view, while the counselor may be seen as quite unrealistic from the teacher's point-of-view.

The wise counselor recognizes that, generally, teachers and adminis-

200 Anthropology in Education

trators, although trying to do the best job they can, respond to all manner of pressures and drives other than those related to the best education for children. If he is really wise the counselor will be able to assess his own limitations in this regard in the same terms that he assesses those of others. Before assuming their ineptitude or lack of interest, he will look for a "sociological" explanation rather than a more individual one for an existing irrationality, and on this basis seek a way to overcome the obstacle.

Arensberg, C. M., and Niehoff, A. H. *Introducing social change, a manual for Americans overseas.* Chicago: Aldine Publishing Company, 1964.
Davis, A., and Dollard, J. *Children of bondage.* New York: Harper & Row, 1940.
Fuchs, E. *Pickets at the gates, a problem in administration.* New York: Free Press, 1966.
Guidance of children in elementary schools. Curriculum Bulletin, 1955–56, No. 13, Board of Education of the City of New York.
Hollingshead, A. B. *Elmtown's youth.* New York: Wiley, 1949.
Jahoda, M. *Current concepts of positive mental health.* New York: Basic Books, 1958.
Klugman, S. F. The effect of money incentives versus praise upon the reliability and obtained scores of the revised Stanford-Binet test. *Journal of Psychology,* 1944, 30, 255–269.
Merton, R. K. *Social theory and social structure.* New York: Free Press, 1964.
Purcell, T. V. The hopes of Negro workers for their children. In A. B. Shostak and W. Gomberg (eds.), *Blue-collar world.* Englewood Cliffs, N.J.: Prentice-Hall, 1964.
Sexton, P. C. *Education and income, inequalities of opportunity in our public schools.* New York: Viking Press, 1961.
———. *The American school, a sociological analysis.* Englewood Cliffs, N.J.: Prentice-Hall, 1967.
Wrenn, C. G. *The counselor in a changing world.* Washington, D.C.: American Personnel and Guidance Association, 1962.

Banfield, Edward C. *The unheavenly city: the nature and future of our urban crisis.* Boston: Little, Brown, 1970. (See especially chap. 7: "Schooling versus education.")
Burnett, Jacquetta H. "Pattern and process in student life: a study of custom and social relationship among the students in an American high school." Unpublished dissertation, Teachers College, 1966.
Eddy, Elizabeth M. "Anthropology and guidance," in T. C. Hennessy (ed.), *Interdisciplinary roots of guidance.* New York: Fordham University Press, 1966.
Landes, Ruth. "An anthropologist looks at school counseling," in Stanten W. Webster (ed.), *The disadvantaged learner.* San Francisco: Chandler Publishing Company, 1966.
Leacock, Eleanor B. *Teaching and learning in city schools: a comparative study.* New York: Basic Books, Inc., 1969.
Lohman, Joseph D. *Cultural patterns in urban schools: a manual for teachers, counselors, and administrators.* Berkeley: University of California Press, 1967.

15

*A commitment to understanding the "whole" of relationships — social,
economic, political, and others — which mark the situation of any human
population in time and space underlies anthropology. As Redfield restates this:
"The classroom is important only as it is understood in its relation to the
society and culture of the children who occupy it, and teaching will be
effective only as it is related to society and culture." His position may not
reveal as much of the urgency many feel about some of the dire relationships
between the classroom and our society. Nor might it impress upon the reader
a sense of the need for us to consider alternatives to merely receiving
America, any more than the "middle-classness" of it, as its definitive expression. Yet the late Mr. Redfield recognized that until (and unless) these
relationships are systematically examined, a good part of the essential dy-
namism of teaching and learning, today, will continue to be dissipated in the
uncertainties of exactly what kind(s) of society for which we are educating the
young. It is to the systematic exposure of the relationships between a classroom and the society and culture(s) of which it is part that anthropology is
also committed. Redfield, who was Robert M. Hutchins Distinguished Professor of Anthropology, University of Chicago, speaks for all the authors in
Part Two by stressing for intending educators the perspective of teaching and
learning in the context of human community.*

ROBERT REDFIELD

A Contribution of Anthropology to the Education of the Teacher

This is far from the first time that an anthropologist has spoken as
such about education and teaching. Two other such occasions have fallen
within my own direct experience in recent years, and I have consulted the
records of these occasions to learn what I should say on this present occasion. The first occasion was a symposium on "Education and the Cultural
Process" held at Fisk University in March, 1941, and the other was a
symposium on "Environment and Education" held at the University of
Chicago in September of that same year. Altogether nine anthropologists
contributed ten papers [1, 2] to these two symposiums — all on some aspect

From *School Review*, vol. 53 (November 1945), published by The University of
Chicago Press. Copyright 1945 by The University of Chicago.

[1] *Education and the Cultural Process.* Papers presented at a symposium commemo-
rating the seventy-fifth anniversary of the founding of Fisk University, April 29–May 4,
1941. Edited by Charles S. Johnson. Reprinted from the *American Journal of Sociology,*
XLVIII (May, 1943). Individual papers of special interest to educators are:
Mead, Margaret. "Our Educational Emphases in Primitive Perspective," pp. 5–11.

of education or teaching as looked upon by an anthropologist. On reading over these papers, I receive a strong impression that, in spite of their apparent diversity, all these anthropologists are, at bottom, saying the same thing. Consequently I am led to entertain the idea that this is perhaps the only thing that anthropologists have to say, or perhaps that it is the most important thing, and that in either case it is what I had better try once more to say.

BASIC IDEA OF "A CULTURE"

This basic anthropological idea is that every individual lives within something called "a culture" — a body of customs and beliefs which provides satisfaction to his human needs and adjustment to his environment. This culture is thought of as something special to each of the many societies in which mankind lives, and it is the many special cultures, separable and comparable, which these anthropologists are usually thinking about when they talk about education. The people of the Trobriand Islands live within or in terms of a culture which is notably different in content from the culture of the Dakota Indians, and yet it is reported or assumed by these anthropologists that the Trobriand culture does the same thing for the people who happen to live as Trobrianders as that which is done by Dakota culture for the people who happen to be Dakota Indians.

A reading of these ten papers makes it evident that all the contributing anthropologists regard each of these cultures as having a necessary and important character: integration, or wholeness. In words used by Malinowski in his paper, each culture is "an organic unit." The customs and

---

Redfield, Robert. "Culture and Education in the Midwestern Highlands of Guatemala," pp. 12–20.

Malinowski, Bronislaw. "The Pan-African Problem of Culture Contact," pp. 21–37.

Watkins, Mark Hanna. "The West African 'Bush' School," pp. 38–47.

Mekeel, Scudder. "Education, Child-training, and Culture," pp. 48–53.

Benedict, Ruth. "Transmitting Our Democratic Heritage in the Schools," pp. 94–99.

Herskovits, Melville J. "Education and Cultural Dynamics," pp. 109–21.

Powdermaker, Hortense. "The Channeling of Negro Aggression by the Cultural Process," pp. 122–30.

[2] *Environment and Education.* A symposium held in connection with the fiftieth anniversary celebration at the University of Chicago. *Supplementary Educational Monographs,* No. 54. Chicago, 1942. Papers presented at the symposium are:

Burgess, Ernest W. "Educative Effects of Urban Environment," pp. 1–15.

Warner, W. Lloyd. "Educative Effects of Social Status," pp. 16–28.

Alexander, Franz. "Educative Influence of Personality Factors in the Environment," pp. 29–47.

Mead, Margaret. "Educative Effects of Social Environment as Disclosed by Studies of Primitive Societies," pp. 48–61.

Alexander, Franz. "Additional Remarks," pp. 62–66.

beliefs which are the parts of the whole are consistent with one another and depend on one another. Mekeel refers to such a culture as "an operational totality" and declares that every culture has "a matrix, a configuration, into which the pieces fit." He denies that a culture "is an index of easily movable items" and tells us that "it must be viewed as a meaningful whole." The Dakota Indians serve chicken and dog meat at a wedding feast, not simply because the two are palatable and available, but because chicken symbolizes the American way of life and dog meat the Indian way; in their situation, marginal to two cultures, both configurations are represented by meaningful symbols in the form of food. Mekeel goes on to tell us that even the ways in which very young children are trained in their excretory habits are consistent with the type of character which is adaptive to, or consistent with, their adult life and that, therefore, these ways of infant training are also parts of the culture, the integrated whole.

Plainly these anthropologists regard integrated culture with favor. They are not indifferent to it; they think it good that there be consistency and wholeness in the culture in terms of which the individual lives his life. The thing which it is thought that a culture does for an individual is a good thing. It is thought that the culture provides the individual with goals, with purpose and significance for his actions, and with the sense that all the activities he carries on are contributory toward realization of these goals. In such a culture the individual knows what he ought to do and finds himself doing it. Conversely, these anthropologists view with alarm attempts to educate without due reference to effects of the education in making the culture less integrated, less whole. Malinowski writes that "the anthropologist recognizes more and more fully how dangerous it is to tamper with any part or aspect of culture, lest unforeseeable consequences occur." As an example he chooses sorcery among African natives, advises caution to anyone trying to educate the natives out of a belief in sorcery, and tells us that, examined in its cultural setting, African sorcery turns out to be a crude but often effective way of managing misfortune, disease, and death and that the natives would be worse off without the sorcery than they are with it. He advises the teacher in Africa to abstain from trying to teach natives not to believe in sorcery, but rather to leave it alone until, by gradual introduction of hygiene and other security-giving modifications, the culture no longer has any place for sorcery, which will of itself disappear. Thus the picture we get of a culture is that of a complex structure in which all the parts are fitted together. The anthropologist tells us not to try to pull out a few pieces that we do not like lest the whole come tumbling down; he wants us to understand the relations of the parts to the whole and, guided by this knowledge, to accomplish a change in manner of life through gradual substitutions.

This conception of "a culture" is, it seems, a peculiar contribution of anthropology to the understanding of human behavior. It is a conception certainly related to, but not the same as, the conception of "human culture" — that aggregate of invention and institution which began when the first stick or stone was kept and its use was explained by one ancient primate to another. Culture in the general and singular serves to set off all mankind as against all animals. Culture in the particular and the plural serves to set one society off as against another. The idea of separate and comparable cultures, one to a local community, is an outgrowth of intimate study of tribal and peasant life in the past two or three generations. You do not find the conception in the pages of Edward Burnett Tylor or in those of Sumner's *Folkways*.[3] It appears in the detailed accounts of special primitive groups, finds its most eloquent and persuasive statement in the works of Malinowski, and is expressed also simply and compellingly in Ruth Benedict's *Patterns of Culture*.[4] As it is an idea that would naturally develop out of the study of the various primitive societies, it has been anthropologists who have developed it.

Significance to Education of Idea of Integrated Culture

If this is *the* important, or at least *an* important, contribution of anthropology to the understanding of human living, my assignment is to provide an answer to the question: What is the significance of the conception of integrated cultures to the training of teachers? Fortunately there is guidance in the papers of the symposiums to which I have referred. I will, however, state the matter as I see it and use the suggestions of these other anthropologists without making them responsible for the formulations that I reach.

In the first place, I assert that, merely because each of us, with few exceptions, grows up in one of these cultures and by this fact is limited in his understanding of his own conduct and that of other people, the coming to know another culture than our own should be a great liberalizing experience. I think, therefore, that the giving of this experience is a task of those who shape the programs of general education. The point I here make is thus a point for teachers in so far as teachers, like everybody else, should have a general education of which this element should be a part, and also for teachers in so far as teachers make the programs of general education for other people.

The end in view here is to bring the young person to understand that every normal human being is reared in a society with ways of life characteristic of that society; that these ways "make sense" as one way is seen

---

[3] William Graham Sumner. *Folkways: A Study of the Sociological Importance of Usages, Manners, Customs, Mores, and Morals*. Boston, 1907.
[4] Ruth Benedict. *Patterns of Culture*. New York, 1934.

to be related to the next, consistent with it and supporting it; that the motives which people have and the values which they embrace are derived, generally speaking, from this traditional culture. The further objective is to lead the young person to look back upon his own culture from the vantage point secured in the understanding gained of other cultures and thus achieve that objectivity and capacity to consider thoughtfully his own conduct and the institutions of his own society which are, in part, a result of thinking as if within another culture. On the one hand, the end is to cause the individual to see that there are ways other than his own which are compatible with human needs and with the dignity of the individual; on the other hand, the end is, through comprehension of another way of life, to develop the power to think well about one's own way of life so that that way may be improved. To some degree the study of anthropology provides this liberalizing experience through the acquaintance it gives with cultures other than our own, and much of the appeal which anthropology has for young people in schools and colleges comes from the fact that it provides such experience. I think this contribution primarily belongs, however, not in the training of anthropologists but in the general education of everybody. How to get it there is something that is yet to be determined.

Because we cannot move a tenth-grade class every afternoon to China or Central Africa, we shall have to teach about these countries chiefly through books and pictures. A principal requirement is time: vicarious acquaintance with, say, Chinese village culture might be sufficiently achieved in one or two years of persisting attention to the subject. I am sure that almost nothing is accomplished toward the end I have in view by the current practice in primary and secondary schools of dividing a year of social studies into short periods in each of which a new subject is taken up, at fortnightly intervals, from Russia to money or minority groups — and, indeed, I doubt that anything very important is accomplished toward any good end. In place of this succession of bowing acquaintances with miscellaneous subjects which are connected, I suppose, in one way or another with the modern world, I suggest the possibility of substituting a persisting and penetrating consideration of some society and culture notably different from our own and well provided with documentation. This might be a principal part of the social-studies curriculum at some place between the ninth and twelfth school years.

Significance to Teachers of Idea of Integrated Culture

This suggestion is an application of the conception of integrated cultures to the making of a curriculum in general education. I turn now to other ways in which the conception may be relevant to teaching. An application may be made of the conception of an integrated culture to the teaching activity itself. If cultures consist of an integration of customs and institutions, then teaching itself may be looked at as one such element more or less integrated in the culture of the community in which the teaching is carried out. This point is, indeed, made in several of the anthropological papers contributed to the two symposiums that I mentioned at the beginning of my remarks. Seeing formal education in its relation to other aspects of culture, these anthropologists are struck by its relative unimportance. They remind us at the beginning of their discussion that schooling is only a small part of education in the broad sense, "the process of cultural transmission and renewal." By the time the child comes to the teacher, he has already passed his most formative years, and the informal instruments of education have already largely shaped his world. What the school can do after that is correspondingly limited. Furthermore, what the school can do continues to be limited by the more powerful influences of the home, the play group, and the neighborhood. Do not expect to accomplish more than is possible, say these anthropologists to the teacher, and you may successfully teach that which finds some support, some basis of consistency, with the culture as it is transmitted in informal communication outside the schoolroom. So Mekeel is not surprised that Indian children, after many years of residence in government schools, in which attempts are made to teach the ways of white men, so often return to Indian life. So Malinowski warns the teacher in Africa not to separate, by his teaching, the child from the native community where he enjoys the warmth and security of life in an integrated culture. The lesson for the teacher from such observations is that teaching is not to be regarded as a technique of inculcation or of stimulation learned from books or from other teachers and thence applicable to a classroom, as medicine may be administered to a sick man, or fertilizer to a farmer's field. The suggested application is that teaching is effective in so far as it tends toward the development in the young person of a coherent body of attitudes and values adequate to the life-needs in his particular community. The classroom is important only as it is understood in its relation to the society and culture of the children who occupy it, and teaching will be effective only as it is related to society and culture.

Being established in the viewpoint of culture as an organic unity, anthropologists seem to be calling upon the teacher to understand, not so much teaching methods, as the community in which the teaching takes place. The real nature of effective teaching, these anthropologists are in effect declaring, lies, not in ways of preparing instruction units nor in devices for testing reading comprehension, but rather in the part played by the school and by what goes on in the school in the cultural life of the children's community. I suspect that in this the anthropologists are telling the teachers to look to matters which teachers in fact do constantly look to because they cannot help it, even though these are not matters that bulk large in the formal training of teachers. In one of the symposium papers Warner looks at the school in the community as he would look at initiation rites in a primitive society, as from the outside. He finds that the high school in the American towns that he has studied is one of many institutions which express and maintain, among other things, the system of ranking according to social status which characterizes the society. The lower-class pupils study commercial and technical courses. The upper-class children takes courses that prepare them for college. The children of each class are taught what will fit them for the station in life which it is expected they will assume. Moreover, he finds a marked tendency to classify children in supposed intelligence groups according to the social positions of their parents, so that a child from the upper class is not put in the lowest intelligence group even if his individual performance might put him there. Still further, he finds that what teachers do to warp theoretically impartial educational procedures to fit the local cultures is done largely because the same result is accomplished anyway by the informal groupings of children in and out of the school. The children's cliques bring about an assorting of children according to their parents' social positions, and the school, in effect, is conforming to these other less visible institutions. Warner is thus applying the conception of an integrated culture to the school and its community. "Understand these," he seems to say to the teacher, "if you would understand what your teaching does, can do, and cannot do."

Significance of Idea of Culture in Modern Schools

The possibility that teaching will not be integrated with the rest of the cultural life of the child is, obviously, increased to the degree that the teacher represents a way of life different from that of the child. The possibility will be very great when an outsider comes to teach in a native community, whether the community be one of Africans or Indians or Kentucky mountaineers. Missionary teaching is often ineffective or disintegrating because it is not related or is unwisely related to the local culture. But the same danger exists, in compound form, in urban schools where the children represent not one integrated culture but many disintegrated cultures, and the teacher not only does not, but could not, teach to develop a single coherent integration if he wanted to. What, then, is the significance of the conception of the individual in one integrated culture in connection with teaching in a society where there is no integrated culture? What is the value of this anthropological conception, developed in primitive society, in modern urban society? It is all very well for the anthropologist to advise the teacher what he may do or even should do in teaching Indians or native Africans, but what can the anthropologist helpfully tell the modern teacher in a modern school?

Half of the answer depends on the extent to which the modern city community is like an Indian tribe or an African village, and part of this half of the answer is given by Warner when he, in effect, urges the student of teaching to study the school in its community. If the student does so, he will find the extent to which the school is integrated with other institutions and helps to perpetuate a local culture. Part of this same half of the answer is expressed in Mead's paper read at the Fisk University symposium. This anthropologist considers the function, not of the school in the community, but of the whole institution of education in modern society, as if she were studying warfare in New Guinea. She finds that its function is different from the function of education in primitive societies. In primitive societies education depends, she says, on the will to learn something that everybody assumes one would want to learn. In modern society it depends on the will to teach something that somebody thinks ought to be taught, even though not everybody wants to learn it. This different nature of education in modern society leads, she goes on to tell us, to a conception of education as something that may not so much perpetuate an old society as make a new one. The society it may make is so new that none of us living now is able to say what it will be, and yet it is supposed that these children whom you and I educate, or their children, will make that society and that the kind of education we give them will somehow fit them for doing so. This is indeed a far cry from the way in which a tribal Indian or isolated African native would look at the educational institutions of his own society. He thinks of education, so far as he thinks of it at all, as something that will perpetuate the kind of life which he has always known. Mead is telling us that, just as modern society is different, in kind, from all primitive societies, taken as another kind, so education is and must be different.

What is this difference in the two kinds of societies or cultures? In the paper that she contributed to the Chicago symposium, Mead enumerates three differences: (1) Primitive cultures are homogeneous, while ours is heterogeneous. (2) Primitive cultures change very slowly, while ours changes rapidly and constantly. (3) The population stocks of primitive societies are relatively less diversified than are ours. Mead thereby recognizes that modern urban culture is different in kind from all primitive societies. As the culture is changing rapidly and constantly, there cannot be one well-integrated culture. What children do is different from what adults do, and indeed adults come to think — some of them — that it is right that children do something different. Moreover, the changes come so rapidly that during the school years of one individual he may be taught completely inconsistent ideas. Benedict, in her paper, makes this point.

There are periods when we tell children to be saving of money; there are others when it is a public duty to spend. There have been recent periods when war was unexceptionally evil and "the earth was unanimous for peace," and there have been more recent periods when, as she says, you might go to jail for saying so. As our culture is always changing and is never integrated, Benedict concludes that "education in our world today must prepare our children to adapt themselves to unforeseeable conditions."

At this point it is apparent that the conception of an integrated culture has undergone some significant alteration. The anthropologists to whom we have looked for guidance began by telling us that every individual lives in a well-integrated culture. Now some of them seem to be confirming our suspicions that, in the case of our own society, no individual does. The question may then be repeated: What is the significance of the conception of the individual in one integrated culture in connection with teaching in a society where there is no one integrated culture? Again, the first half of the answer may be repeated: In some degree, as in Warner's studies of the place of the school in the status system, there is integration in modern society, and the school is part of that integration. But the other half of the answer may be given also. The value of the conception of the individual in a well-integrated culture lies, in part, in the suggestive contrast between our own case and the case of the stable primitive societies. We should not so well see the peculiar problems and responsibilities of modern education if we did not see modern education as a special and variant case of education in all societies. That it is special and variant is expressly stated by Mead. In stable societies with well-integrated cultures, all educative influences, she says, operate simultaneously and consistently upon the individual, and she has illustrated this fact vividly in her series of photographs showing the treatment accorded babies in Bali. But in our heterogeneous and changing society there is a qualitative difference, she says; what the radio says may be quite unrelated to what mother says to baby, and what mother-in-law over in the corner manages to convey by a gesture is emphatically in contradiction. It is the inconsistencies, the lack of integration, that make our society different from stable primitive societies. In a sort of definition by indefinition, it is this lack of integration which gives our society its character. Interestingly enough, of all the contributors to these two symposiums, it is not an anthropologist but a psychiatrist, Franz Alexander, who says this most plainly. "Paradoxically stated," he says, "the pattern of our world is that it has no fixed pattern." For the psychiatrist the significance of this conclusion lies in the need to study individual careers in terms of individual life-histories. For the teacher the significance lies in the need to develop the capacities of the individual to deal with circumstances which the teacher cannot foresee.

THE TEACHER'S TASK

The conception of one integrated culture leads, therefore, to a view of the task of the teacher which sees it as double. The conception is helpful to the teacher, in part because it is directly applicable to the child in "this" school in "this" community. The conception is helpful, in part because it is not directly applicable. The apparent contradiction is resolved by distinguishing the short run in time and the local setting from the long run in time and the wider setting. So far as the short span of years is concerned, and in the local neighborhood (especially if that neighborhood be in one of the more stable towns and not in a community of rapidly changing population), the school will be found reasonably well integrated with the rest of the cultural life, and what can be accomplished by the teacher will be limited by these relationships which it is, therefore, necessary for him to understand. On the other hand, the school is an instrument for social change and is accepted as such, both by laymen and by educational leaders. For example, while it is true, as Warner says, that the high school perpetuates the status system of the community, it is also true, as Mead says in her paper read at Fisk University, that education is a recognized means by which the individual may leave his social rank and move to another. For the more remote future, education, to us, exists to develop powers to deal with contingencies beyond our powers of prediction. Children are to be educated so as to find what personal and cultural security they can find in the communities that now exist, and they are also to be educated to make, by effort and understanding, new integrations out of whatever pieces of living the future may bring them. The teacher today is both a perpetuator of an old integration and a builder of the power to meet disintegration. If a paradox remains, it is not one that I have invented; it exists in the nature of modern life.

FURTHER READINGS

Carse, William. "Teacher education in culture change," in Joseph C. Finney (ed.), *Culture change, mental health, and poverty*. Lexington: University of Kentucky Press, 1969.

Deutsch, Martin. *Minority group and class status as related to social and personality factors in scholastic achievement*. Monograph No. 2, Society for Applied Anthropology, 1960.

Hall, Edward. *The silent language*. Garden City, N.Y.: Doubleday, 1959.

Labov, William, and Clarence Robins. "A note on the relation of reading failure to peer-group status in urban ghettos," *The TC Record*, vol. 70 (February 1969).

Stenhouse, Lawrence. *Culture and education*. New York: Weybright and Talley, 1967.

PART THREE

ANTHROPOLOGY OF EDUCATION

Anthropology is a means to information; it is an inquiry. Anthropological inquiry has both a descriptive and an analytic side. Its descriptive activity is distinguished, most would agree, by three features: it is localized, it is prolonged, and it is intense. This is to say that anthropological description results from research which is done on site, for extended periods of time, and, in theory, to the exclusion of all other interests.

The descriptive activity of anthropology is observational; anthropology disdains experiment and only admits survey and other research methodologies selectively, utilizing these where the context of information gained (or checked) by them is established, usually by prior observation. Anthropological inquiry also eschews conceptual overloads, choosing to travel light in constant expectation of organizing ideas that emerge, as if jumping out, from gathered data. Culture is one of the few concepts with which anthropologists enter field situations, and it acts as the primary device of description.

Educational encounters, whether these occur in formal or informal settings, tend not to repeat laboratory models — if indeed they will submit, in some of their respects, to satisfactory models at all. They are moments of action and response, fluid and sometimes nonverbal. And, although their caprice has been overstated, the events of teaching and learning do manage to trouble even the most precise, comprehensive research strategies, as any educator who has attempted classroom observation will attest.

Nonetheless, conventional research and evaluation procedures in education exploit arbitrary environments, statistical measures, and "problems" in seeking (often basic) information about what goes on in educational encounters and in building knowledge of educational processes and structures. Anthropology offers a considerable expertise to traditional educational research in this regard. One distinction of anthropological inquiry is that it describes "natural" environments and ground-level behavior. The descriptive activity of anthropology concerns what people are observed to *do*, not simply what people *say* they are doing or what they claim *ought* to be done. Much educational research (and particularly evaluation — formative or summative) suffers the confusion of actual behavior and normative behavior. In a sense the problem of relevance in contemporary American public schooling is, in fact, a failure on the part of schoolmen to recognize the inconsistencies, contradictions, and paradoxes youth confront in trying to make sense of differences between actual and normative behavior. Further, the disposition of traditional educational research to generalize, and attempt application of, findings from the study of arbitrary environments and normative behavior to "natural" environments of "real" behavior is much less a tendency *of the past* than contemporary technically impressive research methods and sophisticated analyses of data would have us believe.

If the craft of anthropological inquiry applies to educational research, it is also true that a great deal of the anthropology of education answers mostly to the profession of *anthropology*. The anthropology of education is considered to be, in the eyes of the discipline, "real" anthropology. The largely parochial perspective of professional anthropology views those who perform as anthropologists *of* education to have convenienced themselves by choosing educational settings and problems, rather than economic, legal, or political settings and/or problems. Most anthropologists whose primary interest is the anthropology of education are inclined to reciprocate this view. They have a marked tendency to assess their work as *anthropology*; they have in their view a prior and fixed commitment to the discipline and to whatever will advance disciplinary interests, theoretical or practical.

All this, one might expect, sustains (at best) a delicate and guarded cooperation between educators and anthropologists in educational research and (at worst) barely submerged antagonisms between the two professions that are expressed, frequently, as emotional contrasts between "them, the educationists" and "them, the anthropologists." It has made, and continues to make, cooperative research difficult.

The two groups of writings that comprise Part Three refer to the anthropology *of* education. It is editorial bias that these selections do not correspond to the situation of extremes just discussed. The intention of the editors is to suggest, through the following articles, some of the range, depth, and possibilities of the anthropology of education — *both* to educators and anthropologists. Meaning to accomplish this, we find that additional biases are at work: first, in the selection of these articles; second, in the judgment that these articles do represent, or *can* be referred to as, the anthropology of education — a bias which the authors, here, may or may not share.

As in Part Two, space limitations have prevented including several basic writings.[1] The articles that follow have been selected for their expression of the range, depth, and possibilities of the anthropology of education and, also, for the variety of educational topics and techniques of anthropological inquiry they articulate. The first section selections exemplify general approaches of anthropology to education, its processes and structures, and relationships between education and the complex of behavioral institutions that characterize society.

Mr. Kimball, thus, elaborates what he identifies as the "educative process" in treating the sociocultural context of learning. Similarly, Mr. Wallace relates kinds of educational emphases to phases of societal development. The contribution of Mrs. Rosenstiel, restates much of the assertion of anthropological relevance to the study of education, while introducing its (mostly unrealized) potential to early childhood education. The approach that Mr. Freedman and Mr. Omark use, more controversial and perhaps more indefinite than any of the others, explores the biosocial nature of human development, seen comparatively, to formal schooling.

The writings of the second section exemplify specific approaches to studying problematic educational phenomena. Though the articles in both sections of Part Three balance description and analysis, those of the second section favor analysis. The analytic activity of, or dimension to, anthropology — its systematic attempt to elucidate sociocultural phenomena, to manipulate descriptive data gained largely through observation in such a way (or ways) as to not only explain behavior but also to *predict* behavioral outcomes or consequences — differs significantly from that of the remaining social sciences. The capacity of anthropology for prediction is, by comparison, small, and the discipline seems constantly to threaten to be inconclusive altogether.

Yet, anthropology is mainly *retrodictive*. The discipline fundamentally engages in predicting "backward," that is, in specifying events, processes, system interactions, material conditions, or other structures of behavior that causally relate to *known*, usually contem-

---

[1] The most noteworthy of these is Jules Henry, "A Cross-cultural Outline of Education," in *Current Anthropology*, vol. 1, no. 4 (July, 1960) pp. 267–305.

porary, behavior — physical anthropology and archaeology being exceptions — to the observer. In this sense anthropology is a form of history (or, some argue, vice versa).

The second section articles, favoring analysis, tend to be more conclusive, which is in part a function of the problems each author sets out to inform, if not to solve. The specificity of the articles is also due in part to the less than wide scale of the research reported or of the behavioral phenomena in focus, and in part to the concern of the authors to detail research tactics.

Both Mrs. Burnett and Mr. Lacey, for instance, delineate the procedure of their inquiry, and both work to define the conceptual organization of their studies. Mr. Wax, in his discussion of American Indian education, scrutinizes current and historical policies and practices of the "superordinate" society to which the Indian is subject in seeking precise understandings of the dilemma of Indian education. Wax's analysis leads to a model of cross-cultural education in much the same way that Mr. Gallaher selects out a strategy for effective educational change from an initial array of contextual insights into the change process and the nature of formal organization.

The interest that has grown about classroom observation, formative evaluation, and such programmatic efforts at teacher behavior modification as micro-teaching is increasingly informed by anthropological inquiry — in both its dimensions. The influence of anthropological field techniques is a particular example. At the same time, larger numbers of anthropologists are finding, if not seeking, the behavioral expression of "classic" research interests in schools and the processes of schooling.

The articles in Part Three indicate the kinds of expertise anthropology offers to educational research. They also convincingly display the diversity and challenge of behavioral problems that education provides anthropologists. The anthropology *of* education that continues to result from these mutual opportunities — antagonisms and disciplinary imperatives aside — ultimately benefits those who learn as well as those who teach. These articles were written in the spirit of that vital promise, and, in the conviction that such a promise is "real" and not an empty claim, they are included here.

A. SOME GENERAL APPROACHES

16

The activity of teaching and learning, wherever situated, is influenced partly by the cultural patterns it promotes, repudiates, or in which it otherwise traffics, and partly by the structure of its social organization. Mr. Kimball, Graduate Research Professor, University of Florida, articulates some fundamental relations by and through which these influences are realized. His expression of concern that the ways we generally organize teaching and learning in our society may in effect be subverting meaningful learning experiences is repeated, today, in discussions of curricula of "affect," "open" classrooms, and countless other devices of reform and renewal. The basic restructuring of teacher-learner relationships, of the environment of learning, remains problematic and subject still to visions like that of Kimball and Mead (Part One). Why that is so deserves anthropological explanation among those of the other social sciences, and Mr. Kimball offers one route to such explanation here. A respected and frequent contributor to the body of published work in anthropology and education, Mr. Kimball is General Editor of the Series in Anthropology and Education published by Teachers College Press.

SOLON T. KIMBALL

An Anthropological View of Social System and Learning

The recent stirrings among groups of educators to reexamine their basic concepts and techniques and to look to the social and behavioral sciences for new ideas is of interest to those of us who work in the beha-

Reprint with permission of the publisher from Esther Lloyd-Jones's *Behavioral Science and Guidance: Prospects and Perspectives* (New York: Teachers College Press, 1963).

215

vioral sciences. The receptivity of educators offers an unusual opportunity to the various social science disciplines to make known their special qualifications and, cooperatively, to advance the cause of education.

As an anthropologist who, for several years, has been concerned with applying the principles of anthropology to educational problems, I welcome this specific opportunity to present to a group so strategically related to the educational enterprise some remarks about the field of interest, research methods, and point of view of anthropology.[1] After briefly describing the range of subjects with which anthropologists deal, I shall concentrate upon the educative process. In particular, I wish to examine the relation between organizational environment and learning, since this is a crucial and, until recently, neglected area.

THE FIELD OF ANTHROPOLOGY

Anthropology is the study of man. Its main focus has always been on elucidating the linguistic, interpersonal, and technical patterns man exhibits in his religious, social, and economic behavior; on relations between cultural behavior and prevailing conditions; and on the processes that explicate change. Of necessity, our search has carried us into areas of interest that we share with other disciplines. Our concern with man as a physical organism links us to biology and physiology; we overlap with psychology in the study of learning and personality; we possess a common field with sociology in the study of social systems. Our concern with symbolic behavior and cultural development gives us ties to the humanities through history, literature, religion, and the arts.

Our historical attention to relatively simple cultures possessing limited population has enabled us to develop techniques which permit us to encompass the whole of their lives and to seek for the interdependencies which unite the disparate elements into a cohesive whole. In recent years, some of us have brought our methods and points of view to the study of complex civilizations like our own and have reached a stage where we are ready to make predictions and propose courses of action for cultural and organizational modification. This last activity we label *applied* anthropology.

Anthropology is a field science. We are skeptical, if not downright contemptuous, of the armchair scholar. We insist that one can learn only by dealing with real people in their native setting. This bias has limited our use of the experimental method, which we are likely to look upon as a contrived approach in which the results may or may not be applicable to

---

[1] George Spindler (ed.), *Education and Anthropology* (Stanford, Calif.: Stanford University Press, 1955).

an existing situation. Actually, we should utilize experiments to a greater extent, but up to now the great variability in the cultures of the world has provided us with those data needed for cross-cultural, comparative analysis. We are not opposed to quantification, but we use it very little, and, as a consequence, we do not rely upon statistical analysis. Instead, we seek to work out cultural patterns or social systems by examining the traits or components and the relationships which unite these.

Anthropology's scientific tradition comes from biology rather than from physical science. Hence, it emphasizes the inductive approach and utilizes the natural history method in examining systems as events in a time span which stretches from origin to infinity. Its analytical techniques organize data in two different ways: (1) by grouping them as types or classes in taxonomic schemes; and (2) by describing them as whole systems.[2]

From this emphasis upon the whole has come the organization and content of our many studies of tribal and community life. In them we have made explicit the relationships which join individuals together in familial, economic, political, or religious groups and activities. We have also classified groups by cultural and biological qualities, such as sex, age, status, and other identifying characteristics. But we have also been concerned with the processes of change in the lives of individuals and of groups. For the individual these are contained within the dynamics of enculturation and socialization, and in the stages which accompany the progression from birth to death ceremonially observed in rites of passage.[3] For the group, change may be primarily the rhythmic recurrences of seasons celebrated in rites of intensification,[4] or it may be the more far-reaching disturbances that arise from environmental or human causes.

Attention to the organic unity of individual, system, or group is an essential component of the anthropological point of view. But the anthropologist pursues also a cosmic interest and seeks, through time and variability, to distinguish the relative from the universal aspects of human behavior and socio-cultural systems. Hence our concern with probing the past and our comparisons between contemporary cultures and institutions.

The Potential of Anthropology for Educational Research

First, the fusion of the humanistic and scientific traditions in anthropology, which is a concomitant of its concern with all the aspects of

[2] Solon T. Kimball. "The Method of Natural History and Educational Research," in George Spindler, *op. cit.*, pp. 82–85.

[3] Arnold Van Gennep. *The Rites of Passage* (Chicago: University of Chicago Press, 1960).

[4] E. D. Chapple and C. S. Coon. "Rites of Intensification," in Chapple and Coon (eds.), *Principles of Anthropology* (New York: Henry Holt, 1942), Chap. 21, pp. 507–528.

culture, offers a way to overcome the limiting and crippling effects of their separation, described by C. P. Snow in *The Two Cultures*.[5] An anthropological analysis of educational practices could bring the excessive fragmentation which characterizes so much liberal education today into clearer focus, and set up counteracting forces. The end result could be to reinvigorate general education from the uneasy sterility into which it has fallen.

Second, the nature of the anthropological perspective itself presents provocative possibilities for analysis, research and interpretation in education. Foremost among the many elements incorporated in this perspective are its cosmic panorama which encompasses human activity from the far reaches of man's origin to the present; its conscious and careful endeavor to achieve nonjudgmental treatment of practice and belief among varied peoples; its search for fundamentals in structure and symbol; its ascription of dignity to all peoples; and its retention of a sense of wonder in the orderliness of the universe. From these elements of the anthropological perspective emerge, many believe, more comprehensive explanations of the behavior of individuals and groups, past and present, and a brighter illumination of the events of "the now."

A third potentiality of anthropology lies in the recently initiated application of the natural history method of data analysis to the teaching-learning situation. When this new application of the natural history method is fully developed and in operation we will possess our first truly scientifically derived method for studying pedagogy as a totality.[6] And the possible utilizations of this anthropological method are not limited to research within the classroom. All educational problems that require, for their solution, research on the operation of on-going systems are accessible through this method. These range from the elucidation of clique arrangements of students and teachers, to the analysis of subcultural age groups, or to the study of educational progression as a series of transitional stages which may be marked by rites of passage.

These, then, constitute three of the general potentialities that anthropology holds for educational research. But, before considering the more specific applications of any one of them, we need to demonstrate in more detail the apposition between anthropological concerns and contemporary educational problems. To that end let us examine briefly the relation between learning as a universal cultural process and the formal educational system as it is organized in our society.

[5] C. P. Snow. *The Two Cultures and the Scientific Revolution* (New York: Cambridge University Press, 1959).

[6] Solon T. Kimball. "Darwin and the Future of Education," *The Educational Forum*, XXV, Nov. 1960, pp. 59–72.

The Educational Process in Anthropological Perspective

The educational process has always been a central concern of anthropologists. Transmission, diffusion, and innovation are terms which refer to activities in which there is an implicit assumption that skills, knowledge, and values are acquired by one group from another. Explanations for the dynamics of cultural persistence and change have been sought by anthropologists within the mechanisms whereby one generation transmits its culture to another and modifies or innovates cultural practices — whether through borrowing from other societies or through the indigenous invention of new cultural practices.

When examined analytically, however, the transmission of the cultural heritage is no simple procedure, even among small, non-literate tribal groups. To seek out its particulars one must specify who teaches what to whom, how, where, and under what circumstances. One must also observe the situations in which there is no apparent effort to teach, but in which the uninstructed successfully imitate the behavior they have witnessed. We know that in the unconscious acts of parents and older siblings toward the very young bases for apprehending and interpreting later experience are laid. These predispositions, induced during infancy, are thought to provide the hard core of personality manifest through later life and passed on to their own children through the subtle process of child rearing.[7]

Nor do these infant learnings exhaust the range that can profitably be studied by anthropological methods. In play and peer-group activities a strange intermixture of conscious aping of adult ways combined with an apparently spontaneous, age-graded behavior is found. Behavior must progressively be learned and then abandoned as the child moves inexorably through adolescence to adult stature and ultimately to old age and death.

Much of the content of anthropological studies of learning in small, non-literate tribal groups seems fully applicable to the study of the educative process in contemporary America. One main and crucial difference in the two situations, however, must be taken into account. In tribal and agrarian societies, practically all the child needs to learn in order to assume full adult status is obtained outside the purview of a conscious, planned, and deliberate educational program. Only among those groups that devote brief periods of instruction preparatory to initiation ceremonies, or in the extended relationship of neophyte to priest or medicine-man,

[7] Geoffrey Gorer. "The Concept of National Character," in Clyde Kluckhohn and Henry A. Murray (eds.), *Personality: In Nature, Society and Culture* (New York: Alfred A. Knopf, 1953), pp. 246–259.

do we have a situation which resembles our own. By contrast, we hold our young captive for many years in an elaborately contrived system to prepare them for participation in the essential activities of society.

We are agreed that this system of education is the crucial and central instrument through which we gradually separate our children from home and family and equip them to establish themselves in the public world in whatever role and place their opportunity and destiny may determine. Yet we may not be fully aware of its structural position in the counterpoise of the nuclear family and the complex of social superstructures. Education's pivotal position becomes clearer if we search for the linkage which unites the private world of the nuclear family and the public world of the great superstructures, for we then discover that education is the major connection between the two. The organizational patterns of the schools are in effect bridges and the educative process provides the skills which our children must gain in their movement out of youth into full adulthood. Thus, in both its structural and functional aspects we must view the school as unique among our great social superstructures.

That our formal, institutional organization of education is unique and essential in our society becomes clear when it is regarded in the context of our other institutions organized for economic, political, religious, familial, or other purposes.

I have already remarked that informal educative processes — which take place in family, peer group, and locality and which mold perspective, shape character, and determine behavior — are one dimension of cultural learning and take place in all societies. Extensive, formal education, on the other hand, arises from the demands of a complex society and serves other purposes. It acts something like the locks of a canal — taking individuals by sequential stages from their family and friendship groups to the public world of work and social responsibility.

The structure and the function of the system of formal education will be molded both by the current demands of the other social superstructures and by the pattern of their development over time. Ours is now a cosmopolitan society, industrial in its technological orientation, pragmatic in outlook and scientific in spirit. The Main Street towns and their symbiotically related rural neighborhoods, which for over half a century following the Civil War held the essence of the national spirit, have now become residual. With their decline has come the loss of the cohesive community with its internal status-differentials expressed in social classes. In place of the cohesive community we now possess the sprawling metropolitan aggregate in which the central portion of the older cities is gradually reforming itself into a mosaic pattern of cultural enclaves, and, while dispossessed agarians are feeding into and perpetuating older slums, the middle class is withdrawing to the sanctuary of the burgeoning suburbs.

Nearly all of our behavior takes place within one or another of two principal types of social groupings — within the nuclear family of parents and children or informal clusters of peers on the one hand, or in one or more of the great corporately organized superstructures of education, business, government, industry, or health, on the other. It is through this latter series of interconnected, interdependent organizations that we discharge our public or societal responsibilities, and through them we in turn receive those innumerable goods and services by which we sustain life, derive comfort and pleasure, and strive to fulfill our hopes and aspirations. We are all members of the great cooperative enterprises through which these tasks are accomplished and goals realized. It is the mission of the schools to prepare us for this membership.

CRITICISMS OF THE EDUCATIONAL ENTERPRISE

If we took seriously all that the critics have said about education during the past ten years, we might give over to despair. The effectiveness with which our schools fulfill their mission has been questioned at many levels and from many sources. Some critics have hacked at bits and pieces of the educational edifice, exposing deficiencies and nonsense; others have leveled charges that are broad, sensational, and frequently ill-informed, if not irresponsible; others have struggled to evolve constructive reforms. All, however, appear unconscious either of the social issues which are currently agitating our society or of the relation between these issues and the process of cultural transformation which has generated them. They seem not to understand the interdependence between school organization and educational process, nor even, perhaps, the unique and solitary responsibility of the schools as the means of transition between the nuclear family and corporate organization.

In general, their narrow and completely erroneous assumption is that all we need do, to put our educational system in good order, is change what happens in the classroom. They further assume that what happens in the classroom can be changed simply by reorganizing the curriculum, beefing up the substance in subject matter, and modifying the methods of instruction. No one will deny that substantial improvement in these areas should be achieved, or minimize the thoughtful and sincere efforts of those who have directed their attention to the possibilities.[8] But no anthropologist could accept the implicit assumption that the educative process is divorced from its social environment. The learning situation is very far from being the atomistically conceived procedure implied by this approach.

[8] William VanTil. "Is Progressive Education Obsolete," *Saturday Review*, Feb. 17, 1962, pp. 56–57, 82–84.

RESEARCH AND THE EDUCATIONAL ENTERPRISE

It is logical to assume that, in a scientifically oriented society such as our own, plans for modifications and changes in a system will be based on the results of research. A major difficulty with most of the available educational research until very recently has been that it has been as atomistic in conception as the attacks leveled by education's critics. Educators in the past have not turned to research to settle broad policy questions — questions critical for every aspect of the educational enterprise. Innovations have been primarily trial-and-error responses to changing conditions, as these conditions were viewed by the innovators, and has included both wholesale borrowing and indigenous developments.[9] Research which might have placed these conditions and their implications for education in a clearer light, thus giving direction to change, and research which would have assessed the effects of innovation has, for the most part, not yet been undertaken.

The available research has tended to be marginal or subsidiary to the over-all problem. School surveys, statistical compilations, and attitudinal studies, which abound, for example, tend to be marginal in their usefulness. Psychological research, whose contributions outweigh those of any other field, has resulted in valuable findings which are, however, subsidiary to the major problems of system, and the implications of which have not been carefully assessed. Thus, the tests and measurements which have been widely adopted for differentiating student capabilities and performances have come under heavy attack from many sources and the next ten years will doubtless witness radical changes in their form and use. Results of experiments in learning, perception, and reading have been applied in programming for machine teaching, in the construction of textbooks, and in teaching methods.

Until the last few years, the chief contributions of the other social sciences have been a brief splurge in the now moribund use of sociometrics and an awareness of the significance of social class background to school performance.[10] In addition, of course, sociology and anthropology have indirectly influenced the viewpoint of teachers and subject matter in ethnic and racial relations, socialization of the child, personality, cultural relativity, and so on. To the extent that these fields have broadened the perspective of teachers and enriched academic programs, the results should be counted as positive.

[9] Lawrence A. Cremin. *The Transformation of the School* (New York: Alfred A. Knopf, 1961), chap. II, "Education and Industry," pp. 23–57.
[10] W. Lloyd Warner, Robert J. Havighurst, and Martin B. Loeb. *Who Shall Be Educated?* (New York: Harper and Brothers, 1944). A. G. Hollingshead. *Elmtown's Youth* (New York: John Wiley and Sons, 1949).

The significant areas of community relationships and functions, administration and school organization, curriculum, subject matter organization and content, social influences on perception and learning, are vital factors in the educational enterprise which have just begun to attract the attention of research in the social sciences. Most of such research is in the developing stages and sociological in orientation. It is too soon to assess its utility or its impact, and educators still seem disinclined to seek our social scientists to conduct research for or with them when they face problems in these areas. The collaboration of the social sciences with public health, agricultural extension, and industry has been far more extensive and richer in results than has similar collaboration in education.

An Anthropological Approach to Research in Education

Clearly we have not gleaned enough information from research to formulate a far-reaching program of educational change. We do possess, however, the conceptual tools to frame the problems about which research should be done, and the conceptual tools of anthropology are particularly well adapted to the formulation of problems which are fundamental to the educational enterprise.

Educational institutions and processes lend themselves to anthropological analysis because (1) they focus upon the intimate relation between the social forms in which a people group themselves and the other aspects of their cultural system — an interdependence which is shown in the connections between technology, customs, beliefs, and even patterns of settlement and land use; and (2) there are available documents and other evidence to reconstruct the stages of transformation through which a society has moved for the purpose of elucidating the principles of change.

In the analysis which follows I propose to apply this approach to an examination of our educational system. Earlier mention was made of the rapid transformation of our society from rural-agrarian to urban-industrial. Between 1870 and 1920, the change was manifest in the rapid growth of cities, whose population increment resulted, in large part, from the arrival of millions of European immigrants; by the development and spread of a new technology in transportation, manufacturing, and services; by the spread of the factory system as the organizational form for production; and by the proliferation and growth of corporations as the system of managerial control and capital concentration.

The corporate form was an extraordinarily efficient and socially revolutionary way of assembling capital, skill, and manpower for production and distribution. It was able to concentrate massive energies upon the solution of a given problem; it developed and maintained orderly processes for achieving its goals; and it had a large degree of flexibility. Centralization of control and dispersion of operation through a hierarchy of differentiated positions, each charged with special but complementary functions, were the structural properties through which its results were realized. The capacity of the corporate system to evolve in response to a changing environment led to the expansion of its activities both in scope and size and to the exertion of its influence over other institutional arrangements, including education. Through the institutionalization of research, it has stimulated rapid and continuous technological change, and there is an increasing attention to its problems of organization, all of which has important implications for education.

Even before 1900, the effect of societal transformation had begun to be felt in the public school system, especially in the cities. Expanding populations, higher requirements for work skills brought on by technological advance, universal education, and an increasingly larger proportion of students who continued their education into high school brought sharp increases in enrollments. These in turn created enormous pressures for new facilities, changed programs, and a suitable organizational structure.

The little red school house of agrarian America presented no problems of school administration and curriculum organization. This school was basically an extension of family and community and, as the subjects taught indicated, it had no need to prepare its students for participation in a large, complex, and changing society. As an educational enterprise, it was part of a unit that included the family and other community institutions, such as the church. It offered no pattern for meeting the educational demands of the emerging urban-industrial society.

Thus the sheer magnitude of the new educational task called for radical departures in educational organization. These took, in the public schools, the direction of an expanding departmentalized bureaucratic superstructure. The once direct relationship between teacher and a board of education representing citizens and parents gave way to a many-tiered line organization in which the pupil occupied the lowest status.

Although, since 1900, there has been a proliferation of personnel through the addition of supervisors, counselors, and specialists in more and narrower fields of subject matter and services, the educational structure as we know it today is essentially the structure that had been developed by 1900. The focal point of the system is the school superintendent who acts as executive officer of the board of education, to whom he is responsible as administrator of a departmentalized bureaucracy. The line of command runs from him through assistant superintendents to principals, and on down.

Considerations of length prohibit me from also including a careful analysis of higher education, but I must touch on this subject briefly for purposes of contrast. The organizational structure of American colleges and universities did not respond to cultural transformation in the same manner as did the public school systems. There are some similarities, but the differences are much more significant. Bureaucratization has been minimal in higher education and relegated largely to housekeeping rather than pedagogical functions. Both teaching and research are functions of the faculty, which jealously guards its prerogatives against administrative encroachment through mechanisms which are well developed in most colleges. The principle of academic freedom remains firmly established. The structure of authority is diffused rather than centralized and horizontally segmented along departmental lines rather than vertically hierarchized, so that the colleague relationship is valued more highly than the supervisory one. The area of student personnel administration may be more bureaucratized in higher education than is the area of curriculum and instruction. This is a question that would lend itself well to anthropological or sociological research. Suffice it to state here that as a structure remains flexible it retains greater capacity to incorporate new functions without disturbing either the central purpose of the institution or its form of organization. How may we account for the sharp contrast between the type of structure usually found in higher education and the structure used by public school administration, and what is its significance?

The easiest explanation is that differing types of educational enterprises require different kinds of organizational structure. Evidence can be adduced to support this conclusion, but only if we disregard two generally held and important premises — first, that the educative process is central to both universities and public schools, and, second, that some environments are presumably more favorable to its realization than are others.

How do we explain the organizational evolution of the urban public schools? It seems reasonable to suppose that public education, which has long been an adjunct of local government, has followed an organizational pattern similar to that of the other expanding municipal services in the big cities. We do know that during the days of urban boss rule, and still today in some large cities, the school system has provided a source of patronage and even graft.

The great corporations might have provided an alternative structural type since their rise also coincided with the growth of the cities. It seems unlikely that the corporations served as the original models from which school organization was deliberately copied. On the other hand, the parallels between the bureaucratic structure of the two are sufficiently striking in their similarity that those who taught future school administrators, beginning in the second decade of this century, extolled corporate organization as a model to be followed. The corporate board of directors has been equated with the board of education, the stockholders with the citizens, and the excutive officers with their counterparts in large corporations.[11] The analogy between teachers and students with foremen and workers has not always been made explicit, but the following statement, written in 1916, is quite clear in its intent:

> Our schools are, in a sense, factories in which the raw products (children) are to be shaped and fashioned into products to meet the various demands of life. The specifications for manufacturing come from the demands of twentieth-century civilization, and it is the business of the school to build its pupils according to the specifications laid down. This demands good tools, specialized machinery, continuous measurement of production to see if it is according to specifications, the elimination of waste in manufacture, and a large variety in the output.[12]

That this point of view was not unique can be amply documented. By 1915 a number of the larger cities had already established "efficiency bureaus," which — through survey, measurement, and testing — were to apply the "lesson of the business world, from which we have much to learn in the matter of efficiency. . . ." [13] A determined band of pioneers, among them Terman, Ayres, and Thorndike, had already provided the educational world with tests and measurements. Industrial efficiency was being spurred by the principles enunciated by F. W. Taylor, whose *Principles of Scientific Management*, published in 1911, brought a surge of time-and-motion studies and rearrangements to work organization in factories. School administrators were urged to employ efficiency to bring about scientific school management.

Those who advocated that education borrow rational and organizational form from industry apparently perceived no dangerous incompatibilities. Efficient utilization of labor in machine production is clearly not the same process as the slow acquisition by the young of intellectual skills. In adapting mechanical processes to education, emphasis is apt to be laid upon rote learning and fact acquisition through repetition, including the inculcation of patriotism with flag drill. Stress on efficiency as the ultimate goal is apt to divorce education from human values.

In addition, the educational system does not have built into it those safeguards which limit corporate excesses in society as a whole — militant unionism and legislative enactments. Teachers have neither the tools nor the understanding to protect the cause of learning against bureau-

---

[11] Ellwood P. Cubberly. *Public School Administration* (Boston: Houghton Mifflin, 1916).
[12] *Ibid.*, p. 338.
[13] *Ibid.*, p. 335.

cratic regimentation. And citizens who are disturbed about the educational system direct their complaints not at educational organization but at practices and teachers. All these factors have tended to foster the persistence of our bureaucratical, hierarchical structure of public education.[14]

If, using the natural history method in the manner I have followed here, we reach the conclusion that our public school system has developed into a bureaucratic, hierarchical structure, the next question an anthropologist asks is: Does such a bureaucratized, hierarchical organization of large school systems serve or defeat the goals of education in our society? This question is based on the anthropological assumption that there is a relation between the learning process and the environment in which it occurs.

While a theory of learning based upon anthropological premises has yet to be explicitly formulated, such a theory is implicit and its outlines discernible in all descriptions of enculturation and socialization. Learning is a function of biological and cultural variables whose interrelations are so complex that in most instances they can only be inferred. Stimulus to learning can come from two sources: from the environment, and from within the individual. Each person, however, interprets new experience through already established categories of understanding, and new learning consists of the modification of the old or creation of new categories. This psychic process patterns experience and gives to the individual his basis for comprehending the world and his place in it. Rote learning, or fact acquisition as an end in itself (the quiz-kid mentality), does not, however, require this patterned internalization, and, in a strict sense, such learning can have little meaning for the individual.

The educative process, to be effective, depends upon the learning process — the internalization and ordering of experience by the individual. Among simpler societies, where education is usually not institutionalized, this results in the repetitive recreation in each generation of those who resemble the preceding. In complex societies, in contrast, a formal system of education can and usually must be deliberately designed to produce successive generations which differ from their antecedents.[15]

Thus, although the learning process is similar in both simple and complex societies, the fact that in complex societies the child can learn *only*

[14] *The New York Times*, Feb. 12, 1962, p. 25. A news report of a new program by the National Education Association "to help big-city teachers solve problems of their own and of the urban areas they serve." Although many problems are listed including "the quality of the teaching profession" there is no intimation that a major culprit is the system of administration to which the teachers are subject.

[15] Margaret Mead. "Our Education Emphasis in Primitive Perspective," *Amer. J. Sociol.*, XLVIII, May 1943. Dr. Mead emphasized the discontinuities which modern education engenders in contrast with the generational sequence of primitive societies.

through *formal* education what he needs to know to become a fully participating member of adult society is of great significance. For this reason, the teacher-learner relationship is crucial in our complex society. When it is used for purposes other than the development of the cognitive capacities, then it has been corrupted. The danger of such corruption mounts with increasing bureaucratization of schools. This becomes clear through an examination of the functions of other types of relationships in institutional organizations.

In all line organizations the directional responsibility from above to below is expressed through the supervisory relationship. Thus, the teacher who follows the instructions of a principal or his supervisory aide responds in a manner equivalent to that of a sergeant or foreman who obeys an order of his captain or manager. When the teacher *directs* students in their activities, she is supervising. In addition, the exercise of custodial responsibility in schools represents an extension of the supervisory relation. Of utmost importance is the fact that directional activity always assumes previous learning; any new learning is an accretion incidental to the event.

When administrators or teachers meet with their own kind to work out a common problem, we speak of a colleague relationship. In contrast, the business man who serves a customer, or a lawyer who offers advice is in a client relationship. There are aspects of both relationships in the classroom, but it is in the dominance of the custodial and the supervisory relationships that the danger to learning activity is most acute.

Supervisory techniques can be used to demand and train for appropriate responses from children, from dogs, and from pigeons (à la Pavlov and Skinner), but these forms of transferred behavior fall far short of the human capacity for learning. Adequate human learning requires the use of cognitive processes in a relationship in which the learner retains autonomy for self-initiation. This potentiality is absent under complete custodial care and severely reduced in a supervisory relationship.

Teaching as an act of supervision may lead to successful achievement of rote learning and fact accumulation, since the system of rewards and punishments, tests and measurements, is geared to recognize and sanction such. But it is the development of the capacity for seeking relationships and dynamics of systems which is central for our type of civilization. This, I must reiterate, can be accomplished only within the context of formal education, since parents and peers do not possess substantive knowledge required for teaching. But as educators we possess no objective means for either discovering or rewarding the accomplishment.

What happens in the school today is crucial. It is the child's first experience as a participant in a corporately organized system. Whatever other qualities his earliest teachers may have, they represent for him the other world, the non-familial public arena toward which he has begun the long years of preparation for eventual induction. The success with which he masters his school environment — in other words, internalizes its learnings — foretells, in most cases, the degree of success with which he will master his public adult environment, although it has little demonstrable relation to the satisfactions he gains in his private life. Internalization of learning then, not acquisition by rote, is the goal of education.

To this end we have dedicated vast efforts to the extension of professional competence to even larger numbers of teachers. There may have been a real need for extensive supervision in the early decades of the century, when many teachers had little, if any, professional training — so that Cubberly could argue that the ideal school system had a superintendent who viewed his responsibility as similar to that of the principal of a normal school. But the urgency of such a procedure must have declined as the proportion of well trained teachers has steadily increased.

More important, the supervisory system as we know it, may defeat the goals of our educational enterprise — the development of the individual creativity and autonomy upon which the continuance of our complex, mobile, and dynamic society depends. We remain, it is true, fairly naive about the learning that comes from participating in a complex organization versus that which we label mastery of subject matter and for which we test continuously. Is the truant or rebel who evades or rejects the system protesting the controls or the academic requirements or both? Industrial research suggests to us that it is not the task, however difficult or onerous, that contributes to worker malaise — for work can be a challenge or it can be endured — but that it is the sometimes-unbearable weight of a supervisory system which restricts the autonomy and creativeness of the individual.[16] This insight should give us pause for in the educational hierarchy teacher and pupil are at the bottom of the system; they are the recipients, not the originators, of the messages which flow along the line of command.

To sum up, an anthropologist considers as interdependent the relation between the educative process in our society and its social system, and the structure of our educational system in relation to its function. Will research turn up the evidence that educational bureaucratization has subverted the teacher-learner relationship into a supervisory one with its consequent corruption of the function of education in our society? If we grant that the central function of our schools is their fulfillment of the transitional role through the educative process, we must focus our attention upon the teacher-learner relationship, but always in the context of the larger system.

[16] Chris Argyris. *Personality and Organization* (New York: Harper and Brothers, 1957).

Further Readings

Bernstein, Basil. "A socio-linguistic approach to social learning," in Julius Gould (ed.), *Penguin survey of the social sciences 1965*. Baltimore: Penguin Books, 1965.
Bienenstok, Theodore, and William C. Sayres. *Contributions of sociology and anthropology to education*. Albany: The University of the State of New York, 1962.
Eggan, Fred. "Social anthropology and the educational system," *School Review*, vol. 65 (Autumn 1957).
Gearing, Frederick O. (ed.). *Proceedings: the national conference on anthropology and education*. Miami Beach, Fla., 1968.
Nicholson, Clara K. *Anthropology and education*. Columbus, Ohio: Charles E. Merrill, 1968.

17

Mr. Wallace examines relations between what he terms the "matter and circumstances of learning" and the "value orientation" that prevails for any society at a given time in its social history. In a manner similar to Herskovits (Part One), Wallace treats schooling, education, enculturation, and learning itself as successive categories of "circumstance." He classifies the "matter" of learning as involving technic, morality, and intellect. Claiming three distinct phases in the cycle of sociocultural change, Wallace assigns to each "value orientation" a representative stress on one or the other of these learning "matters." The contemporary American case of "value orientation," and its representative stress, Wallace relates with a sense of urgency (and cheerless consequence) comparable to that of Kimball, previously. Mr. Wallace's published work includes Culture and Personality *(New York: Random House, 1961). He is Professor of Anthropology, University of Pennsylvania.*

ANTHONY F. C. WALLACE

Schools in Revolutionary and Conservative Societies

Introduction

There is a great debate in this country today about schools. In what degrees should they stress the intellectual, technical, athletic, and social

From Frederick C. Gruber (ed.), *Anthropology and Education*. The Martin G. Brumbaugh Lectures, Fifth series. (Philadelphia: University of Pennsylvania Press, 1961), pp. 40–54. Reprinted by permission of the author and publisher.

development of the student? Should the approach of the teacher to the pupil be didactic or persuasive? Should schools be integrated or segregated, by race, by religion, by intelligence, by social class? The very existence of debate, and the acrimonious language in which it is conducted, poses an interesting problem for the social scientist. We live now in a world society which is rapidly changing, both collectively as a result of the on-going world-wide industrial revolution, and severally, nation by nation, in consequence of the more particular pressures of local cycles of revolution, conservatism, and reaction. May not some of the local American argu-ments, and their acrimony, be merely the expression of conflicts which arise, lawfully and predictably, from strains inevitably generated by those cyclical processes of cultural change the major phases of which we call revolution, conservatism, and reaction? That is the question which this essay will undertake to discuss.

THE KINDS OF LEARNING

Let us begin, pedantically, by defining the word *school*. We shall say that a school is an institution which deliberately and systematically, by the presentation of symbols in reading matter, lectures, or ritual, at-tempts to transform from a condition of ignorance to one of enlightenment the intellect, the morality, and the technical knowledge and skills of an attentive group of persons assembled in a definite place at a definite time.

Schools are virtually ubiquitous. It is nearly impossible for a human being to avoid attending school, whether he live in jungle or on desert, in city or in hamlet, or even in hospital, jail, or concentration camp. In America, and in all industrial societies, there are schools of six major kinds: (1) compulsory schools for that general transformation of youth into a qualified citizenry which occupies the childhood and adolescence of most young persons; (2) degree-granting schools (generally called col-leges and universities) for advanced and specialized training of young adults; (3) religious (or political) schools for young and old; (4) military schools; (5) vocational and job-training schools; and (6) a vast miscellany of schools which impart what may be described as occasional knowledge, of such widely various subjects as first aid, Zen Buddhism, and the manu-facture of compost. Even in the most primitive societies, where schools of a kind familiar to us would be difficult to maintain, schools there are nonetheless of a particular kind: the mystery schools. Mystery schools would seem to be of three main types: the "bush schools" which indoctri-nate pubescent males and females with the secret lore of adults; the religious schools which induct novitiates into religious cults and secret societies; and the professional schools which instruct young shamans in the arts of their profession. These schools have developed out of rites of passage, particularly initiation rituals, and hence are sometimes called initiation schools: they elaborate their socially useful function around joints in the tree of maturation, and always retain as much interest, if not more, in testing and celebrating the human transformation as in shaping the transformation itself. But they fit the definition: they are definite in place and time and membership, and concerned with communicating in symbols their definite bundles of information. Our schools differ from the primitive schools, apart from obvious discrepancies in size and plant, in the degree to which they are divorced from the process of celebrating the more or less spontaneous transformations of human experience, and in the extent to which they aggressively produce the transformations necessary to cultural continuity. Our schools profess, at least, to teach us almost everything we know.

Yet, as we all realize, even in our own scholastic society, schools are able to impart only a fraction of what any man learns. Any one of us can testify to this poignant truism. Like most of my readers, I, for instance, as an American professional man, have been continuously entangled with some school or other since the age of five. I have, in fact, spent nearly all of my life flitting in and out of schools, as full- or part-time student or teacher. Let me enumerate "my" schools as I recall them. As a student I attended kindergarten, grade school, junior high school, Sunday school, high school, liberal arts college (leading to Bachelor of Arts degree), basic military training, Army Specialized Training Program (one semester of engineering), military radio operators' school, Armed Forces Institute correspondence school (mathematics), graduate school (leading to the Master's degree and doctorate in anthropology), and the Rorschach Institute Summer Workshop; and followed the didactic curriculum at the Philadelphia Psychoanalytic Institute. As a teacher, I have instructed illiterate soldiers in the basic arts of reading, writing, and arithmetic; I have taught various social science subjects in three departments in two institutions of higher learning; and I have given occasional lectures to students in several curricula at various institutions. Now to be sure, many persons of my age, in this society, have attended more schools and also have taught for longer periods of time in a greater number of schools; and furthermore, while I have done a certain amount of teaching, I do not regard myself as, primarily, an educator. My major commitment thus far has been largely to research and the administration of research. So perhaps there are others who have learned in school relatively more than I of what they know, value, and can do. But for my own part I am sure that a very large proportion of what I know, value, and can do I learned apart from any school. I learned to speak a language before I went to any school; I learned to feed myself, walk, drive a car, play tennis, scrub my ears, and write halfway decent prose outside of school; I absorbed a large proportion of useful technical knowledge by reading and in conversation outside of school. Most of what little I do know about the problems I spend most of my time thinking about now, I learned after I emerged from the cocoon of graduate school, chirping like a green locust, clothed in the loose folds of a damp Ph.D.

The point is an obvious one, but its obviousness should not tempt us to leave it out of consideration: that learning in school is only one kind of human learning; and that human learning is simply a complex form of an activity in which all animals (and an increasingly large number of machines) engage. It is convenient to arrange the circumstances of human learning in the form of a scale of generality, each category of which is contained in, and implied by, its succeeding category. If we take *schooling* as the initial category, it is followed by *education,* then *enculturation,* then *learning* itself. Schooling is the learning that is done in a school; and a school, as before, is an institution which deliberately and systematically, by the presentation of symbols in reading matter, lectures, or ritual, attempts to transform from a condition of ignorance to one of enlightenment, the intellect, the morality, and the technical knowledge and skills of an attentive group of persons assembled in a definite place at a definite time. Education is all learning (including but not confined to schooling) obtained from reading or from listening to formally prepared symbolic presentations. Enculturation is all learning enjoined on the person with a particular status as a member of a particular culture-bearing society, and thus includes, in addition to schooling and education, such homely but essential skills as knowing a language or two; observing the proper times, places, and techniques for the execution of such malleable bodily processes as urination, defecation, breathing, walking, eating, sleeping, and sexual intercourse; the securing and effective use of clothing, shelter, transport, weapons, and help; even the manner of communicating emotion and other information by facial expression, body posture, and other kinesic devices. Learning, of course, is the cover term, embracing all of the foregoing, and also those idiosyncratic learnings which every person accumulates throughout his lifetime and which may or may not be transmitted to others.

Let us now classify learning in a different way, by matter rather than by position on a scale of circumstance. In any situation of learning, three matters can be learned. These are the matters of *technic,* of *morality,* and of *intellect.* And since the bulk of this essay will concern the content and priority of these matters under various conditions, we shall now discuss these three matters of learning in some detail.

Technic is the most conspicuous matter of learning. And it is the teaching of technic which has been the subject of the most intensive analysis by psychologists and educationists. The most widely used paradigm for the learning of technic has been the stimulus → cue → response

→ reinforcement structure (the so-called S-R type of learning). This paradigm describes an animal which acts after it has been "stimulated" (i.e., after an environmental process has produced a change in its internal state). It has an opportunity to do various things, but at least one of these things will be followed by a "reinforcing" (i.e., punishing or rewarding) change of the organism's internal state. Furthermore, each action is performed in a context containing perceptible "cues." Experience shows that for almost any species it is possible to select some combination of stimuli, cues, and reinforcements in the matrix of which the animal will with increasing reliability perform some one action. The process of reliability increase is called "learning" because the observer feels that he too, if he were in the same spot, would perform that act as soon as he discovered that it was more frequently followed by a reward, or at least by the negation of punishment, than any other alternative. In naïve language, the animal "learns how" (i.e., learns the technique) to secure reward and/or to avoid punishment. It is easy to infer from this what corresponds to common belief, namely that people, dogs, and rats all learn best when they are "motivated." It is also easy — but not necessarily valid — to infer that people, dogs, and rats will learn best what *is* reinforced, directly, personally, and materially.

Technic, therefore, is "how to" learning by reinforcement. It includes such things as learning how to talk, how to extract the square root of a number, how to dance, how to harpoon a walrus, how to play a piano, how to decorate an apartment, how to cook a meal, how to balance a budget, how to identify a witch, how to get to heaven. From this standpoint, even the rote learning of information — dates, names, events, formulas, art work, institutional structures, store prices, fashions, and the like — is "how to" learning, for the motive lies not in the acquisition of the information but in the use to which it may be put, whether to impress the neighbors, to win prizes, to fill out the image of the "intellectual," or whatever. And even values — such as standards of beauty, tastes in music, concepts of the good life — may be learned, both by rote, as when one learns first the symbols for the rewarded values, and later, by performing the act that earns the reward.

Morality, on the other hand, deals not so much with "how to" as with "what." Furthermore, in my usage here, morality concerns, not just positive and negative goals, not just values, not even all socially approved values, but one particular kind of socially approved value. This kind of value is the conception that one's own behavior, as well as the behavior of others, should not merely take into consideration the attitude of the community, but should actively advance, or at least not retard, its welfare. *Morality* is thus to be sharply distinguished from mere propriety, conformity, and respectability, although it is not necessarily non-conformist.

Morality, in this sense, is most *conspicuously* exemplified by such heroic actions as the soldier's who throws himself on a hand grenade in order to smother the blast and save his buddies; as the statesman's who suffers political oblivion rather than betray his country's interests; as the tribesman's who gives himself up to the enemy for punishment in order to prevent retaliation upon his whole people. It is also most *commonly* practiced in the humble endurance of discomfort, protracted over decades, by inconspicuous people in positions of responsibility.

Now it is, to my way of thinking, questionable whether this kind of morality can be adequately explained by any *simple* learning-by-reinforcement model. Although morality is not necessarily accompanied by sacrifice, in any particular case its criterion is its potentiality for sacrifice. And sacrifice seems to fly in the face of the law of effect. Indeed, the American academic psychologist is apt to deny that moral behavior in this sense can exist in a sane person. I recall once hearing such a psychologist argue with a psychiatrist on the point. The psychologist had posed this extraordinary question: Suppose that a man and his wife were in some dangerous situation such that the husband could only escape with a whole skin if he abandoned his wife to her death; but he could save them both if he suffered a mutilating injury which deprived him of his genital organs. The psychologist argued that the normal husband would inevitably abandon his wife. The psychiatrist asserted that only an immature man would place a lower value on his wife's survival than on his own sexual anatomy. Yet anyone who has observed men in combat, who has seen the religious or the political devotee in action, who has watched a family holding together in adversity, must realize that morally altruistic behavior is possible. And it is hard to escape the inference that such persons, on such occasions, have not learned to sacrifice their own interests in favor of their conception of the interests of other persons merely by passing through some adroitly arranged sequence of Skinner boxes.

The third of our matters of learning is *intellect.* By intellect I do not mean intelligence, nor do I mean intellectualism. As Jacques Barzun has lucidly and at considerable length explained, intelligence is not necessarily governed by intellect, nor is the intellectual, as a social type, necessarily a custodian of the "House of Intellect." Intellect is, as he puts it, an "establishment":

> That part of the world I call the House of Intellect embraces at least three groups of subjects: the persons who consciously and methodically employ the mind; the forms and habits governing the activities in which the mind is so employed; and the conditions under which these people and activities exist. . . .
> Intellect is the capitalized and communal form of live intelligence; it is intelligence stored up and made into habits of discipline, signs and sym-

bols of meaning, chains of reasoning and spurs to emotion — a shorthand and a wireless by which the mind can skip connectives, recognize ability, and communicate truth. Intellect is at once a body of common knowledge and the channels through which the right particle of it can be brought to bear quickly, without the effort of redemonstration, on the matter in hand.

Intellect is community property and can be handed down. . . .

That is why I have used the image of a house. I would speak of the *realm* of mind — limitless and untamed — but I say the House of Intellect, because it is an establishment, requiring appurtenances and prescribing conventions. . . .

From the image of a house and its economy, one can see what an inquiry into the institution of Intellect must include. The main topics are: the state of the language, the system of schooling, the means and objects of communication, the supplies of money for thought and learning, and the code of feeling and conduct that goes with them. When the general tendency of these arrangements makes for order, logic, clarity, and speed of communication, one may say that a tradition of Intellect exists.[1]

Intellect thus is, to begin with, a social tradition, an aspect of culture, if you please. The core of this tradition is the proposition that if a subject is worthy of consideration at all, it should be considered in a particular cognitive form. That particular way of proper consideration may vary considerably from one society to the next, and, in a complex society, from one group to the next. To the humanist, the approach of *intellect* involves the careful and exact use of a language: the use may or may not be conventional in lexicon or even in grammar, but it must be as little ambiguous, self-contradictory, and flabby as possible. In the tradition of intellect, language *is* thought, and therefore there is no such thing as a strong thought lamely expressed; lame language is lame thinking. To the Western humanist also, a willingness to range widely for quotation, for metaphor, and for illustration is a *sine qua non* of intellect; a provincial intellect is a contradiction in terms. In discussion, or even in argument, a man of intellect is ready to be bound, as well as to bind his opponent, by rules of logic; the *non sequitur* and other absurdities are inadmissible tools even if in the course of their use a valid statement happens to be constructed. The concern with logic reaches its highest refinement, however, not among humanists, but among scientists, who strive for the precision of mathematics, not because mathematics is numerical, but because it is logical. Where rigorous logic can be applied to non-quantitative observations, the scientist may — depending on the nature of his problem — be glad to work without numbers. But he too is conscious of living *in* a tradition of thought.

---

[1] Abridged from pp. 3–6 *The House of Intellect* by Jacques Barzun. Copyright © 1959 by Jacques Barzun. Reprinted by permission of Harper & Row, Publishers, Inc. and Martin Secker & Warburg Ltd.

Like the humanist Barzun, the physicist Oppenheimer uses the metaphor of the house to describe the world of the scientific intellect; and it is, as he says, "a vast house indeed." Oppenheimer, in contrast to Barzun, is fascinated by the fluidity, the boundlessness, the openness of "the house called science" — and, most of all, by the ceaseless work that goes on there. He introduces us, first, to one

> relatively quiet room that we know as quantum theory or atomic theory. The great girders which frame it, the lights and shadows and vast windows — these were the work of a generation our predecessor more than two decades ago. It is not wholly quiet. Young people visit and study in it and pass on to other chambers; and from time to time someone rearranges a piece of the furniture to make the whole more harmonious; and many, as we have done, peer through its windows or walk through as sightseers. It is not so old but that one can hear the sound of the new wings being built nearby, where men walk high in the air to erect new scaffoldings, not unconscious of how far they may fall. All about there are busy workshops where the builders are active. . . .
>
> It is a vast house indeed. It does not appear to have been built upon any plan but to have grown as a great city grows. There is no central chamber, no one corridor from which all others debouch. . . . It is a house so vast that none of us know it, and even the most fortunate have seen most rooms only from the outside or by a fleeting passage, as in a king's palace open to visitors. It is a house so vast there is not and need not be complete concurrence on where its chambers stop and those of the neighboring mansions begin. . . .
>
> We go in and out; even the most assiduous of us is not bound to this vast structure. One thing we find throughout the house: there are no locks; there are no shut doors; wherever we go there are the signs and usually the words of welcome. It is an open house, open to all comers.[2]

It is, as C. P. Snow reiterates, one of the tragedies of our time that the house of the humanistic intellect and the house of the scientific intellect seem so often to be, to one another, mutually barred and hostile citadels. It is possible that this conflict of the "two cultures" is more in the nature of a civil war than of a struggle between two establishments, and that the House of Intellect is one divided against itself; and conceivably, it is the relative poverty of this house, in our own society, which has made it difficult for its occupants to get along with one another.

But we should not confine our discussion of intellect to the last few centuries of western Europe and the Americas. There was, for instance, a scholastic intellect which developed in the medieval religious tradition. There was a tradition of the intellect among the followers of Mohammed;

---

[2] J. Robert Oppenheimer, *Science and the Common Understanding* (New York: Simon and Schuster, 1954), pp. 82–85. Copyright © 1953, 1954 by J. Robert Oppenheimer. Reprinted by permission of Simon and Schuster, Inc. and Joan Daves.

and, likewise, among Indian, Chinese, and other civilized peoples. It would be possible, indeed, to argue that intellect has its own tradition and its own problems, in most if not all cultures, even though its house may be small and contain only a few specialists in law, religion, politics, warfare, irrigation technology, astrology, or what have you. For the utility of intellect springs from the fact that it is the only truly universal tool, capable of maintaining and restoring human arrangements against the erosions of time, capable of recognizing and solving new problems as well as learning the answers to old ones. And it does this intensely human task by requiring its users to practice what is sometimes, and paradoxically, described as an inhuman detachment from the technics and morality of the moment.

We may take a schema to represent the divisions of learning which we have so far discussed. In Figure 1 are shown the three matters of learning and the scale of the circumstances of learning.

What Should a Man Learn?

The obvious answer to the question of what a man should learn has already been taught us by the anthropologists. Manifestly, what it is needful to learn in one society is not necessarily needful in another. Cultural differences demonstrate that there is no absolute set of things to be learned; what a man should learn is a function of his culture.

But concealed behind this principle lies a corollary: in order that noticeable cultural differences shall exist at all, there must be a significant

FIGURE 1
The divisions of learning

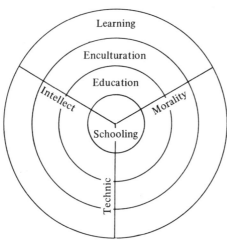

degree of conformity to norm within each society. And this prevents us from going on to assert that what a man should learn is a matter for him alone to decide. There is, in fact, no human society on the face of the earth which concedes to *any* individual the right to learn anything he chooses. And furthermore, it is the school which is established by the community — not, be it noted, by the family — to ensure that the individual learns what he must know.

The values which guide the group in its choice of what learnings to impress on the individual are legion, and they may be described on many levels of complexity; but for our purposes three contrasting value orientations are most significant: the revolutionary, or utopian, orientation; the conservative, or ideological, orientation; and the reactionary orientation. What a man is expected to do in his life will, in part, depend on whether he lives in a revolutionary, conservative, or reactionary society. And what he is expected to do determines what he is expected to learn. Furthermore, not merely what a man should learn, but whether he should learn it in a school, or from his parents, or from his peers, or by casual reading, conversation, and attendance at entertainments, will be in part determined by whether he lives in a revolutionary or a conservative or a reactionary society.

We are asserting, in other words, that the value orientation of the society — in the tripartite sense given above — will determine not only the content of what a man is expected to learn, but whether he is expected to learn it in a school or under some other circumstances.

Now the utility of the three value orientations as a means of classifying each of several contemporaneous societies is unquestionable. Without much difficulty one could, for instance, label China and Cuba today as revolutionary societies; the United States and Great Britain as conservative; and Portugal and the Union of South Africa as reactionary. China and Cuba are deliberately and forcibly replacing old institutions with new ones organized in a new way according to a plan. The United States and Great Britain are, in regard to domestic policy, conservative in the sense that the existing institutions are considered to be adequate, not perfect, but perfectible, and hence in need not of replacement but of repair. Portugal and the Union of South Africa are reactionary in the sense that their leaders' internal policies have been warped by an intention to ward off internal attack from groups which threaten to replace existing institutions with new ones. While no society can be wholly one thing or another, everywhere, in all of its aspects, at any one time, it seems reasonable to consider one value orientation or another as predominant in a given group, such as the political, economic, or religious leadership, during a stated period. The precise content of these values, of course, will vary: thus a revolutionary society may be communistic, capitalistic,

Muslim, nativistic, or whatever, depending on local circumstances; and a comparable variety of conservatisms and reactions are also available.

But we may also use this tripartite classification for different time periods in the same society. Here one may expect that the orientations will change in a definite order: a society which is now revolutionary will, if it changes, become conservative, next reactionary, and again most probably revolutionary. Thus, over centuries or millennia, any one society is apt to follow a roughly cyclical path through revolution, conservatism, and reaction, over and over again. This subject has been approached by scholars and scientists in various ways and is one of the classic problems of the social sciences. My own approach to it has been via the study of what I call revitalization movements, particularly of a religious variety.

Thus one may, with regard to any one society, expect to find that the content and circumstances of learning will vary with the varying predominance of its value orientation. And now we may go to the crux of the matter. It would appear that with each of the major value orientations there is associated a philosophy of schooling which characteristically assigns priorities to the matters of learning in schools. It is to the elucidation of the association between these priorities and the value orientations that the remainder of this essay will be devoted.

The Revolutionary Society

Let us consider first the dynamics of a revolutionary society. A revolutionary society is a society dominated by a revitalization movement, which may be defined as a deliberate, organized, conscious effort by members of a society to construct a more satisfying culture. It may in the extreme be either religious or political, but is usually a combination of both. The code of the movement defines the previous state of society as inadequate, perverse, even evil, and depicts a more or less utopian image of the better society as the goal culture toward which the *ad hoc* and temporary social arrangements of the present transfer culture is carrying the society. Generally, a revitalization movement must pass through six stages in order to create a truly revolutionary society:

Formulation of the code. Mere dissatisfaction with the existing state of affairs does not launch a revitalization movement. A prophet, political party, or clique must formulate explicitly the nature of the existing culture's deficiencies, the nature of a desirable goal culture, and the nature and mode of operation of the transfer culture. This formulation must be more than an exercise of intellect: it must be passionately moral.

Communication. The formulator must preach his code to other people. This communication must emphasize the moral obligation of the bearer to subscribe to this new code and render service to the movement.

Organization. The converts made by the formulator organize into a hierarchical system, with a prophet or other titular head, an elite group of disciples who constitute an executive praesidium, and a rank and file who carry out but do not make policy.

Adaptation. As the movement's challenge to the existing leadership of the society is met, by counter-propaganda or by force, the movement will be required to enlarge, modify, specify, and otherwise adapt the code to the circumstances of survival. The process of reformulation is continuous from this point on, for new situations constantly arise not anticipated in the code; and it lasts long after political victory is complete. This process of doctrinal elaboration is a work of disciplined intellect, and high value is accordingly placed on intellect, which can perform such work (whereas technic cannot).

Cultural transformation. When social power falls into the hands of the movement (the revolution is "won"), the movement is able to carry out directly the cultural transformation of the society. In this process, morality and intellect are more valuable than technic, for technic tends to be conservative, and intellect will discern that a new technic will have to be invented to meet new tasks.

Routinization. As the movement's immediate aims are realized by the acquisition of power and the establishment, if not of the goal culture, at least of the transfer culture, the organization of the movement per se tends to contract into the form of a church, or a behind-the-scenes party, which attempts to *maintain* the ongoing transfer culture. At this point the society has become conservative, with a division of role between the executive and the morality-maintaining functions.

The present world, no less than past human history, affords numerous examples of revolutionary societies. We have already cited China and Cuba as examples. Communist nations form a large class of revolutionary societies today, but many other kinds exist: for example, a revitalization movement among the Manus, off the coast of New Guinea, described at length in Margaret Mead's book, *New Lives for Old*; the numerous "cargo cult" and "marching rule" movements delineated in Peter Worsley's study of Melanesian cults. *The Trumpet Shall Sound*; the nationalisms, Egyptian, Algerian, and contemporary African; the new India and Indonesia; and so on. Much of contemporary world history can best be understood in terms of revitalization theory.

With respect to schools and schooling, one inference is paramount: that in a revolutionary society (i.e., society in the process of cultural transformation under the leadership of a revitalization movement) the primary concern of schools must be the *moral* transformation of the population. Next in order of priority will be intellect; and last of all, technic (despite the often critical need for technically trained personnel to carry out the program of the transfer culture). The reason for this priority list — morality, intellect, and technic — is that the moral rebirth of the population and the development of a cadre of morally reliable and intellectually resourceful individuals to take over executive positions throughout the society is the immediately necessary task. This is a capital investment, so to speak, and from which interest in the form of technical skills will ultimately be generated. The moral intellectuals produced by revolutionary schools may, to conservative eyes, appear to be fanatics and theoreticians who fumble badly on technical tasks. But they are necessary, during the temporary period of revolution, in order to do the work of converting the populace, developing large plans, and adapting the code to local and temporal circumstances. If they do their work well, they will develop a base upon which later expansions of technic can build without fear of counter-revolution, apathy, and lack of foresight.

The most conspicuous example of the revolutionary priority scale in schools is the Chinese Communist educational program, including the so-called "brain-washing" programs not only for prisoners of war and political enemies but also for new cadres. Moral reform comes first; training in the work of intellect (in order to explicate and apply political theory to local situations) falls second; and finally come technical skills; this is the order of emphasis. It is also noteworthy that Communists, at least in the preparation of a revitalization movement in a non-Communist country, work busily to develop cadres at universities in order to transform, in effect, the schools from institutions emphasizing technic into institutions emphasizing morality. The school thus becomes, willy-nilly, the moral battleground for the rest of the society, and (without necessarily having the blessing of faculty or administration) therefore functions as a moral and intellectual training center for both revolutionary and reactionary factions.

THE CONSERVATIVE SOCIETY

A conservative society is a society in which a revitalization movement has won its battle with reaction and has established a successful new culture. This new culture may, in terms of the revitalization code, be only a transfer culture, but since the process of transfer may, even in theory, take a long time, it can become a stable way of life. Being secure and successful, the old movement does not need to preoccupy itself with combat against reaction or against new revitalization movements. The problem is to keep the machine going as efficiently as possible, with occasional improvements, and possibly with smoothly programmed shifts from one stage to another on the path toward the goal culture.

With respect to morality, the transformation of the society is sufficiently complete for severe moral non-conformists to be treated as delinquents, criminals, or victims of mental illness. The reform, rehabilitation, or control of these people can be safely left to the police, the courts, the medical profession, and (most importantly) to the informal sanctions of the family and the community itself. All communication media are saturated with applications of the new code. Society as a whole can therefore communicate the moral values necessary to the maintenance of the transfer culture, and thus to the achievement of the goal culture, through multiple channels of communication as part of the general process of education and without extreme dependence on schools. It is even possible to permit a degree of open non-conformity, of a less severe kind, to be sure, in order to avoid the inconvenience of exercising close surveillance over individuals and the expense of deliberate schooling. A conservative society is, paradoxically, also a liberal society, precisely because the elite is secure enough that it can afford to learn from its critics and even to absorb them into the ranks of conservatism as a "loyal opposition."

With respect to intellect the conservative society is tolerant, but since the work of code formulation and its application has been largely accomplished, the skilled practitioner of intellect is not necessary to the regime. Intellect becomes a rather special tradition, relatively free from constraint, but without access to power because, in a political sense, it has little power to offer. Thus the schools see relatively little need to force intellect even upon the intelligent. Intellect becomes a career in itself, self-sought and guild-protected, with the members of the guild practicing partly for the fun of it and partly as professional men selling their services to the highest bidder (and not necessarily, alas, for a high price). Under such circumstances, remarkably "pure" intellect can develop, producing vastly significant contributions to knowledge, and ultimately perhaps exerting considerable social power. But this power is exerted in an amoral manner, as in the creation of new weapons and technologies, new philosophies of the mind, new mathematics, and so forth. The *morally* concerned "intellectual" is apt (in a statistical sense) to be no intellectual at all, but a taker of unconventional moral and aesthetic stands in a stereotyped conventional way, a snob, a *poseur* who pretends that what is different from mass behavior must be based on superior values. The "intellectuals" and the practitioners of intellect are generally rather distinct groups in conservative societies, the true practitioner of intellect being a professional, ruthlessly severe in competence, and relatively indifferent to the moral implications of his work, even though his life as citizen, parent, and friend may be highly moral. Indeed, for some professionals of this type, the work of intellect is in itself morally good, provided it is competent work: this the scientist, if not the humanist, maintains. The "intellectual," by contrast, is likely to be an amateur, a dilettante, a poor painter, a sloppy writer, and an incompetent musician, whose noisy revolt against conventional morality and technical materialism is supported for its entertainment value by materialists, condemned by moralists, and largely ignored by practitioners of intellect.

But the divorce of intellect from morality, ending a marriage which was consummated in revolution, makes the house of intellect itself appear to the outsider to be merely a specialized machine shop of technic, and transforms the orientation of the school toward it. The school now emphasizes technic as its primary mission. It first of all trains people to do jobs. The jobs may be closely defined: bookkeeping, automobile driving, jousting with a lance, praying correctly; or they may be vaguely defined: being able to vote intelligently in elections, handling human relations smoothly. The demands of morality come next, for morality is considered, in a negative sort of way, to be necessary to keep society from falling apart. (In the revolutionary society, morality was supremely necessary, both to prompt the destruction of the old society and to guide the building of the new one.) Intellect is respected, but it is also recurrently confused with native intelligence, with the pseudo-intellectualism to which we alluded earlier, with some sort of impotent disloyalty, with stuffiness, with an inhuman lack of concern for human values, or even with immorality and cruelty. As such, it may be allowed to develop spontaneously but will not be supported by the state, for fear of developing something dangerous at the expense of undeniably useful technic and unquestionably desirable morality.

THE REACTIONARY SOCIETY

The reactionary society is a post-conservative society. The conservative order, having been challenged by a budding revitalization movement (i.e., by what it regards as a treasonable, heretical conspiracy imported from abroad), adjusts its posture to minimize the effectiveness of its competitor's propaganda and to mobilize counterattacks. In the interest of preserving the same values that an earlier revitalization movement established in pain and sweat, and which the conservative society cherished and elaborated, the reactionary society subverts its own way of life in order to deliver telling blows against the enemy within. In so doing it may destroy the very social structure which it is defending; and it becomes, because of the growing discrepancy between ideal and practice, and because popular confidence in its values begins to erode, rapidly moribund, an eminent subject for revitalization.

The reactionary society thus, in the area of learning generally, has two paramount concerns: first, to combat the alien heresies by revealing the inadequacy of their values and the poverty of their practice; and second, to recapture the moral enthusiasm of its earlier, revitalization phase. Consequently, the reactionary society shares with the revolutionary society a supreme concern with *morality*: a paradox of social history, which is apt to puzzle the sophisticated conservative in the middle, who finds it difficult to understand the extremists, who seem to understand each other very well. This concern with morality is reflected in a re-emphasized religiosity, a refurbished political ritualism, repressive laws, an oppressive police, and — in the schools — a conviction that the moral education of the young must take precedence over all else. This anxiety lest the young can be morally seduced requires, as in revolutionary societies, the schools to take over from the family, from industry, and from other social groups the responsibility for the moral development of the young, and to place extreme emphasis on the human environment of the school child. The moral purity of his teachers and his schoolmates comes to be more important than the content of instruction, or even than school itself, and if either knowledge or rectitude must be sacrificed, it is knowledge whose immolation is certain.

Although they share a preoccupation with morality, the reactionary and the truly revolutionary society differ in their evaluation of intellect. In the logic of revolution, morality and intellect are believed to be linked in a pact with the future. Hence, as we have suggested, the revolutionary society will place intellect before technic in its scale of priority: the cultivation of intellect becomes a kind of capital investment in people. In the reactionary society, by contrast, intellect is feared as a potential enemy because, in the preceding conservative phase, it has acted as endowed critic of the conventional wisdom, charged with responsibility for pointing out pathways to improvement; and because, in the competing contemporary revolutionary organization, students and mature intellectuals are conspicuously influential. Thus the reactionary society will favor technic over intellect, will redefine tasks which previously were regarded as intellectual in order to make them technical, and will redefine relatively harmless aesthetic diversions as "intellectual." The cost of this scholastic reorganization, however, is apt to be very great, since the derogation of intellect will reduce the number of persons in the reactionary society who are capable of thinking coherently, purposefully, and creatively on matters of public concern. The ultimate consequence to a reactionary society of neglecting the cultivation of intellect is collapse before the onslaught of a revitalization movement which is guided by intellect (Figure 2).

CURRENT APPLICATIONS

Today our society here in the United States is conservative. We went through our major revitalization movement nearly two hundred years

FIGURE 2
The matters of learning

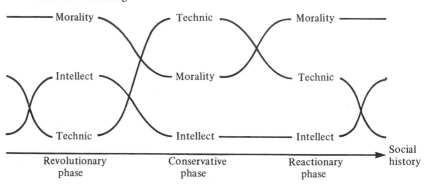

ago; we have elaborated and refined the principles established during our revolutionary period — principles thought out by men of intellect and codified in the Declaration of Independence and the federal Constitution — and have since that time worked to preserve and perfect a way of life guided by these principles. Under the pressure of internal strains and foreign wars, cold and hot, we have so far avoided becoming truly reactionary.

There is a clear danger, however, that the external pressure of a revolutionary Communist philosophy, even though its internal influence is very small, may provoke the unwary into adopting a reactionary posture. Nowhere is this danger more present than in regard to the schools. Our schools have traditionally been, as must be the case with any conservative society, less interested in intellect than in technic, but nonetheless more interested in intellect than in morality. Elaborate precautions have been taken to prevent the excessive intrusion of overt religious or political interests into the public and private schools. But by placing control of schools in the hands of all too often technically, rather than intellectually, committed educators and practical business and professional men, equally elaborate efforts are made to ensure that technic takes precedence over intellect. This situation in itself has brought cries of alarm from many people — admirals and parents, laymen and college deans — who recognize the inherent danger to our rocket program in raising generations of children who are not intimately acquainted with the obligations of intellect, who have been trained to do everything well except thinking. The intellectual unpreparedness of many college graduates is certainly an obvious problem to anyone who contemplates the large number of unsuccessful candidates for the degree of Doctor of Philosophy. Contributing to failure, in many of these cases, is an inability to construct a coherent paragraph, to design a dissertation, to understand even the most elementary operations of formal logic, or to distinguish the interminable presentation of disconnected observations, obtained with elaborate instrumentation and offered in a pretentious technical jargon, from disciplined scholarly or scientific investigation. It is also a critical problem in recruiting scientists for both fundamental and applied research, which, contrary to popular mythology, does not proceed automatically, guided by the goddess of wisdom, but stumbles along at best, and at worst wastes millions of dollars on hastily planned and illogically conceived assaults on empty problems. The question is not one of intelligence, but one of intellectual, as opposed to merely technical, training. Graduate schools are not intended, and should not serve, to convey training in intellect: they must depend on secondary schools and colleges to provide them with candidates for specialized training whose intellects are at least somewhat disciplined, if not altogether mature.

But danger resides, not merely in the practical consequences of the present dilapidated condition of the house of intellect, but in the likelihood that this unsatisfactory state of affairs will become even worse. Loyalty oaths, the censoring of libraries, the singling out of teachers and scientists as a group for investigation, the cramming of curricula with courses in sex, marriage, automobile driving, citizenship, and political right thinking, and the willingness of a considerable part of the white population to do without schools rather than sit next to Negroes — these are signs of a reactionary panic which, if it spreads, will inevitably destroy the intellectual base of an entire nation, and leave it, within two generations, blind in a revolutionary world.

Thus, in the view taken in this essay, the school problem of the contemporary United States does not arise from some inexplicable deterioration of moral and intellectual stamina, related to a Spenglerian decline of the west. Nor is it the consequence of any particularly perverse philosophy of education. The progressive schoolman and the fundamentalist in education — neither of whom want precisely what I want, but who are nonetheless likely to be skilled, devoted, and self-sacrificing public servants — are both at the mercy of innumerable semi-educated electorates and their politically affiliated school boards, of state and federal educational bodies, of legislatures, of boards of trustees, of colleges and foundations, all of whom are exquisitely sensitive to dangers to the conservative position, and many of whom will soon be all too ready to insist that the schools' first duty is to develop moral and well-trained citizens and soldiers, and that its last duty is to discipline the mind.

Let me suggest what, in a conservative society intending to survive in a revolutionary world by refusing to freeze into the reactionary posture, the value hierarchy of the schools should be. The cultivation of intellect should come first, technic second, and morality last. Intellect should be cultivated in all persons, to the limit of their abilities, and those whose abilities are least should learn to respect and admire the achievements and the rewards of those more fortunate. (This is not a psychological impossibility, nor need it be traumatic: athletic sports are not prohibited as mentally unhygienic simply because ability and hard work are conspicuously rewarded, while the vast majority are left to watch delightedly the feats of the stars.) Far from supinely assuming that the rigor of logic and mathematics and of language studies does not generalize to anything but itself, such rigor should be required in work on all other subjects, both humane and scientific. The goal should be a citizenry who feel an obligation to be rational in their thinking on personal or public affairs as well as in their technical work.

Let me cite a humble example. I would like to see a generation of high-school graduates who are *all* willing to reject a conclusion reached via a demonstrated *non sequitur*. Surely it is not asking too much of an educational system to train all of its graduates to recognize and reject at least a simple *non sequitur!* There is no sacred spark in human nature which would be tragically extinguished if, because of his intellectual training alone, a man did not feel free to conclude that because all Communists, let us say, believe in racial equality, then all those who preach racial equality must be Communists! Indeed, I will go on to assert, quite seriously, that a readiness to squeeze a *non sequitur* out of a simple syllogism can ruin a person's, or a nation's, career as surely as bullets or hydrogen bombs. A general tendency to reject conclusions offered by, or tentatively drawn from, use of the *non sequitur*, is not a matter of morality, nor of technical skill in symbolic logic, nor of innate intelligence alone. It is a matter of intellect, of acquired tradition, of learning through instruction and experience that one is rewarded less often for choices based on a *non sequitur* than on those based on correct logical form. It is, indeed, a principal component of intellect precisely because it is a general tool which is applicable to any problem whatsoever.

Now this, to my mind, is the kind of thing that intellect is all about. Intellect is a cultural matter; it must be learned; and, for survival, it must be used. Our country's survival as a conservative society — or, indeed, as any kind of society — depends radically upon maintaining a system of schools which teaches the tradition of intellect as its primary obligation.

REFERENCES

Barzun, Jacques. *The House of Intellect.* New York: Harper & Brothers, 1959.
Mead, Margaret. *New Lives for Old.* New York: William Morrow & Company, 1956.

Oppenheimer, J. Robert. *Science and the Common Understanding.* New York: Simon and Schuster, 1954.
Snow, C. P. *The Two Cultures and the Scientific Revolution.* Cambridge: Cambridge University Press, 1960.
Wallace, Anthony F. C. "Revitalization Movements." *American Anthropologist,* vol. 58 (1956), pp. 264–81.
Worsley, Peter. *The Trumpet Shall Sound.* London: Macgibbon & Kee, 1957.

FURTHER READINGS

Dahlke, H. O. *Values in culture and classroom.* New York: Harper and Brothers, 1958.
Eckstein, Max A., and Harold J. Noah (eds.) *Scientific investigations in comparative education.* New York: Macmillan, 1969.
King, Edmund J. *Other schools and ours,* rev. ed. New York: Holt, Rinehart and Winston, 1965.
Service, Elman R. "The law of evolutionary potential," in Marshall D. Sahlins and Elman R. Service (eds.), *Evolution and culture.* Ann Arbor: University of Michigan Press, 1960.
Wallace, Anthony F. C. *Culture and personality.* New York: Random House, 1961.

18

Freedman and Omark use perhaps the most general approach to education in Part Three. It stresses two relatively new specialties in anthropology: comparative ethology and behavior genetics. Benjamin Bloom's pivotal study, Stability and Change in Human Characteristics (New York: Wiley, 1964), provides a ready framework for much of the argument developed here. Other aspects of Freedman and Omark's discussion are not so conveniently referred, and deserve careful reading. The implications of studies of human behavior that "see" man as an animal species are, in vital part, untold. The physical study of man tends to be so emotionless as to seem inhumane, and inevitably expectations are raised of dry, immediately (or forever) impractical research, shot through with statistics. Fundamental issues in education today revolve about questions of educability and the nature of the learning process, however, and these concerns are also central to the lines of inquiry drawn by Freedman and Omark. Genetic difference and relationships between genetic and cultural influences upon human behavior are key matters in comprehending, as Kimball put it, the "educative process." The authors hold teaching and research positions at the University of Chicago, where Mr. Freedman is also associated with the Committee on Human Development.

DANIEL G. FREEDMAN AND DONALD R. OMARK

Ethology, Genetics, and Education

INTRODUCTION

We realize that it is an unusual paper which can say something fresh about education, and only someone new to educational literature, as is our case, would even try. We plan in Part One to look at human development over the first six years or so within the context of comparative ethology, drawing comparisons between *Homo sapiens* and other species wherever appropriate. Part Two falls into the realm of behavior genetics, and is concerned with *within-species* variations.

If we acknowledge at the outset that our comparisons of human and animal development must stand as analogies rather than homologies, or, at best as rough examples of phylogenetic progression, perhaps we can avoid considerable bickering. To take sexual dimorphism as just one example, our logic goes something like this:

If all the birds and mammals which have been closely studied show some degree of male-female behavioral dimorphism, how likely is it that *Homo sapiens* does not? Are we born psychosexually neutral as Hampson and Hampson (1961) assert, and must we depend completely on the fortunes of experience to acquire our sexuality? The answer which we accept is that it is not very likely that XX chromosomal constitution as opposed to XY is behaviorally meaningless, and in fact considerable evidence may be mustered for all sorts of built-in male-female behavioral differences (Diamond, 1965; Hamburg and Lunde, 1966).

If such differences are found, we should consider such manifestations among hominids as no less biological than, say, among rhesus. Similarly, because nearly all social mammals thus far studied show some form of dominance-submission hierarchy, again with sexual dimorphism, it seems reasonable to look for similar behavior in man. There is, of course, considerable sustaining evidence for this as well (Freedman, 1967a; also see the following).

Reprinted with revisions from Frederick O. Gearing (ed.), *Proceedings: The National Conference on Anthropology and Education* (1968), pp. 21–42.

The following illustrations in this article are reprinted by permission: Fig. 1: J. P. Scott, *Science*, 138 (Nov. 1962) 949–958, fig. 1. Copyright 1962 by the American Association for the Advancement of Science. Fig. 2: Erlenmeyer-Kimling and Jarvik, *Science*, 142 (Dec. 1963) 1477–1479, fig. 1. Copyright 1963 by the American association for the Advancement of Science. Figs. 6–11: Lesser, Fifer, and Clark, *Monographs of the Society for Research in Child Development*, 30, no. 102 (1965) 63–68, figs. 1–6. © 1965 by the Society for Research in Child Development. Figs. 12–14: Stodolsky and Lesser, *Harvard Educational Review* 37, no. 4 (1967) 546–593. © 1967 by the President and Fellows of Harvard College.

A problem in accepting this line of reasoning is that despite the general acceptance of evolutionary theory, many scientists cannot in fact accept man as part of the evolutionary story. There is, for example, the avowed or implicit dualism of many of our leading biologists, e.g., Sir John Eccles, Julian Huxley, and T. de Chardin, but a discussion on this topic is not particularly appropriate here. We have only to say that ours is a monistic position which asserts the singularity of mind and body and that, in our opinion, this is the only logically defensible position to hold.

EARLY DEVELOPMENT: CURIOSITY AND FEAR

In general, we can say that in the animals which we shall mention, familiarization and attachments to parents come first, followed by a rising fear of strange stimuli, and especially fear of strange organisms. At the same time there is a development of curiosity and investigativeness, and much of what follows will describe these opposing forces of curiosity and investigativeness on the one hand and fear of the strange on the other.

Animal Infancy

In all animals which are cared for, protected, and led or carried by a parent, e.g., anatidae, canidae, monkeys, etc., the initial period after birth is spent exclusively with the parental animals and siblings, and almost all responses are directed to the parents. The most famous example is imprinting in anatidae, where the precocial hatchlings follow the adult with an intensity that often brings identificatory tears of laughter to human viewers. So strong is the drive to follow that, as is well known, the initial following response can even be elicited by a human surrogate parent.

Only after some time, after the bond has become fast and youngsters have matured somewhat, do the young start investigating the rest of their surroundings. This trend is far more striking in mammals than in birds, but all animals who are under predation pressure must eventually learn about the stable, "usual" state of their environment; the implication of this last remark is that a fear of the unusual or strange has been phylogenetically adaptive, and indeed, the evidence for this is fairly incontrovertible (e.g., Hediger, 1964; Freedman, 1961).

At first the major effort, aside from feeding, is toward learning about the nest and the caretaker, and fear seems quite absent. Many nesting birds, for example, will respond to a proffered finger after hatching, but after a time only the usual stimulus (e.g., parent) draws gaping and chirping whereas the finger results in their ducking low and freezing. Similarly, in precocial anatidae, after imprinting occurs, all strange stimuli tend to result in startled and quick grouping behind the parent.

It is easy to observe the development we are talking about in precocial birds, because their foraging (protocuriosity?) carries them farther and farther from the nest, but never too far! At the slightest departure from the familiar, they scurry back.

Canid pups are rather less nervous, but the pattern is precisely the same (Freedman, King, and Elliot, 1961). In our study, litters of beagles and cockers were reared in acre pens that turned out to be fairly good simulations of wild conditions. At four weeks the pups remained in the nest; at five they ventured a few yards from it, and at six, up to 50 feet. At the same time they developed an increasing fearfulness of strange organisms, especially large ones, so that curiosity became tempered by fear (Figure 1).

Small organisms such as insects frequently drew playful growling and mock hunting behavior from the pups, but the appearance of a man or a strange dog, after six weeks of age, resulted in mad flight for cover (in our experiment the favorite hiding place was under the nest box). Schenkel's description of the development of lion cubs at the Nairobi National Park in Africa (1966) is very similar, even as to ages.

At the level of the primates, Harlow and Harlow's description of rhesus development (1959, 1962, 1966), Jay's of langurs (1963), and the studies of home raised chimps (Kellogg and Kellogg, 1933; Hayes, 1951) all show similar developmental patterns [1]: The secure home base (mother) is the first order of business, followed by increasing curiosity and investigativeness, then play with mother, objects, and small living things. These activities are always tempered by a fear of strange objects, particularly if they move *toward* the animal (Schiff et al., 1962) and most particularly if they are large.

Human Infancy

The infant is a social being before anything else. The infant begins absorbing the living persons about him through his senses, especially his eyes, although sound and touch are of great importance. Sometime in the second month the *en face* smile appears, soon accompanied by cooing and other sounds. The caretaking adult finds all this irresistible, joyous, if not emotionally overpowering, and considerable interaction with the adult begins to occur. It should be emphasized that much of this is initiated by the infant!

The importance of mutual smiling for eventual attachment is suggested by the following observation:

> Jock is seven weeks old. E enters his room and Jock looks past him at the window. E speaks and Jock looks at E, but only briefly. E walks back and forth before Jock's crib, but Jock does not follow with his eyes.
>
> E then bends over Jock and starts baby talk. Jock soon fixes on E's

---

[1] Such a list could grow quite long, and would additionally include such studies as Jolly's on lemurs (1966), Schaller's on the mountain gorilla (1963), and Van Lawick-Goodall's on chimpanzees (1967).

FIGURE 1
Timing mechanisms for the critical period in puppies. The period is initiated by positive behavior mechanisms, such as playful fighting, which result in attraction to a strange individual, and it is brought to a close by the development of a fear response which causes the attraction to decline. The optimum period for rapid and permanent socialization comes shortly after the appearance of prolonged avoidance reactions (From Scott, 1962).

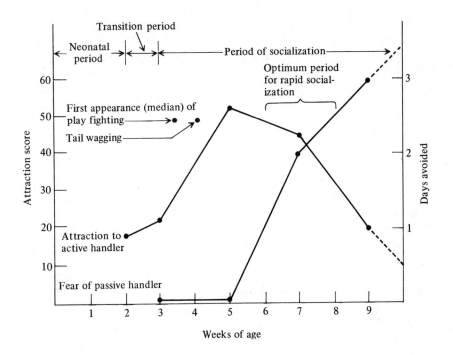

Weeks of age

face, staring intently for a full 20 seconds, and then smiles. Several more smiles are similarly elicited.

E again walks back and forth before Jock's crib, but now Jock follows him visually everywhere he goes, even craning his neck when E wanders out of sight. This continues over the 10-minute observation period.

For his part, E reports feeling much closer to Jock now that Jock has returned his cooing and smiling in kind and is following him with his eyes.

In the early months a definite preference for the primary caretakers appears, while there is a tolerance, if not as great an attachment, for all those who appear frequently before the distance receptors of the helpless human infant (Walters and Parke, 1965).

Usually by the fifth month, strangers, particularly large strangers (Cagen, 1966), begin to elicit fear responses even as they also elicit a sort of fascination, to judge by the fixed stare which precedes outright crying. A number of recent studies bear this out, i.e., older infants confronted by a familiar and an unfamiliar person spend most of the time watching the stranger (Morgan and Ricciuti, 1969; Caldwell and Honzig, 1969; Ainsworth, 1967, 1969; Rheingold, 1961; Freedman, Loring and Martin, 1967). Of course, if the strangers draw too close, vigilance is replaced by panic, crying, and turning toward mother.[2] It certainly looks as if the infant's attention to the strange is an attempt to cope with and master it while simultaneously exhibiting built-in vigilance to potential danger.

A host of studies on "perceptual preferences" of infants (cf. Fantz, 1963; Fantz et al., 1962; Line, 1931; Spears, 1964, in humans; and Sackett, 1966, in rhesus monkeys) yields a complementary picture. Presented with various patterns, human infants up to about three months of age prefer to look at that which is familiar, that is, the process of familiarization seems most important at the beginning of life; toward six months however, novel stimuli are much more interesting in that older infants tend to look at novel stimuli and turn away from familiar ones (e.g., Lewis, 1967).

It is quite clearly a phylogenetically adaptive mechanism to be highly curious about all that is new — new objects, new people, new places — and almost all higher animals share similar traits. As regards new places, the whole issue of territoriality, which we can only mention, appears to involve a basic need to become familiar with one's surroundings. Where other species might render a strange area familiar by scent markings, the normal human child or adult is usually highly wary and explorative until familiarized with a new place. Good teachers, of course, are highly cognizant of this phenomenon, especially at the start of the school year, and Spock has noted that pediatricians see this suspiciousness in their offices as early as five months of age.

Thus, curiosity in early childhood and thereafter most often has the double aspect of interest and wariness. With regard to pathology of the capacity for curiosity, we know that it can be greatly reduced, if not destroyed, if there is no emotionally secure home base developed from which one may then wander.[3] Thus in some orphanage raised infants,

---

[2] Schaller (1963) has described what must be a similar reaction in himself on accidentally coming *en face*, at only a few yards distance, with a fully grown female gorilla. He suspects the gorilla was just as frightened and just as relieved as he on turning away. The reaction of the infant, it would appear, is potentially with us the rest of our lives, but fortunately it is usually experienced in much milder terms because of the increased capacity to cope.

[3] Erikson (1950) has called this process the formation of "basic-trust" and Ainsworth (1962) has recently summarized a substantial body of supporting evidence. In the same vein, several reviews of literature on environmental correlates of obedience in children (Hoffman, 1963; Kohlberg, 1963) conclude that obedience in our culture is dependent on a base of love and the concomitant appearance of empathy in parent-child com-

rocking and self-stimulation may substitute for exploration with eyes, hands, and feet or, as in the case of experimentally deprived rhesus monkeys, similar behavior takes the place of physical incursions into the environment. This is too well documented to go into here (Harlow and Harlow, 1966; Ainsworth, 1967), other than to point out how well the animal and human data fit.

The most obvious lessons for education from all this is: (1) Youngsters are naturally curious; conversely, curiosity does not have to be taught. (2) Fear can obliterate curiosity, and it is the role of the empathizing adult (teacher or parent) to recognize when this is happening and to help reduce the child's anxiety.

Please note that this position is essentially that of Rogers, Maslow, Holt, and others: given understanding adults, it is impossible to prevent learning and growth. We would go a step farther to say that in most children the urge to "find out" is so strong that it would take an enormous amount of mishandling to eliminate it. It is perhaps ironical that the environmentalist tradition that insists that man is infinitely malleable must, if only as corollary, show little faith in what man will do if left to his own devices.

One reads such dramatic book titles as *Death at an Early Age* (Kozol, 1967), by which the author means slum children lose their curiosity through the mishandling of teachers and school systems. We have yet to see an uncurious slum child. It is just that they are not curious about what goes on in the classroom. Some of the issues this brings up will be discussed in the last section.

Play. In humans, as in all mammals who engage in play, it starts early in life and expands considerably before the serious business of adulthood begins. It is clearly a most marvelous way to discover the specifics of one's fellows and one's surroundings, and has the great adaptive advantage of fostering such learning anew in each generation.

In general, it is in the spirit of play that the first imitations of adult gesture occur, e.g., pat-a-cake almost always first appears in the midst of a joyous encounter with the mother or a befriended adult, with accompanying smiles and with eyes on the face rather than the hands (Freedman, 1963). Strangers, as we have implied, will only inhibit the child by offering it gestures or sounds to imitate.

Consider, however, that if the mother or caretaker is not interested in playing and talking to the infant in this way, it follows that fewer gestures and sounds will be absorbed (as seems to be the case in the

---

munication. In the training of dogs, too, there is ample evidence that an initial emotionally positive base between the dog and a human maximizes later obedience (Freedman, 1967b) and results in improved guidedogs (Pfaffenberger and Scott, 1959).

Mayan village investigated by Brazelton et al., 1967). It certainly would appear that the *playful* mother is the best teacher and the best source of early stimulation, and it is our suggestion that, in considering the importance of early stimulation, we should think first in terms of adult-infant play and only secondarily in terms of mobiles over the crib, flashing lights, and other similar gimmicks intended to raise the cognitive level.

From our own observations, it is clear that the great majority of nursery schools teach via play, but that far too soon in a child's educational career play becomes restricted to recess, and the classroom becomes a terribly serious place. There is then the very long wait until graduate school, where, if one is lucky, he meets a creative instructor who still believes, as did Carl Lashley that our important discoveries come while "playing around." [4]

Discipline. By eighteen months considerable motor independence has been achieved, and along with this blessing comes the necessary problem of discipline — the perennial "don'ts."

For one thing, it is clear to us that both obedience and disobedience are necessary phases of human adaptation. Parental watchfulness of a temporarily "fearless" toddler is always represented, on the toddler's part, by a modicum of fear and respect for directives coming from the adult. Some toddlers and children are more amenable to the adults' injunctions than others, but complete obliviousness to adult demands is clearly non-adaptive and pathological (see especially Levy, 1943).[5] At the other extreme, too great a fear of authority would tend to obliterate initiative, reduce curiosity, and eat into courage. Thus, as always, some balance of two opposing forces needs to be achieved, and a good American parent is one who properly senses when and when not to put pressure on his child, given the nature of that child.

In many other cultures, however, the major source of affection and the major source of rules are formally separated (Levi-Strauss, 1967), as between the father and uncle among the Trobrianders. Until recently this was true of our culture as well in that mothers and fathers frequently took the respective roles of fount of affection and source of rules, with a certain amount of overlap to be sure. However, in recent years the tendency has been for all adults — mothers, fathers, and teachers — to embody both roles. As a consequence most Americans we know are perpetually worried

---

[4] When Kurt Goldstein, the great neurologist, came to this country in 1938, he visited Lashley and asked what he was doing. "Just playing around," was the response. In the same vein, Lorenz has reported that Von Frisch made all of his basic discoveries when home, relaxing and "fooling around" with his beehives.

[5] Although Levy deals primarily with environmental causes, he nevertheless asserts that such "psychopathy" usually involves a genetic x environmental interaction.

as to whether or not they are striking the right balance between affection on the one hand, and restriction and imposition on the other.

This perhaps proves anew that almost all things are possible for the human species, or at least that given such antinomies as obedience vs. egoism and disciplinary vs. laissez-faire upbringing, a great variety of possibilities can be generated. As American parents, we are as confused about the "right" way as the next person, and we can only note that the psychological, psychiatric, and educational literature is similarly at odds with itself.

For example, Bereiter and Engelmann (1966) have been emphasizing the *authority accepting* tendency of children in their instructional method by shouting and asserting grown-up power, and they report substantial results doing it that way. On the other hand, Holt (1965) seems to eschew all authoritarianism in favor of respectful guidance in the hope that children will experience the emergence of their own interests and powers; again marvelous results are reported.

For parents there is obviously a time for each attitude, and it is similarly difficult to believe that either a relentless authority or an all-loving "saint" could make a good all-around teacher. Perhaps each is suited to certain types of children, or perhaps the basic common denominator in both of these styles was a "positive transference" to the teacher. This gets us into the question of the creative teacher, and unfortunately, there are no formulas for how to achieve that remarkable state of grace.

SEXUAL DIMORPHISM: DEVELOPMENT OF NEGATIVISM, COURAGE, PLAY WITH PEERS, AND DOMINANCE HIERARCHY

All cared-for animals must eventually relinquish dependence on their parents, and each species has built-in mechanisms for achieving the separation. Usually there is mutual accommodation between mother and child. In the rhesus, for example, the four- to five-month old wanders farther and farther from mother, and she in turn is less inclined to fetch him back. Slowly he becomes interested in other youngsters, and by the time he is a yearling, play in the peer group takes up most of his time. If, for some reason he persists in his dependency and continues on the teat, a few well-placed bites help to send him out into the extrafamilial world (Harlow and Harlow, 1966).

It is at this time, too, in the rhesus, that clear-cut differences between male and female behavior appear. Male youngsters enter into rough and tumble games while females tend to gather elsewhere in far less active groups. Among the males, rough and tumble fun becomes progressively more serious, and during the second year serious biting indicates the dominance hierarchy is well underway. Females usually find their way into the hierarchy only after sexual maturity via their male consorts (Hall and

De Vore, 1965).[6] As for the development of courage, if not foolhardiness, one has only to watch Koford's films (1963) of the juvenile rhesus of Cayo Santiago diving from high trees into a shallow lagoon — apparently with the sole purpose of splashing one's playmates. There seems little doubt, although no data are reported, that these displays result in respect, not only from the watching human audience, but among the monkeys themselves, and that they help to sort out the dominance order. Finally, it is well established over many species that physical strength, particularly as evidenced by weight, correlates highly with ultimate position of dominance.

Now what has all this to do with human development and human educability? First, what characterizes sexual dimorphism among humans? We now have considerable data that newborn girls are already different from newborn boys on a number of behavioral measures.

Infant girls are more responsive to touch, less angry and demanding when hungry or thwarted, more given to steady gazing at various stimuli, especially the human face, and less prone to search for novelty. They are also more fearful of strangers. Infant girls relate more through vocalization and later in the first year, through verbalization; boys do more watching and manipulation.

By thirteen months more girls show a preference for things they can care for and for fine muscle tasks, while more boys prefer mechanical cars and gross muscle tasks. Even when both sexes are given baby dolls, boys tend to use them as inanimate playthings, girls as real babies. Thirteen-month-old girls are more fearful in a strange place, investigate less than boys, and stay closer to mother. Male toddlers will wander away from home more frequently and take more physical chances, as in climbing ladders. Toddler boys are, additionally, more negativistic — a trait which is doubtless related to self-assertion and courage. By four years it is clear that boys are far more aggressive, given to temper outbursts, as well as to displays to bravado. If one reads Mead's *Male and Female* (1949) carefully, six of the seven cultures she knew showed similar behavioral dimorphism. (The Tchambuli, a society in the process of decay, was the one exception.[7])

We have been watching children between three and six years and find that boys engage more in rough and tumble play by four, and that by six

---

[6] In the lemurs *P. verreauxi* and *L. macaco* the male-female ratio in a troop is commonly greater than one, and the aggressive-passive dichotomy is apparently reversed (Jolly, 1966).

[7] This emphasis on what we call *phylogenetically adaptive behavior* (Freedman, 1967) is not meant to deny that familial and cultural institutions do indeed differentially influence the behavior of the sexes. In our view, however, such institutions only support or shape such differences and do not create them, as it were, out of the blue.

years they have formed quite definite dominance-submission hierarchies. As in rhesus, this is not true of girls (Omark and Edelman, 1969).

When two boys at four years are asked "Who is toughest?" each one replies "I am." By 5½, however, both agree that one or the other is tougher, and they also can rank the entire class on "toughness," "smartness," and "tallness" with considerable agreement and accuracy among all the boys. This study, incidentally, was made within a nongraded class, and it appears that the notion of ranking becomes meaningful and important to five-year-old human males with or without the encouragement of adults.

Although more data are needed, it nevertheless appears that, as in rhesus, males and females are different from the very start, and that they gravitate gradually but definitely, into quite different social patterns by 5½ years of age.

It is of historical importance to realize that this apparently phylogenetically derived competitiveness among males is precisely the phenomenon which Freud dubbed the Oedipus complex: For example, in 1½-year-old rhesus males and 3- to 5-year-old human males, there is often a physical challenge made toward adult males (e.g., the father, uncle, in humans) and the usual response on the part of both rhesus and human adults can best be classified as bemusement. In human boys, of course, the challenge is often fantasied or play-acted. Later, when these youngsters are juveniles and challenge the adult, adult bemusement turns to irritation, and when the challenger is near-adult, irritation can turn to severe anger. The parallel between rhesus and humans, we would venture to say, is nearly exact.

We would venture further that these patterns are similar in all societies, but unfortunately we have yet to find an ethnography which supplies information on the development of hierarchization. Fortunately, we do have a colleague in the field (Nigeria), Jerome Barkow, who is studying this process among three- to six-year-olds in a Hausa village, and who plans then to watch the same age group in a contrasting African society (as yet undetermined because of the political situation there). We also have data, and we are gathering more, in the continued boy-girl differentiation play engaged in throughout the grammar school years. Table 1 is a simplified "box score" based on recent studies (Maccoby, 1966). From this chart we see that, in addition to contrasting social development, males and females differ in many abilities, again apparently on an epigamic basis.

What do these data on sexual dimorphism suggest for educational practices? Here we are on unsure ground and we do not, as yet, have much to say. Some United States studies show grammar school instruction to be more effective in classes separated by sex.[8] Apparently the goody-good

---

[8] S. F. Yolles (1967) reported an experiment near Washington, D.C., where educators decided to have separate elementary school classes for boys and girls. One teacher

TABLE 1
Summary of Research on Some Sex Differences

	Male	*Female*	*No difference*
Aggression	44	4	8
Dependency			
Self-report and projective			
measures (Older Females)	0	5	0
Conformity and Suggestibility	2	14	11
Nurturance and Affiliation	5	45	6
Anxiety			
(Paper and pencil tests)	2	18	12
Guilt	0	8	1
Verbal Cognitive Abilities	14	62	25
Other Cognitive Abilities			
Mathematical reasoning	11	1	9
Spatial	12	0	6
Perceptual speed (clerical)	0	8	2
Cognitive Styles			
Field independence	11	1	1
Conservatism in judgment and			
risk-taking	0	5	0
Breaking set and restructuring	5	0	2
Conservatism in affective			
judgments and expression	5	0	1
School grades	0	5	0

Extracted from R. M. Oetzel, "Annotated Bibliography," in E. Maccoby (ed.), *The Development of Sex Differences*, 1966. Each unit equals one study.

girls and the more noisy, adventuresome yet highly organizable boys are best off apart so that the implicitly different social approaches do not grate on each other. On the other hand, there are cogent arguments for not separating the sexes, and what one recommends in this regard will doubtless depend on what one's aims and values are, and on the particular school setting. Perhaps the knowledge that minor curriculum changes make very little difference, no matter what they are (Stephens, 1967), has made us extremely discreet about entering into that cauldron.

However, we can offer parents and teachers a note which follows from the hierarchical organization of groups of six-year-olds and older. Children

---

said: "I learned things about boys and girls that I had never understood before. I had spent years trying to keep boys from disturbing everyone. This was just wasted effort. I found that boys can still concentrate even when they are noisy. You can learn to work in a boiler factory, if you have to, and that is just what I have done."

Another said: "I always liked girls best until I got a whole classful of them. In the beginning of the experiment, it dawned on me that the girls were not doing their own thinking. Parrot-like, they repeated everything that the teacher had ever said. What are we doing to these girls, I began to wonder, to make them so conforming?"

The results of the experiment were impressive. Both sexes did significantly better in their studies. The boys became much more interested in school. The girls grew more independent and original in their thinking.

are often found to complain of unhappiness with school, but persistent questioning reveals only that it is not the subject matter nor the teacher which is bothersome. With sensitive rather than persistent questioning one finds, more often than not, that the trouble lies in the child's perception of being on the low end of a same-sex hierarchy. "Everyone hates me," "they all laugh at me," usually means "I'm fairly far down on the social scale and not in with the leadership." Unfortunately this is not the place for an extended discussion of therapeutic strategies for raising a child's hierarchical position and self-esteem, but such discussions are available.

Judging from our own studies, the hierarchical scale in the early grades seems to primarily involve physical toughness in boys and what we can call friendship-orientation in girls, with various other subsidiary hierarchies possible (Freedman, 1968). Whereas toughness has been important in all the male peer groups we have studied, regardless of socioeconomic class, whether or not "smartness" is status enhancing depends on the peer-group ethic. In some peer groups, abilities in school subjects are not considered important, and then we get the frequently experienced teacher's reaction often heard from white teachers of lower class black students (cf. Jensen, 1967), "I can't seem to get to them," or "they've shut me out." Needless to say, strategies for getting around such an impasse is one of the burning topics of our times, and we humbly defer its discussion to another time.

Umwelt

We should like, in closing this section, to briefly describe the very useful ethological concept of *Umwelt*, or the "perceived world," first developed by Jacob von Uexkull (1967). Von Uexkull might have asked, for example, how is the classroom situation perceived by the child? What are the forces there which are meaningful to him? How would one reconstruct a child's day at school, from his point of view? With these questions in mind we have started asking three-, four-, and six-year-olds about school. One has to interpret their answers, because they are always terribly idiosyncratic, but one can nevertheless see developmental trends. When asked about school, 3½-year-old Gregory, for example, talks only of his friends, so that we can assume making friends is most important for him. Six-year-old Tony, on the other hand, talks of being able to count to a thousand and, knowing him as we do, this indicates his need to do big things, and that school is a way of becoming more powerful. One could use this methodology in a great variety of ways, e.g., comparing the perceptions of children of different economic classes, different ethnic backgrounds, different schools, different teachers, and so forth. While time-consuming and perhaps not amenable to elegant statistical methods, befriending and talking to children can be a most gratifying mode of research. It also helps eliminate the adult distortions of what is really going on.

BEHAVIOR GENETICS

Our discussion of sexual dimorphism has already involved us with the field of behavior genetics. However, the more usual message of the geneticist working with behavior is to stress that 2^{23} gametic combinations result in near infinite variation, and that we need not be surprised that each individual poses unique problems for the teacher, and so forth. It is now clear, at least to behavior geneticists, that all aspects of human behavior — abilities, talents, temperament, personality, and pathology — have genetic components (Erlenmeyer-Kimling and Jarvik, 1963; Vandenberg, 1966; Gottesman and Shields, 1967), but since this contention is probably still unconvincing to many, we will illustrate it with some data.

Erlenmeyer-Kimling and Jarvik (Figure 2) summarize fifty-two studies of intelligence among individuals of progressively closer genetic relationships. It is very clear that, as genetic identity is approached, in a range from nonrelatives to identical twins reared apart or together, the correlation progressively increases.

In our own work with twins in their first year of life, that is before

FIGURE 2
Correlation coefficients for "intelligence" test scores from 52 studies. Some studies reported data for more than one relationship category; some included more than one sample per category, giving a total of 99 groups. Over two-thirds of the correlation coefficients were derived from IQ's, the remainder from special tests (for example, primary mental abilities). Midparent-child correlation was used when available, otherwise mother-child correlation. Correlation coefficients obtained in each study are indicated by dark circles; medians are shown by vertical lines intersecting the horizontal lines which represent the ranges (From Erlenmeyer-Kimling and Jarvik, 1963).

Category		0.00 0.10 0.20 0.30 0.40 0.50 0.60 0.70 0.80 0.90	Groups included
Unrelated persons	Reared apart		4
	Reared together		5
Fosterparent-child			3
Parent-child			12
Siblings	Reared apart		2
	Reared together		35
Twins Two-egg	Opposite sex		9
	Like sex		11
Twins One-egg	Reared apart		4
	Reared together		14

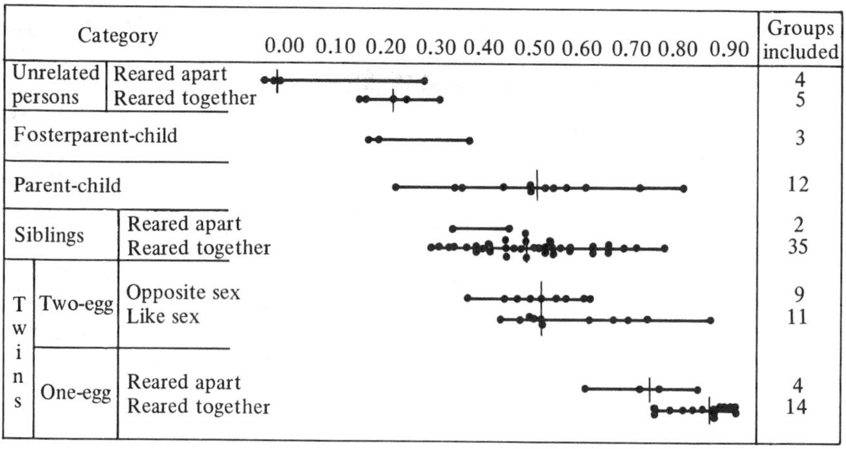

FIGURE 3
Twin behavior investigated on the Bayley Mental and Motor Scales. There is considerably more difference in individual behavior of fraternal twins than of identical ones (In Freedman, 1967b).

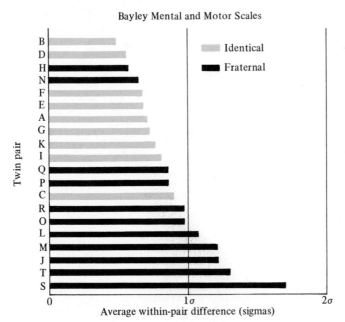

mutual imitation could effect differential performance, we found a similar picture (Figure 3; Freedman, 1967b). Thus, mutual imitation can now probably be ruled out as a major bias of twin studies, because about the same order of concordance occurs in infant twins as in older twins.

With regard to personality items, Vandenberg (1966) lists a substantial number of twin-studies which have used different measures of personality but with the same general outcomes, i.e., identicals are more concordant than fraternals. To give a few examples, Gottesman (1963, 1965) used the Minnesota Multiphasic Inventory in two separate populations and found all F ratios but one, based on

$$\frac{\text{variance of dizygotic pairs}}{\text{variance of monozygotic pairs}} \; (\sigma_{DZ}^2/\sigma_{MZ}^2)$$

were well over unity, with only one scale significant at the .01 level; when these data are combined with those of Reznikoff and Honeyman (1966) all MMPI scales are over unity, three surpass the .01 level and two the .05 level of statistical probability (Table 2). The implication is that the

TABLE 2

F Ratios of DZ Within-pair Variances for Twins from Minnesota, Massachusetts, and Connecticut on the Minnesota Multiphasic Personality Inventory[a]

	34 DZ, 34 MZ Gottesman (1963)	68 DZ, 82 MZ Gottesman (1965)	16 DZ, 18 MZ Reznikoff and Honeyman (1966)	118 DZ, 134 MZ Combined data
Hypochondriasis	1.19	1.01	2.33[b]	1.21
Depression	1.81[b]	1.82[b]	1.62	1.53[c]
Hysteria	.86	1.43	2.70[b]	1.23
Psychopathic deviate	2.01[b]	1.63[b]	1.54	1.39[b]
Masculinity-femininity	1.18	1.41	2.37[b]	1.10
Paranoia	1.05	1.61[b]	1.78	1.27
Psychasthenia	1.58	1.46	.82	1.52[c]
Schizophrenia	1.71	1.49[b]	1.40	1.36[b]
Hypomania	1.32	1.15	1.65	1.21
Social introversion	3.42[c]	1.49[b]	2.02	1.59[c]

[a]Last column is based on all three studies, averaged after z-transformation. Note that the study with the largest N (Gottesman, 1965) has the greater number of scales which proved significant. Further, when the studies are combined, the level of significance in three scales is raised (after Vandenberg, 1966).

[b]$p < .05$

[c]$p < .01$

greater the number of twins in a study, the greater are the number of items which will be found significantly "heritable." [9] The recent study by Nichols (1966), using the test responses of 850 pairs of high school twins, bears this out. Aside from finding that many of the factors (cohesive groups of items) on his tests were significantly "heritable" (Table 3), a large number of relatively unimportant individual items were also highly "heritable" (e.g., the answers to Do you bleach your hair? or Do you want to be a judge?).[10]

It appears that when one gets into very large numbers of twins, one taps into heritable aspects of a large and unpredictable number of items. This has led us to speculate that with an infinite number of twins, all aspects of behavior would be adjudged "heritable." Such an expectation seems in keeping with a monistic position on the heredity-environment issue, that is, a position which holds that these are not antinomies but different angles on the same system.

Again, our study of infant twins tends to back up the data gathered on older twins (Freedman, 1965). Using repeated administrations of the Nancy Bayley Infant Behavior Profile over the first year, we found greater concordance in our identical pairs (Table 4; Figure 4). In an especially well controlled aspect of this study, independent judges rated monthly films which had been taken of these infants, again using the Bayley Infant Behavior Profile. In order to avoid a "halo" effect, each judge rated but one member of any twin-pair, and again intrapair differences among fraternals were distinctly larger (Figure 5). Thus, on viewing the available data to this date, there can be no reasonable question about the genetic mediation of intelligence, abilities, and personality.

We should like now to briefly touch on the problem of "continuities over the life span" as it relates to behavior genetics. Needless to say, maturational changes and ontogenetic adaptations are at odds with continuity, and the findings of most longitudinal studies are therefore sparse in this area (e.g., Kagan and Moss, 1962; Thomas et al., 1963; Bayley, 1964). Nevertheless, on close analysis, we have found many interesting continuities from infancy through five and six years of age (the length of our study thus far) in our twins. Let us illustrate with a rather straightforward observation based on films taken during our studies.

> Arturo and Felix, a fraternal pair of twins, showed striking dissimilarity in their threshholds to smiling, as early as two months of age. At that age, Arturo would smile, with his eyes closed, to the stroking of his cheek, a

---

[9] "Heritability" here refers to a significant F ratio and merely means that it is probable that heredity plays a significant although unknown role in the realization of the phenotype in question.

[10] Also, note the behavioral sexual dimorphism in Table 3.

TABLE 3

Statistically Significant Twin Correlations from the California Psychological Inventory Scales[a]

	Males			Females		
	Intraclass correlation			Intraclass correlation		
Scale	MZ (N = 207)	DZ (N = 126)	t	MZ (N = 291)	DZ (N = 193)	t
Significant for both sexes						
Sociability	.53	.25	2.94	.54	.33	2.80
Social presence	.51	.15	3.64	.55	.31	3.19
Self-acceptance	.43	.16	2.55	.54	.37	2.39
Sense of well-being	.54	.33	2.28	.45	.27	2.12
Self-control	.56	.27	3.15	.57	.36	2.81
Achievement via conformance	.49	.06	4.11	.44	.25	2.41
Factor I (value orientation or social adjustment)	.55	.28	2.97	.55	.34	2.86
Factor II (person orientation or extraversion)	.56	.19	3.88	.59	.39	2.79
Rigidity	.47	.13	3.34	.47	.23	2.98
Managerial	.61	.23	4.13	.56	.42	1.97
Significant for males only						
Dominance	.58	.13	4.68	.50	.36	1.88
Capacity for status	.57	.36	2.30	.60	.54	.86
Responsibility	.57	.29	3.02	.43	.40	.45
Socialization	.53	.15	3.79	.55	.49	1.03
Tolerance	.59	.30	3.26	.48	.39	1.13
Achievement via independence	.58	.36	2.54	.52	.42	1.45
Intellectual efficiency	.59	.27	3.43	.47	.38	1.08
Acquiescence	.47	.09	3.69	.39	.23	1.86
Social desirability	.47	.22	2.48	.49	.39	1.27
Significant for females only						
Good impression	.48	.32	1.64	.46	.28	2.26
Communality	.32	.24	.75	.40	.12	3.22
Psychological-mindedness	.47	.28	1.95	.36	.19	2.03
Flexibility	.43	.25	1.81	.51	.18	4.05
Not significant						
Femininity	.43	.27	1.65	.31	.14	1.92

[a]The value of t used to classify scales into the various significance groups was 1.96. Since only cases where r_{MZ} was greater than r_{DZ} would be considered significant, this was a one-tail test at the .025 level.

TABLE 4

Nancy Bayley Infant Behavior Profile (Survey of Individual Items)[a,b]

	P
1. *Social orientation:* responsiveness to persons.	.005
(1) Does not modify behavior to persons as different from objects.	
(9) Behavior seems to be continuously affected by awareness of persons present.	
2. *Object orientation:* responsiveness to toys and other objects.	.02
(1) Does not look at or in any way indicate interest in objects.	
(9) Reluctantly relinquishes test materials.	
3. *Goal directedness:*	.02
(1) No evidence of directed effort.	
(9) Continued absorption with task until it is solved.	
4. *Attention span:* tendency to persist in attending to any one object, person or activity, aside from attaining a goal.	.02
(1) Fleeting attention span.	
(9) Long-continued absorption in a toy, activity, or person.	
5. *Cooperativeness:* (Not relevant most of first year).	
6. *Activity:* inactive-vigorous.	N.S.
(1) Stays quietly in one place with practically no self-initiated movement.	
(9) Hyperactive: can't be quieted for sedentary tests.	
6.1 *Activity:* level of energy (low to high).	N.S.
6.2 *Activity:* coordination of gross muscle movements for age (smooth functioning to poor coordination).	N.S.
6.3 *Activity:* coordination of fine muscles (hands) for age (smooth functioning to poor coordination).	.04
7. *Reactivity:* the ease with which a child is stimulated to response, his sensitivity or excitability. (May be positive or negative in tone.)	.04
(1) Unreactive; seems to pay little heed to what goes on around him. Responds only to strong or repeated stimulation.	
(9) Very reactive; every little thing seems to stir him up; startles, reacts quickly, seems keenly sensitive to things going on around him.	N.S.
8. *Tension:*	N.S.
(1) Inert, may be flaccid most of the time.	
(9) Body is predominantly taut or tense.	
9. *Fearfulness:* (e.g., reaction to the new or strange: strange people, test materials, strange surroundings).	.05
(1) Accepts the entire situation with no evidence of fear, caution, or inhibition of actions.	
(9) Strong indications of fear of the strange, to the extent he cannot be brought to play or respond to the tests.	
10. *General emotional tone:* unhappy-happy	N.S.
(1) Child seems unhappy throughout the period.	
(9) Radiantly happy; nothing is upsetting; animated.	
11. Endurance or behavior constancy in adequacy of response to demands of tests.	N.S.
(1) Tires easily, quickly regresses to lower levels of functioning.	
(9) Continues to respond well and with interest, even with prolonged tests at difficult levels.	
12. *Sensory areas:* preoccupation or interest displayed (none to excessive).	
(a) Sights: looking	.025
(b) Sounds: listening	N.S.
(c) Sound producing: vocal	N.S.
(d) Sound producing: banging, or other	.005
(e) Manipulating (exploring with hands)	.02
(f) Body motion	N.S.
(g) Mouthing or sucking: thumb or fingers	N.S.
(h) Mouthing or sucking: toys	N.S.

In Freedman, 1965.

[a]Probabilities are from Mann-Whitney one-tailed tables and refer to items in which identical twin pairs exhibit significantly greater concordance than fraternal twins over the first year. In no case was the opposite true

[b]Each item was rated along a scale from "deficient" to "overendowed," with five steps usually spelled out; a nine-point scale was obtained by adding half steps. The first and last steps are supplied to clarify the items.

FIGURE 4
Twin behavior investigated on the Bayley Infant Behavior Profile (In
Freedman, 1967b).

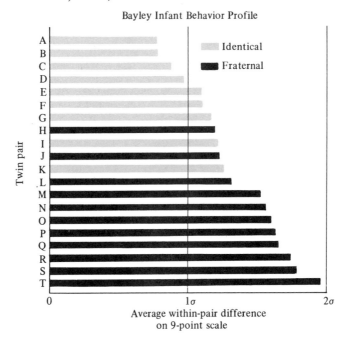

Bayley Infant Behavior Profile

soft voice, or the tinkle of a bell. Felix rarely smiled, but by contrast was
alert and unusually observant. At nine months, when confronted by a
stranger, both seemed equally uncomfortable. Arturo, however, tried to
smile, despite his fear, while Felix simply kept his eyes from meeting those
of the stranger. At the 5½-year follow-up, the persistence of these differences in interpersonal approach were striking. Felix exhibited only one full
smile during the entire interview, while Arturo smiled constantly over the
entire time. Such striking differences were never seen among our identicals, and we must conclude that different genotypes were ultimately responsible.

What does all this mean for educators? For one thing, we have no re-
course but to acknowledge that we are all genetically unique, and that this
fact enters into all phases of our phenotypic uniqueness. However, the
implications are not novel, and any method which openly appreciates
individual uniqueness, such as the Montessori (when properly practiced),
computer-regulated progress (Atkinson, 1968), or differential tutoring
(Bloom, 1968), seems to be suggested by them.

The more important implication of genetical logic for anthropology

FIGURE 5
Within-pair differences on the Bayley Infant Behavior Profile, based on 8 consecutive months of filmed behavior (either months 1-8, or months 5-12. (In Freedman, 1967b).

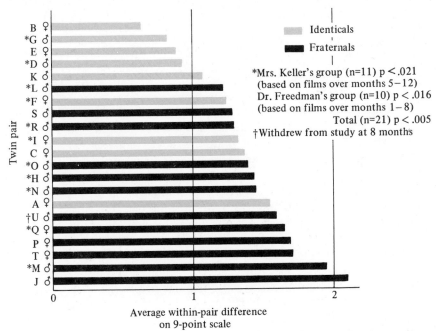

and education, however, is that ethnic groups and societies can differ from one another on a genetical basis, that is, on the basis of differential gene frequencies and in genetic combinations available. Dobzhansky, the usual person to be quoted in this area (e.g., Dobzhansky, 1962), has frequently made the first point regarding differential gene frequencies, and emphasized the overlap between groups. However, he has seen fit to be discreet about the second point, that which emphasizes the presence of unique genetic combinations within relatively closed groups.

Ginsbury and Laughlin (1967) have pointed out that in the feedback that inevitably occurs between society and the gene pool, there is selection for a phenotypic norm or norms. These phenotypic norms can be achieved in many genetic ways, or, so to speak, via different genetic packages. When we talk of genetic differences between societies, we therefore do not necessarily mean these differences are due to the presence of different genes, but we refer instead to the unique gene combinations that a particular society tends to exhibit and support as its norm.

These ideas, coupled with the probable fact that most societies had relatively few founders and that some degree of inbreeding is the rule, leads to the expectation that relative isolates are both culturally and genetically differentiated one from the other. It also follows that the culture developed by an isolated group is particularly adjusted to the gene-pool of that group, and that Balinese culture, for example, is in harmony with the Balinese gene-pool. One might add that not just anyone (any arbitrary genotype) is capable of becoming a viable member of Balinese society. Bateson, incidentally, agrees, largely on an intuitive basis (personal communication), and Mead and MacGregor (1951) apparently considered this a distinct possibility.

For those who equate the genetic approach with notions of unchangeability, we must stress (along with Ginsburg and Laughlin, 1967) that in any *large* society there is probably sufficient genetic variation so that, hypothetically, any phenotype present elsewhere in mankind could be reproduced within that population, and without resorting to outbreeding. This malleability of the genetic structure within a group is, in fact, the basis of evolutionary change, and, in this view, phenotypic differences between human groups exist primarily because of differential adaptions to different environments (see especially Brace and Montagu, 1965).

It is time now to present some data which will support these essentially logical assertions. Most data on genetic differences between populations stem from the physical measurements popular before the 1930's, and on the more precise monogenic blood groupings which have been popular since. Unfortunately, at the level of behavior, monogenic effects are of little interest for they are inevitably related to enzyme defects and neural pathology. On the other hand, since complex behavior is inevitably affected by the cultural surroundings, what are we to do?

Looking at newborns is one possibility. For example, at least five studies show that Negro infants are at birth and throughout the first year motorically advanced over Caucasians (Bayley, 1965; Curti et al., 1935; Geber and Dean, 1966; Knobloch and Pasamanick, 1958; Walters, 1967). Brazelton et al. (1967) have recently found that a group of one hundred Mayan infants were substantially different from a Caucasian sample in temperament and coordination throughout the first year, again starting with data obtained immediately following birth. For one thing, the Mayan neonates exhibited almost none of the normally occurring spasmodic movements so common in Caucasian newborns, and maintained smoother gross motor measurements throughout the first year. Marshall, a pediatrician with twenty-five years experience in Hawaii, has noted (personal communication) consistent differential reactions to shots at three months between his Japanese and Polynesian patients: Japanese babies are far more reactive and, unlike the Polynesian babies, their fear persists on subsequent visits. We plan to follow this up with a controlled study.

Freedman and Freedman (1969) compared twenty-four newborn Chinese-American infants with twenty-four European-American infants, controlling for hours of age, type of delivery, amount of medication, socioeconomic status and birth order. While there was almost complete overlap in the range of scores between the two groups, the Chinese infants were significantly quieter, less perturbable, and easier to calm once they were upset. Similar temperamental differences seem to characterize these two ethnic groups in San Francisco grade schools, so that there is little choice but to hypothesize inherited temperamental differences as characterizing the two groups.

As one can see, data are minimal, largely because few workers have thus far examined newborns and infants cross-culturally. It would seem a logical second step, once extensive data on infants are collected within a society, to trace lines of development longitudinally to see how they become part of the societal pattern, even as we have done in making a case for genetically mediated individual differences within our twins (e.g., the case of Arturo and Felix).

Again, we may ask what practical difference does all this make, particularly for education? In answering this, we should like to present data from a study by Lesser, Fifer, and Clark (1965) on Chinese, Jewish, Negro, and Puerto Rican grade-schoolers in New York City (Figures 6–11). Verbal, reasoning, numerical, and spatial abilities were measured, and, as is apparent in the curves, overall social class difference is significant and shows no interaction with specific abilities. On the other hand, ethnic groups not only differ in overall ability, but show significant strengths and weaknesses on specific abilities.

Because of the unusual consistency of these findings, Stodolsky and Lesser (1967) repeated the tests with Chinese and Negro children in Boston, with the results as indicated in Figures 12, 13, and 14. Once again, while there are obvious displacements up and down between the New York City and Boston samples, the patterns of strengths and weaknesses are strikingly consistent. However, since the environment within an ethnic group, whether in New York City or Boston, may be very much the same, these data are only weakly indicative of *inherited* differences.[11] If we indeed wanted to pursue the problem of the differential inheritance of abilities, probably the best data would come from an adoption study where a substantial number of infants of one ethnic group are adopted

[11] Many social scientists feel that ethnic groups such as Jews and Chinese are not gene pools in any useful sense of the word. To a human geneticist, however, these groups do indeed show different *frequencies* of various gene controlled traits, such as blood groups, diseases such as diabetes and Tay Sachs syndrome, as well as frequency of twinnings and numerous other nondisease characteristics. Although ethnic comparisons are crude compared to studies of inbred strains of animals they have been the basis for hundreds of scientific reports.

FIGURE 6
Pattern of normalized mental-ability scores for each social-class group, all ethnic groups combined. (From Lesser, Fifer, and Clark, 1965.)

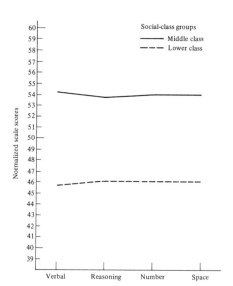

FIGURE 7
Pattern of normalized mental-ability scores for each ethnic group. (From Lesser, Fifer, and Clark, 1965.)

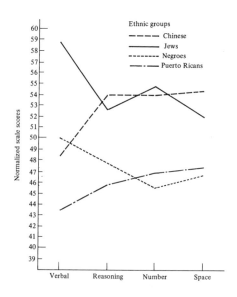

FIGURE 8
Patterns of normalized mental-ability scores for middle- and lower-class Chinese children. (From Lesser, Fifer, and Clark, 1965.)

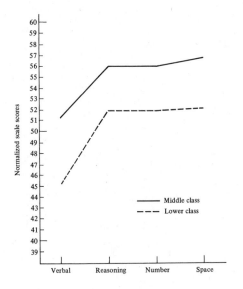

FIGURE 9
Patterns of normalized mental-ability scores for middle- and lower-class Jewish children. (From Lesser, Fifer, and Clark, 1965.)

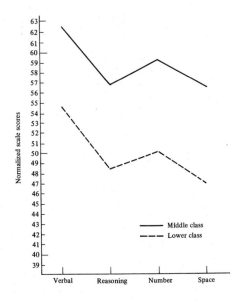

FIGURE 10
Patterns of normalized mental-ability scores for middle- and lower-class Negro children. (From Lesser, Fifer, and Clark, 1965.)

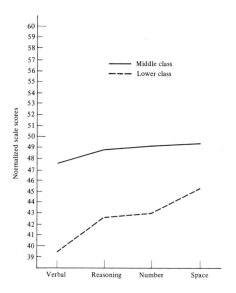

FIGURE 11
Patterns of normalized mental-ability scores for middle- and lower-class Puerto Rican children. (From Lesser, Fifer, and Clark, 1965.)

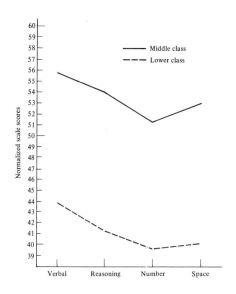

FIGURE 12
Patterns of mental ability for Chinese and Negro
children: NY vs. Boston. (From Stodolsky and
Lesser, 1967.)

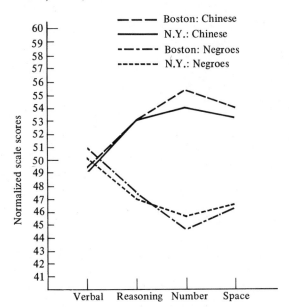

into families of a second ethnic group. At least two studies of this kind
are underway, both with adopted American Indian children, but as yet
no publications are available.[12]

---

[12] We are very cognizant of the controversy which has arisen recently upon presentation of similar data, as for example, following Shockley's paper to the National Academy
of Sciences (1966), and the condemnation of his views by various groups, including the
entire genetics department of his own University. Our position is the same as that of the
sociologist Bressler (1968):

> Only pluralists could maintain a substantial measure of composure if the statistical
> distribution of socially valued characteristics were not identical for all groups. Their
> participation in the broader society would persuade them that none had a monopoly
> on virtue, vice, or talent. At the same time, pluralists would be confident that each
> group, out of the totality of its experiences, could make its own *distinctive* contribu-
> tion to the intricate texture of American life. Some groups might be more heavily
> represented in the arts, others in the sciences, and still others in equally valuable pur-
> suits. And since every identifiable group is the product of a unique history, which may
> have included exposure to differential selection processes, it would not be surprising
> if genetic rather than environmental influences sometimes explained a higher propor-
> tion of the variance in observed behavior.
> The capacity of any minority to accept serenely the fact of resemblances and dif-
> ferences among people presupposes that the majority will not frustrate their aspira-

FIGURE 13
Patterns of mental ability for Chinese children;
middle- and lower-class, NY vs. Boston. (From
Stodolsky and Lesser, 1967.)

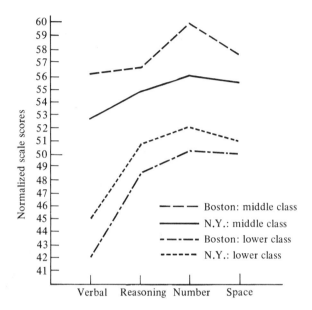

With regard to the socioeconomic differences apparent within each ethnic group in the Lesser et al. data, Jensen (1968) has pointed out that it
is a reductio ad absurdum to take the position that *individual* differences
are largely determined by heredity but that *social class* differences are not,
and he cites statistical evidence based on regression to the mean to sup-

---

tions for full emancipation. There are differences in average IQ scores among white
ethnic groups, but the origin and nature of Irish characteristics, for example, are not
a matter of public debate or anxious self-scrutiny, precisely because a once-persecuted
minority has now been absorbed — despite an unfavorable stereotype — into the
mainstream of American society. In this connection, the Stanford geneticists seem to
believe that any appearance of scientific support of a doctrine of intrinsic race differences might have unfortunate effects on the attitudes of the white population. It
would presumably reduce the fervor of the virtuous, justify the passivity of the un-
committed, and provide moral succor to the bigot. These defensible expectations must
be balanced against countervailing considerations. An ideology that tacitly appeals to
biological equality as a condition for human emancipation corrupts the idea of freedom. Moreover, it encourages decent men to tremble at the prospect of "inconvenient"
findings that may emerge in future scientific research. This unseemly anti-intel-
lectualism is doubly degrading because it is probably unnecessary. From M. Bressler,
"Sociology, Biology and Ideology" in D. C. Glass (ed.), *Genetics* (1968). Reprinted
by permission of Rockefeller University Press.

FIGURE 14

Patterns of mental ability for Negro children; middle-
and lower-class, NY vs. Boston. (From Stodolsky and
Lesser, 1967.)

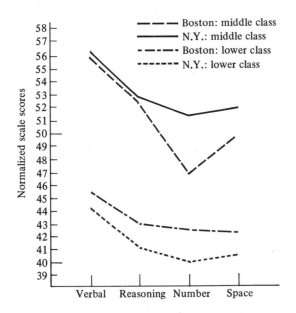

port this contention. In addition we may consider the fact that the same
environmental enrichment of preschoolers seems to benefit children in
higher socioeconomic levels as much or more than it does children in lower
socioeconomic levels (Bettye M. Caldwell, personal communication about
unpublished data). Thus, so-called cultural or environmental deprivation
seems to apply about equally to most of our society, and these terms become robbed of any meaning whatsoever.[13]

[13] A creative teacher, e.g., one who is able to operate *solely* out of respect for his
students, can help children of any social class, but he seems about equally rare in lower
or middle-class schools (Stodolsky and Lesser, 1967). The real deprivation of the lower
classes involves *injustice* rather than low test scores. So long as one group devalues another, so long shall we have the problem of an "inferior" class. It is also clear that indig-
nation and anger by the "one down" group is frequently the only way to make a "one
up" group respectful. Thus, in our view, it is legal and moral justice and not IQ points
that our lower classes need and are rightfully demanding, and what they are fighting for
in the streets. Part of that justice, in a nation as rich as ours, is the availability of free
pre-schools for lower classes, as in Project Headstart, in reaching for certain minimum
standards of achievement no matter what the cost, in full employment, a minimum income, open housing, and in other programs aimed at eliminating second class citizenship.

We cannot leave this subject without remarking on Jensen's much maligned article (1969). This paper, which purports to show, among other things, that educational difficulty within lower class blacks is largely attributable to an inherited inability to use the abstract mode of thought, came at a most unfortunate time in history, i.e., when black Americans are finding joy, for the first time, in being who they are. The Jensen paper thus came as a stab in the back for many, and the response was predictably angry.

The major problem of the Jensen article, in our opinion, has nothing to do with the worth of his statistical arguments, most of which appear reasonable. For example, Jensen's evidence has been criticized as indirect and circumstantial, but the criticism can be made of any study in which direct experimentation (e.g., Mendelian crossing) is not permissible or feasible, and this includes most studies with humans. (It should not be surprising that whites and blacks differ significantly in averages on IQ tests. One could most probably demonstrate significant differences in IQ between residents east of the Mississippi and those west of the Mississippi. See especially Bakan [1966] for a discussion on the vagaries of statistical significance between any two large groups.) As already indicated, the real issue involves the feelings of humiliation and anger on the part of black readers who, in their struggle to achieve equality in America, have felt another white boot forcing them down. When Jensen points out, logically enough, that it can only help blacks to know where their deficiencies lie, it is easy to see why blacks deeply resent his "helpfulness." It is clear that this problem looms too large for simplistic answers, and we hope that, out of the many discussions which have since arisen, some new ideas will emerge.

In any event, it should be perfectly clear that hereditary variation in abilities does not mean that some children are *predestined* to lower achievement than others. Perhaps, given school systems in which all children are taught the same lessons and at the same pace, we can speak of such "predestination." But there are other possibilities. Bloom (1968), for example, points out that the

> basic task in education is to find strategies which will take individual differences into consideration but which will do so in a way as to promote the fullest development of the individual. . . . Thus, we are expressing the view that, given sufficient time (and appropriate types of help), 95 percent of students (the top 5 percent plus the next 90 percent) can learn a subject up to a high level of mastery. We are convinced that the grade of A as an index of mastery of a subject, can, under appropriate conditions, be achieved by up to 95 percent of the students in a class.
>
> It is assumed that it will take some students more effort, time, and help

to achieve this level than it will other students. For some students the effort and help required may make it prohibitive. Thus, to learn high school algebra to a point of mastery may require several years for some students but only a fraction of a year for other students. Whether mastery learning is worth this great effort for the students who may take several years is highly questionable. One basic problem for a mastery learning strategy is to find ways of reducing the amount of time required for the slower students to a point where it is no longer a prohibitively long and difficult task for these less able students.

We should like to emphasize that this can as well be a geneticist's as an educator's point of view. Geneticists know from studies with inbred strains of animals that changes in environment can alter a phenotype, sometimes quite drastically (e.g., Freedman, 1958; Ginsburg, 1967). They know further that if they are to discover the phenotypic parameters of inbred strains, only a random sample of environments for each genotype would be totally satisfactory. This is, of course, an impossible demand, and it assures us, in fact, that the nature-nurture controversy will never be resolved. For there is always the possibility that some as yet untried environment will extract either desired or unexpected phenotypic changes from the genotype under study.

In closing, we quote again from Bressler (1968):

> The ultimate prize to be gained from more sympathetic contact between social biology and sociology is a unified life science that would define the nature and limits of human variability. In the short run, we might clarify a great number of questions to which we are now offering incomplete answers. The fear that greater attentiveness to ethological and genetic findings compromises liberal values is an anachronistic response to a bygone era which both of these disciplines now disavow. The contributions of social biology to the understanding of social behavior should be judged by the ordinary criteria of science rather than by the irrelevant standards of outmoded polemic. And if, perchance, greater familiarity with ethology and behavior genetics should impel us to reconsider our most cherished formulations, this change in sociology should not be mistaken for a crisis in the ethical universe.

References

Ainsworth, M. D. "The effects of maternal deprivation: a review of findings and controversy in the context of research strategy," *Public Health Papers*, 1962, vol. 14. Geneva: World Health Organization.

———. "Patterns of infantile attachment to mother," in Y. Brackbill and G. G. Thompson (eds.), *Behavior in infancy and early childhood*. New York: The Free Press, 1967.

——— and Wittig, B. A. "Attachment and exploratory behavior of one-year-olds in a strange situation," in B. M. Foss (ed.), *Determinants of infant behavior,* vol. IV. London: Methuen, 1969; New York: Barnes and Noble, 1969.

Atkinson, R. C. "Computer based instruction in initial reading," in *Proceedings of the 1967 conference on testing problems.* Evanston: Educ. Test. Service, 1968.

Bakan, D. "The test of significance in psychological research," *Psychology Bul.,* 1966, 423–437.

Bayley, N. "Consistency of maternal and child behaviors in the Berkeley growth study," *Vita Humana,* 1964, vol. 7, pp. 73–95.

———. "Comparison of mental and motor test scores for ages 1–15 months by sex birth order, race, geographical location, and education of parents," *Child Develop.,* 1965, vol. 36, pp. 379–411.

Bereiter, C., and Engelmann, S. *Teaching disadvantaged children in the preschool.* Englewood Cliffs, N.J.: Prentice-Hall, 1966.

Bloom, B. S. "Learning for mastery," in B. S. Bloom et al. (eds.), *Formative and summative evaluation of student learning.* New York: McGraw-Hill, 1971.

Brace, C. L., and Montagu, M. F. A. *Man's evolution.* New York: Macmillan, 1965.

Brazelton, T. B., Robey, J. S., and Collier, G. A. Infant development in the Zenacanteco Indians of Southern Mexico, 1967. Mimeographed.

Bressler, M. "Sociology, biology and ideology," in D. C. Glass (ed.), *Genetics.* New York: Rockefeller University Press and Russell Sage Foundation, 1968.

Cagen, J. Unpublished data. University of Chicago, 1966.

Caldwell, B. M., and Honzig, A. S. "Visual following, attachment and alerting," in B. M. Foss (ed.), *Determinants of infant behavior,* vol. IV. London: Methuen, 1969.

Collins, S. D. *The health of the school child.* Washington, D.C.: U.S. Public Health Service, 1931.

Curti, M., Marshall, F. B., Stegerrda, M., and Henderson, E. M. "The Gesell schedules applied to one-, two-, and three-year-old Negro children of Jamaica, B.W.I.," *J. Comp. Physiol. Psychol.,* 1935, vol. 20, pp. 125–56.

Diamond, M. "A critical evaluation of the ontogeny of human sexual behavior," *Quart. Rev. Biol.,* 1965, vol. 40, pp. 147–73.

Dobzhansky, T. *Mankind evolving.* New Haven: Yale University Press, 1962.

Edelman, M. S., and Omark, D. R. *Dominance hierarchies in young children* (ms., University of Chicago, 1970).

Erikson, E. H. *Childhood and society.* New York: Norton, 1950.

Erlenmeyer-Kimling, L., and Jarvik, L. F. "Genetics and intelligence: a review," *Science,* 1963, vol. 142, pp. 1477–79.

Fantz, R. L. "Pattern vision in newborn infants," *Science,* 1963, vol. 140, pp. 296–97.

———, Ordy, J. M., and Udelf, M. S. "Maturation of pattern vision in infants during the first six months," *J. Comp. Physiol. Psychol.,* 1962, vol. 55, pp. 907–17.

Freedman, D. G. "Constitutional and environmental interactions in rearing of four breeds of dogs," *Science,* 1958, vol. 127, pp. 585–86.

———. "The infants' fear of strangers for the flight response," *J. Child Psychol. Psychiat.,* 1961, pp. 242–48.

———. 16 mm. sound film: *Development of the smile and fear of strangers.* PCR-2140. University Park, Pa.: Psychol. Cinema Reg., 1963.

———. "An ethological approach to the genetical study of human behavior," in S. G. Vandenberg (ed.), *Methods and goals in human behavior genetics.* New York: Academic Press, 1965.

———. "A biological view of man's social behavior," in W. Etkin (ed.), *From fish to man.* Chicago: University of Chicago Press, 1967a.

———. "The origins of social behavior," *Science Journal,* Nov. 1967b, pp. 69–73.

———. "A biological approach to personality development," in S. Washburn (ed.), *Perspectives in human evolution,* vol. I. New York: Holt, Rinehart and Winston, 1968.

Freedman, D. G., and Freedman, Nina A. "Behavioral differences between Chinese-American and European-American newborns," *Nature,* vol. 224 (1969).

———, King, J. A., and Elliot, O. "Critical period in the social development of dogs," *Science*, 1961, vol. 133, pp. 1016–17.

Geber, M., and Dean, R. F. A. "Precocious development in newborn African infants," in Brackbill and Thompson (eds.), *Readings in infancy and childhood*. New York: The Free Press, 1966.

Ginsburg, B. E. "Genetic parameters in behavioral research," in J. Hirsch (ed.), *Behavior-genetic analysis*. New York: McGraw-Hill, 1967.

——— and Laughlin, W. S. "Genetic potential and social structure," *Columbia University Forum*, Fall 1967.

Gottesman, I. I. "Heritability of personality: a demonstration," *Psychol. Monogr.*, 1963, vol. 77, p. 9, whole number 52.

———. "Personality and natural selection," in S. G. Vandenberg (ed.), *Methods and goals in human behavior genetics*. New York: Academic Press, 1965.

——— and Shields. "A polygenic theory of schizophrenia," *Proc. Nat'l Acad. Sci.*, 1967, 58:1, pp. 199–205.

Hall, K. R. L., and DeVore, I. "Baboon social behavior," in I. DeVore (ed.), *Primate behavior*. New York: Holt, Rinehart and Winston, 1965.

Hamburg, D. A., and Lunde, D. T. "Sex hormones in the development of sex differences in human behavior," in E. Maccoby (ed.), *The development of sex differences*. Stanford: Stanford University Press, 1966.

Hampson, J. L., and Hampson, J. G. "The ontogenesis of sexual behavior in man," in W. C. Young (ed.), *Sex and internal secretions*. Baltimore: Williams and Wilkins, 1961.

Harlow, H. F., and Harlow, M. K. "Social deprivation in monkeys," *Scientific American*, 1962, vol. 207, pp. 137–46.

———. "Learning to love," *American Scientist*, 1966, vol. 54, pp. 244–72.

Harlow, H. F., and Zimmerman, R. R. "Affectional responses in the infant monkey," *Science*, 1959, vol. 130, pp. 421–32.

Hayes, C. *The ape in our house*. New York: Harper, 1951

Hediger, H. *Wild animals in captivity*. New York: Dover, 1964.

Hoffman, M. L. "Child rearing practices and moral development," *Child Devel.*, 1963, vol. 34, pp. 295–318.

Holt, J. C. *How children learn*. New York: Pitman, 1967.

Jay, P. C. "Mother-infant relations in langurs," in H. L. Rheingold (ed.), *Maternal behavior in mammals*. New York: Wiley, 1963.

Jensen, A. R. "Social class, race and genetics: implications for education," *Amer. Educ. Res. J.*, 1968, vol. 5, pp. 1–42.

Jensen, A. R. "How much can we boost I.Q. and scholastic achievement?" *Harvard Ed. Review*, 1969, vol. 39, p. 123.

Jolly, A. *Lemur behavior*. Chicago: University of Chicago Press, 1966.

Kagan, J., and Moss, H. A. *Birth to maturity*. New York: Wiley, 1962.

Kellogg, W. N., and Kellogg, L. A. *The ape and the child*. New York: McGraw-Hill, 1933.

Knobloch, H., and Pasamanick, B. "The relationship of race and socio-economic status to the development of motor behavior patterns in infancy," *Psychiat. Res. Rep.*, 1958, vol. 10, pp. 123–33.

Koford, C. B. 16 mm. sound film: *Rhesus monkeys of Cayo Santiago island*. Atlanta: National Institute of Neurological Diseases and Blindness, 1963.

Kohlberg, L. "Moral development and identification," in L. H. Stevenson (ed.), *Child psychology*. Chicago: University of Chicago Press, 1963.

Kozol, J. *Death at an early age*. New York: Bantam Books, 1967.

Lesser, G. S., Fifer, G., and Clark, D. H. "Mental abilities of children of different social-class and cultural groups," *Monog. Soc. Res. Child Devel.*, 1965, vol. 30, p. 4.

Levi-Strauss, C. *Structural anthropology*. New York: Basic Books, 1963.

Levy, D. M. *Maternal overprotection*. New York: Basic Books, 1963.

Lewis, M. Infant attention: response decrement as a measure of cognitive processes, or what's new, Baby Jane? Paper presented at the Society for Research in Child Development Symposium on *The Role of Attention in Cognitive Development*, New York, March 1967.

Line, W. "The growth of visual perception in children," *Brit. J. Psychol. Monogr. Suppl.* XV, 1931.

Mead, M. *Male and female.* New York: W. Morrow and Co., 1949.

——— and MacGregor, F. C. *Growth and culture: a photographic study of Balinese childhood.* New York: Putnam, 1951.

Morgan, G. A., and Ricciuti, H. N. "Infants' responses to strangers during the first year," in B. M. Foss (ed.), *Determinants of infant behavior*, vol. IV. London: Methuen, 1969.

Nichols, R. C. "The resemblance of twins in personality and interests," National Merit Scholarship Corp. *Research Reports*, 1966, vol. 2, no. 8.

Oetzel, R. M. "Annotated bibliography," in E. Maccoby (ed.), *The development of sex differences.* Stanford: Stanford University Press, 1966.

Omark, D. R., and Edelman, M. S. The development of early social interaction — an ethological approach. Paper presented to the National Lab. on Early Childhood Education, Chicago, January 1969.

Pfaffenberger, C. J., and Scott, J. P. "The relationship between delayed socialization and trainability in guide dogs," *J. Genet. Psychol.*, 1959, vol. 95, pp. 145–55.

Reznikoff, M., and Honeyman, M. S. "MMPI profiles of monozygotic and dizygotic twin pairs," *J. Consult. Psychol.*, 1966.

Rheingold, H. L. "The effect of environmental stimulation upon social and exploratory behavior in the human infant," in B. M. Foss (ed.), *Determinants of infant behavior*, vol. I. New York: Wiley, 1961.

Sackett, G. P. "Monkeys reared in isolation with pictures as visual input: evidence for an innate releasing mechanism," *Science*, 1966, vol. 154, pp. 1468–72.

Schaller, G. B. *The mountain gorilla.* Chicago: University of Chicago Press, 1963.

———. "Behavioral comparisons of the apes," in I. DeVore (ed.), *Primate behavior.* New York: Holt, Rinehart and Winston, 1965.

Schenkel, R. "Play, exploration and territoriality in the wild lion," in Jewell and Loizos (eds.), *Play, exploration and territory in mammals.* London: Academic Press, 1966.

Schiff, W., Caviness, J. A., and Gibson, J. J. "Persistent fear responses in rhesus monkeys to the optical stimulus of 'looming,' " *Science*, 1962, vol. 136, pp. 982–83.

Scott, J. P. "Critical periods in behavioral development," *Science*, 1962, vol. 138, pp. 949–58.

Shockley, W. Possible transfer of metallurgical and astronomical approaches to the problem of environment versus ethnic heredity. Speech before National Academy of Sciences, Oct. 15, 1966.

Spears, W. C. "Assessment of visual preferences and discrimination in the four-month-old infant," *J. Comp. Physiol Psychol.*, vol. 57, 1964.

Stephens, J. M. *The process of schooling; a psychological examination.* New York: Holt, Rinehart and Winston, 1967.

Stodolsky, S. and Lesser, G. S. "Learning patterns in the disadvantaged," *Harvard Educational Review*, 1967, 37:4, pp. 546–93.

Thomas, A., Chess, S., Birch, H. G., Hertzig, M. E., and Korn, S. *Behavioral individuality in early childhood.* New York: N. Y. University Press, 1963.

Vandenberg, S. G. *Hereditary factors in normal personality traits.* Research report from the Louisville Twin Study Child Development Unit, Department of Pediatrics, University of Louisville, August 1966.

Van Lawick–Goodall, J. "Mother-offspring relationships in free-ranging chimpanzees," in D. Morris (ed.), *Primate ethology.* Chicago: Aldine Press, 1967.

Von Uexkull, J. "A stroll through the world of animals and men," in C. H. Schiller (ed.), *Instinctive behavior.* New York: International Universities Press, 1957.

Walters, C. E. "Comparative development of Negro and white infants," *J. Gen. Psychol.*, 1967, vol. 110, pp. 243–51.

Walters, R. H., and Parke, R. D. "The role of distance receptors in the development of social responsiveness," in L. P. Lipsitt and C. C. Spiker (eds.), *Advances in child development and behavior*, vol. 2. New York: Academic Press, 1965.

Yolles, S. F. "How different are they?" *The New York Times Magazine*, February 5, 1967.

Further Readings

Cravioto, Joaquín. "Nutritional deficiencies and mental performance in childhood," in David C. Glass (ed.), *Environmental influences*. New York: The Rockefeller University Press and Russell Sage Foundation, 1968.

Freedman, Daniel G. "A biological view of man's social behavior," in William Etkin, *Social behavior from fish to man*. Chicago: Phoenix Books, The University of Chicago Press, 1967.

Mason, William A. "Early social deprivation in the nonhuman primates: implications for human behavior," in David C. Glass (ed.), *Environmental influences*. New York: The Rockefeller University Press and Russell Sage Foundation, 1968.

Montessori, Maria. *Pedagogical anthropology*. New York: Lippincott, 1913.

19

The predicament of Angelo that Mrs. Rosenstiel describes is shared by a nation of Angelos, Alicias, and Willie Maes. It seems a simple misunderstanding, and easily righted. It is neither. The assumption that Angelo, too, can open his window at night, or will, in the interests of "good" health, associates with other assumptions about Angelo — many of which are similarly uninformed. These assumptions accumulate to attitudes and expectations whose eventual aggregation is often phrased in terms of "cultural disadvantage," "compensatory education," and "the inner-city child." It is too late for many educators to indulge simple misunderstandings. The problem of sensitivity to cultural difference is complex, deeply rooted in the American conscience, and awesomely expressed as both educational policy and classroom practice. Mrs. Rosenstiel, chairman of the Behavioral Sciences Division, Mills College of Education, New York City, is a concerned anthropologist whose professional interests and writings are remarkably prescient.

ANNETTE ROSENSTIEL

Anthropology and Childhood Education

In this era of rapid technological and social change, the problem of maintaining the equilibrium of teacher-pupil relationships has become increasingly important. The wide diversity in the cultural background of today's school children makes it imperative for the teacher to understand the motivations of child behavior in terms of varying cultural norms.

Anthropology gives the teacher a broader cultural perspective, making it possible to eliminate ethnocentrism and to create a classroom atmosphere conducive to the free interchange of ideas that is the goal of good teaching. A knowledge of anthropology provides the teacher with a keen perception of man's biological limitations, as well as an appreciation of the tremendous range of his capabilities. Similarly, through a heightened awareness of the cultural conditioning in her own background, the teacher achieves a better understanding of her own relationship with the student and of the student's relationship with the total school environment. In this way, too, hidden or covert prejudices, which tend to color and distort interpersonal and intergroup relationships, can be objectively revealed and studied and appropriate measures taken to eliminate them.

A recognition of the significance of cultural differences gained through the principles of anthropology helps the teacher overcome in her personal experience many of the stumbling blocks that impede intercultural understanding. The same result can be secured for students whose educational experience is obtained in an atmosphere of intercultural acceptance.

Although cultures may vary widely, they have much in common. For instance, there is no culture in which the family does not play a part. No culture is without religion, or education, or some form of economic life. A knowledge of the many ways in which these aspects of culture have developed throughout the world, and a realization of the fact that to be different does not necessarily make one inferior, will aid the teacher greatly in recognizing and accepting the values behind the sometimes apparently strange behavior of people from other cultures.

To illustrate with an actual classroom situation, there is the case of Angelo, a six-year-old Sicilian-American boy in the first grade of a large urban school. Anxious to impress upon the children the importance of good food, fresh air, and the other concomitants of good health, the teacher centered her classroom work around this topic. The class learned

From *School and Society*, vol. 87, no. 2162 (November 21, 1959), pp. 482–483. Reprinted by permission.

that it was good to drink orange juice, brush your teeth, and, above all to sleep with the window open. The children sang songs about these activities and learned a little pantomime dance to go with the songs. They enjoyed the activity immensely. When asked how many had done what the song said about opening the window, all the children but Angelo raised their hands. How was he to explain to his teacher that his father had taught him never to open the window at night, because the open window lets in the evil spirits?

A lack of understanding of the cultural factors involved here, of the conflicts which develop in a child torn between two cultures, might very well cause confusion for the teacher as well as for the child. How was the teacher to know that in malaria-ridden Sicily, where there were no screens for windows, the belief was current that malaria was caused by evil spirits that roamed about at night and came in through the open windows?

In this case, an anthropological orientation would help the teacher ascertain the facts and avoid possible mishandling of the situation. Such knowledge not only will help the teacher evolve basic principles for her own behavior, but also can considerably enrich the curriculum which she presents to her students, for she can draw many examples and parallels to arouse their interest and to encourage new projects and independent thinking.

Anthropology is interested in the process of culture change and is vitally concerned with what happens when peoples meet. The teacher who is aware of the processes involved in this social phenomenon will be better able to anticipate student reactions in her class and can better help students through the difficult period of cultural adjustment.

Today's child is interested not only in the present and in the future, but, to a surprising degree, in the past as well. His intellectual curiosity impels him to learn anything and everything about himself. Museum exhibits and children's books deal more and more with those aspects of the prehistoric past which have scientific and social significance for today's world. The teacher who is aware of these trends and who is equipped to provide authentic information in this important area of knowledge can thus be in a position to fill a very basic educational need.

Some of the most insistent questions in the young mind are: "How did life start on earth?" "How did the first man come on earth?" "Why are there so many different kinds of people in the world?" The teacher with a knowledge of the theory and data of anthropology is qualified to clarify these questions and many more. She is able to provide scientific answers, for anthropology provides data regarding the evolution of man and the development of culture, as well as many clues to the puzzling problems of race and cultural differences.

This approach can be vividly demonstrated in such classroom activities as the study of the American Indian. Presented in an anthropological framework, a knowledge of the cultural patterns of Indian life can help the child acquire a true perspective of the historical past of his own country and the ways in which the meeting of the white man and the Indian have affected not only each other, but also the complex American culture which has developed as a result of this continuing contact.

If we are to develop in the present young generation a sense of perspective, an understanding of other points of view, and a spirit of mutual cooperation and trust, it must be done through our educational system. Beginning at a very early age, false attitudes must be eliminated and behavioral patterns established which will be compatible with the goals and the values of our democratic system. Consequently, a knowledge of anthropology becomes absolutely basic and essential for the teacher who aspires to the highest ideals of modern education.

FURTHER READINGS

Bronfenbrenner, Urie. *Two worlds of childhood: U.S. and U.S.S.R.* New York: Russell Sage Foundation, 1970.

Kimball, Solon T. "Cultural influences shaping the role of the child," *Those first school years.* Washington, D.C.: NEA, Department of Elementary School Principals, XL, 1960.

Rosenstiel, Annette. "Educational anthropology: a new approach to cultural analysis," *Harvard Educational Review,* vol. 24 (1954).

West, James. "Childhood education in rural America," in Walter Goldschmidt (ed.), *Exploring the ways of mankind.* New York: Holt, Rinehart and Winston, 1960.

Whiting, John, and Beatrice B. Whiting. "Contributions of anthropology to the methods of studying child rearing," in Paul H. Mussen (ed.), *Handbook of research methods in child development.* New York: Wiley, 1960.

B. SOME SPECIFIC ANALYSES

20

Although teaching and learning reach the larger society and back, their locus remains the classroom, where most children first and last encounter formal education; there, the actual drama of education is played out. Methods of inquiry into classrooms vary. Some are integrated as methodology, others refer less to a defined, replicable set of concepts and postulates than they do to outlines of procedure. Anthropological inquiry into classroom behavior ranges from traditional treatments of classrooms and their native people, large and small, as a convenient sort of "tribe" to views of the classroom as a kind of sociocultural coral reef, where the interrelation of teaching and learning may be examined in ecological detail. Mrs. Burnett employs a mixed method, "seeing" the classroom as a behavioral "stream" and stressing local observation of events as these occur in classroom context. Her use of network analysis not only obviates assumptions of the classroom as a "microcosm" — as simply the whole of society writ small — but also provides a positive structure for the scrutiny of relationships between home and school. Mrs. Burnett, a practicing anthropologist and Associate Professor of Education, University of Illinois, suggests that "microethnography" is more than a means to behavioral data. Her skillful integration of in vivo description, network-type analysis, and conceptualization of the classroom as a course of events leads to a comprehensive research strategy in which anthropological inquiry is methodologically central.

JACQUETTA H. BURNETT

Event Description and Analysis in the Microethnography of Urban Classrooms

Doing ethnography in the modern city is somewhat like trying to stay afloat on a stormy sea. People, problems, factors, and variables seem

Reprinted by permission from a paper originally presented at the Annual Meeting of the American Anthropological Association: Seattle, Washington, 1968. Revised for this edition. © Jacquetta H. Burnett, 1969.

to come in waves breaking over the mind, tearing at one's feeble efforts to make sensible statements about attributes, components, or relationships in answer to one's questions. In this circumstance some unit or unitary percept of this sea of data is a minimal necessity to keep one's senses from drowning in disorientation.

The objective of the EPIC (*Estudio de Problemas Interculturales*) is to study the intercultural process and problems in migration, education, and occupation of Puerto Rican youths in Chicago. The first set of questions asked by the researcher concerned whether cultural factors and differences were one major source of the educational problems experienced by Puerto Rican youths in United States schools. A second set of questions asks how the educational problems and cultural factors affects occupational socialization and access to occupations for Puerto Rican youths in an urban setting in the United States. The household of a Puerto Rican youth is regarded as the domain and conservator of a characteristic Puerto Rican culture. At the same time, the school, in this case one elementary school comprised of grades one through eight, is viewed as the domain and conservator of a dominant and characteristic North American culture. Peer relations is a third domain, potentially of great relevance to acculturation of youth, but its cultural character or characteristics was an unknown that had to be discovered.

In the urban setting of our research, no neighborhood segments, or community units, were small enough, bounded clearly enough, or understood sufficiently well for use as a sample system through which to approach our research objectives. A study of families would not necessarily get us into the school. A study of school classrooms and associated families, when each classroom might have thirty-five to forty-four pupils, would overtax our resources. If we were to study cultural factors and differences *in vivo*, we needed a new research strategy. Our solution, then, was to bring together two separate streams of conceptual development in social anthropology, egocentric network models and event analysis, to develop a new variant on earlier methodological strategies for doing ethnographic studies in urban settings.

We decided to study a sample of egocentric networks. The networks began with thirty egos who were selected by stratified random selection from one grade level, the seventh grade of 1967–68, in one large urban elementary school. We planned to follow the sample of egos and parts of their networks over a period of approximately two and one-half years, from seventh grade through the first year of secondary school (that is, through the ninth grade, which is part of secondary school in our city).

We chose seventh grade because this was the point at which the effects of cultural difference came into full expression, or so the literature and the private accounts of teachers and of Puerto Rican community leaders told us. Moreover, starting with a group at this grade level we could examine the effects of a difference in experience with school cultures. We included in the randomly selected principal sample five girls and five boys who had attended Puerto Rican schools for at least five years of their school careers before coming to Chicago, five girls and five boys from Puerto Rican families who had spent all their school careers in Chicago schools, and five non–Puerto Rican girls and five non–Puerto Rican boys. The last ten provide us with a comparison for sorting out factors that are endemic to the inner city — socioeconomic level, broken homes, etc. It will help to keep us "honest" and self-critical about what is poverty and urbanism and what is cultural difference.

EGOCENTRIC NETWORK ANALYSIS

This paper is mainly concerned with event analysis, but some attention to network analysis is necessary to show the special nature of the methological linkage between the two areas. The concept of network or egocentric network as developed by Barnes (1954), Bott (1957), Epstein (1961), and Mayer (1966) is based on the image of points connected and interconnected by lines in lattice-like patterns.[1] The points represent persons (Epstein, 1961; Barnes, 1954) or household groups or other groups (Bott, 1957). The lines represent relationships of some sort such as person-contacts, friendship, or even a range of several different sorts of relationships. Barnes emphasized the linkages of friendship, acquaintanceship, and kinship of persons with other persons; Bott emphasized whether other persons or households in a network were acquainted or connected with one another, as well as with the family of origin — i.e., the point-of-origin of the network; and Mayer used the concept to depict and explore linkages of political support for three different egos as the relationships were enacted or manifested in an election in Madhya Pradesh State in India.

When we began our study we drew on this development of egocentric network concepts to define where and with whom we should begin our study. So, in the early stages of the research, in the spring of 1968, we selected thirty seventh-grade children, or thirty egocentric networks. We wanted to study their networks, in particular, that part of each network that manifests itself in the household, in the school and classroom, and in relations with peers outside the classroom and school.

[1] If you will think of an ego-centered sociogram, this will give you a quick idea of the imagery involved. Given a field of persons represented as points in two dimensional space, select one point as an ego; then draw a line to represent a primary linkage to every person-point with whom he has face-to-face and *regular* contacts.

After selecting our sample, we followed the plan of the network and contacted the household adults. Moreover, then and now we go only into those classrooms that our sample of egos attend and where we have been doing regular participant observation and taking ethnographic accounts of events. In the households we are doing interviews and trying to establish close enough relations to do participant observation. In our storefront neighborhood research center we have invited our sample and their friends, or more accurately, the youths and their friends in the classrooms we observe, to afternoon recreation time.

In our observations and interviews with household adults and teachers we plan to follow out certain secondary linkages, where we can, into the area of the network that is unbounded from ego's point of view. Beginnings with links from ego to teacher and then following these secondary linkages of the teacher to other teachers carries us into the study of school culture. The secondary linkages of parents can lead us to relatives, leisure-time companions, and on-the-job relationships. The question of whether the linkages of the household are close-knit or loose-knit networks (Bott, 1957) shall interest us from the point of view of acculturation of household patterns to North American patterns, to maintaining island patterns, or to developing idiosyncratic family practices. Studying the cultural character of these linkages and of the cultural characteristics of three organizational contexts in which they manifest themselves is our central objective. But we study the linkages and their social contexts through more than interviews; we use participant observation and ethnographic description of *observed events* to explore the linkages.

Although our network sample defined who and where we were to begin our study, it left us with the question of how and what we planned to observe and study. The problem of being explicit on this point loomed larger for us than for most ethnographic studies, since the research was being carried out not by a single ethnographer, but by a team of field-workers. Moreover, the style of the division of labor led to ethnographic accounts that were interdependent, rather than merely parallel or related. We faced a serious problem of clear intersubjective communication in comparing one classroom with another, a household with a classroom, and life in peer groups with life in a household and in school. We were looking at numerous streams of behavior in various different locales. From the point of view of our egos, we were observing egos and their networks in events — human behavioral events.

Events As Segments

Regarding the classroom — where we began the research — as a stream of behavior, we could perceive phases or segments of that stream that seemed to have natural breaks, at least in temporal dimension. Although the concept of event has had a different emphasis and a somewhat more macrocosmic meaning in anthropological literature, the author thought, for several persuasive theoretical reasons, that we would label as "event" that segment with a certain "natural" or "easily developed" sense of integrality to it, and thus preserve what Barker (1963) regards as the primary attribute of the behavior stream — its arrangement in time. The event we speak of here is a microevent; but our unit of description can logically and with theoretical significance, be linked to macroevents of the order of a festival, a community ceremonial, a health survey, or longer and more complex constellations of human behavioral processes and elements (Kimball and Pearsall, 1955).

An event begins with the entry into a specific place by a person, or sets of persons, and their engagement there in actions, including interactions. The event ends when the person, or at least one complete set of the various sets of persons engaged in behavior, changes his place, either by departing from that place, or by manipulating the place defining objects so that the location is transformed from one place type to another. In Puerto Rico, I saw classrooms of students transformed into a partial school assembly by simply moving the partitions between four classrooms and reorienting the chairs toward the stage on one end. On the other hand, the mere movement of personnel or part of the personnel in and out of a place where an event is occurring, doesn't necessarily constitute the end point of an event. This is clearly the case in our urban classrooms where students move in and out of the classroom at a bewildering rate for special classes, monitor duties, service to the school, safety patrol duties, etc. But when one teacher goes out and another teacher comes in one has completely changed the membership of one set, although the actor-type of the set does not change. This then amounts to a *new* event. In like manner, keeping the same teacher in the same place, but changing the class of students entirely, constitutes the ending of one event and the beginning of another. At this time, this is our working definition of the beginning and ending of an event. It has proved usable so far.

Isolating events in an urban school is often easy. For example, as the warning bell ending lunch recess rings, students line up, by room and sex, outside the building and enter together by classroom groups. If the teacher isn't there, they assemble around the door until the teacher comes with the key and they enter to take their seats. For one teacher, after the final bell, as regular as morning prayers in a nunnery, the teacher says, "Girls, put up your wraps," pause while girls get up and hang up wraps they don't want to wear, "Boys, hang up your coats," pause while the boys who have wraps put them in the cloak room. "Now get out your homework papers," and so the new event proceeds. Most regular, recurrent events in the school begin and end with a ritual phase. Other events like school assemblies are highly ritualized throughout.

Let's follow out the stream of behavior over a period of time. After morning recess and the assembling ritual just described, in a given classroom there will be minor changes in personnel from time to time and day to day, but the place is the same and set of actors and actor types are common from event to event. As time moves through its cycle, objects, actions, and messages interrelate to produce what we can abstract as *activities*. Some activities become salient and so the event comes to be named after them — "the spelling hour." A bell near noon initiates a series of actions that begin with "Put your books and things away" from the teacher. Pause. Teacher, "Girls get your wraps and form a line, by twos." Action by girls. "Now boys, get your wraps and form a line by twos." The girls and boys form a line at a 45° angle to one another, at the corner of the room where the door is. (I've never observed a class in this school where the door is in any other position than in the corner.) The teacher stands near the origin of the angle, waiting for the bell to signal time to lead them out. They move out in a line of twos, usually girls first, then boys. The teacher moves out last and closes the door, and checks to see that it is locked. They move on, stopping at the top of the stairs, then down two flights of stairs, pausing at every landing, and around to the door. As they get near the double door their line disappears into a sea of students surging through the double doors. This happens the same way when school is out. At noon, however, the teacher walks them to the door, *then* turns to her left and goes into the cafeteria.

I compared these events day after day for one classroom I observed regularly. Then I observed another room, another place (but the same place-type) and another teacher (but the same actor-type), etc. Usually there was a ritual episode to begin an event and a second ritual episode to end an event. The particular event I discussed above was continuous from recess to noon. Other events during the day began with the same ritual episode of entry and later terminated with the ritual episode just described. Sometimes new instances of events were initiated by a change in the teacher, and often the teachers exchanged places. On other occasions a class group terminated one event and began another by shifting from classroom to gym, or to library, or to home mechanics room.

I compared my field notes with the accounts of two other field observers. It became clear that, although all events in the day did not begin and end in the same way, beginnings and endings were highly regularized for a given event that recurred at the same time, in the same place, and with the same actor sets.

ELEMENTS AND COORDINATES OF EVENTS

We describe an event by describing *where* it is, *what* objects are involved, *what* actions and what interactions occur and *who* participates, and *when* these elements appear, in the order of their appearance. . . . Actions are carefully distinguished into verbal action and nonverbal action. The messages of the verbal action are recorded, either in English or in Spanish depending upon which code is used. To get a full verbal account in the classroom, however, at least a tape recorder is necessary. In addition to using actions, verbal and nonverbal, as elements in the microanalysis of an event, we used scene coordinates of the actions, that is, the elements that set the scene for the action which include actor types, place-space types, object-types and absolute and relative time (Harris, 1964). Actor types are defined by physical features, behavioral features, and combinations of both types of features. Object-types, too, can be defined by physical or behavioral features, or a combination of both. But object types also help to define place-space. So, for example, the difference in a classroom and a school library may be based on the differences between types of objects present rather than in macro-place features such as room size. However, providing an inventory of all objects or artifacts before entering into descriptions of behavior is probably unnecessarily tedious. The degree of refinement in characterization is necessary to describe behavior, distinguish places, events, and classes of actions intersubjectively.

At the first level of abstraction on action, one can distinguish interaction, which is, of course, interdependent, ordered actions of two or more persons. Thanks to early, careful work on the part of Chapple and Arensberg (1940) to develop a data language and system of notation for interaction, we can be fairly precise when we wish to focus on the interaction dimension of the event. We can include a fairly precise account of interaction in the direct observation of events.

We have included on our observation form a place for entering guides or paradigms that apply to the action and relations that take place in the event. This is not to be recorded during the observation, because such statements are often several logical steps and a few inductive leaps away from direct accounts of the behavior stream. These constructions, however, do provide for the logical, structural account of the system. The provision on the form for placing these formulations in juxtaposition with the descriptive account of the event readily allows us to index the empirical bases for those constructions.

The conceptualization of *activities* is another reconstruction of descriptive data several logical steps removed and, therefore, at a further level of abstraction from the coordinates of the scene and the stream of action. Goodenough (1963) suggests that because activities are organized with reference to intended goals, they, like sentences in speech, have recognizable beginnings and endings, which make them readily isolable as natural behavioral entities for analysis. Plainly, they are likely to be behavioral entities that have significance and meaning in the minds of members of a culture. The concept of activity bridges the level of description involved in microevents with the level of symbolic meaning and manifest function of the culture in which the events take place. Thus, we adopt Goodenough's formulation (1963, p. 324), that whether the activity is customary (that is, "designed to accomplish recurring purposes . . . where the same means for accomplishing the purpose continues to be available. . . .") or whether the activity is *ad hoc* (that is, "designed to accomplish unusual ends or to deal with conditions where common means are unavailable. . . .") all activities involve these three features: actors of certain types; a set of procedures that can be formulated as recipes and rules; and one or more purposes or goals from the views of the actors. Actors and other people are aware that the effects of goals and purposes contribute to the activity's meaning to them. The effects of purposes, however, whether or not the people are aware of all of them, produce the activity's functions in their lives and in the event. . . .

Making sense out of activities involves relating the action to intended consequences, usually by asking, "Why are you doing that?" or, placing more emphasis on procedure, asking, "Why are you doing that *that* way?" (Goodenough, 1963, p. 325). For a given cultural group, finding purpose for activities gives one a picture of the cognitive maps the members of a group have of their physical, social, and even historical environment. These maps are what Levi-Strauss (1964) calls "folk-models." In earlier behavioral science terms, they were labeled the desires and values of a people. So beyond the descriptive account of the events themselves for our Puerto Rican and non–Puerto Rican egos and their networks in the domains of home, school, and peerdom, we have been inquiring about peoples' procedures and purposes in their activities and about their perceptions of their own and others' purposes. We have been comparing them with one another to reveal culture differences and unrecognized sources of conflict.

Event Typologies

Returning once again to the task of event-focused descriptive ethnography, we now turn to the questions of the relationships among events and to questions of classes and types. Whereas events are described and characterized by the elements we have just discussed, the *relationships* among events can be of several varieties. One important relationship is temporal-spatial scheduling, a relationship that underlies the typology of events we are using at this stage in our research. This typology will be discussed below.

Another way of comparing events is through *feature overlap,* or the amount of common features among events which can be specified in terms of actors and actor types; place and place types; actions, interactions, or their abstractions as activities, particularly customary activities; and relevant object-types. It is through feature overlap that we decide whether one instance of an event is sufficiently like another instance of an event to be classed as the "same" event. Events may be *complementary* to one another with respect to features; i.e., they complete one another in some fashion. Thus the actor composite of the school may be divided up among simultaneous events; e.g., teachers in the cafeteria and pupils on the playground during recess.

Events are often *contingent* upon one another, one being instrumental to another. The contingency relationship is of special interest to us because some of our proposed explanations for commonly known conflicts suggest that some events in the households have contingencies with some events in the school, and one of our problems is to discover those contingencies. For the school to attain certain goals, certain outcomes, it may depend on and require certain contingent conditions to exist in the homes of its students, in the form of certain activities or procedures for carrying out activities. When the conditions are not present, or when carried out by different procedures than those assumed in schools which the children attend, then schools find themselves unable to meet their goals. They may rationalize the failures by viewing the home as deprived or disadvantaged when in actuality it should be more properly regarded as *different* in customary goals, meanings, and purposes. Another way to view this problem is to view the school as disabled, disadvantaged, and in need of rehabilitation to adapt to the conditions of its parental constituency, because its activities are contingent upon the presence of certain activities and certain customary procedures in the homes of its student clientele if it is to attain the goals related to its key social functions. From the point of view of the event typology, contingency of events in different domains points up the practical applications of topology that includes this relationship.

One can analyze events according to how nearly they comprehend or include all the actors and actor-types in the system or organization in question. Events that function as rites of intensification for a system should be found to include representatives of all actor types in the system or organization, even if not all the individual actors. The relative frequency of events with different degrees of comprehensiveness might be found to relate to such concepts of group climate as "cohesiveness." Comprehensiveness, of course, can vary from a single-person event, to partial assembly, to full assembly of the complement of actors — both for school, household, and peer-network. The composition and frequency of partial assembly, relative to full assembly and to single-person event is a numerical relationship of some importance. Another dimension of comparison is event complexity. Complexity of an event varies with the variety of different activities, actor types, semantic domains, sequencing of activities (and episodes), and object-types that are involved in the course of an event.

We have adopted temporal scheduling of an event as a basis for our first typology. *Recurrence* means that an event type recurs on a cyclical basis such that one can specify its occurrence in that cycle, and at what point in the cycle it will occur — diurnally, weekly, monthly, seasonally, etc. *Regular events* are predictable events, but predictable within stated limits. Speaking in terms of the typology, events are *recurrent-regular* in that they are highly predictable and have a very specific, sequential place in the cycle. Some events are *recurrent, but irregular* in that one knows they will happen within the interval of a temporal cycle, but just when they will take place in the cycle is uncertain. *Nonrecurrent-regular* events cannot be anticipated in terms of cycle, but are predictable within an interval period. Finally, *nonrecurrent-irregular* events are happenings which are unpredictable from within the system. An example of this nonrecurrent-irregular event in our school system was the death of the principal and the memorial event held in his memory. In the social system of the school, his death is a nonrecurrent-irregular event.

Using as our basic dimension a schedule of events by time cycles and by absolute time we can provide proper time orientation to our model of the behavior stream. We may subdivide any given one of these types according to varieties of place types, actor types, and activity types. Under the general recurrent-regular type events or Type I, we might list subtype *a* events that could be labeled *daily-morning/teacher-student/in-classroom/ doing-math event*. Recurrent-regular subtype *b* events might be *daily-afternoon/student/playground/recess;* and subtype *c* event could be scheduled at the same time as subtype *b* where subtype *c* is *afternoon/ teacher/cafeteria/drinking-coffee event*. Type I, subtype *b* and *c* are related to one another by being complementary to one another.

Recurrent-irregular types of events, or Type II, might have subvarieties as subtype *a, weekly/sixth, seventh, eighth, teacher-student-administrator/ auditorium/having-program*. The point is that this event subtype will happen some time during the week, but specification of when it will occur on a smaller time scale, such as a daily time scale or relative time within the daily time schedule is impossible. Within the nonrecurrent-regular event type one might have such subvarieties, *teacher-student/adjustment-office/for sanctioning*. This type happens often and regularly, but not on a recurrent cycle. Several days might go by without the occurrence of this type of event and then three such events like this could occur in one morning.

Nonrecurrent and nonregular events such as the appearance of a crew of research workers on the scene to do ethnographic research, of course, are important types of events that can't be predicted from internal knowledge of the organization. Another example of this type of event might be a student demonstration that hasn't as yet become regular, let alone a recurrent kind of event in the school in which we are doing a study. High school students in some predominantly black high schools in Chicago did try to put demonstrations on a recurrent weekly basis for a period, but they weren't able to maintain recurrent regularity.

We emphasize that we are working toward a usable typology of events by working inductively. Even our four-member typology based on schedule came about inductively because it is important to develop the capability of predicting events in order to be there to observe them, or even to make work plans. We rounded out our typology beyond our inductive recognition of two types by generating four types and discovering real events that fit the theoretical categories. We could develop a theoretical typology based on our event coordinates types and activity types, but by this procedure we would have a grid with many thousands of cells and types. The most fruitful strategy seems to be that of working from our four schedule types, and on an inductive basis make further decisions about types of event characteristics.

The contour of events in the school is based on a basic pattern of four events that are very similar in beginning and ending episodes, and three other *periods* in which events are diffused into different place-types and among the actor-types in the system. The first four we ordinarily call "class," the other three periods are "recess." Weekly recurrent variations are introduced into the daily cycle — weekly events in the library, in the gymnasium, in the home mechanics shop, and as a special teacher for art and for music.

Although the schoolwork processing events and their cyclical variations have repetitive beginnings, endings, place-types, actor-types, and even *procedures of activities*, there *is* great variety in interaction and particularly in the verbal messages that make up the information flow. Some indication already shows that household and peer behavior are characterized by proportionately fewer recurrent-regular events. Seemingly there is more recurrent-irregular scheduling of events, and many nonrecurrent-regular events in household and peer relations. One can anticipate, however, less complexity and variability in messages and code, and perhaps even less variation in interaction.

An Example

Perhaps an example can be used here to illustrate our approach. On a particular Wednesday morning in November, I had entered the classroom at 10:45 A.M., as the class returned from recess. My commentary was as follows:

> The boy in the blue shirt wads a sheet of paper up in his hand, swings his knees around under the edge of the desk, gets up, walks to the front of the room, then turns left across the front of the room in front of the desks over to the waste basket under the windows. He walks leisurely and deliberately. He unhurriedly drops the wad of paper into the waste basket, turns and walks slowly back across the front of the room in front of the desks, apparently on his way back to his desk. At this point the teacher says to him, "Julio, *what* are you *doing?*" "Taking that scrap paper to the waste basket, Teacher." Teacher says, "You *know* you are not to get up and *wander* around the room. *Remember* that!" Boy in blue shirt (Julio) returns to seat in a less leisurely, but still not completely hurried fashion, puts his hands on his desk and whirls himself around them, throwing himself into the seat and stares up at the teacher momentarily (I can't see his face nor the expression on it). Then he picks up his pencil and begins writing on a sheet of paper at his desk.

This account includes two activities, one of which interrupted the other. Julio stated his purpose was to throw away waste paper. The teacher may have had a different idea of his purpose. Her actions also follow a definite procedure, a "verbal-spear" with the purpose, apparently, of controlling his behavior, and of explicating a rule of behavior.

In the account please note that the actions are described not only in terms of when each occurs relative to other actions, but also how it occurs; that is, for example, in terms of the volume of voice with which certain parts of the message are emphasized. All this is the procedural part of an activity. In giving attention to the *procedure* we are well within the cultural realm; that is, specifying a style or a rule for the style of a set of actions that are interrelated with respect to a purpose. One can move on in the cultural realm here and talk about the conceptualization or cognition of purpose. The teacher, on being interviewed, could specify her notion of Julio's purpose, a statement of purpose that predictably will differ very radically from his. She might have said, "He got up because he seems unable to concentrate, and wanted to pass the time." The observer may specify certain goals or a goal that he thinks the behavior leads to; but in addition, he must derive from the verbal messages, or from accounts in interviews, what the actors regard as the explicit goal-objectives of the activity's procedure from the actor's point of view. Within his own analysis and concept of a dynamic activity, the observer may have some theory of implicit or latent purposes or objectives which could be served by the procedure of the activity.

An observer's view of purpose, however, should take into account the full course of activity that took place throughout the event that he was describing. For example, having observed the activity we have just mentioned in the context of the full event — from the point at which the whole class and the teacher entered the room — I knew that an earlier episode had begun with a "public" remark by the teacher: "Who is using Susan's desk as a waste basket?" Susan, who was absent that day, sits in the desk behind Julio. On top of her desk, around the old-fashioned ink well, several wads of paper were piled. Very obviously Julio was the culprit. As the teacher stared at him with a pursed-lip, accusing expression, Julio gathered up the wads of paper and quickly walked over to the waste basket, threw them in and walked back to his desk. When later in the course of the same event, Julio got up to take *one* piece of paper to the waste basket, he may have been responding to the earlier episode. In an interview with Julio one might establish that the earlier episode was part of the context of the episode that we related here.

It is our hunch that most North American female teachers try to establish an interactive style with boys, including older Puerto Rican boys, that challenges the latter's sense of masculinity. This arouses them to do battle with the female teachers to maintain their self-concept of having arrived at manhood, in the Puerto Rican terms. If our comparisons suggest that that relationship is plausible then we can pursue it into the realms of cognition, self-concept, interpersonal identity, etc.

As an example, consider the fact that the episode involving Julio is a kind of activity we've noticed occurring with great frequency between certain teachers and older Puerto Rican boys in the school. When involving Puerto Rican boys of fifteen or sixteen the interaction we described is usually only the first phase of a more extended episode that includes both verbal and physical action on the part of the Puerto Rican boy to defy the directive of the teacher. In contrast, the North American boys and the younger and smaller Puerto Rican boys generally do not work themselves up to the point of continuing the episode into actions of defiance. They capitulate or at least appear to capitulate, although this doesn't deny them the privilege of heated and colorful descriptions of their concept of the teacher outside the context of the episode. During these types of encounters with older Puerto Rican boys suspense builds up over who is going to *win*. As time goes on and more of these episodes occur between a given pair, a teacher and a Puerto Rican boy, the teacher may be forced to take the boy to the office to win. But she has "lost" to some degree because she resorted to the larger system of arrangements for social control that is not of her own design.

With respect to the question of conflicts between Puerto Rican boys and North American teachers, our research task is to select a sample of events, *not a sample of individuals*, and to be sure that the events vary according to actor type. We could take a random sample of Type I recurrent-regular events; e.g., math in the morning, but stratify that sample by the sex of the teacher; e.g., male and female. Or we could collect descriptions of the nonrecurrent-regular event, *teacher-student/adjustment-office/behavior sanction*, that took place over a given period of time, say a four-week period, and analyze them for actor-type characteristics and for the event-type that just preceded the nonrecurrent-regular type that we are sampling. By checking back on the event-type that just preceded this nonrecurrent-regular event, we are checking out contingencies, of course.

If we establish the plausibility of this type of interaction and contingency in the school, our next step is to follow the network of those Puerto Rican boys in our principal sample who fit the age range of boys involved in this type of event. We turn to their households and to events in that household in order to see whether the pattern of interaction and the procedural aspect of activities directed toward sanctioning and toward inhibiting violations of behavior rules seem to follow the same procedures as those we have seen in school. In particular, we would want to look at the same activity sequences involving Puerto Rican adult women and Puerto Rican boys to find out if there is a sharp contrast between the procedures in their interactions, with the procedures in activities involving the same Puerto Rican boys and their female teachers. If contrast is sharp then we can pursue the question through interviews with informants concerning how these behavioral procedures and their differences affect them and strike them in emotive and in value terms.

We could carry on the analysis of these two episodes and of other episodes in the same event, but I think this example carries the burden of expressing part of our rationale for using behavioral events. As we have specified, it is a segment of the stream of behavior that we can use as an integral context for the behavioral items we are interested in — from object types to the semantic analyses of the messages that occur in the event.

One other very important point should be made in terms of the limitations of sheer human energy. For example, it's important to recognize that within the classroom there are simultaneous currents of activities. The current of activities that involves the teacher can be quite different from the current of activities that involves the students with one another, although both are going on during the same event. Moreover, a teacher may interrupt one activity, introduce another and complete it, and then go back to the first. While an observer may be in the class throughout the course of the day, the amount of attention demanded in the accurate report of the behavior stream would not allow one to continue this kind of close observation necessary throughout the day. So, one's recording may be in terms of *events*. Two carefully described events in the course of the morning while the other events are briefly sketched in, according to the order in which they occurred, how they began and ended, is, we think, an orderly and sensible way to develop a store of data. Several people are able to orient themselves quickly with respect to each other's ethnographic work.

A serial, contingent, and complementary arrangement of events has long been recognized in the analysis of ritual and ceremony. (Radcliffe-Brown, 1922; Chapple and Coon, 1947). Sometimes a set of serially related microevents has been referred to as *event* in the singular (Kimball and Pearsall, 1955). For our purposes that collection of microevents is a "serial event set," not a single event. Nor do we wish to simplify events to the point of singling out only one factor, in variant aspects, as the unit (Chapple and Arensberg, 1940). In contrast to that emphasis, the descriptive segment that we call a microevent is a complex of component parts or factors, each of which may take variable form. The component variations amount to cultural difference when they reach a certain order of variation. Our approach is more analogous to a molecular than an atomic approach to units of description.

The level at which the discovery of difference will be a most potent base from which to suggest changes in organization, and behavior will be at the level of activities and interactions. We anticipate finding differences between household and school in the conceptual domains of socialization, schooling, and occupational socialization. Feature overlap of activities in an event — that is, the recurrence of similar activities in different instances of an event — is one relation out of which an event typology based on activities can be generated. Insofar as our rapport with the households permit us, we are trying to get accounts of streams of behavior in that context to compare with our classroom behavior. We feel it is at this level of activity that we can fruitfully compare patterns of behavior in the home and in the school, both in terms of procedure and in terms of goals and purposes. Moreover, interviews around these activities are the common referent points with respect to which we can compare the cognitive maps and conceptualizations of different members and different segments of the egocentric networks.

A more general but equally important objective of event description and analysis is to secure descriptive data that can be used for cross-cultural comparison of schools and for comparing schools in the same cultural system. The criteria for satisfactory description go beyond that of satisfying our own anthropological research demands, however. We are involved in action-generating research, and eventually we must have descriptions and comparisons that meet and satisfy instrumental criteria for modifying teacher behavior, administrative procedure, and even student behavior so as to make a genuine difference in the satisfaction of Puerto Rican children within United States schools.

To reiterate, a description of event types presented in terms of the time cycles by which they occur can provide the general contour of the pattern of schooling, as well as of the household and of peerdom. The main advantage that we now derive from the approach outlined here is that the team of field workers has a way of orienting themselves to each other's work. Each has an idea of from where in the complex stream of behavior the other has chosen to draw in order to get a participant observer description. We have intersubjective navigational points, so to speak. The microdescriptions of particular behaviors and verbalization in particular classrooms can then be placed into a temporal sort of macromodel of the organization or of the group into which ego's network has led us.

In summary, we are studying a sample of egocentric networks using participant observation, interviews, and basic ethnographic description, but the accounts are conceptualized as accounts of events. We are studying the linkages in the networks through their manifestations in events. We can follow these egos into the classroom, as well as into household and peer contacts, and do ethnographic accounts of their experience in the classroom. Putting our accounts in terms of a cluster in the stream of behavior, which we call "events," allows us to study the peer linkages and the teacher linkages as they manifest themselves in these events. Examination of these events may even allow us to study the effects of teachers' secondary linkages on the teacher's primary links with the sample egos. We submit that using this approach to allow us to combine participant observation with network analysis in terms of event description resolves on the one hand the object-sample problem posed by the very complex urban setting and on the other still permits us to utilize the *in vivo* observational study of complex processes of acculturation.

References

Barker, Roger G. *The Stream of Behavior.* New York: Meredith, 1963.
Barnes, J. A. "Class and committees in a Norwegian island parish," *Human Relations* 7:39–58, 1954.
Bott, Elizabeth. *Family and Social Network.* London: Tavistock Publications, 1957.
Chapple, Eliot, and Conrad Arensberg. "Measuring human relations," *Genetic Psychology,* monograph 22, 1940.
Chapple, Eliot, and C. Coon. *The Principles of Anthropology.* New York: Wiley, 1947.
Epstein, A. L. "The network and urban social organization," *Rhodes-Livingstone Institute Journal,* 29:29–62, 1961.

Goodenough, Ward. *Cooperation in Change*. New York: Wiley, 1963.

Harris, Marvin. *The Nature of Cultural Things*. New York: Random House, 1964.

Kimball, Solon T., and Marion B. Pearsall. "Event analysis as an approach to community study," *Social Forces*, 34, 1955.

Lévi-Strauss, Claude. "Social structure," in *Anthropology Today*, A. Kroeber (ed.). Chicago: University of Chicago Press, 1953.

Mayer, A. C. "The significance of quasi-groups in the study of complex societies," in M. Banton (ed.), *The Social Anthropology of Complex Societies*. London: Tavistock, 1966.

Radcliffe-Brown, A. R. *The Andaman Islanders*. Cambridge: Cambridge University Press, 1922.

Smith, Louis, and William Geoffrey. *Complexities of the Urban Classroom*. New York: Holt, Rinehart and Winston, 1968.

FURTHER READINGS

Barker, Roger G. *Ecological psychology*. Stanford: Stanford University Press, 1968.

Kimball, Solon T. "Education," in Otto von Mering and Leonard Kasdan (eds.), *Anthropology and the behavioral and health sciences*. Pittsburgh: University of Pittsburgh Press, 1970.

Moore, Alexander. *Realities of the urban classroom: observations in elementary schools*. Garden City, N.Y.: Doubleday, 1967.

Smith, Louis M., and Paul A. Pohland. *Grounded theory and educational ethnography: a methodological analysis and critique*. St. Ann, Mo.: Central Midwestern Regional Education Laboratory, 1969.

Warren, Richard L. *Teacher encounters: a typology for ethnographic research on the teaching experience*. Research and Development Memorandum No. 45. Stanford: Stanford Center for Research and Development in Teaching, Stanford University, 1969.

21

Mr. Lacey's microsociological investigation of social mechanisms and processes operant in an English grammar school compares with the inquiry reported by Burnett. The approaches of the two researchers are remarkably similar. Each contrasts learner behavior which is accountable to class or cultural factors outside the school with that which is accountable to the sociocultural milieu of the classroom. Each obtained data through intensive, local observation. Each, it develops, is concerned with the ultimate functioning of educational policy — "academic streaming" in the Lacey selection, and, by implication, "education for the disadvantaged" in Burnett — especially as that policy affects individual and groups of learners. It may be, in short, that there are fewer differences of method (and finding) between the research strategies of Burnett and Lacey than the terms "microethnography" and

*"microsociology" imply. Mr. Lacey represents a sociological tradition distinct
in some ways from the American; it is also true that he and Mrs. Burnett chose
quite similar problems to research. Yet clear and critical likenesses remain.
If Burnett has pointed the way toward a methodology grounded in anthropological inquiry, so does Lacey argue, in effect, for a strategy that balances
in vivo data with its quantification, which integrates ethnographic description
and analytic models. Mr. Lacey, formerly Lecturer in Sociology, Manchester
University, is at present associated with the Center for the Study of the Social
Organization of Schools, Johns Hopkins University.*

C. LACEY

Some Sociological Concomitants of Academic Streaming in a Grammar School

A great deal is now known about the macro-sociology of secondary
education in this country. Recent studies [1] focusing on selection for entry
and on the performance in secondary schools of pupils with various
social and psychological characteristics have sketched in the major dimensions of the problem. This paper, on the other hand, which is an early
report on one aspect of the research in the sociology of education, being
undertaken at Manchester University,[2] is an attempt to lay bare some of
the micro-sociological mechanisms within one school and dwells primarily
on processes of differentiation and subculture formation. It must therefore
be seen against the background of well-established findings in the field.

The paper contains three sections:

1. A description of some of the sociological characteristics of boys entering the school.

2(a). A descriptive analysis of some aspects of the developing informal
structure of one class in the school, with particular reference to two case
studies.

From *The British Journal of Sociology*, vol. 17, no. 3 (September 1966), pp. 245–
262. Reprinted by permission of the author.

[1] See, for example, J. E. Floud, A. H. Halsey and F. M. Martin, *Social Class and
Education Opportunity*, 1956; J. W. B. Douglas, *Home and School*, 1963; Central Ad-
visory Council for Education's Report of 1954, *Early Leaving*.

[2] This is the first report on research financed by a grant from the Ministry of Education to the Department of Sociology and Social Anthropology in the University of
Manchester. A team of three research associates (Mrs. Audrey Lambart, Mr. David
Hargreaves and myself) was appointed to undertake research in different schools. The
work of the team was coordinated by Drs. R. Frankenberg and V. G. Pons and owes a
great deal to the interest of Professors M. Gluckman, P. Worsley and Dr. A. H. Halsey
of Oxford University, who acted as consultant to the scheme.

(b). An attempt to establish a model which describes the passage of pupils through the school.

3. An attempt to verify the model through the use of quantitative indices — in particular, the concepts of differentiation and polarization which are developed in section 2(b).

The overall aim is to provide a picture of the stratification and subsequent sub-culture development, associated with academic streaming.

Section 1

The Intake

The grammar school is a highly selective institution. To start with, therefore, it is important for us to investigate the ways in which this selection affects the composition of the newly recruited first-year classes. It is only possible to talk about subsequent subcultural development if the initial characteristics of the group are clear.

The particular factors that will concern us here are:

(1) The way selection restricts the intake to a particular type of student.
(2) The way selection isolates the successful candidate from his fellow pupils and friends at his junior school.

1. Though not completely conclusive, the evidence gathered supports my contention that the new intake to a grammar school will consist largely of 11-year-olds who have been accustomed to playing what I have called "best pupil" role in their junior schools, and are, in their new environment, often separated from their former school friends. The extent to which this is true in any grammar school will, of course, depend on a large number of factors, such as the percentage of grammar school places available and the number and the size of junior and grammar schools in the catchment area.

It is useful to look at Hightown Grammar School [3] as an illustration of the way the selection process works.

The Local Education Authority of Hightown sends about 15 per cent of its 11-year-olds to grammar schools each year. This clearly does not imply that 15 per cent of the pupils in *any* junior school in the town will find themselves in the same grammar school. There are six grammar schools in Hightown and these are specialized in a number of ways; there are two Roman Catholic grammar schools (one for boys and one for girls) which serve the separate R.C. education system in Hightown and the surround-

---

[3] Hightown is a pseudonym for the town in which the school is located and I therefore refer to the school itself as Hightown Grammar School. I conducted eight months full-time and ten months part-time fieldwork in the school. In all I have been associated with this school and others in the area for 3½ years.

ing area; and four L.E.A. grammar schools (two for girls and two for boys) which draw their pupils almost exclusively from Hightown. For non-Catholic, 11-year-old boys in Hightown there are then three possible grammar school avenues; entry to a direct grant school outside the town, Hightown Grammar School and Hightown Technical Grammar School. (A very small fraction attend public schools.)

The distribution of boys between these avenues is, however, complicated by the unequal reputation of the schools to which they have access. A few of the most able boys compete successfully for places in direct grant schools, the bulk of the most able enter Hightown Grammar and the remainder enter Hightown Technical Grammar.

Table 1 shows that the boys entering Hightown Grammar are selected from a large number of junior schools, and that the selection test tends to scoop a few pupils from each school. Over half the boys come from schools that send six or less pupils. Evidence from a variety of sources (junior school reports, autobiographies and the statements of junior school teachers etc.) clearly shows that these contingents include the vast majority of top scholars, team leaders, school monitors, head boys and teachers' favourites. In short they are the "best pupils."

2. The relative isolation of pupils from their former schoolmates is only partially illustrated in Table 1. When the boys arrive at Hightown Grammar they are divided at random into four classes. These classes are also House Groups. The pupils in them remain together for prayers, school meals and registration as well as lessons.

A more comprehensive picture of the degree of isolation of the first-year boy, on his arrival at Hightown, must therefore take into account the effect of the school organization. In order to do this I used "friendship choice" questionnaires, from which it was possible to extract the number of boys who had friends in their first-year classes who had attended the same junior school as themselves. This showed that 58 boys out of 118 questioned had no friend from the same junior school in their class. Thus almost half of the first-year intake spend the great majority of their time at school in a class in which they are isolated from their previous friends.

TABLE 1
1962 Intake to Hightown Grammar Classified According to Size of Junior School Contingents

Mean size = 3.5 boys per contingent

	Size of contingents				
	1-3	*4-6*	*7-9*	*10-12*	*Total*
Number of junior schools	24	5	4	2	35
Number of pupils	42	25	30	21	118

It can be seen from the foregoing analysis that any batch of new boys assembling at Hightown Grammar School are likely to make up a highly selected and homogeneous group. The annual intake being about 120, they represent under 4 per cent of their age group in the community and all are boys who have ostensibly been selected on the basis of their sex, religion and academic achievement. Only the direct grant grammar schools are more selective; their pupils are likely to have achieved a higher academic standard and to find themselves even more isolated from their junior school friends.

The homogeneity of the intake and the relative isolation of individual new boys from their junior school friends are both important factors affecting patterns of behaviour in the first-year classes. The first-year pupils show a high degree of commitment to the school. School uniform is rigidly adhered to; caps and blazers are proudly displayed, school functions and clubs are attended disproportionately by first-year boys. Their behaviour in the classroom is characterized by eagerness, cooperation with the teacher and a high degree of competition among themselves. "Please sir, Willy Brown is copying my sums" is a remark that could only come from a first-year boy. I once tried to measure the response rate to a narrative and question-and-answer lesson given by a History teacher. So many responded to each question that I could not record them. As the tension mounted boys who did not know the answers looked around apprehensively at those who did. These were in a high state of excitement and they smiled triumphantly at those who did not know the answers, they stretched their arms and bodies to the utmost as they eagerly called "sir," "sir," "sir," every time the master glanced in their direction. When the master said "All right, Green, you tell us," there were quiet sighs and groans as those who had not been called upon subsided into their seats. The whole performance was repeated as soon as the next question was asked.

During such spells the desire to participate was so great that some boys would put up their hands and strain for notice, even though they had no idea of the answer. And, if asked to give the answer, they would either make a gesture suggesting that they had suddenly forgotten, or else subside with an embarrassed and confused look, to the jeers and groans of the rest of the class who would then redouble their efforts to attract attention.

The type of enthusiasm characteristic of a first-year class was occasionally found in second- or third-year forms but there were a number of observable differences. The second and third forms were more likely to "play dead" and to allow five or six people to "do all the work"; and, even if the master succeeded in getting a larger proportion to participate, there was always a residue of boys who hardly participated or who only did so by giving obviously wrong or funny answers. Finally there was the possibility that the form would use any excitement of this kind to sabotage the lesson or to play the fool. For example, a boy will stretch so hard that he falls out of his desk, another will accidentally punch the boy in front as he puts up his hand and the form's "funny man" will display his wit in response to an ambiguous question — sometimes isolating the teacher from the class by referring to a private class joke.

First-year forms are thus widely regarded by teachers as the easiest and most rewarding to teach. They are typically allocated to young inexperienced masters or to masters who have difficulty with discipline. Misdemeanours are largely the result of high spirits, overeagerness or forgetfulness rather than conscious malice. Hopes are high and expectations as to school performance and subsequent careers are unrealistically rosy.

Section 2(a)

The Informal Structure — Two Case Studies

As soon as this highly selected first-year population meets at Hightown Grammar School and is allocated to the four first-year classes, a complex process of interaction begins. This process takes place through a variety of encounters. Boys talk and listen to each other, talk and listen to teachers, listen to conversations, notice details of accent, gesture, clothing, watch others at work and at play in various situations and in innumerable different permutations.

During the first few days much of this interaction appears to take place in a fairly random way influenced mainly by the physical and organizational arrangements. Soon, patterns of selection begin to emerge. Various initial interactions yield information and experience, which are retained by the individual and provide some basis for the interpretation and partial control of other interactions. This partial control is extremely important because it soon gives rise to a recognizable, although unstable and changing structure.

When I started observing the first-year classes in March 1963, the members of each class had only been together for about six months, but each class already had a definite structure of which the pupils clearly had detailed knowledge. When a master called a boy to read or answer a question, others could be seen giving each other significant looks which clearly indicated that they knew what to expect.

On one occasion, for example, a master asked three boys to stay behind after the lesson to help him with a task calling for a sense of responsibility and cooperation, the master called "Williams, Maun and Sherring." The class burst into spontaneous laughter, and there were unbelieving cries of "What, Sherring?" The master corrected himself. "No, not

Sherring, Shadwell." From the context of the incident, it was clear that Sherring's reputation was already inconsistent with the qualities expected of a monitor. On another occasion, Priestley was asked to read and the whole class groaned and laughed. Priestley, a fat boy, had been kept down from the previous year because of ill health (catarrh and asthma) and poor work. He grinned apprehensively, wiped his face with a huge white handkerchief and started to read very nervously. For a few moments the class was absolutely quiet, then one boy tittered, Priestley made a silly mistake, partly because he was looking up to smile at the boy who was giggling, and the whole class burst into laughter. Priestley blew his nose loudly and smiled nervously at the class. The teacher quietened the class and Priestley continued to read. Three lines later a marked mispronunciation started the whole class laughing again. This performance continued with Priestley getting more and more nervous, mopping his brow and blowing his nose. Finally, the master with obvious annoyance, snapped "All right, Priestley, that's enough!"

This short incident, one of several during the day, served to remind Priestley of his structural position within the class and to confirm the opinions and expectations of the class and the teacher towards him. Priestley's behaviour was consistent with his performance in the examinations at the end of the Autumn Term when he was ranked twenty-ninth out of thirty-three.

During this period of observation I also noticed the significance of the behaviour of another boy, Cready. Cready first attracted my attention because, although his form position was similar to Priestley's (twenty-sixth) he habitually associated with a strikingly different group. He behaved very differently in class, and had a markedly different reputation.

Cready was a member of the school choir and it so happened that the English master, whose classes I was observing, was also the music teacher and he had arranged the class so that the members of the school choir sat in the row next to the piano and his desk (row 4). To be a member of the choir one had to have a good voice and be willing to stay in school to practice during dinner time and at four o'clock, once or twice a week for certain periods of the year. In the next two rows were members of the first-form choir. To be in this a boy had only to be willing to sing. In the last row (row 1) were boys who could not or would not sing.

During the first three lessons I observed Cready answered four of the questions put to the class. On two of these occasions he had, before putting up his hand, discussed the answer with the boy next to him. If Cready got an answer wrong he was never laughed at. Priestley answered two questions in the same period. He got one of these wrong and was laughed at by the class. Also as I observed later, if Priestley attempted to discuss an answer with the boy next to him, he was reprimanded.

TABLE 2
Record of Teacher-pupil Interaction—Average for 3 Lessons

Type of interaction	Row number			
	1	*2*	*3*	*4*
Answers to questions (per boy)	.5	.7	1.3	3.6
Rebukes (per boy)	1.6	1.2	.5	.4
Questions from boys (totals)	3	1	2	10

Table 2 illustrates how the seating arrangements in the class affected the pattern of interaction with the teacher.[4]

A sociogram for the class showed an apparent inconsistency. In class Priestley was frequently in the middle of a group of mischievous boys. If there was trouble Priestley was in it. I expected him to be fairly popular with some of the boys who led him into trouble, but none of them picked him as a friend. He chose five boys as his friends but the only boy to reciprocate was the other Jewish boy in the class.

The other boys used Priestley to create diversions and pass messages, and because he was so isolated he was only too pleased to oblige. He could never resist the temptation to act as if he was "one of the boys." However, when he was caught out they deserted him and laughed at him rather than with him. He was truly the butt of the class.

These incidents, seen in the context of the structure of the class, show how Priestley had fallen foul of the system. He was not in control of his own situation, and anything he tried to do to improve his position only made it worse. His attempts to answer questions provoked laughter and ridicule from his class-mates. His attempt to minimize the distress this caused, a nervous smile round the class, a shrug of the shoulders, pretending either that he had caused the disturbance on purpose or that he did not care, served to worsen his position with the teacher.

He compensated for his failure in class and lack of academic success by learning the stocks and shares table of the *Financial Times* every week. This enabled him to develop a reputation in a field outside the sphere in which the school was competent to judge. He would emphasize the *real* importance of this in his future career and thus minimize the effect of his scholastic failure. Even this did not improve his standing in the school, especially with the staff. It served only to explain his laziness, his bad behaviour and lack of concern with school work. "Oh Priestley,

---

[4] This pattern holds good for other lessons I observed in this class. However, I do not wish to imply that this relationship between seating, class position and interaction is typical of the school as a whole. Other classes had different patterns.

he is just biding his time with us, from what I hear his future is assured anyway." "He is just lazy," said the English master.

If I had had to forecast the future performance of these boys on the evidence I would, of course, have expected Cready to do better in the following examinations and Priestley if anything, worse:

Examination results:

		First-year exams				Second-year exams	
		Autumn	Spring	Summer		Autumn	Spring
Priestley	1A	29	30	26	2C	12	27
Cready	1A	26	10	10	2E	11	12

It is interesting to note the family background of these two boys. Priestley is Jewish, second in a family of three and lives in an area of expensive detached houses. His father is a clearance stock buyer. Cready on the other hand lives on a council estate, is fourth out of six in the family and his father is a quality inspector in an abrasives factory.

Cready and Priestley do not, therefore, conform with the established correlation between academic achievement and social class. Cready, a working-class boy from a large family on a council estate, is making good, while Priestley, an upper-middle-class boy from a smaller family, is failing academically. However, this negative case highlights the point I want to make; there was a measure of autonomy in the system of social relations of the classroom. The positions of Cready and Priestley are only explicable in the light of an analysis of the system of social relations *inside* the classroom. This system is open to manipulation by those who are sensitive to its details. Hence Cready, who had all the major external factors stacked against him, was able to use the system of social relations to sustain and buoy himself up, while Priestley, despite all the advantages that he brought to the situation, had fallen foul of the system and was not only failing but also speedily losing any motivation to succeed in the sphere in which the school was competent to judge him.

I reiterate that this is not an attempt to disprove the general established trend but to highlight the fact that there are detailed social mechanisms and processes responsible for bringing it about, which are not completely determined by external factors. By studying these mechanisms it will be possible to add a dimension to our understanding of the general processes of education in our schools.

SECTION 2(B)

Differentiation and Polarization

It is important to discuss these processes in a more general way and set up a model which describes the passage of pupils through the grammar school. To do this, I will need to introduce two terms — "differentiation" and "polarization."

By differentiation is meant the process of separation and ranking of students according to a multiple set of criteria which makes up the normative academically oriented, value system of the grammar school. This process is regarded here as being largely carried out by teachers in the course of their normal duties.

Polarization on the other hand is regarded as a process taking place within the student body, partly as a result of differentiation but influenced by external factors and with an autonomy of its own. It is a process of subculture formation in which the school-dominated normative culture is opposed by an alternative culture which I will refer to as the anti-group culture. The content of the anti-group culture will, of course, be very much influenced by the school and its social setting. It may range from a folk music, C.N.D. group in a minor public school to a delinquent subculture in a secondary modern school in an old urban area. In Hightown Grammar School it fell between these extremes and was influenced by the large working-class and Jewish communities of Hightown.

There are a number of scales on which a master habitually rates a boy. For the purposes of the analysis I will consider two:

(a) Academic Scale.

(b) Behaviour Scale. This would include considerations as varied as general classroom behaviour and attitudes, politeness, attention, helpfulness, time spent in school societies and sports.

The two are not independent. Behaviour affects academic standards not only because good behaviour involves listening and attending but because a master becomes favourably disposed towards a boy who is well-behaved and trying hard. The teacher, therefore, tends to help him and even to mark him up. I have found in my own marking of books that when I know the form (i.e., good and bad pupils) I mark much more quickly. For example, I might partly read the essay and recognize the writing: "Oh, Brown. Let's see, he tries hard, good neat work, missed one or two ideas — 7/10" or, "This is a bit scruffy, no margin, not underlined, seems to have got the hang of it though. Who is it? Oh, Jones, that nuisance — 5/10!"

There is another reason why good behaviour is correlated with academic achievement. A boy who does well and wishes to do well academically is predisposed to accepting the system of values of the grammar school, that is he behaves well. This is because the system gives him high prestige and it is therefore in his interest to support it; the membership of the choir illustrates this point. He is thereby supporting his position of prestige. On the other hand a boy who does badly academically is predisposed to criticize, reject or even sabotage the system, where he can, since it places him in an inferior position.[5]

A boy showing the extreme development of this phenomenon may subscribe to values which are actually the inverted values of the school. For example, he obtains prestige from cheeking a teacher, playing truant, not doing homework, smoking, drinking and even stealing. As it develops, the anti-group produces its own impetus. A boy who takes refuge in such a group because his work is poor finds that the group commits him to a behaviour pattern which means that his work will stay poor and in fact often gets progressively worse.

The following extracts, from an essay entitled "Abuse" and written by a first-form boy for his housemaster, illustrates a development of anti-group values of an extreme nature for a first-year pupil.

> I am writing this essay about abuse in the toilets. . . . What they (the prefects) call abuse and what I call abuse are two different things altogether.
>
> All the people where I live say I am growing up to be a "Ted" so I try to please them by acting as much like one as I possibly can. I go around kicking a ball against the wall that is nearest to their house and making as much noise as I can and I intend to carry on doing this until they can leave me alone. . . . It seems to me the Grammar School knows nothing about abuse for I *would much rather be a hooligan and get some fun out of life than be a snob always being the dear little nice boy doing what he is told.*

In Section 1 we saw that at the beginning of the first year, the pupils constitute a relatively homogeneous and undifferentiated group. They are uniformly enthusiastic and eager to please, both through their performance of work and in their behaviour. The pupils who are noticed first are the good pupils and the bad pupils. Even by the Spring term some masters are still unsure of the names of quiet pupils in the undifferentiated middle of the classes they teach.

It is fairly rare for an anti-group to develop in the first year. Although one or two individuals may develop marked anti-group values, they are likely to remain isolates. In the 1962 first year, I was able to recognize only one, Badman, quoted earlier. He wished to be transferred to a secondary modern.

The more usual course of events associated with a marked degree of (relative) failure in the first year is for the child to display symptoms of emotional upheaval and nervous disorder and for a conflict of standards to

[5] For a fuller exposition of this argument specifically related to delinquency, see A. Cohen, *Delinquent Boys.*

take place. Symptoms that occurred in the first-year intake of 1962 included the following:

> Bursting into tears, when reprimanded by a teacher.
> Refusal to go to school or to go to particular lessons, accompanied by hysterical crying and screaming.
> Sleeplessness.
> Bedwetting.
> Truanting from certain lessons or truanting from school.
> Constantly feeling sick before certain lessons.
> One boy rushed to stage in assembly clutching his throat and screaming that he could not breathe.
> Consistent failure to do homework.
> High absence record.
> Aggravation of mild epilepsy.

The 15 cases recorded probably represent all the cases of major disturbance but a large number of the cases of minor disturbance probably never became known to the school.

The individual significance of these cases cannot be discussed here but their general significance is important to the model under discussion. We have seen that the 11+ selects the "best pupils" from the top forms of the junior schools. These forms have been highly differentiated in preparation for the 11+ examination. The pupils have, in many cases, been "best pupils" for some time and have internalized many of the expectations inherent in the position of "best pupils." Their transfer to the grammar school not only means a new environment, with all that such a change entails — for example, new class-mates, new teachers and new sets of rules — but also for many of them a violation of their expectations as best pupils. It is when this violation of expectations coincides with "unsatisfactory" home backgrounds that the worst cases of emotional disturbance occur.

In the second year the process of differentiation continues. If streaming takes place between the first and second years as it did in the year group I am studying it helps speed the process and a new crop of cases of emotional disturbance occur. In the 1963 second year most of these cases were associated with boys who were failing to make the grade in the top stream and boys who were in the bottom half of the bottom stream. After six months in the second year this bottom stream was already regarded as a difficult form to teach because, to quote two teachers:

(i) "They are unacademic, they can't cope with the work."
(ii) "Give them half a chance and they will give you the run around."

The true anti-group starts to emerge in the second year, and it develops markedly in the third and fourth year. It is in the third and fourth years that strenuous efforts are made to get rid of anti-group pupils. Considerable pressure is put on the Headmaster by the teachers that take the boys and the Head in turn transmits this to the Board of Governors. In most cases application to leave will also be made by the boy and his parents. However, the Board of Governors are often loath to give permission for a boy to leave or transfer for two reasons: (i) The governors are also the governors for the secondary modern schools in the area and cannot readily agree to passing on discipline problems from the grammar school to the secondary modern. (ii) They are generally very suspicious of grammar school teachers and feel reluctant to risk an injustice to a pupil who is often a working-class boy.

However, there are some requests that cannot easily be refused, for example, cases of ill health, family hardship or consistent truanting. There are also a number of cases of unofficial leaving. In these cases the boy has actually left school and taken a job but is still being marked as absent in the register. It is difficult to estimate accurately the extent of the total loss but in two years somewhere between 10 and 15 pupils left or were transferred from each year before taking "O" level or reaching the age of 16.

A similar process can be observed in the sixth form and results in a crop of leavers in the first-year sixth. The extent to which differentiation develops and is internalized in the sixth is illustrated by the following remark made to the Economics master. He had just rebuked a boy in the Upper Sixth Modern and told him that unless he worked harder he would not pass Economics "A" level: "Well, the way I look at this: If some of the boys in the General [6] form can get it and they usually do, then I should be all right."

Section 3

The indices developed in this part of the paper are prepared from two questionnaires completed by all members of the 1962 intake. One questionnaire was given at the end of the first year and one at the end of the second. The indices are designed to illustrate the processes of differentiation and polarization.

On both occasions the boys were asked who had been their close friends over the last year. They were asked to restrict themselves to boys in the school and to six choices, unless they felt they definitely could not do so.

There was virtually no difference in the average number of choices *received* per boy in the four *unstreamed* first-year classes (Table 3).

[6] The general stream is the bottom stream in the sixth form.

TABLE 3

1A	4.1 choices per boy
1B	4.1 choices per boy
1C	4.2 choices per boy
1D	4.5 choices per boy

When the boys were streamed on academic criteria at the end of the first year these same friendship choices were related to the new forms 2E, 2A, 2B, 2C [Table 4(a)].[7]

TABLE 4
Average Number of Friendship Choices Received per Boy After Streaming: First Year and Second Year

	Average number of choices per boy in each class	
	(a) 1st year	*(b) 2nd year*
2E	4.8	5.0
2A	4.5	4.5
2B	3.9	3.9
2C	3.3	4.3

Not only do the figures reveal striking differences but these differences are related to academic achievement. At the end of the first year, the higher up the academic scale a boy was placed, the more likely he was to attract a large number of friendship choices.

At the end of the second year the boys were asked the same question. The response was equally striking. Column (b) of Table 4 shows that the year spent among a new class of boys has hardly changed the overall positions of 2E, 2A and 2B, although the actual friendship choices for any one boy will have undergone considerable change. However, 2C has undergone a substantial change. The increase from 3.3 to 4.3 for 2C represents an increase of something like 30 choices, in a class of 30 boys. That the new popularity of the boys in 2C is brought about by the growth of a new set of norms and values or the beginnings of the anti-group subculture is demonstrated by Table 5. The boys of 2C have become popular for the very reasons that they were unpopular in their first year.

The boys of 2E and 2A who according to our hypothesis *should* be positively influenced by the academic grading, since they are successful in relation to it, show that it does in fact have a marked positive influence

[7] Approximately the top one-quarter of each first-year form went into 2E, the second quarter into 2A and so on.

TABLE 5
Distribution of Friendship Choices According to Class: Second Year, 1963
(1962 Intake at End of Second Year)*

Number in each class in brackets	2E	2A	2B	2C	Others	Total of choices made	% of choices in own class
2E (31)	96	24	13	7	11	151	63.2
2A (31)	28	94	16	6	14	158	59.5
2B (28)	20	17	63	23	20	143	45.6
2C (30)	9	4	18	92	13	136	67.2
Totals (of choices received)	153	139	110	128	58	588	

*Read across for choices made, down for choices received by each class

TABLE 6
Distribution of the Sons of Non-manual Workers
Between the Four Second-year Streams

	Non-manual manual ratio	Ratio
2E	18/14	˙1.3
2A	18/13	1.4
2B	13/14	0.9
2C	8/23	0.3

on their choice of friends (e.g., 2E make 24 choices into 2A, 13 choices into 2B and only 7 into 2C). There is no element in the organization of the school that could bring this about.

In 2B a change takes place. Their choices into 2E and 2A have the expected form but there is an unexpectedly large number of choices into 2C, i.e., 23, more than into either 2E or 2A. Similarly, the boys of 2C show a marked tendency to choose their friends outside 2C, from 2B rather than 2E and 2A. There must be a basis, other than the school-imposed academic values, on which these friends are chosen. This alternative set of norms and values I have already referred to as the anti-group subculture.

Table 6 shows that in the second year academic achievement is related to social class. To some degree this is a problem of working-class and middle-class culture.[8] That this is not the whole answer, is demonstrated

[8] See D. N. Holly, B.J.S., June 1965, for analysis of the effect of social class on performance in a comprehensive school.

by reminding ourselves of Table 4(a) and (b) where it is clearly demonstrated that this anti-group development took place between the ends of the first and second year. If it were solely a social class phenomena it would have been apparent at the end of the first year.

This analysis is confirmed by another set of data (Table 7) which is in many ways complementary to the first. In the second-year questionnaire I asked "What boys do you find it difficult to get on with?" Once again I allowed them to put up to six names unless they felt they could not possibly confine themselves to six. This time, however, many boys refrained from putting any names down and only a few put six. Enough names were mentioned to establish a pattern of unpopularity. Once again the largest number of choices were made into the informants' own class.

TABLE 7
Distribution of Choices of Unpopular Boys: Second Year, 1963

	2E	2A	2B	2C	Others	Prefects	Total of choices made	Average number of choices received
2E	38	4	4	26	3	0	75	1.71
2A	5	33	1	9	22	1	51	1.45
2B	7	4	24	20	1	0	56	1.14
2C	3	4	3	42	3	6	61	3.23
Totals (of choices received)	53	45	32	97	29	7	243	

The number of choices made into other forms was always less than 7 with one notable exception — 2C received 26 from 2E, 9 from 2A and 20 from 2B and so received the highest number of unpopularity choices, 97 compared with 53 for 2E which is the next highest.

The preponderance of choices into 2C is explained by the anti-group development in 2C. These boys are now regarded as bullies and "tough eggs" who in Badman's terminology would rather be hooligans and have a good time than be nice little boys. They are aggressive, loud-mouthed and feared by many who are successful in terms of the dominant school norms.

An expectation that is considerably altered by academic streaming is the school-leaving age. Boys who are successful will expect to continue after "O" level at 15 or 16 into the sixth form.

At the end of the first year the boys were asked "At what age would you like to leave school?"

The results demonstrate the overall optimism of the first year. Only 25 per cent wanted to leave at the end of the fifth year, 75 per cent desiring a sixth-form career. In practice only something like 50 per cent ever achieve this. When the figures are broken down into the second-year classes they reveal, even so, considerable foresight (Table 8).

TABLE 8
Average Age at Which the Boys in Each Class
Would Like to Leave School

	Before streaming at end of first year	After streaming at end of second year
2E	17.4	17.4
2A	17.7	17.3
2B	17.3	17.4
2C	17.0	16.7

Even the relatively low value of 2E compared with 2A is fairly realistic in that since 2E take the G.C.E. at the end of four years compared with the normal five for 2A, B and C, many will expect to complete their sixth-form career at 17½ compared with the normal 18½. The fact that at this stage in their school career they had not been told officially that they would be going into 2E in the following year only marginally affects the situation because by this time the process of structuring and differentiation had gone on sufficiently for most boys to know whether they would go into 2E or not. In the same questionnaire 28/32 of the boys who eventually went into 2E indicated that 2E was the second-year class of their choice.

By the end of the second year, the averages of the desired leaving age revealed a number of puzzling features.

2E remained the same while the average age for 2A fell below 2B. 2B's average in fact increased to the same level as 2E, 2C's average value decreased, but not as much as one might expect. The situation has been complicated by an additional factor which I have called "streaming reaction."

When the top seven or eight boys from each of the first-year housegroups are put into 2E it is fairly obvious that most of them are not going to be able to maintain a high position in the form. In fact Table 9 shows that only two were able to maintain their position, the rest were all placed lower in 2E than in their first year class. This was less marked in 2A with only 16 boys doing less well. It was reversed in 2B and 2C.

The depressing effect of streaming reaction on the Express form is unlikely to influence their estimates of the length of their school careers to any great extent, because all the E stream are expected to go into the sixth form and they are told this constantly throughout the year. A typical remark would be, "All of you will be expected to go on into the sixth form and *many* of you will I hope go on to university." Streaming reaction is very marked in the E stream but it takes on a different form (see later).

TABLE 9
Examination Performance Before Streaming
Compared with Examination Performance
After Streaming

	Number of boys who were placed higher in second year than first year	Same	Number of boys who were placed lower in second year than in first year
2E	0	2	28
2A	7	4	16
2B	17	2	6
2C	15	0	2

2C is also affected by its polar position. It is not much to a boy's credit to have got a higher place in the class if that class is 2C. Masters discussing 2C with me put it bluntly. "There is not one boy in the class who has any sort of academic ability. In fact most of them shouldn't be in the school at all. It's not fair on them and it's not fair on the school." Remarks of this sort were frequently made while talking to me in front of the class and were obviously audible to the front rows of boys, as well as to myself. The low prestige of 2C therefore minimized the correcting effects of streaming reaction, with respect to leaving age.

It was in 2A and B that streaming reaction had its maximum effect. The relative positions of the two forms were for a long while ambiguous, since the Head had not made it clear. Some masters thought that 2A and 2B were on the same level, others that 2A was better than 2B. Only one master thought that 2B was academically better than 2A but it is significant that he was able to make the mistake and hold to it for a considerable length of time.

In these two classes then, streaming reaction was a major factor in affecting the length of time that the boys wanted to stay in school.

Another demonstration of "streaming reaction" is shown by the personal assessment of success table (Table 10). The boys were asked "Do you consider that the past year at school has been a success?"

The difference between 2A and 2B is not significant but the difference between 2E and 2C is, especially when one considers the way in which the staff assess the "success" of the two forms in tackling academic tasks. This difference can only be accounted for by the past experience of the

TABLE 10
Personal Estimate of Success in Second Year

	Regarded the past year as a success	Couldn't say	Regarded the past year as unsuccessful
2E	19	1	11
2A	24	–	7
2B	21	–	7
2C	24	2	4
Totals	88	3	29

two groups, the different sets of standards they have acquired and the way in which their new experiences measure up to those standards. This is confirmed by an analysis of the experience of the eleven boys who regarded themselves as unsuccessful in 2E. On average, they dropped 16 places in their second-year exams compared with their first-year exams. On average the rest of the class dropped eight places. During the year two of these boys had been considerably emotionally disturbed — crying in lessons, crying before school and refusing to come to school. A third went through a similar period and his father wrote the school complaining that "the boy is utterly demoralized." The only other category of boys to yield so large a number of disturbed cases in the second year was the bottom of 2C!

Finally Table 11 shows another area of activity that is affected by streaming. The boys were asked to estimate the average length of time spent on homework each evening. Streaming has given rise to distinctly different climates of expectation with relation to homework. Although there is considerable overlap in the estimates given by individual boys in the four classes (which of course deserves further analysis), the table does give a convincing demonstration of another aspect of the process of differentiation.

TABLE 11
Estimate of Length of Time Spent on Homework
Before and After Streaming

	Estimated average time spent on homework each night: first year	Estimated average time spent on homework each night after streaming: second year
2E	1 hr. 3 mins.	2 hrs. 0 mins.
2A	1 hr. 4 mins.	1 hr. 43 mins.
2B	1 hr. 10 mins.	1 hr. 18 mins.
2C	1 hr. 1 min.	1 hr. 7 mins.

Conclusion

In this article I have attempted to develop a model which describes the internal processes of a grammar school in terms of sub-culture formation, differentiation and polarization. The indices presented in the last section are an early attempt to verify quantitatively some of the impressionistic data of Section 2. The research is, however, still continuing and a great deal of the material already collected is still at an early stage of analysis.

It is expected that material, yet to be collected, as well as that already in the pipeline, will clarify and modify this early formulation. Nevertheless the evidence presented here seems to indicate that the relationship between the internal organization [9] and development of pupil subcultures [10] is an important factor in the process of education that warrants careful examination in further research.

Further Readings

Frankenberg, Ronald. *Communities in Britain*. Baltimore: Penguin Books, 1966.
Gross, Morris. *Learning readiness in two Jewish groups: a study in "cultural deprivation."* New York: Center for Urban Education, 1967.
Jackson, Philip W. *Life in classrooms*. New York: Holt, Rinehart and Winston, 1968.
Singleton, John. *Nichu: a Japanese school*. New York: Holt, Rinehart and Winston, 1967.
Wolcott, Harry F. "Concomitant learning: an anthropological perspective on the utilization of media," in Raymond V. Wiman and Wesley C. Meierhenry (eds.), *Educational media: theory into practice*. Columbus, Ohio: Merrill, 1969.

22

The lucid discussion of directed educational change that follows differs in approach from either of the two previous articles. First, Gallaher phrases culture as a corpus of ideas, and not as patterned behavior. Second, the author focuses on "target systems," rather than upon the actual behavioral domains of classrooms; and third, he attempts to relate an array of concepts that refer variously to the nature of organizations and the change process, in contrast to the data-specific development of a few selected concepts in each

---

[9] B. Jackson, *Streaming: an Education System in Miniature.*
[10] See J. S. Coleman's *Adolescent Society.*

of the two previous articles. Generally, the consequence of a change can be taken as a function of the extent to which that change violates or compromises an established order. Changes in relatively "closed" social organizations, as Gallaher notes, characteristically reflect on and have implications for the whole of the organization, not just a part (or some parts) of it. Today's schools represent "closed" social organizations, and changes in schools, whether in instructional program or in the environment of instruction, tend to be promoted or repudiated in terms of the total school enterprise. This is a structural bias. Many educational changes, both minor and major, are in fact resisted not so much for reasons particular to the substance or rationale of those changes, but rather because of their expected consequences to other aspects, directions, or procedures of school life — especially to the sense of custody that yet prevails in contemporary schooling. If meaningful changes are to take place, knowing what constitutes the established order of the school then becomes critical. Mr. Gallaher, who is Professor of Anthropology and deputy director, Center for Developmental Change, University of Kentucky, is persuaded by the efficacy of the insights he presents, here, into the social constitution of the school.

ART GALLAHER, JR.

Directed Change in Formal Organizations: The School System

In the paper that follows I shall examine certain limited phenomena and raise a number of issues that seem relevant — always from the viewpoint of an anthropologist — and I shall make a number of suggestions which, when recast in your own frame of reference, will serve as positions for discussion. I propose to do this by first examining the nature of change as it is viewed by anthropologists. In this discussion I will emphasize the role of advocate because I believe it is crucial. This will be followed by an examination of the concept "formal organization," with some attention turned on the organizational peculiarities of the school and the implications of these for understanding directed educational change. I shall then comment briefly on what seems to me the crucial problem . . . the potential of the school administrator in the role of advocate.

The Nature of Change

When the anthropologist talks of change he speaks of change in culture because the latter, more than any other concept, focuses the great

From *Change Processes in the Public Schools* (Center for the Advanced Study of Educational Administration, University of Oregon, 1965), pp. 37–51.

number of diverse interests which characterize anthropology as a behavioral science. By culture is meant those ideas, socially transmitted and learned, shared by the members of a group and toward which in their behavior they tend to conform.[1] Culture, then, provides the selective guidelines — ways of feeling, thinking, and reacting — that distinguish one group from another. This is true whether by group we refer to large social systems, such as nation-state societies, or, more relevant for our purposes, to smaller social systems, formal organizations such as a hospital, a labor union, or a school system in a given community. As a convenient way of denoting a lower level of conceptual abstraction, the latter are sometimes called "subcultures."

The preoccupation with culture by anthropologists rests on a number of basic premises, two of which are especially germane to our interests. . . . One is the belief held by anthropologists that culture, since it is socially transmitted and learned, and since it is a major adaptive mechanism of man, is bound to change.[2] Very early in their empirical data anthropologists became aware of the *normative* quality of culture, that is, in a given social situation the carriers of a culture can define the *ideal* behavior pattern that is called for. It was apparent just as early, too, that there were gaps between the ideal and the *actual* patterns of behavior. The significance of this finding ultimately led to the premise that a given culture is bound to change with time because (1) man's adjustment to his non-human environment is never fully complete, what Wilbert Moore calls *the constant environmental challenge*,[3] and (2) no known group is free from social deviation though such information does not always find its way into the monographs written by anthropologists. If we want to view this in a slightly different way, the sociocultural systems developed by man are tension-producing as well as tension-reducing, and the attempts

---

[1] For the many ways in which culture has been defined by anthropologists and other behavioral sciences, see A. L. Kroeber and Clyde Kluckhohn, *Culture: A Critical Review of Concepts and Definitions*, Papers of the Peabody Museum, vol. XLVII, no. 1, Harvard University, 1952. This volume lists some 160 definitions and groups these according to the qualities of culture that are emphasized. This particular work demonstrates what a tremendously rich and fluid concept culture really is.

[2] This belief has not always characterized anthropology; many of the early field-workers, who studied mainly isolated societies, accepted a model of culture as essentially stable. However, as culture came to be understood better this interpretation proved so inadequate that some theorists asserted the other extreme, that every culture is, in fact, in a constant and continuous state of change. Without qualification, the latter position is as misleading as the former. Most contemporary anthropologists would accept Keesing's suggestion as more in line with the facts; that is, "Proper perspective on this problem must see forces making both for stability and change." See Felix M. Keesing, *Cultural Anthropology*, Rinehart & Co., New York, 1958, p. 384.

[3] In an unpublished paper titled "Developmental Change in Urban-Industrial Societies." This paper will be published in a volume of essays on developmental change, edited by Art Gallaher, Jr.

to manage tension are productive of innovation and its acceptance.[4] I am, therefore, suggesting that a tension-managemeent organizational model is useful for culture change purposes because, among other reasons, it implies the viewpoint that change is a natural consequence of human social life.

Though it was recognized early in anthropology that changes in culture could be internally derived, as through *invention* and *discovery*, the greater attention by far has been paid to changes that accompany contact between groups. Two of the more important concepts developed to explain contact changes are *diffusion*,[5] which refers to the transfer of culture elements from one group to another, and *acculturation*,[6] which refers to changes occurring in the culture of one group in contact with another. Out of the research focused on these two concepts came the distinction between *non-directed* and *directed* culture change.[7] It is the latter, of course, that is important to us.

By directed culture change is meant a structured situation in which an advocate interferes actively and purposefully with the culture of a potential acceptor. In this situation an advocate consciously selects elements in a *target system* (that which is to be changed) and by stimulating the acceptance of innovations, inhibiting the practice of prior patterns of behavior, or, as is frequently the case, doing both of these things simultaneously, he manages the direction of change. The success

[4] Ibid.

[5] Diffusion in anthropology has been concerned mainly with the distribution of elements of culture as opposed to a concern with diffusion as process. The latter is much more identified with rural sociologists. See Everett M. Rogers, *Diffusion of Innovations,* The Free Press of Glencoe, New York, 1962, for a good statement by a rural sociologist; see also Herbert F. Lionberger, *Adoption of New Ideas and Practices,* Iowa State University Press, 1960. For a statement by an anthropologist, see the last three chapters of Ralph Linton, *Acculturation in Seven American Indian Tribes,* Appleton-Century Co., New York, 1940. A number of other general works in anthropology, published during the 1930's and later, include sections of diffusion.

[6] Acculturation is one of the major concepts used by anthropologists in their studies of change process. One of the first attempts to systematize the concept was by a Social Science Research Council Sub-Committee on Acculturation, composed of Melville Herskovits, Robert Redfield, and Ralph Linton. The results of the seminar were published in 1937 and were recently made available again under the original title, *Acculturation: The Study of Culture Contact,* by Peter Smith, Publisher, Gloucester, Mass., 1958. The bibliographic reference is to Melville J. Herskovits. Another Social Science Research Council Seminar grappled with the concept in 1953. The results of that seminar are reported as "Acculturation: An Exploratory Formulation" in the *American Anthropologist,* vol. 56, no. 6, pt. 1, 1954, pp. 973–1003. Another useful publication is *Acculturation Abstracts,* ed. Bernard Siegel, Stanford University Press, 1955.

[7] For an early statement regarding this distinction, see Ralph Linton, *Acculturation in Seven American Indian Tribes,* op. cit., chap. 10. For a more recent statement on types of contact change, see Edward H. Spicer, "Types of Contact and Processes of Change" in *Perspectives in American Indian Culture Change,* edited by E. H. Spicer, University of Chicago Press, 1961.

with which this is done depends mainly on (1) how the advocate plays his role, particularly his use of authority, and (2) the behavior of those who make up the target system. We shall return to the matter of change shortly, but before talking of the second major premise that we need to have in mind, let me emphasize that I believe the way that the advocate plays his role is one of the more crucial variables in the success or failure of attempts to direct change.

A second premise regarding the nature of culture that is particularly important to us is the belief held by anthropologists that parts of a culture, however conceptualized, are linked to other parts and, therefore, any element of culture is comprehended fully only by understanding its relationship to other simultaneously present, relevant facts. This is, of course, the *structural-functional viewpoint*,[8] and if we keep in mind that the interdependence of parts that is implied is not absolute but is rather a matter of degree, it is a view that is not only useful but one that I believe necessary for understanding the full ramifications of change processes.[9] In line with this, the distinction between manifest and latent functions is especially relevant for understanding directed sociocultural change situations.[10] I say this because, in directed change, purpose should be made explicit, and it is precisely at the manifest-latent level of analysis that we confront directly the matter of purpose. By manifest function we shall refer to those objective, hence intended, consequences of whatever part of culture we define; by latent we shall refer to the unintended and unrecognized consequences of the same order.[11] For example, in a rural community that I once did research in I found that the manifest function of membership on the school board was to serve the school by working with the superintendent in budget and other policy matters. At the same time, a latent function of membership on the board was the acquisition of a kind of political power that had nothing whatsoever to do with education, but which, when exercised, was very often detrimental to the manifest objectives of the school system.

We can now turn our attention to some of the variables viewed by anthropologists as influencing the acceptance or ultimate rejection of in-

---

[8] This refers to the basic premise of functionalism. For an excellent summary of the concept see Raymond Firth's "Function," in *Current Anthropology*, edited by William L. Thomas, Jr., University of Chicago Press, 1955. See also Laura Thompson, *Toward a Science of Mankind*, McGraw-Hill Co., 1961, p. 9. Also, see Harry Johnson, *Sociology*, Harcourt, Brace and Co., New York, 1960, pp. 48–63.

[9] See Robert K. Merton, *Social Theory and Social Structure*, Free Press, 1957, pp. 25 et seq., and Alvin W. Gouldner, "Reciprocity and Autonomy in Functional Theory," in L. Z. Gross, ed., *Symposium on Social Theory*, Row, Peterson, 1958.

[10] Neal Gross makes this point for educational sociology in "The Sociology of Education," in Robert Merton et al. (eds.) *Sociology Today*, Basic Books, 1959.

[11] See Robert K. Merton, op. cit., pp. 61–66.

novation. In order to facilitate our understanding of these variables let me first introduce a conceptual framework within which we can perceive them as related. In this regard it will be useful for us to have in mind what is meant by a *culture change cycle*. The latter is viewed by anthropologists as involving three broadly conceived processes. These are: (1) *innovation*, the process whereby a new element of culture or combination of elements is made available to a group; (2) *dissemination*, the process whereby an innovation comes to be shared; and (3) *integration*, the process whereby an innovation becomes mutually adjusted to other elements in the system.[12] In our discussion here, attention will focus mainly on the more significant concepts and variables by which we understand innovation and dissemination.

Homer Barnett, who has authored the most extensive anthropological treatise on innovation, sees it as a mental process, and makes the point that every man is a potential innovator. Barnett is concerned essentially with the creative act of innovation, and he turns most of his attention on delineating the cultural and psychological variables which underlie specific innovative processes.[13] I do not believe, however, that our concern . . . is in that direction. Rather, we are more concerned with the introduction of changes in ways that will best gain their acceptance. It will be useful for us, then, to distinguish between the term *innovator*, which we will reserve for the individual or agency responsible for the conception of an innovation, and *advocate*, which we shall use to refer to individuals or agencies who sponsor an innovation for the express purpose of gaining its acceptance by others.[14] Thus, in the directed change situation we can assume that the role of advocate is always a purposive one. With these few comments out of the way, we can turn our attention to some of the variables which influence the definition and enactment of the advocacy role.

Elsewhere I have suggested that there are two major role models for advocacy,[15] that the distinction between these is one of means rather than ends, and that in each case the conception of means for gaining acceptance derives from assumptions about the nature of change. The model that I call the *pragmatic advocate* prescribes a role concerned mainly with creating a climate conducive to acceptance; the view of the culture change cycle is global, acceptance is to be achieved, but the *processes*

[12] Ralph Linton, op. cit., last three chaps.

[13] Homer Barnett, *Innovation: The Basis of Culture Change.* McGraw-Hill Co., New York, 1953, especially chaps. 2–6.

[14] Ibid., pp. 291–95.

[15] Art Gallaher, Jr., "The Role of the Advocate and Directed Change." Paper read at the University of Nebraska Symposium on Identifying Techniques and Principles for Gaining Acceptance of Research Results. To be published in a volume edited by Wes Meierhenry.

of acceptance are accorded signal importance. This model rests on the premise that success or failure in directed change is referable mainly to the advocate's understanding of the content and internal organization of the pattern where change is sought.

The *Utopic model* defines the advocate's role mainly as one of manipulation to gain the acceptance of an innovation; the view of the culture change cycle is myopic, it focuses almost exclusively on the *act of acceptance*. There is a basic premise that one can achieve results best by doing things to, or planning for, people rather than with them.

For most cases I believe the pragmatic model is the best for achieving genuine change; that is, acceptance that is valued. I believe it is best because it is based on complete and detailed knowledge of the target system, and in the directed change situation there is no substitute for that. There is, in fact, a large body of research to support the basic assumptions underlying the pragmatic model, that is that people will more readily accept innovations that they can understand and perceive as relevant,[16] and secondly, that they have had a hand in planning.[17] Working from this model, and with these two assumptions in mind, the task of the advocate is made easier if he is prestigeful in ways that are valued by the target system. Related to the matter of prestige, and very often a function of it, is the more important variable of the *dependence upon authority* [18] that is shared in the target system. This is a simple and practical matter of the following order: in a given community are potential acceptors willing to adopt an innovation in the public school system advocated by a school administrator, or will they follow the lead of a physician or a political pressure group of "super-patriots," or other source of opposition? Who are those who command some kind of authority and who, because of it, can be expected to serve logically as emulative models in the dissemination of an innovation?

In the directed change situation I believe that dependence upon authority is one of the more crucial variables. I would urge those who must plan educational change in our society to give careful consideration to

[16] The list of sources is long. The following, taken from research done in management and industry, support this hypothesis. Robert A. Goodwin and Charles A. Nelson (eds.), *Toward the Liberally Educated Executive*, the New American Library, New York, 1960; Auren Uris, *The Management Makers*, The MacMillan Co., New York, 1962, pp. 91–164; Harold Koontz and Cyril O'Donnell, *Principles of Management*, McGraw-Hill Book Co., Inc., New York, 1959, pp. 359–85.

[17] Again, the list of sources to support this hypothesis is long. A representative sample would include the following: Georges Friedman, *Industrial Society*, The Free Press, Glencoe, Ill., 1955, pp. 261–372; Kurt Lewin, "Group Decision and Social Change," in T. Newcomb and E. Hartley (eds.), *Readings in Social Psychology*, Henry Holt and Co., New York, 1949, pp. 330–44; Edward H. Spicer, *Human Problems in Technological Change*, Russell Sage Foundation, 1952, cases 7, 8, 11, 14.

[18] Homer Barnett, op. cit., chap. 3, for a discussion of this variable in connection with innovation.

the kinds of authority to which innovations are tied. It may be that conventional authorities already present are inadequate. We may need to invent new ones, and with the assistance of mass media and other devices by which we manage such things, endow them with the kind of prestige and other qualities necessary to get the job done.

Viewed in a different way, the matter of authority assumes added relevance. If we view authority as the control that some members in the group have over the activities of others, it follows that those with rank and power in an organization control rewards. Rewards are, in fact, a major mediating factor in the reciprocity that characterizes the social relationship of those with power and those without it. Stated bluntly, those in authority can sometimes effect change by denying customary reciprocity; that is, by manipulating rewards in ways that deny the target system an expected gratification.[19] We must keep in mind, however, that the distinction between those with authority and those without it is not always clearly defined; in a given organization there may exist checks and balances on the definitions and use of authority. In this regard, Howard Becker's research on the authority systems of the public school is very interesting.[20] So far as the professional functionaries are concerned, and here we are talking of administrators and teachers, each controls sanctions that permit some control over the other's behavior. However, I shall later make the point that authority in the educational organization, because its goal is service, derives its significance more at that point where the organization articulates with the client group.

There is another variable that I should like to stress as especially crucial in the success of an advocate in a directed change situation and that is *the expectation of change* [21] shared by members of the target system. It is important for an advocate to know the areas of culture where people value change and where they have come to expect it. These are channels into which innovations can be fed with the greatest chance of success. On the other hand, if such expectations are not present, or if innovations cannot be tailored to fit those that are, the advocate may find their creation essential to his long-range task. In line with this, an important quality for the target system to have is the capacity for criticism.[22]

---

[19] For a good discussion of this point see Charles P. Loomis, "Tentative Types of Directed Social Change Involving Systemic Linkage," *Rural Sociology*, vol. 24, no. 4, Dec., 1959, pp. 383–90.

[20] "The Teacher in the Authority System of the Public School," in Amitai Etzioni (ed.), *Complex Organizations: A Sociological Reader*, Holt, Rinehart and Winston, New York, 1961, pp. 243–55.

[21] Homer Barnett, op. cit., chap. 2 for a discussion of "expectation of change" as a cultural variable in innovation.

[22] See Margaret Mead, "Changing Culture: Some Observation in Primitive Societies," in *The Human Meaning of the Social Sciences*, ed. Daniel Lerner, Meridian Books, 1959. In this article Dr. Mead explores the variables which cause people to reflect on culture change.

It may well be that this capacity is not present, and that it will have to be encouraged. A corollary that the advocate should keep in mind here, however, is that the *margin of security* for many in the target system may be very low, hence an alternative in the form of an innovation becomes doubly threatening. This is somewhat contrary to the long-held view that those who derive security from an organization are reluctant to change the vehicle of their success. I am suggesting that in formal organizations of a service variety, such as educational systems are, the opposite might well be true — those who are secure can sustain the threat of examining alternatives, whereas those whose margin of security is low will resist changing a system that has *accommodated to them*. In practical terms, within our present frame of reference, I am posing the hypothesis that the better teachers in a given school system are more likely to accept innovations than are the poorer ones; the more educationally secure members of the client group are more likely to accept innovations in the system than those who are less familiar with the intricacies of the educational process.

A number of other variables that influence the acceptance and rejection of innovation involve the general matter of *scale*. For example, what is the extent of the target system's *felt need* for change? Is the *time factor* right; that is, is the system already undergoing change, or is there a target system apathy induced by previous innovative failures? There is also the matter of size in the system to be changed, and the associated organizational complexity that it varies with size. The latter bears importantly on communications effectiveness, which in turn relates to the problem of determining the most viable unit for effecting change. It might be that even when the entire target system is scheduled for change, it can be done best by changing smaller, more manageable components one at a time.

One further point regarding communications should be emphasized and that is, the advocate in his concern with the formal properties of communication systems should not ignore the informal, less structured channels for moving information. In formal organizations the social cliques that develop among work associates or around some other common interest can be invaluable channels for communicating information *so that it will be accepted*.

The Nature of Formal Organizations

By formal organization we shall mean one that is deliberately conceived and planned for the explicit purpose of achieving certain goals. All organizations have social structure and they can be viewed as subcultures. If they are of any considerable size the most significant aspects of social structure are typically a centralized authority and an ordered status hierarchy. Viewed as a subculture, the formal organization has at minimum a normative system that defines the purpose, the *goal-orientation*, of the personnel who occupy the specialized statuses and perform specialized roles within the organization. At its most formal level the dimensions of the subculture are prescribed in the organization's official body of rules. Though the structural and cultural aspects of organization seem obvious, we must make sure that they are not so obvious that we lose sight of them. In directed change especially we should continually explicate these two dimensions and keep them conceptually separate. We must know which we plan to change. For example, do we want to modify structure to more efficiently attain goals in the system, or do we want to maintain a structure and innovate new goals? Above all, an advocate must never assume that change in one aspect will necessarily lead to desired change in the other. Depending on the organization in a change situation, culture and social structure may each manifest peculiarly stubborn strains toward autonomy.

So far as directed change is concerned, those aspects of formal organization that are most important are the authority that we attach to the structure and, from a cultural standpoint, the matter of a goal-orientation and normative procedures for arriving at defined goals. The dimension of authority which has received the most attention in the formal organization literature is legitimation. The latter, which can be crucial in directed change situations, has been a topic of some concern by social scientists, especially since Max Weber addressed himself to the subject. Weber believed that authority in organizations is legitimated in three ways: (1) by the sanctity of tradition, (2) by values that derive from conceptions of the divine or supernatural power (the Charismatic leader), and (3) by a belief in the supremacy of the law.[23]

There is no need for us to elaborate these categories here. Rather, we can agree with Gouldner [24] when he says:

> The authority of the modern administrator is characteristically legitimated on the basis of his specialized expertise; that is, administrators are regarded as proper incumbents of office on the basis of what they know about the organization or their professional skills, rather than whom they know.

Since we have suggested earlier that the tension-management model is a good one for understanding the dynamics of change, it is interesting to note here that Gouldner [25] also sees the problems surrounding authority as constituting a major factor in organizational tension.

[23] See H. H. Gerth and C. Wright Mills (trans. and eds.), *From Max Weber: Essays in Sociology*, New York, Oxford University Press, 1946, pp. 196–204.

[24] Alvin W. Gouldner, "Organizational Analysis," in Robert K. Merton et al. (eds.), *Sociology Today*, Basic Books, New York, 1959, pp. 413.

[25] Ibid., pp. 413–16.

From the standpoint of directed change the matter of authority in formal organizations derives its importance from factors other than mere legitimation. For example, in a formal organization what statuses are most likely to be extended to encompass the advocacy role? A logical hypothesis is that statuses with the most authority legitimated around the goals of an organization are the ones that advocacy responsibility is most likely to be attached to. Among other things, such statuses presumably have more sanctions vested in them than do others. However, successful innovation often is achieved only in the absence of formal sanctions, in which case persuasion or other methods are employed. Therefore, viewed from the perspective of the target system we need to ask the following: does the target system view the role of authorities legitimated by the functional requirements of the organization as including also the responsibility for innovation? They may not. In fact, their perception of the legitimated authority's role set may emphasize the opposite so strongly that they will not tolerate a redefinition of it to include innovative responsibility. Those who direct change in formal organizations should keep in mind the formal properties of a system do not tell the whole story; in the matter of authority just mentioned, for example, recipients can and do organize in ways that enable them to resist pressures placed by formal authority.

It seems appropriate at this point, then, to emphasize that the formal aspects of social structure and culture which characterize an organization are always accompanied by networks of informal relations and unofficial norms. The informal relations that emerge are, of course, related to the nature of the organization and they, in turn, mold the behavior of functionaries in ways which obviously influence the formal properties of the system. In short, there are in all formal organizations elements of structure that are organizationally unprescribed, such as cliques and informal status structures, but which are not unrelated to the formal elements of structure. For example, a clique of work associates can easily resist pressures placed on them to increase production, accept innovations, and the like,[26] and it is a fortunate school administrator, indeed, who has not had to contend with the passive resistance techniques of teachers.[27] We know group cohesiveness to be one of the most important aspects of the informal structure.

Concomitant with the informal structures are elements of culture, that is, patterns of belief and sentiment, that are also organizationally unprescribed. For example, in a given school system there is every likelihood

---

[26] See especially F. J. Roethlisberger and William J. Dickson, *Management and the Worker*, Cambridge, Mass., Harvard University Press, 1939.

[27] Howard K. Becker, "The Teacher in the Authority System of the Public School," op. cit.

that one will find the unofficial norm that one teacher must never question another's grade, even if it is known that the grade is unjustified. To do so is to threaten the authority system that the teachers are attempting to define.[28] Again, it is worth reiterating that those who direct change in formal organizations will find it imperative to have knowledge of both the formal and informal aspects of the target system.

Another feature of formal organizations that must always be kept in mind is that they never exist in a social vacuum, but rather are linked to other organizations in a larger social system. From an analytical viewpoint we must, then, establish the parameters within which the formal organization derives its significance; that is, the boundaries within which authority is legitimated, goals are defined, and decisions are made. It is important to keep in mind that there is no inherent congruity between these three levels of action; one may rest on the local autonomy of the organization itself, whereas the other two may derive significance mainly from the external environment.

In a very worthwhile article on organizational analysis, Gouldner [29] casts linkage not in the conceptual framework of integration of the parts, but rather from the vantage point of "the functional autonomy of organizational parts." Again, with our tension management model in mind, he offers the interesting hypothesis that ". . . the structure of complex organizations . . . serves to maintain and protect the parts from others within the same system, at least in some degree. Thus organizational structure is shaped by a tension between centrifugal and centripetal pressures, limiting as well as imposing control over parts, separating as well as joining them." More than any other formal organization that I can presently think of, an understanding of the adjustment of the school to its external environment is crucial for those who would guide us to innovations in education.[30] This becomes even more relevant when we understand some of the peculiar qualities that characterize the school system as a formal organization. I am referring to the peculiarities associated with the two aspects for formal organization — authority and the establishment and maintenance of goals — that I have identified as crucial in directed change. We now turn our attention to these considerations.

COMMENTS ON THE SCHOOL SYSTEM AS A FORMAL ORGANIZATION

Viewed from a global perspective, the most significant quality of the school as a formal organization to keep in mind is that it is a *service*

---

[28] Ibid.

[29] Alvin K. Gouldner, 1959, op. cit.

[30] Neal Gross, op. cit., makes the point that this is an area that needs research by those interested in the sociology of education.

organization.[31] This means that the prime beneficiary of the organization is the client group, which in turn becomes a crucial variable in determining the limits and kinds of authority that are developed, and the goal orientation that the organization will take.

The professional functionaries in the school, that is administrators and teachers, confront continually the dilemma of legitimating their authority to determine goals in the system.[32] By all of the rights of passage, whether administrator or teacher, theirs is a specialized expertise that presumably equips them to determine the client beneficiaries' own best interests. However, I believe we should have to look long and hard to find a client group — those served by hospital, mental health, social work organizations, to name a few — that more aggressively questions professional authority than the one served by education. This is not new, it is a traditional matter. With a wide spectrum of values to draw from, many of which are anti-intellectual and not the least of which is local autonomy, the client group has, indeed, insisted upon a system which permits formal control to rest in the hands of laymen.[33] This control is given its most explicit symbolic representation in that major structural link between the school and its external environment, including the client group itself, the school board. As Gross [34] suggests, we need to understand this phenomenon better. For example, if the manifest function of a school board is to establish policies governing a local public-school system, what are the latent functions of a school board? It is not hard to receive the impression in many communities that the board has as its main function the protection of the community from the schools.

It is true that the power to legitimate authority and to establish goals is not as much in the local community or school district today as formerly. Much, in fact, has been relinquished to the state. However, enough is there to make this one of the very real problems for planning educational change. This is true because *so many problems currently defined in local school systems, and the innovations necessary to solve them, today owe their relevance to larger systems, such as the region or the nation-state,* more than at any prior period in our history. At the same time, because of racial integration, the prayer decision, and other political developments in our society, there is the greatest possible concern with local autonomy. There are, in fact, disturbing reports from teachers in all sections of the country that their professional status is increasingly

---

[31] Peter M. Blau and W. Richard Scott, *Formal Organizations,* Chandler Publishing Company, San Francisco, 1962, chap. 2.

[32] Ibid., pp. 51–54. The point is made that service organizations commonly face the problem of becoming captives of the client group.

[33] This point is also made by Neal Gross, op. cit., p. 137. He suggests this as an area that needs research in the sociology of education.

[34] Ibid., p. 133.

threatened, especially by reactionary political elements that hope to reduce alternative goals in education. The client group's new and vigorous interest in local autonomy could not come at a time when it is more out of touch with the sociocultural reality in which education must find its place. This seemingly paradoxical situation — *the concern of local client groups in the power to legitimate authority, a centrifugal tendency, contrasted to the centripetal one of problems in the local system, and the innovations necessary to solve them, deriving from larger systems — could well be the most difficult problem area for educational innovators.* Its importance should not be underestimated.

The task of professional functionaries is probably more difficult in service organizations than in any other kind. They must serve the collective interests of the client group and at the same time retain their authority and not become subservient to the demands of the client group.[35] I need only remind you that surrender to the client is not unknown in education. Many administrators and teachers take the line of least resistance and there are cases known where systems have surrendered to the client group.[36]

From the positive side, though, educational planners can derive some comfort from the knowledge that traditionally Americans have kept a kind of flexibility in their thinking about education and certainly a predisposition to change content and method. I am not sure that this predisposition to weigh alternatives is so evident when goals are involved, but then the latter are not always explicit. We might, in fact, say that more attention should be given to explicating viable goals in education, especially if we are to turn more of our attention on planning for change. Nevertheless, the process of education has been tied one way or another to related considerations of change, such as the dominant concern with social mobility, and this has led to something of an expectation of change in education. Those who direct innovations should be alert to this and, whenever possible, take advantage of it. Again, a word of caution is in order: the concern for local autonomy that I have mentioned may not permit this expectation of change to carry over into problem areas that derive their significance from beyond the local area or region.

THE SCHOOL ADMINISTRATOR AS ADVOCATE

The research in anthropology points to two classes of people as those most likely to be successful in bringing about change. Barnett,[37]

[35] Peter M. Blau and W. Richard Scott, op. cit., pp. 51–54.

[36] See especially Burton R. Clark, *Adult Education in Transition: A Study of Institutional Insecurity,* University of California Press, 1956.

[37] Homer Barnett, "Personal Conflicts and Culture Change," *Social Forces,* vol. 20, pp. 160–71.

who believes that the essential element in the innovative process is dissatisfaction, suggests four categories of people as innovators; these are also the ones most likely to initially accept an innovation. However, we have distinguished conceptually between the role of innovator and that of advocate and have indicated that it is the latter that concerns us. I would question that the success of the advocate is related to dissatisfaction; rather, it derives more from other qualities and dissatisfaction may or may not be present. As I have already indicated, I am inclined to the view that it is more important for the advocate to have prestige,[38] and/or that members of the target system depend upon his authority in matters of change.[39]

With these few comments out of the way we can turn our attention now on the role of the school administrator as it presently stands, and offer some comment on his potential as an advocate. I am referring, of course, to the generalized status and role of school administrator, recognizing that there are individual exceptions to the rule. If I had to summarize the school administrator's role in one phrase, it would be *he is the man in the middle*.[40] He stands between the client group, technically represented by the school board, and professional and other functionaries who comprise the educational system. "He faces towards several different audiences, each with different sets of demands — school boards, parents, parent groups, teachers, and students — as well as other administrators. He has to play his role appropriately in the light of all these demands." [41]

From a functional viewpoint our "man in the middle" has what Spindler [42] calls a *balancing role*.

> His job is in large part that of maintaining a working equilibrium of at best antagonistically cooperative forces. This is one of the reasons why *school administrators are rarely outspoken protagonists of a consistent and vigorously profiled point of view*. Given the nature of our culture and social system, and the close connection between the public and the schools *he cannot alienate significant segments of that public and stay in business.* (Italics mine.)

Because his role is a balancing one, and because I see nothing in our sociocultural system to indicate that the linkage of the public and the

[38] Richard N. Adams, "Personnel in Culture Change: A Test of a Hypothesis," *Social Forces*, vol. 30, pp. 185–89.

[39] Homer Barnett, *Innovation: The Basis for Culture Change*, McGraw-Hill Book Co., New York, chap. 3.

[40] For a good discussion of the "man in the middle" see John Useem, John D. Donoghue, and Ruth Hill Useem, "Men in the Middle of the Third Culture," *Human Organization*, vol. 22, 1963, pp. 169–79.

[41] George Spindler (ed.), *Education and Culture: Anthropological Approaches*, Holt, Rinehart and Winston, New York, 1963, p. 142.

[42] Ibid., p. 238.

schools will tolerate any other, I have strong reservations that the school administrator status is the one to assign advocacy functions to. I have already indicated that there seems to be a centrifugal tendency toward local autonomy in legitimating authority, and that at the local level the client group traditionally manages authority. *If* the problems in education were those that could be solved at the local level, *if* the client group was capable of structuring innovative procedures for meeting such problems, and *if* the client group maintained its traditional controls, the school administrator would automatically advocate innovations to other functionaries because of his position in the status hierarchy of the organization. But the system is not that way, and fortunately so. The problems of the local school, and the solutions to these problems, as we have indicated, come from centripetal forces that are pulling each local system out of its environment and into systems that are broader in scale. The sources of local client-centered authority may not be aware of the significance of the larger system or, what is worse, may not even care or resist the fact that it exists. Under these conditions they are not apt to permit advocacy as part of the administrative role. And since the role of advocate is purposive and one that involves commitment that, even under the best of change circumstances, sometimes involves conflict, the school administrator might reduce his balancing role effectiveness if he assumes advocacy. I do not mean the administrator should avoid any concern with change, because that is impossible. Rather, I am asserting that I do not believe the problems of change should rest mainly in the administrator's status.

I suggest that we are at an appropriate juncture in our society, meaning that the problems of education viewed from whatever perspective are of sufficient magnitude, to innovate positions that have as their special role function the management of educational change. This could be a special unit called Experimental Education, Planning Division, or by some other innocuous title, built into systems that could afford it. For those that could not meet the expense of such a unit, we should begin to think in terms of a model, perhaps patterned along the lines of agricultural extension. An *educational extension* with a research program focused on creating alternatives and an action program to prepare change agents to assist school systems with innovation, dissemination, and integration problems, is well worth considering. Change is a natural and inevitable consequence of the sociocultural and physical worlds within which our collective lives are acted out and it should be just as natural and just as inevitable that we should give some attention to managing the direction of that change. In line with this, one final word of caution — planning is not something to be taken lightly or as something that just happens; rather, *planning is activity and in and of itself is process.*

Further Readings

Atwood, Mark S. "Small-scale administrative change: resistance to the introduction of a high school guidance program," in Matthew B. Miles (ed.), *Innovation in education.* New York: Teachers College Press, 1964.
Jensen, Gale Edw. *Problems and principles of human organization in educational systems.* Ann Arbor, Mich.: Ann Arbor Publishers, 1969.
Miles, Matthew B. "Some properties of schools as social systems," in Goodwin Watson (ed.), *Change in school systems.* Washington, D.C.: National Training Laboratories, NEA, 1967.
Sieber, Sam D. "Organizational influences on innovative roles," in Terry L. Eidell and Joanne M. Kitchel (eds.), *Knowledge production and utilization in educational administration.* Columbus, Ohio, and Eugene, Oregon: University Council for Educational Administration and Center for the Advanced Study of Educational Administration, 1968.
Storey, Edward. "Concomitant outcomes: change strategies and their sociostructural consequences." Paper read at the Annual Meeting of the American Educational Research Association, Minneapolis, Minn., 1970.

23

The transforming of American Indian education, Wax observes,

> *from a process, over which the Indian had had some control and which he might have viewed as a device for helping himself and his people, into an instrumentality of the superordinate white and directed punitively at the sense of Indian identity,*

is a despoiling familiar to subjugated peoples the world over. It also, he suggests, partly results from the confrontation of "educators of one cultural tradition [with] pupils of another," where effective and final control over schooling remains to the educator and the cultural interests he represents. Bohannan, earlier, remarked that two cultures were seldom an either/or proposition, that their meeting is communication, faulty or not. Mr. Wax describes the meeting of two cultures as a transaction, the key item in which is "de facto control of the educational process." In seeking to isolate the reasons why Indian education fails, Wax eschews political and moral issues, although clearly the subordination of American Indians is a political matter and the result of expediencies that Wax takes care to note. Similarly, moral judgments intrude upon his discussion. These aside, Mr. Wax argues convincingly for reconstructed views of the education of cultural "minorities," by which the integrity of a people, their way of life and sense of community is neither dismissed, ignored, nor patronized, but truly shared. Wax is Professor of Sociology, University of Kansas, and immediate past president of the Council on Anthropology and Education.

MURRAY WAX

American Indian Education
as a Cultural Transaction

If during the several centuries in which they have been in contact, much of the interaction between American Indians and whites (Europeans) has centered about trade, welfare, and the eviction of the Indian peoples from their homelands,[1] an equally constant theme has been education. From the Spanish and French missionaries until the present day, the whites have been concerned to educate the Indian.[2] Usually, this has implied not simply the imparting of literacy, technical skills, or academic lore, but the transmutation of his culture and personality — from a heathen into a Christian, from an economic collectivist into an individualist, and, in the case of the nomadic groups, from a hunter into a settled and diligent farmer.

Interested in the technological accomplishments of the whites, the Indians quickly accepted a number of them. Their adoption of the domesticated horse, for example, was so thorough that the mounted warrior has become the popular stereotype of the true Indian. We can no more think of the traditional Navaho without his sheep (domesticated in Europe) than of the Pilgrim fathers without maize and pumpkins (domesticated in the Americas). Indians were also attracted to the formal learning of the whites, and during the period of European exploration and early settlement of this continent, several of the independent tribal units were hospitable to the founding of schools. The Cherokee nation became an outstanding case, establishing its own school system, operating a national newspaper, and spreading literacy more widely among its people than the neighboring white states did among theirs. Within a short time, a sprinkling of Cherokee were college graduates, so that it and related Indian nations of the south were referred to as "civilized tribes." Had they or other tribes, then receptive to formal learning, been given even another genera-

From *Teachers College Record*, vol. 64, no. 8 (May 1963), pp. 693–704. Reprinted by permission of the author and publisher.

[1] An excellent, but brief, history of Indian and white contact in North America is Hagan (1961); it also has some bibliography. The student interested in ethnographic detail on particular tribal groupings will find invaluable the extensive bibliography collected under the supervision of Murdock (1961).

[2] Adams (1946) is a short and colorless history of Indian education, containing an extensive bibliography. Sketches of article length will be found in Thompson (1957), Fey and McNickle (1959), and Lesser (1961). Beatty (1956) reviews the period of his own activity as an administrator from the late 1920's until the reversal of policy under the Eisenhower administration.

tion in which to absorb, diffuse, and integrate Western knowledge into their cultures, the results might have been surprising. But the lawless and violent frontier, with its hordes greedy for land, advanced too swiftly. Perhaps, also, the very learning of the Cherokee was too gentlemanly for the contest. They might have been better off if their young men had learned the baser arts of metallurgy and chemistry, the manufacture of guns and gunpowder; instead, they learned how to argue and win a case before the United States Supreme Court and then found their cause lost when President Jackson ignored the decree protecting their national rights.

EXPLOITATION AND EDUCATION

The hunger of the whites to exploit the resources of the frontier could not be slaked, and as the power of the United States increased relative to its Indian neighbors, it embarked on a final series of efforts designed to exterminate them as separate peoples or assimilate them forcibly into the general population. The Indian Removal actions of the nineteenth century and the Reservation system broke the power of the independent tribes and brought them under severe control. Allotment of reservation lands in severalty usually led to further disorganization and impoverishment.

As the tribes were forced to surrender most of their political independence, so too did they surrender any effective control over the formal education of their children. It was not merely that white administrators regarded them as incompetent to operate schools, but that they felt that contact between Indian parents and their children would corrupt the latter into "Indianness." So, during the latter part of the nineteenth century, children were virtually kidnapped from their homes to be incarcerated in boarding schools where they were subjected to a severe discipline in order to mold them into "whites." Education was thus transformed from a process, over which the Indian had had some control and which he might have viewed as a device for helping himself and his people, into an instrumentality of the superordinate white and directed punitively at the sense of Indian identity.

Since that time, of course, there have been a variety of important changes in governmental policies. Before mentioning some of those pertinent to education, it will be useful if we first obtain some kind of picture of the kind of Indian community that has resulted from this earlier era of conflict, brutality, and repression.

Indian communities today are of several different forms. At one pole are the rather small groups who have lived intimately with white society for generations, possessing little autonomy and actually preserving more in the way of outmoded European practices than of native Indian ones.

At the other pole is a diversity of tribes, relatively autonomous and isolated bodies, and preserving a great many native practices and customs even while selectively adopting many of the technological complexes of the larger society. For many of these people, the native language is the primary one within the household and the first learned by the child; likewise, the native religion continues to regulate the habits of the family and community, even when a veneer of Christianity has been applied. Despite the persistence of native traits, theirs is not the aboriginal culture but a "reservation culture," a distinct and novel form, adapted to their peculiar mode of existence (Witthoft, 1961). It is the groups with these "reservation cultures" that constitute what is referred to as the "Indian problem," and it is their community dynamics that we shall now review.

CONSERVATIVE VS. PROGRESSIVE

Most of these communities are divided into two basic factions, those known as "fullbloods" and those known as "halfbreeds." The true difference between them is cultural and ideological, rather than racial. Because interbreeding with persons of European descent has been going on since the earliest days of exploration and trade, I refer to the first group as *conservatives* (or traditionalists) and to the second group as *progressives*. Both are dissatisfied with their present condition of poverty, social disorganization, lack of autonomy, and general cultural depression.

Responding to these evils, the conservatives turn toward the past and cherish memories of ancient glories. (A minority of extreme traditionalists believe that ultimate relief depends on supernatural intervention, which may be facilitated by reviving and maintaining tribal rituals and customs.) As to proposals for current reform, the conservatives are thoroughly skeptical of anything issuing from the whites or modeled upon them. In their judgment, the white is the alien, the enemy, and the intruder, who has brought the Indian people only misery. "Acting white" is the most stinging epithet in their vocabulary. They are not sure how to improve the lot of their people, but they find only further malaise in most suggestions emanating from the white and his administrative agencies.

The result is a negativism in which the energies of the conservative population are devoted to preserving a style of life that represents a sorry amalgam of impoverished white and deteriorated Indian cultures and with which they themselves are impatient. The more the administrators criticize and pressure for reform, the more they identify their true "Indianness" with the refusal to budge, even to improve their condition. (A good proportion of their white neighbors is ever happy to agree that the Indian cannot learn and will not change.) Their syndrome of economic impoverishment, isolation from other cultures, and blind conservatism is self-reinforcing, and the greater the pressure upon them to change, the more they resist and withdraw. As only one of many possible illustrations, there are fewer fullblood Cherokee who are literate today than there were a century ago, when they were part of a flourishing and independent Indian nation.

PROGRESSIVE ASSIMILATION

In contrast, the progressive faction of the community is oriented toward the white society and the acquisition of white customs, values, and manners; their aim is assimilation. Most of them, however, have a limited perception of the nature of the larger American society. Their view of it is based not on direct vision, but on refraction through the dicta and preachments of a highly mixed crew of administrative officers, school teachers, and missionaries. Ordinarily, the sole corrective available to the progressive is actual experience with neighboring white society in the form of small Western towns, usually provincial and often contemptuous of all things "Indian." In any case they are not particularly helpful as preparation for metropolitan areas where a variety of employment and economic possibilities are to be found.

The one experience that has truly enlarged the horizon of some Indians during the past generation is military service. Through it, they have come into contact with a diversity of peoples in a diversity of situations: conquerors and conquered, technologically advanced and retarded, pro- and anti-Americans. Some of these young Indian men and women, returning to their home communities, have been acting as a leaven. But, it is still generally true that the viewpoints of both conservatives and progressives in most Indian communities are extremely limited, with neither having any true conception of the richness, flexibility, and vitality of the aboriginal societies nor of the fantastic variability and potentialities of the Western civilization to which their peoples have been marginal.

For the white person dealing with conservative Indians, it is important to know that voluntary cooperation has been the basis of most Indian societies. Those disapproving of a project simply withdrew and refused to participate, and the tactic has been and is employed today when conservatives deal with whites and progressives. Withdrawal and negativism have allowed Indians to be defrauded of property and rights on innumerable occasions, and have likewise caused them to reject projects demonstrably to their benefit; but they have also served as mechanisms for perpetuating some recognizable fraction of a unique culture and kind of personality.

INDIAN UNDER-EDUCATION

So far, I have postponed the presentation of statistics: proportions of children enrolled in school, grades completed, and the like. The reasons for this are severalfold. To begin with, I know personally some of the best Indian college students in the country. On first meeting, many were highly intelligent and original, but were shockingly provincial and miseducated, compared to college students elsewhere. Even their knowledge of American and Indian history, which one might have expected to have some depth, was of the level of American popular culture (R. Wax, 1961). For the moment, we are not concerned with questions of cause or responsibility for this condition but only wish to remind the reader of what he well knows — that merely serving time within school walls is not equivalent to education.

Also troublesome for utilizing and interpreting educational indices is the problem of deciding who is an "Indian." The Bureau of Indian Affairs compiles its statistics with regard to those persons over whose property it has the status of trustee or regarding whom it has legal grounds to assume some of the role of guardian. Courts of law are oriented toward issues of inheritance and tend to grade Indianness in "quanta of blood" according to the registration of forbears; the courts have been indifferent to the question of "way of life" and have scarcely had to deal with a fraction of the chicanery and evasion of the nineteenth century, when whites claimed to be Indians and Indians claimed to be whites in an effort to participate or withdraw from the reservation system and land allotment (Pope, 1958).

From even the official figures for federally recognized tribes, however, the educational situation is deplorably poor (U.S. Census, 1953; Anderson, Collister, and Ladd, 1953). As of 1950, the median number of school years completed among Indians 25 years of age and older was less than six. The comparable figure for the white population was over nine years of schooling. In interpreting the figure for the Indians, we should bear in mind that for a large number, education was offered in a language that was totally or partially foreign, so that much of the effort in the earlier grades was devoted simply to instruction in English (and the routine of a school from an alien culture). Moreover, the low median level has also meant a paucity of persons gaining any sort of advanced education, so that Indian communities have lacked leaders who were broadly educated in the intellectual traditions of the larger society.

In the far past, and even yet today, the simple fact of tribal geography has contributed to educational difficulties. The large tribal groupings of reservation culture are located in barren and inhospitable areas of the country. Thinly scattered, in regions of poor roads, they have been difficult of access for any administrative purpose, including schooling. (This has tended to justify the use of boarding schools from an early age onward.)

More and Less Fortunate

When we come to the current situation of the education of young Indians today, the picture is considerably more complex because of the variation among regions and tribes. Some tribes have had the good fortune to fall heir to wealth recently, in a period when society at large has assisted them to retain it rather than conspired against them. An outstanding case is the Navaho, who, a decade ago, had virtually no exposure to formal education; today, all manner of ambitious programs for educating Navaho youth are flourishing. As they are among the largest of tribal units and with a high rate of natural increase, their change in status will have a great effect on over-all Indian statistics; until now, they have often not been included in totals and averages. At the opposite pole are tribes like the Sioux of the Dakotas, who were poor and still are poor, who were poorly educated and who remain in that state. Unlike the Navaho, they have been within reach of schools for some time, but attendance and enrollment remain major problems, with only 83 per cent of the children, enumerated as Indians within the Aberdeen Administrative Area, enrolled in school (U.S. Bureau of Indian Affairs, 1959). Perhaps the most depressing areas — and also the least known — are the remnants of the tribes once termed "civilized" in eastern Oklahoma and elsewhere. Because the federal government withdrew its trusteeship a half-century ago, while at the same time destroying the tribal government and distributing tribal lands, no formal statistics on the conservative (fullblood) group have been reliably kept. As an ironical commentary on the relationship between progressive and conservative factions, some prominent halfbreed political figures have publicly and vociferously denied the existence of educational or economic problems among the conservative Cherokee of Oklahoma. (Fortunately, the Principal Chief of that tribe is far above such nonsense, but his is a limited role, deriving from federal appointment and having the shadowy authority of heading a tribe that was officially dissolved years ago.)

In estimating the scope of the Indian educational problem and the efficacy of various programs for education and betterment, it is important to keep in mind the high rate of natural increase of this population and especially of its conservative core (Hadley, 1959). A certain proportion of the young people have been achieving some degree of education, migrating from their home community, even assimilating into the larger population, without significant effect on the social and educational status of the residue. Any permanent "solution" to the Indian "problem" — any amelioration of the conditions of economic, social, and psychic depression — must reach the vast majority of each community. It is arguable that the migration of the youthful, energetic, and better educated has actually accentuated difficulties by depriving their communities of persons who might be able to serve as a bridge between the conservatives and the external society. It is also arguable that the effect of boarding schools is pernicious in that, by educating the child away from home, it unfits him for sympathetic and cooperative action with his kith and kin on return as an adult.

CROSS-CULTURAL EDUCATION

American Indian education is, of course, but one instance of the widespread phenomenon of cross-cultural education.[3] Some of its problems are not particularly the fault of either Indian or white, but arise whenever educators of one cultural tradition confront pupils of another (Henry, 1967; M. Wax, 1961). A key variable in this transaction is the locus of power — the *de facto* control of the educational process — which may lie with the educators, the pupils, or elsewhere entirely. Within Western history, an early instance of the powerful pupil is Philip of Macedon, who hired an Athenian named Aristotle to instruct his heir, a wild but talented lad, in the intellectual accomplishments of a defeated and politically subordinate people. A more equable balance is manifest in the custom of European aristocrats of the past few centuries, who hired alien tutors of good (though poor) families to instruct their children in the languages and customs observed in other civilized lands. The configuration, now so common, in which the pupils stem from a subordinate or socially disadvantaged stock, seems to be part of the movement for public education, which is a recent development within Western civilization.

As an aspect of that movement, our metropolitan public schools have been geared to educating and "Americanizing" the children of impoverished immigrants, whether from foreign countries or from our own native areas where a distinct subculture has maintained itself, as among the Negroes of the Deep South or the whites of the Middle Southern hills. Even where the ethnic stock of a community is reasonably homogeneous, there are still significant differences in culture and political power among the various classes (Hollingshead, 1949; Warner et al., 1949). Thus, we are accustomed to a tripartite educational configuration in which ultimate

---

[3] The author would be grateful for bibliography on studies and informal descriptions of cross-cultural education in various areas of the world.

control rests with a school board derived from the higher reaches of community status and power; day-to-day regulation rests with administrators and teachers of a middle level of status and power, and the parents of the pupils — many of whom represent the lower levels of the community — have little or no voice as to what is taught their children or how it is done. Because we take this configuration so much for granted, it is worthwhile reminding ourselves that, especially in the cross-cultural situation, it is neither natural nor inevitable that the recipients of the education lack control over the school system. This is of some international significance. In the countries that were formerly colonies, the nationalistic drive for independence has also affected the educational institutions; rather than being the targets of the educational missions of more advanced peoples, these new nations wish to operate their own schools and to utilize foreigners as advisers only.

SCHOOL AGAINST PARENTS

The goal of the educational process is another issue which likewise affects that of the locus of control. Traditionally, formal education has had modest or specialized goals, such as furnishing the populace with the rudiments of literacy so that they could read Holy Scriptures or giving them the simple intellective skills basic to the common manual arts; only an elite was given prolonged, intensive training of an abstract sort. With the public education movement, the school has been assigned, or come to inherit, the task of fully socializing children through adolescence, with, as a corollary responsibility, the assimilation of children of "deviant" ethnic backgrounds into the common American world. Where socialization and assimilation are the educational goals — rather than, say, vocational training — the school becomes in effect a challenge to the authority and wisdom of the parent generation. If some degree of control over the educational process remains with the parent group, the conflict may be meliorated. But when the locus of control is elsewhere, then the schoolroom may become the focal point of all manner of tensions, complicating the simple transmission of knowledge. On the one hand stand adults who represent a particular, superordinate, civilized tradition; on the other hand sit pupils who are to be inculcated with customs, values, and thoughtways different from and antagonistic toward those of their elders.

Both parties to the cross-cultural school exercise selectivity with regard to the content of the educational transaction. From the variety of his own civilized society and its intellectual traditions, the educator selects customs, creeds, and knowledge which are moral and proper or the effects of which will, he hopes, be salutary. In this fashion, he tends to draw an unrealistic picture of his society and, if his goal were simply assimilation, he would have ill prepared his audience for the actualities of life.[4] Conversely, most pupils tend to cling to the customs and values practiced in their homes and to view the subject matters of their curriculum with the detached eye of the practical man: How can this be of any use to us. (It is notorious that the traits most easily adopted in cases of cultural contact are those of immediate utility and gratification, so that on the American frontier, the Indians quickly learned the use of iron kettles and alcohol and the whites the use of canoes and tobacco.) Within the educational situation, most pupils are oriented not toward assimilation and the discarding of native ties, but toward sharing in the material benefits associated with the culture of the teacher.

An additional element in the cross-cultural transaction is the impact of the school as a social institution. The more the school and its educational processes encompass the child, the greater is their impact, if for no other reason than that they thereby isolate him from other associations and relationships. Most Americans have come to take for granted and to regard as normal and wholly desirable a system of formal education that physically separates child from parents for most of the hours of the day and most of the days of the year. Where the child of a primitive society would early have been given responsibilities within his kin group — caring for those younger than himself, garnering food, herding flocks — here he is sorted and segregated by age level, isolated from external responsibilities, and devoted solely to his own educational development. Without entering into the merits and demerits of this system, it is plain that its introduction into Indian society is thoroughly disruptive of traditional patterns of socialization, social control, and familial labor.

SCHOOL QUALITY

Evaluations by outside authorities of federally operated schools for Indian children have tended to rate them as being technically adequate (Anderson et al., 1953; Peterson, 1948; Coombs, 1961). Assuming this to be so, it follows that the current state of Indian educational problem cannot be attributed to schools that are deficient in personnel or facilities. The evaluations acknowledge that the schools are not ideal in terms of their task or in terms of their numbers or convenience of location to the various Indian communities. Some people still lack a proper number of schoolrooms per capita, and the choice still seems to be one between day schools with long bus rides or boarding schools some distance from the home

---

[4] Foster is the first anthropologist to call attention to the mechanics of this selective transmission by a study of the Spanish influence upon the Americas (1960).

community. (This situation may be an ideal one for experimenting with television and other electronic and mechanical teaching aids as a substitute for the cost, regimentation, and familial disruption of boarding establishments.) As to the quality of the curriculum, the Bureau of Indian Affairs has taken the realistic attitude of trying to make its schools comparable in aims and techniques to those of the public schools of the states in which Indians reside (Howard, 1949). If the white children of neighboring communities perform better on standardized achievement tests than do the Indians — and these differences have been measured — then the fault cannot be said to rest with the school systems as such (Coombs, 1961; Coombs et al., 1958).[5]

For some time, the Bureau of Indian Affairs has aimed at eliminating the special school system for Indian children and having them attend the public schools of their region. The principal area of dispute has been the rate of this change. Especially under the Eisenhower administration, the policy tended to be one of terminating the federal schools as rapidly as possible. Advocates of this policy have contended that the informal learning that then occurs between Indian and white child is important, and some have also declared that schools for Indians alone constitute a form of segregation which the federal government must not practice. Opponents of this policy have contended that the Indian child of conservative parents is not prepared for so drastic a change and is competitively and culturally so much at a disadvantage, especially when confronted with teachers who know nothing of Indian ways, that dropout is likely (Jones, 1953). Nevertheless, there is little warrant in the available evidence from which to infer that the cause of the Indian educational problem is the technical inadequacy of the school system.

ABILITIES OR VALUES?

A second factor to be ruled out is the possibility that the Indian child is incapable of mastering the educational tasks in question. Unquestionably, the child of conservative Indian background starts school at a disadvantage compared with a child of the white middle class. His native tongue is not English (nor related to Indo-European languages), and the practices of his family do not involve much use of literacy or other scholastic skills. Yet this lack of background has been successfully overcome in other American cross-cultural situations. During the past half-century and more, many children have been reared in homes oriented about the values of the "old country," and even nurtured on its language, and yet

---

[5] I deal here only with the scientific issue of the cause of Indian educational deficiencies and not with the political or moral issue of whether it might be wise or expedient to improve Indian schools greatly, regardless of parity with neighboring communities.

gone on to respectable achievement, educationally and vocationally. Following Havighurst and Neugarten (1957; 1954), we can assume that by the time the Indian child enters school, he will have developed skills and sensibilities superior to the whites in some areas and inferior in others, but that over-all, he should be capable of educational achievement, provided other factors do not interfere.

While the cultural difference between school and the Indian home may be of minor significance in preparing the child *intellectually* for his educational tasks, it is my hypothesis that this difference is of great significance in terms of the disparity and conflict of *norms* and *values*. This hypothesis, which may be denominated *cultural disharmony* or *cultural shock*, derives from the well-established facts that conservative Indians train and discipline their children in quite different fashions and concerning quite different areas of life than do most whites (Wax and Thomas, 1961; Joseph, Spicer, and Chesky, 1949; Leighton and Kluckhohn, 1947; Macgregor, 1946; Thompson and Joseph, 1944). Indian children thus experience the ordinary American school as individualistic, competitive, intrusive, regimented, immoral, and emotionally frigid, compared to life in the home circle. Conversely, the inexperienced or strait-laced teacher finds her Indian pupils to be unresponsive, intractable, lacking in scholastic initiative, and morally delinquent.[6] This conflict will, of course, be exaggerated in boarding schools as compared with day schools. Cultural disharmony was noted and emphasized in a variety of researches conducted a generation ago. Since then, there have been many changes in Bureau policies and in the living conditions of some tribes, so there may have been considerable improvement.[7] It would be of special interest to study the devices by which this cultural disharmony may have been minimized in some cross-cultural schools.

IDENTITY IN CRISIS

A second, positive hypothesis as to the causes of Indian educational problems concerns the attitude of the elders of the community toward the school system. Insofar as they feel that the schools are instrumentalities

[6] Erikson's account (1939) permits one to discern the horrified shock of some teachers and boarding school personnel when they encounter the sexual behavior of the Sioux, which is governed by standards that are loose and precocious when compared to those of the middle-class white. Briefer, less interpretive accounts, describing the difficulties of sympathetic educators, confronted with the behavior of children from conservative Indian families, will be found in Fey and McNickle (1959); Page (1953); Pratt (1957).

[7] Since it is sometimes thought that hiring Indians for administrative or educational positions eliminates the problem of cultural shock, it should be pointed out that the effect may be the reverse. If the Indians hired are aggressively "progressive" and assimilationist, they may be less tolerant of conservative practices and more hostile toward conservative elders than were their white predecessors.

of the whites, designed to inculcate Indian children with alien values and to transform them into "whites," they are antagonistic. This notion of a threat to Indian identity poses the question of the extent to which conservative Indians feel that schools are punitively directed against their very being rather than designed to help them, as Indians, to improve their lot.

Comparatively, we should again bear the immigrant case in mind. The urban school was, in effect, a challenge to the authority of the first generation of family elders and to the values of the ("old country") society from which they had sprung. They could tolerate this challenge only because they had already accepted the goal of adaptation to the larger society with its accompanying social and financial gains. For religious reasons, some immigrant groups have not wished their children to assimilate into the larger society, and where they have settled in relatively dense and self-sufficient communities, highly integrated about their own institutions, they have been notably successful in resisting the assimilative force of public education. The parallel between such communities as those of the Amish and Hutterites and those of the American Indians is highly stimulating and again suggests that some of the educational difficulties have little to do with the intrinsic nature of Indian personality and values.

Third, the degree of participation or exclusion from the process of decision-making on educational matters varies among tribes but is typically low. Parmee (1961, p. 23) has been studying one problem case, the San Carlos Apache, and I can do no better than to quote from his (oral) discussion:

> Many Apaches object strongly to the fact that they have almost no voice in the planning and operation of their educational school program, of their reservation school program, and yet they are expected to give it their full and complete support. Apaches say that they are continually told that some day they will have to run their own affairs, but they are given few opportunities today to learn how to manage such a program through experience gained by taking part in its present operation. Large numbers of Indian parents on the reservation have only a meager background in education and almost no contact with the schools that their children attend. Communication between parent and child on school matters appears to be surprisingly limited. As a result, many aspects of a school program are neither known nor understood by the parents even though they are required to give it their full support.

CAREER IGNORANCE

The fourth and last hypothesis is one of *career ignorance;* it states that Indians lack understanding of the economic potentials of the larger society and of the careers and vocations that might be available to them were they to seek them and acquire the requisite training. Throughout, I have stressed the practical orientation of the Indian peoples when they are not disturbed by ideological conflicts over their identity and values. Indians would like to improve their economic situation, and, as Hoyt (1961) has noted, their children are much concerned about obtaining jobs on leaving school. The isolation and provincial quality of their environment, however, limits their knowledge both of the sheer variety of occupations and of their educational prerequisites.

In the past and still today, the federal government has tried to steer Indians into careers which seemed appropriate in terms of their limited skills, the nature of local resources, and the needs of the total economy. However, the position of authority of the federal officials vis-à-vis the reservation peoples has created a strong tradition of suspicion. The most unfortunate situations are those where *career ignorance* is combined with the factors involved in the other hypotheses, *cultural disharmony* and *threat to Indian identity*. When the guidance given to Indians is designed not to enable them to improve their economic status, but to push them out of their home communities and toward some version of assimilation, then the counselors and their advice are most likely to be regarded with antagonism. Parmee's report (1961, pp. 24–25) on the Apache is again appropriate:

> A . . . reason for . . . resistance and lack of interest on the part of some Apaches concerns the possibility that one of the chief goals of the educational program for the Apaches is aimed in direct opposition to the real desires of a large number of people. This goal, which has been openly stated by . . . administrators and is supported by the nature of the program is simply this — to get Apaches away from the detrimental influences of life on the reservation and to train them for assimilation into off-reservation communities. Most Apaches . . . seem anxious to keep the reservation, to live on it, and to prosper from its resources in modern, comfortable, and distinctly Apache communities. Nevertheless, there is much evidence to indicate that economically, socially, and educationally, such goals that Apaches have are not being encouraged.

Even if or where this type of antagonism and striving at cross-purposes did not exist, school and employment counselors would still be greatly limited in what they could do for their Indian clients. With any group, much of job-getting takes place through informal channels of communication, a tradition of "savvy" or "know-how" about some area of the economy or region of the country, and just plain chance. Typical of this process is the success of the Caughnawagas in high steel (Mitchell, 1960); to my knowledge, no counselor had ever explicitly oriented Indian youth toward this kind of valued and remunerative occupation.

In the long run, the Indian must himself make the basic choices, judging his own interests and abilities and needs. To do this wisely, he must be able to perceive the connection between childhood education and adult vocations. Meanwhile, so long as he does not understand — or is so threatened that he understandably refuses to understand — that the schooling open to his children may lead them toward novel careers that are remunerative, personally satisfying, and suitable to their values, he will simply not make the sacrifices required; nor will he encourage his children to do so.

REFERENCES

Adams, Evelyn C. *American Indian education*. New York: King's Crown Press, 1946.
Anderson, K. E., Collister, E. G. & Ladd, C. E. *The educational achievement of Indian children*. Washington, D.C.: U.S. Bur. Indian Affairs, 1953.
Beatty, W. W. Twenty years of Indian education. In Baerreis, D. A. (Ed.) *The Indian in modern America*. Madison, Wis.: State Hist. Soc., 1956, pp. 16–49.
Coombs, L. M. Implications of the achievement level of Indian students. In *Annual Conference of the Co-ordinating Council for Research in Indian Education*. Phoenix: Div. Indian Educ., Ariz. State Dept. Publ. Instr., 1961.
Coombs, L. M., Kron, R. E., Collister, E. G., and Anderson, K. E. *The Indian child goes to school*. Washington, D.C.: U.S. Bur. Indian Affairs, 1958.
Erikson, E. H. Observations on Sioux education. *J. Psychol.*, 1939, 7, 101–156.
Fey, H. E., and McNickle, D'A. *Indians and other Americans*. New York: Harper, 1959.
Foster, G. M. *Culture and conquest*. New York: Viking Fund, 1960.
Hadley, J. N. Demography of the American Indians. *Ann. Amer. Acad. Pol. Soc. Sci.*, 1957, *311*, 23–30.
Hagan, W. T. *American Indians*. Chicago: Univer. Chicago Press, 1961.
Havighurst, R. J. Education among American Indians: individual and cultural aspects. *Ann. Amer. Acad. Pol. Soc. Sci.*, 1957, *311*, 105–115.
Havighurst, R. J., and Neugarten, Bernice L. *American Indian and white children*. Chicago: Univer. Chicago Press, 1954.
Henry, J. A Cross-cultural outline of education. *Current Anthropol.*, 1960, *1*, 267–305.
Hollingshead, A. B. *Elmtown's youth*. New York: Wiley, 1949.
Howard, H. H. *In step with the states*. Washington, D.C.: U.S. Bur. Indian Affairs, 1949.
Hoyt, Elizabeth. An approach to the mind of the young Indian. *J. Amer. Indian Educ.*, 1961, *1*, 17–23.
Jones, C. F. Notes on Indian education. *J. Educ. Sociol.*, 1953, 27, 16–23.
Joseph, Alice, Spicer, Rosamond, and Chesky, Jane. *The desert people: a study of the Papago Indians*. Chicago: Univer. Chicago Press, 1949.
Leighton, Dorothea C., and Kluckhohn, C. *Children of the people: the Navaho individual and his development*. Cambridge: Harvard Univer. Press, 1947.
Lesser, A. *Education and the future of tribalism in the United States: the case of the American Indian*. New York: Phelps-Stokes Fund, 1961.
Macgregor, G. *Warriors without weapons: a study of the society and personality of the Pine Ridge Sioux*. Chicago: Univer. Chicago Press, 1946.
Mitchell, J. The Mohawks in high steel. In Wilson, E. *Apologies to the Iroquois*. New York: Farrar, Straus & Cudahy, 1960.
Murdock, G. P. *Ethnographic bibliography of North America*. (3d ed.) New Haven: Human Relations Area Files, Yale Univer., 1961.
Page, Marge. Schoolhouse in the desert. *J. Natl. Educ. Assn.*, 1953, 42, 514.
Parmee, E. Social factors affecting the education of the San Carlos Apaches. In *Annual Conference of the Co-ordinating Council for Research in Indian Education*. Phoenix: Div. Indian Educ., Ariz. State Dept. of Publ. Instr., 1961, pp. 22–26.

Peterson, S. *How well are Indian children educated?* Washington, D.C.: U.S. Bur. Indian Affairs, 1948.

Pope, R. K. The withdrawal of the Kickapoo. *The Amer. Indian,* 1958, 8, 17–27.

Pratt, W. T. Living beside us — worlds apart. *Childhood Educ.,* 1957, 34, 1965–1968.

Thompson, H. Education among American Indians: institutional aspects. *Ann. Amer. Acad. Pol. Soc. Sci.,* 1957, 311, 95–104.

Thompson, Laura & Jospeh, Alice. *The Hopi way.* Chicago: Univer. Chicago Press, 1944.

U.S. Census Bureau. *Non-white population by race.* Washington, D.C.: Govt. Print. Off., 1953.

U.S. Bureau Indian Affairs. *Statistics concerning Indian education.* Lawrence, Kans.: Haskell Institute, 1959.

Warner, W. L., et al. *Democracy in Jonesville.* New York: Harper, 1949.

Wax, M. More on cross-cultural education. *Current Anthropol.,* 1961, 2, 255–256.

Wax, Rosalie H. A. brief history and analysis of the workshops on American Indian affairs conducted for American Indian college students, 1956–1960, together with a study of current attitudes and activities of those students. Mimeo. 1961.

Wax, Rosalie H., and Thomas, R. K. American Indians and white people. *Phylon,* 1961, 22, 305–317.

Witthoft, J. Eastern woodlands community typology and acculturation. In Fenton, W. N., and Gulick, J. (eds.) *Symposium on Cherokee and Iroquois culture.* Bur. Amer. Ethnol., Bull. 180. Washington, D.C.: Smithsonian Inst., 1961.

Further Readings

Herzog, John D. "Deliberate instruction and household structure: a cross-cultural study," in Max A. Eckstein and Harold J. Noah (eds.), *Scientific investigations in comparative education.* New York: Macmillan, 1969.

Kluckhohn, Florence R. "Variations in value orientations as a factor in educational planning," in Eli M. Bower and William G. Hollister (eds.), *Behavioral science frontiers in education.* New York: Wiley, 1967.

Savard, Robert J. "The basic attitudes of minorities toward opportunity for educational advancement: the American Indian," in *Educationally disadvantaged students in social work education.* New York: Council on Social Work Education, 1968.

Wax, Murray L., Rosalie H. Wax, and Robert V. Dumont, Jr. *Formal education in an American Indian community.* SSSP Monograph No. 1, *Social Problems,* vol. 2 (Spring 1964).

EDUCATION IN OTHER CULTURES

The selections in Part Four refer, in the scheme of this book, to the anthropology of education. They are studies of the ways education occurs in cultural contexts other than our own; as such, these writings represent what is popularly believed to be the majority contribution (and basic relationship) of anthropology to education: the provision of substantive understandings about how, to what ends, and with what effect cultural others educate and are educated.

Each article is an attempt to arrange similar kinds of understandings about aspects of education that are *locally* problematic. The value of such understandings is, chiefly, twofold: by access to the processes, intentions, meanings, and structures of education, we are informed about the culture in the context of which these occur. The "vantage point," as Comitas phrases it, of education permits us certain insights into systems of culture. It allows us a more thorough comprehension of *any* culture — reason to stress the extreme utility of the study of education and educational encounters to anthropological fieldwork.

Also, with access to the policies, real and normative, and the observable practices of education in *other* cultures, we are better prepared to describe and explain our *own* culture. The value of data generated from studying education in other cultures is both a function of the extent to which educational processes, intentions, meanings, and structures among human groups elsewhere are comparable to our own, *and* of our willingness to entertain some or all of these other ways as alternatives.

In this latter sense, anthropology acts less to provide information about how other peoples behave educationally than as a resource for alternative ways of teaching and learning and of the human experi-

355

ence of these. And, that special potential is reason to emphasize the utility of anthropological descriptions and analyses of education and educational encounters to educators.

The five articles that follow typify case studies in anthropology and education. They also closely resemble those portions of standard ethnographies which detail the system of education, formal or informal; characteristic mode(s) of socialization, enculturation, or patterned child-rearing; or relationships between education and other institutions of behavior in a given culture, or set of cultures. Mr. Hanks, Mr. Parmee, Mr. Comitas and Mrs. Ramcharan-Crowley, for instance, use considerable observational data to support their analytic arguments. Even Mrs. Hodgkin's multifaceted account systematically relates each cultural context with which she deals, in contrast to usual discussions of international or "overseas" student-host interaction, in which specification of the cultural systems of student, host, or of both is incomplete, if not selective to the point of distortion.

Studies of education in other cultures deserve their popularity. Their practical effect is broad, and their appeal often genuine. Whether they enable us to sense the teaching and learning experience of rural Thai, Apache, Bolivians, Malaysians, or Dominican Creoles, as here, or of any other human group, is next in importance to the opportunities they provide for engaging other educational ways and, in engaging these, to see them as credible alternatives.

24

*The "apathetic reception" given a modern, national system of education by
a rural, rice-farming Thai community reported here by Mr. Hanks recalls Wax's
account of "conservative" Indian responses to American public education.
Hanks finds that the primary source of local indifference in Bang Chan was
the "failure of the school to conform with traditional [Thai] assumption concerning education." The author explains traditional expectations as being
substantive and practical to the point of paying ". . . direct heed to the
problems of the farmer." The modern school, in policy and practice, violates
this set of expectations; worse, perhaps, it raises false expectations of alternatives to an agrarian life. Mr. Hanks, Senior Research Associate, Cornell
Thailand Project, Cornell University, asserts that so long as systems of local
apprenticeship, folk transmission, and the authority of convention remain
intact and otherwise persuasive, modern schooling in traditional, nonurban
contexts may anticipate a limited clientele, which surely holds for developing
societies the world over. His assertion implies, too, to the relevance of traditional schooling in contemporary contexts, in which case apathy, indifference,
and other less passive responses are problematic student behaviors.*

L. M. HANKS, JR.

Indifference to Modern Education in a Thai Farming Community

Programs which seek to "modernize" the school systems of foreign
countries must, inevitably, reckon with the indigenous assumptions concerning education. The following essay enquires into a cluster of assumptions found in Thailand, which establish the nature of knowledge,
teaching, and learning. With these concepts as defined in Thai culture, we
seek to account for the apathetic reception of modern education among
the rice-farmers of Bang Chan, a community of some 1600 people in the
central plains near Bangkok. The data were collected during a study of this
community in 1953–54, sponsored by Cornell University. We refer especially
to Bang Chan, although conditions there differ only in detail from neighboring Thai communities. Our first section describes the traditional assumptions concerning education in general and then we turn to the
sequence where Bang Chan meets the various steps toward compulsory
education promulgated by the central government. A third section dwells
on the interaction of government, teachers, farmers, and pupils in the

From *Human Organization*, vol. 17 (Summer 1958), pp. 9–14.

current scene and, finally, we reconsider the assumptions concerning education to explain the evident indifference of Thai farmers.

THE EDUCATIONAL TRADITIONS

For centuries, Thai education resembled a medieval guild or monastic order, with learning only for the initiate. A prospective pupil petitioned a master, who first satisfied himself of the applicant's wit and moral worth, and then might accept him. Obeisance to the master began and ended every teaching session. On completing his instruction, the pupil became a disciple and was obliged to pay ceremonial thanks to the master whenever he drew on his knowledge. Should the pupil enter actual practice, he was, in certain cases, addressed by a special title and, as his reputation increased, might accept pupils of his own.

Whether the subject matter was technical, religious, or military, the relationship of pupil to master was always sacred. Indeed, the Lord Buddha announced himself primarily as a teacher, rather than as a prophet, savior, or god. So, today, duty bids the priests at the Buddhist temple, like their predecessors who were the first disciples of the Buddha, to teach the doctrine to all young men (women were excluded) who petition for learning. They teach that virtue or "merit making" mitigates suffering in life and that leading a virtuous life will break the cycle of rebirths. All considered this was the most important lesson, in fact, a prerequisite for responsible adulthood and, hence, for most further learning. To receive this moral knowledge, a young man beseeched the assembled priests to be admitted to the monastic order. Often he had previously served as a temple-boy, helper or servant to a priest, yet without the vows of a priest or novice, he could not receive instruction. After receiving it, however, he could ask release from his vows at any time.

Where a teacher lived, were it temple or bamboo hut, there was a center of learning, yet temples were always the great centers. A teacher served his community as a practitioner of astrology, medicine, or other magical art. He taught by reciting crisp aphorisms or metrically phrased statements, which were memorized by the pupil and pondered at length. For moral instruction, a pupil learned, for instance, the Five Sacred Precepts or the Noble Eight-fold Path. A pupil in medicine might memorize the varieties of a particular disease and a medical formula for curing each kind. When the essential texts were committed to memory, the pupil had completed his instruction.

The rationale for this system of learning rested on the peculiar concept of knowledge. Real knowledge was assumed to be both substantial and practical, like a tool which copes with one of life's difficulties. Without this knowledge or the aid of a practitioner, one was as helpless as a person required to drive a nail without a hammer. The moral law, by showing how to mitigate suffering in life, also provided a formula for lending success to one's undertakings. Astrology, more particularly, assisted farmers to know the propitious day for planting or the hour for marrying off their daughters. Even in music, the Thai thought, not of developing a skill, but of instructing how to play a certain piece on a particular instrument. Similarly, one read a given book rather than learned to read, and, though having learned one book helped with the next, the knowledge of the book constituted the desired gain. Of course, parents trained children in desirable habits, and an individual might profit by experience, but these were not education. Education dealt with important knowledge which was discovered only by heroes or saints, not by ordinary mortals. Such knowledge had to be obtained from one who had received it through the chain of teachers leading back to the original hero or saint. This kind of knowledge alone was education. A teacher's reluctance to pass these often dangerous tools to unscrupulous hands, and a pupil's gratitude, followed from this view of knowledge. Nor did a teacher assume that knowledge per se equipped one to practice well; instead, he was responsible for giving it to no one who might distort it or whose personal characteristics might jeopardize it.

Departure from this conception of education, though presaged by earlier events, began to gather momentum when King Chulalongkorn proclaimed, in 1885, his intention to make literacy universal among his subjects. His proclamation implied the breaking of a monopoly where esoteric knowledge was to become secular. Concurrently, the world expanded to include more knowledge, and this new knowledge, outside the control of the priests, helped to redefine the character of the old. Learning continued to mitigate suffering, but the moral rationale was diluted with pragmatic, technical considerations. To this upheaval must be added the social repercussions of new occupations and institutions which arose to transmit knowledge to the nation.

EDUCATIONAL SEQUENCES IN BANG CHAN

Prior to 1908, few rice cultivators conceived reading possible, or even desirable, for themselves. There was a large fund of good farming techniques which we would call a knowledge of agriculture but it escaped their notice because of its ubiquity. For them, farming was training in habit since "anyone could farm." Whether one brought a good crop to the threshing floor or harvested a mere handful, "depended on one's virtue." The way to accumulate this virtue or merit, so that one might enjoy good crops and happiness in present or future existences, was the particular traditional religious knowledge to be acquired at the local Buddhist temple, preferably by a year or two spent in the priesthood. Whoever could be spared from tilling the fields might learn this essential knowledge. Then he was fit for marriage and life's responsibilities. Women, and those sons who could not be released from work, would have to accept their lot patiently. Maybe with effort in this life, it would be better in the next. Occasionally a Bang Chan boy might linger at the temple a few years, learn to read Pali or Cambodian script, and assist his community additionally by announcing the auspicious day for the new plowing or by giving the blessing for a new house.

Other intentional education did occur outside the temple. Midwifery and preparing corpses might be learned from local practitioners by serving them as apprentice-helper. Anyone could weave a mat, build a house, or make a boat of sorts, but it took special knowledge from a kinsman to repair the temple or build the better boats. Some parents instructed their children to dance or to sing songs which would enliven a neighborhood celebration. And certainly a knowledge of magic formulas to increase one's success in gambling or love passed quietly between boys. But none of this folk-knowledge could be dignified by the term *education* in the Thai meaning of the word.

Temple Schools

A year or two before his death in 1910, King Chulalongkorn's literacy program reached Bang Chan. It took full advantage of existing circumstances by offering temple boys the opportunity for instruction by the priests in reading and writing. Study of the educational level achieved by age-groups in the population suggest that some years passed with little regular instruction and, even in the years when classes did occur, only 15 to 40% of the eligible boys attended. Judging also by tales of the temple schools, attendance was voluntary or easily by-passed:

> When young I went three years to school at Wat Noj. I was always absent from classes because the teacher, my father's brother, was very severe. While we were studying in the classroom, this priest slept in the adjoining room, but he could tell whether a pupil was reading or not. He beat those who did not read with a fish tail.

The resistance of this pupil to instruction may have contributed to this teacher's ire, for teachers presumed receptive learners. In turn, receptiveness often may have perished in classes with incompetent teachers charged by head priests with keeping the school going.

Bangkok temples, close to the eye of the king's ministers, fulfilled the educational aims more adequately than those in the provinces. The few boys from Bang Chan lucky enough to have a priest in Bangkok as a relative might spend a few years serving this priest and might attend a school which prepared for state examinations. The successful candidate could enter the king's service, and two or three of Bang Chang's sons reached prominence through this route. Most, however, moved no farther from home than the local temple where they lived a few years, serving the priests and attending classes until they returned home to aid their parents. Thereafter, at twenty-one, almost all the men entered the temple as priests for a year or two to listen to the sacred texts and those who could already read might extend their knowledge. In consequence of this program, piety flourished, the temple grew, and, although only a few took advantage of it, one suspects that the population had more than its former share of curers, astrologers, and ceremonialists.

As literacy mounted, the importance of reading and writing must have become more apparent. Farmers, who once could only hear the chanted words of a sermon, began to read the very words of the text undiluted by paraphrase. Many houses had kept a sacred book for its benign effect, but, with literacy, it could be read to family members on some leisure day during the rainy season. By buying one of the newly printed almanacs, one could himself determine, without having to ask a neighbor trained in lore, the propitious day to begin transplanting. If one were learning a formula from some teacher, it could be written in a notebook without the need to trust one's memory. Then there was no danger of a misstep, with the inevitable unfortunate results.

Some of these advantages must have occurred to the little group of farmers who, because they lived very far from the temple, founded a private secular school near their homes. In 1932, they invited a man with his son to move into their area to teach. Sixty pupils came for instruction in arithmetic, as well as in reading and writing, and the course was limited only by the time it took a pupil to learn to read the small collection of books and to master elementary arithmetic. Perhaps as a result of the latter experience, the value of arithmetic also became apparent to a few who needed no longer mutely to accept the money given by the rice dealer for their harvest. In any case, the patrons continued their support for the few years until the advent of the revised governmental program.

State Education

By 1953, three years after the overthrow of the absolute monarchy, the new constitutional government's program reached Bang Chan. Attendance became compulsory for girls as well as boys between the ages of 8 and 12, and truant officers, established in offices a few miles from the community, enforced attendance. Lay teachers were paid by the government to instruct in the three R's, morality, history, geography, and scoutcraft. By passing the state examinations for the first four elementary grades, pupils became eligible to continue their education into the six years of middle school, although this higher level remained (and still remains) beyond state minimum requirements.[1]

In Bang Chan a small minority welcomed the change, organized co-operative labor to construct a school building outside the temple, and gave their moral support to the new regulations. They looked approvingly at their daughters, as well as their sons, sitting with twenty to fifty children at their benches in the classrooms or running among two hundred or more children on the playground outside the iron-roofed school house. Of course it was good to know that some of these teachers had formerly taught as priests in the temple schools, but they raised no questions when women later came to instruct their sons in one or more of the six classrooms. The majority, however, grumbled at having children distracted from their proper contribution to the household but, in the face of a government order, they could only shrug their shoulders helplessly. They also complained of the trouble and cost of having to dress a child in the prescribed manner every day for school. Furthermore, each child had to buy paper and pencils and, perhaps, even had to be given a few cents for cakes to eat at noon. Many parents could not spare a boat to send the children along the canals to school and depending on a neighbor for this favor was often awkward.

These immediate difficulties would have been compounded had a parent attempted evaluation of the new program. Parents who had attended school under the priests would have recognized with approval the daily obeisance to the teacher. Copying letters of the alphabet from the blackboard into notebooks, chanting a text, or reciting the Five Noble Precepts would also have seemed appropriate. Saluting the flag may have reminded some fathers of their service in the army but it was certainly novel to require this of children. The remainder, with the possible exception of arithmetic, made little sense. Geography, history, and scoutcraft lay beyond their ken. Though any one of these subjects might have been explained by an interested person, the whole did not fit the recognized province of education and parents quickly left school affairs to the teachers.

Parents, nevertheless, might express opinions about the value of school. A small conservative group deplored the slighting of religious affairs. Hearing a teacher read stories from the life of the Buddha a few times a week and reciting the credo did not suffice. Moreover, they no longer sent their sons to serve a priest at the temple; only the unruly

---

[1] The precise age of required attendance, together with details of curriculum, have changed from time to time under various ministers of education; for a review of these, cf. M. L. Manich Jumsai, *Compulsory Education in Thailand*, UNESCO, 1951. Particularly p. 47 and p. 89.

boys, or those from starving families, resided there. An elder, schooled at an earlier period, observed:

> Parents want their children to know Pali, Thai, and Cambodian because some books are written in these languages, such as Phra Naraj's book describing sin and merit. Everyone used to have to know this text, but some knew it better than others. Now only the old people can read it because of the Cambodian writing. At every funeral there ought to be a reading of this text. Today the text is brought but nobody reads it.

For this group, reading was desirable because, although it did not help to grow rice, it taught virtue, on which success of every sort depended.

Others disregarded morality but questioned the utility of school for the present life. They merely asserted that farming requires no training:

> My children have passed the fourth grade already. It cannot help them earn a living. When they are through, they can only help their parents farm.

This man presupposed the utility of education but saw little of value in the new school. Some conceded minor value to literacy, like the man who found it helpful to read signs when travelling, but who otherwise saw no gain from education for farmers.

Contemporary Response and Educational Policy

Less than fifteen years after the government school building had been erected, a strong blast of wind during a storm collapsed the building. No one was in the school at the time, but teachers and local education officials soon were streaming toward it to survey the damage. The entire structure needed to be rebuilt but no one knew how. The Ministry, with their funds already promised to other projects, could not help. In this desperate moment, the head priest offered to shelter the school again in the temple. Not only this, but he recalled, in a special sermon, a precedent established by King Vajiravudh (1910–1925); the king, seeking to modernize the nation, broke with tradition by founding schools instead of temples. Of course, few in Bang Chan knew of this precedent nor of the head priest's source in pronouncing that making merit by building schools equals the merit of building temples. Nevertheless, the message was effective, for merit makers soon had assembled a temporary shelter in the temple, with the beams and roofing salvaged from the old building. Once classes were reconvened, the head priest turned to the new school. At his direction, the lay elders, a group until then concerned only with temple affairs, met with teachers to determine how to raise money. Their efforts were no doubt catalysed by the presence of foreign anthropologists whose interest in education was undisguisable. But all these efforts in a prosperous time could not gather more than a tenth of the money needed, so interest declined after the departure of the anthropologists. The satisfaction of having the school back "where it belonged" stifled further efforts.

Four years later, the school project revived with the return of the anthropologists. Teachers and temple elders quickly reconvened to arrange a token beginning of the school with the accumulated funds and thus reassured the community that the collected funds were still available for the purpose and had, in fact, increased by accumulated interest. In the midst of this work, a high official from the Ministry of Education visited the community. He had come at the request of one of the anthropologists to see what could be done to bridge the gap between present funds and a final new building. Surveying the scene of work, he asked succinctly the number of children in the present school and was told three hundred; he then asked the number of rooms planned and was told three. A little later he threw the assembled teachers and temple elders into consterna-tion by brushing aside their efforts. The school would have to be twice the size planned and would cost four times the maximum which the committee had calculated, he told them. The hearts of his listeners sank at this impossible goal but they did not realize the meaning of crowding a hundred pupils into one room. Fortunately the official showed com-passion by offering to shoulder the entire cost and by accepting local offers of labor to raise a dirt mound above the high-water level for the foundation. The community could, and did, join the short-term effort by the temple elders and, in 1955, the new building was officially opened on a spot next to the temple. The school was reestablished as a separate building but had acquired the backing of the temple elders.

Parents

It is too early to assess the effects of this new school in the com-munity, although we would expect enthusiasm for education to mount at a faster rate in the future than it did during the two decades after 1935. Some of the people had begun to value education as a means of advancing to another occupation, like the widow who, having lost her legacy of land, observed:

> Since I have no land to give my children, the best I can do is to see that they get an education. That will help them most in life.

Two of her sons have found positions in commercial firms, while a third has become a teacher. Poverty, however, is only one basis for valuing education; others find learning an arduous occupation:

> Our children wanted this education because they did not like farming. They were raised here in Bang Chan, and we parents worked in the fields,

but they never did. They all started at the Bang Chan school, went to Middle School in Minburi, then to Cha Choeng Sao where they stayed with their oldest sister who was teaching.

Such parents as could sympathize with their children's ambitions could labor in the fields with a will and make the needed sacrifices. Indeed, it is a sacrifice to send children to middle school especially. A boy or girl who must leave the community to attend these middle schools, becomes occupationally unfitted for farming, and remains as a costly dependent longer than the ordinary child. Some estimate the need to spend as much as a quarter of their annual income on tuition, books, clothing, transportation, and food. As a result, some say that middle school is "only for children of rich families."

Although parental wish to give children an easier life accounts for the majority of the school backers, the occasional farmer catches something of King Chulalongkorn's view. The king had sighted, back in the nineteenth century, some of the reservoirs of knowledge necessary to run a modern state and had opened the conduits to this source. One farmer translated this view into his own experience on the land:

> Education is to help the people who have increased in number while the land remains constant. Now one needs more education to make a living. In the future, every person will have to be a more skillful worker than now. Even in digging earth, one will have to learn how to dig.

This man perceived the need to equip one's self with knowledge if one were to make an adequate living and even farming, not to mention the many new occupations, requires knowledge.

Yet the number of parents with enthusiasm for education continues low. While the new school building provided a frequent topic of conversation in 1954, householders in one hamlet were asked to state, for a survey, what value they saw in education for the future. Of thirty-nine householders, only fifteen replied to this question. The majority acted as if they had never given a moment's thought to the topic. Among those who replied, six saw no value to education "because farmers do not need to read." The others recognized some worth in literacy or arithmetic, although they conceded it "would not help much later."

The Ministry

If Bang Chan farmers are preponderantly indifferent to, or non-comprehending of, the school, the Ministry of Education has replied by asserting the need for more numerous and effective schools. From an earlier emphasis on literacy alone, the task has ballooned, with the further aim of advancing Thailand in a world of rapacious nations. The official program holds that the knowledge and habits of a modern nation must be built into a population only recently disinterested in the world beyond the national borders. For this task, education is primary; men must hold a deep loyalty to the nation beyond their personal fealty to the king; old superstitions must be replaced with a knowledge of science; "out-moded" living habits must yield to modern practices. Beyond such pronouncements the Ministry has done little to explain the new purposes and forms of education.

According to most Bangkok people, the backwardness of the nation centers in the countryside, and some of the Ministry's ends are reinforced in the city. A young Bangkok woman, while visiting in Bang Chan, apologized to one of the foreign anthropologists:

> Children in villages are stupid; they cannot read. When the government school was built, parents did not send their children until they were forced to. In the village, there are only four grades and the children are taught, but they soon forget. Thailand is different from foreign countries. It only just got civilization from them.

Such comments overlook the strength of Thai tradition and reveal a frequently found urban feeling of urban superiority but of national inferiority, along with a sense of urgency to overtake the Occident in technical knowledge.

The Teachers

The burden of this program lies with the teachers. They receive, through the official hierarchy, their instructions on what to teach, along with precise specifications on time and method for the job. Improvements in curriculum or method are communicated in periodic conferences and in-service refresher courses. Inspectors from the district office check on the program's progress, and state examinations for promotion to the next grade gauge a teacher's effectiveness.

Bang Chan's teachers recognize and accept their role in remaking the nation. Like their superiors in the Ministry, they recognize the limitations of insufficient textbooks, maps, and other equipment for the job. Without certain of these aids, teachers draw on newly written aphorisms such as "Buy Thai goods; love Thailand and love to be a Thai. Live a Thai life, speak Thai, and esteem Thai culture." [2]

Teachers probably are more conscious than the Ministry of the difficulties of their tasks. Although attendance records are filed with the district office for official scrutiny, the teacher understands them more vividly when he must face half-filled benches for a week after vacation. He experiences the aches of preparing a pupil for the annual state exami-

---

[2] Translation of a civics text for Grade 3, by courtesy of the United States International Cooperation Administration.

nation, only to find that pupil absent on examination day and to discover later that the child overslept because a parent took him to an all-night ceremony. A teacher observed that she had to work single-handed:

> When I ask parents to help their children by doing home reading and things like that with them, they say, "Don't ask me to do that. It's your job. What are you being paid for?" So there is no cooperation from parents usually but some parents are helpful.

When the Ministry takes pride in its latest book on hygiene, the teacher recognizes that telling children to brush their teeth twice a day avails little in a community with scarcely a dozen toothbrushes. He knows that the regulations require each child to dress in a clean uniform and that the inspector will report unfavorably when one-third of the children wear none. Yet teachers do not insist on the letter of the rule, for they understand the inability of many families to provide even one uniform, let alone such an extra one to wear while this one is being washed. In such little ways, the teacher mediates between the community and Ministry expectations.

Indeed, he must avoid antagonizing the community for, as we have seen, he depends upon community good-will to support the school. Even before the school building collapsed, teachers made annual rounds of homes asking for a little money, rice, or labor to help repair some desks, to clean the pond where drinking water is stored, or to patch a leaky roof. They know the reluctance of indifferent farmers to contribute to the school: a teacher estimated that, for every five *baht* of cash, or five baskets of rice given to the temple, only one goes to the school. This must be set against a background of a community very short of cash, though fortunately quite well-fed.

Youth and the Family

While the new school was being considered, only three of fourteen fourth-grade boys and four of fifteen girls said, in reply to a questionnaire, that they wished to farm for a living. The majority thought of becoming soldiers, government officials, doctors, and nurses. In such a group of farm children, we can only reckon these preferences as dreams, yet these dreams have moved a step closer to reality for these children than for their parents who, a generation ago, could not have presumed to dream of a living except from the land.

The realization of these dreams depend largely on parents and opportunities. Literate parents may reinforce the school tasks as illiterate parents could not. Yet even illiteracy does not mean indifference. All parents make sharp, clear judgments when children are very tiny as to who is bright enough to continue his education and who is fitted only to be a farmer. For most, the need of another field hand makes the decision easy; the child cannot be spared. Children of resourceless farm laborers must become independent as quickly as possible by going to work with a neighbor who has land, or by taking a job in a factory. A few girls venture into Bangkok as domestic servants and parents breathe more easily knowing that the child is cared for and might even send a little money home. But, where the decision on education is real, choice is often difficult. In addition to the loss of manpower and the extra expense of sending a child to middle school, parents must forego an ideal where children and grandchildren continue to live in the same household and care for their aging parents. When children depart from home, they feel absolved from supporting their parents. Although people say only the rich can afford to send their children beyond the elementary grades, a penniless boy, who was sent to a kinsman priest in Bangkok, earned a scholarship to a famed preparatory school. His mother sends rice to the family which boards him, with a little cash from her fees as a spirit medium, and eagerly searches out new listeners to hear of her son's accomplishments. Children of such parents begin school at an earlier age than the majority and, at the age when others are released from attending school, these children have already spent several years in middle school.

On these various accounts, the majority leave school after fulfilling minimum requirements. The record, however, shows a small increase each year of those who continue to middle school. Some children of ambitious parents have become teachers, and four of the six teachers in Bang Chan's school grew up in the community. Approximately an equal number is teaching elsewhere. More have found employment outside the community, like the young man who learned about electricity and came to serve as electrician in the king's household, or the members of one family who, having learned to make bronze cutlery, now work in a small factory in Bangkok run by the family. Others have learned their skills away from home and have returned to Bang Chan where they sew shirts on a sewing machine or assemble and repair radios when not busy in the fields. Such artisans are more numerous than teachers but the majority without special knowledge must earn its living by farming. According to a 1954 population sample of Bang Chan, 65% of the men between 14 and 30 are in agricultural occupations and the remainder serve as soldiers, service employees, or factory workers. Of those men over 30, the percentages would be more like 95% farmers. Of the women, a slightly larger fraction (68%) continues to farm, while the remainder has married into a city household, works in a factory, or is in domestic service. The majority of youth still considers itself fit only for farming, since only a few have ventured seriously into the increasing variety of new occupations. An "easier" occupation is more often dreamed than realized.

THE SOURCES OF INDIFFERENCE

The new educational program has appealed little to the rice farmers and, despite twenty years of exposure, the community continues unenthusiastic. In the West, we look to schools as agents of national progress; these institutions serve to fit each new generation for its duties as citizens. Indeed, Bang Chan schools are modeled on these schools of the West but national advancement, judging by changes on the land, has come independently rather than through the schools. How may we account for this result?

We may grant that no country can develop overnight the personnel, buildings, or equipment necessary for a brand new kind of school. No doubt in 1935 there was a national shortage of teachers, and textbooks had not been printed in adequate numbers to serve all the entering school children. In Bang Chan, however, if these difficulties were present, they did not seriously impede the operation of the school. Classes took place regularly, sometimes with more competent teachers and more ample materials, but never did a lack necessitate closing the doors.

It is also difficult to account for indifference to the school on economic grounds. Vacations are arranged so that the children can assist their parents during planting and harvest. Moreover, in an earlier day, when families were more dependent than at present on manpower to raise their crops, they readily sent sons to the temple to become priests. That people still contribute to the temple more readily than to the school also argues that Bang Chan lacks the will, rather than the resources, to back the school.

This lack of will does not arise from eschewing learning per se. The man who can read and write enjoys a certain prestige in the community. A portion of the respect for priests and teachers may be traced to their greater than average knowledge. Moreover, young people are encouraged to apply themselves to learning, as where an elder deplored the inability of the young to read Pali and Cambodian texts. An elderly woman recalled the pleasure of hearing her father read portions of a traditional epic poem and she further observed that literate neighbors still borrow these books.

Instead, we would point to the failure of the school to conform with traditional assumption concerning education. Let us first observe some of the ways in which the present school conforms to the traditional standard. Some vestiges of the original religious character have been maintained by locating schools in the vicinity of a temple; this is deemed the appropriate location. Although teachers no longer dress in yellow robes, obeisance to the teacher occurs daily preceding classroom recitation. A more elaborate, traditional paying-of-respect to teachers by both pupils and teachers is a standard annual feature of the school calendar.

In addition, although teachers no longer have the privilege of selecting their pupils from among the petitioners, they encourage and attend to the needs of the most devotedly industrious, preserving, in this manner, the assumption of worthiness to receive attention. Then, in permanent debt for this special help, these pupils of special industry continue as followers of a teacher, ready to assist him when needed. In this informal manner a teacher's moral leadership is preserved.

Although such features doubtless help to retain some semblance of education, certain indispensable features are lacking. As knowledge is assumed to be both substantial and practical, a considerable portion of the curriculum stands functionless in the eyes of the community. Parents understand moral education as practical education for, through acting virtuously, one may improve one's lot. Such people would insist that education should present the important sacred precepts. Other parents also understand that education may be more directly and implementally practical and they would insist on subject matter paying more direct heed to the problems of the farmer. This is the conclusion of the people who think of knowledge in substantial and practical terms, so that text-books telling simple stories in order to sharpen the skills in reading, as we in the West have directed, have no relevance. A pupil should learn the letters and the words of a text with direct bearing on his needs. Should he fail to understand the meaning of the words at the moment of learning, by committing the text to memory and, by having it with him, he may still stumble on its pertinence some time in the future. On these grounds, the tales in a reader about the visit of a nephew and uncle to the zoo, tales from Thai history, and descriptions of remote lands may possibly be acknowledged as worthy, but certainly not as education helpful for farmers.

Thus the school is judged according to its contribution to morality or to aiding the life of farmers. Morality has been absorbed into a curriculum as one of many subjects, and, although a priest addresses an occasional sermon to the school children, this, with three hours per week devoted to moral instruction looks inadequate to those who judge by ethical standards. On the other hand, the school's contribution to making a better living requires the student to recognize social mobility as personally possible. Though many have the dream of becoming government officials, they have not fitted the passing of examinations clearly into a step toward realizing this dream. The majority, as a consequence, finds few benefits in schooling. Yet this group would doubtless turn more enthusiastic if the school helped them to grow more rice or to build better houses.

And one may find some justification in the majority position. Bang Chan does not resist change. Elders point to the progress they have witnessed over the past decades: Crops are larger; weeds are fewer; old pests have disappeared; people may light their houses brightly at night and irrigate their fields in a few hours with a motor. Where individual initiative is responsible for these advances, people have learned the lessons as folk knowledge transmitted by neighbors and kinsmen. The school has brought none of these benefits.

The other great point is: Over the world, schools have grown in importance where they have begun to establish a monopoly on knowledge and on certification of competence. As long as folk transmission, apprenticeships, or seniority of experience offer dignified alternatives, schools serve a limited clientele. In Thailand, the monopoly is growing with the advent of new technological knowledge and the government's control of schools, as well as certification of competence for its own service. Until a farmer's child can no longer make a living on the land and can escape his plight only through school examinations, public education in the countryside will remain functionally limited.

FURTHER READINGS

Bharati, Agehananda. "Formal education as tradition-enhancing input in modern India." Paper read at the Annual Meeting of the American Anthropological Association, San Diego, California, 1970.
Burling, Robbins. *Hill farms and padi fields: life in mainland Asia.* Englewood Cliffs, N.J.: Spectrum Books, Prentice-Hall, 1965.
Hanks, Lucien M. "American aid is damaging Thai society," in Robert Jay Lifton (ed.), *America and the Asian revolutions.* Chicago: Transaction Book, Aldine, 1970.
Ingersoll, Jasper. "Fatalism in village Thailand," *Anthropological Quarterly*, vol. 39 (July 1966).
Kaufman, Howard. *Bandkuad, a community study in Thailand.* Locust Valley, N.Y.: J. J. Agustin, 1960.

25

Mr. Parmee uses four individual histories to help the reader "visualize more clearly the relationship between the problems of Apache teen-agers in school and those experienced at home on the reservation." He discusses economic and social dilemmas of the San Carlos, dynamics of Apache family organization, and the configuration of public and government-administered education as related and often contradictory influences upon maturing Apache youth.

Wax in Part Three identified differences between conservative and progressive outlooks in the Indian community in sensitivity to tribal tradition, attitudes toward assimilation, and the felt value of formal education. Mr. Parmee specifies these differences not only to the San Carlos but also to the institutional context of Apache family, "Anglo" schooling, and government dependency. His elaboration of the raveled network of expectations to which many Apache teen-agers are subject is in effect an exposition of the interface of "two worlds" — theirs and the white — which these young adults constantly occupy, with understandably problematic results. Mr. Parmee's article appears as a chapter in his study, Formal Education and Culture Change: A Modern Apache Indian Community and Government Education Programs *(Tucson: University of Arizona Press, 1968).*

EDWARD A. PARMEE

Factors Affecting the Education of Apache Youth

The discussion of factors contributing to the academic and personal problems of Apache teen-agers will be divided into three main parts: (1) problems stemming from the community, (2) problems stemming from the family, and (3) problems stemming from the education program. Before getting into the first of these topics, however, a sample of case histories illustrating some of the more significant problems and their underlying causes . . . will be reviewed. Interviews and personal records from school and agency files were used to compile more than 30 detailed case histories, from which the four presented here were selected.

CASE HISTORY NO. 1: "DANNY" [1]

Danny was born in 1944, the illegitimate son of his unwed Apache mother and Anglo father. He never saw his father, but he did vaguely remember the man his mother married shortly after Danny was born. He was a Navajo. When his mother went off to live with her Navajo husband, Danny was left behind at San Carlos to be raised by his maternal grandparents. Once in a great while Danny's grandparents were visited by his mother and her husband, but he did not care for either of them and

By permission from *Formal Education and Culture Change: A Modern Apache Indian Community and Government Education Programs,* Edward A. Parmee, Tucson: University of Arizona Press, copyright 1968.

[1] All names presented in the four case histories below are fictitious.

was glad they had left him at San Carlos. Although his grandparents were old and nearly blind, they showed their love for him; and even as a little boy, he felt responsible in caring for them.

The home that Danny shared with his grandparents was a small wooden frame house with a single room 12′ x 14′ located on a barren plot of ground at Gilson Wash. There was no gas or electricity, and water came from an outdoor tap. Heating and cooking was done on a wood stove. They had no car, and getting around to the store, the church, and the hospital took many hours of walking. Out of the small pension Danny's grandfather received, they purchased the barest essentials. Sometimes when this was not enough the local welfare agent helped them out.

Danny attended a variety of schools before entering the school program at Globe. He attended the local mission school, the government school at San Carlos, and for brief periods two public schools. His attendance was good, according to the records, and his teachers spoke highly of him. They said he was "quick to learn," "speaks English well and like[d] numbers," and that he was a "top student in class" when he was in the sixth grade at San Carlos. But when Danny entered the seventh grade in Globe the record of his achievements fell.

At Globe Junior High Danny did so poorly the first year that he was conditionally promoted to the eighth grade. In the eighth grade his marks improved slightly, but still he got mostly 4's. Danny explained his problem basically in these terms:

1. When he left the reservation Indian school and entered the integrated public school, he realized he was far behind the non-Indians in his class. It took him a great deal of effort to catch up and to try and keep up with the others.

2. There was no encouragement to study at home. There was, in fact, no place to study. Thus he seldom studied at home. His grandparents did not compel him to study; when his chores around the house were done, he simply went off to "goof around with the other kids."

Throughout, Danny's attendance was excellent. His I.Q. and achievement test scores were approximately average, which was higher than other Apaches. In 1960, however, his mother returned to the little house at Gilson Wash with a Pima man, her husband having died earlier of TB. One night she received an almost fatal beating from this man, the result of excessive mutual drinking, and was rushed to the hospital. The Pima man was banished from the Apache reservation by tribal authorities.

By now Danny had made friends with his high school music teacher, Mr. Donald, who had befriended the boy on numerous occasions. When the crisis at Danny's home occurred, it upset the boy greatly, and the local authorities agreed to permit Danny to live with the Donald family in Globe. Danny worried about his grandparents, but the Donalds took him to visit them often. He also visited his mother at the hospital, but this he soon stopped. Mr. Donald said it depressed Danny greatly each time.

Danny's grades finally began to show signs of improvement. A simple inquiry brought a rather enthusiastic response: "Man, you should see what I have now," he said. "I've got my own room, my own desk, my own lamp, and everything! We even have a set of encyclopedias in the house, and I use it all the time. Sometimes when I don't want to study they (the Donalds) make me study. They *push* me into it!" Danny's tone evinced his approval.

Danny liked the attention the Donalds were showing him. "Whenever I have a problem, I just go to Mr. Donald and he helps me." He never had a father or maternal uncle to turn to before. Other Apaches shunned him because he was a "half-breed" and not one of them. It hurt him at first, but he did not seem to resent this as much as one might have expected. In fact, he felt sorry for the other Apache children. They seldom discussed their personal lives with their parents, he said, and their parents did not inquire. School matters were almost never mentioned unless a child was sick. "The parents aren't interested in their children," he rationalized. "They don't care what their kids do. They tell him, 'You can go out and work as a cowboy, it doesn't matter.' They don't care if their kids do well in school or not."

It was not long before the Donalds adopted Danny. He went less often to the reservation and worked in Globe during the summers. He even started dating an Anglo girl, after the Donalds had pacified her parents. Donald felt that adult Anglos were far more prejudiced than their children. Apache students resented Danny's behavior and rejected his friendship, but he did not seem to care any more.

CASE HISTORY NO. 2: "BERT"

Bert was the oldest boy and fourth in a line of eleven children. His father was the son of an early Apache scout who, while in the service of Captain Crawford during the late 1800's, aided in the capture of Geronimo, and was later assigned to guard the fallen leader in his eastern prison camp in Oklahoma. In 1960 the family lived in pleasant surroundings at Seven-Mile Wash, in a better-than-average three-room frame house, as well as two additional houses. The grounds were well kept, and the family enjoyed electricity, running water, and the use of radios, a washing machine, and two pick-up trucks. Bert's father was a steady, reliable worker, holding a rather prominent position in community health services. He had the equivalent of an eight-grade education, but was considered by his employers to have learned far more through his own personal efforts since the time of his school training.

Bert's parents were strongly education-oriented. He and his brothers and sisters all had excellent attendance records throughout their school careers. Nearly all had average or better than average achievement records, and one of Bert's older sisters even went on to junior college, but she found it quite difficult. Their home life was exceptionally stable and harmonious in spite of the size of the family — a result of the father's firm discipline and strong sense of family responsibility.

Bert stayed in Indian schools until he was in the seventh grade. Then he started attending school at Globe. He said that the transition for him was very hard. For the first time he had to do homework, and his parents provided a place for him to study at home. His marks were very poor that year and his attendance was far below his average for the other years. The non-Indians, he said, were hard to compete with and he found English difficult.

Bert was promoted to the eighth grade, and when his work did not improve, he was granted a "social promotion" to grade 9. He took remedial English his freshman year in high school but failed it along with general math, business, and world geography. He was held back at the end of the year, and after taking over some of these courses, was allowed to become a sophomore in 1960. His grades remained poor and it was obvious from the interviews that he was discouraged. His father, in fact, had expressed deep concern about the boy's future. He blamed Bert's troubles on a newly acquired interest in girls, and he made formidable efforts at breaking up all possible romances, convinced that only firm discipline would get the boy's mind back on his education, "where it should be." But all of Bert's problems were not female, and the following incident, revealed at an interview, illustrates a rather frequent occurrence among Apache students in school.

During an interview, Bert announced one day that he was going to fail biology. The class had been assigned a semester project, and Bert had chosen to write a 7,500 word paper on radiation biology. He picked this topic because it had sounded interesting to him, but when he learned how complex a subject it was, he knew he could not handle it. Two weeks later he asked to have his topic changed, but the instructor refused. Now, the day before it was due, Bert had not written a single word.

A subsequent inquiry revealed that had Bert made an attempt at completing his project, he might have passed the course, but he had not discussed this possibility at the time with his instructor. He had also failed to approach the Indian student counselor with his problem and, in fact, appeared to be ignorant of the man's function in the school program. Bert had not mentioned a word of his dilemma to his parents.

When asked if he ever confided in others concerning his own personal matters, Bert replied that he sometimes wanted to talk to someone about such things very much, but he knew of no one in whom he could confide. He did not talk to his parents because he was certain they would not understand. His good pal, Harry, was a quiet fellow and they seldom talked about personal matters; so Bert kept most things to himself. If a guy went around with a girl, he said, most (Apache) people said they should get married. It was hard to go dating like the white boys and Mexicans. There was really no one a guy could confide in, and he just did not "have the guts" to ask people for help.

When told that he would probably have to take biology over again, Bert replied smiling, "Oh, I don't mind. It's one of my favorite subjects." Later he added, "I'm gonna be 18 this August. Maybe I'll just quit an' stay around home like the other guys."

Case History no. 3: "Lydia"

Lydia lived in Bylas, and in 1960 attended the seventh grade class at Ft. Thomas. Her father had been a part-time laborer all his life, except when he was an Army scout in 1928. Both her father and her mother had been previously married and had large families.

According to the local welfare worker, Lydia's parents had never really maintained a stable home for their children The family income had for years been sporadic and seldom sufficient to meet the barest needs. They were often dependent on welfare and assistance from relatives, and the children had to be "farmed-out" whenever one or both parents were jailed for drunkenness. When sober they talked about education, but they seemed to prefer to send their children off to boarding school where others could take care of the task. Nearly all of Lydia's older sisters were married now, but the rest of her siblings were still in school as she was, making failing grades and showing poor attendance. Their life together as a family was to "live and shift" (social worker) from one day to the next.

In 1960 Lydia had to borrow clothes in order to go to school. With no home to go to each night, she would "run around," as Apaches would say, going from house to house with friends — some of whom were in the same plight as she — and with the groups of boys who dared to disobey the curfew. Sometimes Lydia would stay with an older sister, but her sister's husband was out of work most of the time, and occasionally he spent some time in jail. She claimed she saw little of her parents.

Lydia said she liked school but found it very hard. Her father and her sister wanted her to stay in school. She said she liked her father because he bought her clothes now and then, but her mother wanted her to quit school because she was ashamed of what people were saying about Lydia's nighttime habits. Lydia did not like her mother and tried to ignore what she said. She said her mother never did anything for her. Lydia preferred to be with her two girl friends most of the time, even though they teased her when the other Apaches did. But they were the only two girls she could talk to, she said.

Lydia was two years over the Apache age norm for her grade. Her marks were mostly failures, and her teachers complained that she was a "complete blank" in class, never responding to anything they said or tried to do. She seldom spoke to Anglos and stayed mostly with other Indian students. She was accused by her teachers of not caring about school and having no pride in her appearance. She was known to drink whenever she could obtain liquor, and sometimes after drinking too much she would go to the homes of friends for food and shelter.

As might be expected, Lydia had very little to say about her own future. She said if she could not stay in school, she would simply "stay at home" — wherever that might be. She admitted, though, that there was nothing for her to do at home. Probing deeper than this only provoked a sad and silent response, a response that answered no questions, but succeeded nearly always in curtailing any further discussion.

CASE HISTORY NO. 4: "JED"

Jed was the third oldest boy out of nine children. His father was a high school graduate and a prominent tribal leader from Bylas, active in politics, law, and church functions. His mother was a quiet, unassuming woman, devoted to her family. They had a larger than average home of brick construction with most household conveniences. In recent years up to 1960 the family enjoyed a steady income and an exceptional degree of harmonious stability, in spite of the father's occasional political battles.

Jed's academic achievement over the years was exceptional. In the seventh grade at Ft. Thomas his lowest grade was a 3— (1 is excellent) in geography. In the eighth grade his marks were mostly 1's and 2's. His lowest mark in the ninth grade was a 3+ in history. In the tenth grade at Ft. Thomas he had nearly a 1 average in all of his "solid" courses. His lowest grade in the eleventh grade was a 2. Jed managed a straight 1.0 grade-point average in English since the eighth grade! His total attendance record was excellent. Among Indians and non-Indians, Jed was considered by his teachers to be an outstanding student, both intelligent and very diligent.

Jed was aware of his accomplishments and did not hesitate to discuss them with the author, although he was never boastful. He attributed his success to plain hard work. He said he studied in school and at home every day, even though some of the other Apache students chided him for it. He blamed the failures of many Apaches in school on the fact that they gave up too easily when in competition with non-Indians. Jed seemed convinced that many Apaches could do as well as he if only they would put aside their defeatist attitude and work harder at their studies.

This was one reason why Jed did not pal around with other Apache boys. He felt that their interests differed from his. They only wanted to "fool around" and had no interest in school or the future. They had, as he put it, "nothing to offer" him. Jed's best pal was a scholarly Mexican boy from whom he learned Spanish and better English. In spite of the resentment expressed by his Apache peers, Jed remarked confidently, "I can handle myself. I'm not afraid of what they say."

Others were also aware of Jed's exceptional standards, and it was usually easy for him to find a job during vacation periods. His relations with his family seemed good, although he preferred to confide more in an older sister or his mother than with his father. The only thing he would say about his father was to admit that he gave Jed money when needed. When Jed announced to his parents his desire to become a lawyer, he was disappointed that his father, at least, had no comment to make and no encouragement to offer. What, then, did motivate Jed to work so hard at his studies?

Jed unhesitatingly replied that he was in heated competition with the non-Indian students in his school. They were out to beat him, he asserted, but he was not going to let them get ahead of him. He realized how much hard work had accomplished, and he was determined to stay on the top of the heap. Much of the time during each interview was spent discussing his plans for college and the many opportunities available for scholarships.

The above case histories represent a very small sample of the many, many similar cases encountered by the author and his research team during the two and one-half year period of the study. The incidents and views described are merely intended to illustrate some of the more typical findings revealed through hundreds of personal interviews with parents, teachers, community service offices, and students, in order that the reader might visualize more clearly the relationship between the problems of Apache teen-agers in school and those experienced at home on the reservation.

"Danny" and "Lydia" represent those Apache youngsters with poor home and family backgrounds — a lack of parental love (although Danny at least had his grandparents) and responsible care, economic instability, and moral depravity where parental guidance and discipline should have prevailed. But Danny's outlook and academic achievement did not parallel Lydia's.

For one thing, Danny was a boy and in Apache society he could move about more freely than Lydia, with less to fear from public criticism. "Runnin' around at night" was a criticism far less consequential for boys than for Apache girls. Lydia was socially "branded" as a bad girl, and even though people might admit that she was not entirely to blame for her situation, mothers of other boys and girls had already "blackballed" her as an undesirable companion for their own children. Her chances of eventually marrying into a good local family were seriously limited, if not altogether lost. Apache boys, on the other hand, involved in the same activities when youths, would sooner or later be pardoned because of the prevailing attitude among Apaches that "boys will be boys." [2]

Although Danny spoke of himself as an Apache, he realized that his half-white heritage (his physical appearance was predominantly Caucasian) would always be a barrier to his complete acceptance by Apaches. This enabled him to rationalize more easily any rejection that he experienced, for he could not blame himself for the folly of his parents. The fact that Anglos — his adopted parents in particular — were willing to accept him gave him an opportunity to develop new interests, goals, and values. His new home, with its relatively luxurious surroundings and facilities, and more importantly, the abundance of close personal attention received from his new parents, gave Danny a new sense of personal worth and pride. It afforded him an opportunity to achieve success as defined by his Anglo parents, and in so doing, to please those for whom he now had a strong feeling of affection and responsibility.

Lydia was not so fortunate. There was really very little hope for her to regain all that she had lost as long as she remained among her people. This is not to say that being adopted into an Anglo family like Danny would be the best solution for all such teen-agers, but rather that as long as Lydia remained in Bylas, she would always have the stigma of her wayward youth, a serious obstacle for her or any Apache girl in her predicament. As it was, she had little in life to look forward to and consequently less cause to strive for improvement, though under the circumstances improvement would have been exceedingly difficult. There were, regrettably, a great many Apache teen-age girls in Lydia's category.

Both "Jed" and "Bert" had stable home lives, with Apache fathers of notable community rank and personal achievement. There were also

---

[2] A more striking example of this phenomenon occurred when a teen-age Apache girl was one night raped by a half dozen Apache youths. The boys were later brought before the local tribal magistrate on charges initiated by the girl's parents. But the boys' families brought counter-charges against the girl. The hearing proved that even though the girl willingly got into the boys' car "to go for a ride," she was forcibly molested by the older boys who overpowered her. The boys' parents, however, charged that she was a "bad girl" for being out at night and agreeing to go with the boys. The hearing ended with the judge sentencing the girl to a term in jail and criticizing her for being an evil influence in the community. The boys were released into the custody of their parents and told not to associate with such bad girls (Parmee, 1959–1961a: 209–211).

older brothers and sisters in both families who had attained comparatively good high school records and were now holding steady jobs. On the
surface, at least, it appeared that both boys had equal opportunities for
personal academic advancement, and yet their respective views towards
the future and records of success were entirely different. Why?

Personality differences are clearly evident when comparing these two
boys, although it is difficult to determine at this point whether the
differences in personality contributed to the differences in achievement,
or vice versa. Jed expressed personal confidence, strong motivation, and
even aggressiveness, a rather atypical trait for Apache teen-agers in general.
Bert, on the other hand, was rather timid in front of Anglos, showed
very little self-confidence about his ability to improve in school, and had
the more common Apache-student tendency to retreat from problems,
rather than to attempt a partial success or to ask for aid.

Although Jed was not accepted by Anglos in the same manner as
Danny was, his attitudes and achievements were clearly recognized by
his teachers and non-Indian peers. He preferred this kind of recognition
to recognition from other Apache boys, many of whom scorned his "White
man's ways." Instead of retreating from competition, Jed regarded it as a
means to obtain personal satisfaction. His closest friend, a Mexican boy,
was his staunchest competitor.

Both Bert and Jed had since childhood been strongly encouraged by
their families to "get a good education." For some reason, Bert had failed
to respond to the opportunities afforded him by his family. Unfortunately,
there was no psychological test of proven reliability available that could
have been used to evaluate any differences in the potential intellectual
aptitude of the two boys, for it would have been difficult to ascertain
how much of the results was attributable to differences in individual
English language abilities.

Bert acted discouraged, as if he had already "tossed in the towel," and
resigned himself to whatever fate had in store for him. Jed, however, was
definitely goal-oriented. He wanted to be a lawyer. Even more he perhaps
wanted to prove to others that all Apaches were not "dumb" and "lazy,"
and that with persistent efforts, he could equal or even better his Anglo
competitors in a world of their own design.

Factors Within the Community Environment

Economic Problems

Earlier in this report some effort was made to point out the serious
unemployment problem existing on the San Carlos Apache Reservation.
It is a problem that was carefully studied by the Stanford Research Insti-
in 1954 (Robison et al.), that also prevailed on the reservation during

the period of this study from 1959–61, and that still persists (Arizona Commission of Indian Affairs, 1964b).

Such widespread Apache unemployment has come about as the result of a number of factors:

(a) Full-scale development of the reservation economic resources has not been achieved. Enterprises such as mining and large-scale farming have died out, and timber harvesting has been extremely limited due to the inaccessibility of much of the forested areas (Robison et al., 1954: 129–131). Leasing contracts, and power and water problems have plagued efforts to attract light industry. Tourism is growing, but heavy investments are necessary to make good roads into the higher mountain areas, which are more suitable for camping, hunting, and fishing. Cattle-raising has been the tribe's chief industry, but even that has not been developed to its most lucrative limits:

> Thus it becomes evident that, through the years, traditional values have operated to prevent the San Carlos from becoming aware of a necessary shift in work habits, orientation to kin, and sociability if a successful cattle enterprise is to develop. In place of sustained work and thrift, which alone can contribute capital for present and future needs, they retain a traditional work pattern based on periodic and irregular activity. Instead of stressing individual enterprise and responsibility for personal needs within a narrow family unit, they emphasize voluntary cooperation and the sharing of surplus within extended kin groups. And, when isolation on the range is essential to future benefits, they are prone to remain within comfortable range of neighbors and kin. San Carlos Apache values are in direct opposition to the demands of the market economy (Getty, 1961–62: 185).

(b) During the period of this study it was observed that individual commercial enterprises among Apaches were rather rare. Commercial enterprises throughout the reservation was dominated by tribal interests, managed by tribal employees, and directed by council authority. According to the 1964 San Carlos Survey only 40 to 45 Apaches were employed by the combined Tribal Council and Tribal Enterprise system (Arizona Commission of Indian Affairs, 1964b). Individual commercial enterprises were usually discouraged by the dearth of individual capital resources, and the unavailability of loans for such purposes. Some tribal leaders admitted that the tribal enterprise system itself defeated potential individual enterprises by the very fact that it was such an overpowering competitor with strong political backing. This was in part a result of the fact that the tribal council budget came primarily from the income procured through tribal enterprises.

(c) . . . The lack of suitable occupational training among Apaches greatly reduced the number of possible job holders on the reservation, and non-Apaches had to be brought in to fulfill most skilled and technical positions.

(d) Apaches, on the whole, were opposed to moving off the reservation to procure jobs. Efforts in the past to relocate Apaches never fully succeeded (Parmee, 1961: 24–25) in spite of tribal efforts to encourage this program (Arizona Commission of Indian Affairs, 1964b). Apaches preferred living in their own communities, regardless of the economic deprivations, to living isolated in distant non-Indian communities (Parmee, 1959–1961a: 127–135).

Although there are no family economic surveys known to this author for the San Carlos Apaches, one can safely surmise from the data presented thus far that family poverty among these people was not uncommon. The effects of this upon the individual families and the lives of each family member will be discussed later; here the concern is the reservation community as a whole.

Many Apaches were in the position of supporting three governments out of their income taxes: federal, state, and tribal. A low income and a large family spared many from doling out funds to the first two governments, but since about 1960 all cattle sales were taxed 2½% to help defray tribal council costs. Many Apaches opposed the passage of this bill, but at the time the council was desperately in need of additional funds.

In recent years the Apache tribal council continually struggled to keep its budget in the black. Caught between the desire to enact new programs for the improvement of reservation conditions and the threat of economic bankruptcy, the tribal council nearly every year found itself dependent upon alien sources for support of its programs. Federal agencies such as the BIA and the U.S. Public Health Service spent millions on the San Carlos Reservation within the past decade to provide a multitude of community service: i.e., roads, welfare, range and agricultural improvement, education, hospital care, water and sanitation, disease control, etc. State welfare services also were at work on the reservation, and private charitable organizations each year lent their financial support to youth projects and individual needy families.

In the field of education the Apache tribe had for years been almost entirely dependent upon the BIA for financial aid and technical assistance. Consequently, Apaches had very little to say about the design and operation of their school programs. Requests by tribal leaders for improvements in the schools were continually held in abeyance by federal regulations, fiscal policies, and the opinions of BIA officials.[3] Even many of the basic

---

[3] For example, pre-school classes for 5-year-olds, more on-reservation day schools, language specialists, etc. (Wesley, 1961: 4–7).

goals of the program were of Anglo rather than Apache origin, and most decisions concerning operational or policy changes were entirely in the hands of the BIA.

Such conditions caused tribal leaders to appear impotent in the eyes of their people and they caused the people to harbor resentment toward the federal government, or Anglos in general, for what was felt to be social and political suppression (Parmee, 1959–1961a: 241–245). Equally unfortunate was the fact that continued dependency of this sort produced apathy and ignorance among the Apache people. . . . Unable to think of the program as their own, many Apaches merely paid it a kind of lip-service that was neither uncooperative nor affirmative. As a result of this attitude, attempts at community-school activities (PTA organizations and the like) often failed. The sole exception to this was the tribal education committee.

This tribally-appointed voluntary committee . . . was, at the time of this study, a partial success. Taking its various functions point-by-point:

(a) It provided educational loans for needy students, but the funds were very limited (a revolving fund of less than $6,000), and usually the committee had a very difficult time getting loans returned and keeping political influences from creeping into application approvals. The Committee also heard many complaints from parents against the school program, but seldom could facilitate any reciprocal action without the consent of the BIA.

(b) Community projects such as sporting events, the local newspaper, summer camp programs, and scouting activities were usually sponsored by the tribal education committee, but its very limited funds, derived at the time solely from its own resources, hindered the committee from taking much more than a kind of diplomatic role in any of the larger projects.

(c) The committee aided in the disbursement of private welfare funds to families with needy school children. Very often the degree of committee influence or popularity with the people was directly proportional to the extent of its control over potential welfare resources.

(d) The tribal education committee acted as a very important liaison service between the common people and educational officialdom in the various separate school systems. It also provided — when funds or borrowed transportation permitted — many Apache parents with the opportunity to visit their children in distant schools. Occasionally Apache high school students were taken to visit a variety of colleges and training schools.

Some Apaches and Anglos laughed at this committee, pointing out its numerous weaknesses and informalities, but it was, in fact, at that time the most significant recent attempt on the part of Apaches to initiate some degree of constructive, active participation in a program of vital importance to their future social and economic progress.[4]

Social Problems

Unlike many rural American communities that thrive in an atmosphere of PTA's, school and social clubs, civic committees, and adult-sponsored youth activities, Apaches found it difficult to establish enough volunteer citizenship aid to meet growing community needs. Attempts by some to organize civic support in this manner failed numerous times during the period of this study.

In San Carlos, for example, unsuccessful attempts were made from time to time to organize a PTA group including both Anglo and Apache parents. Anglos blamed it on Apache parental apathy. Apaches said it was because Anglos dominated all of the meetings and that the group had no influence with the agencies operating the school program. The tribal education committee, they said, at least had the ear of the council and was run by Apache leaders (Parmee, 1959–1961a: 23–24).

In 1960, however, there were other tribally appointed committees that did not function as effectively as the education committee, which met at least once every month and had year-round projects under way. A great deal depended upon the individual leadership of the committees, and although some of it was very weak, few Apaches were willing to openly criticize the councilmen who were in charge. The fact was, some Apaches did not understand this Anglo-American concept of civic and committee leadership, and for this reason hesitated to take active command of their assigned positions (Parmee, 1959–1961a: 94–95).

Even among the few citizens' groups that did exist at San Carlos during the time of this study (i.e., women's hospital auxiliary, Boy Scouts, church parish clubs), cooperative activities seldom occurred and inter-group channels of communication were very weak or non-existent.

The management of law and order on the San Carlos Apache Reservation was a major responsibility of the tribal council. Each year it involved the largest council expenditure, which included the salaries of Apache judges, jailers, policemen, and juvenile officers, plus all of their operational and vehicular expenses. From the many interviews with reservation officials, families, and tribal leaders, it was evident that alcoholism and its concurrent side-effects comprised one of the greatest law and order problems for the San Carlos Apaches (Parmee, 1959–1961a: 36–38). As

---

[4] From a personal letter by the author to Marvin Mull, Chairman, San Carlos Apache Tribe, March 8, 1962.

will be seen from the summary of court records below, juveniles (ages 10–17 years) as well as adults were affected.

In June of 1959, a survey of juvenile court records was made covering the period of June 1, 1958, through May 31, 1959. The following is a summary of these findings:

(a) Out of more than 90% of all juveniles arrested, 26% were 16-year-olds, 25% were 17-year-olds, 25% were 15-year-olds, and 14% were 14-year-olds. The remaining 8% or so included age groups 10 through 13 years.

(b) April, May, June, July, August, and December had the highest rate of arrests, averaging 27 cases per month.

(c) The range of charges for arrest ran as follows:

—disorderly conduct, drunkenness, disobedience [5] 55%
—curfew violation 7%
—assault 6%
—carrying a concealed weapon 6%
—theft 5%
—smoking, failure to go to school, running away from home, traffic violation, illicit cohabitation, vandalism, resisting arrest, escape from jail, and parole violation . . . each less than 5%

(d) Out of 180 recorded court decisions, 90 juveniles were given probation, 76 were given jail terms ranging from 10 to more than 120 days, and 14 were given into parental custody. Appeals from parents or relatives often released children before the completion of their terms, but it was the policy of the tribal court to keep each juvenile sentenced to jail at least a few days in his cell in order to "teach him a lesson" (Parmee, 1959–1961a: 80, 82).

Various types of social pressures, derived from remnants of traditional Apache customs and beliefs, frequently caused families and individuals to become discouraged when trying to modernize or improve their home or personal conditions. More traditionally oriented Apaches would accuse such people of being traitors to their God-given culture and becoming like "Whites." If the accused were at all sensitive to such criticisms they sometimes left the reservation or gave up their desires for modernizing (Parmee, 1959–1961a: 95).

. . . Such pressures existed on many reservations, inhibiting attempts at personal achievement among students as well as adults. Both "Danny"

[5] This charge was primarily used against juveniles who had been drinking, causing disorder, and illegally procuring liquor.

and "Jed" had apparently felt the sting of such reprimands. Some Apaches, in fact, were convinced that these social pressures were responsible in part for the low number of Apache college graduates and trained Apache reservation employees (Parmee, 1959–1961a: 95). Understandably, however, not all Apaches heeded these sanctions.

Political Problems

On most reservations as in many non-Indian communities, economic power and political power went hand-in-hand. The San Carlos Reservation was no exception. Agencies like the BIA and Public Health Service were permitted no part in tribal politics; but, by the mere fact of their economic potential, they acted as powerful governing forces on the reservation. The Apache tribal council, on the other hand, as was pointed out earlier in the discussion of community economic problems, was often frustrated in its efforts to legislate new programs or changes in existing ones because of its own economic impotence and its consequent dependency on alien assistance.

To the average Apache reservation inhabitant this gave not only the feeling of being dominated and of being forced into a way of life not of his own choosing, but it also had the demoralizing effect of making him feel helpless and inferior as he watched his elected leaders make often futile demands upon alien people directed by unknown or incomprehensible laws and regulations originated in a place called "Washington."

Many Apaches today have very meager knowledge of the basic principles and designs of democratic community government. Although their traditional forms of social and political organization have long ago been changed, little has been done to teach them the fundamental tenets of the new forms of government. As a result, some Apache leaders today are not informed adequately so that they can function effectively as legislative representatives of their own local districts. This has its deleterious effects upon the people as a whole.

In 1960–61, for example, nearly every Apache interviewed was highly critical of his council. Typical comments included: The council's activities are suspect; sometimes it appears disinterested in its own people; some leaders are self-centered; it doesn't do anything; it is often helpless in times of need (Parmee, 1959–1961b: 27–29). This was more than ordinary bellyaching. It was the result of a continual lack of opportunities for the Apache people to participate in democratic government. It reflected public disfavor over the few local district meetings and the many closed council sessions; over the little effort to inform the public of the "hows" and "whys" of government operations, new programs, and changes in longstanding policies; and over much high level manipulation (Parmee, 1959–1961a: 237–46, 254–56, 272–72a).

Factors Within the Family Environment

Widespread Poverty

At the time of this study, federal, state, and private welfare programs on the San Carlos Reservation spent great sums of money to alleviate the extremely low or non-existent incomes of hundreds of Apache families.[6] The largest of these programs was operated by the local BIA welfare department. Not all Apaches agreed with the manner in which this program functioned, however. Criticism was chiefly aimed at the apparent lack of constructive operational goals and case records, which resulted in a rather arbitrary disbursement of funds (Parmee, 1959–1961a: 154–57). There was also no apparent provisions in the program for the eventual reduction in welfare dependency among Apaches. This writer, for example, observed no efforts being made to assist families in the efficient management of their available incomes, even though it was clearly obvious that such assistance would have helped many cases.

While much of the existing poverty on the San Carlos Reservation was the result of deflated cattle incomes and higher costs of living, as well as widespread unemployment, many families became welfare cases perhaps sooner than necessary because of poor financial planning. Many incurred heavy debts through unwise buying and the over-extension of their credits at the local stores. The following actual case study will illustrate some of the demoralizing effects experienced by many Apache families through the excessive use of credit resources and public welfare.

> The "A" family was once financially solvent. They handled most of their purchasing through one or two of the local traders who conveniently managed most of the family's financial affairs. Mrs. "A" went to the traders' stores and bought what she needed. When Mr. "A" received his cattle check twice each year he simply went to each trader and paid off his entire bill, seldom fully aware of what his money was spent for. He usually was able to cover the bill and that was all that concerned him. He felt pretty good, in fact, because at times there was some cash left over for pocket money, or perhaps for a new car or pickup. Occasionally, when Mr. "A's" bill was very high and there was not going to be much pocket money left over, he simply informed the tribal office to have his check turned over to the stores (this usually happened with a bill at some large store like the Tribal Store) and this way he did not have to bother making the transaction himself.
>
> The "A" family managed well until the prices of cattle dropped. There was a drought and the sales had to be postponed. Then came the day

---

[6] Regrettably, no per capita or total annual expenditure figures were available, but nearly all boarding school children came from welfare recipients. Elderly folks were generally on welfare.

when Mr. "A" could no longer pay off as many of his bills as he had before, and his credit limit was severely curtailed. This put a crimp in the "A" family's style, because they were used to much freer spending, and in fact, it took them some time to adjust to the situation. Now they had accumulated such heavy bills — in comparison to their decreased income — that the traders were forced to curtail the "A" family's credit more and more, and requested that Mr. "A's" income checks be withheld from any member of the family for fear that they would be spent before some of the bills were paid off. From this time on, Mr. "A" was lucky to even see one of his income checks, much less have the pleasure of owning it for a while. This made him very bitter.

As the years passed, Mr. "A's" family grew, and his needs increased — as did his bills — but his income from cattle did not. He worked part-time now to help out a bit, but there simply was not much work he could do on the reservation. His relationship with the traders was no longer very friendly, and he and his wife had to fight for every penny of credit they could get. Sometimes they even tried trading elsewhere, but the other traders on the reservation knew the "A" family's situation and saw that they were poor credit risks. Their requests were gracefully turned aside.

Then Mr. "A" lost his part-time job. It seemed as if Mr. "A" and his family were to face starvation. The little help they formerly received from Mrs. "A's" relatives was now turned down because they were becoming too much of a burden. There were arguments and a few fights — and that ended that. Mr. "A" cursed the stinginess of Mrs. "A's" folks and the two families refused to speak to one another. The one who felt worst of all was Mrs. "A," who was ashamed of their helplessness and sorry for the rift between their families.

Mr. "A" vented more of his anger on the traders who stoically received his abuse but offered him no further credit. Each knew he had already given in to Mr. "A" more than was good for either party. Mr. "A" even made a plea to the tribal council for a horse or a tractor so he could do some farming to help with his family's needs for food — but then he also needed seed, fertilizer, etc., etc. The council was unable to help him. Mr. "A" returned home very dejected, wondering what good the council was if it could not help him.

Mr. "A's" economic problems finally reached a climax when the new school year began. The children needed new shoes, dresses, levis, jackets, etc. and the family simply did not have the funds to cover these new items. Mr. "A" informed Mrs. "A" that she would have to pay a visit to the Welfare Office and ask at least for new clothes. Mrs. "A" was not very happy about this because she had heard that it was not easy to convince that "welfare lady" that help was needed — and besides, she was a bit ashamed to have to sit with all those other women in the waiting room, hearing their gossip about others, and knowing that they would gossip about her as soon as she had gone. Mrs. "A" had never cared to associate with them before, and now it seemed they were all in the same predicament.

It was a bit of a struggle — with the embarrassments, the language problems, and all — but Mrs. "A" finally managed to get some help from welfare. She even managed to get a couple of the older children off to boarding school. They usually kept the food bills so high and were getting a bit hard to handle, anyway, she thought. But Mrs. "A" was sorry to have to send the oldest girl away. She had become a real companion now that the family was no longer on such good terms with her relatives. Mr. "A" appeared to be getting more and more despondent, more bitter and quite complaining. He could not find a job and soon got tired of sitting around the house listening to the children make noises and Mrs. "A's" incessant chatter. He knew she was unhappy about the fight with her relatives and having to accept welfare, but there did not seem to be much he could do about it. To him, it seemed like a dirty deal all the way around: no more herd, no jobs, and the traders turning their backs whenever they saw him coming. Sometimes it all made him so mad and disgusted that he would leave his home and go off to visit with some of the other men who were hanging around like him. Some of them had the same hard-luck stories he had to tell, so at least they were sympathetic company. Once in a while if anyone had a few extra dollars, they even went over to the bootleggers and bought a few bottles of "brew." It was something to do, anyway.

The following year Mr. "A" tried to send off two more of the older children to boarding school, but he was told that the schools were all filled up. These two now had to go to public school. Mrs. "A" was really glad. She did not care to be separated from her children, even though Mr. "A" did not seem to mind it in the least. During the first week of public school it seemed as if everything was going to work out quite well, for the kids seemed to enjoy their new experience. The delight was short-lived, however, for one day one of the children brought home a bill for books and supplies. The other said he needed a special kind of gym shoes.

The children were afraid to go back to school without the money so they stayed home for the next few days while Mr. "A" went to see the chairman of the education committee and the reservation principal. He did not trust his wife in this important matter, and besides, he felt it was about time he gave those people a piece of his mind and told them what he thought of their education program. He did, too. He told them that he was a high school graduate. He was not uneducated like "some of these Indians around here." He even learned a trade. But what good did it do him? He had no job, no money. His wife had to ask for welfare. His children needed new clothes, they wanted more meat to eat — and that public school had the nerve to ask him for $12 for books and $6 for special gym shoes! What kind of a gym did they have down there, anyway, that his boy had to have special shoes to walk on it? That must be for rich people, for white people! What happened to our own high school? Everything was better then.

But Mr. "A" did not return home dissatisfied. The chairman of the education committee talked the credit manager into letting Mr. "A" have enough credit to buy the gym shoes and some more food besides, and the reservation principal called the public school and asked them to waive the costs of the books. They reluctantly complied. During the next few months when Mr. "A" received a dividend check for some special VA benefits, he and Mrs. "A" kept it a secret even from their friends, and then went out and spent it as they pleased. It was a long time since they had had the pleasure of such freedom. The creditors could "scratch for the money" as far as Mr. "A" was concerned. They controlled all of his cattle income by now, anyway, he lamented.

Mr. "A" and his friends complained vehemently when the tribal council tried to pass a bill for income taxes on cattle sales, but it went through. Some political machine, that council, Mr. "A" and his friends thought. There was no doubt in their minds that it was in cahoots with the trading enterprises and the public schools to exploit unfortunate Indians like themselves. They agreed such things deserved as little of their support as possible (taken from Parmee, 1959–1961c: 11–17).

The ability to plan an efficient family budget is not an inherent characteristic among any people. It is a learned behavior; and many people the world over, even in countries where thrift is a matter of national pride, find it difficult to effectively assimilate this behavior. So much more difficult was it then for Apaches, who, less than four generations ago, "had been a subsistence-oriented group, operating on a seasonal basis, placing little value on thrift or on sustained labor throughout the year . . . [after which] being placed on the reservation, most of the Indians lived almost thirty years on rations provided by the United States Government" (Getty, 1961–62: 185).

When, in addition, one considers the tradition of economic inter-dependence within extended family and clan relations . . . as well as the apparent absence of opportunities to learn about new forms of family economics, it is of little wonder that many Apaches were inexperienced and inept in the art of budgeting. Coupled with generally low incomes and large numbers of children, such conditions caused many Apache families to be hard pressed for school clothes, books and supplies, and adequate household facilities for homework and study. It seems altogether possible that existing welfare services on the San Carlos Reservation may perpetuate the economic dependency of Apache families unless changes are made in some of its fundamental practices.

Breakdown in Traditional Apache Family Relations

[The present disintegration of] . . . the traditional Apache gotah system of family authority and inter-dependency . . . was evidenced by the literature (Kaut, 1957: 84; Marinsek, 1960: 37–38) and illustrated by some of the data regarding family economics (the case of the "A" family). In addition to the obvious material effects produced by such changes, it was apparent from much of the interview data that Apache methods of childrearing — particularly at the teen-age level — had changed considerably in form, if not in function.

It was interesting to note that while Apache parents frequently criticized teachers and school officials for reprimanding Apache children in class, many of the same parents used almost identical methods of discipline — not within the traditional setting of the gotah or household, but in the setting of the tribal court system modeled after Anglo-American patterns of jurisprudence. It was not uncommon for a parent experiencing difficulty in disciplining a teen-age child to call upon the tribal court to deal firmly with the youth; even if it meant issuing a jail term. The judge would comply; then when it was thought that the child had served long enough to have "learned a lesson," he was released into the custody of his parents (Parmee, 1959–1961a: 80, 82).

The traditional element of public ridicule entered into this picture at the juvenile court hearing when parents of accused children were asked to testify against them before the entire courtroom assemblage, including judges, police officers, and other arrested youths and their parents. The following actual court incident will help to illustrate this form of behavior:

> The mother was asked to testify against her daughters. This she did with no restraint. I don't know what she said but frequently the two girls would glance at their mother with rather hurt expressions on their faces, and once in a while they would look at the floor and shake their heads negatively. Both girls were quite nervous and one was on the verge of crying, but she tried hard not to.
>
> Both were neatly dressed and sat close to one another. When the sentence was passed, the one girl nearly burst into tears, but after a few words from her sister (who seemed older) she subsided. At one time the older sister even made the younger one smile. There was obvious comradeship here and mutual support.
>
> After giving testimony, the mother simply turned her back on the two girls and walked out the door. They looked after her with blank expressions. Then, after the hearing the girls walked away towards the prison together, arm-in-arm (Parmee, 1959–1961a: 83).

Parental rejection of the two sisters was evident in the above case, but it appeared to be offset somewhat by sibling "esprit de corps." In some cases, however, the parents seemed almost vengeful by the severity of their testimonies. As one Apache court employee put it:

> Often when the mother comes into court to testify against her daughter, she tries to be mean and says all sorts of things so her daughter won't disobey again. This morning, that mother told the judge all of her daugh-

ter's private affairs; what boyfriends she had, how she acts, and all kinds of things like that in order to embarrass the girl. That's not right. Those are private matters. Those are family matters which should not be discussed here in court in front of all these people. The daughter tries hard not to cry though (Parmee, 1959–1961a: 84).

Apache court discipline was also used for drop-outs and for children delinquent in school. In fact, during the spring of 1959, when teen-age drop-outs had become particularly prevalent, the tribal education committee agreed to place the full responsibility for this problem in the hands of the tribal judge, who promptly announced that he would put the parents as well as the students in jail if they refused to comply with school attendance regulations (Parmee, 1959–1961a: 71–74).

Opinions regarding the constructive effectiveness of this system of discipline varied greatly at the time. Some Apache leaders agreed with it whole-heartedly, as the decision of the education committee indicated. Most Anglos felt it was a cruel and rather unconstructive way to deal with adolescents, predicting that it would have serious harmful effects on their personalities.[7]

This last view appeared quite plausible, when considering the many juvenile cases in which it was evident that current values, behavior patterns, and institutions had failed to adequately replace their earlier traditional forms; failed for parents as well as children, but primarily for the children who were expected to endure these conflicts and still return to school each day with minds at ease, eager to assimilate the teachings of an alien culture.

FACTORS WITHIN THE PROGRAM OF FORMAL EDUCATION

Special Needs of Apaches at Primary Grade Levels
Inadequately Met By Schools

As a starting point for the discussion of this topic, the author again cites the words of the recent former chairman of the San Carlos Apache Tribe:

> . . . I suspect our schools are not beginning to tackle adequately the basic difficulties of language — the simple problem of communication — of understanding and being understood — which confronts on all sides, the non-acculturated Indian child as he gets further along in school where both ideas and vocabulary become increasingly complex. I suspect that this failure to comprehend on the part of the Indian child accounts in large measure for the lessening of interest and enthusiasm for school,

---

[7] Opinions expressed primarily by school administrators and the local welfare worker.

which I am told begins for Indian children along about the fifth grade (Wesley, 1961: 4).

The findings of this study indeed bear out the suspicions of Wesley quoted above. With the project office located at the San Carlos federal day school for several months, the author had many opportunities to observe the methods used in teaching Apache elementary students. All of the teachers at that time, even the most dedicated ones, lacked special language training to aid their Apache-speaking pupils. Even those teachers working with the Beginners' classes (in which nearly every enrolled pupil knew almost no English at the start) admitted that what they themselves lacked in training, they had to make do with ingenuity. Teachers' meetings were seldom held and virtually no assistance was given to the teachers during the school year.

As the youngest Apache students moved from grade to grade, their difficulties with language compounded as the work became more demanding. Competition at the Indian schools was relatively light, however, since most of the teachers were taught that Indians disliked competition, although occasionally favors or prizes were won by high achievers. Low achievers were made to feel as good as the rest even though the teacher had little time to spend giving them remedial work.

Some teachers solved the problem by dividing up the classes into various ability groups for reading, arithmetic, and other subjects. In one of the classes where this author did some substitute teaching, there were no less than five such groups for reading and arithmetic. It was extremely difficult to keep four of the groups actively working while testing the recitation of the fifth group. Many were left to idle away their time after completing desk assignments. Statements made by the reservation principal at that time supported these observations.

> . . . Some of this lack of interest and progress in learning is definitely the teachers' fault. Every time I walk into a class up here — and I do mean it has been the same every single time — I come in and find at least 50% of the students drawing pictures or just wasting time. And I've done this dozens of times, and it has always been the same. I think a lot of those kids are just passing the time of day (Parmee, 1959–1961a: 188).

Charges and counter-charges kept shifting the blame for the slow academic progress of Apache students in the reservation day schools. Teachers blamed it on the lack of proper teaching aids and classes that were too large for the amount of remedial work needed by the students.[8] Another BIA educator of rank returned much of the fault to the teachers, some

---

[8] At San Carlos Day School the classes averaged between 25 and 35 students in 1960.

of whom, he said, had a "very poor" knowledge of correct English. In confirmation of his argument he recalled watching one teacher make grammatical errors in no less than eight out of ten sentences that had been written on the blackboard for students to copy (Parmee, 1959–1961a: 187).

To what extent were Apache students entering the public schools after the fourth grade actually retarded? A Globe grammar school official stated that most entering Apache pupils were ill-prepared for public school work. Their knowledge of English was so poor that it was difficult to teach them anything new. Although remedial reading courses were offered in the Globe and Ft. Thomas schools, many Apaches apparently refused to take advantage of them (Parmee, 1959–1961a: 196).

The inadequate preparation of Apache teen-age students in the higher grade levels was evident to some degree from their low grade-point averages and the extent of the age-grade lag in grades 4 through 12. One further attempt was made in 1961 to test the validity of these findings after the project staff fell heir to a considerable body of materials from one of the federal reservation school fourth grade classes; the materials consisted of the pupils' entire year's work in art, mathematics, spelling, theme-writing, English grammar, geography, and science.

This material was brought for analysis and appraisal to the 1961 Workshop for Teachers of Bilingual Students, at the University of Arizona. Three public school teachers of the intermediary grade level (grades 4–6) spent several hours reviewing the work of every pupil, and came up with the following conclusions concerning both the extent of the students' scholastic progress and the nature of the teacher's techniques for instruction.

The Performance of the Class. (a) The students with the lowest achievement test scores appeared to be "down-right illiterate," responding in a manner that was "far below the fourth grade level."

(b) Those students with the highest achievement test scores produced work that might be considered to be on a par with average non-Indian public school students, but they would probably find it difficult to compete in next year's fifth grade public school class, where the competition would be greater and the work somewhat more advanced.

(c) Many of the middle-ranking students of this class did work that was far below the normal fourth grade level, especially in English and mathematics. Some of their work indicated only a first grade arithmetic concept level.

(d) Much of the work of the class showed "great numbers of errors, which indicated either a real lack of understanding of fundamental concepts, or carelessness from poor motivation, or both." Many of the pupils "obviously did not comprehend or try to follow the teacher's instructions on worksheets and tests."

(e) According to the standard performance indicated by these materials, the evaluation committee decided that the class as a whole was "poorly prepared for fifth grade public school work."

An Evaluation of the Teacher's Techniques. The panel of three public school teachers admitted that they were being highly critical of the teacher's techniques, by basing their judgment on the recommended standards of teaching, which are for any teacher difficult to follow precisely. They also admitted that this was not entirely an equitable appraisal because it was based primarily on the written work in class only, and not on the oral and illustrative work that presumably complemented the former in the classroom. In spite of these shortcomings, some interesting insights were revealed by the panel:

(a) Judging by the written material that was presented to the class throughout the year, the teacher seemed to be "lost, groping around, and having great difficulty in coping with his pupils' academic problems."

(b) His methods seemed inconsistent, unimaginative, and often confusing to the pupil; on the whole, poor planning was evident.

(c) None of the tests or papers showed any corrections of the errors that were made in great numbers.

(d) Some of the tests that were given to the pupils contained language errors that were made by the teacher. On the whole, the work that the teacher had prepared for his class was sloppy.

(e) No apparent attempt had been made by the teacher to insist on following instructions — or if he did, there was no noticeable improvement throughout the year.

(f) Many of the work sheets that were made up for the class were so poorly worded that their instructions were unclear.

(g) According to the available material, no apparent effort was made on the part of the teacher to encourage his pupils to express themselves in terms of elements from their own cultural background.

From these statements, made by the experienced teachers of the fourth grade level, one could conclude that this particular class of pupils was poorly prepared to meet the demands of the integrated class in public school the following year. By the end of the year, many were not even capable of doing fourth grade work and their teacher was apparently unable to cope with the serious problem of academic retardation that faced him. The outlook for his pupils' success in the higher grade levels appeared rather dim, indeed.

Deficiencies in the Education Program at the Junior and Senior High School Levels

As can be seen from the enrollment figures presented earlier in this report, the BIA San Carlos Agency was increasingly successful in its efforts to enroll Apaches in boarding school. Between 1958 and 1961, federal boarding school enrollment expanded 51.3%, until it included more than 16% of the total student population on the reservation. While some agency officials (i.e., the reservation principal and the social worker) acclaimed this as an achievement, one Area Office administrator expressed concern and disapproval:

> "I realize only too well that home conditions on the San Carlos Reservation are as bad as you could find anywhere, but there are altogether too many Apaches being sent to boarding school."
>
> It was this person's opinion that the federal boarding schools were "a blessing" to many unfortunate youngsters from poor homes, but such schools were not the panacea for all the ills of Apache youngsters. It would be better, he said, to have more of them living at home, attending public school in the normal fashion with the availability of a stronger guidance program to help those who are having serious difficulties. He concluded by saying that the primary field for the solution of the educational problems at San Carlos was right on the reservation itself (Parmee, 1959–1961b; 211–12).

Public school officials expressed an even dimmer view of local agency policies regarding boarding school enrollment. One administrator went so far as to say that Apaches should quit seeking "the easy way out" by going to all-Indian boarding schools, and should instead learn to "cut the mustard" in the public schools along with everyone else (Parmee, 1959–1961b: 215).

Basically, the three chief criticisms against the boarding school program were:

(a) Apaches in boarding schools were isolated from non-Indians, socially as well as competitively. This isolation would eventually prolong the process of integration into Anglo society, which non-Apaches felt was a desirable thing. . . . Even some tribal officials agreed that school integration was an essential factor in the improvement of Apache education (Wesley, 1961: 5).

(b) None of the public school people interviewed felt that the academic standards at the boarding schools were as high as those of the average public day school. The then chairman of the tribal education committee also expressed the view that boarding school training was inadequate to meet the requirements for college preparatory training.[9]

(c) One shortcoming in the boarding school program, criticized at various times by Apache leaders, is the lack of special facilities for the emotionally disturbed Indian child (Wesley, 1961: 6–7). Each year found teen-agers with serious personal problems being dismissed from public, mission, and even boarding schools. They returned to the reservation to generally poor home conditions and no future for which to live. Most of these students soon wound up in jail, incurring on occasion lengthy sentences, when instead they needed psychiatric care and a more constructive environment (Parmee, 1959–1961a: 24, 59–60).

At the time of this study in 1960, most Apache teen-agers were attending public schools; and, as already seen from the analysis of school records, many were in serious academic trouble. Aside from the various existing personal and home environmental factors over which the schools had no control, there were factors in the public school program itself which obstructed the successful education of Apaches. It should be stated at the outset, however, that the public schools were not entirely to blame for these deficiencies. A part of the fault lay with those who maneuvered the change-over from reservation Indian schools to public schools: namely, the Bureau of Indian Affairs and Apache leaders, who supported the plan without raising serious objections to its shortcomings.

Although the change-over . . . had begun and ended long before this study began, there was ample evidence from the interviews with school officials indicating that prior to the arrival of the first large influx of Apache students after 1949 no significant preparation had been made in the way of extra remedial facilities, curriculum adjustments, or teacher orientation. As one school administrator put it:

> We first knew about it three months before school got out. That was in the spring. In the fall of that year we had them in our schools. There wasn't any preparation — other than physical and financial [10] — made for the change-over. It happened all at once (Parmee, 1959–1961a: 199).

Considering the inadequacies in the program of the on-reservation government schools, it is not difficult to understand the extreme handicaps many Apaches must have felt in the public school education program without any of the provisions mentioned above. Even by 1960, nearly

[9] Personal conversation with the author.
[10] Referring to enlargement of the physical plant and staff, and establishment of Johnson-O'Malley support.

ten years after the first large group of Apaches had entered the public high schools, little had been achieved in the way of devising special academic programs for the Indian students beyond the limited acceleration of remedial reading facilities (Parmee, 1959–1961a: 196).

Instead of tribal, BIA, and public school cooperation in a planned program that might have aided Apache youngsters with the transition from federal to public schools, the public schools were apparently left on their own to make the best of it. Some did by putting Apaches in so-called "slow-groups" (Parmee, 1959–1961a: 197–98), and by granting social promotions to a large number. At Globe the guidance counselor was expected to allot half his working time to Indian student problems, while at Ft. Thomas the school superintendent-principal made himself available at all times for such purposes.[11]

In spite of the available counseling services in the public schools, the standard methods for evaluating the nature and extent of Apache personal and academic problems and the techniques for measuring individual Apache potentials and interests seemed quite inadequate. Bernardoni's findings . . . at least showed the shortcomings and pitfalls inherent in tests like the Lorge-Thorndike series, when using them to compare Indians with non-Indians (Bernardoni, 1960: 11). Where language differences made comprehension of the test difficult for the student and the lack of a double set of known cultural standards obstructed the testor's comparison of the responses, such devices could only be partially successful in achieving the goals for which they were intended.

It was also evident at the time of this study that some of the schools, and especially the BIA agency, were not maintaining adequate records for the purpose of periodically evaluating the students' progress and the program's effectiveness. All of the data summaries presented thus far, with the exception of the school enrollment figures and the Lorge-Thorndike test results, were collected and organized by the project staff. Although each student had his individual record file at the school he was currently attending, the author knew of no efforts on the part of school administrators to compile such records into periodic summaries for the purposes of trend evaluations [12] (Parmee, 1959–1961b: 1–6).

At times it appeared that school staff evaluations of Apaches expressed

---

[11] The guidance counselor at Globe was reputed to have spent very little time doing any counseling at all (Parmee, 1959–1961a: 196–97). In fact, he himself admitted to the author once that very few Indian students (boys in particular) ever came to him with problems [notes from case history of "Bert"]. This perhaps explains in part why some Apache students like "Bert" did not even know of the counselor's services.

[12] The record of one year's total absences by the Bylas school principal was the sole exception known.

more of personal views and impressions than validated findings. A brief sample of collected comments should suffice to illustrate this point:

> They [Apaches] could work as well as other students if they would get out of their I-don't-care attitudes (public school teachers) (Parmee, 1959–1961a: 193).
>
> Apaches are one of the smartest Indian tribes in the Southwest, and also one of the most hostile, most stubborn, and meanest. . . . They are a bit lazy, too (public school employee) (Parmee, 1959–1961a: 213–14).
>
> The trouble is, these [Apache] people don't want education. They think it's poison. They hold ceremonies every year to do away with all the evils their kids have picked up in school! (reservation school principal) (Crumrine 1959: 29).
>
> Apaches are at the bottom of the barrel as far as Indians go. They are the dumbest and worst off economically. They don't want to be educated, and they don't want to get out from under the government (public school counselor) (Crumrine 1959: 40).

It would have been difficult to estimate how many non-Apache school personnel shared these views, but it was plain enough to see that prejudice was not restricted to any one school or occupational level. Some of these views among public school people remained because few ever came on the reservation to see things for themselves. Out of the few who did, some went back with their suspicions even more strongly confirmed than before — or so they said.

Conflicts Arising out of the Orientation of the Education Program

Thus far, much has been said about the lack of Apache participation in the operation of the education program. This alien management of a key reservation development program did not permit Apaches to guide the fate of their own future, nor did it provide them with the opportunities for learning how to do so (Wesley, 1961: 7). Apaches resented being denied this privilege and did what they could to fight against it (Parmee, 1959–1961a: 230–309).

A second fundamental criticism that Apache leaders expressed again and again in opposition to the education program evolved out of a conflict of basic goals for the program.

> I realize the fact that there are people who talk about integration, assimilation, acculturation, first class citizenship, etc. But you know the American Indians have something different that was bestowed upon them by the grace of God, such as our songs, tribal dances, arts and crafts, our religion, games and stories. Some of these are fast disappearing and my question is: are we going to continue to lose these precious gifts through

this process of education or becoming White men? Or should we continue to identify ourselves as Indians, which to me is no disgrace (Wesley, 1961: 7).

The "people" Wesley referred to were the administrators of agencies managing Indian affairs, school officials, and off-reservation politicians. It was these people, who by means of their economic and political power and their educational advantage held the fate of many reservation programs in their hands. Directing programs of integration to facilitate the earliest possible assimilation of Indians into the larger American culture was a primary orientation of their thoughts and actions.

This orientation was expressed in their public speeches (Head, 1960: 24), in their programs of relocation, public school integration (Parmee, 1959–1961a: 197, 301), and tribal government, and in their day-to-day dealings with Indians (Parmee, 1959–1961a: 301). Tribal leaders like Annie Wauneka (1963) and Clarence Wesley (1961) tended to react negatively to this imposed Anglo orientation of Indian programs, as did many of their followers, even though they worked hard to bring such programs to their respective reservations. Thus, while they feared the implementation of these programs might on the one hand accelerate the extinction of Indian culture, they also could not deny the fact that formal education was a key factor in solving existing social and economic problems, by raising the educational standards of their people.

Apache teen-agers did not express the same fears as the older generation. From the many student interviews and case histories, like those presented in this study, it was evident that some were not so concerned about the future — not even their own, much less the future of their whole tribe. On the other hand, others, such as "Jed," felt they could be educated and still remain Apache. To them "Apache" had a different meaning from that of the "old folks." It was less characterized perhaps by ancient ceremonials, mythology, and socio-religious customs, but it meant "Apache" nevertheless, and its principal features were clearly modern. As the new-generation Apache tribal chairman described it:

> If we have better housing, health, better jobs on the reservation, does this mean that we won't be Indians anymore? No, it doesn't. If an Indian wants to be an Indian he can be one all of his life. You don't forget your Indian upbringing easily, even when you have the highest education (Mull, 1963: 30–31).

Older, more tradition-oriented Apaches like Wesley failed to see things quite this way. Much of their lives' efforts were spent in trying to preserve the many unique traditional aspects of Apache culture that were "bestowed upon them by the grace of God" (Wesley, 1961:7). Less educated Apaches, however, could not always, like Wesley, see the positive as well as the negative effects of education, and their resistance to many programs of modernization directly influenced the lives of their children, for it made understanding difficult between the young and the old, and added further to the already staggering proportions of existing teen-age problems.

REFERENCES

Arizona Commission of Indian Affairs. *Survey of the San Carlos Reservation*, 1964.

Bernardoni, L. C. Analysis of results of Lorge-Thorndike Intelligence Tests with Apache students. Personal communication, 1960.

Crumrine, L. S. Field notes from San Carlos, 1959. Arizona-Sonora Files. University of Arizona, Tucson.

Getty, H. T. "San Carlos Apache Cattle Industry," *Human Organization*, vol. 20, no. 4 (1962).

Head, W. "The Navajo People and the Future," *Third Annual Conference on Navajo Education*. Flagstaff, Ariz., 1960.

Kaut, C. *The Western Apache Clan System*. University of New Mexico Publications in Anthropology, no. 9. Albuquerque: University of New Mexico, 1957.

Marinsek, E. A. *The Effect of Cultural Difference in the Education of Apache Indians*. Albuquerque: University of New Mexico, 1960.

Mull, M. Mimeographed speech. *Fourth Annual Indian Education Conference*. Arizona State University, Tempe, Arizona, 1963.

Parmee, E. A. San Carlos Field Log. Ms. Arizona-Sonora Files, University of Arizona, Tucson.

———. San Carlos Report. Ms. Arizona-Sonora Files, University of Arizona, Tucson.

———. Basic Outline of San Carlos Report: Topic III. Ms. Arizona-Sonora Files, University of Arizona, Tucson, 1959–61.

———. "Social Factors Affecting the Education of San Carlos Apaches," *Annual Conference of the Coordinating Council for Research in Indian Education*. Phoenix, Ariz., 1961.

Robison, H. E., E. H. Spicer, et al. *The San Carlos Apache Indian Reservation: A Resources Development Study*. Stanford Research Institute, Phoenix, Ariz., 1954.

Wauneka, A. Recorded speech. *Fourth Annual Indian Education Conference*. Arizona State University, Tempe, 1963.

Wesley, C. "Indian Education," *Journal of American Indian Education*, vol. 1, no. 1 (1961).

FURTHER READINGS

Hobart, C. W., and C. S. Brant. "Eskimo education, Danish and Canadian: a comparison." *Canadian Review of Sociology and Anthropology*, vol. 3 (May 1966).

Jocano, F. Landa. *Growing up in a Philippine barrio*. New York: Holt, Rinehart and Winston, 1969.

Spindler, George D. *Urbanization and education in a rural German village*. Stanford: Department of Anthropology, Stanford University, 1969 (mimeo).

Wolcott, Harry F. *A Kwakiutl village and school*. New York: Holt, Rinehart and Winston, 1967.

Wylie, Laurence. *Village in the Vaucluse*. New York: Harper & Row, 1957, 1964.

26

Comitas describes the "almost perfect congruence" between the structure of education and pattern of social stratification in prerevolutionary Bolivia. Postrevolutionary "divisions in Bolivian education," he finds, "correspond closely with the old social divisions of Bolivian society," especially in that "the rural segment is virtually barred from participation on . . . secondary and university levels." The Bolivian revolutionary politic is sustaining, in effect if not by design, prerevolutionary distributions of power and privilege through educational structure. One argument to explain this seeming anomaly is that the revolutionary order has not yet succeeded in "revolutionizing" education; another (preferred by Comitas) is that the revolution was perhaps meant only to succeed a given social apparatus, and not thoroughly reform it. The result, either way, is a disaffected segment of the population, and Comitas draws the implications of that sentiment both to theoretical interests in revolutionary relationships of education and social reordering, and to the sociopolitical future of Bolivia. Much of the minority concern in America with the implications of current trends in "compensatory" and bilingual education and of the practical, if benign, "oppression" of our part-societies — Chicano, black, Indian, et al. — to our future, educational and otherwise, parallels his insights into the Bolivian condition. Mr. Comitas is Professor, Department of Anthropology, Columbia University, and Teachers College, Columbia University. Among his publications is Caribbeana 1900–1965: A Topical Bibliography *(Seattle: University of Washington Press, 1968).*

LAMBROS COMITAS

Education and Social Stratification in Contemporary Bolivia

The Bolivian Revolution of 1952 is regarded by many as the only significant social revolution in contemporary South America. Whether or not this revolution effected any radical change in the stratification system, however, still remains open to question, since Bolivia has received a minimum of scientific attention in comparison with most other Latin American countries. This paper attempts a limited analysis of this critical question through the examination of one key area of social activity, that of education. While the dangers of a relatively narrow focus on a multi-faceted problem are many, I should stress, in defense of the procedure, that the core importance of education makes it a productive point of entry for the study of complex social systems. As anthropology shifts to

From *Transactions* of the New York Academy of Sciences, vol. 29, no. 7, pp. 935–948, L. Comitas. © The New York Academy of Sciences; 1967; Reprinted by permission.

research of complex sociocultural units, the theoretical and methodological necessity for the systematic development of such vantage points becomes obvious.

To place the substantive argument which follows in clearer perspective, I must first deal briefly with two linked issues — first, the functions of education in society; and, second, the social structure and stratification system of traditional Bolivia.

In any social system, those institutions integrally involved with education can have but one of two basic social functions. The first and most significant function is to maintain and to facilitate the existing social order. This function appears to have been operative in the overwhelming majority of societies known. Education, in these cases, provides a fundamental mechanism for maintaining the sociocultural status quo through systematic and culturally acceptable training of the young for effective participation in the system. In general, the more stable and enduring the society and its culture are, the more congruous is the fit between education and the total system. Where stability is the operative function, any disjunction between education and the social system is predictably remedied through reform of the educational institutions and not through reform of the society. The objective of such institutional reform is to correct the balance and congruity, thereby readjusting the threatened social equilibrium.

In a number of relatively rare cases, the function of education is revolutionary in nature — to promote and secure the restructuring of a given society through the deliberate introduction of a type of education significantly different from that offered to the older generation. In these cases, educational change historically has followed drastic social, political, and economic upheaval and has been utilized by the new leadership to consolidate, to protect, and to refine the revolutionary gain. Education, in these instances, plays a more dynamic and creative social role, helping to reformulate the structure and reorient the values of society. This is a more positive and, I believe, a more defensible view than that taken by Talcott Parsons, who argues that the extreme concern of revolutionary regimes with "education" reflects their need to "discipline," in terms of revolutionary values, the population over which they have gained control but which did not participate in the revolutionary movement (Parsons, 1951, p. 528).

Historic examples of the revolutionary function of education are relatively uncommon. Certainly for the 20th century there are only limited examples even though this century has probably experienced more "revolutionary" activity than any comparable period in the past. Turkey under Kemal Ataturk in 1923, the Soviet Union in the 1920's, present-day China with its Red Guards, and drastic educational upheaval, and undoubtedly

Castro's Cuba, supply us with illustrations of thoroughgoing revolutionary systems of education. In these nations, as in a few others, education was or is being used to carry forward the social restructuring by preparing young citizens for life in a manner and with a content which radically breaks with traditions of the past. In essence, a true revolution requires the development of a new education to help build the new society as well as to safeguard against social reaction and regression and the possible collapse of the new system. However, if over a period of time, the revolution is consolidated and protected, the function of education shifts from revolution back to one of social maintenance — to help assure the stability of the new order. Consequently, while the revolutionary function in education is of fundamental importance in any radical and permanent reformation of society, it is, almost by definition, transitional in nature. The social raison d'etre for its existence diminishes once the social reorganization has been established. If this argument holds, every "revolutionary" society, to be in fact revolutionary, needs to initiate and support a revolutionary education, even if only for a relatively limited period of time. It follows then that an analysis of education in a society labeled "revolutionary" should be uniquely suited to assess the intensity and social impact of any centralized attempts to change the traditional patterns of stratification since such attempts are the keys to a successful and completed revolution and education an integral part of the process. In addition, through the examination of the organization, operation, objectives and content of education, a significant portion of the conscious and unconscious intent of a "revolutionary" regime can be gauged. It is with these particular ends in mind that I turn to an examination of pre- and post-revolutionary Bolivia.

Bolivia has an estimated population of only 3½ million, one of the smallest in South America, despite the fact that it is the fifth largest country on the continent. In economic terms, it competes with Haiti as the poorest nation in the New World, with an estimated per capita income of approximately \$150 a year.[1] Culturally, Bolivia is almost prototypical of the Indo-American culture area as defined by Elman Service (1955). Fully two-thirds of the population are racially and culturally identifiable as Aymara or Quechua Indians, the impoverished descendants of the Incaic high civilizations of aboriginal America. The high density of this indigen-

---

[1] Accurate economic statistics for Bolivia are difficult to obtain. However, the 1966 edition of the Gallatin Annual of International Business puts Bolivia's per capita income at about \$154, the second lowest in Latin America, Haiti being the lowest. This positioning compares favorably with that established in Mikoto Usui and E. E. Hagen's reliable 1957 survey, *World Income*, which lists Bolivia's per capita income as \$99, the lowest in Latin America, and Haiti's at \$100, the second lowest.

ous population at the time of conquest, the complexity of the pre-Hispanic Indian societies, the harsh nature of the highland environment and the specific forms of socioeconomic exploitation were all significant variables in the formation of a social system which existed throughout much of the country's colonial and Republican history, and in some aspects persists to the present day.

Following the Conquest, a sharply segmented society developed consisting, at first, of two absolutely differentiated, hierarchically placed social sections, articulated only through the economic and regulative pressures of the socially superordinate segment, which was and remained numerically very small. Composed of the original Spanish settlers and their descendants and of a small but steady infusion of other Europeans, this superordinate group was the carrier of either Hispanic or Western European culture or the creolized variants of it. With its control of the latifundia and the other strategic resources of the territory, with its domination of a theoretically centralized but essentially loosely integrated political system, and with its preference for Castillian to the almost total exclusion of native languages as mediums of communication, this closed social segment developed aristocratic values and the behavior to match. Not unexpectedly, then, the sociocultural gulf between the groups and the requirements of the economic system gave rise to upper segment convictions and rationalizations that Indians were subhuman, no more than beasts of burden, and carriers of a culture that could only be despised.

The subordinate segment was totally Indian, and it included the vast majority of the colonial population. Its adaptation to European cultural patterns was selective and incomplete. Only those European elements necessary for social and economic survival were assimilated or syncretized. Consequently, a considerable portion of the culture of this social segment remained indisputably either Aymara or Quechua and, over time, even European-derived patterns developed an identifiably Indian cast.

As in the rest of the Andean highlands, two organizational alternatives were possible for the rural indigenous population, depending to a large degree on local circumstance. For inhabitants of economically marginal lands, the modal reaction to the Conquest was social retreat and coalescence into substantially closed, corporate communities with the concomitant development of defensive attitudes and behavior. For the indigenous inhabitants in fertile and accessible regions there was no choice; forced labor on the latifundia was the rule. In either situation, the Indian population was relegated to subordinate, sometimes almost slavelike, positions in the social hierarchy, positions which generated deferential cultural attitudes and styles toward members of the upper segment. Deference and servility were the reactions to force, and there is no evidence to indicate that this behavior and the accompanying values demonstrated even grudging acceptance of or consensus about the rightness of the social system. A peasant, speaking of the life of less than twenty years ago, said:

> Before we were slaves because we were stupid, we didn't understand what was going on. We didn't have anybody to defend us and we were afraid to do anything for fear that the patron would beat us. We didn't know why we were beaten. We didn't know about our rights (Muratorio, 1966, p. 5).

Throughout almost all of its post-Conquest history, Bolivia was socially and culturally segmented: The *blancos*, or masters and exploiters, were culturally European, and they occupied the highest status points in the society; the *Indios*, or exploited workers, were culturally Aymara or Quechua, and they filled the lowest status position of the system. A structurally intermediate social segment developed later. Generally referred to in Bolivia as *cholos*, the members of this stratum are analagous to the *mestizos* and *ladinos* of other Latin American countries. Primarily town and city dwellers, *cholos*, of either Indian or mixed descent, have taken much of Hispano-Bolivian national culture, but they are not culturally homologous to the superordinate segment. Concentrating on small businesses, middlemen operations and transport, *cholos* traditionally have been disliked by the elites, feared by the Indians, and avoided by both.

In political terms, early Bolivia and the viceroyalty of which it was a part can best be categorized as a conquest state with a stratification system based on the unilateral application of force. Later developments during the Republican period did little to effect fundamental changes in the bases of social inequality. Social accommodations to force did not lead to acceptance of the system. In this regard, Bolivia was never feudal, as was Medieval Europe, where unequal distribution of opportunity could be part of the normal order of things and where social consensus could validate inequality (Smith, 1966, p. 166). In a recent article, M. G. Smith has referred to a variety of basically nonconsensual societies as "unstable mixed systems." He notes for the Latin American variants in this category, among which I would include Bolivia, that:

> Systems of this sort may endure despite evident inequalities, dissent and apathy, partly through force, partly through inertia, partly because their organizational complexity and structural differentiation inhibits the emergence of effective large-scale movements with coherent programs (Smith, 1966, p. 172).

For present purposes, it is not necessary to find the precise sociological label for traditional Bolivia. It suffices to state that rigid stratification was at the root of the system, that aspects of cultural and social pluralism were evident, and that the structure successfully inhibited social mobility. Status in traditional Bolivia was characteristically ascriptive, based on birth into a particular social stratum and community. Differential rewards accrued to each social segment, and the system of distribution of such rewards was first protected by naked force and then by a juridical and political system dominated by the elites.

In such a social framework, it is not difficult to understand why systematic formal education for the Indian population was not considered a necessary governmental or social function for well over four centuries. The efforts made in education, particularly on the university level, were essentially reserved for the children of the social elite and were located in urban centers of population. Urban education in Bolivia has long continuity.[2] Aside from occasional lip service to the idea of Indian education and the occasional mission or parochial school in the countryside, almost no educational facilities were extended to the Indian until 1929. In that year, the State decreed that agricultural proprietors with more than 25 workers were obliged to establish primary schools on their estates for the Indians and that these schools were to be under the direction of the Minister of Public Instruction and the Rector of the University (Flores Moncayo, 1953, pp. 340–43). From the little evidence available, and given the temper of the majority of landholders, the edict had little practical effect. From the early 1930's through 1951, there was growing agitation from the more socially conscious members of the elite for the development of educational facilities for the rural masses. In part, this agitation stemmed from the socially broadening experiences of the Chaco War (1932–35), in which Indians were taken into the army and, for the first time, left the Altiplano and the high valleys (Quiton, 1963, p. 2). For some Bolivians with high status, the unique experience of fighting alongside the Indian against a national enemy allowed for the development of more benign attitudes toward the indigenous population. It is during this difficult period of Bolivian history that the problems of the Indian began to be considered seriously by the intelligentsia and that the first hesitant action was taken to provide the Indian with a modicum of education. Just prior to the war, in 1931, WARISATA, the forerunner of the *Núcleos Escolares Campesinos*, or Indian nuclear schools, had been opened (Pérez, 1962, pp. 80–95). The nuclear model, a radical concept in rural training, provided for a central

---

[2] During the Colonial period, educational institutions, located principally in the cities and large towns, were under the direction of the Roman Catholic Church. With independence, public education became the responsibility of the government. At this time, Marshal Sucre promulgated legislation establishing primary, secondary and vocational institutions in all capitals of departments. During the first decade of the 20th century, the structure and content of Bolivian education, still primarily located in areas of large population concentration, was strongly influenced by a Belgian educational mission led by Dr. George Rouma, a pupil and colleague of Dr. Ovidio Decroly, the noted Belgian educator.

school which was located generally in a large *pueblo* and which supported a number of smaller and more limited sectional schools in surrounding villages and hamlets. In 1935, a supreme decree authorized 16 such nuclear clusters throughout Bolivia, a very limited step towards the solution of the problem of Indian education. Nevertheless, the rhetoric and stated intent of this decree is of significance in that the lack of social cohesion in Bolivia is clearly enunciated and the value of education in effecting a change is posited:

> It is the obligation of the State to integrate the native classes into the life of the country, invigorating their education in all the centers of the Republic and to assist equally the different ethnic groups that comprise the nation (Flores Moncayo, 1953, p. 349).

In the early years, from 1931 and up to 1944, the curriculum of the nuclear school was formal and academic, similar to that of the urban primary schools and the other rural schools maintained for non-Indians. It had little or no specific relationship to the need of the *campesinos* (Nelson, 1949, p. 22). In 1945, however, on the advice of an American educational mission,[3] all rural education was reorganized. While retaining the nuclear school format, the basic objective became preparing Indians for rural life. In theory, these schools offered to the *campesino* child a four-year curriculum emphasizing agricultural and vocational subjects and personal hygiene and giving secondary importance to reading, writing, and arithmetic. The language of instruction in these schools tended to be Spanish. Justification for a markedly different system and content of education from that offered to the urban population was seen in the distinct needs of the *campesino*, ". . . a man who works the land, who holds the spade and plow and who has a different life from the urban man" (Quitón, 1963, p. 2).

Despite these stirrings, the expansion of educational facilities in the countryside before 1952 was fundamentally limited. Up to 1946, only 41 nuclear centers with 839 small sectional schools had been established (Nelson, 1949, p. 16). On the eve of the Revolution, these numbers had not changed significantly. By 1951 (and here I must utilize unreliable government figures), only 12.9% of the rural school-age population — ages five to fourteen — had ever been matriculated at any school (Plan Bienal,

---

[3] In September 1944, an agreement was signed between the Bolivian Ministry of Education and the United States Government creating the Cooperative Educational Program to assist in the development of Bolivian education. In 1948, this organization was replaced by the Interamerican Educational Cooperative Service (SCIDE), which was sponsored, in conjunction with relevant Bolivian ministries, by the United States' International Cooperation Administration. SCIDE gave technical assistance in rural education, industrial education, and agricultural vocational education.

1965(?), p. 10). At that time, the official illiteracy rate for Bolivia was about 70%, from which I estimate an illiteracy rate for the rural population of well over 90%. Linguistically, the process of *castellanización*, or the attempt to make Spanish speakers of the Indians, had made little headway. Few rural Indian women knew Spanish, and a very large majority of men remained monolingual in either Aymara or Quechua. Semitrained teachers, an emasculated curriculum, lack of financial and political support from the government, and attacks from local landlords kept expansion and progress to a minimum. From all indications, it can safely be concluded that the impact of formal rural education in pre-Revolutionary Bolivia was weak, that it had little apparent effect in integrating the social segments, and that it had accomplished little, if anything, towards the amelioration and economic uplifting of *campesino* life. In the Bolivia of 1951, there remained an almost perfect congruence between the pattern of social stratification and the marked differences in the national allocation and use of educational resources.

In 1952, a combination of social and economic events forcibly propelled Bolivia into the 20th century. After a series of coups and countercoups, the Nationalist Revolutionary Movement (MNR) [4] assumed power. The MNR, a party of urban intellectuals and politicians with widely differing ideologies, led, guided and occasionally diverted the several elements in Bolivia clamoring for change and recognition. With a sweeping platform of social reform, in total opposition to the ideas and wishes of the traditional elite, the MNR had to assure itself of the support of the Indians, that social segment which until this time had never been allowed participation in Bolivian national life. To ensure this support, a number of basic socioeconomic actions were taken which transformed the power shift of 1952 into a frontal attack on the traditional order of Bolivian society. First, universal suffrage was granted to all adults, with no requirements for literacy or understanding of Spanish. Secondly, pressured by the tin miners, the most highly politicized workers in the country, the MNR nationalized the vast holdings of the three most important tin barons. Finally, and most importantly, propelled more quickly by the extralegal seizures of latifundia lands by organized *campesinos*, the government legislated a national agrarian reform, returning to the Indians land that once belonged to their forefathers. Through this legislation and its execution, the government, supported by *campesino* strength, weakened the power of the superordinate segment. The partial redistribution of the country's national

---

[4] The *Movimiento Nacionalista Revolucionario* was founded in 1940 by Victor Paz Estenssoro and Hernán Siles Zuazo with a platform of social change and nationalism. In 1951, the MNR unexpectedly received the largest number of votes in the general election, but the takeover of the government by a military junta prevented the party from taking power at that time.

resources and the newly mobilized, but politically potent, force of the *campesinos* formed the scene for social change.

Although the social fabric of Bolivia was unquestionably altered during the 12 years of MNR control, the extent and form of this restructuring is as yet unclear. In addition, significant questions still remain as to how far the revolutionary leadership intended to carry its reform, to what extent it was willing to institutionalize and legitimatize change, and to what degree they were ready and able to incorporate the Indian into the new system so as to permit his free competition for position in society. In short, was the government the fulcrum for deliberate change of the traditional principles which regulated access to advantageous status positions? [5] Satisfactory answers to these questions are difficult to find; inadequate and sometimes misleading national statistics, lack of archival research, and the pervasive fog of official propaganda tend to obscure the issues, as important as they are to both scholar and administrator. However, as I have already indicated, an examination of education since the Revolution of 1952 should suggest some answers. Theoretically, if the political transformation of 1952 was revolutionary in its essence, education should clearly reflect this fact.

Despite the social and economic crises which beset the new government, by 1955, it had implemented a new Code of Education, laying out the structure of an educational system which exists to the present. The basic goal of the new education was to integrate the nation. In the words of President Paz Estenssoro in 1955, "The educational system which we are introducing corresponds to the interests of the classes which constitute the majority of the Bolivian people" (SORO, 1963, p. 206.)

Organizationally, the Code provides for a multiple division of educational responsibility, allocating such responsibility to a number of governmental and quasi-governmental bodies. In this schema, the Ministry of Education, for example, has direct authority only for urban education — the formal schooling of children living in the cities, the capitals of departments and provinces, and other large population centers. In this urban system, legal provision is made for pre-school, primary, secondary, technical-vocational and university cycles for the clientele which it serves. Furthermore, the Ministry has the additional responsibility of training teachers for its own school system, of preparing the curriculum, of setting the length of the school year, and of almost all other academic and administrative matters. Philosophically, the objectives of urban education are little different from those of pre-Revolutionary days and fall well within the Western tradition from which they were derived. On the primary

[5] Utilizing one issue, these are the same fundamental questions raised by Richard W. Patch (1960) and Dwight B. Heath (1963) in their debate over whether agrarian reform in Bolivia was a result of grassroot pressure or of central government action.

school level, for example, the school is seen as the catalyst for the cultural formation of the child, taking into consideration its idiosyncratic characteristics and its biological, physical and social needs. The social structural significance of this practically independent section of Bolivian education is that it coincides, to a very considerable degree, with the Spanish-speaking sectors of the population and with those geographical areas dominated by the descendants of the traditional elites, the small and amorphous middle class, and the *cholos*. In this regard, the urban system continues, with minor modifications, the Bolivian tradition of a classic, academic education for the socially and economically privileged segments of the nation.

The Ministry of *Asuntos Campesinos*, or Peasant Affairs, is responsible for the education of the rural population as well as for other activities directly relevant to rural life. Through fundamental education, the goal is to train the *campesino* child to function in his milieu and to aid in the uplifting of the rural community. Deliberately, all instruction is given in the Spanish language, continuing the policy of *castellanización*, so that eventually, in theory, a common language will unify the nation. Provisions are made for nuclear schools, sectional schools, vocational-technical schools, and rural normal schools, but none for secondary schools or for university level work. The stated objectives of rural education are basically different from those of urban education: to develop good living habits in the *campesino* child; to teach literacy; to teach him to be an efficient agriculturalist; to develop his technical and vocational aptitudes; to prevent and to terminate the practices of alcoholism, the use of coca, the superstitions and prejudices in agronomy; and finally to develop in the *campesino* a civic conscience that would permit him to participate actively in the process of the cultural and economic emancipation of the nation (Ministerio de Educacion y Bellas Artes, 1956, p. 136). This system of rural education, in essence, is a continuation and expansion of the experiments of the 1930's and 1940's. While it is a system designed for the cultural and economic uplifting of the *campesinos*, significantly, it provides no mechanism for the movement of the rural student into the secondary and university cycles. Structurally, except for the possibility of limited training in the rural normal schools or through migration to the cities, the *campesino* terminates his education at the end of the primary cycle, if he is fortunate enough to reach that stage.

Several numerically less important systems of primary education also exist. For example, the *Corporacion Minera de Bolivia* (Comibol), the national mining corporation, administers and supports schools in the mining areas, and *Yacimientos Petroliferos Fiscales Bolivianos* (YPFB), the national oil corporation, is responsible for schooling in the oil and oil-refining territories. Although an educational coordinating council exists,[6] with representatives from all agencies concerned, in fact, each agency with educational responsibility has de facto control of the educational destinies of its clientele.

With well over a decade having elapsed since its inception, what have been the results of this educational structure for rural Bolivians? Most importantly, there has been a substantial physical expansion of the rural school system. By 1965, there were 5,250 government and private schools in the countryside, a fivefold increase over pre-Revolutionary days. Admittedly, many of these schools are little more than crude adobe shelters. Nevertheless, by 1964, 38.2% of the rural school-age population was registered at school, an increase in enrollment of about 250% since 1951 (Plan Bienal, 1965(?), p. 10). In six Altiplano and Yungas communities with rural schools which were studied by anthropologists during the period from 1964 to 1966,[7] the percentage of inhabitants who claimed any elementary schooling ranged from 31.3% to 49.4%, with a mean of 43.4%. However, few *campesinos* in these communities progress further than the second year. For example, in one Yungas high valley community from this sample, composed of long-resident Negroes and transplanted Aymara, the mean number of years of education for ages 12 to 22 is 2.2 years for the Negroes and 2.0 years for the *campesinos*. The mean number of years of education for those over 22 years, and therefore less affected by the educational reform of the MNR, is 0.12 years for the Negroes and 0.71 years for the *campesinos* (Newman, 1966, p. 78).

One sign of the value placed on education by Indians is that the majority of rural schools have been constructed by *campesinos* with materials donated and gathered by the community and with only limited State aid. Schweng reports on Pillapi, an expropriated hacienda near Lake Titicaca:

> . . . the interest in education the *campesinos* showed was moving. After the first school was built in 1955 at the expense of the project, the other schools were built by the *campesinos* themselves. They made the

[6] The purpose of the *Consejo de Coordinación Educacional* is to ensure the basic unity of Bolivian national education. It is chaired by the Minister of Education and includes, among others, the Director General of Education, the Director General of Rural Education, the General Inspector of Education for the Schools of the State Mines and Petroleum areas, the National Director for the Protection of Minors and Children, and the Director of Vocational Education. Other interested ministries are also represented.

[7] This is a three-year project of the Research Institute for the Study of Man under Peace Corps Grant No. PC(W)–397. The basic objective of this anthropological-epidemiological study are to assess the impact of Peace Corps public health programs in Bolivia and to provide social scientific guidelines for future public health programming in Bolivia and in structurally similar contexts. The research included intensive community studies of Sorata, Coroico, Reyes, San Miguel, Compi and Villa Abecia, as well as several shorter, selected studies of surrounding villages.

adobe bricks, leveled the ground, dug the foundations and provided all the unskilled labor (1966, p. 54).

However, a serious drawback is that over 90% of these schools lack adequate furniture and sufficient teaching materials. The rural normal schools lack laboratories and libraries; the few industrial schools lack machinery for practical lessons and, as a result, students and student teachers learn only theory without practical experience.

Despite rudimentary facilities, however, the educational aspirations of the *campesinos* are very high. Many *campesinos* perceive education as the catalyst for social mobility, as the means by which they or their children will escape from the hard and unremitting toil on the land. Theoretically, by learning Spanish and attaining literacy, they can more readily move to the urban centers and find better employment; if they choose, they can begin the process of becoming *cholos*. Others see education as a general panacea for their life condition but have little idea as to what specifically can be gained from it. For some in this group, education is endowed with magical qualities. There are even a few *campesinos* who view education as necessary for the preservation of a traditional way of life. This particular point of view was lucidly presented by a *jillikata*, or leader of a traditional *ayllu* in an isolated community in the hills overlooking the Altiplano.[8] His position, while simple, was structurally revealing: Since the central government requires literacy as a prerequisite for holding local political office, the paucity of eligible candidates makes it possible for traditionally unacceptable persons to be selected. This often has lead to intracommunal clashes between the official and the traditional systems of authority. Consequently, in one old man's opinion, schools were necessary to provide a supply of literate and traditionally acceptable leaders. In essence, he was choosing to change just enough so as not to have to change. Formal education, where it exists, may well have different meanings for the population. Nevertheless, as noted by Olen E. Leonard in a recent study of the Altiplano:

> The school is the source of greatest pride in each community. Almost all the heads of families seem to admit that the improvement of their educational system has been one of the better attainments of communities during the last decade (1966, p. 26).

However, for the less than a third of the rural school-age population

---

[8] This is a community in the Province of Carangas situated at approximately 14,000 feet above sea level. It is possible, from the *pueblo* site, to view almost the entire Altiplano region of the Andes. The community is part of an enclave of Aymara-speaking *campesinos*, partly surrounded by Quechua populations. Archeologically and anthropologically, this relatively inaccessible and little studied section of Bolivia offers much to the serious scholar.

attending school,[9] the possibilities for learning are limited. To begin with, the teacher is required to teach in Spanish even though he may be less fluent in the language than in his native Aymara or Quechua. The non–Spanish-speaking Indian children are instructed in the first grade, therefore, in a language they cannot understand. To compound the problem, an extreme form of rote instruction is utilized: As the teacher speaks, the child copies the words into his course book, which is graded for accuracy, neatness and artistic quality. Memorization and recitation are uniformly stressed almost to the complete exclusion of the use of observation and experimentation. Lack of equipment and lack of training on the part of the teachers effectively preclude any vocational or technical training, so that the student generally receives only rudimentary instruction in the fundamentals of reading, writing, and arithmetic. With the language barrier, which is never completely surmounted, much of even this hard-learned literacy is eventually lost. Schweng makes much the same point for his Altiplano community:

> In their educational effort, the schools were handicapped by the Government's insistence on using the schools as an instrument of "castellanizacion," for forcing the use of Spanish on non-Spanish speaking Indians to the exclusion of their native tongue. The mother tongue of the children of Pillapi was Aymara and no other language was spoken at home; the women spoke Aymara only and there were only a few fathers who spoke even a little Spanish. But in the schools, from the first grade, the language of instruction was Spanish and Aymara was not taught at all. The continuation of this policy after the Revolution was in strange contrast with the cult of the Indian encouraged by the Government and the freedom given for the use of Indian languages, Aymara and Quechua, in politics. Forcing Spanish made teaching very difficult and the educational effort wasteful. Without opportunity for using the language most children soon forgot the little Spanish they picked up at school in the two years they customarily attended. They learned less than would otherwise have been the case (1966, pp. 54–55).

The policy of *castellanización* has also compounded problems of cultural and ethnic identity. If one of the basic objectives of the rural school is to cultivate a sense of pride in being an Indian and a *campesino*, then instruction in Spanish, a language inextricably associated with the superordinate elements of Bolivia and of little direct value in an Aymara or Quechua community, widens rather than narrows the social gap. The language of instruction in this case tends more to divorce, rather than weld more

[9] Although in 1964, 38.2% of the school-age population in the rural areas were officially counted as being registered in schools, the number actually in full attendance was and continues to be much lower. One estimate for 1961 (SORO, 1963, p. 199) is that only about one in ten rural children attended school.

closely, the student and his rural context. In any case, the goal of making Spanish the cornerstone of national cohesion is far from being realized. For example, of the four basically Aymara communities in the study sample, none had more than 1.2% monolingual Spanish speakers, and these were almost always government officials assigned to the community. Aymara monolinguals ranged from a high of 84.4% in one community to a low of 42.5% in the most acculturated village. Self-professed bilinguals in Spanish and Aymara ranged from a low of 10.5% to a high of 49.6%.[10]

Aside from linguistic barriers and a truncated and unrelated curriculum, the low quality of rural education is also a function of the inadequacies of rural teachers. While urban teachers are required to have a secondary school and a normal school diploma, rural teachers need only a primary school certificate, plus six months in a rural normal school. In many cases, even these minimal requirements are not met, so that a large number of rural teachers have not completed the primary school. Teachers' salaries are low in all parts of the country, averaging about $40 a month. As a result, teachers' attendance in school is often sporadic, since other work is sought to augment the income. This is particularly true of male teachers. In addition, with a politically strong teachers' union which makes it almost impossible to fire a teacher, the educative process stagnates. A normally short school year is shortened further by student participation in scores of national and religious holidays which require days of special preparation before the event, by political crises which close the schools, by teachers' strikes, and by teacher absenteeism.

As a consequence, the *campesino* child receives, from the rural school system, little formal preparation for modern life, and this is clearly reflected in the educational statistics. Student absenteeism rates are very high and usually attributed to the need for the child to assist in family work, but they are also related to the actual, as opposed to the stated, content of the programs, the lack of teacher preparation, and the scarcity of teaching aids and classrooms. The desertion or dropout rate is extraordinarily high. Of each 100 *campesino* children ages five to seven years, only 37 enter the first grade, and six complete the sixth terminal year (Plan Bienal, 1965(?), p. 15). Finally, the problem of illiteracy has not been solved. While the official illiteracy rate has been modestly reduced from 68.9% in 1950 to 63.0% after 14 years (Plan Bienal, 1965(?), p. 5), I would speculate that even this limited gain was made in the urban areas.

In providing expanded educational opportunities for the *campesinos*, the

[10] Data on language were generated from a census collected at an early date in all communities studied by the Research Institute for the Study of Man. A comprehensive sociological survey, which included a long section on language and education, was undertaken at the close of the field study in 1966. These data are currently being computer processed and will be utilized as the basis for several forthcoming papers and reports.

MNR corrected what it believed was a glaring injustice of the old order. As far as a limited economy permitted, the *campesino* was granted the right of formal schooling, which in the past had been essentially reserved for the privileged classes. In this regard, the government provided an institutional structure to help meet the rising aspirations and demands for education. In many of the remote areas of Bolivia, the school, for the first time, became a factor in the socialization of the *campesino* child. Abstractly then, the very extension of educational services to the rural masses can be considered revolutionary.

An analysis of the structure and content of rural education, however, leads to diametrically opposed conclusions. The balkanization of the educational enterprise, the multiple allocation of responsibility, the differing educational goals for different socioeconomic groups, in my opinion, lead inevitably to further qualitative distinctions between these groups. In fact, the more efficient each section of the total educational system is in the training of its wards, the more distant becomes the ideal goal of integration through education. Furthermore, since the divisions of Bolivian education correspond closely with the old social divisions of Bolivian society, and since the rural segment is virtually barred from participation on the secondary and university levels, the effect is to institutionalize, in education, the stratification patterns of the past. Given the structure of education, there is no opportunity, short of physical relocation and cultural transformation, for the *campesino* to receive that level of training which will allow him to compete successfully for the advantageous positions in society. It is of more than academic interest to note that most of the sharply stratified societies which have made resolute moves toward modernization and toward a consensual form of social structure select unitary systems of education to aid in the process.

Conservative rather than revolutionary thought is also seen in the content of rural education. Subject matter and mode of instruction reflect both patronizing and paternalistic features. A leitmotif of the educational philosophy is the suppression of all cultural elements in *campesino* life which are considered dysfunctional, but little is offered to replace that which is suppressed. When this is combined with the central decision to give highest priority to training for rural life, the *campesinos*, from an educational perspective, are sealed off from social movement in the society. A short-run gain for the national economy is a long-run investment in the continuance of a sharply stratified state. I do not argue here for absolute homogeneity for all sectors of Bolivian education, but for Bolivian youth to have institutionalized opportunities to move, if qualified, from one differentiated educational sector to the other. This would provide an important condition for an open society and would decrease the social dangers which will ensue when unrealistic aspirations hinged to education are not realized.

This cursory review suggests that, in education, the Revolution of 1952 and the 14 years of MNR dominance did little to modify the hierarchical order of the socially significant segments of Bolivian society and did little, if anything, to provide new, institutionalized forms of social articulation. It is obvious that, whatever else the directives were that emanated from the center of the system, they were not revolutionary in effect. The considerable social change which Bolivia has experienced during the last 14 years seems to be more the result of a partial splintering of the traditional order than a thoroughgoing social reform. It is a change generated, in the main, by an uncoordinated but mass pressure from a discontented social base. One can then speculate that the post-1952 phase of Bolivian history represents a period of *campesino* coalescence and emergence which, if not diverted, will lead to serious upheaval before resulting in reform and social regrouping. In this present process of coalescence, any opportunity for formal education is of value. This is perhaps the true legacy of the present system. . . .

REFERENCES

Flores Moncayo, José. 1953. *Legislación Boliviana del Indio: Recopilacion 1825–1953.* La Paz, Bolivia.
Heath, Dwight B. 1963. "Land reform and social revolution in Bolivia." Paper read at 62nd Ann. Meeting, Am. Anthropological Assoc. Mimeographed.
Leonard, Olen E. 1966. *El Cambio Economico y Social en Cuatro Comunidades del Altiplano de Bolivia.* Mexico: Instituto Indigenista Interamericano Serie Antropologia Social, No. 3.
Ministerio de Educación y Bellas Artes. 1956. *Código de la Educación Boliviana.* La Paz, Bolivia.
Muratorio, Blanca. 1966. "Changing bases of social stratification in a Bolivian community." Paper presented at 65th Ann. Meeting Am. Anthropological Assoc. November 17–20, Pittsburgh, Pa. Mimeographed.
Nelson, Raymond H. 1949. *Education in Bolivia.* Federal Security Agency, Office of Education, Bulletin No. 1.
Newman, Roger C. 1966. "Land reform in Bolivia's yungas." M.A. thesis, Columbia Univ., New York, N.Y.
Parsons, Talcott. 1951. *The Social System.* Free Press, New York, N.Y.
Patch, Richard W. 1960. "Bolivia: U.S. assistance in a revolutionary setting," in *Social Change in Latin America Today.* Richard W. Adams, ed. Random House, New York, N.Y., pp. 108–176.
Pérez, Elizardo. 1962. *WARISATA: La Escuela-Ayllu.* La Paz, Bolivia.
Plan Bienal. 1965(?). Plan del Sector de Educación y Formacion Profesional, 1965–66. La Paz(?), Bolivia. Mimeographed.
Quitón, Carlos. 1963. "Proceso de la educación rural y educación fundamental en Bolivia," *Boletin Indigenista,* April, No. 1.
Schweng, Lorand D. 1966. "An Indian community development project in Bolivia," in *A Casebook of Social Change,* Arthur H. Niehoff, ed. Aldine Publishing Co., Chicago, Ill., pp. 44–57.
Service, Elman. 1955. "Indian-European relations in colonial Latin-America," *Am. Anthropologist* 57(3): 411–425.
Smith, M. G. 1966. "Pre-industrial stratification systems," in *Social Structure and Mo-*

bility in Economic Development, Neil J. Smelser and Seymour M. Lipset, eds. Aldine Publishing Co., Chicago, Ill., pp. 141–76.

SORO (Special Operations Research Office). 1963. *U.S. Army Area Handbook for Bolivia*. The American University, Washington, D.C.

FURTHER READINGS

Becker, Howard S. "Schools and systems of stratification," in A. H. Halsey, Jean Floud, and C. Arnold Anderson (eds.), *Education, economy, and society*. New York: Free Press, 1961.

Bruner, Edward M. "Cultural transmission and cultural change," *Southwestern Journal of Anthropology*, vol. 12 (Winter 1956).

Illich, Ivan. "Commencement at the University of Puerto Rico," *New York Review of Books*, October 9, 1969.

Johnson, John J. (ed.) *Continuity and change in Latin America*. Stanford: Stanford University Press, 1964.

McPherron, Stasé P. "Changing teacher role under school self-management in Yugoslavia." Paper read at the Annual Meeting of the American Anthropological Association, San Diego, California, 1970.

27

The term cross-cultural education *refers to three, quite different phenomena. It characterizes, first, formal or informal educational encounters that involve cultural difference. Second, the term describes formalized teaching and learning experiences in which cultural difference is presumed, or known, to be problematic. And, third, cross-cultural education circumscribes the field of study that compares educational processes and structures* across cultures. *Mrs. Hodgkin's sensitive discussion of the differential impact of Western-oriented Australian education upon Chinese-Malaysian, Indian-Malaysian, and Malay students notes the "tendency to see the processes of cross-cultural education in terms of total 'assimilation,' rather than as a matter of temporary adjustment and selective acceptance of certain techniques, knowledge and behaviour." The impermanent, transient status of cross-cultural educational encounters such as those Mrs. Hodgkin examines in anthropological context, here, prompts the exchange of stereotyped, surface, or even discriminatory impressions between the cultures represented. She urges a transcultural perspective of such encounters, which not only voids superficial exchange but also provides for the full expression of mutual benefit in relationships between students, teachers, and local hosts. A frequent contributor to educational literature, Mrs. Hodgkin is associated with the University of Western Australia.*

MARY C. HODGKIN

Cross-Cultural Education in an Anthropological Perspective

Cross-cultural education, formal and otherwise, has become increasingly important in the years since World War II. For centuries, students have travelled to foreign parts in order to supplement their academic and technical knowledge, but it is only within the last two decades that this exchange has reached proportions sufficiently great to attract general attention. Increase in means of travel and communication throughout the world is, of course, partly responsible for this expansion, but the most striking and significant factor is the need in newly developing countries and nations for technical skills and academic knowledge which cannot yet be obtained within their own boundaries.

Australia, together with New Zealand, has become a major area for providing facilities for tertiary and also secondary education for students from Southeast Asia. In 1963 there were over 12,000 Asians studying in Australian schools, technical colleges, and universities.

The failure rate in most Australian universities is high (Rowley and Ironmonger, 1963), but as far as has been ascertained up to the present the proportion of Asians who fail is no greater than that of Australians.[1] However, no records have so far been published of the number of Asians who come to Australia to obtain academic qualifications and then fail to matriculate or to complete the course to which they originally aspired; these figures would not be easy to obtain because the majority transfer from course to course, from institution to institution, and even from State to State before they ultimately return home with, or without, some sort of qualification.

Concern has been expressed in various quarters at the dissatisfactions and disappointments that result from these failures, to say nothing of the waste of money and time. It is sometimes suggested that stricter measures for screening and selection should be employed in the students' home countries before they are permitted to go overseas, or that higher standards of admission should be applied in Australia. However, the students come

Reprinted by permission of the General Editor, *Anthropological Forum*, 1964, vol. I, no. 2, pp. 232–247. This journal is published by the University of Western Australia Press.
[1] Cf. the observation "that the rate of progress of Asian students is lower than for Australian students, and suggests that the higher failure rate occurs among those students . . . without adequate qualifications, and without adequate language skills" (Caiden, 1964:46).

from a variety of linguistic and educational backgrounds; they apply for a wide range of courses in both secondary and tertiary institutions; and any form of pre-selection would be difficult to implement and not necessarily acceptable to the educational establishments in Australia. Furthermore, it would appear to be an infringement of personal freedom if a parent who was prepared for the necessary expenditure were prevented from sending his son overseas, provided entry into a foreign school or college were available.

Asian parents are usually unacquainted with the standards and requirements of overseas study, and like parents anywhere are often unduly optimistic about the abilities of their offspring. Many students are sent to study courses for which they have neither the inclination nor the ability. This underlines the necessity of guidance before such students embark upon their studies. The majority of private students who come to Australia do so in the hope of obtaining a matriculation pass in order to qualify for a university course. It is at this point, between the Matriculation examination and university or technical entrance, that there is the greatest need for guidance and advice.

One important research problem in this field hinges on the fact that tests of educational ability or personality traits which are employed to measure "intelligence" or aptitudes of Western-educated students have proved inadequate to predict the achievements of Asian students. In the first place, differences in language affect performance in those tests which are verbally oriented; secondly, the majority of suitable instruments of measurement presuppose some familiarity with a Western cultural background. In every society persons are taught to perceive and define social and natural phenomena and assess the relationships between them in varying ways. Thus argument by analogy, in terms such as "leg is to foot as arm is to . . . ," which is a characteristic feature of certain Western type verbal tests of "intelligence," is likely to be quite unfamiliar to some students.

Any person who undertakes to advise students from societies other than his own should have some knowledge of the values, attitudes and general way of life in those societies. He should also have an appreciation of the social background of his subjects, and of the economic situation in their home countries, so that he can suggest courses which will be relevant to future prospects of employment and social requirements. For example, it would be unrealistic to recommend that a student should study for a degree in biochemistry or microbiology when the facilities for work in these fields are as yet scarcely developed in his country — unless he is an exceptionally gifted student who could serve as a "pioneer" or a spearhead of change in that direction.

It is not always easy to determine whether failure on the part of an Asian student is a consequence simply of lack of ability, or of other factors.

Certainly in a number of cases language difficulties, methods of study, or interpersonal problems appear to have been responsible. The majority of these can be traced to cultural differences between the student's home environment and the one in which he is temporarily living.

Relationships between teachers and students are significant in this connection. Quite apart from linguistic troubles there are problems of values and attitudes, as well as pre-conceived assumptions which inhibit communication and may lead to mistakes in teaching procedures, in educational administration, and in advice given to students. These can easily contribute to a student's difficulties and in extreme cases may lead to acute individual stress or "alienate" him, emotionally and intellectually, from the country in which he is undertaking his study.

It is sometimes assumed that cross-cultural (or transcultural) education will lead inevitably to improved international relations. That this is not necessarily so has been pointed out by several authorities (e.g., Du Bois, 1956; Sellitz et al., 1963). Complex forces are involved in such an exchange, and it is clear that persons responsible for the planning and implementation of any cross-cultural educational programme should possess a sensitive knowledge and understanding of cultures other than their own, as well as of the mechanisms of social and cultural change.

Education in broad terms can be defined as the transmission from generation to generation of the culture of a given society or part of that society. It can be assumed that an educational system is in some way functionally related to the values and norms of the particular group in which it operates; otherwise it would cease to contribute to the continuity of social life. Although it can be defined more generally and in more impersonal terms, for the purpose of this paper acculturation can be taken as the process which is set in train through association between persons with different cultural backgrounds. The exchange of students between one educational system and another represents one of the most potent vehicles of such acculturation. In many situations in which such exchange occurs, there are on one side members of a non-literate society, and on the other members of a politically complex or highly industrialized society who are more often than not in a dominant position. The changes which represent one aim of the exchange, or are anticipated as side effects, may be presented as beneficial to the material advancement of the non-literate group.

The case of overseas students is somewhat different. Such persons usually come from literate societies, though possibly from what have been called underdeveloped nations. They are, ideally, in a position to make a fairly careful selection of techniques and knowledge which they see as necessary to themselves or their own societies, and also to adopt only temporarily those aspects of the foreign culture which appear to be essential to the acquisition of the desired techniques. This is quite unlike the situation of such peoples as the Australian Aborigines, for whom there is, practically speaking, little alternative to attempting a permanent adjustment to life within the society of the dominant group.

Malinowski and others, in writing about the study of culture change, have emphasized that it is essential to take into account the societies on both sides of the contact as well as those persons directly concerned in the contact situation. To understand the impact of cross-cultural education as a particularly powerful agent of change, all those who are interested in the results of the exchange, whether they be anthropologists, politicians, or educators, should be alert to the differences as well as the similarities between the societies involved.

Social Anthropology can be of positive use here, in contributing answers to questions about the relevance of modern education in ideal and in practice, in content and in techniques, not only in what have been, traditionally, non-literate societies but also in our own (cf. Berndt, 1956). Any teacher who has to cope with factors of adjustment to changing circumstances, whether it be in a monocultural or a cross-cultural situation, needs more than superficial acquaintance with the values of those he (or she) would reach. There are often discrepancies between the informal education or socialization which takes place in primary groups, the formal education in school in a familiar environment, and the further education which is provided in a foreign setting.

The stimulus for writing this paper came from problems and questions encountered in the course of research and welfare activities bearing directly upon one field of cross-cultural education at the secondary and tertiary levels in Western Australia, and specifically in Perth. The paper takes up a number of issues connected with such problems, looking at them in the light of statements which have been made about them by anthropologists and others. These statements vary greatly in quality. The difficulties involved in using them are mainly methodological ones. Some, persuasive as they may seem, are grounded in nothing more substantial than hunches or impressions, others are based on solid research, and perhaps most are a mixture of both in varying degrees. On the face of it, it is not easy to distinguish what has gone into such a statement — how much is clearly factual evidence and how much "interpretation," or speculation.

The majority of the students with whom I am specifically concerned in this paper come from what is now known as Malaysia, especially from the territories of Malaya and Singapore: Chinese,[2] Indian, and Malay. A variety of subcultures is represented in this population, some retaining

---

[2] Except where otherwise stated or implied, the term "Chinese" in this paper refers to Chinese-Malaysian, and "Indian" to Indian-Malaysian.

much of the traditional orientation of their particular "ethnic" category or group, and others showing the influence of the changing patterns of urban life in a society which is being rapidly altered by the impact of the West. It is easy but quite misleading to make sweeping generalizations on the basis of facile assessment of "national characteristics," or in the very questionable framework of "racial stereotypes." In any case, identification of cultural patterns in such broad terms tends to be highly subjective. However, it is true that there are cultural continuities among the major Asian ethnic groups, which have been manifested in identifiable behaviour and belief patterns as well as in the field of social structure and organization over the centuries. (Cf. Sharp, 1962, for comment on this theme.)

Some Cultural Characteristics

Chinese

Of the 1,200 Asian students in Perth in 1963, more than 1,000 were Chinese. Over 900 of these came from Malaysia. Two main subdivisions could be delineated here: those whose education at home had been primarily in schools developed on Western patterns where the linguistic medium was English, and those educated in Chinese-medium schools where the teaching was based largely on traditional methods and conservative values. Many of the students in both came from homes where English was not spoken, and where traditional, past-oriented, attitudes were still dominant.

The majority of Chinese in Southeast Asia migrated within the last century from rural areas in Southeast China. Here the localized lineage structure was stronger than in other parts of China (Freedman, 1958); and the overseas Chinese have retained many of these family traditions, extending the clan structure to a system of surname and district groupings as a putative overseas substitute for the original kinship groups. The ideal of the joint or extended family still has some counterparts in actuality; even if this is not a co-resident unit under present-day conditions, the values associated with it still affect the behaviour of its members. Characteristic of such a grouping are attitudes of mutual interdependence, relying on primary group alignments for assistance and support and tending to ignore wider bonds of community and nation.

Chinese students overseas, especially those from Chinese-language schools, on the whole show little interest in such national groupings as the Malaysian Students' Association, or in clubs and similar bodies which emphasize interests shared with Australian students. They form closed "old school" associations which take the place of the kin group in matters of mutual aid and social interaction generally, and prefer to lodge in rented houses with schoolmates rather than in the homes of Australians or with other Malaysian students.

Financial support of a Chinese student is in many cases arranged by several members of his family in Malaysia, who pool resources to send one member overseas. This arrangement is consistent with the ideal of kin group interdependence, and, as in all such transactions, it involves obligations for the student on his return: for example, he may have to repay relatives, or friends of his father, or contribute toward the education of younger members of the family. In view of these commitments, failure to complete courses or even a temporary setback involves a circle very much wider than the individual student. Murphy (1959) has indicated that such obligations place an especially heavy burden on an eldest son. In several instances, students have had to give up their studies and return home on the death of the head of the family in order to shoulder the responsibilities of the kin group.

Educators who do not understand the ramifications of Chinese primary groupings fail to appreciate the tension and frustration, which sometimes amounts to actual dysphoria, when a student's poor grades result in his being excluded from a course or even being sent home. This, accompanied by fear of shame and disgrace to the family, is a major cause of attempts to manoeuvre teachers and administrators, to exploit personal contacts, and to obtain concessions, such as are often displayed by Chinese students in Australian institutions.

During the past three years the Perth Technical College has instituted a system of notifying parents when students are not "making the grade," with a warning that unless the student improves during the year he will not be re-admitted for the next year. This approach is extremely unpopular among the students, and for some of them has resulted in severe emotional stress. Protests have been made on the grounds that it is a threat to their independence as adults — an argument which, they feel, will be more readily understood in terms of Australian mores than other reasons they might put forward. When parents, who may be illiterate or at least unable to read English, receive the official communication, they may infer that the disgrace involves not only study or class assignments, but some moral lapse as well. Many traditionally oriented Chinese suppose that earnest and continuous application to study is all that is required for success. This is probably connected with the method of learning by rote, and is reinforced by anxiety that sons and daughters who have been released from stern parental discipline may consequently neglect their studies. The immediate reaction of such parents is to curtail the student's allowance, on the assumption that the less money he receives the less he will be influenced by the temptations of social life. Hardship in living conditions may result, or else the student adds indebtedness to his academic problems.

In the traditional Chinese family, and to some extent even in those with a more Western outlook, the father is a figure of authority and his displeasure a thing to be avoided at all costs. This is an added reason why adverse reports sent home cause such deep concern. One factor which influenced the authorities in notifying parents was the discovery that many students who had failed had deceived their relatives into believing they were doing well.

One girl who had failed to matriculate, home on vacation, said she would be returning to Australia to take a course at the University. Her relatives and friends celebrated her success with a large dinner party. She was then faced with the necessity of returning and re-enrolling at some institution in order to maintain this fiction. Another student who was not permitted to re-enroll at the University remained in Perth for several months allowing his parents to assume that he was still attending classes. It was not until the Department of Immigration checked with the University and wrote to his father that the truth finally came out.

In a rapidly changing society where many parents are less well-educated than their children, the ordinary tensions of personal growth and development are often overlaid with the strains of social growth. When security and solidarity are represented by a relatively closed kin system, as among the Chinese, there is a natural desire to avoid or minimize such tensions where possible. In Chinese society where the young are taught that age indicates wisdom, and parents represent authority, it is upsetting to discover, in the light of better education, that the ideas of one's parents are regarded as crude and old fashioned. It can, even, lead to a feeling that any form of authority should be opposed and rejected. Such an attitude may be in part responsible for the open defiance of parents and teachers which has broken out from time to time in Chinese-medium schools in Singapore (Wells, 1956). Such defiance was no doubt exploited for political ends in Malaya, but it could explain some of the difficulties encountered with Chinese students in Australia.

A concomitant of the traditional Chinese pattern of respect for age and the authority of the elders is the method of learning employed in the older type of Chinese-medium schools. This consisted of learning and repeating by rote the sayings and writings of Chinese sages, and the meticulous copying of Chinese calligraphy (Weakland, 1950). There was a perpetual striving for perfection in reproducing the ancient classics. Although this type of teaching is changing rapidly under the influence of Western education, there is still a strong tendency among Chinese students, especially, to attempt to memorize appropriate parts of their textbooks. Many teachers in universities and technical colleges can give instances of students who have reproduced whole sections of books in response to examination questions. It is exemplified also by the frequent distress evinced by students when given alternative references or a choice of reading matter on a particular subject.

On one occasion two different editions of "The Tempest" were available to matriculation students, and several enquired from the teacher which of these would be used in preparing the examination — since they would need to learn the footnotes to answer any questions on the text.

In another case a student who suffered extensive injuries to an eye in an accident the day before an examination was advised by his doctor and teachers to sit for a later examination, but insisted on attending, and managed to pass in four of the five subjects. He said that he had memorized the information for the examination and knew that he would forget before the next opportunity to sit for it. He attributed his failure in the fifth and last subject to the fact that with an injured eye he had been unable to refresh his memory at the last minute.

It has been said that in a society which places stress on the authority of parents or immediate kin, and on respect for conformity to tradition, originality and initiative are not encouraged. Although there are outstanding leaders in every walk of life among the modern Chinese in Malaysia and elsewhere, there is still a tendency among Chinese students to be diffident in expressing their own ideas or making a critical assessment of a teacher's statements or matter found in books. One student remarked, "Questions which begin with describe are easy, but I find it very difficult to answer those that say 'Discuss.' "

Even in English-medium schools in Malaya, there is still a much more authoritarian attitude to education than is found in Australian schools. Questions are largely discouraged, outside reading is rare, and the ideal of "originality" is seldom stressed. Social distance between teacher and student is still wide; and with large classes and few libraries there is little opportunity for experience in discussion or in the gathering of a range of opinions on any subject.[3]

One interesting sidelight in this connection is the general observation that of the students who come to Australia many of those from Chinese-medium schools prove to be good in mathematical subjects and in the theoretical aspects of the natural sciences. Whether this is because set problems in mathematics can be handled more readily on the basis of

---

[3] Flecker (1959) has suggested that the only personality attribute differentiating between students who passed and those who failed was conservatism — i.e., lacking in an experimental and critical approach.

memory, or because there is skilled basic instruction in these subjects in such schools, is a question on which further investigation would be useful.

It has been suggested that "the Oriental" way of thinking is different from that of the West (Needham, 1956; Northrop, 1960; Abegg, 1952); for example, that the Chinese see the universe as a circle of components which influence each other rather than as a sequence of causal relationships. This is a sweeping statement, and especially so if applied to modern educated Chinese, some of whom have become outstanding scientists on Western lines; and in any case such statements would appear to be oriented in terms of philosophical speculation rather than of scientific investigation which is closely grounded in empirical enquiry. However, it would be interesting to explore this matter in relation to the teaching of scientific subjects to Asian students in Australian universities and schools.

One of the most important concepts of Chinese culture is that of "face" (*lien* or *mien* in Chinese). In summary, this has to do with the respect or esteem accorded a person's reputation, moral character, dignity and status. Loss of face is regarded as more serious than any other form of personal disgrace. It can affect the nervous system more strongly than actual physical fear (Hu Hsien-chin, 1956).

Fear of losing face influences the actions of students who fail in examinations or have to return home without credentials for which they originally came to Australia; the tensions and frustrations caused by adverse reports of progress have already been mentioned. It has also an important bearing on interaction between teacher and pupil, and between Chinese and Australian students. To guard against the possibility of slight or rebuff in face-to-face relations and dealings with other people, many Chinese engage the assistance of a third party or "go-between" to mediate in any situation which could involve failure or rejection. This is a characteristic of social transactions in traditional Chinese society and is still prevalent among business men and others even in the modern cosmopolitan cities of Asia. In dealings with teachers and administrators in Australia some Chinese students prefer to ask a third person, even another student, to approach someone from whom they wish to receive a favour or concession, and when a direct approach has to be made they usually prefer to bring a third person into the situation to assist in shielding them from the embarrassment of a direct refusal.

This attitude has some bearing also on teaching and learning problems. A member of staff who reprimands a student in class so that he loses prestige in the eyes of his fellows is likely to be exceedingly unpopular. Teachers frequently complain of the difficulty of obtaining replies from Chinese students to questions asked in class, and their lack of response in university seminars during general discussion. One reason is undoubtedly reluctance to lose face by making a statement which is inadequate or incorrect. A number of instances where failure to answer questions has been attributed to a language barrier could well be due to this.

Standards of morality vary, of course, not only between societies but also within them, on the basis of different subcultures or even different situations. So do definitions of "truth," where ideal and practice may diverge quite conspicuously — in Western European type societies no less than in others. It has been suggested that the Chinese tend to have a more pragmatic attitude to this and to be less concerned with absolute standards of truth than are societies steeped in the Western European tradition. In actual circumstances, the "truth" of a report as presented in court by a witness may be governed to a large extent by fear of the consequences — for example, penalties for perjury. Realistic appraisal of a situation may enter into it, too — as in the question, "How far can I get away with this account, in contrast to that?" Because the subject is so complex I shall not discuss it here, but merely note that in order to avoid loss of face or other forms of social rejection a Chinese student may experience few qualms in changing his version of reality to suit the occasion.

A Chinese Malayan student, arrested for stealing, made a statement admitting his guilt. He was released on bail, and with the help of his friends and the Chinese student whom he had robbed concocted a story which was designed to prove his innocence when he appeared in court the next day. Objections by his lawyer and others on the grounds that this was not true completely failed to impress them. However the argument that the story was not sufficiently convincing to deceive the magistrate eventually succeeded in persuading him that he would be wiser to plead guilty.

Chinese attitudes to kinship obligations, as essentially reciprocal, extend to transactions in the wider society. Gifts may be made simply in order to achieve some return in the way of concessions or assistance, although not necessarily directly or in the immediate future; and the expectation of return benefit may be measured quite frankly and realistically in terms of the monetary or other value of the gift. This kind of reciprocal expectation is a normal feature of most human societies, but the checks, safeguards and "screens" associated with it vary a great deal. If framed too blatantly, or allowed to intrude into areas of behaviour where it is considered to be inappropriate, it shades into what in Western societies is regarded as bribery and usually strongly condemned, at least at the verbal level. However, the practice is an approved part of business exchange in the Chinese commercial world. Many persons who deal with Chinese students in Australia are embarrassed by gifts and hospitality, especially when other students draw their attention to the implications, or suspicions are voiced that concessions are the result of such actions. The principal of one college has stated that he now refuses to accept any invitations from his

Asian students because he has found that such acceptance is expected to involve him in obligations to make concessions or relax rules in return.

Indians

The majority of the Indian students from Southeast Asia are Hindus whose forbears came originally from southern India or from Ceylon.

In Hindu families in Malaysia the father is the authoritarian head of the household (Wells, 1956), although the mother has some autonomy in the domestic sphere. The ideal of joint residence is still upheld, although there is rarely more than a stem family unit in the urbanized conditions in which most Indians, other than plantation workers, live in Malaysia. They are isolated from the extended kin group, having migrated overseas within the span of one or two generations; and responsibility for education in Australia usually rests with the parents alone and does not extend to the wider kinship unit as with the Chinese.

Indian students appear to maintain closer ties with their families at home than do many of the Chinese students and show less concern that problems and difficulties which affect them should be withheld from their parents. Hsu (1963) has suggested that Hindus show diffuseness in their dependence relationships and a negative attitude to personal ties which stem from their feeling that the world is only an insignificant part of the universal design, and the family merely a temporary point of reference rather than the focus of their activities as it is to the Chinese. It is true that in the overseas situation Indian students seldom appear to form close cohesive groups among themselves, and are much more frequently seen with members of other ethnic categories than are the Malays and Chinese. However, in proportion to their numbers they show a great deal more interest in student associations at a national or institutional level, and, possibly because they are in the minority among Asians both in Western Australia and in Malaysia, have an appreciation of the ways in which formal associations can exert pressure on the authorities to procure concessions and benefits.

When an Indian student considers that he has been treated with injustice he may become excited and emotional, but he usually lacks the staying power and implacability of the Chinese in battling for his rights. He is more likely to turn to administrative or government authority, for example guidance officers, than to members of his primary or peer group for assistance in times of trouble. Hsu (1963) again suggests that Hindus are more likely to make unilateral demands on those in superior positions and tend to expect more of their government than do the Chinese.

Indians from Malaysia experience much difficulty in the search for employment on return home. This is due partly to the preference accorded Malays in government positions and partly to the fact that few of the southern Indians are involved in private commercial enterprises (Hodgkin, 1963). In consequence there is some insecurity in respect of their future prospects, and a definite possibility that on returning home they may find themselves low in the prestige hierarchy or even without employment. Du Bois (1956) has related difficulties of future upward mobility to frustration and alienation in the overseas situation. Indian students who fail to make the grade are often resentful that they have not been given further opportunities to try again, and blame the Australian authorities.

The majority of Indian students from Malaysia have had the greater part of their formal education in the English language, and therefore usually have fewer linguistic difficulties than many of the Chinese and Malays. Because responsibility for their maintenance overseas is in the hands of the nuclear family there are relatively few Indians able to take advantage of foreign education as private students; and on the whole, perhaps because of their small numbers and the fact that those who take this step need a fairly strong incentive to do so, their standard of ability seems to be higher than in the case of the other ethnic categories. Failure is therefore more likely to be due to social or interpersonal upsets rather than academic disabilities. In addition, most of those who come here have fathers who have had a Western-type education, many for one of the professions, so that there is a greater degree of understanding of overseas educational requirements and more appreciation of living problems here, both on the part of parents and among the students before they leave home.

Among the problems which affect the progress of Indian students, those of personal relationships cause the greatest stress. They appear to need, even more than others do, the satisfaction of close personal ties, and, far from viewing these negatively, to depend on them for emotional support; and it is here that danger lies in the foreign setting. Australians are friendly, as a rule, but this is often at a superficial level. Deeper emotional ties are harder to establish. In the words of one Indian student, "It is easy to be friendly with Australians but difficult to find a friend." Breakdown of the ties they do manage to form brings corresponding disillusionment and unhappiness. Where these relationships involve members of the opposite sex, there are greater hazards. Religious differences create problems if marriage with an Australian is contemplated, and the reactions of relatives at home add to these difficulties. Indian parents usually expect to arrange marriages on a basis of family, caste, and income criteria and it is not unusual for a Hindu family to disown a son who marries an Australian girl. This possibility, as well as that of friction with the girl's family on the grounds of "colour prejudice," is a source of strain and worry to a student caught up in such a situation.

One of the characteristics of Hindu society in India, and to some extent in other parts of Asia, is the influential part played by the "guru" or teacher. Traditionally the guru is a religious teacher and, in a sense, a bridge between the illusory life of the world and the life of the gods. Some of this respect for the guru has devolved on the secular teacher, and tends to inhibit discussion and critical analysis of material in lectures and books; in other words, as in the case of the Chinese, cultural factors, still influential in a new environment, continue to militate against expression of "originality" and "initiative" except within the bounds of tradition.

Malays

A few of the Indian students from Southeast Asia are Muslims, but all the Malay students profess this religion. Those from the northern and more rural states of Malaya appear to take their religious beliefs more seriously than those from the more sophisticated urban areas. Because of the political emphasis on encouraging the development of the Malays from more "backward" areas, more of these are going overseas for further study, many with the assistance of Government or State scholarships.

Difficulty was recently experienced in an Australian boarding school when the headmaster ruled that five Malay boys must attend Sunday chapel. He had not enforced the order until he found them disobeying school rules during this period when they were unsupervised. He also felt that isolation from this service might create an Asian bloc in the school. The boys wrote to their parents, one of them was removed from the school, and complaints were made at a national level through the respective High Commissioners. A compromise was reached when the Malays were permitted to study either the Koran or their school books at the back of the hall during the service.

One important tenet of Islam is the doctrine of predestination. Failure in an examination can be attributed to the will of Allah, in accordance with the view that it is idle for human beings to make any effort to combat destiny. This is not necessarily a matter of conscious rationalization at the time; but it supplies a convincing excuse for failure, in the eyes of kin who are in a rural environment at home, and means that a Malay who has not completed his course need have little fear of "losing face" on his return home. As he also has little difficulty in obtaining employment in Malaysia in the present political situation, he is not faced with the same threat to his chances of upward mobility as are the Indians. Consequently many Malay students in Australia have a light-hearted attitude to study problems and are easily deflected by sociable diversions. They are warm-hearted and responsive to overtures of friendship. Ability and interest in sport and a keen sense of humour make them popular with young Australians, but often with those whose interest in formal education is negligible, so that temptations are great to spend more time than they can afford away from study.

Possibly because a young Malay is likely to have come from a nuclear family home where he has had a strong tie with his mother (Djamour, 1959), he readily develops similar relationships with his landlady or other Australian persons who show a motherly attitude toward him. This can facilitate his adjustment to life in a foreign environment (Du Bois, 1956).

It has often been said that Malays do not show a great interest in commerce and have little wish to acquire wealth or save money (Djamour, 1959). There have been many attempts at the political level to create an interest among the Malays in the economic development of their country. This is probably the reason why most of those who are sent overseas with government assistance enroll for degrees in economics or commerce or take up accounting. A lack of personal interest in these fields may be one reason why so many of them find it difficult to concentrate on their studies, and why the failure rate among them is high.

Differences in Cultural Backgrounds Are Crucial

Variations in cultural and subcultural background among the Asian students who come to Australia make it clear that they cannot, with advantage, be classified in a single category. Apart from differences between nation-states themselves, many of the developing nations of Southeast Asia could be called, in Furnivall's terms (1948), "plural societies"; and although they are all trying to unite their peoples into coherent entities this aim is still a long way short of realization. Malaysia is possibly the most prosperous and highly developed among these states, and its political organization is based on a "democratic" system which bears some resemblance to that of Australia; yet the cultural divergences among its peoples are far greater than those found in Australia, where the population is predominantly of Western European origin.

All too often, persons who are concerned with the education and social-personal adjustment of students from these Asian countries regard them as a relatively homogeneous group labelled "Asians," or, rather more specifically, as "Malaysians"; and they assume, accordingly, that a uniform approach to them will suffice. There is also a tendency to see the processes of cross-cultural education in terms of total "assimilation," rather than as a matter of temporary adjustment and selective acceptance of certain techniques, knowledge and behaviour. It has been suggested, by Australian teachers and administrators, that the really successful foreign students are those who enter the educational system at the secondary level and who emerge from the "operation" as "Westerners" in all but physical appearance. This side-steps the serious issue of re-adjustment when such students return home, and, especially in Australia, where the official immigration policy precludes permanent residence for most Asians, overlooks the primary aim of providing educational facilities to assist not only individual persons but, more generally, the developing nations from which they come.

COMMON PROBLEMS

There are, however, some problems of cross-cultural education which confront all the students who come from these newly developing countries.

In any educational experience, motivation or incentive is a key factor in relation to success or failure. Young persons who are sent away from home to study need strong motivation to withstand the strain of changes in cultural behaviour, of loneliness, and lack of primary group support, as well as difficulties of language and new study procedures. Those who come from societies or subcultures where parental authority is restrictive and largely unquestioned may have no interest in the actual subject matter of the courses they undertake. In the case of the Chinese and Indians, future careers have usually been mapped out for them by parental ambition or by family pressures. Their concern for academic achievement thus has to do with the culturally defined goals of prestige, wealth, and family pride rather than with the desire to become qualified in a profession for its own sake. In Malaysia there is some anxiety that the Malays should achieve educational advancement rapidly in order to be able to compete with the Chinese; for them, therefore, the pressure is usually phrased as one of national or political necessity, and very often their choice of career is dictated by the type of scholarship offered by a Malayan State or the Malaysian Federal Government.

Western education, particularly if acquired in a foreign country, is an instrument of social and economic advancement whether in relation to the family or at an individual level. However, it is usually far removed from social reality in the community from which the student comes. Many Western educationalists continue to pay lip service, at least, to the scholarly ideal of learning for its own sake, although for the "man in the street" it is becoming increasingly a matter of obtaining qualifications for more material ends. For the young Asian, as for many Australian (and other) students, the immediate problem is rather that of mastering the knowledge required to answer examination questions. This is perhaps more important in the overseas situation, where so often the actual content of what is learnt bears little relation to future needs in professional service at home. Consequently it is almost impossible to persuade the Asian student to follow trails which might develop a wider range of interests but which have little direct bearing on his immediate objective of acquiring the degree or diploma or certificates he wants. If he can do so by the traditional method of learning by rote the night before he takes the test, he is unlikely to follow the advice of his teachers and counsellors to try any other system of study.

Technical skills alone do not have the same prestige value at home as academic qualifications, so that even if a young Asian has aptitude and abilities which would ensure him a rewarding future in some technological field he is likely nevertheless to struggle to achieve entry into an academic profession for which he is little suited. Thus several students whose interests led in the direction of journalism or commercial art have been forced by parental pressure or by their own fears of future status problems to try to obtain accountancy qualifications, or degrees in engineering or law.

At the present time numbers of students come from rural or working class backgrounds where the technical skills of their parents or relatives have brought sufficient prosperity to finance their overseas study. But Western education and the prestige accorded to students in developing Asia alienates them in some degree from their "uneducated" relatives. They therefore lack cues for conduct in the new situation even in their own country. In these circumstances their anxieties are intensified by criticism, and their confidence undermined. Some teachers feel that continual urging is necessary to improve results through increased application to study. Often these exhortations take the form of criticism of learning methods and attitudes which are imputed to them on the basis of "racial stereotypes," without an appreciation of the actual situation or of its cultural complexity. This damages the students' self esteem and estranges them emotionally from those teachers, and from Australians in general (Roucek, 1958; Du Bois, 1956). Moreover the overseas student's living quarters may be such that he comes into contact, outside his school or class environment, with a different subculture, where formal education, particularly at the tertiary level, is not highly valued, where little prestige is accorded to students as such, and where academic qualifications do not necessarily bring increased social prestige. In such a subculture he is much more likely to find unfavourable or intolerant attitudes toward his nation or ethnic group than among the better educated members of the host society. All these factors have been mentioned, by social scientists who have studied cross-cultural exchange, as contributing to alienation and stress among overseas students (Roucek, 1958; Morris, 1956).

It has been observed that, on the whole, students at the university level appear to have fewer problems of adjustment than do those in the secondary and technical establishments. This may be attributed in part to greater maturity, but greater satisfaction in terms of prestige and status probably helps. In addition, social intercourse with better educated persons has a bearing on the situation; and possibly wider appreciation of cultural differences on the part of university staff members may be an important contributory factor in facilitating the students' adjustment.

The role of the educator in programmes of cross-cultural exchange, then, is by no means an easy one. It is fallacious to assume that nothing but good can be the outcome of translating a large number of young people from one cultural background into the educational system of another without making the necessary allowances or alterations. Where failures occur there is a tendency to place the blame entirely on inadequate selection procedures in the underdeveloped countries, or differences in educational standards there. These, however, represent only part of the problem; and if the maximum benefit is to be achieved in personal and national assistance, as well as in the broader field of international relations, the implications must be considered in their wider aspects. An educator cannot expect to make much headway unless he appreciates the gaps between the cultural background of his pupils and the types of learning process, both formal and informal, to which they have been subjected at home as well as abroad. He must be able to interpret to them the differing systems of rewards and relationships which apply in the new situation, and he must understand problems of adjustment which may have a vital effect on the students' ability to take advantage of the educational facilities which are offered. In this connection it should be added that, despite the increasing number of formal surveys and questionnaires, not enough is known about the actual behaviour of Australian students, so that comparisons are apt to be sketchy and impressionistic: more research is needed, to clarify the picture of cultural and subcultural contrasts — and similarities; for example, what is involved in the general role of simply being a student.

There is much to be said for the system of orientation of foreign students in specialized courses which are included in some programmes in the United States. This, however, presents difficulties in a country such as Australia which is itself in a relatively early stage of industrial development and economic growth. In Western Australia a beginning has been made in the introduction, in 1964, of short orientation courses of a few days or weeks for newly arrived students in both the University and the Technical Colleges.

However, the wider training of teachers in cross-cultural understanding would benefit not only overseas students but Australians as well. There is need for all members of the host society to appreciate cultural differences and, what is more, to consider them objectively. For Australians, whose social and cultural orientation has hitherto been limited mainly to Europe, but whose horizons are rapidly widening to include the nearer nations of

Southeast Asia, this expansion of outlook is not only desirable but vital to future survival.

REFERENCES

Abegg, L. *The Mind of East Asia*. London, New York: Thames and Hudson, 1952.

Berndt, R. M. Anthropology and Education. *The Educand*, vol. 2, no. 3, 1956.

Caiden, N. Student Failure in Australian Universities, *Vestes*, vol. VII, no. 1, 1964.

Djamour, J. *Malay Kinship and Marriage in Singapore*. London: Athlone Press, University of London (London School of Economics, Monographs on Social Anthropology, no. 21), 1959.

Du Bois, C. *Foreign Students and Higher Education in the United States of America*. Washington, D.C.: American Council on Education, 1956.

Flecker, R. Characteristics of Passing and Failing Students in First Year University Mathematics. *The Educand*, vol. 3, no. 3, 1959.

Freedman, M. *Lineage Organisation in Southeastern China*. London: Athlone Press, University of London (London School of Economics Monographs on Social Anthropology, no. 18), 1958.

Furnivall, J. S. *Colonial Policy and Practice*. Cambridge: Cambridge University Press, 1958.

Hodgkin, M. C. Aspects of Australian Education for Asians. *Journal of Higher Education*, vol. 1, no. 2, 1963.

Hsu, F. L. K. *Clan, Caste and Club*. Princeton: D. van Nostrand, 1963.

Hu Hsien-chin. The Chinese Concepts of Face. In *Personal Character and Cultural Milieu* (ed., D. C. Haring). New York: Syracuse University Press, 1956.

Morris, R. T. National Status and Attitudes to Foreign Students. *Journal of Social Issues*, vol. 12, no. 1, 1956.

Murphy, H. B. M. Culture and Mental Disorder in Singapore. In *Culture and Mental Health* (ed., M. Opler). New York: Macmillan, 1959.

Needham, J. *Science and Civilisation in China*, vol. 2. Cambridge: Cambridge University Press, 1956.

Northrop, F. S. C. *The Meeting of East and West*. New York: Macmillan, 1960.

Roucer, J. S. The Sociological Implications of Studying Abroad. *Journal of Human Relations*, vol. 6, no. 2, 1958.

Rowley, S., and Ironmonger, D. S. Graduation Rates in Australian Universities. *Vestes*, vol. VI, no. 3, 1963.

Sellitz, C. et al. *Attitudes and Social Relations of Foreign Students in the United States*. Minneapolis: University of Minnesota Press, 1963.

Sharp, L. Cultural Continuities and Discontinuities. *Journal of Asian Studies*, vol. 22, no. 1, 1962.

Weakland, J. H. The Organisation of Action in Chinese Culture. *Psychiatry*, vol. 13, 1950.

Wells, A. F. Patterns of Authority in the Family in Malaya. *Transactions of the Third World Congress of Sociology*, 1956.

FURTHER READINGS

DuBois, Cora. "Some notions on learning intercultural understanding," in George D. Spindler (ed.), *Education and anthropology*. Stanford: Stanford University Press, 1955.

Epstein, Erwin H. "Cross cultural sampling and a conceptualization of 'professional instruction,' " *Journal of Experimental Education*, vol. 33 (Summer 1965).

Gezi, Kalil I. "Factors associated with student adjustment in cross-cultural contact," *California Journal of Educational Research*, vol. 16 (May 1965). (Reprinted in Gezi, Kalil I., and James E. Myers (eds.), *Teaching in American culture*. New York: Holt, Rinehart and Winston, 1968.)

Hippler, Arthur E. *Barrow and Kotzebue: an exploratory comparison of acculturation and education in two large northwestern Alaska villages*. Minneapolis: Training Center for Community Programs, University of Minnesota, 1969.

Spaulding, Seth, John Singleton, and Paul Watson. "The context of international development education," *Review of Educational Research*, vol. 38 (June 1968).

Taba, Hilda. "Cultural orientation in comparative education," *Comparative Education Review*, vol. 7 (February 1963).

28

There is, to some extent, a necessary "reality gap" between school and the (cruel) world outside it. Formal education may in fact be defined by its discontinuity with the otherwise real world. Learning a foreign language, for example, is a discontinuous experience by definition. Formal schooling and its clientele suffer, and the real world tolerates, discontinuities to a point. Thus, one usual complaint about foreign language instruction is that it is too discontinuous — it no longer relates, or, it does not last the distance from school to home. Mrs. Ramcharan-Crowley, who was formerly headmistress of Naparima Preparatory School, San Fernando, Trinidad, argues that the systems of education that are colonial legacies to the island societies of St. Lucia and Dominica base themselves in cultural discontinuities excessive to the point of human waste and abuse. She is plainspoken about effective alternatives. In describing the dilemma of island students who, having been schooled to perform on academic examinations as remote in practical benefit as the off-island opportunities in higher education they represent, "face a lifetime of ill-paid and despised subsistence agricultural or urban labor," Mrs. Ramcharan-Crowley remarks a discontentment that is, in part, global. The late Adlai Stevenson phrased its thrust as a "revolution of rising expectations." Fueled by intolerable discontinuities in systems of formal education, perilous to standing social arrangements, the revolution may only await the "local patriotism" Mrs. Ramcharan-Crowley suggests is emerging among St. Lucian and Dominican Creoles.

PEARL RAMCHARAN-CROWLEY

Creole Culture:
Outcast in West Indian Schools

For the past century and a half, colonial educational policies in St. Lucia and Dominica have been designed to eradicate the local Creole cultures. These policies have resulted in a wide gulf between formal education and everyday life. An anthropological study of these island cultures suggests changes that might be made in school programs to meet present and future needs, and to serve better the goals of the new Federation of the West Indies.

The islands of St. Lucia and Dominica lie in the southern section of the chain of the Lesser Antilles and are separated from each other by the island of Martinique, which like Guadeloupe to the north is a *departement* of France. Although St. Lucia, Dominica, Martinique, and Guadeloupe once shared the same culture and language, the divergent regimes of Britain and France over the past hundred and fifty years have caused considerable cultural variation. Today St. Lucia and Dominica are British islands, and they form two of the ten administrative territorial units in the Federation.

Dominica, with an area of 305 square miles, has a population of sixty-five thousand; while the smaller island of St. Lucia, with an area of 233 square miles, has a population of ninety thousand. Both populations are overwhelmingly of mixed European and African origin, with a few hundred local and foreign whites in each island, plus several thousand Christian East Indians in St. Lucia and a handful of Caribs in Dominica.

Both islands were originally inhabited by Caribs and Arawaks, who successfully resisted European settlement until the seventeenth century, when France and Britain began an extended naval and military struggle for supremacy. Before final British conquest at the beginning of the nineteenth century, Dominica changed hands five times and St. Lucia, thirteen times.

The resulting Creole culture is a strange mixture of African and provincial French elements plus influences from the colonial British and the nearly extinct Caribs. French traditions linger in the legal code, in formal religion, in dress, in cuisine, and in vocabulary; but the heritage of Africa and of slavery continues in magic practices, in mating patterns, in family structure, in music, in folklore, in attitudes and in values. These islands

From *School Review*, vol. 69, no. 4 (Winter 1961), published by The University of Chicago Press. © 1961 by the University of Chicago.

are not only poor and isolated, but also deeply different from the French and the British islands around them. In a hundred and fifty years of persistent effort, the British authorities have failed to replace the local Creole culture with more generalized British colonial patterns of behavior.

In St. Lucia and in Dominica, as in other islands of the West Indies, the earliest schools were established by religious denominations. But in recent years schools have come more and more under government control. Today most of the fifty-two primary schools in St. Lucia are run by the Catholic Church, several are run by Protestant groups, and only one is a government school. However, all receive government funds. In Dominica there are forty-four government schools and only three government-aided religious schools.

In spite of compulsory attendance laws in both islands, about 25 per cent of the children, most of them in rural areas, are not in school at all. If these children chose to attend, there would be no place for them in the schools, and there is little prospect that the governments and the churches will be able to finance schools for all the children in the foreseeable future.

The spoken language of these islands and of nearby Martinique and Guadeloupe is Creole, known locally as *patois*, a French vocabulary with a simplified grammar containing some African elements. Taylor (1955), Verin (1958), and Alleyne (1961) have recently studied Creole linguistic structure and the cultural effects of its rivalry with English. Without a knowledge of Creole, neither French nor British colonizers could hope to understand the island cultures. Even today English-speaking government officials and professionals who are unfamiliar with the Creole language are out of touch with the life of the people.

The educational systems of these islands have aimed at substituting so-called culturally rich English for Creole. As early as 1844 Henry Breen, a British civil servant in St. Lucia, spoke of the benefits to be gained by the universal adoption of English in the schools (1844). Yet today in St. Lucia 40 per cent of the people speak only Creole. In Dominica 25 per cent speak only Creole.

Since Creole is an unwritten language, these people are illiterates. The illiteracy rate for St. Lucia is 45 per cent and for Dominica, 35 per cent. The rates include illiterates who speak English. These two islands have the highest illiteracy rates in the Caribbean with the exception of Haiti, where the rate is 89 per cent and where Creole is also spoken.

The local English, which is spoken with Creole intonations, is interlarded with Creolisms, which have been partially translated (It makin' hot, oui!). This colloquial English is commonly spoken even by highly educated islanders. For they, too, use Creole by choice in everyday life.

According to contemporary learning theory, a foreign language is best learned through vernacular instruction in the early years of schooling.

Yet Creole has traditionally been forbidden in elementary schools, although of necessity this rule is often broken with the younger children who speak no English.

The exclusive use of English as the medium of instruction has proven something of a farce. In spite of its practicality and increasing prestige, there is no indication that English is replacing Creole in the community. Rather, children from their earliest years are forced to live two lives: the permissive, fun-filled daily round of Creole life and the rigid, stultifying school life, where language expression is inhibited and parrot reading is the practice.

These people should be encouraged to be bilingual — literate in English while still speaking their mother tongue. Although Antillean Creole can easily be written in the McConnell-Laubach orthography used in Haiti, local patriotism has not yet developed sufficiently to demand that this system be taught in the schools.

The moral code as propounded in the schools is also at variance with local practice. Formal marriage, legitimacy, and the patrilineal family are held up as the desirable patterns for children, 80 per cent of whom are born out of wedlock and live in matrifocal families marked by frequently changing common-law unions.

In these poor and undevelopable agricultural islands, unattainable foreign living standards are presented as standards for the students to strive toward. Courses on domestic science are pathetically unrealistic in terms of local products, tastes, needs, and equipment. Few girls in St. Lucia in their hillside shacks equipped with coalpots and homemade furniture will need to know how to prepare an elegant tea with full silver service. But they will need to know the rudiments of nutrition and child care. This gulf between what is taught in school and how life is lived at home drives deep into almost every aspect of living.

Less than 3 per cent of the population get a high-school education. Those who do graduate consider agricultural labor and craft work degrading, and aim at government service and other white-collar employment. Whenever possible they leave the islands to pursue careers abroad.

High-school education aims primarily at preparing students to pass British External Examinations, which qualify students for further schooling in England. Thus, disproportionate stress is placed on high attainment in academic subjects, since the reputation of a school is based on the number of its students who pass these British examinations. As a result, most of the students are denied a curriculum in keeping with local knowledge, interests, and expectations. West Indian parents fiercely resist any attempt to change these unrealistic and undemocratic examinations because they fear the loss of standards and prestige, and the difficulty of transferring credits abroad.

Consequently, there are almost no vocational courses, no mechanical or technical training courses, no opportunities to study crafts, agriculture, or husbandry. Few attempts are made to attract students to careers in these useful fields. The lack of business courses combined with the local practice of mutual financial responsibility among all of one's relatives discourages individual efforts in trade. The result is that most of the local business enterprises are controlled by foreigners. Understandably, the young people are discontented when they realize that they can never obtain the handful of professional and white-collar jobs available in the community, and when they see that they face a lifetime of ill-paid and despised subsistence agricultural or urban labor.

The people, particularly the teachers in these islands, are sharply conscious of the demoralized state of their educational system, and there is considerable public and private discussion and criticism. If these islands are to take their place in the new Federation, their people must be educated more effectively for the lives they are to lead in a democracy. Children must be taught the duties and the responsibilities of citizenship in their new country. Illiterate adults who cannot speak English are at the mercy of unscrupulous exploiters of all kinds and have no chance to share in the life and the wealth of their nation.

The most obvious difficulty inhibiting reform is the shortage of financial resources available to the schools. Foreign missionary groups are not interested in converting people who are already Christian, especially when the government pays the teachers and proclaims its right to control what is taught in the church schools.

Neither island has a teacher-training institute. A few teachers are sent to normal schools in Trinidad and Barbados. Teachers are recruited through a pupil-teacher apprenticeship system. An older teacher is asked to train a young recruit in educational theory and practice, and both take occasional examinations designed for British teachers in a similar apprenticeship system.

In an attempt to upgrade the training program, British teach-yourself textbooks were introduced in St. Lucia, but unfortunately the language and the concepts in the books proved to be beyond the comprehension of the average West Indian adolescent. Under these circumstances it is not difficult to see why few of the better minds are attracted to the teaching profession.

However, each island does have a group of devoted and professionally alert teachers whose vision comes from long years of practice rather than from formal training. More often than not, these teachers find themselves in conflict with a harried administration. A few years ago they forced the dismissal of the director of education in St. Lucia. They considered his teach-yourself system of training impractical and disapproved of his uncompromising attitude toward the use of Creole in the early grades and his policy of keeping foreign-trained teachers in administration rather than releasing them for teaching in the schools (Simmons, 1958; Walters, 1958).

West Indian educators must ultimately recognize that the centuries-old program of total Europeanization has been a failure. Creole culture has been remarkably tenacious in the past and gives every indication of being durable in the future.

A more realistic syllabus must be created, and the parents, the churches, and the island governments must be persuaded to accept it. Along with more buildings, up-to-date West Indian textbooks, and better teacher recruitment and preparation, the schools of the islands need courses that interpret the world in local terms, courses that incorporate local materials and terminology, courses that give the child information that he will find attractive because he can see its usefulness.

Because West Indians are hungry for education and have strong traditions for co-operative activity, these problems can be solved. In the mild Caribbean climate school buildings need not be elaborate. Reasonably functional open-air structures of tapia (clay mixed with grass) with floors of pounded earth, roofs of thatch or galvanized iron, and outdoor sanitary facilities can be built inexpensively with few imported supplies and possibly even with volunteer labor, as churches often are.

There are foreign-trained West Indian professionals qualified to write local textbooks that could easily gain government support. If the governments improved teacher preparation and raised teachers' salaries, more and better teachers would be attracted to the profession. In the village, the teacher's prestige is second only to the priest's; and, as secularism grows, the teacher will tend to replace the priest as the authority on the power structure and the outside world.

Since World War II, Belgian nuns in Dominica have attacked the problem of a realistic syllabus. Their convent high school, originally open only to legitimate upper-class Catholic girls, was converted into a less selective school open to nearly all girls who apply. For those who do not specialize in academic subjects, the school offers classes in domestic science and crafts.

One nun who had considerable training in art experimented with native materials and resurrected an almost extinct island technique for making rugs, mats, and other objects from palm, sisal, and other local fibers. Old Dominican women, who were paid for their work, were brought in to train the girls, and country women were remunerated for gathering and preparing the palm and other materials. An outlet for the finished products was found in a tourist shop in Barbados. Tourists and wealthy local people proved willing to pay relatively high prices for these rugs, and they are now shipped all over the world. This craft has even been commemorated on a Dominican postage stamp. The nuns not only support their schools and other charity work on the proceeds, but point out that the craft school is doing what the convent school failed to do: providing incomes for young girls so they can resist the economic blandishments of men.

More programs of this sort could use local skills and artistic talent, develop healthy small industries, attract tourists and income, and direct the West Indian urge for education into fruitful channels.

REFERENCES

Alleyne, Mervin. "Language and Society in St. Lucia," *Caribbean Studies*, I (April, 1961), 1–10.
Breen, Henry H. *St. Lucia: Historical, Statistical, and Descriptive* (London: Longmans, 1844), p. 169.
Simmons, Harold F. C. "Lucia in Wonderland," *Voice of St. Lucia* (January 18, January 25, February 1, 1958).
Taylor, Douglas MacRae. "Phonic Interference in Dominican Creole," *Word*, II (April, 1955), 45–52.
Verin, Pierre. "The Rivalry of Creole and English in the West Indies," *West-Indisohe Gids*, XXXVIII (December, 1958), 163–67.
Walters, Elsa H. "Lucia in the Looking Glass," *Voice of St. Lucia* (April 5, 1958).

FURTHER READINGS

Hood, Catrions, T. E. Oppe, J. B. Pless, and Evelyn Apte. *The children of West Indian immigrants: a study of one-year-olds in Paddington.* London: Institute of Race Relations, 1969.
Landy, David. *Tropical childhood: cultural transmission and learning in a rural Puerto Rican village.* New York: Harper and Row, 1959, 1965.
Oxaal, Ivar. *Black intellectuals come to power: the rise of Creole nationalism in Trinidad and Tobago.* Cambridge, Mass.: Schenkman, 1968.
Rubin, Vera (ed.) *Social and cultural pluralism in the Caribbean.* Annals of the New York Academy of Sciences, vol. 83 (1960).
Smith, Michael G. "Education and occupational choice in Jamaica," *Social and Economic Studies*, vol. 9 (1960). (Reprinted in Smith, *The plural society in the British West Indies.* Berkeley: University of California Press, 1965.)

PART FIVE

ANTHROPOLOGY AND EDUCATION: SOME ISSUES

Hunger, bad housing, medical neglect, racism, underemployment, religious bias, and miseducation *happen* in America. They are day-by-day miseries for a great many Americans, and the chance of these marginal peoples to be finally free of such oppressions seems small and trite.

The professional response of educators and social scientists to the array of social problems that attend America varies. This reflects, first, differing perceptions of (or beliefs in) *what* it is that is problematic in American society and *to whom*. Second, it represents the differing degrees to which individual educators and social scientists — and associations of them, local and national — are committed to act on those same perceptions or faiths. And third, it signals a constant debate over the nature of a humane and less than problematic society, American or otherwise.

In some views, for instance, social problems are seen as pathologies of specific groups in American society. In other views social problems are seen as expectable, if not the inevitable outcomes of a society that has been built on inequity and which is now subject to the inhuman terrors of a pernicious technology.

The variety of professional response to social problems is also conditioned by the roster of choices, situational or doctrinaire, in appropriate courses of problem solution. Basic convictions tend to divide three ways: some feel change best occurs in slight and progressive increments, others see hope only in wholesale social upheavals, and still others feel that social problems carry in them the seeds of their own, eventual solution. The view that problems self-correct is too often justification for inaction. It is a rebuke (and sometimes of a very precise sort) to those who *are* concerned and who look to fellow man for the relief of man-made social agonies.

445

The two remaining views are characteristic of two general positions on social problems, one or the other of which is usually assumed by educators and social scientists alike. One of these general positions can be called "established"; the other can be referred to as "critical, engaged." "Established" educators and social scientists, most anthropologists included, tend toward agency solutions and remedial or ameliorative social actions. They are inclined to focus on *mind-*changing. For "established" educators and social scientists, social problems are ultimately corrected in the form of mass, or otherwise conspicuous, *attitudinal* change.

The "established," if not steadfastly conserving, are at least disposed to preserve or to but slightly modify *existing* social structure in dealing with social problems. They prefer "value-freedom" and "ethical neutrality" in their relationships as professionals where social problems are concerned, and it can be suggested that their prior commitment is to an as objective as possible and vigorously nonpartisan profession, be it education, social science, or an accepted integration of the two.

"Established" educators and social scientists are dramatically distinct from the "critical, engaged." These latter educators and social scientists, fewer in number and including a very few anthropologists,[1] tend toward solutions to social problems that suppose *agencies* — the schools, the courts, the systems of welfare — *to be a significant part of social problems* and in no way the exclusive right to their solution. They favor social action more radical than remedial. They are inclined to focus on changing the *structure* of American society. Social problems, in their vision, are solvable by the circuitry of a *restructured* American society.

"Critical, engaged" educators and social scientists, if not liberal in their outlook and personal politics, tend at least to view *access to scarce resources* as the most important dimension of social problem-solving. They repudiate the logical possibilities of "value-freedom" and "ethical neutrality," arguing that a profession which takes *no* social positions (in order to maintain its research freedom and to secure its commitment to objectivity in the pursuit of "truths") in conducting its intellectual business is in effect opting for the social *status quo*, which is an advocacy — however sublime or unwitting. They are committed to a social action craft or discipline: education, social science, or a partisan and often circumstantial match of the two.

---

[1] A more detailed discussion of social problems, especially as viewed by contemporary anthropologists, appears in Edward Storey (ed.), *An Uncertain America*. Boston: Little, Brown (in press).

"Critical, engaged" educators and social scientists would agree, more or less, that

> There is lamentably little recognition of the crisis in education. There is smugness where there should be concern; complaining "jams" the few voices urging true innovation and change. The moderate and the mild control the destiny of education. They have deluded themselves that blunted emotions signify maturity. They desire change but the change is only some modest tinkering. They wish to repair the system by replacing worn-out parts. In training teachers to work with the disadvantaged they may add a course or two, or bring to the faculty a person who claims expertness in this area. All too often the instructional program reinforces the notion of cultural deprivation and as such may be a negative rather than a positive influence on the teacher.[2]

That public education is in the hands of "established" educators (and those social scientists allied with them) is a capture of some good with bad. Many "established" thinkers are of course cognizant of the crises in education. Some are themselves victims of these; others are acting out genuine commitments to progressive change. But many more (front-line teachers as well as administrators) *are* smug, and it is the grip of their attitude that has provoked most of the writings in Part Five.

Smugness is not always willful. It can be due to plain ignorance and social insensitivity as well as to an indifference and complacency about the folds of false promise and bureaucratic privilege that wrap the school experience. Smugness has done much to breed the notion of "cultural deprivation." The notion is, itself, illogical. A culture — that is, a set of patterned behaviors distinctive to a human group — does *not* deprive. If anything, it *provides* or *facilitates meaning* in the personal and public lives of the people who share it.

A culture is not *in its own right* depriving. A society or social order judges the patterned behaviors of a member group to be depriving, to the extent that these influence persons away from or in opposition to established, mainstream, or otherwise desired ways.

The idea of "cultural deprivation" is handy then to those whose culture they believe to underwrite school success, if not also to stand as *the* most worthy, indeed, the *standard* of behavior to which all

---

[2] Smith, B. Othanel, in collaboration with Saul B. Cohen and Arthur Pearl, *Teachers for the Real World*. Washington, D.C.: The American Association of Colleges for Teacher Education, 1969, p. 8.

cultural others should aspire. When schools and schooling, as in America, are under the social auspices and effective political and economic control of such an authoritative standard, "cultural others" are offered little choice but to adapt to, adopt, parody, and perhaps finally rebel against that "standard." School success is not only most easily achieved by and through the repertoire of "standard" behaviors: *school success is in fact defined by them.*

It is a (mostly) white and "middle-class" game, and its whole has rapidly come to be seen as loaded — in its present form — by the millions of cultural others in our society. The alternatives these groups represent contain possible solutions to the socially problematic circumstances of American public education. It is characteristic of vanguard educational change and reform programs today that this potential is being acted on, that differing cultural influences are being accepted *as relevant* to problems of the school and schooling, not as deterrents to their resolution.

No effect of anthropology in relation to education seems quite so worthwhile as that which works to resolve the human problems of a system of public education become inhumane. That effect is an outcome of insights into *what* it is that is humanly problematic in contemporary American education. It is also a result of determinations to do something about these problems, whether structural faults or group insensitivities.

The articles in Part Five communicate the kinds and scale of insights that are possible by (though not exclusive to) anthropological inquiry into schools and schooling. The articles do not exhaust anthropological approaches to either the human dilemmas generated by current educational practices or the policies of inequity that sustain those practices. Nor are these writings always in complete agreement on the manner and intensity of professional involvement that is adequate to effective engagement of education as a *social* problem. Though not all the authors are equally "critical" or "engaged," none are mistaken as "establishment."

The authors share commitments to act beyond perfunctory performances of anthropological research in education. That stance structures Mr. Gans' satire and it is explicit in Mr. Bruner's informed discussion of the educational politic, even as these two nonanthropologists make expert and creative use of anthropological perspective in treating contemporary educational problems. A commitment to action may be seen by some to be unduly harsh and strident in the Henninger-Esposito selection; it is as an underwater wave in the deliberate essay by Mr. Lesser.

A decision to personally involve oneself in correcting the deep-seated biases of organized testing may, for some, emerge from the report of research offered by Miss Cohen, while the very nature of professional "responsibility" to and for public education in America is Mr. Lindquist's special focus. These last two writers, one concerned with conflicts resulting from cultural differences in cognitive styling, the other with anthropological caring, reveal much of the substance and spirit of anthropology as it relates to education in this final, and perhaps most vital, dimension — education as a social enterprise.

29

His tongue not so completely in cheek, Mr. Gans imaginatively probes a contemporary learning environment. He reports "artifacts" and structural "remains" uncovered by the "Center for Urban Archaeology." His deft use of archaeological method extends to inference, phrased here as a set of engaging hypotheses. Mr. Gans asks oblique but deadly serious questions — questions which, for all their familiarity, plainly need answering, nuclear holocaust or no. Gans is particularly concerned, as was Mead (Part One), with the anachronistic institution of secondary education. A special effect of his imaginary "dig" is to insinuate how little of what we do know about optimal learning environments is actually subject to practice in education today. Mr. Gans' published work includes People and Plans *(New York: Basic Books, 1968). Formerly Senior Research Associate, Center for Urban Education, Gans is presently associated with the Joint Center for Urban Studies of the Massachusetts Institute of Technology and Harvard University.*

HERBERT J. GANS

Report of the Center for Urban Archaeology

This report describes the preliminary findings of excavations conducted by the Center for Urban Archaeology in a suburban American settlement of the Early Atomic Age (*circa* 1950 to 2100). The year's "dig" was highly successful, for we uncovered a large building approximately 900 years old, probably erected at the beginning of the E.A. Age. Detailed analyses to determine the purpose of this structure are now underway.

The building consisted of nearly 50 rooms, all on one floor, with a central wing and two long perpendicular wings to form the letter H. Except for some large rooms in the central wing, almost all rooms were uniformly of the same size. In two of these, part of the flooring has been sufficiently preserved to suggest that a group of people gathered there frequently. We think that these people were arranged in rows facing toward an inside wall, where a special person or machine may have stood to lead the group in a common activity.

The very largest room was built on an incline, sloping down toward a smaller room with a raised floor. Another large room contained remains of primitive wood and metal working tools; in yet another we found three metal casings, on which we believe the inhabitants started fires with the

From *The Urban Review*, November 1968, a publication of the Center for Urban Education.

aid of a gas. Three rooms held fragments of what must have been scientific equipment, but of an earlier era and no longer used by the scientists of the period. One such room was littered with fish skeletons, the bones of small domesticated birds and animals, and large numbers of glass fragments.

The most interesting of the large rooms had a very high ceiling, and large metal rings and bars of various sizes were evidently attached to the walls. Immediately adjacent we uncovered two identical smaller rooms, probably encased in porcelain, in which a liquid was dispensed from metal pipes in the ceiling.

The building was entered from the central wing; its wall construction suggests many doors, as if masses of people had normally come in at the same time. Nearby were a number of smaller rooms. In one we found an almost perfectly preserved table; the fact that it was made of mahogany, even then a rare wood, suggests that an important functionary occupied the room. An antechamber contained a small locked metal case which held a few coins; its cover was inscribed in raised letters. The only letters still identifiable were "Pt" and "csh."

As far as we can tell, the building was not in full use at the time of its destruction, for we found parts of only three skeletons, male, probably 13–17 years of age, all of them in the room with the metal rings and bars.

Because of the sparsity of skeletons and artifacts, we can only guess at the purpose of this structure, and the team is currently considering a number of hypotheses to guide the analysis. Some team members believe the building was a prison, the series of uniform rooms housing groups of prisoners, each overseen by a guard. The rooms with the metal rings and pipes could have been used to torture prisoners. The advocates of this hypothesis also support their argument by the location of the structure on a large open space some distance from other buildings as if to isolate it from the rest of the settlement.

This writer doubts that the structure was a prison, for we found no evidence of the barred windows and towers used in this era to prevent prisoners from escaping; and preliminary chemical analyses have indicated no trace of human blood anywhere, thus ruling out torture. It is, of course, possible that the building was an institution to rehabilitate young prisoners, for we know that the elders of this culture were enmeshed in bitter conflict with their young. It may be that the various instruments we excavated were used for milder, nonlethal forms of torture.

Other team members believe that the structure served the community as a meeting place, either for religious or political functions. The big room with the sloping floor may have been used by priests or tribal leaders for community-wide gatherings or rites; the uniform rooms, for meetings of clans or other subgroups. The proponents of the religious hypothesis suggest that the room with the metal rings was designed for orgiastic exercises; the metal pipes may have supplied alcohol, a liquid depressant widely used by this culture for mind-expansion. They also speculate that the letter H may have had a sacred meaning. The advocates of the political explanation argue that the firemaking artifacts and the animal bones point to the serving of food, a popular practice at community gatherings of the culture. They add that the metal box contained "Political Cash," used to reward leaders for making the desired public decisions.

I find neither hypothesis persuasive. We know that the religious and political rituals of this culture did not involve wood or metal working tools, and its political ideology was egalitarian, so that the community could not have been segregated into nearly 50 subgroups.

Two younger team members think that the building was used to educate the age group represented by the skeletons we excavated. They suggest that the young people were required to assemble in the uniform rooms each day where they were taught by an elder specially trained for this purpose, and that the other rooms were devoted to special schooling in the use of tools, scientific instruments, methods of food preparation and animal killing. It is thought that the room with the metal rings provided muscular training to prepare young people for hand-to-hand combat in intertribal wars.

Although this theory offers explanations for almost all the foods uncovered by our dig, I frankly find it indefensible. For example, since the outside walls of the uniform rooms were evidently constructed of window glass, it is hard to believe that the young people would have paid much attention even to a specially trained elder; they must have spent most of their time watching the activities going on outside. Moreover, it seems highly unlikely that the relatively advanced culture of the Early Atomic Age would have instructed its young people in the use of tools and scientific instruments already anachronistic at the time.

However, my main objection to this hypothesis is that no archaeological studies of yet earlier cultures have ever found a special building devoted to educating the 13–17 age group. In these earlier cultures, as in our own, young people of that age were educated by involvement in the life of the community, by working in various productive and public service activities to learn how the community functioned, what work opportunities were available to them, and what types of work they found most suitable to their own personalities. In preindustrial cultures, where occupational roles were limited, they were simply fitted into a slot and then learned the traditional ways of filling it. This contrasts with our own era, in which the work experience, combined with a couple of hours of daily reading and discussion, helps them learn to understand themselves and adult society, and prepares them for benefiting maximally from the general education and specialized occupational training of the universities when they are 18.

It is simply inconceivable to me, therefore, that the Early Atomic Age, would have used special educational institutions which segregated, physically and socially, this alert and vital age group from the everyday life of the community. Surely the culture was sophisticated enough to know that Man learns best by doing and problem solving in an ongoing enterprise, that the 13–17 age group is much too energetic to spend its days cooped up in training rooms, and that youngsters of any age learn best from each other, and not from an elder, who, by necessity, must impose his own ways on them.

The young team members argue, and rightly so, that one cannot assume other cultures to have cherished the values that we consider rational. They also suggest that the building was similar to our own childhood training laboratories for instruction in graphic, visual, oral and mathematical modes of communication. I feel, however, that the differences outweigh the similarities. Our laboratories may segregate young people for educational purposes, but only from ages 4 to 12. During these years, they are best able to learn communication skills, but are still too inexperienced in social living to benefit materially from social studies and other academic methods for understanding self and society. Moreover, the laboratories use teaching machines, informal learning groups and individual tutoring; they certainly do not force youngsters, who are still quite asocial, into formal groups for instructional purposes.

My own hypothesis is that the building was a relic from the Machine Age which immediately preceded the Early Atomic Age. Probably built as a prison, it no longer served a regular purpose in the settlement and may even have stood empty. After all, despite its size, the structure contained only three skeletons and just a handful of the millions of artifacts extant in this period. We know that the culture preserved outdated buildings as part of its worship of history; we also know that its young people often had to isolate themselves in unused structures for sexual rites and other forms of play which were outlawed by the elders.

There is not enough evidence to prove this, or any other, hypothesis, and further excavations of similar structures are needed. If we can obtain the necessary research grants, we shall look for other American communities of this period that are better preserved. If only Nuclear War I had not so completely obliterated so many of these settlements.

FURTHER READINGS

Gans, Herbert J. *The uses of television and their educational implications: preliminary findings from a survey of adult and adolescent New York television viewers.* New York: The Center for Urban Education, 1968.

Henry, Jules. *Culture against man*. New York: Random House, 1963.
Janowitz, Morris. *Institution building in urban education*. New York: Russell Sage Foundation, 1969.
Pettitt, George A. *Prisoners of culture*. New York: Charles Scribner's Sons, 1970.
Willower, Donald J., Terry L. Eidell, and W. K. Hoy. *The school and pupil control ideology*. University Park: Penn State Studies, Monograph no. 24, 1967.

30

"If we insist on replacing the culture of poverty with something precious to us but alien to them," Mr. Ianni claims, on evidence, "we can expect disquieting and even disastrous consequences." Although the notion of a "culture of poverty" is in dispute (see Leacock, Part Two), the imposition upon minority (hence culturally different) Americans of a behavioral regime standardized to the majority white is no longer even contended. It is recognized as being at the heart of the most pervasive contemporary educational crisis. Making one's culture irrelevant; placing groups of American youth at almost overwhelming behavioral "disadvantage"; and, in effect denying the culturally different the dignity of their difference are hardly functions of a responsible universal system of formal education. Yet these functions are everyday performances of our schools. Recognition is not the problem — eyes have been opened that wide — as much as it is their solution. What can be done to reform schooling? to upset these functions? and by whom? through which media? Mr. Ianni elaborates one possibility here: the deliberate involvement of socioeducational change in the arts. Such an involvement would act, in his view, directly (and positively) on established minority cultural motifs; it would assure some continuities where behavioral discontinuities yet prevail. Mr. Ianni was Deputy Associate Commissioner for Research, Office of Education, HEW. He is currently director, Division of Educational Institutions and Programs, Teachers College, Columbia University.

FRANCIS A. J. IANNI

Cultivating the Arts of Poverty

In the great debate about how we should educate the poor, one central question is rarely asked: "What should we educate them for?" Do we want to prepare the poor for roles in middle-class, white society or do

From Francis A. J. Ianni, "Cultivating the Arts of Poverty," *Saturday Review*, June 17, 1967. Copyright 1967 Saturday Review, Inc.

we hope somehow to work within the bounds of their own cultural world? Having rejected the idea of making them middle class, we toyed for awhile with the idea of helping them develop a sense of pride in their natural worth and origins until black nationalism worried us and Black Power became a threat. Right now, however, we have no clear-cut objectives and we don't seem very inclined to search them out.

Our recent experience with science and technology seems to have convinced us that we can do anything we want to, given the time and the notion. This same self-assurance and continuance have led us to one of the great mythologies of our time: the belief that the good things in life — beauty, truth, security, and love — are now almost within our grasp. We have only to apply ourselves, our knowledge, and our skills and the Great Society is ours. And not content to enjoy them alone, we actually presume to believe that we can somehow distill all of these joys and pleasures into some opiate, yet palatable form, and dispense them like wonder drugs to those less fortunate than we.

We give proud names to programs designed to prescribe and distribute this American middle-class psychodelica — Upward Bound, Head Start, Higher Horizons, and *Alianza para Progreso*. We plan the campaign to eradicate misery and ignorance —which we equate — and to destroy the automobile graveyard and the slum with all the precision and paraphernalia of a military operation. The strategy is clear; it remains now only to decide on the tactics, and on the character and composition of the occupation once the battle is won.

We know that education is to be the major weapon and we need only decide how we are going to use it. And yet, we might well ponder the terrible consequences of victory, for what, in fact, do we have to offer as a replacement for the culture of poverty? In the cognitive domain we have some evidence that better schooling can lead to better jobs, but what are the affective consequences of the cultural revolution we propose? Will we make use of existing cultural motifs in the lives of these people or will we, confident in our own excellence, find new ways to assert our cultural advantage?

There is abundant evidence from similar attacks on a "cultureless" or "deprived" people to indicate that if we insist on replacing the culture of poverty with something precious to us but alien to them, we can expect disquieting and even disastrous consequences. In Africa and Asia, for example, the effects of efforts by colonial administrators to give to indigenous peoples a share in English or Dutch, Spanish or French cultures are now evident in the problems of developing nations in these areas. The more fully the African or the Asian became immersed in the foreign culture the more he felt and continues to feel the helpless loneliness and rage of the man without a past. For whatever the motivation of the European educator in imparting *his* culture to the native peoples, he was assuming that his past would become theirs and, except for a few interesting archaeological ruins, that their history began on the day of contact.

The consequences of coercive cultural change can, in fact, be horrendous if the destruction of the old culture reaches deeply into the ethos of that society. W. H. R. Rivers, in his *Essays on the Depopulation of Melanesia*, pointed out the destructive results on the unifying ethos of Melanesian culture and society when the British imposed their own cultural norms and prohibited head hunting. Each head-hunting expedition took years to plan and accomplish, and the activity of the preparations and aftermath was the glue that held Melanesian social organization together. Without the stimulation of these ritual functions the Melanesians literally died of a sense of futility and boredom. They had nothing to live for. Someone else must ponder the question of the justification of the British in abolishing what was to them an abhorrent, nasty habit but which actually took fewer lives in the long run than resulted from its abolishment. My interest in recounting it here is to indicate that social "betterment," even planned social "change" and "reform," can be disastrous unless we consider and appreciate how it is perceived by those undergoing change and how the change relates to what went before.

There appears to be rather consistent agreement among anthropologists and artists on the role of the arts as agents of social change; many see the arts — whether in their developmental force, in the "inner logic of art forms themselves," in the art tradition, or in a "world soul" — as the spirit and image of a particular culture or society. The artist experiments, innovates, and rebels within the bounds of the culture that has conditioned him. The art historian, for example, who describes the Italian futurists as rejecting the Italian culture which they found around them in museums and decaying *palazzi*, must look to social and political developments in Italy and realize that this was a culture seeking a new, twentieth-century identity, and the futurists were but part of this movement. Today's rash of rebellious innovative art forms — Pop art, junk sculpture, and the "happening" — is a brazen reply to a jaded public that demands both individualism and conformity from the artist.

In these new art forms today's artist replies to John Dewey's stern dictum that "art is experience" with a thumb-to-the-nose reply that all of culture is up for grabs and "all experience is art." But this rebellious attitude is peculiarly associated with other forms of protest, from civil rights to sexual freedom and from anti-war protests to justice for Timothy Leary. Here I am saying two different but related things: (1) The question of whether art and artists "lead" or follow social change is, for me at least, an unanswerable and unimportant question; and (2) regardless of whether art leads or follows, stimulates or responds, it is conditioned by the culture which mediates it. When we speak of "art *for* the culturally disadvantaged," we admit by the term itself that this age of American culture has nothing better to offer them as a cultural milieu than what they already have.

Three orders of evidence support what I have said. First, in my experience with the "disadvantaged," I have seen very few programs in the arts which do not attempt to take the best of what "we" have to offer in order to help "them" fit better into our world. It is the same old story of the colonial administrator we saw earlier. At its best this means an attempt to reproduce the art forms of middle-class, white America in a form that is both acceptable and comprehensible to individuals who are not a part of this cultural heritage. At its worst it means a patronizing attempt to uplift the art consciousness of a people who are, again, "culturally disadvantaged."

Sometimes we go to the other extreme. If modern American middle-class culture is alien to them, we argue, and if the legends of our national history are lily white, then let's build up both race pride and self-image by using the medium of great Negro figures in American history and the glory of ancient African kingdoms. Does it really create a new self-image for a Harlem youngster to know that there was a Negro named Matthew Henson present at the discovery of the North Pole? And how can this same youngster from Harlem identify with the glories of ancient Aksum or the greatness of the kingdom of the Ashanti? These are as alien to him and as little a part of his sensed cultural history as they are to us. It is absurd to assume that there is some multigenerational cultural *élan* dormant in the Negro's genes which can be sparked to life by primitive African art or culture history.

In either case, we are usually dealing not with the current or folk culture of the group under contact but rather we are acting as purveyors of our own popular culture or attempting to spawn a meaningless nativistic cult. I would not make the term popular culture synonymous with mass media; rather, I would distinguish folk from "popular culture" by indicating that in folk culture there is a creative sharing of a *cultural value* or an art form based upon common tradition among those who feel some involvement in what is produced. Popular culture, on the other hand, I would describe as the logical companion of mass production that has its vital force in entertainment rather than in creativity. It is assembled *for* somebody.

Examples of folk culture abound in primitive society where art is expressive of group relationships and in the personal contact of the producer and the consumer of art. In popular culture, however, we seem to have lost the artist, any creative elite, or indeed, despite the fact that they call the tune in terms of what gets produced, even a creative audience. By and large, the audience is present to be entertained, amused, or in some way "enriched." Their involvement in any sense of understanding, feeling or re-creation of the culture which produced art form is, at best, minimal.

Art is to me both a re-creation of what it is like to be alive and an intensely personal experience. Art, like love, can be sensed and experienced only as an intense personal relationship. Art, again like love, cannot be contrived or manufactured to suit someone else's taste. When this becomes necessary, art becomes entertainment, and this is what present popular culture has become. Created on schedule as a response to the demands of the popular art market place, it neither amplifies nor negates our cultural world — it just makes it absurd. It doesn't even offer an escape anymore. Let me confess that when things get dull or bothersome, I dream of escaping the lonely life in the crowd by escaping popular culture as well as material wants and drives. I see myself living in the richness of the moment, on a sun-drenched beach and running my toes through the waters, sensing and immersed, not entertained and amused. But such experiences are rare, and I cannot tell you what the feeling is like or re-create it for you.

Here is the ultimate in the absurdity of trying to act as an agent for substituting one cultural mode for another. It is what Camus saw as absurd in modern man's attempt to exist among the confusion of values which is our popular culture. It is what Heraclitus meant many years ago when he observed that man is estranged from that with which he is most familiar and that he must continuously seek to rediscover it. It is what I suggest the artist can do if he does it with, rather than for, the poor.

If I were a Negro in Bedford-Stuyvesant or a Puerto Rican in East Harlem, I would not for one moment consider giving up my rich — if disadvantaged — culture for the lonely general culture. Oscar Lewis has done a brilliant job of showing how rich and comforting the culture of poverty can be, and repeatedly illustrates that what causes the disjunctures and the disharmonies is our attempt to tell the disadvantaged that they don't know what they are missing. One need only spend some time in the culture of poverty to realize that there is a cultural stimulation — in fact, it can be a source of uninhibited pleasure. But in this puritanical age we distrust pleasure because it suggests triviality. Just as learning which is fun is suspect, living *dolce far niente* is condemned unless you can afford it. Our world forces us to think clearly and logically, and to live as if we enjoy it, or it does not permit us to survive.

If the artist wants to act as an agent of social and cultural change he must work with and within the society and the culture he hopes to change. He, like the anthropologist, must become as much a part of it as he can and build from within rather than attempting to impose from without.

And to do this we must understand — not appreciate but understand — the present culture of poverty.

How well, for example, do we understand the culture of the American Negro? We have been looking at the Negro in this country for 300 years and yet we continue to see only what we want to see. And now he shows us only what we want to see. We see him, we hear him, we may even appreciate him as an artist, but we seldom if ever get a glimpse through the window of black culture in this country. Consider, for example, the simple fact that Negro entertainers, no matter how well established, no matter how successful, have developed the maddening knack of giving us only what we think we like to hear and see. Their real virtuosity is incredible, and yet they entertain us with a parody of what our popular culture really is. Listen carefully to Ella Fitzgerald or Pearl Bailey burlesquing a romantic ballad, or watch the Harlem Globetrotters buffoon and make a mockery of a game of basketball. They burlesque the Negro as an athlete but they also always manage to defeat their foil, an all-white team.

Negroes purvey our popular culture for the commodity it is. They know its cheapness, its unreality. Their persons having been sold, literally, in our society, they have some acquaintance with commercialism; they know how to sell, and are in a better position to learn what is not for sale. This is what Mahalia Jackson seems to mean in singing only spirituals, although she sings them with a jazz beat. As a veteran performer, the Negro is, in his very existence, the most sophisticated critic of our romanticism, our social etiquette, our ethics, our fashions, and our enthusiasms. He cannot even deceive himself completely when he becomes bourgeois; it is all too new. Negroes as performers add an extraordinary dimension to ordinary activities. Their involvement is not conscious and contrived but spontaneous and mimetic, issuing out of the ambivalent experience that every actor has of the act and of reality.

Stanley Diamond has illustrated the farcical Theater-of-the-Absurd quality of Negro involvement in the popular culture. He describes as follows that great cultural *double entendre*, the second heavyweight championship fight between Sonny Liston and Cassius Clay. First, both men are, in our cultural world, self-acknowledged professional outsiders, members of what one might call the "Establishment of the outside." Liston is an ex-convict and scofflaw. Clay (Muhammad Ali), the star performer, is a Black Muslim who has made the pilgrimage to Mecca and a celebrated trip to Africa. Like Liston, he is unschooled, although obviously clever, and manifestly rejects the white world. He even managed to fail the Draft Board intelligence test twice. Now, having refused induction into the Armed Services, he identifies increasingly with the racial as well as the religious objections to the draft.

Born in the South, Clay has successfully turned himself into an Aesopian, a fabulous character. His famous rhymes and manufactured rages against opponents have a bowdlerized folk quality. One senses a kind of reverse Uncle Remus in Clay's act. Each of his opponents has been characterized as an animal: Liston is a bear, Floyd Patterson, a rabbit. The characters fight among themselves but they always outwit the white man. Clay embraces them all and draws them into his fabled world, precisely because he, alone, in his exuberance, exposes the absurdity of their professional lives in white society. He can do this because he is young, rich, and has, by means of his new religion, apparently withdrawn from the phantom circle of statuses conferred by whites.

Liston simply plays it cool, speaking astringently and tersely when questioned, uninterested even in appearing interested in the conventional opinion of mankind. Both are champions — arrived, glorified puppets of the white crowd, but puppets who have learned to pull their own strings, each in his peculiar way.

The event began under a flood of extremely powerful and hot television lights and was over about two minutes later, with Clay knocking Liston out. So far as their behavior on stage was concerned, intuition, improvision, and mutual interest provide the clue; no precise battle plan was necessary.

The question remains why the whole affair was executed so unimpressively, so transparently. But that was part of the farce. In retrospect, it appears as a near-perfect burlesque of a heavyweight championship fight. There was no visible punch, no bruises. The actors know their audience. They have known it for generations. The audience will fill in what it pleases. As usual, we will ascribe to it the Negro behavior which fits our assumptions. We will insist that the affair was either a fix, or a mysteriously authentic fight (one veteran white sportswriter described the perfect punch in detail; a well-known sporting journal tried to photograph it as such). What we will resist seeing is that two physically tremendous men put on an entertainment for a society in which they do not believe. With due consideration for themselves, they refused to batter each other into the ground for the pleasure of a predominantly white audience, according to white rules of the game, for prizes which they had already achieved by other means.

If what Diamond describes here is characteristic of much of Negro-white relations in popular culture, there are, however, happier encounters in which artists can work with the "disadvantaged" to create and re-create a new cultural world which has all of the comfort of the old along with the security-producing elements of the new. My colleague at the Horace Mann–Lincoln Institute for School Experimentation, Herbert Kohl, has been tremendously successful in working with children from a "disadvantaged culture," developing a pride in the old as well as an understanding of the general culture. One of his early experiences was with the reaction of the Establishment to two poems written by two different eleven-year-old girls in his class. One poem, called "Shop with Mom," received high praise and was published in the school paper:

> I love to shop with mom
> And talk to the friendly grocer
> And help her make the list
> Seems to make us closer.

The other, "The Junkies," was bitterly condemned when Kohl tried to have it published in the same paper. It was full of misspellings and grammatical errors, didn't rhyme, and besides, it was on a subject the teacher-editor said an eleven-year-old "just could not know anything about":

> When they are
> in the street
> they pass it
> along to each
> other but when
> they see the
> police they would
> run some would
> just stand still
> and be beat
> so pity ful
> that they want
> to cry.

Eventually, Kohl was able to work with the children by casting aside the Establishment view (and leaving the school system in the process). For anyone interested in working with youngsters from "disadvantaged" areas, the story of his learning of their culture and their acceptance of the new patterns he developed with them makes fascinating and intensely valuable reading.

What is important here is that eventually he and they were able to create a new set of patterns which did not negate the old culture but still gave them a window into our world. For example, after a long series of experiences with reading classical mythologies and creating their own myths (the kids made up some wonderful mythical characters with names like Skyview, Missile, and Morass), an eleven-year-old created a fable which illustrates the mixing of cultural worlds:

> Once upon a time there was a pig and a cat. The cat kept saying old
> dirty pig who want to eat you. And the pig replied when I die I'll be made

use of, but when you die you'll just rot. The cat always thought he was better than the pig. When the pig died he was used as food for the people to eat. When the cat died he was buried in old dirt. Moral: Live dirty die clean.

As Kohl points out, this fable exudes the exhilaration felt by children when they are allowed freedom to create after being stifled in the classroom. But it also illustrates what is most challenging in the involvement of the artist in the world of the "disadvantaged" — the ability to help create a new reality. Artists have always created their own reality, and I suppose that when you do this in social and political rather than esthetic terms you are really designing utopias. Perhaps that is why utopias are usually full of artists. If utopias have failed in the past, I don't think this should cause too much concern. The real value of a utopia, after all, has always been what happens once it is disassembled and everyone goes back into society carrying with him elements of what he learned.

Further Readings

Cohen, Rosalie, Gerd Fraenkel, and John Brewer. *Implications for "culture conflict" from a semantic feature analysis of the lexicon of the hard core poor.* Pittsburgh: Learning R & D Center, University of Pittsburgh, 1967 (mimeo).

Eddy, Elizabeth M. *Walk the white line: a profile of urban education.* Garden City, N.Y.: Doubleday, 1965.

Goodman, Mary Ellen. *Race awareness in young children.* New York: Collier Books, 1952, 1964.

LaBelle, Thomas J. "The school: center of cultural conflict and learning," *TC Record,* in press.

Valentine, Charles A. *Culture and poverty: critique and counter-proposals.* Chicago: University of Chicago Press, 1968.

31

Systems of schooling, although generally detached from working politics, can scarcely be thought apolitical, being the primary means of allocating power and privileged position in most contemporary societies. Mr. Bruner discusses the political premises of instructional theory, especially as pedagogy regards "who shall be educated and to fulfill what roles?" He sees the social politic to intrude on the popularly accepted "purity" of academic theories of instruction. Bruner sees trends in instructional form as responsive both to evolving, societal situations of human learning and to sociopolitical expediencies — brutal and benign. Where Ianni, in the previous article, questioned the social wisdom and, by implication, the instructional theory of imposing alien behavior patterns and expectations upon the culturally different, Bruner asks: "how can the power and substance of a culture be translated into an instructional form?" Making cuturally patterned behaviors relevant, rewarding, and otherwise effective in instructional context, Bruner and Ianni might insist, is to seek the instructional form inherent to them and not to distort these behaviors to precut dimensions. Mr. Bruner, widely known for his contributions to instructional theory, is Professor of Psychology and Director, Center for Cognitive Studies, Harvard University. He collaborated in writing Studies in Cognitive Growth *(New York: Wiley, 1966).*

JEROME S. BRUNER

Culture, Politics, and Pedagogy

Despite the books and articles that are beginning to appear on the subject, the process of education goes forward today without any clearly defined or widely accepted theory of instruction. We have had to make do and are still making do on clever maxims and moralistic resolutions about what instruction is and should be. The controversy that swirls around this tortured subject is a mirror of larger discontent with our culture and our morality. And so it should be — but not to the exclusion of dispassionate appraisal of the means whereby the sought-after ends might be achieved. And perhaps that, too, is overly much to expect, for if the past decade has taught us anything, it is that educational reform confined only to the schools and not to the society at large is doomed to eventual triviality.

There are a number of reasons why a theory of instruction may have little effect on educational practice. First, it could be that the theory is wrong — yet it is difficult to find a theory that is flat wrong and won't have some reasonable proposals to make. A second reason might be that it is inappropriate to the central problems of practice. For instance, a theory that is clearly excellent in respect to the instruction of children who are already motivated to learn may prove ineffective in dealing with the alienated Negro students of the inner-city school. A third reason might be its unmanageability — one aspect of which is obscurity in the path from the abstract to the concrete. No matter how deeply one is moved by the

From Jerome S. Bruner, "Culture, Politics and Pedagogy," *Saturday Review*, May 18, 1968. Copyright 1968 Saturday Review, Inc.

spirit of Froebel's theory, for example, it is difficult to know what one does to assure, in his metaphor, that a child be nurtured like a plant lest he be choked by the weeds of circumstance.

But even if a pedagogical theory is correct, relevant, and manageable, it may be practically ineffective when it fails to relate to the urgencies of a society.

While American society in the first decades of the twentieth century was deeply concerned with the problems of acculturating new waves of immigrants, the favored theory was once more concerned with the teaching of content per se, with minimum emphasis upon formal discipline or the training of mental faculties. Those theories were perhaps too closely related to the education of special elites. Today they are popular again.

A theory fares well when it accords with a culture's conception of its function. Each culture has conceptions of the nature of a child, some conceptions of what constitutes good adults. It also has, at some implicit level, some conceptions of what it regards as the appropriate means of getting from the nature of a child to the nature of an adult. If a pedagogical theorist is to move that culture, he must forge a theory that relates to that range of acceptable means. The failure of a theory may be that it fails to accord with or overcome or relate to the "range of acceptable means" of a culture.

The net outcome of our probing is, I think, the realization that a pedagogical theory is perforce quite different from, and hardly as neutral as, the usual type of scientific theory. Indeed, it is even questionable whether it is principally a scientific theory in the explanatory sense. Nor is it a purely normative theory such as a grammatical theory, prescribing rules for reaching specified goals (such as "well formed sentences"). A theory of instruction is a political theory in the proper sense that it derives from consensus concerning the distribution of power within the society — who shall be educated and to fulfill what roles? In the very same sense, pedagogical theory must surely derive from a conception of economics, for where there is division of labor within the society and an exchange of goods and services for wealth and prestige, then *how* people are educated and in what number and with what constraints on the use of resources are all relevant issues. The psychologist or educator who formulates pedagogical theory without regard to the political, economic, and social setting of the educational process courts triviality and merits being ignored in the community and in the classroom.

It is neither surprising nor inappropriate, then, that critiques of pedagogical theories are as often as not in the form of social and political criticism and ideological debate. It has been instructive to me to see the manner in which some of these debates take shape. A book of mine,

The Process of Education (1960), has been translated into several languages. In Italy, the book touched off a debate on the problem of revising Italian education to cope with the changing industrial society, and it has been used for clubbing Marxists and classicists alike. In the Soviet Union, one group of social critics has used the book's emphasis on discovery and intuition to castigate the dogmatism of remaining Stalinists who wish to set the dogma of socialism on the line in the classroom. That view has been seconded in Poland, Hungary, and Czechoslovakia.

In Japan, the social critics praise the book for indicating that school subjects that are technical and mathematical need not be without a proper intellectual structure and cultural grace. In Israel, a land surrounded by a ring of hostile nations, the book has been greeted as an invitation to avoid mediocrity in the preparation of new immigrants — a mediocrity that social critics fear will bring Israel to a state of dangerous vulnerability in her present isolated position. In the United States — and perhaps this is the only country affluent enough to harbor such thoughts — the principal social criticism has been a concern for the maintenance of spontaneity of the child. It has been a sobering experience to realize in what degree a book of this sort must perforce serve social and political ends and can never remain a technical book alone.

This brings me to a second conclusion, this time about the role of manageability in the impact of pedagogical theories. Manageability encompasses not only the so-called educational technology of films, books, computers, and the like, but also the scale of the enterprise in terms of people and funds. We have now entered an era in which the federal government, through the Office of Education, has established regional research and development centers to concern themselves with the betterment of our educational effort. They provide a fresh opportunity to explore deeply the feasibility of particular theories, comprehensive or segmental, concerning effective instruction.

I have had the intimate experience over the last five or six years of participating in and observing the attempt to translate a more general theory into one single course in the social sciences, "Man: A Course of Study" (1965), designed for the fifth grade. (It is being developed by what was originally Educational Services, Inc., and has now become the regional center, Educational Development Corporation.) The experience has taught us all not to be casual about means. For it soon turns out that what seems like a simple pedagogical premise would, if implemented, produce a minor revolution in teacher training or in film-making or in school budgeting. This is the engineering part of what is properly called the theory of instruction. It is something that we are only now beginning to understand. Innovation, by whatever theoretical derivation, involves vast development and engineering. By past standards of performance, we could not absorb many new innovative ideas. If we learn how to implement these matters in our generation, we shall lay the groundwork for a truly great impact of adequate theories of instruction in the next generation.

These observations on why theories of instruction are ineffective lead to a second question: What is it that is special or different about education in the sense of schooling in contrast to other ways in which we instruct? Consider the evolution of education as a cultural means of passing on skill, knowledge, and values. It is impossible, of course, to reconstruct the evolution in techniques of instruction in the shadow zone between hominids and man. I have tried to compensate for this lack by observing contemporary analogues of earlier forms, knowing full well that the pursuit of analogy can be dangerously misleading. I have spent many hours observing uncut films of the behavior of free-ranging baboons, films shot in East Africa by my colleague Irven DeVore with a very generous footage devoted to infants and juveniles. I have also had access to the unedited film archives of a hunting-gathering people living under roughly analogous ecological conditions, the !Kung Bushmen of the Kalahari, recorded by Laurance and Lorna Marshall. I have also worked directly but informally with the Wolof of Senegal, observing children in the bush and in French-style schools.

Let me describe very briefly some salient differences in the free learning patterns of immature baboons and among !Kung children. Baboons have a highly developed social life in their troops, with well organized and stable dominance patterns. They live within a territory, protecting themselves from predators by joint action of the strongly built adult males. It is striking that the behavior of baboon juveniles is shaped principally by play with their peer group, play that provides opportunity for the spontaneous expression and practice of the component acts that, in maturity, will be orchestrated into either the behavior of the dominant male or of the infant-protected female. All this seems to be accomplished with little participation by any mature animals in the play of the juveniles. We know from the important experiments of H. F. Harlow and his colleagues how devastating a disruption in development can be produced in subhuman primates by interfering with their opportunity for peer-group play and social interaction.

Among hunting-gathering humans, on the other hand, there is constant interaction between adult and child, or adult and adolescent, or adolescent and child. !Kung adults and children play and dance together, sit together, and participate in minor hunting together, join in song and storytelling together. At very frequent intervals, moreover, children are party to rituals presided over by adults — minor, as in the first hair-cutting, or major, as when a boy kills his first kudu buck and goes through the proud but painful process of scarification. Children, besides, are constantly playing imitatively with the rituals, implements, tools, and weapons of the adult world. Young juvenile baboons, on the other hand, virtually never play with things or imitate, directly, large and significant sequences of adult behavior.

Note, though, that in tens of thousands of feet of !Kung film, one virtually never sees an instance of "teaching" taking place outside the situation where the behavior to be learned is relevant. Nobody "teaches" in our prepared sense of the word. There is nothing like school, nothing like lessons. Indeed, among the !Kung children there is very little "telling." Most of what we would call instruction is through showing. And there is no "practice" or "drill" as such, save in the form of play modeled directly on adult models — play hunting, play bossing, play exchanging, play baby-tending, play house-keeping. In the end, every man in the culture knows nearly all there is to know about how to get on with life as a man, and every woman as a woman — the skills, the rituals and myths, the obligations and rights, the attitudes.

The change in the instruction of children in more complex societies is twofold. First of all, there is knowledge and skill in the culture far in excess of what any one individual knows. And so, increasingly, there develops an economical technique of instructing the young based heavily on *telling* out of context rather than *showing* in context. In literate societies, the practice becomes institutionalized in the school or the "teacher." Both promote this necessarily abstract way of instructing the young.

The result of "teaching the culture" can, at its worst, lead to the ritual, rote nonsense that has led a generation of critics to despair. For in the detached school, what is imparted often has little to do with life as lived in the society except insofar as the demands of school are of a kind that reflect *indirectly* the demands of life in a technical society. But these indirectly imposed demands may be the most important feature of the detached school. For school is a sharp departure from indigenous practice.

It takes learning, as we have noted, out of the context of immediate action just by dint of putting it into a school. This very extirpation makes learning become an act in itself, freed from the immediate ends of action, preparing the learner for the chain of reckoning, remote from payoff that is needed for the formulation of complex ideas. At the same time, the school (if successful) frees the child from the pace-setting of the round of concrete daily activity. If the school succeeds in avoiding a pace-setting round of its own, it may be one of the great agents for promoting reflectiveness. Moreover, in school, one must "follow the lesson" which means one must learn to follow either the abstraction of written speech — abstract in the sense that it is divorced from the concrete situation to which the speech might originally have been related — or the abstraction of language delivered orally but out of the context of an on-going action. Both of these are highly abstract uses of language. It is no wonder, then, that many recent studies report large differences between "primitive" children who are in schools and their brothers who are not: differences in perception, abstraction, time perspective, and so on.

As a society becomes yet more technical, there is a longer separation from actual doing, and education begins to take up a larger and larger portion of the life span; indeed, education becomes part of the way of life. More and more time is given over to telling (usually in print), to demonstrating out of the context of action.

We can already foresee a next step in technical progress that will impose further changes on our methods of educating. For one thing, the rate of change in the surface properties of knowledge will likely increase. That is, the theory of circuits will blossom, although likely as not it will do so on the basis of understanding more deeply some principles that are now known but not fully understood. In teaching, then, we shall be more likely to search out the deeper, underlying ideas to teach, rather than presenting the technical surface that is so likely to change. A meta-phoric way of putting this is to say that technical things are more likely to appear changed to an engineer than to a physicist.

There will also be many more aids and prosthetic devices for processing information than ever before. Some of these seem certain already. For one thing, we are organizing our knowledge in a data bank accessible to a user by retrieval techniques inherent in modern computing. This makes knowledge more accessible and less subject to the ancient filing and recall gymnastics of the classical scholar. For another, there will be increasing pressure to reformulate problems in a well-formed fashion in order to make them accessible to the powerful devices of computing. Ill-formed problems do not lend themselves to computing. There are dangers and opportunities in such formalism. Whichever, the trend is already discernible. In general, I think it can be said that we shall in the next hundred years be using many more intelligent and automatic devices that we shall program in behalf of our problem-solving. We need not be Luddites about it, either.

I suspect that there are three forms of activity that no device is ever going to be able to do as well as our brain with its 5×10^9 cortical connections, and I would suggest that these three represent what will be special about education for the future.

The first is that we shall probably want to train individuals not for the performance of routine activities that can be done with great skill and precision by devices, but rather to train their individual talents for research and development, which is one of the kinds of activities for which you cannot easily program computers. Here I mean research and development in the sense of problem-finding rather than problem-solving. If we want to look ahead to what is special about a school, we should ask how to train generations of children to *find* problems, to look for them. I recall that wonderful prescription of the English Platonist, Weldon, to the effect that there are three kinds of things in the world: There are troubles which we do not quite know how to handle; then there are puzzles with their clear conditions and unique solutions, marvelously elegant; and then there are problems — and these we invent by finding an appropriate puzzle form to impose upon a trouble.

What this entails for education is necessarily somewhat obscure although its outlines may be plain. For one thing, it places a certain emphasis on the teaching of interesting puzzle forms: ways of thinking that are particularly useful for converting troubles into problems. These are familiar enough in any given field of knowledge: they are the useful abstractions. What is needed is a sense of how to teach their use in converting chaotic messes into manageable problems. Much of the attraction of the use of discovery in teaching comes, I suspect, from the realization of the need to equip students in this way.

A second special requirement for education in the future is that it provide training in the performance of "unpredictable services." By unpredictable services, I mean performing acts that are contingent on a response made by somebody or something to your prior act. Again, this falls in the category of tasks that we shall do better than automata for many years to come. I include here the role of the teacher, the parent, the assistant, the stimulator, the rehabilitator, the physician in the great sense of that term, the friend, the range of things that increase the richness of individual response to other individuals. I propose this as a critical task, for as the society becomes more interdependent, more geared to technological requirements, it is crucial that it not become alienated internally, flat emotionally, and gray. Those who fret and argue that we are *bound* to go dead personally as we become proficient technically have no more basis for their assertion than traditional romanticism. Recall that the nineteenth century that witnessed the birth of the Industrial Revolution also produced that most intimate form, the modern novel.

Third, what human beings can produce and no device can is art — in every form: visual art, the art of cooking, the art of love, the art of walking, the art of address, going beyond adaptive necessity to find expression for human flair.

These three — research and development, unpredictable services, and the arts — represent what surely will be the challenge to a society which has our capacity to provide technical routine. I assume we should teach the technical routines, for that is built into our evolving system. Will we be daring enough to go beyond to the cultivation of the uniquely human?

Another question we must ask, then, is: How can the power and substance of a culture be translated into an instructional form?

First we must look briefly at what we might mean by the nature of knowledge as such, because this will prove crucial to our concern. Perhaps the most pervasive feature of human intellect is its limited capacity at any moment for dealing with information. We have about seven slots, plus or minus two, through which the external world can find translation into experience. We easily become overwhelmed by complexity or clutter. Cognitive mastery in a world that generates stimuli far faster than we can sort them depends upon strategies for reducing the complexity and the clutter. But reduction must be selective, attuned to the things that "matter." Some of the modes of reduction require, seemingly, no learning — as with our adaptation mechanisms. What does not change ceases to register: steady states in their very nature cease to stimulate. Stabilize the image on the retina by getting rid of fine tremor, and the visual world fades away.

There is another type of selectivity that reflects man's deepest intellectual trait and is heavily dependent on learning. Man constructs models of his world, templates that represent not only what he encounters and in what context, but ones that also permit him to go beyond them. He learns the world in a way that enables him to make predictions of what comes next by matching a few milliseconds of what is now experienced to a stored model and reading the rest from the model. We see a contour and a snatch of movement. "Ah yes, that's the night watchman checking the windows. . . ." It is in the nature of the selectivity governed by such models that we come increasingly to register easily on those things in the world that we expect; indeed, we assume that the expected is there on the basis of a minimum of information.

There is compelling evidence that so long as the environment conforms to the expected patterns within reasonable limits, alerting mechanisms in the brain are quieted. But once expectancy is violated — once the world ceases strikingly to correspond to our models of it (and it must be rather striking, for we ride roughshod over minor deviations) — then all the alarms go off and we are at full alertness. So man can deal not only with information that is before him, but go far beyond the information given, with all that this implies both for swiftness of intellect and for fallibility. Almost by definition, the exercise of intellect, involving as it must the use of short cuts and leaps from partial evidence, always courts the possibility of error. It is the good fortune of our species that we are also highly adept not only at correction (given sufficient freedom from time pressure), but we have learned to institutionalize ways of keeping error within tolerable limits, science being the prime example.

The models or stored theories of the world that are so useful in inference are strikingly generic and reflect man's ubiquitous tendency to categorize. William James remarked that the life of the mind begins when the child is first able to proclaim, "Aha, thingumbob again." We organize experience to represent not only the particulars that have been experienced, but the classes of events of which the particulars are exemplars. We go not only from part to whole, but irresistibly from the particular to the general.

At least one distinguished linguist has argued in recent times that this generic tendency of human intellect must be innately human for, without it, one could not master the complex web of categorical or substitution rules that constitutes the syntax of language — any language. Both in achieving the economy with which human thought represents the world and in effecting swift correction for error, the categorizing tendency of intelligence is central. For it yields a structure of thought that becomes hiearchically organized with growth, forming branching structures in which it is relatively easy to search for alternatives. The blunders occur, of course, where things that must be together for action or for understanding happen to be organized in different hierarchies. It is a form of error that is as familiar in science as in everyday life.

I do not mean to imply, of course, that man structures his knowledge of the world only by the categorial rules of inclusion, exclusion, and overlap, for clearly he traffics in far greater complexity, too. Witness the almost irresistible urge to see cause and effect. Rather, the categorial nature of thought underlines its rule-bound nature. The eighteenth-century assumption that knowledge grows by a gradual accretion of associations built up by contact with events that are contiguous in time, space, or quality does not fit the facts of mental life. There are spheres where such associative laws operate within limits — as, for example, with material that is strange and meaningless (the psychologist's nonsense syllables, for instance) — but in the main, organization is a far more active process of imposing order, as when we form a hypothesis and then check it not so much to be sure but to be clued in.

We do the greater part of our work by manipulating our representations or models of reality rather than by acting directly on the world itself. Thought is then vicarious action, in which the high cost of error is strikingly reduced. It is characteristic of human beings, and no other species, that we can carry out this vicarious action with the aid of a large number of intellectual prosthetic devices that are, so to speak, tools provided by the culture. Natural language is the prime example, but there are pictorial and diagrammatic conventions as well: theories, myths, modes of reckoning and order. We are even able to employ devices to fulfill functions not given man through evolution — devices that bring phenomena into the human range of registering and computing. Today, indeed, we develop devices to determine whether the events we watch conform to or deviate from expectancy in comprehensible ways.

A colleague, George A. Miller, put it well in speaking about computers: "Mechanical intelligence will not ultimately replace human intelligence, but rather, by complementing our human intelligence, will supplement and amplify it. We will learn to supply by mechanical organs those functions that natural evolution has failed to provide."

The range of man's intellect, given its power to be increased from the outside in, can never be estimated without considering the means a culture provides for empowering mind. Man's intellect, then, is not simply his own, but is communal in the sense that its unlocking or empowering depends upon the success of the culture in developing means to that end. The use of such amplifiers of mind requires, admittedly, a commonly shared human capacity, and each society fashions and perfects this capacity to its needs. But there is, I believe, a respect in which a lack of means for understanding one matter places out of reach other matters that are crucial to man's condition whatever his culture.

Consider now the nature of codified knowledge. The past half century surely been one of the richest, as well as the most baffling, in the history of our effort to understand the nature of knowledge. Advances in the foundation of mathematics and logic, in the philosophy of science, in the theory of information processing, in linguistics and in psychology — all of these have led to new formulations and new conjectures.

Perhaps the greatest change, stemming principally from the revolutions in physics, is in our conception of what a theory is. For Newton, inquiry was a voyage on the seas of ignorance to find the islands of truth. We know now that theory is more than a general description of what happens or a statement of probabilities of what might or might not happen — even when it claims to be nothing more than that, as in some of the newer behavioral sciences. It entails, explicitly or implicitly, a model of what it is that one is theorizing about, a set of propositions that, taken in ensemble, yield occasional predictions about things. Armed with a theory, one is guided toward what one will treat as data and is predisposed to treat some other data as more relevant than others.

A theory is also a way of stating tersely what one already knows without the burden of detail. In this sense it is a canny and economical way of keeping in mind a vast amount while thinking about a very little. What is perhaps most important about this way of viewing theory is the attitude it creates toward the use of mind. We now see that the construction of theory is a way of using the mind, the imagination — of standing off from the activities of observation and inference and creating a shape of nature.

There are several conclusions to be drawn from this long excursion into the nature of intellect, into the nature of how one organizes knowledge to fit it. First of all, it becomes necessary to translate bodies of theory into a form that permits the child to get closer and closer approximations to the most powerful form of a theory, beginning with a highly intuitive and active form of a theory and moving on as the child grasps that to a more precise and powerful statement of it. I find no other way of bringing the child through the maze of particulars to the kind of power that would produce the combination of research and development, unpredictable services, and the arts. Second, this means that on a practical level the entire university community — indeed, the entire intellectual community — must have a role in education, that the separate education faculty is a misconception and probably one that requires rearrangement in the future. (Since this was written, Cornell has disbanded its faculty of education and reassigned its responsibilities to the entire faculty of arts and sciences.)

As my colleague, Philip Morrison, put it in respect to his field, there are degrees granted by departments of physics in theoretical physics, in experimental physics, and in applied physics. Why not one in pedagogical physics? Teaching is surely an extension of the general exercise whereby one clarifies ideas to oneself. All of us who have worked on curriculum have learned tremendous amounts about our subject matter simply by trying to convert it into a form that would be courteous and comprehensible to a young learner.

Now if this is the case, if we require that there be pedagogical physics and its counterparts, there is surely some need for a *special* coalition to devise means of teaching the symbolic activity involved in the kind of theory-making we have been discussing. I do not know what to call this coalition of fields; the symbol sciences might be appropriate, but it is an absurd name. Linguists, philosophers of science, philosophers of history, logicians, psychologists, teachers, substantive specialists who most understand the simple structures of their fields, mathematicians — such a coalition might show how a university might express its concern for the symbolic powers inherent in the use of a culture. We obviously do not understand what could be done by a group of this sort. They range all the way from teaching children to be brief and compact when that is needed to hold things in the range of attention, to devising the kind of mathematical program embodied in the report of the Cambridge Conference on School Mathematics (*Goals for School Mathematics*, Houghton Mifflin, 1963).

Finally, we may ask: How is intellectual development assisted by instruction?

Let me focus on the teacher in this process. One immediately invokes the phrase "teacher training." But before we do, consider a few points to be taken into account. We know that children do not readily or easily think in school. By school age, children expect arbitrary and meaningless (to them) demands to be made on them by adults — the result probably of the fact that adults often fail to recognize the task of conversion necessary to make their questions have some intrinsic significance for the child. Children, of course, will try to solve problems if they recognize them as such. But they are not often either predisposed to or skillful in problem-finding, in recognizing the hidden conjectural feature in tasks set them. We know now that children in school can quite quickly be led to such problem-finding by encouragement and instruction.

The need for this encouragement and instruction and its relatively swift success relates, I suspect, to what psychoanalysts refer to as the guilt-ridden over-suppression of primary processes and its public replacement by secondary process. Children, like adults, need reassurance that it is all right to entertain and *express* highly subjective ideas, to treat a task as a problem where you *invent* an answer rather than *finding* one out there in the book or on the blackboard. With children in elementary school, there is often a need to devise emotionally vivid special games, story-making episodes, or construction projects to re-establish in the child's mind his right not only to have his own private ideas but to express them in the public setting of a classroom.

But there is another, perhaps more serious difficulty: the interference of intrinsic problem-solving by extrinsic. Young children in school expend extraordinary time and effort figuring out what it is that the teacher wants — and usually coming to the conclusion that she or he wants tidiness or remembering or doing things at a certain time in a certain way. This I refer to as extrinsic problem-solving. There is a great deal of it in school.

There are several quite straightforward ways of stimulating problem-finding. One is to train teachers to want it, and that will come in time. But teachers can be encouraged to like it, interestingly enough, by providing them and their children with materials and lessons that *permit* legitimate problem-finding and permit the teacher to recognize it. For exercises with such materials create an atmosphere by treating things as instances of what *might* have occurred rather than simply as what did occur.

Let me illustrate by a concrete instance. A fifth-grade class was working on the organization of a baboon troop — specifically, on how they might protect against predators. They saw a brief sequence of film in which six or seven adult males go forward to intimidate and hold off three cheetahs. The teacher asked what the baboons had done to keep the cheetahs off, and there ensued a lively discussion of how the dominant adult males, by showing their formidable mouthful of teeth and making threatening gestures, had turned the trick. A boy raised a tentative hand and asked whether cheetahs always attacked together. Yes, though a single cheetah sometimes followed behind a moving troop and picked off an older, weakened straggler or an unwary, straying juvenile. "Well, what if there were four cheetahs, and two of them attacked from behind and two from in front? What would the baboons do then?"

The question could have been answered empirically — and the inquiry ended. Cheetahs *do not* attack that way, and so we do not know what baboons *might* do. Fortunately, it was not. For the question opens up the deep issues of what might be and why it is not. Is there a necessary relation between predators and prey that share a common ecological niche? Must their encounters have a "sporting chance" outcome? It is such conjecture, in this case quite unanswerable, that produces rational, self-consciously problem-finding behavior so crucial to the growth of intellectual power. Given the materials, given some background and encouragement, teachers like it as much as the students. This is simply an example, and provided in that spirit only.

Let me now turn to dialogue. My colleague, Roman Jakobson, assures me that there is a Russian proverb to the effect that one understands only after one has discussed. There are doubtless many ways in which a human being can serve as a vicar of the culture, helping a child to understand its points of view and the nature of its knowledge. But I dare say that few are so potentially powerful as participating in dialogue. Professor Jan Smedslund, at Oslo, has recently remarked on our failure to recognize that even in the domains of formal reasoning, logic, and mathematics, the social context of discussion can be shown to be crucial.

It is a simple suggestion I am making. Entering the culture is perhaps most readily done by entering a dialogue with a more experienced member of it. Perhaps one way in which we might reconsider the issue of teacher training is to give the teacher training in the skills of dialogue — how to discuss a subject with a beginner.

Pedagogical theory, then, is not only technical, but cultural, ideological, and political. If it is to have its impact, it must be self-consciously all of these. The technical task indeed, is more formidable than ever we suspected, and we may now be operating close to the scale where we can begin to do the appropriate engineering to realize the implications of even utopian theories.

Knowledge, to be useful, must be compact, sensible, and manipulable. Theory is the form that has these properties. It should be the aim of our teaching. But in the evolution of education, it is also the case that as we move to an ever more technical organization of our culture, and now to a period involving the use of information-processing automata, the pattern of education changes. Three uniquely human traits want especial cultivation to increase the human quality of human societies — problem-finding, the provision of unpredictable services, and art in its myriad forms from music to cuisine.

Finally, one of the most crucial ways in which a culture provides aid in intellectual growth is through a dialogue between the more experienced and the less experienced, providing a means for the internalization of dialogue in thought. The courtesy of conversation may be the major ingredient in the courtesy of teaching.

FURTHER READINGS

Bateson, Gregory. *Naven*, 2nd ed. Stanford: Stanford University Press, 1958.
Goodman, Mary Ellen. *The culture of childhood: child's-eye views of society and culture.* New York: Teachers College Press, 1970.
Jones, Richard M. *Fantasy and feeling in education.* New York: New York University Press, 1968.
Storey, Edward. "The classroom and its cultural discontents: some practical alternatives for teachers of English." Paper read at the Annual Meeting of the National Council of Teachers of English, Atlanta, Georgia, 1970.
Whiting, Beatrice B. (ed.) *Six cultures: studies of child rearing.* New York: Wiley, 1963.

32

A "bad" education suffers by hindsight, by example, and inevitably by exposure to a "better" one. But, it is at least an education. To what does a "non-education" compare? To no education at all? Possibly, yet a non-education, the authors remind us, fails as education; its human waste is the more significant in being the product of a process that is specifically intended to provide for human potential. Or is it? Mr. Henninger and Miss Esposito, contributors to The New Republic, are conscientious in their abuse of the conventional education being waged against the American Indian. Beyond the statistics they have harvested is a singularly shining hope: Indian schools that are Indian-inspired, Indian-run, and otherwise accountable to the Indian communities — an antidote to the distressing notion that present-day Indian schools are so many territorial prisons. How much a hope the Rough Rocks, street academies, and other forms of community schooling represent will depend equally on their local accomplishments and on the disposition of white America to cooperate in their local control.

DANIEL HENNINGER AND NANCY ESPOSITO

Indian Schools: Regimented Non-Education

Senator Edward Kennedy has taken over the chairmanship of his late brother's Indian Education Subcommittee, which is soon to release a report recommending basic changes in the ways we educate Indian children. It's about time. The Bureau of Indian Affairs spent $86 million of its $241 million budget in 1968 on the education of 55,000 Indian children, and there's little to show for it.

Nearly 60 percent of these youngsters must attend BIA boarding schools, either because there's no public or federal day school near their home or because they are "social referrals" (BIA jargon for anything from a bilingual difficulty to serious emotional disorders and juvenile delinquency). One percent finish college. In Alaska there is only one federal high school, so two-thirds of the Alaskan Indians are sent to a boarding school in Oregon; 267 others go to school in Chilocco, Oklahoma. The Navajo nation comprises one-third of the BIA's responsibility, and 92 percent of its children are in boarding schools. The schools have a 60 percent dropout rate, compared to a national average of 23 percent.

Assimilation has been the aim of the Bureau of Indian Affairs since the early 1800's. But it no longer expresses that purpose in the embarrassing language of a World War II House subcommittee: "The final solution of the Indian problem [is] to work toward the liquidation of the Indian problem rather than toward merely perpetuating a federal Indian Service working with a steadily increasing Indian population." From the BIA's "Curriculum Needs of Navajo Pupils" we learn that the Navajo child "needs to begin to develop knowledge of how the dominant culture is pluralistic and how these people worked to become the culture which influences the American mainstream of life . . ."; "needs to understand

that every man is free to rise as high as he is able and willing . . .";
"needs assistance with accepting either the role of leader or follower
. . ."; "needs to understand that a mastery of the English language is
imperative to compete in the world today . . ."; "needs to understand that
work is necessary to exist and succeed. . . ."

Often the government places children in federal boarding schools at the
age of six or seven; over 9,000 under the age of nine are so placed. That
quite a few parents resist having their young taken from home for a year
is indicated by a 1966 HEW survey: 16,000 Indian children between the
ages of eight and 16 were not in school.

The Indian school curriculum is standard: ancient history, European
history, American history, geography, arithmetic, art, music (an Indian
"needs training in proper tone production in order to properly and effectively sing Western music"). Not much about *their* history. The Interior
Department investigated Indian schools in Alaska last spring and found
that "education which gives the Indian, Eskimo and Aleut knowledge of
— and therefore pride in — their historic and cultural heritage is almost
nonexistent. . . . In the very few places where such an attempt is made, it
is poorly conceived and inadequate." Most of the boarding school teachers
are aware of the variations in language, dress and customs of their students,
but their sensitivity to the less obvious differences in Indian values, beliefs
and attitudes is peripheral and by the way. Most Indian children speak
English poorly or not at all; communication between teacher and pupil is
difficult or impossible. Yet Bureau schools conduct *all* classes in English.

It doesn't take long to discourage young, dedicated teachers: "Most of
the teachers came to Chilocco because of humanitarian reasons," said a
former teacher at the Oklahoma boarding school. "They saw the pitiful
situation and truly wanted to help, but after months of rejection and
failure, they either quit or they began looking at it as an eight to five
job with no obligation to their students." A teacher at an Arizona school
wrote the BIA last year, suggesting that the inclusion of courses in agriculture and native crafts might arouse his habitually unresponsive students.
"This idea [didn't] set well with many of the 'old hands' among the administrators," he later said. "The only thing that came out of it were some
dark days for me, and a label as a trouble-maker." The turnover rate,
among teachers is double the national average. To an Indian child, the
teacher is a stranger passing through. An obvious remedy is to enlist more
Indian teachers. At present only 16 percent of the Bureau's teachers are
Indian, and with only one percent of the Indians graduating yearly from
college, there is little chance that the percentage will rise.

Estranged from his family, confronted with an alien culture and unable
to talk to his teachers, the Indian's academic performance is predictably

poor. What is harder to explain is the "crossover phenomenon." For the first few years of school, Indian achievement parallels that of white children and then slowly but persistently regresses. An Indian starts to fall behind between the sixth and eighth grades, and if he doesn't drop out finishes high school with a 9.5 grade education. Despite this regression a boarding school student is never held back for academic failure; at the end of each year, he is promoted to the next grade whatever his performance. Summer school programs are scarce. Bureau teachers are contracted by the year, and one-third go on educational leave during the summer while the rest clean up the schools, take inventory and so on. As a result the typical high school class contains highly intelligent students as well as many who should still be in grade school. The teacher tries to compensate by aiming his instruction somewhere between the two extremes, so much of the class drops off to sleep or stares blankly at books.

One would think that after school the children could find some release from his dreariness, in the dorms or in some extracurricular activity. Life at a federal boarding school though, is regimented and arbitrary. Seen from the air, many of the schools look like military installations — complexes of one-color, one-texture buildings set up in the middle of otherwise barren areas. The impression of physical isolation mirrors the cultural isolation in the classroom. The building-complex usually includes dormitories (boys and girls), classroom buildings and housing for the staff. Many of the buildings are in disrepair. In a number of places (Tuba City, Arizona, for example), condemned buildings are still in use. The Fort Wingate Elementary Boarding School in New Mexico uses old Fort Wingate, once commanded by Douglas MacArthur's father. Forty years ago, the Brookings Institution's Merriam Report declared this plant unsuitable.

Even the new buildings are designed to reinforce the numbing sterility. Long, narrow, lifeless dormitories house row upon row of double-deckered iron beds and little else. Windows are sometimes barred. Floors are bare; the vivid personal decorations that are so much a part of many Indian communities are discouraged. Dress, too, is strictly regulated. The system makes individualizing one's appearance or environment fairly impossible. Beneath all the regulation is the Bureau's implicit concept of the children: all Indians are alike. In reality some children are at boarding schools because there is no alternative schooling available, while an increasing number, the "social referrals," come to the schools with serious emotional problems. Dr. Anthony Elite of the Public Health Service's Indian Health Office in Phoenix has said that "with this great change in the profile of the student body, there has not been a concomitant change in staffing skilled workers or training existing personnel to cope with these problems."

Each hour of a child's day is planned by the clock, with strict schedules posted in the dorms. Classes, meals, study periods, chores, free-time, bed —the routine never varies. Frequent headcounts are taken to quickly identify runaways or "AWOLS" as the Bureau calls them. Demerits are handed out for breaking the rules. The demerits can be removed by performing extra chores or by sacrificing privileges like TV, a school movie or snacks. At the Chinle Elementary Boarding School each child has a punchcard fastened to the end of his bed with punched holes representing demerits on one side and merits on the other. A little boy proudly displayed his card to a visitor. He was especially proud of the large number of holes he had accumulated. Most of the holes were on the demerit side. He didn't know the difference. At another school two small boys were seen sitting on the floor, tearing up old textbooks as a punishment.

Dr. Robert Bergman, a PHS psychiatrist on the Navajo Reservation, said, "the somewhat limited social opportunities of the boarding high school give the adolescent students few protected ways of exploring boy-girl relationships. The sexes are pretty well kept separate most of the time, and even casual contact between them is looked on with some suspicion by school officials anxious about possible scandal. A hostile rebellious attitude develops in the students, and they make their own opportunities away from the potential help of adults. Many students make a very abrupt transition from no dating at all to sneaking out to drink and make love." The administration's response to such behavior is more repression and school officials at a number of boarding schools cite discipline as their most important problem. Asked what he would do if given more money, the superintendent at Chilocco said he would build a jail and hire more guards.

To maintain discipline, the school eliminates as many outside or uncontrollable influences as possible. A visitor is discouraged from talking to the children. A child "caught" talking to a visitor gets a sharp warning glance from a school official. Authorities address the children in English and discourage using native language in both the classroom and dorms. Dr. Bergman relates the rather bizarre results of this policy: "I often encounter [dorm attendants] who pretend not to speak Navajo. They have become so convinced that speaking Navajo is a bad thing to do that they often won't admit that they can. [Most attendants are themselves products of boarding schools.] The children learn that what they say in Navajo is effectively kept secret from the authorities even if one of the Navajo-speaking members of the staff hears them, because the Navajo staff member will be too ashamed of having understood to tell anyone."

School authorities in effect dictate when children may go home for weekends and when parents may visit the schools. The Bureau has a *de facto* policy of discouraging such visits, because the children are noticeably upset and troublesome afterwards, and the number of runaways invariably increases. To reach the school, parents must travel long distances over roads that are impassable most of the year. The schools afford them neither accommodations nor transportation. At the easily accessible Fort Wingate school, signs on the dormitory doors announced that no child would be permitted home for two weekends prior to Thanksgiving. A teacher at the Tuba City Boarding School wrote of the problem . . . to Sen. Robert Kennedy, then chairman of the subcommittee on Indian Education: "Most children on the reservation starting at age six only see their parents on occasional weekends, if that often. At these times parents are usually allowed to check out their children — if the child's conduct in school warrants it, in the opinion of the school administration. If he has been a 'problem' (e.g., has run away) parents are often not allowed to take him until he has 'learned his lesson.'" The students' most visible emotional problem is boredom — the deadening routine of marching in line to meals and class, the lack of recreation or an interesting diversion. The letter to Sen. Kennedy summarized the emptiness of life at a boarding school: "The children search everywhere for something — they grasp most hungrily at any attention shown them, or to any straw that might offer some escape from boredom. You can't help but see it in their faces when you visit the dorms of the younger children. At the older boys' dormitories, they are used to the conditions — you can see that, too. They no longer expect anything meaningful from anyone."

Their reaction to this gradual dehumanization is extreme. Recently on the Navajo Reservation, two young runaways froze to death trying to make it to their homes 50 miles away. Escape through glue-, paint- and gasoline-sniffing is as common as chronic drunkenness at the boarding schools. On Easter morning two years ago, authorities at the Chilocco school found a Crow boy who had apparently drunk himself to death. More recently a runaway at the Albuquerque Boarding School was found frozen to death after an alcoholic binge.

Suicide among young Indians is over three times the national average and an even greater problem at the boarding schools. Yet the Superintendent of the Albuquerque school said he had never seen an Indian suicide in any school in his 28 years of experience. Testifying before Sen. Kennedy's subcommittee, Dr. Daniel O'Connell found evidence to the contrary: "The situation as far as suicide is concerned is especially acute among the boarding school children, particularly in high school. . . . In the Busby School in the Northern Cheyenne Reservation, for example, with fewer than 250 students, there were 12 attempted suicides during the past 18 months."

The closest thing the child has to a surrogate parent is the so-called instructional aide or dormitory attendant. Aides are responsible for the children in the dorms and supervise their routine activities — dressing and washing the smaller children, housecleaning and free time. Psychologically, the instructional aide is the most important member of the staff, since the dorm is the closest thing the children have to a home life. But he is the lowest paid and has the lowest status in the school hierarchy. Each aide is expected to care for 60 to 80 children. At a conference with Dr. Bergman, an aide asked for help in getting her 75 first-graders to put their shoes by their beds at night. Every morning is mass hysteria as seven-year-olds scramble for a missing right or left shoe. Night attendants are responsible for 180 to 260 children, so there is rarely someone to comfort a youngster having a normal childhood nightmare.

The instructional aides are not encouraged to take a personal interest in the children. An aide was severely reprimanded for inviting some girls to her room to make Navajo fry-bread. The authorities would prefer that the system's few professional guidance counselors handle the children's problems. The present ratio of students to counselors is 690 to one. One counselor complained that 30 to 40 percent of his time is spent retrieving runaways, another 30 percent supervising housekeeping, leaving little time for serious counseling.

For its more serious problems — the suicide-prone, the alcoholics, the psychotics — the BIA employed one full-time psychologist last year for the entire federal school system. A rebellious or uncooperative student gains a reputation as a "trouble-maker" and is expelled from one school after another until he is old enough to drop out. A Fort Hall boy who has attempted suicide six times was sent to Chilocco last fall for lack of anywhere else to send him. Among the Indians, Chilocco is considered the end of the line.

The Rough Rock Demonstration School in northeastern Arizona is a welcome anomaly in this chain of dead-end desert schools. Jointly funded by the Office of Economic Opportunity and the BIA, the Navajo boarding school is innovative in that it is run by Indians. The seven Indians who comprise the school board set school policy, hire and fire teachers and manage the school's $790,000 budget. The curriculum includes daily instruction in Navajo culture, history and language, and the school's Cultural Identification Center attracts talented Navajo artists and translators to produce meaningful texts for Indian children. Nor is the built-in bleakness of dorm life found at Rough Rock. The school has 10 counselors, and parents are invited to live in the dorms for eight-week periods (reducing the child-adult ratio to 10 to one). The parents work as dorm aides, with pay, and attend adult education programs, since many are less-educated than their children. Students are encouraged to go home on weekends and the school provides transportation for those who would otherwise have to stay at school. The school's teachers make periodic visits to the children's homes to let the parents know how their children are doing. (The parents of many children at other schools haven't the slightest idea of what grade their children are in.) Of the school's 82 full-time employees, 62 are Indians, and for many it is their first permanent job. It is too early to say whether Rough Rock's community-involvement approach is *the* answer to Indian education. The experiment is expensive ($2,500 per student) and the school will have to look elsewhere for support after OEO funding expires. . . . What the Indians at Rough Rock have proved is that given effective control of the immediate forces that shape their lives, they can be a success, qualified in measurable achievement, total in terms of self-respect.

Further Readings

Bergman, Robert, Joseph Muskrat, Sol Tax, Oscar Werner, and Gary Witherspoon. *Problems of cross-cultural educational research and evaluation: the Rough Rock demonstration school.* Minneapolis: Training Center for Community Programs, University of Minnesota, 1969.

Erickson, Donald, and Henrietta Schwartz. *Community school at Rough Rock, a report submitted to the Office of Economic Opportunity.* Contract No. B89-4534 (April 1969).

Levine, Stuart, and Nancy O. Lurie (eds.) *The American Indian today.* Deland, Fla.: Everett Edwards, 1968.

Peterson, John H., Jr., and James R. Richburg. "Evaluation and accountability in Mississippi Choctaw education." Paper read at the Annual Meeting of the Society for Applied Anthropology, Boulder, Colorado, 1970.

33

Mr. Lesser discusses the sociohistorical situation of a native people which has become a misunderstood unconventional minority in its own homeland. The American Indian, as durable as his legend, occupies us as an anthropological subject and at the same time as a social problem. The two human interests are not in every case equally served. Nor are they taken regularly by the same anthropological researchers. Indeed, one interest is considered to be "pure" or "academic"; the other, because the Indian minority experiences low life expectancies, bad housing, depressed occupational chances, racism, etc., is construed to be "applied" or "social action" anthropology. Mr. Lesser, without pumice, attempts to integrate the two interests here. He introduces the extraordinary relationships between Indian communities and the greater American society, and in so doing he steadily sketches the crucial influences of contemporary education on tribal futures as Lesser prefers these to be: matters of decision by and for Indians. Lesser's position is more or less that of Wax (Part Three), Parmee (Part Four), and Henninger and Esposito in the previous article. Professor of Anthropology, Hofstra University, Lesser sets an unusual standard for an anthropology that relates not only as disciplined social science but also as a necessary adjunct to informed social policy, especially in programs for minority education.

ALEXANDER LESSER

Education and the Future of Tribalism in the United States: The Case of the American Indian

To a good many Americans, the American Indians are a "problem," and by no means a simple problem that can be easily solved. This rather common American feeling cannot be accounted for alone by the position of the Indians as a minority or by the disadvantages that go with it. In actual situations of discrimination, the public mood is clear and action prompt. Thus, in Pontiac, Michigan, in 1960, when a Winnebago veteran was denied burial in a cemetery "restricted to Caucasians," the people were indignant and interred him with public ceremony and military honors. This kind of Indian "problem" is unlikely to leave vague discomforts unresolved.

The sense that Indians are a special "problem" comes, I think, from their unique position rather than from their minority situation — their distinctive legal status in relation to the nation and their stubborn insistence on their Indian identity. Neither of these is clearly understood by the public, and the intrusion of either or both may so color a situation that public reaction is confused and uncertain. The recent situation in New York illustrates this. Edmund Wilson in *Apologies to the Iroquois* observed in Niagara Falls that "a good deal of sympathy . . . for the fight of the Tuscaroras" against New York Power Authority plans to take Tuscarora lands for a hydroelectric project "turned into a kind of resentment" when the Indians, invoking tribal rights under treaties with the United States, seemed to be winning; non-Indians in the same predicament

Originally published as "Occasional Paper No. 3" of the Phelps-Stokes Fund. Reprinted in *The Social Service Review*, vol. 35, no. 2 (June 1961), pp. 1–9.

had no such legal argument against condemnation. This kind of situation may not evoke a definitive public reaction; it is more likely to generate uneasiness and leave behind it a sense of "problems" unresolved.

A resolution of this special Indian "problem" is unlikely unless the factors involved in the Indian situation are understood and unless the historical significance of the position of the Indians in the United States is realized.

I

Americans not in direct contact with Indians may not even be aware of their existence most of the time, and the experience of rediscovery, when Indians make headlines, may itself be disturbing. Indians are a reminder of a past that troubles the American conscience. More than that, their existence as *Indians* unsettles the firm conviction that in this country, with its superior institutions, assimilation is proper and desirable and in fact an inevitable, automatic process. Why, after centuries of contact with us, should Indians still feel so separate and aloof?

In 1961, the striking fact is that Indians are not only here with us to stay, in the sense of biological survival,[1] but that there are many thousands of Indians — in 29 of the 50 states — still essentially unassimilated. They have not experienced that identification of interests and outlook, that "interpenetration and fusion," in which they would have acquired American "memories, sentiments, and attitudes" and come to share our "experiences and history" which the late Chicago sociologist, Robert E. Park, saw as the essence of assimilation.

Most unassimilated Indians live in Indian communities. There are many — in twenty-five states. Pueblo and Hopi communities of New Mexico and Arizona and the Navajos are perhaps best known. In the Southwest are also Apache communities, the Pima and the Papago and the Havasupai, among others. But Indian communities are found as well in other parts of the country. To mention a sample, there are the Eastern Cherokees of North Carolina; the Chippewas of Red Lake, Minnesota; the Menominis of Wisconsin; the Sauk and Fox of Iowa; the Hidatsa, Mandan, Arikara, and several divisions of Teton Sioux in the Dakotas; the Blackfeet and Cheyennes in Montana; the Klamaths in Oregon. Other states in which Indian groups survive include Oklahoma, California, Nebraska, Kansas, Wyoming,

---

[1] The census shows a marked increase in Indians during recent generations and a rate of population growth more rapid than that of the country as a whole or of any other identifiable group. There are now between 400,000 and 500,000 Indians in the continental United States and Alaska, and, if the present rate of increase continues, descendants of the original Americans may be as numerous in another generation as their ancestors were in Columbus' day.

Idaho, and Washington. Americans recently became aware of two in New York, the Tuscaroras and the Senecas, when these Iroquois opposed state and federal plans to inundate Iroquois lands by construction of dams for power and flood control. Edmund Wilson, in memorializing these people in *Apologies to the Iroquois*, gives eloquent testimony to the viable group life of these and other Iroquois communities of New York.

In size, these communities range from the Navajos, the largest, with more than 70,000 members, to small communities like the Sauk and Fox of Iowa, who number a few hundred. In culture, there is great diversity, and Indians still tend to identify themselves first as Navajos, Sioux, or Cherokees, and secondarily as Indians.

Indian groups are of course only a handful of the tribes who originally peopled the country. But their endurance, with the deep sense of tradition and identity which many retain, is a remarkable phenomenon. They have survived the exterminations which depleted and destroyed Indian peoples of the Atlantic seaboard and of California; the forced evacuations which took many from their homes into alien country; and the concentration of tribal groups in restricted areas, stripped of their traditional land base. Most important of all, they have survived despite the generations of national effort to force assimilation upon them, for our dominant Indian policy from the beginning has been assimilation. Their existence today reflects the voluntary decision of their members, as citizens of the United States,[2] to maintain traditional group life, in many cases on the homelands of their ancestors — a decision which speaks strongly for the vitality of the Indian way and the values of Indian group life.

How "Indian" is life in these communities? Measured by externals, by clothes and housing, by use of non-Indian technology and gadgets, or by ways in which many now make a living, it may appear that the people of these communities have on the whole adopted our ways. The San Carlos Apaches of New Mexico, for example, raise some of the finest American livestock for market. The Red Lake Chippewas of Minnesota ship fish by refrigerated trucks for sale in Chicago. The Sauk and the Fox of Iowa make a living by working for wages among their non-Indian neighbors. Indian life has not been standing still. The Indians have been making accommodations and adjustments to our society and economy from early times and they continue to do so.

But modern studies of Indian communities show that adoption of the externals of American life is not neatly correlated with accompanying

---

[2] By 1924, more than two-thirds of the Indians were citizens under treaties and agreements. In that year citizenship was confirmed by enactment for all Indians born in the country. Indians have full rights of citizenship, which include, of course, the right to complete freedom of movement anywhere. The time is past when Indian communities can be dismissed as "segregation" or as "concentration camps."

changes in basic Indian attitudes, mind, and personality. Feelings and attitudes, the life of the inner man, change more slowly than utilitarian features of comfort and convenience. Studies among the Cherokees of North Carolina, for example — considered one of the Five Civilized Tribes for more than a century — and among the Navajos of the Southwest reveal the same inner Indian feelings about the world and man's place in nature, the same non-competitive attitudes, the same disinterest in the American drive for progress and change.

The changes these community Indians have made over time, taken all in all, seem selective. Some inner man resisted complete annihilation of self and identity and held fast to values and attitudes acquired in a mother's arms and on a father's knee and chose from us some things of use but not others. They chose principally what we call material culture and technology and little of our sentiments and values and our philosophy of life.

II

Indian non-assimilation in an America which has so largely assimilated many peoples from many lands is an anachronism only if we think of the Indians as merely one among many American minorities and if we look for the same process of cultural change and adjustment in them all. The others are immigrant minorities; with the exception of the Negroes, they came here voluntarily, and their coming, their choice of a new homeland, implies some commitment toward assimilation.

The Indian situation and Indian relations with the dominant culture in America are quite different. The Indians have roots deeply buried in the soil; their communities have a history in the land more ancient than that of the majority people. They can best be compared with European national minorities who became part of an alien country as a result of national expansion or, in North America, with the French-Canadians of Quebec who became part of an English country after 1763. In these cases, as among the Indian communities, the people are resistant to assimilation and try to maintain traditional ways and even traditional language.

What is true of those who remain at home in close association with their own ethnic community, however, is not true of those who may migrate and take up life elsewhere. Members of European national minorities may move into industrial cities or emigrate to America; French-Canadians of Quebec may migrate to western provinces of Canada; American Indians may leave their tribal communities for life in our towns and cities. As in the case of European immigration to the United States, Canada, or Latin America, the migration is a movement of individuals and families.

If they do not return home, these migrants are subject to assimilating influences of a different culture to a degree that their kinfolk at home are not, and they are more likely to be receptive to assimilation. The process takes time and usually takes place over generations. The original migrants achieve only partial assimilation; their children, especially when schooled entirely in the new environment, carry the process further; and in the third generation assimilation becomes virtually complete.

This kind of assimilation has taken place over the years among our Indians, as individuals or families have left their communities and in time severed their tribal connections. How many have left Indianism behind in this way we do not know, for it is difficult to keep an accurate count, but there have been many.

A confusion between this process of assimilation of migrants over a period of generations and that of the adaptive change and accommodation going on in Indian home communities may explain the confident predictions made on more than one occasion that this or that Indian community would become fully assimilated in some definite period of time. The stated period is often twenty-five years, approximately a generation. At the end of that time, however, contrary to predictions, the community is still there, as strong in numbers and as viable and unassimilated as ever. Some members may have left and chosen assimilation, but an increase of the population at home has usually more than made up for the loss. It has become increasingly probable that many of the communities that have endured are likely to be with us for a long and indefinite future unless radical or brutal measures are taken to disorganize and disperse them. We may have to come to terms with a people who seem determined to have a hand in shaping their own destiny.

Nor is the persistence of these Indian communities in an industrialized America a wholly exceptional fact in the modern world. Communities with strong commitments to traditional ways of life are known in industrialized European areas. For example, the Keurs, in *The Deeply Rooted*, describe a traditional Drents community in the Netherlands. More striking are studies in Wales and Cumberland, close to the heart of industrial England, the original home of the Industrial Revolution. Alwyn Rees, in *Life in a Welsh Countryside*, found country neighborhood patterns of life persisting in Wales in 1940 from a pre-industrial past and, in some ways, from a more remote pastoral and tribal past. W. M. Williams, in *Gosforth*, describes Cumberland ways in 1950 still unassimilated by industrial England, still persisting in traditional patterns hundreds of years old.

Such obstinate endurance, with its inner resistance to engulfment by dominant but alien traditions, can be understood, no doubt, as a reflection of the fundamental role of primary relationships — especially that of parents and children — in handing on basic attitudes, feelings, and patterns of interpersonal relations. But it is also a stubborn fact of vital importance in understanding the contemporary world of many peoples and many cultures, each of which may seek from the West ways to improve standards of life, but each of which may at the same time be determined to keep an identity and tradition of its own.

III

The feeling that Indians are a special "problem" is not a reaction only to Indian non-assimilation. The unique legal status of Indians, when it obtrudes and reveals that Indians may have special rights other citizens do not have, is equally disturbing. It offends the American sense of fitness and equality, the feeling that there should be no special groups — none at a disadvantage and none that have advantages over others.

For it is true that the distinctive legal position of the Indians — their primary relation to the federal government — involves what may be called "special rights." The government, as trustee, protects Indian lands and such trust-protected lands are exempt from state and local taxation.[3] The federal government provides services to Indians, including agricultural and soil conservation services and health and education services, that others receive principally through state and local agencies. And Indian communities have under federal law rights of community self-government and the right to organize tribal business corporations.

The federal status of Indian communities began in early times, and it has a long history. For more than a century after colonization, the balance of power was on the Indian side, and the colonists, seeking peaceful relations essential to the survival and expansion of settlement, dealt with the Indian tribes as they found them — autonomous and self-governing. They made treaties and agreements with individual tribes through tribal leaders.

This recognition of the autonomy of the separate Indian tribes became a principle of dealing with them as independent nations which the United States inherited from British colonial rule. Thus, Indian relations were external affairs of the United States — a matter for treaty-making by the nation and not by the states. We "bought the United States" from the Indians, to use a phrase of Felix Cohen's, by treaties with individual Indian tribes, treaties which, as part of the bargain, guaranteed trust protection of remaining Indian lands and freedom from taxation on those lands. When the treaty-making period was ended by Congress in 1871, the Indians, as dependent groups within the nation, remained a federal responsibility and the

---

[3] However, Indians pay all other taxes paid by other citizens, including real estate taxes on Indian-owned land not in trust status.

provisions of treaties made before 1871 became continuing federal obligations to the Indians, the basis of most of the "special rights."

The special status of Indians and their "special rights" not only are themselves annoying to us but seem related to that other needling fact about Indians: the aloof pride with which many have persisted in remaining Indian. For their status and rights set the Indians apart, a unique group of American citizens, and thus aid and abet them in keeping a separate identity. On the whole, however, they help those remain Indian who want to be Indian, who express their wish by clinging together in a community; those who want assimilation can and do leave the community and go their separate ways.

During the more than a century of this country's commitment to a policy of assimilating and absorbing the Indians, the government has not been unaware of the role of Indian community life and the federal Indian tie in thwarting the assimilation process. In 1887, Congress saw Indian patterns of land tenure as the foundation of Indian community institutions and attacked them in the General Allotment Act. That act, by ending communal land tenure and making Indians individual property owners, was intended to break up tribal life and assimilate Indians as individuals; unhappily, when communities disintegrated under its pressures, the detribalized individuals who lost their lands became, not assimilated Americans, but paupers and public charges.[4] As recently as 1953, Congress proposed to terminate the federal Indian tie as rapidly as possible, including termination of trust protection and federal services to Indians. The intent was clear: immigrants do not become fully assimilated as tribal groups and neither would Indians. Although the termination program is at a standstill for the present, two large tribes, the Menominis of Wisconsin and the Klamaths of Oregon, are now going through the last stages of termination procedures enacted in 1954.

If it be admitted that the persistence of Indian communities is related to their federal status, and that Indian rejection of full assimilation is related to the fact that Indian communities survive, there still remains the question: Should the nation's Indian policy be committed to and directed toward assimilation?

---

[4] The act was in force 47 years. During the period, two-thirds of Indian-owned lands of 1887 were alienated from Indian ownership, principally as a result of the procedure of first individualizing land holdings and then removing them from trust status. Some tribes were not subject to allotment, especially tribes in the Southwest. Of the many who were subject to the program but opposed it, few wholly escaped; the Red Lake Chippewas of Minnesota are perhaps the outstanding case. Some of the disastrous effects of the allotment program were remedied in the Indian New Deal period that began in 1934. In 1960, one tribe, the Northern Cheyennes of Montana, was trying to promote a tribal "Fifty-Year Unallotment Program" to return all allotted lands still Indian-owned to tribal ownership.

For a brief period, while John Collier was Commissioner of Indian Affairs (1933–45), this question was courageously answered in the negative. The existence of Indian communities as a reality of the modern world was accepted and a program was designed, partly realized in legislation — the Indian Reorganization Act (IRA) of 1934 and supplementary legislation — to provide Indian communities with the legal status and machinery and the economic resources and opportunities they required to continue their existence for as long a time as they chose. Tribal self-government and tribal business corporations under this program have already been mentioned; the program also included provisions for an adequate land base, financial credit, and adequate training and education.

The charge that this program was intended to halt Indian progress and keep Indians, like museum specimens, in their ancient unchanging ways, stems from a complete misunderstanding of its motivation or from die-hard assimilationism. The program was actually committed to more change and progress toward improved standards of Indian life than had ever been contemplated in the preceding century of Indian affairs. How Indian, in the sense of old Indian ways of life, are the livestock corporations, the farming and husbandry co-operatives, the co-operative tribal stores, or the commercial credit that were essential parts of the Collier program? The program was in fact dedicated to constructive accommodation and adjustment of Indians to modern American life, but also to the idea — unpopular, perhaps, among most Americans — that a decision to become completely assimilated and give up Indian identity and community life was not for the nation or the government to make but for the Indians to make for themselves.

IV

Some Americans see assimilation, and ending Indian communities and special Indian status, as in the best interests of Indians. The legal forms which now safeguard the status of Indian communities are seen as restrictions or limitations of Indian activity and opportunity and not as marks of Indian freedom. The Indian rights of tax exemption on trust property are not ordinarily so characterized, of course; they are usually written off as peculiarities which set Indians apart from others, increasing social distance and the difficulties of intergroup relations. But such features of the trust situation as government control over the use and disposition of trust-protected Indian lands and other tribal assets are seen as hampering and restrictive, as undue paternalism and overprotection which increase Indian dependency and destroy Indian initiative.

Few would deny that overpaternalism has often impaired the administration of Indian affairs. The trustee relation is often ambiguous and difficult; abuse of power on the one hand or over-anxiety on the other both may have damaging effects.

The difficulty is compounded in Indian affairs because the federal government is in a trustee relation to both communities and individuals. The trust protection of individual property is an outgrowth of the federal trust relation to tribal property; tribal property may be individualized, but individual owners may hold restricted titles (in theory, being judged incompetent), rather than unrestricted titles in fee simple. This trust relation to individuals has all too often involved abuses or overprotection, and it may well be that the relation is more restrictive than liberating, especially if individuals have chosen the path of detribalization and assimilation. But it is the federal trust relation to Indian communities rather than individuals that is most germane in this discussion.

In the case of communities, it is doubtful that paternalistic abuses which have occurred are inherent in the federal trust relation. Tribal self-government, for example, since its organization under the IRA, has suffered on a good many occasions from unwarranted government interference. When Indians asked for clarification of their rights under new tribal constitutions, superintendents were often too prone to interpret provisions in favor of their own authority and against that of the tribe. And when graft or corruption is alleged against tribal councils and administration, officials all too often have intervened so eagerly that Indians have had little opportunity to work out democratic processes for themselves. Federal trusteeship can be operated without such abuses.

Perhaps the more important question about the restrictive or liberating character of the protected status of Indian communities is what kind of freedom we are talking about. The freedom of Indians to become as non-Indian and assimilated as they wish cannot be the issue here. The Indians are citizens with the full rights of citizenship, and many have exercised their freedom to become completely Americanized. But there are many who want and need the freedom to be Indian within the framework of America. For them the existence of the community to which they belong is essential to that freedom, and some defined legal status of the community is essential to its continued existence.

The disappearance of our Indian communities by assimilation has a crucial finality that assimilation can never have for other American minorities. Irish, or German, or Scandinavian, or Italian immigrants who become assimilated can still look toward a homeland from which they came, a viable tradition and culture which dignifies their origins. For the Indian, the tribal community is the only carrier of his tradition; if it disintegrates and disappears, his tradition becomes a matter of history, and he loses part of his identity. We are coming to know the importance of this sense of identification with a viable tradition in the meaning of Israel for the American Jew, or of the emergence of free African nations for the American Negro.

There is a tendency for people in the United States to think in 1961 that we may be coming of age as a people, that now we may be able to accept diversity in our midst without condescension, and that we may be ready to accept as sovereign equals the many peoples, of many races and creeds and cultures, who coexist with us in the complex modern world. Such a liberalism, however, is not yet the American mood in Indian affairs.

While we are unable to rise above assimilationism in our attitude to the Indians, the legal forms which now safeguard their community life and their right to be Indian may be essential. No doubt other forms could be developed by them within the framework of American law, such as, for example, corporate community life without a federal tie, but Indians are unwilling to risk such a change. They hold fast, in the assimilationist mood of America, to the historical status which protects them.

In other respects, however, the Indians are changing and ready for greater changes. Still greatly handicapped by their predominantly rural situation in an industrialized America, they seek technical assistance and training if they can secure these without sacrificing the Indian status they have and want to keep.

Outstanding in the change going on among Indians is the sudden appearance in the last decade of a strong urge for advanced education. Less than two hundred Indians were in college in 1950. Yet by 1959 more than 4,300 were attending colleges and universities, and the number seems likely to continue to increase. This changed attitude toward education, which involves not only the young but their parents and families as well, implies other less obvious changes in Indian attitudes toward their life in America.

Higher education means, of course, that more Indian individuals may choose the path of non-tribal, assimilated life. But it also means that Indian community life will soon be in the hands of a generation of educated Indians. Some communities may choose to disband, with their members going their separate ways; others may want to carry on group life for an indefinite future period. In either case, the decision is likely to be made by informed, educated people, aware of their past and also of their possibilities in America.

Meanwhile, the best we can do, as Felix Cohen once put it, may be "to get out of the way" of the Indians, to stop hampering their efforts to work out their own destiny, and especially to stop trying to make them give up their Indian identity. In a world which may be moving toward greater internationalism, in which we hope that peoples, however diverse, will choose the way of democracy, we cannot avoid the responsibility for a democratic resolution of the American Indian situation. Our attitude toward the Indians, the stubbornest non-conformists among us, may be the touchstone of our tolerance of diversity anywhere.

FURTHER READINGS

Aurbach, Herbert, and Estelle Fuchs (with Gordon Macgregor). *The status of American Indian education.* University Park: Pennsylvania State University, 1970.

Berry, Brewton. *The education of the American Indians: a survey of the literature.* Columbus: Research Foundation, Ohio State University, 1968.

Chance, Norman A. *Premises, policies, and practice: a cross-cultural study of education in the circumpolar North.* Conference on Cross-Cultural Education in the North, Montreal, Canada, 1969.

Eggan, Dorothy. "Instruction and affect in Hopi cultural continuity," *Southwestern Journal of Anthropology,* vol. 12 (Winter 1956).

Singleton, John. "Cross-cultural approaches to research on minority group education," *Journal of the Steward Anthropological Society,* vol. 2 (Fall 1970).

34

Arguments regularly wash over matters of test construction, appropriate or inappropriate contexts for assessing "intelligence," purported and actual "intelligence" differences, and normative or ordinal systems of scholastic progress that are variously invested in standardized testing and evaluation. Few of these arguments run as deep or evoke quite the same response as those raising the possibility, from one human group to another, of entirely dissimilar conceptual styles. Explaining such styles as "rule-sets for the selection and organization of sense data," Miss Cohen establishes the empirical point that "culture-free" nonverbal tests of intelligence do not necessarily void bias; instead, these may only remove bias to a higher, thus more subtle, level of abstraction, which penalizes those who differ in cognitive orientation. Cohen's assertions imply much to the array of "intelligence" differences that are commonly attributed to information-poor or otherwise deprived learning environments. That these differences may respond to distinctive conceptual styles, and not uncritically to "race" and other broad-scale social categories, relates to the whole teaching and learning experience, of which test and measurement is but part. Miss Cohen, an associate of the Learning Research and Development Center, University of Pittsburgh, elaborates two conceptual styles, "relational" and "analytic." The latter represents a cognitive "requirement of the school." The two styles being incompatible, Cohen claims, inevitably "relational" stylists experience profound culture conflict, with extremely problematic consequences for learner and school alike.

ROSALIE A. COHEN

Conceptual Styles, Culture Conflict, and Nonverbal Tests of Intelligence

In 1963 a series of studies on the cognitive nature of educational disadvantage was begun at the Learning Research and Development Center at the University of Pittsburgh.[1] A number of studies were completed, and others are still in progress. Some of these investigations have dealt with the generic requirements for pupil performance in school and some with the cognitive framework from which such requirements are derived (Cohen, 1967). Others have dealt with comparative language styles of low-income groups and those used as standards in the school (Cohen, Fraenkel, and Brewer, 1968) with sources of different conceptual styles in primary group participation, with the replacement of socioeconomic status with a discriminator among children from low income homes (Cohen, 1967), with the relationship of conceptual styles to ego-development (Cohen, 1967; 1968a), and with an analysis of programs for the educationally disadvantaged (Cohen, 1965). A common thread through all these inquiries was the two-way analysis of the cognitive requirements of the school and their derivative social and psychological behaviors and those learning characteristics brought to the school by children from low-income homes.

Findings from the above body of research helped to isolate specific areas of response difficulties in these tests, which we have identified as areas of culture conflict, and to define and clarify some of the culture-bound characteristics of nonverbal tests of intelligence. In order to outline the pattern of reasoning used by the investigators, some of the findings from the studies are reported briefly below.

In order to operationalize the middle-class orientation of the school the content of the ten most widely used standarized tests of intelligence and achievement were analyzed, and a sample of the researchers who develop and revise these tests were surveyed (Cohen, 1967). The object of this inquiry was to identify the generic requirements for achievement that such instruments make of the people to whom they are administered. Three types of requirement were isolated: (1) breadth and depth of general information, (2) analytic abstraction, and (3) field articulation (the ability

From *American Anthropologist*, vol. 71, no. 5 (October 1969), pp. 828–856. Reprinted by permission of the author and publisher.

[1] This research and development was performed pursuant to a contract with the U.S. Office of Education, Department of Health, Education and Welfare under the provisions of the Cooperative Research Program.

to extract salient information from an embedding context, as in reading comprehension or in the extraction of an arithmetic problem from a word context). Although information growth with growing maturity is taken for granted, development in analytic abstraction and field articulation is often obscured by the information contexts in which the demonstration of these cognitive skills is embedded.

Standardized tests of intelligence and achievement are made up of items that assess both increasing assimilation of concepts and general information and increasing skills in formal analysis and field articulation. The latter skills are measured by items requiring the subject to derive analogies or "logical" sequences. Here is a sample from the Metropolitan Achievement Inventory (ninth-grade level):

> Chair: sit; bed: . . . (*Chair* is to *sit* as *bed* is to . . .)
> Select from the following: *Lie; bedroom; night; crib; tired.*

To arrive at the appropriate response (lie), the subject must abstract the part of speech required, in addition to other attributes of the choices, in order to complete the logical sequence. Reading-comprehension tests directly measure increasing skills in field articulation, although performance on all sub-tests requires this skill. Thus, the school requires improvement in analytic abstraction and field articulation skills in increasingly measured amounts at each higher grade level as well as a demonstration of growth in pupils' information repertoires. In general, intelligence tests are weighted toward information components; achievement tests are weighted somewhat on "logical" skills, that is, on skills of analytic abstraction and field articulation.

Analytic-abstraction and field-articulation skills require a specific kind of approach to selecting and organizing information. Individuals differ, however, in what they select as salient information in a given stimulus or situation. They also differ in how they classify and generalize that information. Methods of selecting and processing information can be classified in terms of "cognitive styles" or "styles of cognitive control." Some individuals are "splitters," and others are "lumpers." Some individuals think attributes of a stimulus have significance in themselves; others think they have significance only in reference to some total context (Kagan, Moss, and Siegal, 1963). But the school requires one specific approach to cognitive organization — analytic — so the ability to use it well becomes more critical at higher grade levels. Pupils with inadequate development of these skills and those who develop a different cognitive style could be expected not only to be poor achievers early in their school experience but also to grow worse comparatively as they move to higher grade levels.

Having determined that achievement in school requires increasingly sophisticated analytic cognitive skills, a second study inquired into the characteristics of other (or perhaps conflicting) approaches to cognitive organization that might divert, or handicap the development of, analytic skills (Cohen, 1967; Kagan, Moss, and Siegal, 1963; Gardner, Ms). The literature on cognitive styles suggests that at least one clear-cut "other" cognitive style has been observed reliably over time. The nonanalytic cognitive style is called here "relational," although in literature it is more commonly called "self-centered" (as opposed to the "stimulus-centered" character of the analytic style). The literature indicates that cognitive styles are independent of native ability and that they are definable without reference to specific substantive content.

The analytic cognitive style is characterized by a formal or analytic mode of abstracting salient information from a stimulus or situation and by a stimulus-centered orientation to reality, and it is parts-specific (i.e., parts or attributes of a given stimulus have meaning in themselves). The relational cognitive style, on the other hand, requires a descriptive mode of abstraction and is self-centered in its orientation to reality; only the global characteristics of a stimulus have meaning to its users, and these only in reference to some total context (Cohen, 1967; Kagan, Moss, and Siegal, 1963).

In the literature, it was also possible to identify clear-cut social and psychological correlates of both analytic and relational cognitive styles. Marked distinctions between individuals using each of these two cognitive styles have been drawn using a wide variety of tests, as well as through consideration of many of their social and psychological characteristics. Many school-related learning characteristics, such as length and intensity of attention, preferences of optional reading material, and the differential dependence upon primary groups, also distinguish between these two types of individuals (Cohen, 1967; Kagan, Moss, and Siegal, 1963). Their language styles differ as well (Bernstein, 1964a: 288–314, 1964b). Appendix A systematizes these relationships as they have been demonstrated empirically by other investigators.

A new observation that emerged from this study of the literature on cognitive styles was that not only test criteria but also the overall ideology and learning environment of the school embody requirements for many social and psychological correlates of the analytic style. This emphasis can be found, for example, in its cool, impersonal, outer-centered approach to reality organization. Analytic correlates can also be found in the requirements that the pupil learn to sit increasingly long periods of time, to concentrate alone on impersonal learning stimuli, and to observe and value organized time-allotment schedules. In order to appreciate fully the impact of the analytic approach on the school environment, therefore, it is necessary to consider how many of its impersonal behavioral requirements ensue subtly from this analytic frame of reference. So discrepant are the analytic and relational frames of reference that a pupil whose preferred mode of cognitive organization is emphatically relational is unlikely to be rewarded in the school setting either socially or by grades, regardless of his native abilities and even if his information repertoire and background of experience are adequate. It appears that, although relational patterns of response have been known to exist, both the cognitive characteristics of this style and its sociobehavioral correlates have been considered deviant and disruptive in the analytically oriented learning environment of the school.

Although the relationship of the analytic frame of reference to curriculum components has engaged the attention of researchers, possible sources of this and other conceptual styles have escaped systematic exploration. Indeed, the psychological literature suggests that cognitive styles are either predetermined by the nature of the organism or that they are the result of idiosyncratic early experiences that have developed into learning pathways as the result of random trials in problem settings. These explanations do not account for the dominance of relational modes of cognitive organization among individuals from low-income environments [2] and of analytic modes among those of middle-class origins. The absence of normal distributions of these characteristics suggests that such systematic variations may have arisen as a result of different social environments that stimulate, reinforce, and make functional the development of one style of conceptual organization and constrain and inhibit others.

Because low-income environments were known to produce some analytic as well as relational thinkers, a search for within-group discriminators was begun. During a year of observation and interview in low-income neighborhoods in and around Pittsburgh, families, young people, indigenous leaders of poverty communities, and sophisticated principals of schools in these districts all were able to identify certain consistent and definably "deviant" characteristics of family and friendship-group organization in these areas, which were validated by observation.

The structure of these important face-to-face groups and the manner in which critical functions were distributed in them appeared to be quite different from typical middle-class methods of primary-group organization. In the family and friendship groups in certain segments of all these low-income districts, regardless of ethnic differences among them, critical functions such as leadership, child care, and the discretionary use of group funds are not assigned to status roles within the group. Instead, critical functions are periodically performed or widely shared by all members of the group; for this reason they came to be called "shared-function" primary groups. A summary of some of their characteristics are compared with those of a sim-

---

[2] That conceptual style is not a function of deprivation and income inadequacy, however, is supported by the finding that the relational style also characterizes the old-money upper class. Data for this study are still being analyzed.

plified formal model in Appendix B, and discursive commentary and further description of their internal dynamics and their articulation with institutional group structures appear in other papers (Cohen, 1968b, 1968c). Observation indicated that relational and analytic cognitive styles were intimately associated with shared-function and formal styles of group organization. The manner in which critical functions were distributed in them seemed to parallel closely the observable cognitive functioning of their members. When individuals shifted from one kind of group structure to the other, their modes of group participation, their language styles, and their cognitive styles could be seen to shift appropriately to the extent that their expertise in using other approaches made flexibility possible. It appeared that certain kinds of cognitive styles may have developed by day-to-day participation in related kinds of social groups in which the appropriate language structure and methods of thinking about self, things, and ideas are necessary components of their related styles of group participation and that these approaches themselves may act to facilitate or impede their "carriers'" ability to become involved in alternate kinds of groups.

Although our major concern was with the relationships between total primary group configurations and their interarticulation and the development of internally consistent conceptual styles, it was possible to identify comparable methods of group participation and their associated conceptual styles within a single group structure in relatively insulated interaction webs.

Several of the studies that followed made use of multidimensional instruments in an attempt to reduce own-discipline and own-culture bias. They studied the relationships among shared-function and formally organized families and friendship groups, relational and analytic conceptual styles, and school achievement (one case of formally organized institutional involvement).[3] In order to determine whether the response styles that ap-

---

[3] Relationships among the family, the friendship group, and the school represent a useful analytic configuration for several reasons. First, they are major socializing agencies. In addition, because the school has been designed to perform socialization functions for society, the relevance of its requirements to other major institutional frameworks is imposing, both in its impact on learning and behavior and through its sorting and selection functions. In this dual role the school acts as a sluice-gate to participation in other major societal institutions.

Use of the schools as an arena for study also presented strong methodological advantages. Because of compulsory education laws, at least in urban centers, the public, private, and parochial schools provide the only social setting in which total normal school-age populations are available for study, cutting across all relevant demographic characteristics. The schools also provide a reasonably standardized stimulation "input" environment against which performance could be measured. The availability of longitudinal records on each pupil, record and pupil accessibility, and the contributions of other specialized professional staff, such as physicians, psychologists, and social workers, were other advantages.

peared on psychological tests were *dominant* modes of conceptual organization, an effort was made to "triangulate" on mode of conceptual organization through the methods and techniques of several disciplines.[4] Two psychological instruments were used, two conventional linguistic instruments, and a seventy-two item set of attitude scales.[5] A typical outline of an instrument plan follows in Table 1 and is elaborated in Table 2.

TABLE 1
Anticipated Responses in Analytic and Relational
Approaches Conceptual Skills by Conceptual Styles

| | Conceptual skills | |
Conceptual styles	*Mode of abstraction*	*Field articulation*
Analytic	Formal (analytic)	Field independent
Relational	Descriptive	Field dependent

This plan was designed to determine the extent to which a given mode of reality organization is demonstrated persistently — on psychological tests of cognitive style, in language selections and organization, and in attitudes about one's self and one's environment. "Conceptual style," then, is a composite construct that incorporates all three dimensions in each of the two cognitive-skill areas. Dominant patterns of conceptual organization were then related to dominant styles of family and friendship group participation (determined by the distribution of critical functions in these two primary groups and producing a longitudinal component, family impact having occurred earlier in time than that of the friendship group) and to school achievement (as measured by eighteen subtests of the Project Talent achievement inventory, covering the areas of general screening, vocabulary, literature, music, social studies, mathematics, physical science, biological science, scientific attitude, aeronautics and space, electronics and electricity, mechanics, farming, home economics, sports, abstract reasoning,

---

[4] Triangulation through the own-cultural bias of observers . . . requires multiple methods focused on the same construct from independent points of observation. This is required because the sense data or meter readings are now understood as the result of a transaction in which both the observer (or meter) and the object of investigation contribute to the form of the data. With a single observation at hand, it is impossible to separate the subjective and objective component. When, however, observations through separate instruments and separate vantage points can be matched as reflecting the same objects, then it is possible to separate out the components in the data due to observer (instrument) and observed. It turns out that this disentangling process requires both multiple observers (methods) and multiple, dissimilar, objects of study [Campbell, 1964: 34–35].

[5] Attitude statements about perceptions of time, self, social space, and causality were included but not reported here.

TABLE 2
The Test Battery Conceptual Skills by Test Subroutines

| | Conceptual Skills | |
Subroutines	Mode of abstraction (analytic or relational)	Field articulation (field independent or field dependent)
Psychological test responses	Sigel test of conceptual style (adaptation)	Witkin graphic figure embedded test (adaptation)
Linguistic characteristics	Synonym set	"Tell-a-Story" test
Social contexts (attitudes)	Guttman I mode of abstraction	Guttman II field embeddedness
	Guttman III[a] difference-variation	Guttman IV[a] luck-achievement

[a]Second-order derivations.

word creativity, and reading comprehension). Norms had been established for the Talent inventory on a five percent national sample.

All items relevant to each cognitive skill (mode of abstraction and field articulation) were Guttman scaled, changing nominal data into ordinal data. Through the mechanism of discriminant analysis the pupils' conceptual skill scores were ordered on a common baseline, and a neutral point was established. This ordering was related to similar common baselines produced by the pupils' Guttman scaled scores on the shared-function formally organized family and friendship group subroutines and similarly scaled scores on the Project Talent achievement inventory. Some typical analytic and relational responses on these instruments appear in Appendix C. Analysis produced the configuration in Figure 1.

Achievement appears in Figure 1 as two normally distributed populations of "good" and "poor" achievers, rather than as a distribution along a single continuum. (I.Q. is held constant and is discussed in later paragraphs.) The relationships among relational and analytic responses, school achievement, and style of primary group participation are apparent. From this analysis it was possible to isolate four clear response types represented by: (1) high-relational pupils who were poor achievers and who had been socialized in, and were at the time of testing, participating in shared-function friendship groups; (2) high-analytic pupils who were good achievers and who were socialized in and continue to participate in formally organized primary groups; (3) middle-range relational and analytic pupils who were middle-range achievers and who had been socialized in one type of family and were then participating in the other type of friendship group; and (4) a conflict pattern (high-analytic abstracters but high field depen-

FIGURE 1
The construction of response types. Polar
relational: participants in both shared-function
families and shared-function friendship groups;
mixed: one type family, the other type of
friendship groups; middle range: (conflict)
family and friendship group responsibilities
vary by mode of abstraction and field
embeddedness; polar analytic: participants
in both formally organized families and
formally organized friendship groups.

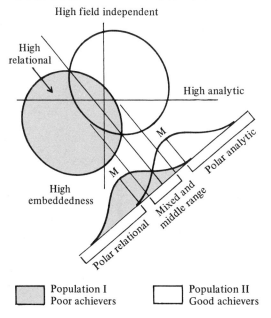

Population I   Population II
Poor achievers   Good achievers

dent) who were middle-range achievers and whose shared-function formal
group style responses were uniquely mixed. Response characteristics of each
of these four groups follows as Tables 3, 4, 5 and 6.

The two polar response patterns — polar analytic and polar relational
— were called "socialization patterns." Pupils with polar response configurations appeared not to be able to synthesize the expectations for either
the alternative kind of group participation or the alternate kind of stimulus analysis. Some pupils, it was hypothesized, had either selected or structured their friendship groups to conform to their conceptual styles.

Among members of the polar response groups, the relationship of
group style to conceptual style was clearly observable in group discussions.
Methods of thinking about group process were very similar to methods of
approaching test items. For example, it was functional for members of

TABLE 3
Relational and Analytic Polar Response Characteristics: Psychological, Linguistic, and Attitude Subroutines, Primary Groups and Achievement

Test subroutines	Response characteristics	
	Polar analytic	Polar relational
Psychological, Linguistic, and Attitude		
Psychological Tests		
Sigel Test of Conceptual Style	High analytic scores	High relational scores
Witkin Figure Embedded Test (Adaptation)	High graphic field articulation scores	Low graphic field articulation scores
Linguistic Subroutines		
Synonym Set (25-word stimulus set)		
Number of words	Average	High
Percent abstracted descriptively	Low	High
"Tell-a-Story" Test	Non-ego-centered	Ego-centered
	Nonembedded	Embedded
Content Analysis	Subject: "reality" or "achievement"	Subject: "luck" or "fantasy"
Attitude scales		
Guttman I Mode of Abstraction		
Guttman II Field Embeddedness		
Guttman III Difference-Variation		
Guttman IV Luck-Achievement	High analytic on all four scales	High relational on all four scales
Response style	Response to style more than eighty percent middle range responses	High polar response style; more than twenty percent "strongly" agree or "strongly disagree"
Primary Groups		
Family	High Guttman formal-family style	High Guttman shared-function family style
Friendship Group	High Guttmann formal-friendship group style	High Guttman shared-function friendship group style
Achievement:	High achievers	Low achievers

TABLE 4
Middle Range Response Characteristics[a] I and II: Psychological, Linguistic and Attitude Subroutines, Primary Groups   and Achievement

Test subroutines	Response characteristics	
	Middle range I	Middle range II
Psychological, Linguistic and Attitude Subroutines		
Psychological Tests		
Sigel Test of Conceptual Style	Middle range	Middle range
Witkin Figure Embedded Test (Adaptation)	Middle range	Middle range
Linguistic Subroutines		
Synonym Set (25-word stimulus set)		
Number of words	Average	Average
Percent abstracted descriptively	Middle range	Middle range
"Tell-a-Story Test"	Non-ego-centered	More ego-centered
	Nonembedded	More embedded
Content Analysis	Subject: "reality" or "achievement"	Subject: "luck" or "fantasy"
Attitude Scales		
Guttman I Mode of Abstraction	Middle range	Middle range
Guttman II Field Embeddedness	Middle range	Middle range
Guttman III Difference-Variation	Middle range	Middle range
Guttman IV Luck-Achievement	Middle range	Middle range
Response style	More than eighty percent middle range, few polar responses, few undecideds	Twenty percent or more polar responses
Additional observations	Strongly desirous of school achievement, good jobs, etc.	Behavior problems in school, gang activities outside of school
Primary groups[b]		
Family	Shared-function	Formal
Friendship group		
Outstanding characteristics	Formal	Shared-function
	Movement from shared function to formal	Movement from formal to shared-function
Achievement	Middle range	Middle range

[a] Outstanding characteristics: Participation in both kinds of primary groups, direction of movement focus.
[b] Family organization was seen as an earlier influence in the lifetime of the individuals tested. In all cases, the direction of movement determined their outstanding behavioral characteristics, i.e., response patterns were more like those of the later (friendship) groups.

TABLE 5
Direction of Movement and Response Characteristics: Nonchoice, Single Type Experience and Choice, Mixed Experience[a]

Experience	Direction of movement	Response characteristics
Socialization pattern		
Nonchoice: single type experience		
Formal family and formal friendship group	No movement	High analytic conceptual style Relative consistency in test dimensions
Shared function family and shared function friendship group	No movement	High relational conceptual style Relative consistency in test dimensions
Choice pattern		
Choice: mixed experience		
Mixed family and friendship group	from: shared-function family to: formal friendship group	Mixed or middle range response pattern; more like analytic conceptual style; candidates for social mobility
Mixed family and friendship group	from: formal family to: shared-function friendship group	Mixed or middle range response pattern; more like relational conceptual style; candidates for mass movement, aggressive in groups, etc.

[a]Conduct pattern excepted.

TABLE 6

Mixed Response Characteristics (The Conflict Pattern): Psychological, Linguistic and Attitude Subroutines, Primary Groups and Achievement[a]

Test subroutines	*Response characteristics*
Psychological tests	
Sigel Test of Conceptual Style	High analytic but vacillating responses
Witkin Figure Embedded Test (Adaptation)	High embedded
Linguistic Subroutines	
Synonym Set	
Number of words	Low
Percent abstracted descriptively	Too low to evaluate
"Tell-a-Story" Test	Ego-centered
	Embedded
	Subject: "Fantasy"
Attitudes	
Response style	High in "undecided's" (some as high as ninety percent "undecided" responses)
Primary Groups	
Family	Mixed responses
Friendship group	Mixed responses
Achievement	Middle range

[a]Outstanding characteristics: conflict in skills, i.e., high analytic scores and high field dependence scores. Theoretically, high analytic skills should also be accompanied by high field articulation skills. In those cases in which these two scores were in conflict there appeared also to be a conflict in reality organization. These pupils were characterized by vacillating responses, high numbers of "undecided" responses, and high levels of anxiety and suggestibility. Almost seventy-five percent were girls despite varied ethnic and social class origins.

shared-function groups to perceive themselves to have relevance only within the contexts of their social groups, and they demonstrated on tests of conceptual style that they perceived parts of standardized stimuli to have relevance only when viewed within their given contexts. They did not extract and specialize functions in their primary groups, and they were not led to extract and organize parts of standardized stimuli on tests. The reverse was true of polar-analytic pupils. Style of primary-group participation appeared to have produced a subtle component of learned behavior that could be viewed in both the development of its related conceptual style and in light of its utility in subsequent group process.

It was found that those pupils with mixed analytic and relational responses had had experience in both types of primary groups. The direction of movement was important in predicting future performance, considering that family impact had occurred earlier in time than that of the friendship group. When movement was from shared-function family to formally organized friendship group, the pupils were more like the polar-analytic pupils both in their test scores and in their social and psychological characteristics. When movement was from formal family to shared-function friendship group, however, pupils were more like the polar-relational pupils. Both groups were flexible in their approach to reality organization; they could become more relational or more analytic at will, within the middle range, and they could participate in both kinds of group organization with some modicum of success. The middle-range achievement patterns with mixed conceptual style response configurations were called "choice patterns." Identification of the factors that had contributed to the pupils' choice when both styles of conceptual organization were possible and both styles of group participation were available was beyond scope of these studies and opened areas for further research.

The conflict-response group of middle-range achievers was of special interest. When analytic skills were high and field dependence scores also high, pupils demonstrated an apparent conflict in reality organization. Pupils with the conflict pattern were highly suggestible and anxious, told fantasy stories, and could not decide how to respond to attitude statements (for example, they returned up to ninety percent "undecided's" on 72-item attitude questionnaires).

Although our major concerns were with the poor participation of the high-relational pupils in the highly analytic school environment, the middle-range achievers — those with mixed skills and those producing a conflict pattern — represented intriguing areas for systematic study. The mixed group, which demonstrated flexibility in their use of relational and analytic approaches to reality organization, was made up of both sexes and varied ethnic origins. The pupils who demonstrated the conflict pattern, however, were seventy-five percent girls. Since embedded responses covered the gamut from abstract categories, through language behaviors, to expressions of embeddedness in their social environments, it is possible that embeddedness may be a distinctive characteristic of female sex-role learning in this society regardless of social class, native ability, ethnic differences, and the cognitive impact of the school.[6] Demonstration of an unique response configuration among girls lent weight to the belief that identifiable subgroup interaction webs can exist within a single social structure such as the family, which can produce, as a result, demonstrable related conceptual patterning.

---

[6] Some items on the subroutines of cognitive style also reflected sex differences. In general, females tended to impute process or motivation to perceived relationships. In addition, girls clustered in the middle ranges on all scales and did not reflect the polar variations of the boys. This may be due to similarity in female role expectations despite other demographic variation.

From the findings reviewed briefly above, conceptual styles had emerged as integrated rule-sets for the selection and organization of sense data. Two definable systems of conceptual organization could be identified and demonstrated, along with several distinctive mixtures, and linked to two different styles of functioning in groups. Within each rule-set certain relationships and patterns of organization are possible and others are not, whether they appear in learning materials or in social interaction. These organized systems had apparently been learned in varied contexts, including group process, but as subliminal components of each context. The many different contexts in which a similar system of relationships could be observed by individuals had acted as examples of the system, reinforcing each other. When they had occurred persistently, they had served to define and reinforce the method of organization, as well as to fix the substantive contexts in which they had appeared in retrievable memory storage (socialization patterns). Persistence in their use appeared to have determined the degree to which an individual believed them to be valid as well as the extent to which he was attached to related social and psychological behaviors and held to values and beliefs associated with them. When the patterns had not been repeated persistently (choice patterns), they had become relevant to certain contexts only. Both the patterns themselves and the sensitive context in which they appeared seemed not to be retrievable except on the denotative level; that is, each context had to be learned separately and not as an example of recurring theme. The necessity for memorizing each context separately was believed to explain in part the characteristic middle-range achievement performance of those pupils with mixed and conflicting conceptual styles.

Methods of selection and conceptual organization, then, are comparatively subtle characteristics of substantive contexts; they are required for successful group participation as well as for structured learning. As such, they are meant to be remembered and transferred to new and unfamiliar situations as well as are the information components in which they are embedded. Indeed, it is the explicit intent of school texts, curricula, and methods to teach the analytic rule-set subliminally in many different contexts; and intelligence and achievement are measured by the school, in part, by how well pupils have learned it. What is less apparent is that the same analytic rule-set is also embedded in formal school organization and in the social settings in which teaching and learning take place. For analytic children the school's formal organization acts as an additional reinforcer of analytic thinking as well as of its related social behaviors. For relational children, however, its impact on conceptual patterning is disorganizing; its climate lacks the cues necessary to understanding, or they are ambiguous; and its requirements for social participation are of low value. When transported to a shared-function environment, both the cognitive requirements of the school and their related social skills are as dysfunctional and disruptive as the relational approach is in the school.

INFORMATION AND CONCEPTUAL SKILLS

The foregoing comment on the relation of conceptual styles to school achievement leaves virtually unanalyzed the information contexts in which styles of reality organization are embedded. It will be remembered that progressive increments in the breadth and depth of the pupils' information repertoires are also required for achievement in school. This third variable accounted for most of the unexplained variance between tested I.Q. and school achievement. This separate yet hitherto confounded component of the achievement profile, when combined with conceptual style performance, produced the combinations in Table 7, which were effective predictors of academic performance.

TABLE 7
Orientation to School Requirements by
Skill-information Combinations

Skill-information combinations	Orientation to school requirements
High analytic skills, high information	High achievement; high I.Q.[a]; high success in school
High analytic skills, low information	High achievement; average I.Q.[a]; anxiety (overachievers)
High relational skills, high information	Low achievement; high I.Q.[a]; behavior problems (underachievers)
High relational skills, low information	Low achievement; low I.Q.[a]; complete inability to relate to the school; withdrawal and drop-out

[a]Tested I.Q.

From this analysis it was possible to clarify the circumstances under which information components enter into academic performance as separate from conceptual style, when native ability is held constant.

Although native ability is not related to the preference of a cognitive style, it does, apparently, affect the size of a pupil's information repertoire, as well as the level of abstraction attainable with either mode of conceptual organization. In a sample of 500 ninth-grade pupils with a full intelligence range from "barely educable" to "gifted," there were found to be sharp differences between the barely educable and the gifted in the size of the information components of their test scores (Cohen, 1968d). There were similar large differences in the levels of abstraction usable by them. Both types of differences appeared on all measures of ability and performance regardless of which conceptual style the pupils used. Native ability, then, may be better defined as the differential ability of individuals to absorb large bodies of information and to reach high levels of abstraction using *either* mode of conceptual organization.

Standardized tests of intelligence and achievement, in their present form, do attempt to identify the relative size of pupils' information repertoires, provided that their frames of understanding overlap or interpenetrate the items used in the test construction, and to measure increments in their ability to use formal analytic methods on higher levels of abstraction. Discrimination in levels of abstraction using relational pathways, however, is not incorporated into their construction plans. Test construction plans also incorporate, as measures of intelligence, some relevant analytic correlates, such as the length of the time frames planned into them for subroutine completion. The time frames, together with information-analytic skill elements, produce their speed-power components. Much of the socialization impact of the school is thus embedded in its cognitive requirements; it may be separated from the information contexts in which it appears. It focuses on the development of social and psychological correlates or derivatives of the analytic approach as major carriers; and it appears on all levels of pupil performance, from test application and response characteristics to classroom management and school administration.

DEPRIVATION, CULTURE DIFFERENCE, AND CULTURE CONFLICT

Once one has become aware of the stringent analytic requirements for performance in school and of the separate information-cognitive skill requirements of standardized tests, it is no longer appropriate to speak of "deprivation," "culture difference," and "culture conflict" synonymously. "Deprivation" and "culture difference" have to do with the information components of these tests and "culture conflict" with different conceptual styles and their conflicting sociobehavioral correlates.[7]

Within the information components themselves two types of distinctions can be drawn — quantitative and qualitative. The term "deprivation" may be used to refer to the quantitative characteristics of a pupil's information repertoire and "culture difference" to its qualitative characteristics.

---

[7] The term "culture conflict" is used in subcultural and subgroup contexts without apology on the basis that similar analytic schemata may be used with varied units of analysis.

When there is a relative lack of the number of concepts and experiences on which a pupil has to draw in order to do well in school, he may be said to be deprived. Limited experience with varied environments and limited access to books and other sources of knowledge may limit the amount of information a pupil has to use. Children from low-income environments may be deprived in this way as a result of their position in society. Institutionalized children or those from other environments that present limited stimulation or those who are sensorially limited, such as blind children, may share this disability. "Culture difference," on the other hand, involves qualitatively different kinds of things and events from those usable in school. A slum child may not know what a refrigerator is, for example, but he may know a great deal about rats. The information repertoires of such children may be sizable but different from those required by the school curriculum.

Neither the quantitative nor qualitative characteristics of a pupil's information repertoire should effectively hamper his ability to communicate with the school environment, however, because neither of them implies incompatibility with school requirements. The school curricula are relatively eclectic in the units of information that are acceptable. In addition, there is no known limit to the number of new concepts individuals can learn. It is, therefore, only when incompatibilities exist (whether or not deprivation and culture difference are also present) that "culture conflict" may be said to exist.

Relational and analytic modes of conceptual organization reflect such incompatibilities; that is, many specific kinds of response characteristics can be factored out of each style that can be demonstrated to impede the development of the alternate kind. Some incompatible response characteristics lie on basic levels of learned behavior, such as conditioned perceptual discrimination and sudomotor reactivity. Others are found in lexical choice and language organization and still others in a wide range of interpersonal and social process behaviors and in many derivative values and beliefs. Each context acts as separate reinforcement of the conceptual process that has been used, and each lower-order derivative of each conceptual style suppresses its alternative. It is to selection and classification rule-sets, then, that many mutually incompatible psychological and social behaviors are tied and not to information components per se. Moreover, because of their integrity relational and analytic rule-sets can, to a great extent, both limit and determine the size and nature of an individual's information repertoire when native ability and environmental stimulation are held constant.

In addition to incompatible selection and classification rule-sets, three other areas of mutual incompatibility emerged from a semantic feature analysis of the lexicon of the hard-core poor. The additional three areas of

incompatibility were in perceptions of time (as a series of discrete moments, rather than a continuum),[8] of self in social space (in the center
of it, rather than in a position relative to others who are passing together
at different rates of speed through social space), and in causality (specific
causality rather than multiple causality) [Cohen, Fraenkel, and Brewer,
1968]. Each of the above categories of thought was closely associated with
relational and analytic styles along several different dimensions; that is,
each reflected a number of rule components in common with its related
conceptual style. For example, the analytic mode of abstraction presumes
a system of linear components. Similar linear components are found in the
perception of time as a continuum or in a linear projection of social space,
and they underlie the notion of multiple causality. This linear component
does not appear among polar-relational children on tests of cognitive style,
in their characteristic language style, nor in the ordering of authority or
responsibility in shared-function social groups. Certain common values and
beliefs follow from such a common component. For instance, without the
assumption of linearity such notions as social mobility, the value of money,
improving one's performance, getting ahead, infinity, or hierarchies of any
type, all of which presume the linear extension of critical elements, do
not have meaning for the relational child. In essence, the requirements for
formal abstraction and extraction of components to produce linear con-
tinua are not logically possible within the relational rule-set.

NONVERBAL TESTS OF INTELLIGENCE

In addition to distinguishing among "deprivation," "culture difference," and "culture conflict," the findings of these investigations also challenge the rationale for the "culture-free" nonverbal tests in current use. It
has been most commonly believed that it is the information (direct experience) components of these tests that carry their culture-bound characteristics. Nonverbal tests concentrate on the ability to reason "logically."
However, it is in the very nature of these logical sequences that the most
culture-bound aspects of the middle-class, or "analytic," way of thinking
are carried. Even more critical than either the quantitative and qualitative
information components of such tests are the analytic mode of abstraction and the field-articulation requirements they embody. Figure 2, taken
from the Lorge-Thorndike nonverbal battery on the ninth-grade level, may
clarify this point.

The logical sequences in Figure 2 are most effectively solved by a parts-
specific, stimulus-centered, analytic mode of abstraction. This strategy
depends upon the ability of the subject to extract and relate relevant parts
of the stimulus. All contextual information has been removed in advance.

---

[8] See the description of the "action seekers" in Gans, 1962.

FIGURE 2

The pupil is instructed to complete the logical
sequences by choosing from the multiple choice
items that are presented.

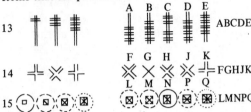

When an entire test battery is constructed of items like the above, as non-
verbal batteries indeed are, analytic-cognitive skills have been separated
explicity from general-information components. If the essential aspect of
"culture conflict" is discrepancy between cognitive modes among pupils,
these tests are even more discriminatory than those formed in part to test
for information growth. Even the best informed and the most widely experienced relational pupil, regardless of his native ability, would score poorly
on such a test.

As a matter of fact, the most intelligent relational pupils score the worst
of all. Their ability to reach higher levels of abstraction through relational
pathways take them farther away from the higher levels of abstraction
reached through analytic pathways. The range of dissociation of the two
paths to higher levels of abstraction can be looked upon as inverted tri-
angles, as shown in Figure 3. Highly intelligent high-relational pupils were

FIGURE 3

Dissociating levels of abstraction through
analytic and relational pathways.

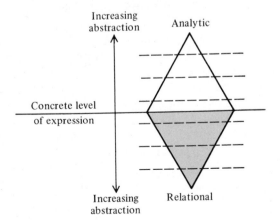

found, in fact, to communicate best with the demands of the school on the concrete level. This was evidenced in our findings in an initial sampling of sixty-six ninth- and tenth-grade pupils of average or better intelligence (Cohen, 1967) and in the markedly better scores of high-relational pupils on two achievement subtests of the Project Talent Achievement Inventory.[9] A content analysis of the Talent battery found that the questions on only these two subtests were framed on concrete levels. Although the more intelligent high-relational pupils scored extremely poorly (15th to 20th percentiles) on the other subtests of achievement, they did extremely well (90th to 95th percentiles) on these two sets of concrete problems. It appears, therefore, that given concrete settings with intelligence held constant, high-relational pupils can compete with analytic ones. It is only when high levels of analytic abstraction are required that their ability to compete is inhibited.

Such findings suggest that in addition to the focused analytic cognitive style requirements of nonverbal tests of intelligence, the level of abstraction they require provides an additional area of difficulty for relational pupils. Since contentless figures are almost completely abstract, they tend to focus on the most extreme levels for the use of analytic cognitive skills. Therefore, not only is the *mode* of cognitive organization required for successful performance on nonverbal tests a critical factor in the inability of relational pupils to deal with them, but the *level of abstraction* on which they focus for the demonstration of these skills intensifies the problems they present to relational pupils.

In addition to illuminating the relationship of the pupils to the tests, the two-way analysis that was followed also cast some light on the relationship of relational and analytic pupils to each other. Not only do relational and analytic pupils communicate with each other best on the concrete level, but the greatest gaps in communication occur between the most intelligent members of the two categories of pupils, as is suggested by the progressively dissociating levels of abstraction illustrated above.

Nonverbal tests of intelligence have not freed themselves, then, of their culture-bound characteristics. Instead, they have focused on one critical aspect of culture — its method of selecting and organizing relevant sense data. Traditional attempts to develop culture-free tests have eliminated their information components in the belief that it is only their substantive experience components that are culture-bound. An additional assumption has been that because they are nonverbal, they are nonstructured. The most culture-bound characteristics of these tests, however, are not

---

[9] This achievement inventory developed norms from a five percent national sample of high school pupils in public, private, and parochial schools. The instrument and a report of findings appear in Flanagan et al., 1964.

their information components but the analytic-logical sequences they require. Both in the mode of abstraction these tests require and in the level of abstraction in which the items are couched, nonverbal tests of intelligence are much more discriminatory against relational pupils than are conventional instruments, which test partly for information growth. Since both the size and nature of a pupil's information repertoire and his native ability are apparently unrelated to his conceptual style, the analytic-relational opposition may be defined as a separate area of pupils' performance. Pupils may be deprived or culturally different from or in culture conflict with the school. They may represent one or two or all these separate kinds of educational problems. Analytic schemata geared to the definition of learning disabilities and programs designed for one type of educational problem cannot hope to deal with the others as well.

SUMMARY

This paper has focused (1) on incompatibility in conceptual styles as a notable indicator of "culture conflict" and on the characteristics that distinguish it from "deprivation" and "culture difference" and (2) on styles of conceptual organization as culture-bound characteristics of nonverbal tests of intelligence. Evidence is also presented of the reciprocal relationships between conceptual styles and styles of primary group process.

Conceptual styles are composites of two cognitive skills — mode of abstraction and field articulation. Along with information growth, these two cognitive skills have been identified as generic components of learning. Conceptual styles are essentially integrated rule-sets for the selection and organization of sense data. Within each rule-set certain assumptions and relationships are logically possible, and others are not. They are definable without reference to specific substantive content and are not related to native ability. They can be identified in the abstract, in language selection and organization, and in attitudes about one's self and one's environment. Associated with these rule-sets, or derivative from them, are a wide variety of social and psychological characteristics in their carriers.

Although there may be more, two conceptual styles have been identified and demonstrated reliably — relational and analytic styles. Relational and analytic conceptual styles were found to be associated with shared-function and formal primary-group participation, respectively, as socialization settings. So intimate were the relationships between primary group styles and conceptual styles that among pupils with experience in both types of groups mixed and conflicting conceptual styles could be observed.

The school was defined as a highly analytic environment in all its salient characteristics and requirements. Many children, however, demonstrate a relational approach to reality organization. Relational and analytic conceptual styles were found to be not only different but mutually incompatible. That is, one approach to reality organization could effectively hinder the development of the other; each could affect its carrier's ability to participate effectively in the alternate kind of group process or to deal directly with its cognitive requirements. In practice it was found that children who had been socialized in shared-function environments could not participate effectively in any aspect of the formal school environment even when native ability and information repertoires were adequate.

The information-cognitive skills requirements for school performance were used to distinguish among the constructs "deprivation," "culture differences," and "culture conflict." "Deprivation" and "culture difference" have to do with the quantitative and qualitative characteristics of the information repertoires of individuals. "Culture conflict" deals with conflicting styles of conceptual organization. Highly relational children in the highly analytic school are thus seen as a case of culture conflict, regardless of whether deprivation and culture difference are also present.

Attention was then directed to nonverbal methods of measuring intelligence and achievement. Nonverbal tests have been designed to reduce their culture bias by drastically reducing their information components. However, they were found instead to deal in a focused fashion with the demonstration of analytic conceptual skills. Rather than freeing themselves of their culture-bound characteristics, they have focused on one critical aspect of it — the analytic mode of selecting and organizing information. When contextual inputs have been held constant, then, nonverbal tests of intelligence are more discriminatory against relational pupils than are the conventional types, which test partly for information growth.

A number of educational problems may be separated out of the above analysis without challenging the relevance of school curricula to future concerns among children. As in any relatively consistent environment in which there are standardized criteria for performance, in which quantity and quality of inputs are relatively standardized, in which a heterogenous population is found, particularly one in which participation is nonvoluntary, as in the school, pupils may be relatively deprived or culturally different from or in culture conflict with it. One, two, all or none of these separate kinds of phenomena may be represented. Although, as they are defined here, deprivation and culture difference may be compensated in part through individualization or variation in the input level of the settings in which pupils learn, culture conflict represents an educational problem of some magnitude. Multiple-method learning environments can be devised. However, they will not only require the development of rules of transformation from one rule-set to another, but they can also be foreseen to produce far-reaching effects on school organization, teacher training, curricula, methods, and materials, the impact of which cannot yet be predicted. Moreover, culture conflict — a transactional concept — does not yield to unimodal analysis. If this is true, procedures for more valid measurement of learning potential and the development of more appropriate learning methods and settings are dependent upon the abandonment of assumptions that there is a single method for knowing.

Although the foci of these studies arose out of practical considerations, the issues that have been explored reflect basic science concerns. If such cognitive mechanisms as styles of cognitive control act reciprocably as mediating factors between social-system characteristics and individual-response characteristics, they are seen as important keys not only to effective program development but also to basic behavioral-science research.

REFERENCES

Bernstein, Basil. Social class and linguistic development: a theory of social learning. In *Education, economy, and society*, A. H. Halsey, Jean Floud, and C. Arnold Anderson, eds. New York: Free Press of Glencoe, 1964a.
——. Elaborated and restricted codes, in *The ethnography of communication*, *American Anthropologist* 66 (6, pt. 2): 55–69.
Campbell, Donald T. Distinguishing differences of perception from failure of communication in cross-cultural studies, in *Cross-cultural understandings: epistemology in anthropology*, F. S. C. Northrup and Helen H. Livingston, eds. New York: Harper and Row, 1964.
Cohen, Rosalie. The value laden contexts in programs for the educationally disadvantaged. Learning Research and Development Center, University of Pittsburgh, 1965.
——. Primary group structure, conceptual styles, and school achievement. Monograph, Learning Research and Development Center, University of Pittsburgh, Studies I, II, III, IV, 1967.
——. Language styles and communication failures in therapy. Paper read at Fourth International Congress of Group Psychotherapy, Vienna, Austria, 1968a.
——. Is formal role analysis generalizable to low income groups? Paper read at the Midwest Sociological Society annual meetings, Omaha, Nebraska, 1968b.
——. Formal role analysis and the culture of poverty. Paper read at the Ohio Valley Sociological Society annual meetings, Detroit, Michigan, 1968c.
——. 1967 Teenage survey. Unpublished paper, 1968d.
——. The relation between socio-conceptual styles and orientation to school requirements. *Sociology of Education* 41:201–220, 1968e.
——, Gerd Fraenkel, and John Brewer. The language of the hard core poor: implications for culture conflict. *Sociology Quarterly* 10:19–28, 1968.
Gans, Herbert. *The urban villagers*. New York: Free Press of Glencoe, 1962.
Flanagan, John C., et al. *The American high school student*. Project Talent, University of Pittsburgh, 1964.
Gardner, Riley. Cognitive control structures and their measurement of preadolescence, in *Programs in cognitive development*. Mental Health Grant 05517, Menninger Clinic, Ms.
Kagan, Jerome, Howard A. Moss, and Irving E. Siegal. Psychological significance of styles conceptualization, in *Basic cognitive process in children*. Society for Research in Child Development monograph 86. Chicago: University of Chicago Press, 1963.
Kelly, E. Lowell, and James C. Lingoes. Data processing in psychological research, in *Computer application in the behavioral sciences*, Harold Borko, ed. Englewood Cliffs: Prentice-Hall, 1962.

Appendix A
Taxonomy of Test Response Characteristics and Sociobehavioral Correlates of Conceptual Styles[a]

Test	Conceptual style	
	Analytic	*Relational*
Cognitive style	Mode of abstraction is stimulus centered	Mode of abstraction is self-centered
	sensitivity to parts of objects	sensitivity to global characteristics
	awareness of obscure, abstract nonobvious features	awareness of obvious, sensed features
	many abstractions based on parts of objects and features of these parts	few abstractions—free association stimulated by stimuli
Sigel test of conceptual style	"arms akimbo . . . etc."	"two boys . . . etc."
Sorting ability	many piles	few piles
Figure sort tests		
Behavior sort test		
Object sorting test	can resort many times drawing new relationships each time	cannot resort—most obvious relationship remains constant
Photo sorting test		
Pettigrew's category width test	groups formed represent minimal conceptual distance from properties of the objects	groups formed represent greater conceptual distance from the properties of the objects
Geometric form drawing test	relative differences are marked by the ratios of the shorter and longer sides	little perception of relative differences
	[emphasized independence of level of abstraction from conceptual style]	
Memory organization	organization of words for commitment to memory based on varied types of relationships	organization of words functional and inferential
Word association	noun-noun sequences; verb-verb sequences	meaning critical inferential sequences recall functionally related words
Psycho-physical judgements requiring selective attention (facilitation-inhibition phenomena), e.g., Embedded Figures Tests, Size Estimation Tests, etc.	good	poor
Perceptual vigilance	high ability to detect changes in monotonous but constantly changing perceptual field over a long period of time	low ability to detect changes in a monotonous constantly changing perceptual field
Serial learning	categorial responses	related words
California test of mental maturity	analytic scores high on nonlanguage sections	analytic scores low on nonlanguage sections
What is learned [parts as whole]	attaches verbal labels to parts as well as wholes of geometric designs	attaches verbal labels only to relevant wholes
Stability of conceptual style after entry into school	stable	creation of more analytic responses and reduction of relational responses

Test	Conceptual style	
	Analytic	*Relational*
TAT	relatively constricted stories containing much description of the properties of the stimuli and minimal creative thematic material	much creative thematic material, little sensitivity to properties of the stimuli
	stories close to physical properties of the pictures (equivalence ranges close)	(wide equivalence ranges)
Rorschach responses	indistinct perceptions infrequent	indistinct perceptions frequent
	high stimulus differentiation	minimal stimulus differentiation
	attends to ambiguous projections of stimuli	ignore ambiguous portions of stimulus
	fewer human responses, whole responses, human vs. mammalian animal responses, human movement responses, color responses	project more life and activity into the inkblots
	and extensor vs. flexor responses	
Reaction time	greater—more time is necessary for scanning	less—time required for response to global characteristics is less
	attitude more reflective	response appears impulsive
Verbal content in personal interviews	reluctant to be dependent on family and friends	dependent on their families as adults
	striving for social recognition	less concerned with the acquisition of recognition goals
	concern for intellectual mastery	
	confident in their approach to challenging intellectual tasks	not confident of ability to solve intellectual problems
	motivated to obtain achievement oriented goals	not motivated to achievement goals
	categorization of statements concerning behavior is highly differentiated	categorization of statements concerning behavior has a low degree of differentiation
Tolerance for unrealistic experiences [e.g., simulation of the effects of motion when movement is not present]	good	poor
Constricted flexible control	flexible	constricted
Impulse control	good	poor
[e.g., Stroop's Color Word Test]	effective use of primary process learning rapid response	ineffective use of primary process thinking, difficulty in inhibiting irrelevant, overlearned, or highly compelling motoric responses (e.g., reading the words while verbalizing the names of the colors)
Learning-related characteristics:		
Attention span	can sit still long time	short attention span
Concentration depth	deep concentration (stimulus remains constant)	shallow concentration
Distractibility	not easily distracted by nonrelevant sounds and movements	easily distracted

Test	Conceptual style	
	Analytic	Relational
Perceptual vigilance	high perceptual vigilance; notice small changes in moving stimulus	low perceptual vigilance
	can do above task without utilitarian purpose	task considered irrelevant
Intensity of attention	deep	shallow
Related school behaviors	sees teacher as a source of information, not individual	sees teacher as individual
	sees teacher as appendage to a problem	
	persistent in task orientation	easily distracted from task
	confident in approach to intellectual tasks	lacks confidence in ability to solve intellectual problems
	motivated to achievement related goals	not motivated to achievement
Optional reading (content)	reality	fantasy
Preferred classroom illustrations (content)	reality	fantasy, humor
Related personality characteristics	stimulus centered activity does not require an affective response	relationship to descriptive characteristics of people and objects requires an affective response
	requires detachment, concentrated attention	global orientation does not require long or concentrated attention
	learning is nonsocial	learning is a social experience
	belief that relationships are "out there" in the stimulus	belief that significant relationships are a product of self and others
	a faith in processes and natural laws	specific causation need not rest on natural laws
	a willingness to listen attentively to differentiate subtle meanings in words, a desire to look for reasons and processes, and to take directions and compare results	primary focus on self, not on stimulus
	ambitious	passive
	independent	dependent
	high spontaneous sudomotor reactivity	less labile sudomotor reactivity
	objective	subjective
	confident of control over the environment	sense of powerlessness
	focus on rules of role performance not individual performance	
	confident in new social situations	anxious in new social situations
		acts as though expecting rejection by new associates
	preference for complexity	preference for simplicity
	preference for social distance	preference for social integration
Behavior plasticity	resist the effect of interfering stimuli	more susceptible to modification by immediate perceptual experience

Test	Conceptual style	
	Analytic	*Relational*
		difficulty in inhibiting reactions to task irrelevant cues
		behavior is more malleable in the face of continual changes in the stimulus field
Sociobehavioral correlates of conceptual style	reflective attitude	impulsive
	a tendency to differentiate experience	less likely to differentiate complex stimulus situation
	ability to resist the effects of distracting stimuli	more reactive to external stimuli
	able to become oblivious of external surroundings	impulsively aggressive
		less likely to withdraw from the group to work on a task
	sedentary	more hyperkinetic
		easily angered by minor frustrations
	capacity for sustained attention	short attention span
		affectionate
		rarely played alone as children
		colorful vocabulary
		easily give up on difficult tasks
Language style		
Lexical; mode of abstraction	analytic abstraction	descriptive abstraction
	words have formal meanings	words have meanings specific to certain contexts; they are concrete with much use of visual and tactile symbols
	[e.g., *money*—coins, cash, currency, etc.; *wine*—port, sherry]	[e.g., *money*—green, bundle, trash, etc.; *wine*—blood, slop, molasses]
		rules for new verbal selections tie actors to action, causes to results, means to ends
		expressions are colorful
		many idiomatic expressions
		low level of generality
Use of synonyms	synonyms used	few synonyms, greatly reduced overlap of semantic ranges
		a great variety of words specific to specific situations or to certain characteristics or functions
Distinctive feature analysis	"token into type" constructions few and used for new developments	"token into type" constructions common for old objects
	depersonalized	personified (reversal)
	euphemisms not very common	euphemisms and reverse euphemisms common
	word choices relate to bundles of features of objects or persons and to prototypical situations	choices relate to individual features of objects or individuals to specific situations

Test	Conceptual style	
	Analytic	*Relational*
	many forms offered for generalization and comparison	few mechanisms for generalization and comparison
	change not too rapid comparatively	rapid change in signifiers of the language
	outer-centered orientation	self-centered orientation
	meaning is not dependent upon extraverbal context	meaning dependent on time, place, authority, and other social relationships between communicants
	critical analysis of meaning verbalized	meaning embedded; not verbalized
Syntax	elaborated code; grammatically complex	restricted code; grammatically simple
	low predictability	high predictability
	sentences of varied lengths	short sentences
	usually finished; good syntax	often unfinished; poor syntax
	periods at ends of thoughts	simple and repetitive use of conjunctions
	many subordinate clauses	little use of subordinate clauses
	integrity of speech sequence	inability to hold a formal subject through a speech sequence
	informational content has integrity	dislocated informational content
	much use of adjectives and adverbs	rigid and limited use of adjectives and adverbs
	discretionary use of impersonal pronouns	infrequent use of impersonal pronouns
	reinforcement is direct and explicit	sympathetic circulatory for reinforcement (e.g., "you know . . .," "don't say a word . . ."
General characteristics	verbally explicit	not verbally explicit
	verbal arrangement closely fits specific referents	structure of speech is simple; the extraverbal component is a major channel for the transmission of individual qualifications
	verbal planning promotes a high level of syntactic organization and lexical selection	
	preparation and delivery of explicit meanings is the major function of the code	meanings may be highly condensed
	the code facilitates the transmission and elaboration of the individual's unique experience	speech is impersonal; it is not tailored to fit a given referent
	the condition of the listener is not taken for granted and the speaker is likely to modify his speech in the light of the special conditions and attributes of the listener	the intent of the listener is taken for granted
	code facilitates the verbal construction and exchanges of individualized or personal symbols	the code facilitates the construction and exchange of communal symbols
	induces in speakers a sensitivity to the implications of separateness	

	Conceptual style	
Test	*Analytic*	*Relational*
	and differences and points to the possibilities inherent in a complex hierarchy for the organization of experience	
	the ability to switch codes controls ability to switch roles	only single code available
Delivery	frequent pauses (hesitation phenomena) for verbal planning	little hesitation; high fluency
Articulation	clear, cool, deliberate	articulatory clues reduced; sloppy; meaning carried in extra verbal channels

[a]This taxonomy is annotated in Cohen 1967. It appears also appended to Cohen 1968c.

Appendix B

Some Important Differentiating Characteristics of Formally Organized and Shared-Function Family and Friendship Groups

Characteristics of the group	*Formally organized*	*Shared-function*
Distribution of critical group functions	Critical functions formally defined and attached to statuses	Widely shared among all members of the group, even children
Interaction patterns	Formally organized and generally understood; relatively constant; attached to status-role coordination	Fluid and changing
Organization of status relationships	Relatively stable; often hierarchically organized	Fluid and shifting; seldom hierarchically organized
Pattern of change in interaction arrangements	Emergent; rationally planned for optimum group efficiency and convenience; change proceeds commonly toward greater specialization of functions	Unplanned and unpredictable; often characterized by disintegration of the organization and restructuring in a fashion similar to the one preceding
Distribution of rewards	Formally set according to analytically abstracted and defined characteristics of the importance of the status and of the position incumbent	Widespread and equal, or snatched through the use of power and thus grossly unequal
Characteristics of leadership function	Leadership often attached to most important status as determined by salient group objectives	Leadership shared along with other group functions, regardless of objectives of the group
Distribution of privilege	Distributed in an orderly fashion; often attached to the hierarchial ordering of statuses	Widely shared or snatched by power and thus grossly unequal in distribution
Reasons for privilege	Privilege attached to occupying an important status	Attached to individual acts of individual persons under idiosyncratic circumstances or to an individual mystique
Generic role expectations	Built around formal functions of each status	Built around identification with total group activities
Scope of role expectations	Necessary expectations are limited to functions defined by specific statuses occupied	Role encompasses all critical functions of the group as well as expectations geared to its sense of group identity

Characteristics of the group	Formally organized	Shared-function
Range of participation in group functions	Intrusions on the functions of other statuses negatively sanctioned	Periodic or continuing participation in all critical group functions positively sanctioned
Status boundaries	Varying degrees of firmness; relationships to each other relatively constant	Loosely held; statuses fluid and shifting in relationship to one another
Latency of role expectations of other statuses	No; individuals are involved in isolated functions assigned to their statuses	Yes; all members ready to act in any capacity at any time
Refusal-to-act privileges	Individual retains the right to refuse to act in any capacity not defined as his job	Individual cannot refuse to act in any critical capacity when called upon to do so
Individual right to challenge group objectives	No, in general, once he has assumed a status; he can leave the status if dissatisfied	Yes
Individual right to challenge current means of attaining group objectives	Variable, depending on the nature of the group	Yes
Use of initiative by individual members	Initiative generally limited to devising new means of performing preset and generally understood functions attached to a status	Permitted both in setting objectives or devising means for attaining them. Either great freedom or great constraint on the use of initiative is positively sanctioned at different points in time
Depth of identification with the group	Casual	Intense
Manner of identification with the group	Marked by commitment to perform a given set of group functions and to the interaction patterns which define the status occupied	Marked by *involvement* in all group functions and in the general sense of group identity
Focus of personal identity	Individual identity partly attached to definable functions which he performs in many groups, and partly to conceptual organizing principles which he uses in co-ordinating these multiple functions	All group members participate in the development of a joint individual-group identity. Reformulation of the group creates a new sense of individual identity
Sense of individual identity	Yes; individual only *participates* in his groups, he does not feel as one with them ("in" the group, not "of" it)	Only as attached to group identity ("of" the group, not "in" it)

Appendix C: Some Typical Analytic and Relational Responses

Words	Analytic responses	Relational responses
Money	coins, currency, medium of exchange, nickels, dimes, etc. (Formal abstraction, i.e., each word has a relatively set meaning which is not dependent upon the circumstances in which it is used. Each set of circumstances is defined in dependent clauses.)	green, trash, bundle, etc. (descriptive abstraction) or bones, berries, etc. (embedded for meaning in the manner in which this money is used) or cabbage, lettuce, etc. (bidimensional: both descriptive and embedded)
Wine	Port, sherry, etc., or selections with alcohol content in common, e.g., beer, whiskey, etc. (formal abstraction)	blood, slop, molasses, etc. (descriptive abstraction)

Words	Analytic responses	Relational responses
Fight	struggle, battle, war, etc. (formal abstraction)	27 different selections, each of which is specific to who the combatants are (males, females, or both; whether they are young or old, gangs or individuals etc.); where the fight takes place (e.g., on a street corner, in one's own territory or elsewhere, etc.), and with what weapons (e.g., fists, brickbats, deadly weapons, etc.) [e.g., "big red rumble"–a routine fight between gangs, using whole bricks; parts of bricks would use the reference, "little red . . . " etc.] (descriptive abstraction and embedded)

Illustration A: Sigel Test of Conceptual Style

Pupil is instructed to choose two of the three pictures on each plate that are alike or that go together in some way and to tell why he selected them. Test consists of 19 plates.

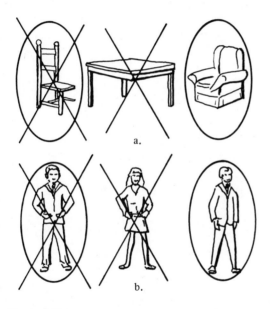

Typical Responses:

(a) *Analytic (X's)* — because a leg is missing from each or because they are wood. Characteristics of response: — stimulus centered; — parts specific.

   Relational (O's) — because they look good together, or because they are both chairs. Characteristics of response: — self-centered; — global characteristics of stimulus have meaning.

(b) *Analytic (X's)* — because both figures have arms on hips. Characteristics of response: — stimulus centered; — parts specific.

Relational (O's) — because they look good together, or because they are both boys. Characteristics of response: — self-centered; — global characteristics of stimulus have meaning.

Illustration B: Witkin Test of Graphic Field Articulation (Adaption)
Pupil is instructed to find the simple figures in the complex ones.
High relational pupils have difficulty finding any simple figures in the complex ones. High analytic pupils find from 15–19 out of a possible 22. Test consists of 7 plates.

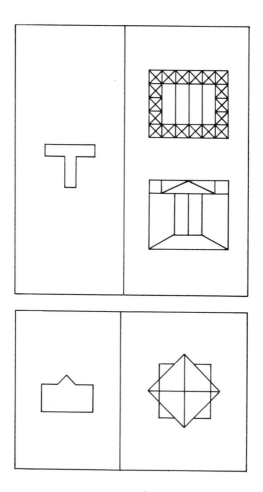

Illustration C: Typical Responses to the Synonym Set
Pupil is instructed to list as many words as he can think of with the same or similar meaning to those used as stimulus items. Test consists of 25 words.

Illustration D: The Attitude Scales

The following are sample items from the scales of descriptive abstraction and field dependence. Pupils were asked to respond to each item on a five point scale from "strongly agree" to "strongly disagree."

Each positive response was scored as indicating a preference for descriptive abstraction in social contexts. Each negative response was scored as a rejection of descriptive abstraction in social contexts. Reverse statement items provided internal reliability checks against negative responses.

A person's outward appearance gives you a good idea of what he is like	Descriptive abstraction
To be like someone you admire, it is more important to imitate his clothes and mannerisms than to copy what he thinks and believes	Descriptive abstraction
How we use words depends mostly on where, when, and to whom they're spoken	Word embeddedness
I wouldn't want to be rich if my family couldn't be rich too	Family embeddedness
You can't depend on knowing how to act when you get out of your own neighborhood	Neighborhood embeddedness
You just can't trust strangers very much	Group embeddedness

FURTHER READINGS

Baratz, Stephen S., and Joan C. Baratz. "Early childhood intervention: the social science base of institutional racism," *Harvard Educational Review*, vol. 40 (1970).

Eells, Kenneth, Allison Davis, Robert J. Havighurst, Virgil E. Herrick, and Ralph W. Tyler. *Intelligence and cultural differences*. Chicago: University of Chicago Press, 1951.

Gladwin, Thomas. *East is a big bird: navigation and logic on Puluwat atoll*. Cambridge: Harvard University Press, 1970.

Masland, Richard L., Seymour B. Sarason, and Thomas Gladwin. *Mental subnormality: biological, psychological, and cultural factors*. New York: Basic Books, 1958.

Segall, Marshall H., Donald T. Campbell, and Melville J. Herskovits. *The influence of culture on visual perception*. Indianapolis: Bobbs-Merrill, 1966.

Vernon, Philip E. *Intelligence and cultural environment*. London: Methuen, 1969.

35

It concerns Mr. Lindquist, in this final article, that "anthropologists, who are notorious conservatives in their advice where primitives are involved, become radical advocates of wholesale change in our own schools." The most frequent involvement of anthropologists in educational policy and practice is at levels removed from and, in his word, "loftier" than the local. It also disturbs Lindquist, Professor of Anthropology, Rhode Island College, that there is an apparent centrism on the part of the anthropological profession as it regards curriculum and curriculum change. Recognizing traditional constraints on the kinds of sociocultural setting and transaction that are taken to be legitimate subjects of anthropological inquiry, Lindquist urges redirecting these troubling tendencies by calling upon the "civic responsibility" of anthropologists to engage public education, its aims and needs, at local levels. His call for anthropological "labor on the local front" suggests that this effort should be less a civic duty than, simply, the ordinary task of anthropology. To construe such activity as anthropology, and not as the "civic responsibility" of anthropologists, is to question the conventions of the discipline, whereby American public schools represent a less significant source of anthropological understandings than the relatively obscure human groups, say, of the Amazon Basin. It may also be to question why anthropologists are "notorious conservatives" in their counsel to any people, simple or complex. And, finally, that a profession which pretends to holism should narrow its vision to its own interests is to question whether it is, itself, following Gearing (Part One), "humanly believable."

LAWRENCE W. LINDQUIST

The Civic Responsibility of Anthropologists to Public Education

The profession of anthropology has succeeded in making its importance known in many areas. It has enlarged its vision, probed its specialities, captured masses of student devotees, become a household word, and developed an "holistic approach" invaluable to the massive study of man.

Physical anthropologists have presented evidence to break down age-old clichés and support scientifically acceptable concepts concerning race and genetics, and archeologists have dramatized the antiquity of man. Both of these branches have been vital in establishing that cultural change is a long-term process frequently correlated with physical and mental modification.

From *Human Organization*, vol. 27, no. 1 (Spring 1968), pp. 1–4.

Cultural anthropologists have contributed to the understanding of man's societies by defining man's culture (usually around the core idea that culture is "learned behavior"), and by probing into its features: its innate "human-ness," its universality, variability, tenacity, and the processes of culture change.

The extent to which anthropologists are committed to a study of their own societies varies considerably — from the view that they should not become actively involved with such analysis to the view that, by virtue of their specialized knowledge, they *must* become a vital part of such study. *Pro* or *con*, there probably would be little argument over the fact that anthropology has something to contribute to the academic preparation of those who are unquestionably suited for such self-directed analysis.

If culture is learned behavior, it would seem that the educative process (formally or informally expressed) necessarily must be inextricably woven into the framework of culture. Even professional anthropologists who stand at the extreme position of doubting the validity of studying their own culture must agree, on the basis of their very discipline, that the society to which they belong transmits its culture from one generation to another. If there are desirable points of value in it, these will be passed on, and their continued acceptance in the society must be enhanced and ensured. The undesirable portions also will be passed on, but their eventual demise should be sought in the interests of future generations. Indeed, the very scholastic climate in which an anthropologist works and desires to work, and which is conducive to reasonably untrammeled investigation, is at stake.

Regardless of the anthropologist's personal role in the formal educative process, there will be teaching and learning — the transmission of cultural patterns — as long as there is human life. As surely as there is an American society, in our modern *milieu*, so there will be manipulation of the educative process, because the American culture has provided for such a pattern. The very concept of a formal educative system with its appointive officials, elected officials, professional administrators and teachers, concerned citizens' groups, parents' organizations and student groups, is indicative of this. In the very thick of the manipulative pattern stand industry, the publishing companies, professional societies, and political groups.

At present most of the academic disciplines have projects committed to secondary or even elementary curriculum building, dedicated in each instance to the proposition that that particular discipline best can serve as a kind of focal point in the school room. Some professional scientists have been asked to serve as consultants and curriculum revisers to professional education groups and local school departments. Currently, it seems proper to profess sympathy with educational program innovations, experiments and revisions, whether or not an actual contribution is intended. This may be the root system which could grow eventually to a desirable sense of civic responsibility toward public education. . . .

There are three great classes of problems evident in curriculum change: (1) the problems of professional revision, (2) the problems of implementation of suggested changes, and (3) the problems of professional and interprofessional consistency.

REVISION

On the matter of revision, consider the paradoxical situation in which we find ourselves. On the one hand, a great deal of energy, time and money are being expended, and resource materials are being produced by some professionals, with or without elementary or secondary program-training. But there is no assurance that these efforts will result in the conversion of appreciable numbers of teachers to the "new" view, or that the innovations necessarily will result in better teaching. On the other hand, consider the pitifully few professionals who check what is being taught in the local school systems, or who trouble themselves to try to correct glaring errors in the existing materials. Anthropologists, because of their normally broad backgrounds, are probably as well qualified as any to recognize errors and inconsistencies in the existing curricula of school systems, from agriculture to zoology. Here lies the primary civic responsibility of anthropologists.

This basic analysis is of vital importance. For even after the curriculum committees of the specialized associations have completed their initial commitments, the programs are not likely to be accepted universally or even throughout an entire state or city. In fact, the present segmented nature of American school systems does not provide for such complete acceptance. The curriculum revisionists are amiss if they do not take into account the extremely local nature of school systems. Regardless of the appeal in producing model materials, plans and units, the fact remains that *individuals* teach in the classroom, and reflect the limits or extent of their own training, and that local school boards and committees have jurisdiction over what will or will not be included in the curricula.

Professional anthropologists, to be effective in public education, must become immersed in local education, for there is no better way of analyzing the needs of school systems. The successful anthropological consultant realizes that no single pattern of education can be universally achieved. To reckon that a program will be adopted and implemented without many changes is to ignore a prime lesson of anthropology: that while culture is a universal phenomenon, it is manifested in as many variations as there are local groupings. For this reason, the anthropologist who wishes to contribute to public education must labor on the local front, regardless of his commitments to projects at loftier levels.

IMPLEMENTATION

Further problems are encountered in the area of implementation. After the "upper-level" revisions have been made by the several disciplines, local elementary and secondary systems must somehow select from these, or reject them. True, curriculum revisions are advocated by most concerned educators. Nevertheless, the implementation of program changes is frequently sabotaged, rejected or severely criticized by those who are antagonistic to innovations, and even by those who advocate revision along different lines from the plans offered. This may be frustrating, but the anthropologist should not be overly surprised — this is just what he has experienced in his analysis of culture change among the Indians, the Africans and the South Sea Islanders.

Anthropologists can offer facts, techniques, and a point of view to students, teachers, counselors and administrators. No doubt we are convinced that whether one administers a large school system or a single classroom, the peculiar probing, analytic system of anthropology can be useful. Whether one is responsible for the psychological testing of a nation of youngsters, or a single class in history, the cultural backgrounds of those tested must be taken into account, even as anthropologists maintain. Whether one is producing an important textbook, or heading a discussion group in Civics I, he can profit by the meticulous care exercised by anthropologists in gleaning facts. Nevertheless, whatever anthropology offers must be instilled in the minds of those involved in education on the local level.

In a sense, we must add salesmanship to our other virtues, if anthropology is to be accepted in the public school system. This cannot be done overnight. While it is well to win devotees among the top-level administrators, the surest way to alienation is to have our contributions imposed on teachers by their administrative superiors: studies in culture contact teach us this! It would seem wiser to introduce the concepts of anthropology in the colleges and universities responsible for training teachers and administrators.

Anthropology must become its own best salesman by convincing members of the profession that such colleges and universities, many of them excellent although less renowned than the so-called major institutions of higher learning, are worthy of their best efforts. It is ironic that in the days of Tylor, anthropologists had to prove that their new specialty was worthy of serious academic consideration to gain a place in the ivory tower, while today many colleges and universities are scrambling to prove their worthiness to employ anthropologists — even new M.A.'s!

Anthropologists need to practice the humility which they are fond of saying their discipline has taught them through the study of alien cultures, by recognizing that public school teachers, a goodly proportion of whom are well-qualified to teach a wide variety of subjects, are the important links in the transmission of the formal patterns of local culture. In this, nothing can take the place of the individual anthropologist laboring on the local level, probing, offering his services, and assisting where possible. Regardless of the perfection of revisions in our school systems, the curricula are temporal phenomena that must undergo constant alterations. Anthropologists interested in local education must face squarely the problems connected with implementation and the continuous up-dating of curriculum content.

Consistency

The final problems are those of sheer consistency. The anthropologist who works with local education needs to bear in mind his professional facts. Cultural anthropologists have proven the value of the "holistic" approach in studying other cultures. To what extent is anthropology, as a professional discipline, "holistic"? We speak in hallowed tones of the contributions of large departments and celebrated institutions, but what do we know of the labors of the single dedicated anthropologist working in the smaller college, yet contributing his share to the total educational program? Indeed, has anthropology become extremely centric of late? What do we know of the curriculum revision achievements in the other professional disciplines, if we are unaware of the total view within our own? Are we conscious of the total needs of local education in the town or state where we live, as well as the full range of needs in the United States? As we work on the high school curriculum, or the curriculum of the lower grades, do we know what exists along the rest of the spectrum? Do we look at the peculiar problems of the ethnic groups, or the academically talented or the slow-learner as well as the ordinary child? Do we know that the handicapped must be educated, too? How provincial are anthropologists, in fact, for all their broadening experiences?

A common device is to present materials to teachers with the expectancy that they will integrate the studies into some meaningful whole. Why should we assume such integration? Even anthropologists frequently remain partisans of their own specialties without attempting broad integration of the total field of anthropology, let alone the areas outside their discipline. Our general cultural patterns do not seem to be conducive to a merging of ideas, and the compartmentalism of subject matter is initiated in the elementary school where science, history, geography, etc., are taught as separate units. This phenomenon continues through the university level, with only occasional use of interdisciplinary approaches.

Furthermore, education-minded anthropologists need to remember the many lessons learned in studies of cultural change. There are many examples of innovations leading to social disintegration and demoralization.

Anthropologists who revise curricula should view curriculum change as culture change and ask how desirable changes can be made most effectively. It may be that from a long range view, the acceptance of certain changes presently thought advantageous will lead to poor results and to a weakening of the educational fiber. Indeed, what psychological effects may lurk in some curricular changes? Yet anthropologists, who are notorious conservatives in their advice where primitives are involved, become radical advocates of wholesale change in our own public schools.

The problems of professional consistency must be viewed on the level where the greatest degree of change through curriculum revision is to be effected. This may not be on the highest administrative level (the Health, Education, Welfare offices in Washington, D.C., for example), since changes are constantly considered there, or in the State Superintendent's office, where curricula may be ground out as the situations arise. It may, rather, have its greatest impact, its most massive wrench, in the second grade of "X" Street school, where Miss Smith has taught her students over a period of twenty-five years.

Nothing, absolutely nothing, can take the place of interested, civic concern by the anthropologist, as citizen and scientist, on the local level.

FURTHER READINGS

Fuchs, Estelle. *Pickets at the gates.* New York: Free Press, 1966.
Kimball, Solon T. "Anthropology and education," *Educational Leadership*, vol. 13 (1956).
Ladd, Edward T. *Sources of tension in school-university collaboration.* Atlanta: Urban Laboratory in Education, 1969.
Mead, Margaret. "The social responsibility of the anthropologist," *Journal of Higher Education*, vol. 33 (January 1962).
Storey, Edward. "Black schools and 'Tom' anthropology." Paper read before the 28th annual meeting of the Society for Applied Anthropology, Mexico City, April 1969.